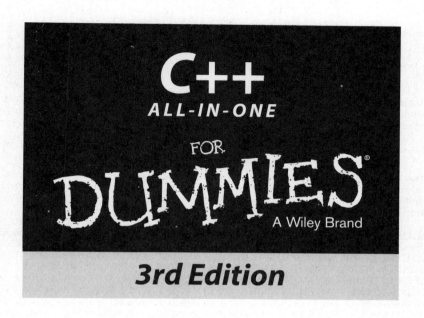

C++
ALL-IN-ONE

FOR

DUMMIES®
A Wiley Brand

3rd Edition

by John Paul Mueller and Jeff Cogswell

FOR
DUMMIES®
A Wiley Brand

C++ All-in-One For Dummies® 3rd Edition

Published by: **John Wiley & Sons, Inc.,** 111 River Street, Hoboken, NJ 07030-5774, www.wiley.com

Copyright © 2014 by John Wiley & Sons, Inc., Hoboken, New Jersey

Published simultaneously in Canada

For general information on our other products and services, please contact our Customer Care Department within the U.S. at 877-762-2974, outside the U.S. at 317-572-3993, or fax 317-572-4002. For technical support, please visit www.wiley.com/techsupport.

Wiley publishes in a variety of print and electronic formats and by print-on-demand. Some material included with standard print versions of this book may not be included in e-books or in print-on-demand. If this book refers to media such as a CD or DVD that is not included in the version you purchased, you may download this material at http://booksupport.wiley.com. For more information about Wiley products, visit www.wiley.com.

Library of Congress Control Number: 2014935515

ISBN: 978-1-118-82378-1 (pbk); ISBN 978-1-118-82379-8 (ebk); ISBN 978-1-118-82385-9 (ebk)

Manufactured in the United States of America

10 9 8 7 6 5 4 3 2 1

Contents at a Glance

Table of Contents

Introduction

C++ is the language of the millennium. Why is C++ so popular?

✦ It's powerful. You can write almost any program in it.

✦ It's fast, and it's fully *compiled*. That's a good thing.

✦ It's easy to use — if you have this book.

✦ It's object-oriented. If you're not sure what that is, don't worry. You can find out about it by reading this very book you're holding.

✦ It's portable. Versions are available for nearly every computer.

✦ It's standardized. The American National Standards Institute (ANSI) and the International Standards Organization (ISO) both approve an official version.

✦ It's continually updated to meet the changing challenges of the computer community.

✦ It's popular. More people are using C++ because so many other people use it.

Sure, some people criticize C++. But most of these people don't truly understand C++ or are just having a bad day. Or both.

No Experience Necessary

This book is not a big rant about C++. Rather, it's a hands-on, roll-up-your-sleeves book, where you will truly *learn* C++.

This edition starts out by helping you get a great C++ installation in place. A lot of readers wrote to tell us that they simply couldn't get C++ to work for them and we listened by adding configuration instructions in Book I, Chapter 1. You can find instructions for working with the Mac, Linux, and Windows throughout the book. The examples are also tested to work on all three platforms.

At the very beginning, we start you out from square one. We don't assume *any* programming experience whatsoever. Everybody has to start somewhere. You can start *here*. Not to brag, but you are in the hands of highly successful C++ users who have shown thousands of people how to program, many of whom also started out from square one.

Great for Advanced Folks, Too!

You already know C++? This book is great for you, too, because although we start discussing C++ from the beginning, we *work all the way through it.*

Want to know how to derive a nontemplatized class from a class template? Check out Book IV, Chapter 5.

Want to see how to create an observer pattern in C++? See Book II, Chapter 6.

Want to find out the difference between deque and vector in the C++ Standard Library? Look at Book IV, Chapter 6.

Want to know how to make a class persistent? Book V, Chapter 5.

Want to know about the Boost library, the library that has added more to the Standard Template Library (STL) than just about any other source? Check out Book VI, Chapters 4 and 5. If you use C++ and don't use Boost, you're really missing out!

This edition also discusses all the latest additions to C++. For example, want to know how to use lambda expressions? Check out Book IV, Chapter 7. In Book VI, Chapter 2, you discover just how useful User Defined Literals (UDLs) can be. You'll also find interesting discussions on debugging applications that rely on command line arguments (Book III, Chapter 2) and dynamic arrays (Book IV, Chapter 6).

For All Computers

C++ All-in-One For Dummies, 3rd Edition, is devoted to working with C++ wherever you want to use it. C++ is now standardized, and you can use the information in this book on many different platforms. We wrote the samples using Mac OS X, SUSE Linux (some of the beta readers used other flavors of Linux), and Windows systems. In order to make this happen, we used a compiler called *Code::Blocks* that runs on almost every computer (Windows, Linux, and Macintosh). It doesn't matter which computer you're using!

All the code in this book has been tested on Mac, Windows, and Linux. (Don't let the Windows screen shots fool you: Code::Blocks works great on just about any platform.) The examples haven't been tested on other platforms, but because C++ has become standard, we're sure you'll be able to use at least the beginning examples wherever you want.

Conventions

As guys who are about to head off to a convention, we thought it would be appropriate to share with you some tidbits about the conventions in this book. However, this time we're talking about the text format:

✦ When you see something in `monofont`, it's a computer word that you *type into the computer or read on a computer screen*. If we discuss a computer term but it's not a word that you *type* into the computer, it is in the usual font. You also see `monofont` for URLs and e-mail addresses.

✦ When you see something in **bold**, you can type it into the computer.

✦ When you see a word in *italics*, it's new and we explain its meaning.

✦ When code is on a single line, it looks like this:

```
MyClass.IsCool();
```

✦ When code appears on multiple lines, it looks like this:

```
MyClass.IsCool();
AndSo.IsYours();
```

✦ Lengthy program listings have a header and a listing number. These are entire programs you can type, and they should run as is. However, you save time and effort by using the code supplied in downloadable form from the publisher's website.

Organization

This book is divided into six minibooks. Each one covers a separate, broad topic, with chapters devoted to individual subtopics.

You can either read this book from cover to cover, or you can look up topics and treat the book as a reference guide — whichever works best for you. Keep it on your shelf, and have it ready to grab when you need to look something up. Here are the six minibooks and what they cover:

✦ **Minibook I, Getting Started with C++:** Here, we start at the very beginning, showing you all you need to know to get up and running with C++. This is also the minibook that gets you started with Code::Blocks. If you don't have a copy of Code::Blocks installed on your system, you definitely want to start by reviewing Chapter 1. This first chapter also takes you on a tour of essential Code::Blocks features.

✦ **Minibook II, Understanding Objects and Classes:** In this minibook, we present all the latest information about object-oriented programming and how to use various diagrams to design your programs. Advanced readers should especially appreciate this minibook because we cover such topics as UML and design patterns. But beginners should be able to understand it, too, and find out how to get up to speed with the best software engineering ideas around.

✦ **Minibook III, Fixing Problems:** Here, we show you how to debug your programs by using a special program called a debugger. If you're a beginner, this minibook gets you started on fixing the problems in your code. If you're advanced, you can appreciate how we use the debugger supplied with Code::Blocks to locate any problems your application might have.

✦ **Minibook IV, Advanced Programming:** In this minibook, we move through advanced C++ topics. After reading Minibook IV, the beginners become intermediate or advanced programmers, and the intermediate and advanced programmers can master the C++ language. This edition of the book contains updated information for the latest version of C++, which includes dynamic arrays, working with unordered data, and using lambda expressions to make your code smaller and easier to read.

✦ **Minibook V, Reading and Writing Files:** Yes, this entire minibook is devoted to the issues of reading and writing files. In this book, we cover stream programming, which is a special way C++ treats files.

✦ **Minibook VI, Advanced C++:** This advanced minibook includes two chapters each on STL (Standard Template Library) and Boost. The STL chapters describe some of the advanced classes not used in other areas of the book and help you create your own templates. The Boost library chapters describe all the tools found in Boost, show how to build a full set of libraries for your own use, and then provide an overview of some interesting Boost capabilities. This minibook also discusses the use of User Defined Literals (UDLs), which is a special way to work with data that makes your application faster and more efficient. You really miss out on a lot if you don't at least visit this minibook after you build your programming skills.

Icons Galore

Hey, what would a *For Dummies* book be without all the great icons? Here's what they mean:

We have lots of experience as both C++ programmers and instructors, and so we pass on tidbits here and there to help you along.

This icon identifies things you may want to remember to do when you're programming.

These icons can save you a lot of headaches. They're suggestions to help keep you from really messing up — the way that we probably already did. You won't cause the computer to explode if you skip these, but you'll sleep better knowing you won't accidentally lose all your code or overwrite a file.

Computer people often search for extra knowledge, even when it may not be necessary. These Technical Stuff paragraphs are fascinating information, primarily to cover your serious curiosity.

What's Next?

If you want to e-mail us, please do! Make sure you send your book-specific requests to:

John@JohnMuellerBooks.com

We both get a lot of e-mail from readers, so we can't always reply, nor can we promise to have a quick-and-easy answer. Please don't be offended if you don't hear back. The blog category at `http://blog.johnmuellerbooks.com/categories/263/c-all-in-one-for-dummies.aspx` contains a wealth of additional information about this book. You can check out the website at `http://www.johnmuellerbooks.com/`.

In the pages that follow, you will see just how easy it is to program in C++. When you finish this book, you will have a full mastery of the language!

Beyond the Book

This book isn't the end of your C++ programming experience — it's really just the beginning. We provide online content to make this book more flexible and better able to meet your needs. That way, as we receive e-mail from you, we can do things like address questions and tell you how updates to either Code::Blocks or the C++ language affect book content. In fact, you gain access to all of these cool additions:

✦ **Cheat Sheet:** You remember using crib notes in school to make a better mark on a test, don't you? You do? Well, a cheat sheet is sort of like that. It provides you with some special notes on things you can do with C++ that not every other developer knows. You can find the cheat sheet for this book at `http://www.dummies.com/cheatsheet/cplusplusaio`. It contains really neat information like the top ten mistakes developers make when working with C++, a list of header files you use in most applications, and some of the C++ syntax that gives most developers problems.

✦ **Dummies.com online articles:** A lot of readers were skipping past the part pages in the book, so we decided to remedy that. You now have a really good reason to read the part pages, and that's online content. Most every parts page has an article associated with it that provides additional interesting information that wouldn't fit in the book. You can find the articles for this book at `www.dummies.com/extras/cplusplusaio`.

✦ **Updates:** Sometimes changes happen. For example, we might not have seen an upcoming change when we looked into our crystal ball during the writing of this book. In the past, that simply meant the book would become outdated and less useful, but you can now find updates to the book at `www.dummies.com/extras/cplusplusaio`. In addition to these updates, check out the blog posts with answers to reader questions and demonstrations of useful book-related techniques at `http://blog.johnmuellerbooks.com/`.

✦ **Companion files:** Hey! Who really wants to type all the code in the book? Most readers would prefer to spend their time actually working through coding examples rather than typing. Fortunately for you, the source code is available for download, so all you need to do is read the book to learn C++ coding techniques. Each of the book examples even tells you precisely which example project to use. You can find these files at `http://www.dummies.com/extras/cplusplusaio`.

Just in case you're worried about Code::Blocks, you can find complete download and installation instructions for it in Book I, Chapter 1. Don't worry about which platform you use. This chapter includes instructions for Mac OS X, Linux, and Windows.

Book I
Getting Started with C++

Visit www.dummies.com for great Dummies content online.

Contents at a Glance

Chapter 1: Configuring Your System

In This Chapter

✔ Getting your own copy of C++ 14

✔ Getting a copy of Code::Blocks

✔ Creating a Code::Blocks work environment on your system

✔ Seeing how Code::Blocks helps you perform tasks

✔ Working with other IDEs

*Y*ou may already have your shiny new copy of C++ installed on your machine. It's possible to get C++ by itself or as part of an IDE. Just how you work with C++ depends on your needs, but if you already have a copy and you're happy with it, then you don't need this chapter — just treat yourself to another cup of coffee and move on to the next chapter, secure in the knowledge that you've already completed a whole chapter of this book with very little effort whatsoever. Before you can do anything interesting at all with C++, you need a copy of it installed on your system. Of course, this means going online, finding the location of the software that's appropriate for your platform, and then downloading it as necessary. If you use an Integrated Development Environment (IDE) such as Code::Blocks (the IDE used throughout this book), you get a copy of C++ with your installation, so you don't need to worry about reading the first section of this chapter. This book relies on your having a copy of C++ 14, which is the latest version of the software available at the time of this writing. However, many of the examples will work with older versions of C++, should you choose to use one.

Even though this book focuses on working with C++ on the Mac, Windows, and Linux platforms, you can actually use the techniques it provides on a great many other platforms, such as certain smartphones. With this in mind, you'll find an overview of using C++ with other IDEs. As your platform becomes more esoteric, you'll find that fewer of the book examples work because your platform may require special programming techniques. The best option for working with this book is using a copy of Code::Blocks 13.12 with C++ 14 support installed on the Linux, Mac, or Windows platform.

Obtaining a Copy of C++ 14

There is no product available named C++ 14. The C++ 14 standard simply says what the language contains and how someone should implement it. In other words, you can't just go online and get a copy of C++ 14; what you need to do instead is get a compiler vendor's implementation of the C++ 14 standard. For example, you can download the Gnu Compiler Collection (GCC) version of C++ 14 from `http://gcc.gnu.org/releases.html`.

Every vendor will have a slightly different interpretation of this standard and could provide additions to the standard. In short, every compiler provides a unique version of C++. However, you also have the choice of not using the special features that the vendor provides, which means your source code is less susceptible to problems that occur when you use multiple compilers. The examples in this book are strictly written to the C++ 14 standard, so you shouldn't have a problem using them anywhere you want.

It's important that you also understand that a compiler is not the same as an Integrated Development Environment (IDE). The compiler is separate from the IDE in many cases and maintained by two separate parties. For example, the Code::Blocks IDE supports multiple compilers, and the GCC compiler works within multiple IDEs. The compiler is the important piece of software that turns your source code into an executable file that the operating system can run to produce the output you want.

The compiler you choose has to support the platforms you want to work with. For example, GCC supports Mac, Windows, and Linux development as well as some Acorn RISC Machine (ARM) processors. In fact, it may support other platforms by the time you read this chapter. Because it works in so many places, this book focuses on GCC, even though the examples will work with other compilers with some modification to overcome compiler differences.

Obtaining Code::Blocks

The Code::Blocks IDE provides an environment in which you can write source code, compile it, test it, and debug it as needed. The IDE doesn't actually compile the source code, but it does provide support for a compiler that does so. (It just so happens it does its job in such a way that makes it appear that the compiler is part of the IDE.) You can choose from a number of compilers in Code::Blocks, but this book focuses on using GCC to ensure that the examples will run on as many platforms as possible. GCC comes with your copy of Code::Blocks when working with Windows, so you don't have to do anything special to work with it except select it during the installation process. (When working on a Mac or Linux system, you must install GCC separately — the compiler doesn't come with Code::Blocks.)

This book is written using Code::Blocks version 13.12. That doesn't mean you can't use it with earlier or later versions of Code::Blocks. However, when working with other versions of Code::Blocks, you may find that you need to modify the code slightly. The modification is required in order to support the compiler that comes with that version of Code::Blocks. The IDE itself won't affect your ability to work with C++ 14.

Code::Blocks comes in both binary form and source code form. You can download either form from http://www.codeblocks.org/downloads. If you're working with a Linux, Mac, or Windows system, you should download the binary version of Code::Blocks from http://www.codeblocks.org/downloads/26. This is the version used in this book. The "Installing Code::Blocks" section of this chapter tells you more about getting Code::Blocks installed on your particular system.

When working with a Windows installation, make sure you use the codeblocks-13.12mingw-setup.exe installer to obtain a copy of GCC with Code::Blocks. If you don't have administrative privileges for your machine, download the codeblocks-13.12mingw-setup_user.exe file instead and make absolutely certain that you don't install it to the Programs folder on your system, because the application won't work there. Create a folder to which you have write privileges and install Code::Blocks there instead.

We cannot stress this enough: Make sure you download the codeblocks-13.12mingw-setup.exe file from the Code::Blocks site. Downloading and installing the codeblocks-13.12mingw-setup-TDM-GCC-481.exe file will create an installation that is unstable and buggy. At least some of the examples in the book won't run with this version of Code::Blocks. The vendor knows about the stability issues and is working on correcting them. Check John's blog at http://blog.johnmuellerbooks.com/ for updates about Code::Blocks as they become available.

Installing Code::Blocks

Before you can use Code::Blocks as your IDE, you need to install it. The following sections describe how to install Code::Blocks on each of the main platforms supported by this book. The instructions in these sections assume that you've downloaded the binary version of Code::Blocks and that you aren't using a custom compiled version of the product.

Working with Windows

Code::Blocks comes with a Windows installer that will make the task of installing the IDE easier. The following steps help you work with the codeblocks-13.12mingw-setup.exe or codeblocks-13.12mingw-setup_user.exe installer:

1. **Double-click the file you downloaded from the Code::Blocks site.**

   You see the CodeBlocks Setup Wizard start.

2. **Click Next.**

   The licensing agreement appears. Read the licensing agreement so that you know the terms of usage for Code::Blocks.

3. **Click I Agree.**

   The wizard displays a series of configuration options, as shown in Figure 1-1. This book assumes that you've performed the default, full installation.

Figure 1-1:
The wizard asks you to select the configuration options to use.

4. **Click Next.**

   The installation program asks where to install Code::Blocks on your system. Unlike many other applications, Code::Blocks will actually write data to this folder from time to time. Unless you have administrative access to the Programs folder on your system, the best idea is to use a folder to which you have write access. To ensure maximum compatibility, the book uses the `C:\CodeBlocks` folder for installation purposes.

5. **Type** C:\CodeBlocks **in the Destination Folder field. Click Install.**

   The installation program automatically creates the C:\CodeBlocks folder for you when it doesn't already exist. You see all of the files installed into the `C:\CodeBlocks` folder on your system.

   The setup wizard may display a dialog box asking whether you want to start Code::Blocks. Click No if you see this dialog box.

6. Click Next.

You see a completion dialog box.

7. Click Finish.

The setup wizard ends.

Working with Mac OS/X

Installing Code::Blocks on a Mac requires a little extra work than it does in Windows. Code::Blocks requires Mac OS/X 10.4 or later to install. The following steps tell you how to get a functional Code::Blocks installation on your Mac system.

1. Download and install Xcode from the App Store to obtain a copy of GCC, if necessary.

You can verify that you have the GNU GCC compiler installed by opening a terminal, typing gcc -v, and pressing Enter. If GCC is installed, you should see some version information along with some compiler instructions.

If you have an older version of Mac OS/X, there is a fee associated with the Xcode download. (Versions 10.6 and later provide free access.) This is a large download of about 1 GB, so allow plenty of time.

2. Extract the Code::Blocks files into a folder.

You see a number of files, including the Code::Blocks application, a readme file containing the latest update information, and a PDF file containing documentation.

3. Open the Applications folder.

You see the applications installed on your system.

4. Drag the CodeBlocks.app file from the folder you used for extraction purposes to the Applications folder.

The operating system adds Code::Blocks to the list of usable applications.

5. Navigate to https://developer.apple.com/downloads/.

This site requires that you sign up for a free developer ID. Simply follow the prompts onscreen to obtain your Apple ID. The sign-up process is free.

6. Click the Command Line Tools for Xcode link.

The operating system downloads the file and displays a package folder for you.

7. Double-click the Command Line Tools package.

The operating system installs the package for you, which enables access to GCC from Code::Blocks.

Using the standard Linux installation

There isn't a single set of steps for installing Code::Blocks on Linux, because each flavor of Linux has its own requirements. Code::Blocks directly support

+ Blag

+ Debian

+ Fedora

+ Gentoo

+ Playpux

+ Red Hat Package Manager (RPM)-based distributions (such as SUSE, Red Hat, Yellow Dog, Fedora Core, and CentOS)

+ Ubuntu

Each distribution type has its own set of instructions that you can find at http://wiki.codeblocks.org/index.php?title=Installing_ Code::Blocks. Make sure you download and install the compiler, debugger, and IDE as needed by carefully following the instructions (typed at the terminal). The file that you download from http://www.codeblocks.org/ downloads/26 contains the packages for a Code::Blocks installation, so you don't need to download each package separately as part of the installation process.

Some Linux installations have special requirements or experience limitations when working with Code::Blocks. The only apparent limitation that affects this book is the lack of Boost support for Red Hat and CentOS. Because of this limitation, you can't use the examples found in Book VI, Chapters 4 and 5. However, if you experience other limitations, please let John know about them at John@JohnMuellerBooks.com and he'll address them as part of a blog post for this book.

Using the graphical Linux installation

All versions of Linux support the standard installation discussed in the "Using the standard Linux installation" section of this chapter. However, a few versions of Debian-based Linux distributions, such as Ubuntu 12.*x* and above, provide a graphical installation technique as well. You'll need the administrator group (sudo) password to use this procedure, so having it handy will save you time. The following steps outline the graphical installation technique for Ubuntu, but the technique is similar for other Linux installations.

1. **Open the Ubuntu Software Center folder (the folder may be named Synaptics on other platforms).**

You see a listing of the most popular software available for download and installation as shown in Figure 1-2. Your list will probably vary from the one shown in the screenshot.

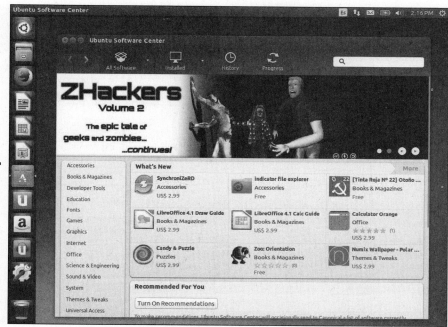

Figure 1-2:
The Ubuntu
Software
Center
contains a
list of the
most popu-
lar software
when you
open it.

2. **Select Developer Tools (or Development) from the All Software drop down list box.**

   You see a listing of developer tools, including Code::Blocks, as show in Figure 1-3.

3. **Double click the Code::Blocks entry.**

   The Ubuntu Software Center provides details about the Code::Blocks entry and offers to install it for you, as shown in Figure 1-4.

4. **Click Install.**

   Ubuntu begins the process of installing Code::Blocks. A progress bar shows the download and installation status. When the installation is complete, the Install button changes to a Remove button.

5. **Close the Ubuntu Software Center folder.**

   You see a Code::Blocks icon added to the Desktop. The IDE is ready for use.

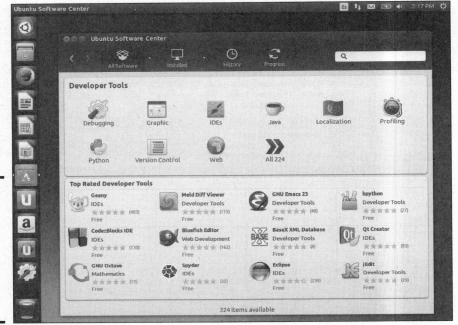

Figure 1-3:
The Developer Tools category contains an entry for Code::Blocks.

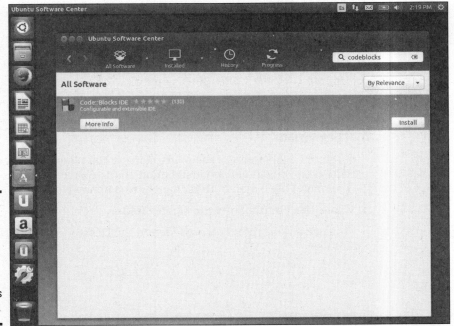

Figure 1-4:
It's possible to obtain additional information about Code::Blocks if necessary.

Touring the Essential Code::Blocks Features

No matter how you install Code::Blocks for your platform, you eventually end up with an IDE with standardized characteristics. This is one of the best reasons to use an IDE such as Code::Blocks — it's possible to use the same IDE no matter which platform you use.

Your screen shots may look different from the ones shown in this book. Even though this book uses screen shots from the Windows version of Code::Blocks, the same features are provided for Code::Blocks installations on other platforms, though the IDE may not look precisely the same on those other platforms. The following sections describe the essential features you need to know about when working with Code::Blocks.

Starting Code::Blocks for the first time

Open the Code::Blocks executable program using the technique your platform usually requires. For example, when working with Windows or the Mac, you double-click the CodeBlocks icon. The first time you start Code::Blocks, you may see a Compilers Auto-detection dialog box. Select the GNU GCC Compiler entry (it may be the only available entry and selected by default), click Set as Default, and then click OK.

At this point, Code::Blocks displays a File Associations dialog box, similar to the one shown in Figure 1-5. It's a good idea to associate the IDE with your C++ files so that opening the file also opens the IDE — making it much easier to write applications and modify them later.

Figure 1-5:
Associate
Code::Blocks
with your
C++ files to
make it
easier to
manage
them.

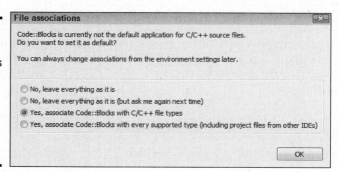

Code::Blocks always begins by opening the IDE and placing a tip dialog box in it, as shown in Figure 1-6. The tip is a random bit of information about using Code::Blocks more efficiently. You can see the next tip in the series by clicking Next Tip or disable the display of tips by clearing Show Tips at Startup. After you read the tip, click Close.

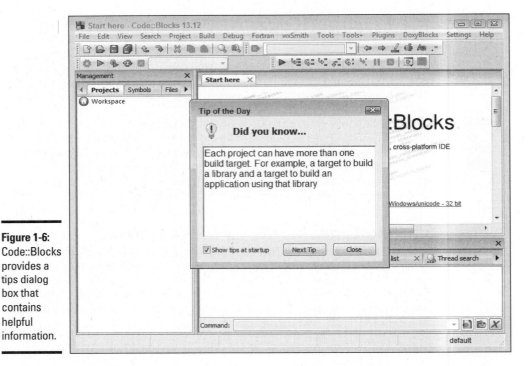

Figure 1-6:
Code::Blocks
provides a
tips dialog
box that
contains
helpful
information.

Select either of the Yes options in this list. It's possible to associate
Code::Blocks with other source code types, but for the purposes of this
book, you only need to associate it with C++ files. Click OK to complete the
action. At this point, you see the IDE.

To make your changes permanent, choose File⇨Quit. The IDE will display a
message similar to the one shown in Figure 1-7. What this message is saying
is that you've made changes to the Code::Blocks configuration. Click Yes to
save the changes.

Figure 1-7:
Save your
changes to
disk.

Windows users may experience a problem at this point. If you install
Code::Blocks in the `C:\Program Files` folder and don't have Administrator
access (or if you simply opened the application as a regular user), you may
find that you can't save any Code::Blocks settings, making using Code::Blocks
an annoying experience. To use Code::Blocks without problems, make sure

you have write access to the folder in which you installed it. The best policy is to install Code::Blocks to the `C:\CodeBlocks` folder on your system. As an alternative, you can right click the Code::Blocks icon and choose Run As Administrator from the context menu to run Code::Blocks with the required permissions.

Opening the sample projects

You obtain the source code for this book from the publisher site described in the Introduction. After you download the .zip file containing the source, you simply extract it to your hard drive.

The source code for this book is divided into books, chapters within books, and examples within chapters. To open the first example found in Chapter 2 of this book, for example, start by locating the `\CPP_AIO\BookI\Chapter02\FirstProject` folder (or the equivalent on your platform). Within this folder is `SayHello.cbp`. The Code Blocks Project (`.cbp`) file extension contains everything that Code::Blocks needs to open the project and present it to you. When you get to this first project, you double-click `SayHello.cbp` and Code::Blocks automatically opens the project for you, as shown in Figure 1-8.

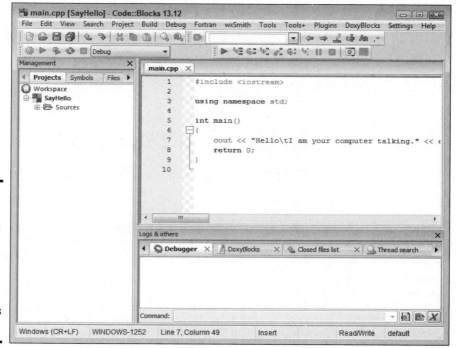

Figure 1-8:
Each example has a `.cbp` file associated with it that opens the example in Code::Blocks for you.

If you have chosen to allow tips, you'll actually see a Tip of the Day dialog box first, like the one shown earlier, in Figure 1-6. Click Close after you read the tip to see the project. Don't worry about the contents of this example for now. You'll discover how it works in Chapter 2. The only thing you need to know for now is how to open a project example so that you can follow along with the examples in the book.

When working with IDEs other than Code::Blocks, you can open the C++ (.cpp) file instead of the .cbp file. Opening the .cpp file will still display the code example for you. C++ stores source code in .cpp files, not as part of the .cbp files.

Viewing the essential windows

There are some windows that you use with every example in the book. As the book progresses, you'll be introduced to other windows, but the ones covered in the following sections are the windows that you need to know about in order to get started with Code::Blocks.

Using the Start Here window

The Start Here window, shown in Figure 1-9, does precisely as its name indicates — it gets you started with Code::Blocks. This window is automatically displayed when you open Code::Blocks directly, without opening a project first. It appears immediately after you clear the Tip of the Day dialog box.

Figure 1-9:
Use the
Start Here
window to
start a new
session.

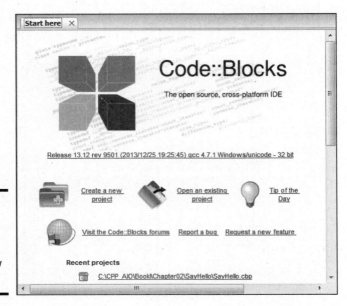

This window is important because it also provides you with access to various Code::Blocks features and makes it possible for you to request changes. Here are the options you can access using this window:

✦ **Create a New Project:** Before you can use Code::Blocks effectively, you need to create a project. A project acts as a container to hold the files used to create the application. It also stores settings used to configure the development environment and present that environment to you in a specific manner.

✦ **Open an Existing Project:** Any time you want to re-create the environment you used during a previous coding session, you open an existing project. The project will automatically open any source code files that you had open and perform other tasks to make it easy for you to start right back up where you left off the previous day.

✦ **Tip of the Day:** If you missed the Tip of the Day or you simply want to reactivate the feature, click this link. Code::Blocks displays the Tip of the Day dialog box, shown in Figure 1-2.

✦ **Visit the Code::Blocks forums:** You can't communicate directly with the makers of Code::Blocks. However, you can communicate directly with other users and get peer support. The makers of Code::Blocks also monitor the forums, and you'll see them actively addressing issues that aren't handled with peer support.

✦ **Report a Bug:** Every application on the planet has bugs (programming errors), including the Code::Blocks IDE. It's important to report bugs when you find them so that they can be fixed.

✦ **Request a New Feature:** Anyone who uses an application long enough will likely come up with a spectacular idea for making it better. The makers of Code::Blocks want to hear your phenomenal idea, so contact them sooner than later.

✦ **Recent Projects:** As you work with Code::Blocks, you'll create more than one project. Rather than look all over your hard drive for the project you need, you can use this feature to find it immediately. To open the project, just click on its link in the Recent Projects list.

Even if you can't see the Start Here window after you open a project, you can always view it by selecting View⇨Start Page. Keeping the Start Here window handy makes it easy to access commonly used Code::Blocks features. However, you can also access these features using menus. For example, to create a new project, you choose File⇨New⇨Project.

Using the Management window

The purpose of an IDE is to help you manage your coding projects in various ways, so it's not surprising that Code::Blocks comes with a Management window, as shown in Figure 1-10. The Management window normally resides on the left side of the IDE's main window, but you can move it where you want by using the title bar to drag the window.

Figure 1-10:
The
Management
window
helps you
manage your
Code::Blocks
projects.

The Management window contains four tabs. The following list describes the purpose of each tab:

✦ **Projects:** Grouping in one place all of the files needed to create an application is a helpful method for managing it. A grouping of applications files is called a *project*, and helping you create and maintain projects is just one way in which Code::Blocks makes application development easier.

✦ **Symbols:** Applications contain a number of symbols, such as the names of functions. You use the Symbols tab to find specific symbols you need within an application. Don't worry too much about symbols now, but eventually you'll find that this tab helps save time and effort by making it easier to locate specific pieces of your application.

✦ **Files:** Locating code and resources you need to add to the current project can be time consuming. The Files tab provides a method for navigating the file system. You can then right-click on files you need and use the context menu entries to perform tasks such as adding the file to your current project.

✦ **Resources:** Graphical applications require the addition of dialog boxes and other visual elements that C++ treats as resources. The Resources tab contains a list of these resources so that you can find them easily and manage them in various ways.

The Resources tab is a feature, used by advanced developers, which you generally don't need to worry about unless you decide to create graphical applications using a combination of C++ and the wxWidgets plugin (installed automatically for Windows developers, but separately for both Mac and Linux developers). An explanation of how to create such applications is outside the scope of this book, but you can see a simple example of such a project at `http://wiki.codeblocks.org/index.php?title=WxSmith_tutorial:_Hello_world`.

Using the Logs & Others window

Code::Blocks helps you track all sorts of activities. For example, when you create a new application from source code you write (a process called building), you see messages that tell you how the process went, as shown in Figure 1-11. The examples in this book will help you understand when to use the various log tab and other tabs (such as the Debugger tab) to better determine how your application works.

Figure 1-11:
Using the
Logs &
Others
window to
understand
how your
application
works.

The tabs you see in this window depend on which options you have enabled in Code::Blocks and what task you're doing. Code::Blocks will usually select the tab you need automatically. If you want to close a particular tab, click the X next to its entry on the tab. To display a tab that you don't see, right-click any tab in the list and choose an entry from the Toggle option on the context menu.

Selecting a compiler

Code::Blocks supports a host of compilers. This book uses GCC because it works on all of the target platforms and it provides great C++ 14 support. Most Code::Blocks installations also select this particular compiler automatically. So there are all kinds of great reasons to use GCC as a compiler. However, you might not have GCC selected on your system, and that could cause problems when running the examples. Not every compiler vendor provides great C++ 14 support, or your compiler vendor might implement a particular detail differently than GCC does. The following steps help you verify that GCC is the compiler selected for your system, and they help you change your configuration if it isn't:

1. **Open Code::Blocks.**

It doesn't matter if you select a project or not. Configuring the compiler will be the same whether you have a project loaded or not.

2. **Choose Settings⇨Compiler.**

You see the Compiler Settings dialog box, as shown in Figure 1-12.

3. **Click Global Compiler Settings in the left pane to display the global compiler settings.**

Figure 1-12:
Set
Code::Blocks
to use the
GCC compiler
to run the
examples in
this book.

4. **Verify that the GNU GCC compiler (or an equivalent for your platform) is actually selected in the Selected Compiler list.**

   The list could contain a number of GCC compiler entries. The best option is the GNU GCC Compiler setting because it offers maximum compatibility with the book examples. If the GNU GCC Compiler option (or an equivalent for your particular platform) is selected, proceed to Step 7.

5. **Select the GNU GCC Compiler option (or the equivalent for your platform) in the Select Compiler list.**

   The Set As Default button becomes enabled after you make your selection.

6. **Click Set As Default.**

   This step ensures that the GNU GCC compiler is used for all of your projects, even if you only want to open the downloaded source code.

7. **Click OK.**

8. **Close Code::Blocks.**

   You see a Layout Changed dialog box.

9. **Click Yes.**

   Your changes become permanent, and Code::Blocks closes.

Using Other IDEs

Even though this book will focus on the Code::Blocks IDE and the GCC compiler combination, the knowledge you gain can be used with any IDE and compiler combination. In fact, all you really need is the compiler. Most developers use an IDE, just because it makes things easy (and we all like things easy). You may find, though, that Code::Blocks simply doesn't provide the functionality you want or that it's too hard to use.

The selection of an IDE is a personal thing, and most developers have specific reasons for choosing a particular IDE. In fact, I use several different IDEs and make my choice based on the needs of a particular project. So it's not even necessary to use the same IDE all the time. IDEs provide management features, while compilers control how the source code is interpreted and turned into an executable file. The two applications perform completely different tasks.

GCC is a great choice for a compiler because a number of IDEs support it. If you decide to use a different IDE from the one found in this book, that's fine with us. In fact, we congratulate you on your desire to take a different path! Here are some alternative IDEs that you might want to consider:

✦ **CodeLite:** http://codelite.org/

✦ **Dev-C++:** http://dev-c.soft32.com/free-download/

✦ **Eclipse:** http://www.eclipse.org/downloads/) when used with C/C++ Development Tooling (CDT) (http://www.eclipse.org/cdt/

✦ **Emacs:** http://www.gnu.org/software/emacs/) when used with the Emacs Code Browser (ECB) (http://ecb.sourceforge.net/

✦ **Netbeans:** https://netbeans.org/downloads/

✦ **Qt Creator:** http://sourceforge.net/projects/qtcreator.mirror/

Chapter 2: Creating Your First C++ Application

In This Chapter

✓ Organizing your applications into projects

✓ Typing code into the code editor

✓ Writing an application that writes to the screen

✓ Doing basic math

✓ Running your application

*I*t's your lucky day. You have decided to learn the most popular programming language on the planet. From the biggest skyscrapers housing huge Fortune 500 companies all the way down to the garages with the self-starting kids grinding out the next generation of software, people are using C++. Yes, there are other languages, but more programmers use C++ than any other language. In this chapter, you start right out writing a C++ application.

As mentioned in Chapter 1, this book relies on your use of Code::Blocks as the IDE and on GCC as the C++ compiler. The procedures are written for the most current version of Code::Blocks (version 12.11) at the time of writing, so you may need to make allowances if you use a different Code::Blocks version, and the procedures won't work if you use another IDE. In addition, you may need to make minor changes to the code as the examples become more complex if you want to use other compilers.

Code::Blocks Creating a Project

Creating a computer application is usually a bigger job than you'd want to organize in your head. Application code is saved in files much like the documents in a word processor. But applications often have more than one source-code file. At big companies in big buildings in big cities, some applications are *really big* — hundreds of source-code files for just one application.

Understanding projects

Applications can contain a lot of source code. To keep all that source code together, programmers use a file that manages it all, called a *project*. A project has a few key elements:

✦ A set of source-code files

✦ (Optional) Resource information such as icons and sound files

✦ A description of how to compile (build) the application

✦ Integrated Development Environment (IDE) settings that tell how to set up the editor you use to write the application

✦ Some general descriptions of the application being built, such as its name and the type of application it is

The *type of application* doesn't mean "word processor" or "really cool earth-shattering software," even if that's what your application is. This book uses *type* to mean your application's overall relationship with other applications:

✦ Does this application run by itself?

✦ Does this application add to or extend the functionalities of another application (such as Firefox)?

✦ Does this application serve as a *library* (a bunch of code that you make available to another application)?

All this information, along with your source-code files, represents a project.

In the Code::Blocks IDE, you create a new project each time you start work on a new application. You provide a little information about the application you're working on, and then you begin writing your code. All the code for your application is stored in one place — in the project.

 This book presents a lot of sample applications, so you may want to create a directory (or *folder*) on your hard drive to house all the applications you create as you work through this book. The downloadable source code uses a folder named CPP_AIO. You can read about how to obtain the downloadable source and other extras for this book in the Introduction.

Defining your first project

To create a new project in Code::Blocks, start Code::Blocks and choose File⇨New⇨Project, or click Create a New Project on the Start Here page that appears when you start the application. A dialog box appears, as shown in Figure 2-1.

Figure 2-1:
The New
from
Template
dialog box
lets you
select a
new project
type.

When you create a project in Code::Blocks, you choose from a list of several types of applications. They're shown as icons in the New from Template dialog box. The following list shows some application types:

+ **GTK+ Project:** This is a graphical application that includes, well, a window. You know the kind: It usually has a menu across the top and something inside it that you can either click or type into. It relies on the Gimp Toolkit (GTK), which provides an incredibly flexible interface that runs on a number of platforms including Linux, Mac, and Windows systems. Read more about GTK in the "What about all of those other projects?" sidebar.

+ **Console Application:** This is an application that gets a paltry Console window instead of a graphical window. *Console* refers to a window with a command prompt. (Folks who recall the old days, before Windows, *call* it a *DOS box,* and you may know it as a *terminal window* when working with operating systems such as the Mac or Linux.)

+ **Static library:** A *static library* is a set of C++ code that you use later in another project. It's like making a really great marinade that you won't use up today. You'll use some of it tomorrow and some of it after that. Same with a C++ library.

+ **Dynamic Link Library:** A Dynamic Link Library (DLL) is kind of like a static library except it is separated from the main application and gets its own file with a `.DLL` extension.

+ **Empty project:** This blank project is as clean as a blank sheet of white typing paper, ready for you to fill 'er up.

  Frankly, it's kind of a pain to use an empty project, because you have to tweak and set a bunch of things. So we never use this option.

What about all of those other projects?

Code::Blocks supports a host of other application types. This book doesn't discuss them, because they won't add to your initial understanding of C++ programming. However, these other projects are valuable in the right environment. For example, the GIMP Tool Kit Plus (GTK+) Project relies on a graphical user interface designed for the X Windowing system (see more at http://www.gtk.org/).

You'll find that Code::Blocks uses a considerable number of acronyms and abbreviations for project and resource names without defining any of them. We define all the acronyms that we employ on first use in the book. However, some of these acronyms and abbreviations go on and on. For example, you might wonder about the GIMP part of the GTK+ definition. GIMP stands for GNU Image Manipulation Program. Of course, now you need to know GNU, which stands for Gnu's Not Unix. Okay, now that we've exhausted that bit of fun, if you ever do run across an interesting acronym or abbreviation, you can always get it defined for you on the Acronym Finder website (http://www.acronymfinder.com/). The bottom line is that you need to research both projects and resources before you use them.

For the samples in this chapter, create a Console Application. Follow these steps:

1. **In the New from Template dialog box, click the Console Application icon found on the Projects tab, and then click Go.**

You see the Welcome page of the Console Application Wizard.

2. **Click Next.**

The wizard asks which language you want to use.

3. **Highlight C++ and click Next.**

You see a list of project-related questions, as shown in Figure 2-2. These questions define project basics, such as the project name.

4. **Type a name for your project in the Project Title field.**

The example uses SayHello as the project title. Notice that the wizard automatically starts creating an entry for you in the Project Filename field.

5. **Type a location for your project in the Folder to Create Project In field.**

The example uses C:\CPP_AIO\BookI\Chapter02 as the folder name. You can also click the ellipsis button next to the Folder to Create Project In field to use the Browse for Folder dialog box to locate the folder you want to use. Notice that the wizard completes the entry in the Project Filename field.

Figure 2-2:
Provide the name of your project for Code::Blocks.

If you made a folder to house all the applications for this book (as suggested in the "Understanding projects" section, earlier in the chapter), put your FirstProject folder in the folder for the book. Make sure you're inside the folder you just created.

6. **(Optional) Type a project filename in the Project Filename field.**

7. **Click Next.**

You see the compiler settings shown in Figure 2-3. Most of the projects in this book use the default compiler settings. However, if you look at the Compiler drop-down list, you see that Code::Blocks supports a number of compilers and you can add more to it. The other settings control the creation and location of a Debug version of the application (the version you use for finding problems in your code) and a Release version (the version that you send to a customer).

8. **Change any required compiler settings and click Finish.**

The wizard creates the application for you. It then displays the Code::Blocks IDE with the project loaded. However, the source code file isn't loaded yet.

9. **Drill down into the SayHello workspace entries on the Projects tab of the Management window and double-click main.cpp.**

You see the source code file loaded so that you can edit it, as shown in Figure 2-4.

Figure 2-3:
Tell
Code::Blocks
where to
place the
Debug and
Release ver-
sions of your
application.

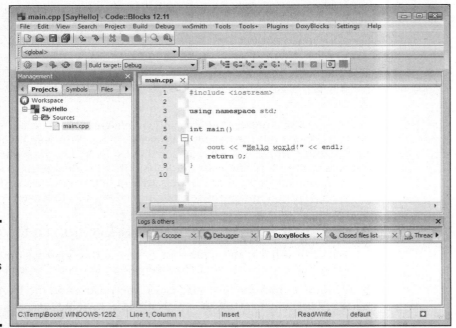

Figure 2-4:
Use the
Code::Blocks
IDE to
interact with
your project.

The project window is organized side by side:

✦ The left side is an Explorer view (called a *tree view*), which represents your project. At the top of the tree view is a workspace — the essential unit of a project. Below the workspace is the name of your project. Underneath that are the components of your project. In this case, only one component exists so far: the source-code file whose filename is main.cpp. Remember that, in order to program in C++, you enter code into a source-code file; this file, called main.cpp, is such a file for your SayHello project.

✦ The right side (which actually takes up about three-quarters of the screen) is the source-code file itself.

This part works much like a word processor or an e-mail editor, and you can type the code into the window. You notice that you already have some code there — a sort of starter code that came into being when you chose Console Application and created the project.

✦ At the bottom of the display are a number of status windows. The Code::Blocks window tells you how the wizard created your application. Don't worry about these windows right now. You see them in action as the book progresses.

Building and executing your first application

Okay, it's time to work with your first application. Use the following steps to save the file, build the application (make it into an executable that your operating system can use), and execute the application:

1. **Save the code file by choosing File⇨Save Everything.**

Saving the files ensures that you have a good copy on disk should something go wrong. For example, you could completely crash the IDE if your application does the wrong thing.

2. **Choose Build⇨Build or press Ctrl+F9.**

This action creates the executable file. Building the code converts words you understand into code that your operating system understands. Notice that Code::Blocks automatically selects the Build Log window for you and you see the steps that Code::Blocks takes to create your application. At the end of the process, you should see 0 errors, 0 warnings (0 minutes, 1 seconds) as the output.

3. **Choose Build⇨Run or press Ctrl+F10.**

An output window like the one shown in Figure 2-5 opens, and you see your first application execute.

4. **Press Enter to stop application execution.**

   The application window disappears and you see the Code::Blocks IDE again.

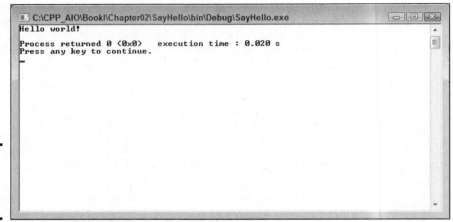

Figure 2-5:
Execute
your first
application.

Well, that wasn't interesting, was it? But that's okay! The application starts out in a basic situation: You have a console window, and then when the application is finished doing whatever it must do, it shows the message `Press any key to continue` — and when you do so, the application ends.

Typing the Code

The rightmost 75 percent or so of the Code::Blocks window is the *code editor;* it's where you type and change your code. Of all the tasks we just mentioned in the first part of this chapter, the nearest equivalent to using the Code::Blocks code editor is composing an e-mail message.

Word movement and selection actions look a bit strange on the screen. They ignore certain characters, such as *braces* — the curly characters { and }.

The code editor works like the editor in an e-mail message. You can

✦ Type code.

✦ Move the *cursor* with the arrow keys (up, down, left, right) to the position where you want to type. The *cursor* is the little blinking vertical bar that shows where your text goes when you type. Some folks call it a *caret* or an *insertion point*.

✦ Click where you want to type. Use the mouse to point where you want to type, and then click the mouse button. The cursor jumps to the spot where you click.

✦ Select text to delete or change. You can select text in either of two ways:

  • Point with the mouse at the first or last character you want to select; then hold down the mouse button while you drag the mouse.

  • Move the cursor to the first or last character you want to select; then hold down the Shift key while you press the arrow keys.

✦ Scroll the text up and down (vertically) or left and right (horizontally) with the scroll bars. The scroll bars work only when there is more text than you can see in the window, just like most other places in the Windows, Linux, and Mac worlds. You can scroll up and down (if there's enough text in the editor) by using Ctrl+↑ and Ctrl+↓ key combinations.

✦ Scrolling changes only what you *see*. You must use the mouse or the arrow keys to *select* what you see.

After you play around a bit with the editor, you can use Table 2-1 to do a few of your favorite tasks. (Of course, if you're new to programming, you may not know yet whether these are your favorites — but they will be soon. Trust me.)

Table 2-1	Navigation and Edit Commands
Command	*Keystroke or Action*
Move the cursor	↑, ↓, ←, or →, Home, End
Move from word to word	Ctrl+← or Ctrl+→
Select with the mouse	Click the mouse in the text, and while the mouse button is down, drag the mouse
Select with the cursor	Shift+↑, Shift+↓, Shift+←, or Shift+→
Select the next word	Shift+Ctrl+→
Select the previous word	Shift+Ctrl+←
Select everything	Ctrl+A
Go to the top	Ctrl+Home
Go to the bottom	Ctrl+End

Starting with Main

When a computer runs code, it does so in a step-by-step, line-by-line manner. But your code is organized into pieces, and one of these pieces is the *main function,* or simply *main().* main() is the part that runs *first.* main() tells the computer which *other* parts of the application you want to use. main() is the head honcho, the big boss.

How does the computer know what is main()? You type lines of code between the *brace* characters, *{* and *}.* Here is the default application that Code::Blocks produces when you create a Console Application project:

```
int main()
{
    cout << "Hello world!" << endl;
    return 0;
}
```

The word main is required, and it tells the computer where main() is. You might also see main() shown as

```
int main(int argc, char *argv[])
```

Don't worry about the words around main() for now. You discover what these words mean later in the chapter. For now, all you need to know is that every C++ application has a main() function.

The computer performs the code line by line. If a line is blank, the computer just goes to the next line. When you write lines of code, you are instructing the computer to do something (which is why some people refer to lines of code as *instructions*).

Showing Information

Ready to type some code and try it out? Let's do it! This code will open the famous console window and write some words to it.

First, make sure that you still have the Code::Blocks IDE open and the SayHello project open, as in this chapter's preceding examples. *If not, follow these steps:*

1. **Start Code::Blocks if it's not already running.**

   You see the Start page for the Code::Blocks IDE.

2. **Click the SayHello.cbp project found in the Recent Projects list.**

   Code::Blocks opens the project for you.

If the `main.cpp` code isn't showing in the rightmost 75 percent of the window, click `main.cpp` in the tree view on the left. It will immediately open. (If you don't see the tree view, click the little tab at the top that says `Projects`; it's next to a tab that says `Symbols`.)

Follow these steps carefully. Make sure that you type everything exactly as given here:

1. **Position the cursor on the line with the opening brace.**

   In this case, that's Line 6. You can see the line number on the left side of the code editor.

2. **Press the Enter key.**

   The cursor should be in the fifth column. If it isn't — if it stays in the first column — then press the spacebar four times.

3. **Type the following line of code exactly as it appears here.**

   Put no spaces between the two less-than (<) symbols. Make sure that you remember the final semicolon at the end. Here's the line:

   ```
   cout << "Hello, I am your computer talking." << endl;
   ```

4. **Delete the line of code that looks like this:**

   ```
   cout << "Hello world!" << endl;
   ```

In the end, your code will look like the following example (the new line that you typed is shown here in bold):

```
#include <iostream>

using namespace std;

int main()
{
    cout << "Hello, I am your computer talking." << endl;
    return 0;
}
```

If you don't type your code correctly, the computer can tell you. This step *compiles* the application: The computer makes sure that what you wrote is okay and then translates it into a *runnable* application. (Don't worry too much about what that means. For now, just think of it as making sure that your application is okay. Appendix A gives you the whole story about compiling.)

To find out whether your application is good to go, choose Build⇨Build.

If all is well, you see a window in the lower-left of the main Code::Blocks window with the really happy message, 0 errors, 0 warnings (0 minutes, 0 seconds). A message like You rock! might be nicer, but 0 errors, 0 warnings (0 minutes, 0 seconds) ain't all that bad.

If you didn't type the line correctly, all is not lost, because the computer will tell you what you did wrong. For example, you might type couts instead of cout. In this case, you will see something like what is shown in Figure 2-6. A list with columns appears at the bottom of your screen.

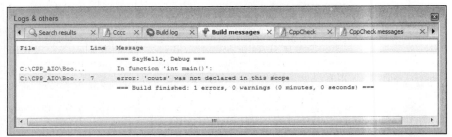

Figure 2-6: Code::Blocks tells you about errors in your application.

+ The leftmost column shows the name of the file where the error was. In this case, the error was in main.cpp, the only file you were working on.

+ The second column shows the *line number* of the problem (in this case, 7).

+ The third column of the list makes a basic attempt to tell you what you did wrong, like this:

```
error: 'couts' was not declared in this scope
```

When the compiler doesn't recognize a word, it says that the word is not declared. In other words, the compiler doesn't know what couts is. (The word should be cout.)

If you want to see the problem, you can point at the error report line and double-click. The bad line appears in the code editor, with a little red box next to the line. The line is also highlighted. As soon as you press an arrow key, the highlight vanishes.

Thus, if you press the → key a few times and get to the word couts and then delete the letter s, you can try again. If you choose Build⇨Build, this time you see the happy message 0 errors, 0 warnings (0 minutes, 0 seconds). Excellent!

No errors means that the application is good enough to run. So run it!

Choose Build➪Run. A console appears with text that looks like this:

```
Hello I am your computer talking.

Process returned 0 (0x0)   execution time : 0.030 s
Press any key to continue.
```

See what happened? There is now a message that says, `Hello, I am your computer talking`. Apparently, the thing you typed caused that message to appear. (Go ahead and press Enter to close the console.)

And in fact, that's exactly what happened. That's how you make a message appear on the console screen. The steps look like this:

1. **Type** `cout`.

   Although `cout` looks like it's pronounced "cowt," most programmers say "see-out." Think of it as shorthand for *console output*. (But don't type *console output* in its place, because the compiler won't accept that.)

2. **After the word** `cout`, **type a space and then type two less-than signs (make sure to leave that single space before them).**

   These less-than signs just mean that *the thing that follows will appear on the console*. The thing that follows, you will notice, is in double quotes. That's the way the computer knows where it starts and ends. The words and stuff inside these double quotes is called a *string* because it's a bunch of letters strung together. (We're not making this up.) The computer knows where the string starts because there's a double quote, and it knows where the string ends because there's a double quote. The computer doesn't display these two sets of double quotes when the application runs.

   Then some weirdness follows. There's another set of less-than signs, which means you want to write more to the console. But what follows? It's `endl`. Notice this is not in quotes. Therefore, we are not saying that we want the strange barely pronounceable word "endl" to appear on the screen. Instead, we're using a special notation that tells the computer that we want to end the current line and start fresh on the next line. And if you look at the output, you'll notice that the words that follow (the message about pressing the any key) are, indeed, on the next line. Note that `endl` is pronounced "end-el."

So that's not so bad after all. Let us recap:

✦ The word `cout` means you want to write to the console.

✦ The `<<` symbols together (with no space between them!) mean the thing that follows is what you want to write.

✦ After the `<<` symbol, you tell the computer what you want to write. It can either be a string of letters, symbols, and other characters (all inside quotes), or it can be the word `endl`.

✦ You can put multiple items in a row and have them appear on the console that way, provided you start the line with `cout` and precede each item with the `<<` symbols.

Oh, and if you have a sharp eye, you may notice one more thing we haven't mentioned yet: We included a semicolon at the end of the line. In C++, every line must end with a semicolon. That's just the way it's done.

Statements in C++ end with a semicolon.

It's not quite accurate to say that *every* line must end with a semicolon. You can break any line into multiple lines. The computer doesn't mind. We could just as easily have written our line as the following two lines:

```
cout << "Hello, I am your computer talking."
<< endl;
```

This is fine, provided that you don't split any individual word (such as `cout` and `endl`) or the `<<` symbols or the string. In effect, any place you have a space occurring "naturally" in the code (for example, between `I` and `am`), you can start a new line, if you want. Then, when the whole *statement* is finished, you end with a semicolon. Think of the semicolon as a signal to the computer that the old statement is finished.

Doing some math

You can get the computer to do some math for you; you can use the same `cout` approach we describe in the preceding section; and you can throw in some numbers and arithmetic symbols.

Although addition uses the familiar plus sign (+) and subtraction uses the familiar minus sign (–), multiplication and division use symbols you might not be familiar with. To multiply, you use the asterisk (*); to divide, you use the forward slash (/).

Table 2-2 shows the math symbols.

Table 2-2	Math Symbols
Symbol	*Function*
+	Addition (plus)
–	Subtraction (minus)
*	Multiplication (times)
/	Division (divided by)

Yep, it's now math-with-weird-symbols time. Continue with the source code you already have. Click somewhere on the line you typed — you know, the one that looks like this:

```
cout << "Hello, I am your computer talking." << endl;
```

Press End so that the cursor moves to the end of the line. Then press Enter so that you can start a new line between the `cout` line and the line that starts with the word `return`.

Whenever you want to insert a line between two other lines, the easiest way to get it right is to go to the first of those two lines, press End, and then press Enter. This will insert a new, blank line in the right place.

After you press Enter, you will notice that something happened: The cursor is not at the start of the newly inserted line; instead, it has four spaces and it's indented flush with the other lines. That's not a mistake. Believe it or not, it's a serious lifesaver. Well, okay, maybe not a lifesaver, but it's almost as good as those little candies that everybody loves. The reason is that often you indent your code (this particular code is indented four spaces); if you're typing lots of code, it's a bummer to have to type four spaces (or press the Tab key) every time you start a new line. So Code::Blocks considerately (and automatically) does the indentation for you.

If, for some reason, your code didn't automatically indent and the cursor is loitering at the beginning of the line, the auto-indent feature is not turned on. It *should* be on by default, but if it isn't, here's how to turn it on:

1. **Choose Settings⇨Editor Options.**

   The Configure Editor dialog box appears.

2. **Make sure that the Tab Indents check box is selected and then click OK.**

3. **Once back in the code, press Backspace to delete your new line and then try pressing Enter again.**

   Behold! The code automatically indents.

4. **After your new, blank line appears and indents itself, type the following:**

   ```
   cout << 5 + 10 << endl;
   ```

   The beginning and the end of this line are just like those of the line you typed earlier. The difference is the middle — instead of typing a string, you type a math problem: 5 plus 10. Note that we put spaces around the 5, around the +, and around the 10 — but not between the 1 and 0. If you put a space there, the computer gets confused (it doesn't know that you meant to write a single two-digit number). When you're finished, your code should look like the following code snippet (here the new line you typed is shown in bold):

```
#include <iostream>

using namespace std;

int main()
{
    cout << "Hello, I am your computer talking." << endl;
    cout << 5 + 10 << endl;
    return 0;
}
```

5. Save your work by choosing File⇨Save Everything.

Instead of choosing File⇨Save Everything, you can recognize that the only thing that changed is the source-code file you're currently working on. If you see the blinking cursor in the code editor, you know that the code editor is active. If not, click somewhere in your code to activate the editor. When you see the blinking cursor, press Ctrl+S. This saves your file.

In the computer world, there's an adage that goes something like this: "Save early, save often." Get in the habit of pressing Ctrl+S every so often. You won't wear out your hard drive, and the keyboard is pretty durable. Every time we type a few lines of code, we press Ctrl+S. Before we compile, we press Ctrl+S. When we're feeling paranoid that the last Ctrl+S didn't stick, we press Ctrl+S. When we're stuck at a traffic light, we press Ctrl+S.

Now you can tell the computer to compile your code. If you haven't saved it, do so now by pressing Ctrl+S. Then choose Build⇨Build. If you typed everything correctly, you should see the magical message 0 errors, 0 warnings (0 minutes, 0 seconds) appear in the Build Log window. But if not, don't worry; you can easily fix it. Look at your code and find the difference between the line we wrote earlier and your code. Here it is again, just for safe measure:

```
cout << 5 + 10 << endl;
```

There is a space after cout, a space after <<, a space after 5, a space after +, a space after 10, and a space after <<. And there is a semicolon at the end. Make sure that these are all correct.

Then when you successfully compile and see the happy message 0 errors, 0 warnings, you are ready to run your application. Choose Build⇨Run.

A console window opens, and you should see the following:

```
Hello I am your computer talking.
15

Process returned 0 (0x0)   execution time : 0.015 s
Press any key to continue.
```

Notice the second line is the answer to the math problem 10 + 5. That means the computer knows how to do math, more or less correctly. (Okay, it had *better be* correct, or we're going to demand a refund from our teachers.)

Ordering the operations

If you want, you can play around with some more complicated problems. For example, you can try something like this:

```
cout << 5 + 10 / 2 * 3 + 25 << endl;
```

What do you think the answer will be? The answer depends on computer rules for the *order* in which it performs math problems. These are called *orders of operation*. Multiplication and division take precedence over addition and subtraction. Therefore, the computer does all the multiplication and division first from left to right; then it does the addition and subtraction from left to right. Figure 2-7 shows the order in which the computer does this particular math problem.

Figure 2-7:
The computer likes to use orders of operation.

$$5 + \underline{10/2} * 3 + 25$$
$$\downarrow$$
$$5 + \underline{5 * 3} + 25$$
$$\downarrow$$
$$\underline{5 + 15} + 25$$
$$\downarrow$$
$$\underline{20 + 25}$$
$$\downarrow$$
$$45$$

Going overboard

The computer actually has various limits, including when it comes to math. If you try something like this:

```
cout << 8762547892451 * 10 / 2 * 3 + 25 << endl;
```

an error message shows up in the error window when you try to compile:

```
error: integer constant is too large for "long" type
```

This message is bad. The reason is that you've gone beyond the limits of what this style of math enables you to do. So be careful.

You can also go too big when you run your application — and (unfortunately) you won't know it. For example, the line

```
cout << 12345 * 12345 * 12345 * 12345 * 12345 << endl;
```

will *compile* correctly — but (aieee!) shows the following result:

```
253233049
```

Nope, it's not correct. Not even a good guess. So the moral here is mainly to use the approach to coding shown in this section only when you're using basic math and don't have to juggle really big numbers. If you're getting over five or six digits, you're getting into too-big territory.

The greatest positive number you can use is 2,147,483,647. The greatest negative number is –2,147,483,647. However, if you're willing to stick to only positive numbers and 0, the computer can make some adjustments inside and handle a higher positive number. In that case, your numbers can range from 0 to 4,294,967,295.

Pairing the parentheses

If you want to get around the order in which the computer does its math, you can add parentheses. For example, if you use the following line, the computer does the final operation (+) before it does the others:

```
cout << 5 + 10 / 2 * (3 + 25) << endl;
```

Whereas previously, without the parentheses, this thing came out to be 45, now it comes out to be 145. First the computer does the 3 + 25 to get 28. Then it begins with the multiplication and division, from left to right. So it takes 10 / 2 to get 5, and then multiplies that by (3 + 25), or 28, to get 140. Then it starts with the addition and subtraction from left to right. So it adds 5 to this to get the final number, 145.

Tabbing your output

Just as you can write a string of letters and numbers to the console, you can also write a tab. For example, change the following line from your application

```
cout << "Hello, I am your computer talking." << endl;
```

to the line shown in bold in the following code:

```
#include <iostream>

using namespace std;

int main()
{
    cout << "Hello\tI am your computer talking." << endl;
    return 0;
}
```

In the preceding code, we replaced the comma and space with a backslash and then a lowercase t. (We also removed the extra line about math, just in case you tried the math from the preceding section.) But when you compile and run this application (remember to *compile it first!*), it won't print exactly what's in the double quotes. Here's what you see:

```
Hello   I am your computer talking.
```

The extra space in the displayed line is a *tab space,* just as if you had pressed the Tab key while typing this. (Is that slick, or what?)

There's a complication to using the backslash: You can't just type a backslash (or a double quote, for that matter) and expect to see it on the screen. A couple of workarounds will show the actual characters:

✦ Really want to display a backslash, not a special character? Use a backslash followed by another backslash. (Yes, it's bizarre.) The compiler treats only the *first* backslash as special. When a string has two backslashes in a row, the compiler treats the second backslash as, well, a backslash.

For example, the following line of code has *two* backslashes:

```
cout << "\\tabc" << endl;
```

The following text shows up at the console:

```
\tabc
```

✦ If a string starts with a double quote and ends with a double quote, how in the world would you actually *print* a double quote? Type a backslash and then a double quote, as in the following code:

```
cout << "Backslash and double quote equal \" in C++." << endl;
```

When that code runs in an application, you see this on the screen:

```
Backslash and double quote equal " in C++.
```

C++ programmers use the term *escape-sequence* to refer to any special character in a string that starts with a backslash. This is an outdated bit of vocabulary — maybe not as old as "methinks," but it does date back to the original C language of the 1970s. Back then, you made special characters appear on console screens by first pressing the Esc key.

Let Your Application Run Away

The word *execute* refers to running your application, but you need to compile (or *build,* using the Code::Blocks terminology) the application before you run it. The compilation process transforms your application into an executable file. An *executable file* is a special type of file that contains an application you can run on your computer. When you run your word processor application, you run an executable file containing the word processor application.

After the computer compiles (builds) your application, it performs a step called *linking*. People often refer to these two steps together as simply *compiling*. Indeed, in this book, we often use the term to mean both steps together. If you're curious about what goes on here, take a look at Appendix A. It has a section devoted to the compiling and linking processes.

Whenever you want to run your application, you first compile it and then you run it. If you make more changes to your application, you must compile it again before running it. Otherwise, the executable file won't have your changes.

Because you almost always use Build and Run in sequence, the kind people who built Code::Blocks included a special menu item called Build and Run on the Build menu. The computer first compiles your code, and then it immediately runs the application if there are no errors. If there are errors, the compiler doesn't run the application, and the errors are reported as usual.

We almost always use the Build and Run option rather than click Build and then Run separately. Sometimes, the old-fashioned approach is more efficient: When we compile and run our applications, we use shortcut keys. It takes a bit of extra time to grab the mouse, move the pointer to a menu, and so on. Instead, we press F9 to compile.

Table 2-3 lists keyboard shortcuts for compiling.

Table 2-3	**Keyboard Shortcuts for Compiling and Running**
Action	*Keyboard Shortcut*
Build	Ctrl+F9
Run	Ctrl+F10
Build and run	F9

Chapter 3: Storing Data in C++

In This Chapter

✔ Using storage bins called variables

✔ Working with integer variables

✔ Using character variables

✔ Manipulating strings

✔ Using Boolean variables

✔ Using conditional operators

✔ Reading from the console

*W*e all love to store things away. The closet is a perfect example of a place to store things. We have boxes in our closets that we have not opened in years. Perhaps we inadvertently created a time capsule. Or just a fire hazard. When you program a computer, you can also store things away. Most people know that a computer has two kinds of memory: memory inside the chip and memory in the hard drive. But most people use the term *memory* in reference to the memory chip; the other is referred to as simply the hard drive. When you type a business letter in a word processor, the letter is stored in the memory. After you choose File⇨Save, the letter gets stored on the hard drive, but as long as you still have the letter open in the word processor, it's generally still in memory.

The best way to think of memory is as a set of storage bins, much like the ones in the closets that we are afraid of. When you write a computer application, you reserve some storage bins, and you give each storage bin a name. You also say what type of thing can be stored in the storage bin. The technical term for such a storage bin is a *variable*.

In this chapter, we show you how you can use these storage bins in your applications.

Putting Your Data Places: Variables

When you write an application, you specify that you want to make use of one or more storage bins called *variables*. You can put different kinds of things in these storage bins. The difference between these computer storage bins and those in your closet, however, is that each computer storage bin can hold only *one thing at a time*.

You can put many different types of things into your variables, too. For example, you can put numbers in a storage bin, or you can put a string in a storage bin. (However, each storage bin contains a unique kind of data — you can't put a number into a storage bin designed for a string.) Book I, Chapter 2 advises that a *string* is simply a bunch of letters, numbers, or other characters all strung together. As for numbers, they can be either *integers* (which are positive whole numbers, negative whole numbers, and 0) or numbers with a decimal point, such as 3.11 or 10.0, which (for various reasons) are called *floating-point numbers*.

The term *floating-point number* refers to a number that has a decimal point and something to the right of the decimal point (even if it's just a 0). When you see the term *floating point*, you can remember what it means by focusing on the word *point* in its name. Think of *decimal point*.

If you are already familiar with the term *variable* from other fields, be careful not to apply their definitions here. Although they're similar, some significant differences are involved. For example, in algebra, a variable represents an unknown quantity, and you can solve for a variable. But in programming, it's simpler than that: A *variable* is simply a storage bin with an associated name.

Creating an integer variable

In your C++ application, you can easily write a line of code that creates a variable. Although what you're doing at that point is simply writing code (and the variable doesn't actually get created until you run the application), people often refer to this process as *creating a variable*. When we are working with another programmer we like, we often say, "*We'll* go ahead and make a variable." What we're really doing is writing code that tells *the computer* to go ahead and make the variable. And, of course, the computer doesn't actually make the variable until the application runs. If, on the other hand, we're working with a programmer we don't like, we probably won't say anything at all.

A variable has three aspects, as shown in Table 3-1.

Table 3-1	A Variable Has Three Aspects
Aspect	*What It Means*
Name	The name you use in your application to refer to the variable
Type	The type of information that the variable can hold
Value	The actual thing that the storage bin holds

The following list describes the items in Table 3-1 in more detail.

✦ **Name:** Every variable must have a name. In your application, you refer to the variable by this name. For example, you may have a variable called `count`, and you may have a variable called `LastName`. Or you could have a variable called `MisterGates`.

✦ **Type:** When you create a variable, you must specify the type of information the variable can hold. For example, one variable may hold an integer, and another variable may hold a single character. After you pick a type for the variable in your application, you can put only things of that type into the variable.

✦ **Value:** At any given moment, a variable holds a single value. For example, an integer variable might hold the number `10`, and a character variable might hold the character `a`. In your application, you can store something in a variable, and later you can store something else in the variable. When you store something else, the variable forgets what was previously inside it. So, in this sense, you can think of a computer as having a one-track mind.

The code for the `SimpleVariable` example, shown in Listing 3-1, demonstrates how to create a variable. This is a full application that you can run.

Listing 3-1:   Creating a Variable

```
#include <iostream>

using namespace std;

int main()
{
  int mynumber;
  mynumber = 10;
  cout << mynumber << endl;
  return 0;
}
```

Take a careful look at Listing 3-1. Remember that the computer starts with the code inside the braces that follow the word `main`, and it performs the code line by line.

The first line inside `main` looks like this:

```
int mynumber;
```

When you declare a variable, the first thing you specify is the type of thing the variable can hold. Here, we used the word `int`. This word is the C++ word for *integer*. Thus, the variable that we're declaring can hold an integer. Next is the name of the variable. This variable is named `mynumber`. Then a semicolon ends the variable declaration.

Notice that, in this line, we have covered two of the three aspects of variables: We have given the variable a name, and we have told the computer what type of thing we want the variable to hold. The order seems a little odd — in C++, we first say the type and then the name. That's just the way it's done in C++, and a good reason stands behind it, which you can read about in "Declaring multiple variables," later in this chapter.

The next line looks like this:

```
mynumber = 10;
```

This line puts something in the variable. It puts the number 10 in it. Because we already said that the variable can hold an integer, you're allowed to put in a 10 because it is an integer. If you had tried to put something other than an integer in the variable, the compiler would have given you an error. The compiler makes sure that you put into a variable only the type of thing that you said you would. The compiler is good at keeping you in line. And of course you noticed that the statement ends with a semicolon. In C++, every statement ends with a semicolon.

To put something in a variable, you type the variable's name, an equal sign (surrounded by optional spaces), and the value. You then end the line with a semicolon. This line of code is an *assignment*. Or you can say that you are *setting* the variable to the value.

The next line is this:

```
cout << mynumber << endl;
```

Book I, Chapter 2 describes what this line does. It's a cout statement, which means that it writes something on the console. As you can probably guess, this code tells the computer to write the *value* of mynumber on the console. It does not write the string *mynumber*. Rather, it writes whatever happens to be stored in the storage bin. The previous line of code puts a 10 in the storage bin, and so this line prints a *10* on the console. When you run the application, you see this:

```
10
```

Think of it like this: When you type the variable's name, you are accessing the variable. The exception to this is when the variable's name appears to the left of an equal sign. In that case, you are setting the variable.

You can do two things with a variable:

+ **Set the variable:** You can set a variable, which means that you can put something inside the storage bin.

+ **Retrieve the value:** You can get back the value that is inside the variable. When you do so, the value stays inside it; you are not, so to speak, *taking it out.*

When you retrieve the value that is in a variable, you are not *removing* it from the variable. The value is still inside the variable.

Declaring multiple variables

Many years ago, when we first learned the original C programming language (which was the language that served as the predecessor to C++), we thought it odd that we had to first say the type of the variable and then the name. But this actually works out well because it makes declaring multiple variables of the same type easy. If you want to declare three integer variables in a row, you can do it all in one shot, like this:

```
int tom, dick, harry;
```

This statement declares three separate variables. The first is called `tom`; the second is called `dick`; and the third is called `harry`. Each of these three variables holds an integer. You have not put anything in any of them, so you may follow that with some code to stuff each of them full with a number. For example, this code puts the number `10` in `tom`, the number `20` in `dick`, and the number `3254` in `harry`.

```
tom = 10;
dick = 20;
harry = 3254;
```

When you run your applications, the computer executes the statements in the order that they appear in your code. Therefore, in the preceding code, the computer first creates the three storage bins. Then it puts a `10` inside `tom`. (Now doesn't that sound yummy?) Next, `dick` gets a `20`. And finally, `harry` consumes a `3254`.

Changing values

Although a variable can hold only one thing at a time, you can still change what the variable holds. After you put something else in a variable, it forgets what it originally had. So when people accuse us of being forgetful, we can just say, "Yes, but you should see that computer we work with all day long!"

You put something new in the variable in the same way you originally put something in it.

Look closely at the code for the `ChangeVariable` example in Listing 3-2. Notice that the first part of the application is just like Listing 3-1. But then we added two more lines (shown in bold) that look pretty much like the previous two: The first one sticks something (20) in the same variable as before, and the next one writes this new value out to the console.

Listing 3-2: Changing a Variable

```
#include <iostream>

using namespace std;

int main()
{
  int mynumber;
  mynumber = 10;
  cout << mynumber << endl;
 mynumber = 20;
 cout << mynumber << endl;
  return 0;
}
```

As before, the line where you put something new in the variable follows the same format: There's an equal sign, with the variable on the left and the new value on the right. As described earlier in this chapter, this statement is an *assignment* statement.

When you see a single equal sign by itself, the item on the left side is the variable or item that receives the information that is on the right side.

Setting one variable equal to another

Because you can do only two direct things with variables — put something in and retrieve the value — setting one variable equal to another is a simple process of retrieving the value of one variable and putting it in the other. This process is often referred to as *copying* the variable from one to another.

For example, if you have two integer variables — say, start and finish — and you want to copy the value of start into finish, you would use a line of code like the following:

```
finish = start;
```

Don't let the language confuse you. Although we said "copy the value of start into finish," notice that the first thing we typed was finish, and then the equal sign, and then start. The left side of the equal sign is what *receives* the value; it is an *assignment* statement.

When you copy the value of one variable to another, the two variables must be the same type. You cannot, for instance, copy the value from a string variable into an integer variable. If you try, the compiler issues an error message and stops.

After the computer runs this copy statement, the two variables hold the same thing. The code for CopyVariable, shown in Listing 3-3, is an example of copying one variable to another.

Listing 3-3: Copying a Value from One Variable to Another

```
#include <iostream>

using namespace std;

int main()
{
  int start = 50;
  int finish;
  finish = start;
  cout << finish << endl;
  return 0;
}
```

Initializing a variable

When you create a variable, it starts out as an empty storage bin. Before it can be of much use, you need to put something in it.

If you try to retrieve the contents of a variable before you actually put anything in it, you end up with what computer people fondly call "unpredictable results." What they really mean to say is, "Don't do this because who knows what's in it." It's kind of like if you go in the attic and you discover that the former owners left behind a big, ominous box. Do you *really* want to look inside it? With variables, the problem you run into is that the computer memory has something stored in that particular place where the variable now sits, and that stored item is probably just some number left over from something else. But you can't know in advance what it is. So always make sure that you place a value inside a variable before you try to retrieve its contents, a process called *initializing the variable*.

You can initialize a variable in two ways. The first way is by declaring the variable and then assigning something into it, which takes two lines of code:

```
int mynumber;
mynumber = 153;
```

But the other way is a bit quicker. It looks like this:

```
int mynumber = 153;
```

This method combines both strategies into one neat little package that is available for you to use whenever you want. You see us initializing variables both ways in this book, depending on how we feel at the moment.

Creating a great name for yourself

Every variable needs to have a name. But what names can you use? Although you are free to use names such as Fred or Zanzibar or Supercount1000M, there are limits to what you are allowed to use.

MyThis and MyThat

As you progress through your computer programming life (which is, we hope, in addition to your life as a millionaire), you are likely to notice that, for some reason, some computer programmers seem to favor variable names that start with the word *My*. Other computer programmers despise this practice and completely distance themselves from it. We have seen such computer identifiers as MyClass, MyNumber, MyHeight, MyName, MyCar, MyWhatASurprise, MyLar, MyStro, and MyOpic. Personally, we have no problem using names that start with *My*, especially in training exercises.

Although most C++ code is in lowercase, you are free to use uppercase letters in your variable names. However, C++ distinguishes between the two. Therefore, if you have a variable called count, you cannot access it later in your application by calling it Count with a capital C. The compiler treats the two names as two different variables, which makes C++ *case sensitive*. But on the other hand, please don't use two separate variables in the same application — one called count and one called Count. Although the compiler doesn't mind, the mere humans that may have to read your code or work on it later might get confused.

Here are the rules you need to follow when creating a variable name:

✦ **Characters:** You can use any uppercase letter, lowercase letter, number, or underscore in your variable names. Other symbols (such as spaces or the ones above the number keys on your keyboard) are not allowed in variable names. The only catches are that

- The first character *cannot* be a number.

- The variable name *cannot* consist of only numbers.

✦ **Length:** Most compilers these days allow you to have as many characters in the variable name as you want. Just to be sure, and to prove we're easily amused, in Code::Blocks we successfully created a variable with a name that was over 1,000 characters in length. However, we wouldn't want to have to type that thing over and over. Instead, we recommend keeping variable names long enough to make sense but short enough that you can type them easily. Most people prefer anywhere from five to ten characters or so.

Examples of acceptable variable names are Count, current_name, address_1000, and LookupAmount. Table 3-2 lists some variable names that are not allowed.

Table 3-2	Examples of Bad Variable Names
Bad Variable Name	*Why It's Not Allowed*
12345	It has only numbers (and it starts with a number, which is wrong as well).
A&B	The only special character allowed is the underscore, _. The ampersand (&) is not allowed.
1abc	A variable name cannot start with a number.

Manipulating Integer Variables

Just like your friends, integer variables can be manipulated. But in this case, manipulation means simply that you can do arithmetic. You can easily do the usual addition, subtraction, multiplication, and division.

In Book I, Chapter 2, we introduce the characters that you use for the arithmetic operations. They are

+ ✦ + for addition
+ ✦ − for subtraction
+ ✦ * for multiplication
+ ✦ / for division

You can, however, perform another operation with integers, and it has to do with remainders and division. The idea is that if you divide, for example, 16 by 3, the answer in whole numbers is *5 remainder 1.* Another way of saying this is that 16 doesn't divide by 3 evenly, but 3 "goes into" 16 five times, leaving a remainder of 1. This remainder is sometimes called a *modulus.* Computer people actually have an important reason for calling it *modulus* rather than *remainder,* and that's because people in the computer field like to use confusing terms.

When working with integer variables, remember the two basic things you can do with variables: You can put something in a variable, and you can retrieve it from a variable. Therefore, when working with an integer variable, the idea is that you can retrieve the contents, do some arithmetic on it, and then print the answer or store it back into the same variable or another variable.

Adding integer variables

If you want to add two integer variables, use the + symbol. You can either print the result or put it back into a variable.

The AddInteger example adds two variables (start and time) and then prints the answer to the console. The addition operation is shown in bold.

```
#include <iostream>

using namespace std;

int main()
{
  int start;
  int time;
  start = 37;
  time = 22;
  cout << start + time  << endl;
  return 0;
}
```

This code starts with two integer variables called start and time. It then sets start to 37 and sets time to 22. Finally, it adds the two variables (to get 59) and prints the results.

In this example, however, the computer doesn't actually do anything with the final sum, 59, except print it. If you want to use this value later, you can save it in its own variable. The AddInteger2 example demonstrates how to save the result in a variable; the storage operation is shown in bold:

```
#include <iostream>

using namespace std;

int main()
{
  int start;
  int time;
  int total;
  start = 37;
  time = 22;
  total = start + time;
  cout << total << endl;
  return 0;
}
```

In this code, you declare the integer variable total along with the others. Then after you store 37 in start and 22 in time, you add the two and save the total in the variable called total. Then you finally print the value stored in total.

You can also add numbers themselves to variables. The following line adds 5 to `start` and prints the result:

```
cout << start + 5 << endl;
```

Or you can save the value back in another variable, as in the following fragment:

```
total = start + 5;
cout << total << endl;
```

This example adds 5 to `start` and saves the new value in `total`.

When you use code such as `total = start + 5;`, although you are adding 5 to `start`, you are not actually changing the value stored in `start`. The `start` variable itself remains the same as it was before this statement runs. Rather, the computer figures out the result of `start + 5` and saves that value inside `total`. Thus, `total` is the only variable that changes here.

Now, here's where things get a little tricky in the logical arena. This might seem strange at first, but you can actually do something like this:

```
total = total + 5;
```

If you have taken some math courses, you might find this statement a little bizarre, just like the math courses themselves. But remember that `total` is a variable *in computer programming,* and that definition is a bit different in the math world.

This statement really just means you're going to add 5 to the value stored in `total`, and you'll take the value you get back and store it *back in* `total`. In other words, `total` will now be 5 greater than it was to begin with.

The `AddInteger3` example shows this technique in action:

```
#include <iostream>

using namespace std;

int main()
{
  int total;
  total = 12;
  cout << total << endl;
  total = total + 5;
  cout << total << endl;
  return 0;
}
```

When you run this application, you see the following output on the console:

```
12
17
```

Notice what took place. First, you put the value 12 inside `total` and print the value to the console. Then you add 5 to `total`, store that back in `total`, and print the new value of `total` to the console.

Now, it's no big secret that we computer people are lazy. After all, why would we own computers if we weren't? And so the great makers of the C++ language gave us a bit of a shortcut for adding a value to a variable and storing it back in the variable. The line

```
total = total + 5;
```

is the same as

```
total += 5;
```

We computer folks also have a special way of pronouncing +=. We say "plus equal." So for this line, we would say, "Total plus equal five."

Think of the `total += 5` notation as simply a shortcut for `total = total + 5;`.

You can also use the += notation with other variables. For example, if you want to add the value in `time` to the value in `total` and store the result back in `total`, you can do this

```
total = total + time;
```

or you can use this shortcut:

```
total += time;
```

If you are adding just 1 to a variable, you can use an even shorter shortcut. It looks like this:

```
total++;
```

This is the same as `total = total + 1;`.

And now the answer to The Great Question

In C++, as well as in the original C language (upon which C++ is based), the operator ++ adds 1 to a variable. So this finally brings us to a point where we can answer The Great Question: Where did the name C++ come from? When the guy who originally designed C++, Bjarne Stroustrup, needed a name for his language, he decided to look into its roots for the answer. He had based the language on C; and in C, to add 1 to something, you use the ++ operator. And because he felt that he added only 1 thing to the language, he decided to call the new language C++. Okay, that's not quite true; Bjarne actually added a great deal to the language. But that entire great deal can be thought of as just one thing made of lots of smaller things. What did he add? The main thing of those smaller things is the capability to do object-oriented programming. That's something we cover in the next chapter. And by the way, the originator of C++, Mr. Stroustrup, is still alive and still doing work for the language at AT&T. You can see his web page at

```
http://www.research.att.
  com/~bs
```

Table 3-3 summarizes the different things you can do that involve the addition of variables.

Table 3-3	Doing Things with Addition
What You Can Do	*Sample Statement*
Add two variables	`cout << start + time << endl;`
Add a variable and a number	`cout << start + 5 << endl;`
Add two variables and save the result in a variable	`total = start + time;`
Add a variable and a number and save the result in a variable	`total = start + 5;`
Add a number to what's already in a variable	`total = total + 5;`
Add a number to what's already in a variable by using a shortcut	`total += 5;`
Add a variable to what's already in a variable	`total = total + time;`
Add a variable to what's already in a variable by using a shortcut	`total += time;`
Add 1 to a variable	`total++;`

Subtracting integer variables

Everything you can do involving the addition of integer variables you can also do with subtraction. For example, you can subtract two variables, as shown in the SubtractVariable example in Listing 3-4.

Listing 3-4:   **Subtracting Two Variables**

```
#include <iostream>

using namespace std;

int main()
{
  int final;
  int time;
  final = 28;
  time = 18;
  cout << final - time << endl;
  return 0;
}
```

When this application runs, the console shows the number 10, which is 28 − 18. Remember that, as with addition, the value of neither final nor time actually changed. The computer just figured out the difference and printed the answer on the console without modifying either variable.

You can also subtract a number from a variable, and (as before) you still aren't changing the value of the variable, as in the following example:

```
cout << final - 5 << endl;
```

You can subtract one variable from another and save the result in a third variable:

```
start = final - time;
```

And you can change the value in a variable by using subtraction, as in the following four sample lines of code. This first subtracts time from start and saves the result back in start:

```
final = final - time;
```

Or you can do the same thing by using the shortcut notation:

```
final -= time;
```

Or you can do the same thing with a number:

```
final = final - 12;
```

And (as before) you can alternatively do the same thing with a shortcut:

```
final -= 12;
```

Finally, as with addition, you have a shortcut to a shortcut. If you want only to subtract 1, you can simply use two minus signs, as in

```
final--;
```

This line is pronounced "minus minus."

Multiplying integer variables

To do multiplication in C++, you use the asterisk (*) symbol. As with addition and subtraction, you can multiply two variables, or you can multiply a variable by a number. You can either print the result or save it in a variable.

For example, you can multiply two variables and print the results to the console with the following line:

```
cout << length * width << endl;
```

Or you can multiply a variable by a number, as in this line:

```
cout << length * 5 << endl;
```

And as with addition and subtraction, you can multiply two variables and save the result in a third variable:

```
area = length * width;
```

And you can use multiplication to modify a variable's value, as in

```
total = total * multiplier;
```

Or, to use the shortcut:

```
total *= multiplier;
```

And (as before) you can do the same with just a number

```
total = total * 25;
```

or this:

```
total *= 25;
```

Dividing integer variables

Although addition, subtraction, and multiplication are straightforward with integer variables, division is a bit trickier. The chief reason is that, with whole numbers, sometimes you just can't divide evenly. It's like trying to divide 21 tortilla chips *evenly* among 5 people. You just can't do it. Either somebody will feel cheated, or everyone will get 4 chips, and 1 will be left over for everyone to fight over. Of course, you could break every chip into 5 pieces, and then each person gets ⅕ of each chip, but then you're no longer working with whole numbers — just a bunch of crumbs.

If you use a calculator and type 21 divided by 5, you get 4.2, which is not a whole number. If you want to stick to whole numbers, you have to use the notion of a remainder. In the case of 21 divided by 5, the remainder is 1, as you figured out with the tortilla chips. The reason is that the highest multiple of 5 in 21 is 20 (because 5 times 4 is 20), and 1 is left over. That lonely 1 is the remainder.

So in terms of strictly whole numbers, the answer to 21 divided by 5 is *4 remainder 1*. And that's how the computer does arithmetic with integers: It gets two different answers: The *quotient* and the *remainder*. In math terms, the main answer (in our example, 4) is the *quotient*. And what's left over is the *remainder*.

Because two different answers to a division problem may occur, C++ uses two different operators for figuring these two different answers.

To find the quotient, use the slash (/). Think of this character as the usual division operator, because when you deal with numbers that divide evenly, this operator gives you the correct answer. Thus, 10 / 2 gives you 5, as you would expect. Further, most people just call this the division operator, anyway.

To find the remainder, use the percent sign (%). This is often called the *modulus operator*.

The `DivideInteger` example shown in Listing 3-5 takes two numbers and prints their quotient and remainder. Then it does it again for another pair of numbers. The first pair has no remainder, but the second pair does.

Listing 3-5: Finding Quotients and Remainders

```
#include <iostream>

using namespace std;

int main()
{
  int first, second;
  cout << "Dividing 28 by 14." << endl;
  first = 28;
```

```
    second = 14;
    cout << "Quotient  " << first / second << endl;
    cout << "Remainder " << first % second << endl;
    cout << "Dividing 32 by 6." << endl;
    first = 32;
    second = 6;
    cout << "Quotient  " << first / second << endl;
    cout << "Remainder " << first % second << endl;
    return 0;
}
```

When you run this application, you see the following output:

```
Dividing 28 by 14.
2
0
Dividing 32 by 6.
5
2
```

Notice, in Listing 3-5, that we used a couple new tricks in addition to (or divided by?) the division tricks. For one, we combined our variable declarations of `first` and `second` variables into one statement. A comma separates the variable names, and we wrote the type (`int`) only once. Next, you combine the output of strings and numbers into a single `cout` statement. We did this for four of the `cout` statements. That's acceptable, as long as you string them together with the `<<` signs between each of them.

You have access to all the usual goodies with both the division (/) and remainder (%) operators. For example, you can store the quotient in another variable, as you can with the remainder:

```
myQuotient = first / second;
myRemainder = first % second;
```

And you have shortcuts available:

```
int first = 30;
first /= 5;
cout << first << endl;
```

In this case, `first` becomes 6 because 30 / 5 is 6.

And in the following case, `first` becomes 3 because the remainder of 33 divided by 6 is 3:

```
int first = 33;
first %= 5;
cout << first << endl;
```

Characters

Another type of variable you can have is a character variable. A *character variable* can hold a single — *just one* — character. It holds a value between –127 and 128 or between 0 and 255. Normally, a *character* is anything that can be typed, such as a letter of the alphabet, a digit, or another symbol you see on the computer keyboard, but a character can also hold nonprintable values.

To use a character variable, you use the type name char. To initialize a character variable, you put the character inside *single* quotes. (If you use double quotes, the compiler issues an error message.) The following is an example of a character:

```
char ch;
ch = 'a';
cout << ch << endl;
```

The character variable here is called ch. We initialized it to the character a, which, you notice, is surrounded by single quotes. We then printed it by using cout.

Null character

One important character in the programming world is the *null* character. Deep down inside the computer's memory, the computer stores each character by using a number, and the null character's number is 0. There's nothing to actually see with the null character; we can't draw a picture of it in this book for you to hang on your wall. (Bummer.) All we can do is describe it. Yes, every once in a while, computer people have to become philosophers. But the null character is important because it is often used to signify the end of something — not the end of the world or anything big like that, but the end of some data.

To notate the null character in C++, use \0, as in

```
char mychar = '\0';
```

Nonprintable and other cool characters

In addition to the null character, several other cool characters are available — some that have a look to them and can be printed and some that do not and cannot. The null character is an example of a *nonprintable* character. You can try to print one, but you get either a blank space or nothing at all, depending on the compiler.

But some characters are special in that they do something when you print, though you can't type them directly. One example is the newline character.

The *newline* character symbolizes the start of a new line of text. In all cases, the computer places the *insertion point*, the place where it adds new characters, on the next line. If you are printing some text to the console and then you print a newline character, any text that follows will be on the next line. Most compilers these days start the text at the far left end of the next line (Column 1), but some compilers start the text in the next column on the next line, as in the following output. In this case, the text appears on the next line, but it starts at Column 4 rather than at the far left end (Column 1):

```
abc
   def
```

Here, you print abc, and then a newline, and then def. Notice that the def continues in the same position it would have been had it been on the first line. For the compilers that we use in this book, however, printing abc, and then a newline, and finally def results in this output:

```
abc
def
```

But to accommodate the fact that some other compilers sometimes treat a newline as just that (start a new line but don't go anywhere else), the creators of the computers gave you another special character: the carriage return. (Can you hear the crowd say, "Ooooh!"?)

The *carriage return* places the insertion point at the start of the line, but not on a new line (which means that if you use just a carriage return on a computer expecting both a carriage return and a newline, you overwrite what's already on the line). That's true with pretty much every C++ compiler.

In Book I, Chapter 2, we describe the tab character and other characters that start with a backslash. These are individual characters, and you can have them inside a character variable, as in the following example, which prints the letter *a,* and then a tab, and then the letter *b.* Notice that, to get the tab character to go into the character variable, you have to use the \ and then a t:

```
char ch = '\t';
cout << "a" << ch << "b" << endl;
```

In Book I, Chapter 2, we mention that to put a double quote inside a string, you needed to precede the double quote with a backslash so that the computer won't think that the double quote is the end of the string. But because a character is surrounded by single quotes, you don't need to do this: You can just put a double quote inside the character, as in

```
char ch = '"';
```

What is that symbol?

Never known to turn down the chance to invent a new word, computer people have come up with names for characters that may not always match the names you know. You've already heard the use of the word *dot* for a period when surfing the Internet. And for some characters that already have multiple names, computer folks may use one name and not the other. And sometimes, just to throw you off, they use the usual name for something. The following are some of the names of symbols that computer people like to use:

  . Dot *(but not* period *or* decimal point*)*

  @ At

  & Ampersand *(but not* and*)*

  # Pound *(but not* number sign*)*

  ! Bang *(though most people still say* exclamation point*)*

  ~ Tilde

  % Percent

  * Star *(not* asterisk*)*

  (Left paren *or* left parenthesis

) Right paren *or* right parenthesis

  [Left square bracket *or* left bracket

  ] Right square bracket *or* right bracket

  == Equal-equal *(not* double equal*)*

  ++ Plus-plus *(not* double plus*)*

  -- Minus-minus *(not* double minus*)*

  / Forward slash

  \ Backslash

  { Left brace *or* left curly brace *or* open brace

  } Right brace *or* right curly brace *or* close brace

  ^ Caret *(though a few people say* hat, *for real — no joke here!)*

  " Double quote

Of course, that raises an important question now: What about single quotes? This time, you *do* have to use the backslash:

```
char ch = '\'';
```

And finally, to put a backslash inside a character, you use two backslashes:

```
char ch = '\\';
```

When the compiler sees a backslash inside a string or a character, it treats the backslash as special and looks at whatever follows it. If you have something like ' \ ' with no other character inside the single quotes following it, the compiler thinks the final quote is to be combined with the backslash. And then it moves forward, expecting a single quote to follow, representing the end. Because a single quote doesn't appear, the compiler gets confused and issues an error. Compilers are easily confused — kind of gives you more respect for the human brain.

Strings

If any single computer word has become so common in programming that most computer people forget that it's a computer word, it's *string*. Book I, Chapter 2 introduces strings and describes what they are, and it gives examples of them. In short, a *string* is simply a set of characters strung together. The compiler knows the start and end of a string in your code based on the location of the double quotes.

You can create a variable that can hold a string. The type you use is `string`. The `CreateString` example shown in Listing 3-6 demonstrates how to use a `string` variable.

Listing 3-6: Using Brackets to Access Individual Characters in a String

```
#include <iostream>

using namespace std;

int main()
{
  string mystring;
  mystring = "abcdef";
  cout << mystring[2] << endl;
```

When you run this application, the string `Hello there` appears on the console. The first line inside `main` creates a string variable called `mystring`. The second line initializes it to `"Hello there"`. The third line prints the string to the console.

Delimiters limit de tokens

When you read an English sentence, you can tell where one word starts and one word ends by looking at the spaces and the punctuation. The same is true in a computer application. Words are normally separated by spaces, but other characters also denote the beginning and end of a word. In a string, this character is the double quote. Such word dividers are called *delimiters* (pronounced "dee-LIM-it-ers"). And just to make sure that you stay confused, computer people use the word *token* to mean the individual words in an application that are set apart by delimiters. However, you won't hear us use that term again in this book, because we prefer the word *word*.

Getting a part of a string

Accessing the individual characters within a string is easy. Take a look at the `IndividualCharacter` example shown in Listing 3-7.

Listing 3-7:   Using the string Type to Create a String Variable

```
#include <iostream>

using namespace std;

int main()
{
  string mystring;
  mystring = "Hello there";
  cout << mystring << endl;
  return 0;
}
```

Notice that the seventh line, the `cout` line, has the word `mystring` followed by a 2 inside brackets. When you run this application, here's what you see:

```
c
```

That's it, just a letter c, hanging out all by itself. The 2 inside brackets means that you want to take the second character of the string and only that character. But wait! Is c the second character? Our eyes may deceive us, but it looks to us like that's the third character. What gives?

Turns out that C++ starts numbering the positions inside the string at 0. So for this string, `mystring[0]` is the first character, which happens to be a. And so, really, `mystring[2]` gets the *third* character. Yes, life gets confusing when you try to hold conversations with programmers, because sometimes they use the phrase *the third character* to mean the third position; but sometimes they use it to mean what's really the *fourth* position. But to those people, the fourth position is actually the fifth position, which is actually the sixth position. Life among computer programmers can be confusing. In general, in this book, we use *fourth position* to mean the fourth position, which you access through `mystring[3]`. (The number inside brackets is called an *index*.)

A string is made of characters. Thus, a single character within a string has the type `char`. This means that you can do something like this:

```
string mystring;
mystring = "abcdef";
char mychar = mystring[2];
cout << mychar << endl;
```

Those strange # lines

Now for those strange-looking lines that start with the # symbol. In Book I, Chapter 6, we talk about how you can divide your code into multiple pieces, each in its own source file. That is a powerful way to create large software applications, because different people can work on the different parts at the same time. But to do so, somehow each file must know what the other files can do. And the way you tell the files about the other files is by putting a line toward the top of your file that looks like this:

```
#include <string>
```

This line means that your application is making use of another file somewhere, and that file has a filename of string. Inside that other file is a bunch of C++ code that essentially gives your

application the ability to understand strings. To see this file in Code::Blocks, right-click the filename and choose Open #Include File: <filename> from the context menu. The line

```
#include <iostream>
```

gives your application the ability to write to the console, among other things.

As you progress through C++, you discover more lines that you can include at the top of your application, each starting with #include and each giving your application more features and capabilities. We use many of these throughout this book. (Now, how is that for a teaser?)

In this example, mychar is a variable of type char. The mystring[2] expression *returns* an item of type char. Thus, the assignment is valid. When you run this, you once again see the single character in the third position:

```
c
```

Changing part of a string

Using the bracket notation, you can also change a character inside a string. The following code, for example, changes the second character in the string (that is, the one with index 1) from a *c* to a *q:*

```
string x = "abcdef";
x[1] = 'q';
cout << x << endl;
```

This code writes the string aqcdef to the console.

Adding onto a string

Any good writer can keep adding more and more letters to a page. And the same is true with the string type: You can easily add to it. The following lines of code use the += operator, which was also used in adding numbers. What do you think this code will do?

```
string mystring;
mystring = "Hi ";
mystring += "there";
cout << mystring << endl;
```

The first line declares the string `mystring`. The second line initializes it to `"Hi "`. But what does the third line do? The third line uses the `+=` operator, which appends something to the string — in this case, `"there"`. Thus, after this line runs, the string called `mystring` contains the string `"Hi there"`, and that's what appears on the console when the `cout` line runs. The fancy programmer term for adding something to a string is *concatenation*.

You can also do something similar with characters. The following code snippet adds a single character to a string:

```
string mystring;
mystring = "abcdef";
mystring += 'g';
cout << mystring << endl;
```

This code creates a string with `"abcdef"` and then adds a `'g'` character to the end to get `"abcdefg"`. Then it writes the full `"abcdefg"` to the console.

Adding two strings

You can take two strings and add them together by using a + sign, just as you can do with integers. The final result is a string that is simply the two strings pushed together, side by side. For example, the following code adds `first` to `second` to get a string called `third`:

```
string first = "hello ";
string second = "there";
string third = first + second;
cout << third << endl;
```

This code prints the value of `third`, which is simply the two strings pushed together — in other words, `"hello there"`. (Notice that the string called `first` has a space at its end, which is inside quotes and, therefore, part of the string.)

You can also add a *string constant* (that is, an actual string in your application surrounded by quotes) to an existing string variable, as shown here:

```
string first = "hello ";
string third = first + "there";
cout << third << endl;
```

You may be tempted to try to add two string constants together, like so:

```
string bigstring = "hello " + "there";
cout << bigstring << endl;
```

Unfortunately, this won't work. The reason is that (deep down inside its heart) the compiler just wants to believe that a string constant and a string are fundamentally different. But really, you don't have a good reason to do this, because you can accomplish the same thing with this code:

```
string bigstring = "hello there";
cout << bigstring << endl;
```

You can do a lot more with strings. But first, you need to understand something called a function. If you're curious about functions, read Book I, Chapter 5, where we cover all the nitty-gritty details.

Deciding between Conditional Operators

One of the most important features of computers, besides allowing you to surf the web and allowing telemarketers to dial your telephone automatically while you're eating, is the capability to make comparisons. Although this topic may not seem like a big deal, computer technology did not start to take off until the engineers realized that computers could become much more powerful if they could test a situation and do one task or another task, depending on the situation.

You can use many ways to write a C++ application that can make decisions; see Book I, Chapter 4, for a discussion about this topic. But one way that is quite handy is the use of the *conditional operator*.

Think about this process: If two integer variables are equal, set a string variable to the string "equal". Otherwise, set it to the string "not equal".

In other words, suppose that you have two integer variables, called first and second. first has the value 10 in it, and second has the value 20 in it. You also have a string variable called result. Now, to follow the little process we just described: Are the two variables equal? No, they are not, so you set result to the string "not equal".

Now do this in C++. Look carefully at the following code. First, you declare the variables first, second, and result:

```
int first = 10;
int second = 20;
string result;
```

So far, so good. Notice that you didn't yet initialize the string variable result. But now you're going to write a single line of code that performs the process we just described. First, look over the following example, and see whether you can figure out what it is doing. Look carefully at the variables and what they may do, based on the process we describe earlier. Then we explain what the code does.

```
result = (first == second) ? "equal" : "not equal";
```

The preceding line is probably one of the more bizarre-looking lines of C++ code you'll see in this book. First, we tell you what it means. Then we break it into parts to show you why it means what it does.

In English, this means `result` gets `"equal"` if `first` is equal to `second`; otherwise, it gets `"not equal"`.

Now break it into two parts. A single equal sign indicates that the left side, `result`, receives what is on the right side. So you need to figure out that crazy business on the right side:

```
(first == second) ? "equal" : "not equal"
```

When you see this strange setup, consider the question mark to be the divider. The stuff on the left of the question mark is usually put in parentheses, as shown in the following:

```
(first == second)
```

This line actually compares `first` to `second` and determines whether they are equal. Yes, the code shows *two* equal signs. In C++, that's how you test whether two things are equal.

Now move to the part on the right of the question mark:

```
"equal" : "not equal"
```

This is, itself, two pieces divided by a colon, so if first is indeed equal to second, `result` gets the string `"equal"`. Otherwise, it gets the string `"not equal"`.

Take a look at the whole thing one more time:

```
result = (first == second) ? "equal" : "not equal";
```

And once again, consider what it means: If `first` is equal to `second`, `result` gets `"equal"`; otherwise, it gets `"not equal"`.

Remember that the storage bin on the left side of the single equal sign receives what is on the right side. The right side is an *expression,* which comes out to be a string of either `"equal"` or `"not equal"`.

The whole `EqualityCheck` example is shown in Listing 3-8.

Listing 3-8:   Using the Conditional Operator to Do Comparisons

```
#include <iostream>

using namespace std;

int main()
{
  int first = 10;
  int second = 20;
  string result;
  result = first == second ? "equal" : "not equal";
  cout << result << endl;
  return 0;
}
```

Boolean variables and conditional operators

You can use Boolean variables with conditional operators. In a conditional operator such as

```
result = (first == second) ?
    "equal" : "not equal";
```

the item (`first == second`) actually works out to be a Boolean value — either `true` or `false`. Therefore, you can break up this code into several lines. We know: Breaking something into several lines seems a little backward. The reason for breaking code into lines is that sometimes, when you are programming, you may have an expression that is extremely complex — much more complex than `first == second`. As you grow in your C++ programming ability, you start to build more complex expressions, and then you start to realize just how complex they can become. And often, breaking expressions into multiple smaller pieces is more manageable.

To break this example into multiple lines, you can do this: `bool isequal;`

```
isequal = (first == second);
result = isequal ? "equal" :
    "not equal";
```

The first line declares a Boolean variable called `isequal`. The second line sets it to the value `first == second`. In other words, if `first` *is* equal to `second`, then `isequal` gets the value `true`. Otherwise, `isequal` gets the value `false`. In the third line, `result` gets the value `"equal"` if `isequal` is `true`; or `result` gets the value `"not equal"` if `isequal` is `false`.

The reason that this code works is that the item on the left side of the question mark is a *Boolean expression*, which is just a fancy way of saying that the code requires a Boolean value. Therefore, you can throw in a Boolean variable if you prefer, because a Boolean *variable* holds a Boolean *value*.

Telling the Truth with Boolean Variables

In addition to integers and strings, another type in C++ can be pretty useful. This type is called a Boolean variable. Whereas an integer variable is a storage bin that can hold any integer value, a Boolean variable can hold only one of two different values: a `true` or a `false`. Boolean values take their name from George Boole, the father of Boolean logic. You can read about him at

```
http://en.wikipedia.org/wiki/George_Boole
```

The type name for a Boolean variable is `bool`. Therefore, to declare a Boolean variable, you use a statement like this:

```
bool finished;
```

This line declares a Boolean variable called `finished`. Then you can put either a `true` or a `false` in this variable, as in the following:

```
finished = true;
```

or

```
finished = false;
```

When you print the value of a Boolean variable by using code like this:

```
cout << finished << endl;
```

you see either a 1 for `true` or a 0 for `false`. The reason is that, deep down inside, the computer stores a 1 to represent `true` and a 0 to represent `false`.

Reading from the Console

Throughout this chapter and the preceding chapter, we give you many examples of how to write information to the console. But just writing information is sort of like holding a conversation where one person does all the talking and no listening. Getting some feedback from the users of your applications would be nice. Fortunately, getting feedback is easy in C++.

Writing to the console involves the use of `cout` in a form like this:

```
cout << "hi there" << endl;
```

Reading from the console (that is, getting a response from the user of your application) uses the cin object. (It's pronounced "see-in," as in "When I see out the door, I'm a-seein' the mountain from here.") Next, instead of using the goofy-looking << operator, you use the equally but backwardly goofy >> operator.

The << operator is often called an *insertion operator* because you are writing to (or *inserting into*) a stream. A *stream* is nothing more than a bunch of characters going out somewhere. In the case of cout, those characters are going out to the console. The >> operator, on the other hand, is often called the *extraction operator.* The idea here is that you are extracting stuff from the stream. In the case of cin, you are pulling letters from the stream that the user is, in a sense, sending into your application through the console.

The ReadString example shown in Listing 3-9 demonstrates how you can read a string from the console.

Listing 3-9:   Using the Conditional Operator to Make Comparisons

```
#include <iostream>

using namespace std;

int main()
{
  string name;
  cout << "Type your name: ";
  cin >> name;
  cout << "Your name is " << name << endl;
  return 0;
}
```

When you run this code, you see the console ask you to type your name, and then it stops. That's because it's waiting for your input. Notice that the insertion point appears immediately after the text "Type your name:". That's because the first cout statement lacks the usual endl. It's normal to leave the insertion point, or cursor, on the same line as the question to avoid confusing the user. Type a name, such as Fred, without spaces and press Enter. The console then looks like this:

```
Type your name: Fred
Your name is Fred
```

The first line is the line you typed (or whatever name you chose to go by), and the second line is whatever appears after you press Enter.

Notice what happens: When you type a word and press Enter, the computer places that word in the name variable, which is a string. Then you can print name to the console by using cout.

You can also read integers, as in the following code:

```
int x;
cin >> x;
cout << "Your favorite number is " << x << endl;
```

This sample code reads a single integer into the variable x and then prints it to the console.

By default, cin reads in characters from the console based on spaces. If you put spaces in your entry, only the first word gets read. cin reads the second word the next time the application encounters a cin >>.

Chapter 4: Directing the Application Flow

In This Chapter

✔ Comparing numbers and evaluating other conditions

✔ Doing things based on a comparison

✔ Repeating code a certain number of times

✔ Repeating code while certain things are true

✔ Repeating code that repeats code that . . . well, you get the idea

As you program in C++, many times you need to present the computer with a choice, allowing it to do one thing in one situation and something else in another situation. For example, you may have an application that asks for a user's password. If the password is correct, the application continues; but if the password is incorrect, the application asks the user to reenter the password. After some number of times — usually, three — the application performs yet another task when the user enters the incorrect password. Such situations are called *conditions.* In the case of the password, the condition is whether the password is correct.

You may also encounter situations where you want several lines of code to run over and over. These are *loops,* and you can specify conditions under which the loop runs. For example, you may want to check the password only three times; and if the user fails to enter it correctly the third time, you may bar access to the system. This is a loop, and the loop runs under the condition that a counter has not exceeded the value of 3.

In this chapter, we walk you through different ways to evaluate conditions within your applications and cause different sections of code to run based on those conditions. We talk about how you can use C++ commands called *if statements,* which are similar to what-if situations in real life. And we show you how to use other C++ statements (such as `do-while`) to perform *loops* (repeating the same application sections a number of times).

To make the explanations clear, this chapter gives you real-world examples that you can feel free to incorporate into your life. The examples usually refer to groups of friends and how you can get money from them. So, you see, the benefits of this chapter are twofold: You find out how to program by using conditions and loops, and you find out how to make money off your unsuspecting friends.

Doing This or Doing That

As you go through life, you're always faced with decisions. For example, when you bought this book, you faced the following decision: Should I buy this great *For Dummies* book where I'm sure to find out just what I need to know, or should I buy some other book?

When you're faced with a decision, you usually have options that offer different results — say, Plan A and Plan B. Making a decision requires making a choice that results in the execution of either Plan A or Plan B. For example, if you approach a stoplight that has just turned yellow, you must either slam on the brakes or floor the accelerator. If you slam on the brakes, the car will stop just in time (you hope). If you floor the accelerator, the car will speed up and you'll go sailing through the intersection just before the stoplight turns red. (Right?) The choice is this: Press the brake, or press the accelerator. And the plan looks like this:

> If I press the brake, I will stop just in time.

> If I press the accelerator, I will speed through the intersection.

Computers are faced with making decisions too, although their decisions are usually a little less exciting and, we hope, don't yield the possibility of police interaction. And computer decisions are usually simpler in nature. That is, a computer's decisions usually focus around such issues as comparing numbers and strings of characters. For example, you may be writing a computer application for a bank where the user of your application (that is, the bank customer) has a choice of Plan A, Make a Deposit, or Plan B, Receive a Cash Withdrawal. If the user chooses to make a deposit, your application adds to the balance the amount of the deposit. If the user chooses to make a withdrawal, your application instead subtracts the withdrawal amount from the balance.

In C++, decisions usually take the form of an `if` statement, which is code that starts with the `if` keyword followed by a condition, which is often a numerical condition wherein two numbers are compared and then two blocks of code appear: one that runs if the condition is satisfied and one that runs if it is not.

Evaluating Conditions in C++

Most decisions that the computer makes are based on conditions evaluated by comparing either two numbers or two characters. For numerical comparisons, you may compare a variable to a number, as in the following statement:

```
x > 10
```

This comparison evaluates whether the variable x is greater than the number 10. If x is indeed greater than 10, the computer sees this condition as true. If x is not greater than 10, the computer sees the condition as not true (false).

Developers often use the word *satisfied* with conditions. For the condition x > 10, if x is greater than 10, we say that the condition is satisfied. It's kind of like, "We're satisfied if our IRS tax refund is five figures." For this, if the condition is x > 9999, and if we did get that much money back from Uncle Sam, the condition is satisfied (and so are we).

For character comparisons, you may compare whether two characters are equal, as in the following statement:

```
mychar == 'A'
```

This comparison evaluates whether mychar contains the letter A. Notice that you use two equal signs, not just one. Using a single equal sign would assign the value A to mychar.

To test whether the character is not equal to something, you use the somewhat cryptic-looking != operator. Think of the ! as meaning *not,* as in

```
mychar != 'X'
```

Finding the right C++ operators

Each statement in the previous section uses an *operator* to specify the comparison to make between the numbers or the strings. Table 4-1 shows you the types of operators available in C++ and the comparisons that they help you make in your applications.

Table 4-1	Evaluating Numerical Conditions
Operator	*What It Means*
<	Less than
<=	Less than or equal to
>	Greater than
>=	Greater than or equal to
==	Equal to
!=	Not equal to

Some operators in this table — and how you use them — can be a bit annoying or downright frightening. The following list gives examples:

+ The operator that tests for equality is *two* equal signs. It looks like this:

    ```
    x == 10
    ```

    When the computer finds this statement, it checks to see whether x equals 10.

If you put just one equal sign in your statements, most C++ compilers will not give you an error — though a statement like x = 10 is not really a condition! Instead, x = 10 is an *assignment,* setting the variable x to 10. When code contains such a statement, the result of the evaluation is always the same, regardless of the value that x has.

✦ The operator that tests for inequality is an exclamation mark followed by an equal sign. For the condition x != 10, the condition evaluates as true only if x is not equal to 10 (x is equal to something other than 10).

✦ When you're testing for greater-than or less-than conditions, the condition x > 10 is not true if x is 10. The condition x > 10 is true only if x is actually greater than, but not equal to, 10. To also test for x being equal to 10, you have two choices:

   • If you're working with integers, you can test whether x > 9. In that case, the condition is true if x is 10, or 11, or 12, and so on.

   • You can use the greater-than-or-equal-to operator to determine equality x >= 10. This condition also is true if x is 10, 11, and so on.

To test for all numbers greater than or equal to 10, the condition x > 9 works only if you're working with integers. If you're working with floating-point numbers (refer to Book I, Chapter 3, for information on the types of numbers you can work with in C++), the statement x > 9 won't work like you want. The number 9.1 is greater than 9, and it's not greater than or equal to 10. So if you want greater than or equal to and you're not working with integers, use the >= operator.

Combining multiple evaluations

When you make evaluations for application decisions, you may have more than one condition to evaluate. For example, you might say, "If I get a million dollars, or if I decide to go into debt up to my eyeballs, then I will buy that Lamborghini." In this case, you would buy the car under two conditions, and either can be true. Combining conditions like this is called an *or* situation: If this is true or if that is true, something happens.

To evaluate two conditions together in C++, you write them in the same statement and separate them with the *or* symbol (||), which looks like two vertical bars. Other programming languages get to use the actual word *or,* but C++ uses the strange, unpronounceable symbol that we call *The Operator Previously Known As Or.* The following statement shows it performing live:

```
(i < 10 || i > 100)
```

This condition is useful for some kinds of range checking where you want to exclude the middle of a range and check only for the extremes. In this case, an i value of 50 (the middle of the range) would evaluate to false. If you use the *or* operator (||), accidentally ending up with a condition that is *always* true is easy. For example, the condition (x < 100 || x > 0) is always going to be true. When x is -50, it's less than 100, so the condition is true. When x is 500, it's greater than 0, so it's true. In addition to an *or* situation, you can have something like this: "If I get a million dollars and I feel really bold, then I will buy a Lamborghini." Notice that we're using the word *and:* In this case, you do it only if both situations are true. (Remember that with *or,* you do it if either situation is true.) In C++, the *and* operator is *two* ampersands: &&. This makes more sense than the *or* operator because the & symbol is often associated with the word *and.* The *and* comparison in C++ looks like this:

```
(i > 10 && i < 100)
```

This example checks to see whether a number is more than 10 *and* less than 100. That would mean the number is in the range 11 through 99.

Combining conditions by using the && and || operators is a use of *logical operators.*

To determine whether a number is within a certain range, you can use the *and* operator (&&), as we do earlier in this chapter.

With the *and* operator, accidentally creating a condition that is never true is easy. For example, the condition (x < 10 && x > 100) will never be true. No single number can be both less than 10 and simultaneously greater than 100.

Including Evaluations in C++ Conditional Statements

Computers, like humans, evaluate conditions and use the results of the evaluations as input for making a decision. For humans, the decision usually involves alternative plans of action, and the same is true for computers. The computer needs to know what to do if a condition is true and what to do if a condition is not true. To decide on a plan of action based on a condition that your application evaluates, you use an if statement, which looks like this:

```
if (x > 10)
{
    cout << "Yuppers, it's greater than 10!" << endl;
}
```

This example translates into English as: If x is greater than 10, write the message

```
"Yuppers, it's greater than 10!"
```

In an if statement, the part inside the parentheses is either the *test* or the *condition.* We usually apply *condition* to this part of the if statement and use the word *test* as a verb, as in "I will test whether *x* is greater than 10."

In C++, the condition for an `if` statement always goes inside parentheses. If you forget the parentheses, you get a compile error.

You can also have multiple plans of action. The idea is simply that if a condition is true, you will do Plan A. Otherwise, you will do Plan B. This is an *if-else block,* which we discuss in the next section.

Deciding what if and also what else

When you are writing the code for a comparison, usually you want to tell the computer to do something if the condition is true and to do something else if the condition is not true. For example, you may say, "If I'm really hungry, I will buy the Biggiesupersizemondohungryperson french fries with my meal for an extra nickel; otherwise, I'll go with the small." In the English language, you often see this kind of logic with the word *otherwise:* If such-and-such is true, I will do this; otherwise, I will do that.

In C++, you use the `else` keyword for the *otherwise* situation. The `IfElse` example demonstrates how to use the `else` keyword, as shown in the following code:

```
#include <iostream>

using namespace std;

int main()
{
    int i;

    cout << "Type any number: ";
    cin >> i;

    if (i > 10)
    {
        cout << "It's greater than 10." << endl;
    }
    else
    {
        cout << "It's not greater than 10." << endl;
    }

    return 0;
}
```

In this code, you test whether a number is greater than 10. If it is, you print one message. If it is not, you print a different message. Notice how the two blocks of code are distinct. The first block immediately follows the `if` statement; it's the code that runs if the condition is true. The next block is preceded by the `else` keyword, and this block runs if the condition is not true.

Think carefully about your `else` situation when dealing with numbers. If you are testing whether a number is greater than 10, for instance, and it turns out that the number is not greater than 10, the tendency of most people is to assume that it must, therefore, be *less than 10.* But that's not true. The number 10 itself is not greater than 10, but it's not less than 10, either. So the opposite of *greater than 10* is simply *not greater than 10*. If you need to test the full range of numbers using a simple if statement, create an if statement that uses either >= or <= (refer to Table 4-1 for a listing of operators).

Going further with the else and if

When you are working with comparisons, you often have multiple comparisons going on. For example, you may say, "If I go to Mars, I will look for a cool red rock; otherwise, if I go to the moon, I will jump up really high; otherwise, I will just look around wherever I end up, but I hope there will be air."

The IfElse2 example, shown in the following code, demonstrates how to combine the if and else keywords to check for multiple alternatives:

```
#include <iostream>

using namespace std;

int main()
{
    int i;

    cout << "Type any number: ";
    cin >> i;

    if (i > 10)
    {
        cout << "It's greater than 10." << endl;
    }
    else if (i == 10)
    {
        cout << "It's equal to 10" << endl;
    }
    else
    {
        cout << "It's less than 10." << endl;
    }

    return 0;
}
```

Here you can see having several different conditions and only one can be true. The computer first checks to see whether i is greater than 10. If i is greater, the computer prints a message saying that i is greater than 10; but if it isn't greater, the computer checks to see whether i equals 10. If so, the computer prints a message saying that i is equal to 10. Finally, the computer assumes that i must be less than 10, and it prints a message accordingly. Notice, for the final else statement, we didn't put a condition (and, in fact, you cannot have a condition with else statements). But because the other conditions failed, you know, by your careful logic, that i must be less than 10.

Be careful when you are thinking through such `if` statements. You could have a situation where more than one condition can occur. For example, you may have something like the example shown in `IfElse3`:

```
#include <iostream>

using namespace std;

int main()
{
    int i;

    cout << "Type any number: ";
    cin >> i;

    if (i > 100)
    {
        cout << "It's greater than 100." << endl;
    }
    else if (i > 10)
    {
        cout << "It's greater than 10" << endl;
    }
    else
    {
        cout <<
            "It's neither greater than 100 nor greater than 10."
            << endl;
    }

    return 0;
}
```

Think about what would happen if `i` is the number `150`. The first condition, `i > 100`, is true. But so is the second condition, `i > 10`. The number `150` is greater than `100`, and `150` is also greater than `10`. So which block will the computer execute? Or will it execute both blocks?

The computer executes only the first condition that is satisfied. Thus, when `i` is `150`, the computer prints the message `"It's greater than 100."` It does not print the other messages. In fact, the computer doesn't even bother checking the other conditions at that point. It just continues with the application.

Repeating Actions with Statements That Loop

Suppose that you're writing an application to add all the numbers from 1 to 100. For example, you may want to know how much money you will get if you tell 100 people, "Give me one dollar more than the person to your left." With a mastery of copy-and-paste, you could do something like this

```
int x = 1;
x = x + 2;
x = x + 3;
x = x + 4;
```

and so on until you get to x = x + 100. As you can see, this code could take a long time to type, and you would probably find it a tad frustrating, too, no matter how quickly you can choose the Edit➪Paste command (or press Ctrl+V). Fortunately, the great founders of the computer world recognized that not every programmer is a virtuoso at the piano with flying fingers and that applications often need to do the same thing over and over. Thus, they created a helpful tool: the for loop. A *for loop* executes the same piece of code over and over a certain number of times. And that's just what you want to do in this example.

Looping situations

Several types of loops are available, and in this section you see how they work. Which type of loop you use depends on the situation. We mention one type in the preceding section: the for loop. The idea behind a for loop is to have a counter variable that either increases or decreases, and the loop runs as long as the counter variable satisfies a particular condition. For example, the counter variable might start at 0, and the loop runs as long as the counter is less than 10. The counter variable *increments* (has one added to it) each time the loop runs, and after the counter variable is not less than 10, the loop stops.

Another way to loop is to simplify the logic a bit and say, "I want this loop to run as long as a certain condition is true." This is a *while loop,* and you simply specify a condition under which the loop continues to run. When the condition is true, the loop keeps running. After the condition is no longer true, the loop stops.

Finally, there's a slight modification to the while loop: the do-while loop. The *do-while loop* is used to handle one particular situation that can arise. When you have a while loop, if the condition is not true when everything starts, the computer skips over the code in the while loop and does not even bother executing it. But sometimes you may have a situation where you would want the code to always execute at least once. In that case, you can use a do-while loop.

Table 4-2 shows the types of loops. In the sections that follow, we show you how to use these types of loops.

Table 4-2	Choosing Your Loops
Type of Loop	*Appearance*
for	for (x=0; x<10; x++) { }
while	while (x < 10) { }
do-while	do { } while (x < 10)

You may want to use these loops in these situations:

✦ `for` **loop:** Use a `for` loop when you have a counter variable and you want it to loop while the counter variable increases or decreases over a range.

✦ `while` **loop:** Use the `while` loop when you have a condition under which you want your code to run.

✦ `do-while` **loop:** Use the `do-while` loop when you have a condition under which you want your code to run *and* you want to ensure that the loop always runs at least once, even if the condition is not satisfied.

Looping for

To use a `for` loop, you use the `for` keyword and follow it with a set of parentheses that contains information regarding the number of times the `for` loop executes.

For example, when adding the numbers from 1 to 100, you want a variable that starts with the number 1; then you add 1 to x, increase the variable to 2, and add the next number to x again over and over. The common action here that doesn't change each time is the "add it to x" part, and the part that changes is the variable, called *a counter variable*.

The counter variable, therefore, starts at 1 and goes through 100. Does it include 100? Yes. And with each iteration, you add 1 to the counter variable. The `for` statement looks like this:

```
for (i = 1; i <=100; i++)
```

This statement means that the counter variable, i, starts at 1, and the loop runs over and over while i is less than or equal to 100. After each iteration, the counter variable increments by 1 because of the i++ statement.

The following list describes the three portions inside the parentheses of the `for` loop:

✦ The *initializer:* You use this first portion to set up the counter variable.

✦ The *condition:* It's the condition under which the loop continues to run.

✦ The *finalizer:* In this third portion, you specify what happens after each cycle of the loop.

Three items are inside the `for` loop, and you separate them with semicolons. If you try to use commas, your code will not compile.

Now the line of code from a few paragraphs back doesn't do anything for each iteration other than add 1 to i. To tell the computer the work to do with each iteration, follow the `for` statement with a set of braces containing the statements you want to execute with each iteration. Thus, to add the counter variable to x, you would do this:

```
for (i = 1; i <=100; i++)
{
    x += i;
}
```

This example would add i to x with each loop. Of course, we didn't start out x with anything in particular, so we should probably include it, too. The ForLoop example demonstrates the for loop in its final form, complete with the way to write the final value of x to the console after the loop is finished:

```
#include <iostream>

using namespace std;

int main()
{
    int x = 0;
    int i;

    for (i = 1; i <= 100; i++)
    {
        x += i;
    }

    cout << x << endl;
    return 0;
}
```

When you run this example, you see an output of 5050. Notice a few things about this block of code.

1. You declare both variables that you're working with: x and i.

2. The for statement initializes the counter variable, specifies the condition under which it continues running, and tells what to do after each iteration. In this example, the for loop starts with i = 1, and it runs as long as i is less than or equal to 100. For each iteration, the computer adds the value of the counter to x; the process that adds the value to x is the code inside the braces.

3. The computer adds 1 to x, which you specify as the third item inside the parentheses. The computer does this part, adding 1 to x, only after it finishes executing the stuff inside the braces.

Meddling with the middle condition

The middle portion of the for statement specifies a condition under which to continue doing the stuff inside the for loop. In the case of the preceding example, the condition is i <= 100, which means that the stuff inside the braces continues to run as long as i is less than or equal to 100.

If you're familiar with other computer languages, the middle condition specifies a condition under which to continue the loop, not a condition under which to terminate the loop. Other languages will say, "Do this until such-and-such is true," but that is not the case in C++.

In our example, we want the loop to iterate for the special case where i is 100, which still satisfies the condition i <= 100. If we had instead said i < 100, the loop would not have executed for the case where i equals 100. The loop would have stopped short of the final iteration. In other words, the computer would add only the numbers 1 through 99. And if our friends are gathering money for us, we would be cheated out of that final $100. And, by golly, that could make the difference in whether we pay rent this month.

The question of when the loop stops can get kind of confusing. If we had gone crazy (but can we really *go* crazy when we're crazy to begin with?) and said that we wanted to add the numbers 1 *up to but not including* 100, we would have wanted a condition such as i < 100. If we had just said *up to* 100, it would not have been clear exactly which we wanted to do — include the 100 or not. If that had been the case and you were writing the application for us, you would want to ask us for clarification. (Unless we're the 100th friend, in which case we may get out of paying our dues.)

In the example we've been using, the condition i <= 100 and the condition i < 101 have essentially the same meaning. If the condition were i < 101, the application would operate the same. But the only reason that's true is because we're working with integers counting up to and including 100. If we were instead adding, for instance, floating-point numbers, and we incremented the counter by 0.1 after each iteration, these two conditions (i <= 100 and i < 101) wouldn't be the same. With i <=100, we would get up to 99.5, 99.6, 99.7, 99.8, 99.9, and finally 100, after which we would stop. But i < 101 would also include 100.1, 100.2, up to and including 100.9.

You can see that the two conditions are not the same by playing with the ForLoop2 example. When you run this example with a condition of i <= 100, the output is 50050. However, when you run this example with a condition of i < 101, the output is 51055.5. (Remember to rebuild the application after you make any changes to it.)

Going backward

If you need to count backward, you can do that with a for loop as well. For example, you may be counting down the number of days remaining before you get to quit your job because you learned C++ programming and you are moving on to an awesome new job. Or you may be writing an application that can manipulate that cool countdown timer that they show when the space shuttle launches. Counting up just isn't always the right action. It would be a bummer if every day were one day more before you get to quit your job and move to an island. Sometimes, counting backward is best.

To count backward, you set up the three portions of the `for` loop. The first is the initial setup, the second is the condition under which it continues to run, and the third is the action after each iteration. For the first portion, you set the counter to the starting value, the top number. For the condition, you check whether the number continues to be greater than or equal to the final number. And for the third portion, you decrement the counter rather than increment it. Thus, you would have this:

```
for (i=10; i>=5; i--)
```

This line starts the counter variable `i` at 10. After each iteration, `i` becomes 1 less, and thus it moves to 9, then 8, then 7, and so on. And this process continues as long as `i` is at least 5. Thus, `i` counts 10, 9, 8, 7, 6, 5. The whole application might look like the `ForCountdown` example, shown here:

```
#include <iostream>

using namespace std;

int main()
{
    int i;

    for (i=10; i>=5; i--)
    {
        cout << i << endl;
    }

    return 0;
}
```

When you run this code, you see the following output.

```
10
9
8
7
6
5
```

Incrementing one step at a time

In previous examples, we declare the counter variable before the for loop. However, you can actually declare the counter variable inside the loop, as in `for (int i = 0; i <= 100; i++)`. The end result is identical to declaring the counter variable beforehand. You must declare the variable every time you use it in a loop, as shown in the following example:

```
int x = 0;

for (int i = 0; i <= 100; i++)
{
    x += i;
}
```

```
for (int i = 200; i <= 300; i++)
{
    x += i;
}
```

In the example in the earlier section "Going backward," you work with integers, and after each iteration, you add 1 to the counter variable. But you can do other things with each iteration. We already hinted that you can work with floating-point numbers and add 0.1 with each iteration. To do this, you can use an application like the ForLoop2 example, shown here:

```
#include <iostream>

using namespace std;

int main()
{
    double x = 0.0;
    double i;

    for (i = 0.0; i <= 100; i+=0.1)
    {
        x += i;
    }

    cout << x << endl;

    return 0;
}
```

Now notice the third item in the for statement: i += 0.1. Remember that this item is the same as i = i + 0.1. Therefore, this third item is a complete statement. A common mistake is to instead include just a partial statement, as in i + 0.1. Unfortunately, some compilers allow that to get through with only a warning. C++ is notorious for letting you do things that don't make a whole lot of sense, though newer compilers tend to fix these errors.

Yes, it's true: The entire statement i = i + 1 is considered to have a side effect. In medicine, a *side effect* is an extra little goodie you get when you take a pill that the doctor prescribes. For example, to cure your headache with medicine, one side effect may be that you experience severe abdominal pains — not something you want. But in computers, a side effect can be something that you may want. In this case, you want the counter to be incremented. The partial statement i + 0.1 returns only a value and doesn't put it anywhere; that is, the partial statement doesn't change the value of i — it has no side effects. (If you try this at home by replacing one of the for loops in the earlier examples with just i + 0.1, your loop runs forever until you manually stop the application. The reason for this action is that the counter always stays put, right where it started, and it never increments. Thus, the condition i <= 100 is always satisfied.)

The final portion of the for statement must be a complete statement in itself. If the statement simply evaluates to something, it will not be used in your for loop. In that case, your for loop can run forever unless you stop it.

Getting sneaky (and too complicated)

If you need multiple counter variables, the `for` loop can handle it. Each portion of the `for` statement can have multiple items in it, separated by commas. For example, the following line of code uses two counter variables. Look carefully at it because it's a bit confusing (in fact, we say a little something about that shortly):

```
for (i = 0, j=10; i <= 5, j <=20; i++, j=j+2)
{
    cout << i << " " << j << endl;
    x += i + j;
}
```

**Book I
Chapter 4**

**Directing the
Application Flow**

To understand this example, look at each portion separately. The first portion starts the loop. Here, the code creates two counters — i and j; i starts at 0, and j starts at 10.

So far, easy enough. The second portion says that the loop will run as long as the following two conditions are true: i must be less than or equal to 5, and j must be less than or equal to 20.

Again, not too bad. The final portion says what must happen at the end of each iteration: i is incremented by 1, and j is incremented by 2.

Thus, you have two counter variables. And it's not too bad, except that you might imagine doing something like this instead:

```
for (i = 0, j=20; i <= 5, j >= 10 ; i++, j=j-2)
{
    cout << i << " " << j << endl;
    x += i + j;
}
```

If you look carefully, you'll notice that aside from i, j starts out at 20 and the loop runs as long as j is at least 10, and that with each iteration, 2 is subtracted from j. In other words, j is counting down by 2 from 20 to 10.

But i is counting up from 0 to 5. Thus, you have two loops: one counting up and one counting down. (Does it seem to you that, just maybe, we're starting to make this a little confusing?)

But wait, there's more. If you think *this* is confusing, take a look at the following gem, which we took great pride in putting together:

```
for (i=0, j=10; i<=5, j <=20 ; i++, j=j+2, cout<<i+j, x+=i+j)
{
}
```

If you type this example, you can see that it does do something. But can you tell what it does just by looking at it? Probably not. (If you can, that's probably not a good thing, either.) The truth is, this kind of code is just too complicated — best to stick with simpler code. Although you may know what this code means, your coworkers will only get frustrated trying to decode it. And if you write code just for fun at home, six months from now — when you go back and look at this code — you might have trouble figuring it out yourself!

Putting too much inside the for statement itself is easy to do. In fact, if you're really clever, you can put almost everything inside the for loop and leave nothing but an empty pair of braces, as we show you in the preceding example. But remember, just because your code is clever doesn't mean that what you did was the best way to do it. Instead, sticking to the common practice of using only one variable in the for statement is a good idea (as is not using multiple statements within each portion).

Keeping your applications clear so that other people can figure out what you were trying to do when you wrote the code is always a good idea. Some people seem to think that if they keep their applications complicated, they're guaranteeing themselves job security. Oddly, all the people we know like that tend to leave their jobs and have trouble getting good references. (Imagine that!)

You may recall that with the ++, you can have both i++ and ++i. The first is a *post-increment,* and the second is a *pre-increment.* You may be tempted to try something like this: for (int i = 0; i <= 5; ++i). Although it looks cool and some people prefer it, the truth is that it doesn't change anything. The ++i still takes place at the end of the loop, not at the beginning, as you might hope. To us, that setup just makes code confusing, so we use i++ in our for loops, and we avoid ++i.

Looping while

Often, you find that for loops work only so well. Sometimes, you don't want a counter variable; you just want to run a loop over and over as long as a certain situation is true. Then, after that situation is no longer the case, you want to stop the loop.

For example, instead of saying that you'll have 100 people line up and each one will give you one more dollar than the person to his or her left, you may say that you will continue accepting money like this as long as they're willing to give it.

In this case, you can see that the condition under which the thing continues to operate is the statement "as long as they're willing to give it."

To do this in C++, you use a while statement. The while keyword is followed by a set of parentheses containing the condition under which the application is to continue running the loop. Whereas the for statement's parentheses include three portions that show how to change the counter variable, the while statement's parentheses contain only a condition.

The `WhileLoop` example demonstrates a simple `while` loop, as shown here:

```cpp
#include <iostream>

using namespace std;

int main()
{
    int i = 0;

    while (i <= 10)
    {
        cout << i << endl;
        i++;
    }

    cout << "All Finished!" << endl;

    return 0;
}
```

This code runs while `i` is less than or equal to `10`. Thus, the output of this application is

```
0
1
2
3
4
5
6
7
8
9
All Finished!
```

The `while` loop is handy if you don't have a particular number of times you need the loop to run. For example, consider a situation where your application is reading data from the Internet. Unless you control the Internet data source, you don't know how much data it can provide. (There are many other situations where you don't know how much data to read, but Internet applications commonly experience this problem.) Using a `while` loop, the code can continue reading data until your application has read it all. The Internet data source can simply *stream* the data to your application until the data transfer is complete.

Often, for this kind of situation, we make a Boolean variable called `done` and start it out as `false`. The `while` statement is simply

```cpp
while (!done)
```

This line translates easily to English as "while not done, do the following." Then, inside the `while` loop, when the situation happens that you know the loop must finish (such as the Internet data source has no more data to read), you set

```cpp
done = true;
```

The `WhileLoop2` example demonstrates how to do this sort of process, as shown here:

```cpp
#include <iostream>

using namespace std;

int main()
{
    int i = 0;
    bool done = false;

    while (!done)
    {
        cout << i << endl;
        i++;
        if (i == 10)
            done = true;
    }

    cout << "All Finished!" << endl;
    return 0;
}
```

In the case of the Internet data example, after you encounter no more data, you would set `done` to `true`. In the case of your friends giving you money, after one of them refuses, you would set `done` to `true`.

If you have worked in other languages, you may have come across the notion of `while` loops always executing at least once. This is not the case in C++. If the condition in the `while` statement evaluates to `false`, the `while` loop does not execute at all.

Doing while

The `while` statement has a cousin in the family: the do-while statement. A loop of this form is similar to the `while` loop, but with an interesting little catch: The `while` statement goes at the end. The `DoWhileLoop` example demonstrates how to use this kind of loop, as shown here:

```cpp
#include <iostream>

using namespace std;

int main()
{
    int i = 0;

    do
    {
        cout << i << endl;
        i++;
    }
    while (i <= 10);

    cout << "All Finished!" << endl;

    return 0;
}
```

Notice here that the loop starts with the `do` keyword, and then the material for the loop follows inside braces, and finally the `while` statement appears at the end. The idea is that you're telling the computer "Do this while such-and-such is true," where *this* is the stuff inside braces and the *such-and-such* is the condition inside parentheses. Because the condition is evaluated at the end, after everything else is done, the output from this example is a little different from the other `while` loop examples:

```
0
1
2
3
4
5
6
7
8
9
10
All Finished!
```

The `do-while` loop has one important caveat: Unlike the `while` loop, the `do-while` loop always runs at least once. In other words, even if the condition isn't satisfied the first time you run the loop, it runs anyway. That can be a problem sometimes, and if you don't want that behavior, consider using a `while` loop instead of a `do-while` loop.

Breaking and continuing

Sometimes, you may write an application that includes a loop that does more than simply add numbers. You may find that you want the loop to end under a certain condition that's separate. Or you may want the loop to suddenly skip out of the current loop and continue with the next item in the loop. When you stop a loop and continue with the code after the loop, you use a `break` statement. When you quit the current cycle of the loop and continue with the next cycle, you use a `continue` statement. The next two sections show you how to do this.

Breaking

Suppose that you are writing an application that reads data over the Internet, and the loop runs for the amount of data that's supposed to come. But midway through the process, you may encounter some data that has an error in it, and you may want to get out of the `for` loop immediately.

C++ includes a handy little statement that can rescue you in such a situation. The statement is called `break`. Now, nothing actually breaks, and it seems a bit frightening to write an application that instructs the computer to break. But this use of the term *break* is more like in "break out of prison" than "break the computer." But instead of breaking out of prison, it breaks you out the loop. This can be any kind of loop — a `for` loop, a `while` loop, or a `do-while` loop.

The ForLoop3 example that follows demonstrates this technique. This sample actually just checks for the special case of i being 5. You could have accomplished the same result by simply changing the end condition of the for loop, but at least it shows you how the break statement works.

```
#include <iostream>

using namespace std;

int main()
{
    int i;

    for (i=0; i<10; i++)
    {
        cout << i << " ";
        if (i == 5)
        {
            break;
        }
        cout << i * 2 << endl;
    }

    cout << "All Finished!" << endl;

    return 0;
}
```

In the preceding code, the first line inside the for loop, cout << i << " ";, runs when i is 5. But the final line in the for loop, cout << i * 2 << endl;, does not run when i is 5 because you tell it to break out of the loop between the two cout statements.

Also notice that when you break out of the loop, the application does not quit. It continues with the statements that follow the loop. In this case, it still prints the message "All Finished!"

You can leave empty the second portion of the for statement (the condition) by simply putting a blank between the spaces. Then, to get out of the loop, you can use a break statement. However, doing this makes for messy code. You should treat messy code like you treat a messy house: Although sometimes we personally don't mind, the truth is that most people don't care to see a messy house. And you really don't want other people to see your messy house — or your messy code. Yes, as a programmer, being a little self-conscious is sometimes a good thing.

Continuing

In addition to the times when you may need to break out of a loop for a special situation, you can also cause the loop to end its current iteration; but instead of breaking out of it, the loop resumes with the next iteration.

For example, you may be, again, reading data from over the Internet, and doing this by looping a specified number of times. In the middle of the loop, you may encounter some bad data. But rather than quit out of the loop, you may want to simply ignore the current piece of bad data and then continue reading more data.

To do this trick, you use a C++ statement called `continue`. The `continue` statement says, "End the current iteration, but continue running the loop with the next iteration."

The `ForLoop4` example that follows shows a slightly modified version of the previous example, in the "Breaking" section. When the loop gets to 5, it doesn't execute the second `cout` line. But rather than break out of the loop, it continues with 6, and then 7, and so on until the loop finishes on its own:

```cpp
#include <iostream>

using namespace std;

int main()
{
    int i;

    for (i=0; i<10; i++)
    {
        cout << i << " ";
        if (i == 5)
        {
            cout << endl;
            continue;
        }
        cout << i * 2 << endl;
    }

    cout << "All Finished!" << endl;

    return 0;
}
```

Nesting loops

Many times, you need to work with more than one loop. For example, you may have several groups of friends, and you want to bilk the individual friends of each group for all you can get. You may host a party for the first group of friends and make them each give you as much money as they have. Then, the next week, you may hold another party with a different group of friends. You would do this for each group of friends. Oh, wait — we just said the word *for,* so that's probably what we're onto with this.

You can draw out the logic like this:

```
For each group of friends,
    for each person in that group
        bilk the friend for all he or she is worth
```

This is a nested loop. But if you do this, don't be surprised if this is the last time your friends visit your nest.

A *nested loop* is simply a loop inside a loop. Because computers aren't good at making friends (although they *can* be used to bilk people), we use an example that's a bit nicer: Suppose that you want to multiply each of the numbers 1 through 10 by 1 and print the answer for each multiplication, and then you want to multiply each of the numbers 1 through 10 by 2 and print the answer for each multiplication, and so on, up to a multiplier of 10. Your C++ code would look like the ForLoop5 example:

```
#include <iostream>

using namespace std;

int main()
{
    int x,y;

    for (x = 1; x <= 10; x++)
    {
        cout << "Products of " << x <<endl;
        for (y = 1; y <= 10; y++)
        {
            cout << x * y << endl;
        }
        cout << endl;
    }

    return 0;
}
```

In this example, you simply have a loop inside a loop. The inner loop can make use of the counter variable from the outer loop. Beyond that, nothing is magical or bizarre about this kind of thing. It's just a loop inside a loop. And yes, you can have a loop inside a loop inside a loop inside a loop. You can also have any loop inside any other loop, like a while loop inside a for loop.

Notice that you have stuff going on outside the inner loop but inside the outer loop. That is, you have a cout call before and after the inner loop. You can do this; your inner loop need not be the only thing inside the outer loop.

Although you can certainly have a loop inside a loop inside a loop inside a loop, the deeper you get, the more potentially confusing your code can become. It's like the dozens of big cities in America that are promising to build an outer loop (a road that surrounds the outside the city to help move traffic faster). Eventually, that outer loop won't be big enough, so the cities have to build another and another. That's kind of a frightening prospect, so try not to get carried away with nesting.

If you put a break statement or a continue statement inside a nested loop, the statement applies to the innermost loop it sits in. For example, the ForLoop6 example that follows contains three loops: an outer loop, a middle loop, and an inner loop. The break statement applies to the middle loop as shown here:

```cpp
#include <iostream>

using namespace std;

int main()
{
    int x,y,z;

    for (x = 1; x <= 3; x++)
    {
        for (y = 1; y < 3; y++)
        {
            if (y == 2)
                break;
            for (z = 1; z < 3; z++)
            {
                cout << x << " " << y;
                cout << " " << z << endl;
            }
        }
    }

    return 0;
}
```

You can see that when y is 2, the for loop with the y in it breaks. But the outer loop continues to run with the next iteration.

Chapter 5: Dividing Your Work with Functions

In This Chapter

✔ Calling a function

✔ Passing things, such as variables

✔ Writing your own great functions

✔ Fun with strings

✔ Manipulating `main()`

People generally agree that most projects throughout life are easier when you divide them into smaller, more manageable tasks. That's also the case with computer programming — if you break your code into smaller pieces, it becomes more manageable.

C++ provides many ways to divide code into smaller portions. One way is through the use of what are called functions. A *function* is a set of lines of code that performs a particular job.

In this chapter, we show you what functions are and how you can use them to make your programming job easier.

Dividing Your Work

If you have a big job to do that doesn't involve a computer, you can divide your work in many ways. Over the years of studying process management, people have pretty much narrowed the division of a job to two ways: using nouns and using verbs.

Yes, that's right. Back to good old English class, where we all learned about nouns and verbs. The idea is this: Suppose that you're going to go out back and build a flying saucer. You can approach the designing of the flying saucer in two ways.

First, you could just draw up a plan of attack, listing all the steps to build the flying saucer from start to finish. That would, of course, be a lot of steps. But to simplify it, you could instead list all the major tasks without getting into the details. It might go something like this:

1. Build the outer shell.

2. Build and attach the engine.

That's it. Only two steps. But when you hire a couple dozen people to do the grunt work for you while you focus on your day trading, would that be enough for them to go on? No, probably not. Instead, you could divide these two tasks into smaller tasks. For example, Step 2 might look like this:

2a. Build the antigravity lifter.

2b. Build the thruster.

2c. Connect the lifter to the thruster to form the final engine.

2d. Attach the engine to the outer shell.

That's a little better; it has more detail. But it still needs more. How do you do the "Build the antigravity lifter" part? That's easy, but it requires more detail, as in the following steps:

2aa. Unearth the antigravity particles from the ground.

2ab. Compress them tightly into a superatomizing conductor.

2ac. Surround with coils.

2ad. Connect a 9-volt battery clip to the coils.

And, of course, each of these instructions requires even more detail. Eventually, after you have planned the whole thing, you will have many, many steps, but they will be organized into a hierarchy of sorts, as shown in Figure 5-1. In this drawing, the three dots represent places where other steps go, but we chose to leave them off so that the diagram can fit on the page.

This type of design is a *top-down* design. The idea is that you start at the upper-most step of your design (in this case, "Build flying saucer") and continue to break the steps into more and more detailed steps until you have something manageable. For many years, this was how computer programming was taught.

Although this process works, people have found a slightly better way. First, before breaking the steps (which are the verbs), you divide the thing you're building into parts (the nouns). In this case, you kind of do that already, in the first two steps. But instead of calling them steps, you can call them *objects*.

One object is the outer shell, and one object is the engine. This way, two different factories can work on these in sort of a division of labor. Of course, the factories would have to coordinate their activities; otherwise, the two parts may not fit together when they're ready to go. And before you figure out exactly how to build each of these objects, it would be a good idea to describe each object: what it does, its features, its dimensions, and so on. Then, when you finally have all that done, you can list the exact features and their details. And finally, you can divide the work with each person designing or building a different part.

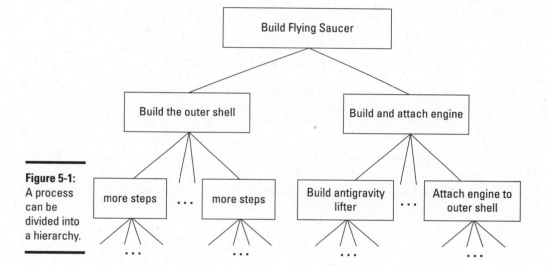

Figure 5-1:
A process
can be
divided into
a hierarchy.

As you can see, this second approach makes more sense. And that's the way programmers divide their computer applications. But at the bottom of each method is something in common: The methods are made of several little processes. These processes are called *functions*. When you write a computer application, after you divide your job into smaller pieces called objects, you eventually start giving these objects behaviors. And to code these behaviors, you do just as you did in the first approach: You break them into manageable parts, again, called functions. In computer programming terms, a *function* is simply a small set of code that performs a specific task. But it's more than that: Think of a function as a machine. You can put one or more things into the machine; it processes them, and then it spits out a single answer, if anything at all. One of the most valuable diagrams we have seen draws a function in this manner, like a machine, as shown in Figure 5-2.

Figure 5-2:
You can
think of a
function as
a machine.

Data goes
into function

Function
(machine)

Possibly one
item comes
out, or no
items come
out.

This machine (or function) has three main parts:

✦ **Inputs:** The function can receive data through its inputs. These data elements can be numbers, strings, or any other type. When you create such a machine, you can have as many inputs as you want (or even zero, if necessary).

✦ **Processor:** The processor is the function itself. In terms of C++, this is actually a set of code lines.

✦ **Output:** A function can *return* something when it has finished doing its thing. In C++, this output is in the form of numbers, strings, or any other type.

To make all this clear, try out the FirstFunction code in Listing 5-1. (Don't forget the second line, #include <math.h>, which gives you some math capabilities.)

Listing 5-1: Seeing a Function in Action

```
#include <iostream>
#include <math.h>

using namespace std;

int main()
{
  cout << fabs(-10.5) << endl;
  cout << fabs(10.5) << endl;
  return 0;
}
```

When you run this application, you see the following output:

```
10.5
10.5
```

In this code, you use a function or machine called `fabs()` (usually pronounced "ef-abs," for floating-point absolute). This function takes a number as input and returns as output the absolute value of the number.

The absolute value of a number is simply the positive version of the number. The absolute value, for example, of –5 is simply 5. The absolute value of 12 is still 12. An absolute value is always positive. And the absolute value of 0 is 0. (The reason for the `f` before the name `abs` is that it uses floating-point numbers, which are simply numbers with decimal points.)

So the first line inside `main()` *calls* `fabs()` for the value –10.5. The `cout` then takes the output of this function (that is, the *result*) and prints it to the console.

Then the second line does the same thing again, except that it takes the absolute value of the number 10.5.

And where is the processor for this function? It's not in your code; it's in another file, and the following line ensures that your application can use this function:

```
#include <math.h>
```

You have seen functions in many places. If you use a calculator and enter a number and press the square root button, the calculator runs a function that calculates the square root.

But functions can be more sophisticated than just working with numbers. Consider this statement carefully: When you are using a word processor and you highlight a word and check the spelling of the word, the application calls a function that handles the spelling check. This function does something like the following:

```
This is a function to check the spelling of a single word.
Inputs: A single word.
Look up the word
If the word is not found
    Find some suggestions.
    Open a dialog box through which you (the user)
        can change the word by either typing a new word
        or picking one of the selections, or just leaving
        it the same.
    If you made a change,
        Return the new spelling.
    Otherwise
        Return nothing.
Otherwise
    Return nothing
```

Notice how we grouped the `if` statements with indentations. The final `otherwise` goes with the first `if` statement because its indentation matches that of the `if` statement.

So that's a function that performs a spelling check. But consider this: When you do not highlight a word but run the spelling checker, the spelling checker runs for the whole document. That's another function. Here it is.

```
This is a function to check the spelling of the entire document
For each word in the document
     Check the spelling of the single word
```

How does the computer do the step inside the `for` loop, "Check the spelling of the single word?" It calls the function we described earlier. This process is called *code reuse*. You have no reason to rewrite the entire function again if you already have it somewhere else. And that's the beauty of functions.

Calling a Function

When you run the code in a function, computer people say that you are *calling* the function. And just like every good person, a good function has a name. When you call a function, you do so by name.

Often, when we're writing an application and write code to call a function, we will say that we are calling a function. This is partly computerspeak and partly a strange disorder in which we computer programmers start to relate just a little *too* much to the computer.

To call a function, you type its name and then a set of parentheses. Inside the parentheses, you list the items you want to send to the inputs of the function. The term we use here is *pass*, as in "You pass the values to the function."

For example, if you want to call the `fabs()` function, you type the name, `fabs`, an open parenthesis, the number you want to pass to it, and then a close parenthesis, as in the following example:

```
fabs(-10.5)
```

But by itself, this line does not do anything. The `fabs()` function returns a value — the absolute value of –10.5, which comes out to be 10.5 — and you probably want to do something with that value. You could, for example, print it to the console:

```
cout << fabs(-10.5) << endl;
```

Or you could store it away in another variable. But there's a catch. Before you can do that, you need to know the *type* that the function returns. Just as with a variable, a function return value has a type. In this case, the type is a special type called `double`. The `double` type is a floating-point type that can hold many digits in a single number. To save the result of `fabs()`, you need to have a variable of type `double`. The `Fabs2` example in Listing 5-2 does this.

Listing 5-2: Seeing Another Function in Action

```
#include <iostream>
#include <math.h>

using namespace std;

int main()
{
  double mynumber;
  mynumber = fabs(-23.87);
  cout << mynumber << endl;
  return 0;
}
```

This code declares a `double` variable called `mynumber`. Then it calls `fabs()`, passing it –23.87 and returning the value into `mynumber`. Next, it prints the value in `mynumber` to the console.

When you run this application, you see the following, which is the absolute value of –23.87:

```
23.87
```

Passing a variable

You can also pass the value of a variable into a function. The `Fabs3` example in Listing 5-3 creates two variables: One is passed into the function, and the other receives the result of the function.

Listing 5-3: Seeing Yet Another Function in Action

```
#include <iostream>
#include <math.h>

using namespace std;

int main()
{
  double start;
  double finish;

  start = -253.895;
  finish = fabs(start);

  cout << finish << endl;
  return 0;
}
```

(We separated the parts of the code with blank lines to make it a little easier to follow.) This code first creates two variables; the first is called `start`, and the second is called `finish`. It then initializes `start` with a value of –253.895.

Next, it calls `fabs()`, passing it the value of `start`. It saves the return value in the `finish` variable, and it finally prints the value in `finish`. When it runs, you see the following appear on the console:

```
253.895
```

Saving a function result to a variable is useful if you need to use the result several times over. For example, if you need the absolute value of –253.895 for whatever reason and then a few lines later you need it again, you have a choice: You can either call `fabs(-253.895)` each time or call it once, save it in a variable, and then use the variable each time you need it. The advantage to saving it in a variable is that you might later say, for example, "Oh, wait! I didn't just want the absolute value! I wanted the negative of the absolute value!" Then you only have to change one line of code — the line where it calls `fabs()`. If, instead, you had called `fabs()` several times, you would have had to change it every time you called it. And by the way, in case you're curious about how to take the negative of the absolute value and store it in a variable, you just throw a minus sign in front of it, like so:

```
finish = -fabs(start);
```

Passing multiple variables

Some functions like to have all sorts of goodies thrown their way, such as multiple parameters. As with functions that take a single value, you put the values inside a single set of parentheses. Because you have multiple values, you separate them with commas. The `Pow1` example shown in Listing 5-4 uses a function called `pow()` to calculate the third power of 10. (That is, it calculates 10 times 10 times 10. Yes, *POW!*). Make sure that you include the `math.h` line in the `include` section so that you can use the `pow()` function.

Listing 5-4:   Seeing Yet One More Function in Action

```
#include <iostream>
#include <math.h>

using namespace std;

int main()
{
  double number = 10.0;
  double exponent = 3.0;
  cout << pow(number, exponent) << endl;
  return 0;
}
```

When you run the application, you see 10 to the third power, which is 1,000:

```
1000
```

You can also pass a mixture of variables and numbers, or just numbers. The following code snippet also calculates the third power of 10 but passes an actual number, 3.0, for the power:

```
double number = 10.0;
cout << pow(number, 3.0) << endl;
```

Or you can pass only numbers:

```
cout << pow(10.0, 3.0) << endl;
```

Writing Your Own Functions

And now the fun begins! Calling functions is great, but you get real power (ooh!) when you write your own, specialized functions. Before writing a function, remember the parts: the inputs, the main code or processor, and the single output (or no output). The inputs, however, are called *parameters,* and the output is called a *return value.*

The AddOne example shown in Listing 5-5 provides both a custom function and code in main() that calls the custom function. (The function is placed outside main() — before it, in fact.)

Listing 5-5:   Writing Your Very Own Function

```
#include <iostream>

using namespace std;

int AddOne(int start)
{
  int newnumber;
  newnumber = start + 1;
  return newnumber;
}

int main()
{
  int testnumber;
  int result;

  testnumber = 20;
  result = AddOne(testnumber);

  cout << result << endl;
  return 0;
}
```

Notice that this example lacks the `#include <math.h>` entry found in earlier examples. You only need to add an entry to the `include` section of your code when you use a feature of that include file. In this case, the example relies on standard math features that are part of the basic C++ language, so you don't need any additional code.

After you get all this code typed in and your fingers are feeling nice and exercised, go ahead and run it. Because there's a good bit of code, you may get some compiler errors at first; look carefully at the lines with the errors and find the difference between your code and what's here in the book.

After you run it, you see

```
21
```

Now, before we explain the code for the function, we'll save the fun for last. Take a look at these three lines of `main()`:

```
testnumber = 20;
result = AddOne(testnumber);
cout << result << endl;
```

You can probably put together some facts and determine what the function does. First, we called it `AddOne()`, which is a pretty good indication in itself. Second, when you run the application, the number 21 appears on the console, which is one more than the value in `testnumber`; it adds one. And that, in fact, is what the function does. It's amazing what computers can do these days.

When you write your own functions, try to choose a name that makes sense and describes what the function does. Writing a function and calling it something like `process()` or `TheFunction()` is easy, but those names do not accurately describe the function.

So now take a look at the function itself. First, here are a few high-level observations about it:

✦ **Position:** The function appears *before* `main()`. Because of the way the compiler works, it must know about a function before you call it. And thus, you put it before `main()`. (You can do this in another way, which we discuss in the section "Forward references and function prototypes," later in this chapter.)

✦ **Format:** The function starts with a line that seems to describe the function (which we explain later in this section), and then it has an open brace and, later, a closing brace.

✦ **Code:** The function has code in it that is just like the type of code you could put inside a `main()`.

After noting these high-level concepts, take a look at the code inside the function. The first part of it looks like this:

```
int newnumber;
newnumber = start + 1;
```

So far, the example is straightforward. It declares an integer variable called `newnumber`. Then it initializes it to `start` plus 1. But what is `start`? That's one of the inputs.

Finally, this line is at the end of the function, before the closing brace:

```
return newnumber;
```

This is the output of the function, or the *return value*. When you want to return something from a function, you just type the word `return` and then indicate what you want to return. From the first two lines in the `AddOne()` function, you can see that newnumber is one more than the number passed into the function. So this line returns the `newnumber`. Thus, all three parts are covered: You have taken the input or parameter; you have processed it by creating a variable and adding 1 to the parameter; and you have returned the output, which is one more than the parameter.

But what is the parameter? It's called `start`. And where did it come from? Here's the first line of the function:

```
int AddOne(int start)
```

The stuff in parentheses is the list of parameters. Notice that it looks just like a variable declaration; it's the word `int` (the type, or integer) followed by a variable name, `start`. That's the parameter — the input — to the function, and you can access this parameter throughout the function by simply using a variable called `start`.

We think that's rather ingenious, if we do say so ourselves. Okay, so we didn't invent it, but, nevertheless, we think it's ingenious: *You can use the input to the function as a variable itself.*

And so, if down in `main()` we had written

```
result = AddOne(25);
```

then, throughout the function, the value of `start` would be 25.

But if we had written

```
result = AddOne(152);
```

then, throughout the function, the value of `start` would be 152.

Arguing over parameters

Technically, the term *parameter* refers strictly to the inputs to the function, from the function's perspective. When you call the function, the things you place in parentheses in the call line are not parameters; rather, they are described as *arguments*. Thus, in the following function header, the variables `first` and `last` are parameters. But in the following call to a function (found in Listing 5-7)

```
ConnectNames("Bill", "Murray")
```

the strings `"Bill"` and `"Murray"` are arguments of the call.

But here's the outstanding thing about functions (or, at least, one of the loads of outstanding things about functions): You can call the function several times over. In the same `main()`, you can have the following lines

```
cout << AddOne(100) << endl;
cout << AddOne(200) << endl;
cout << AddOne(300) << endl;
```

which would result in this output:

```
101
201
301
```

In the first call to `AddOne`, the value of `start` would be `100`. During the second call, the value would be `200`, and during the third call, it would be `300`.

Now take another look at the header:

```
int AddOne(int start)
```

The word `AddOne` is the name of the function, as you've probably figured out already. And that leaves the thing at the beginning — the `int`. That's the *type* of the return value. The final line in the function before the closing brace is

```
return newnumber;
```

The variable `newnumber` inside the function is an integer. And the return type is integer. That's no accident: As programmers have all heard before, friends don't let friends return something other than the type specified in the function header. The two must match in type. And further, take a look at this line from inside `main()`:

```
result = AddOne(testnumber);
```

What type is the `result` variable? It's also an integer. All three match. Again, no accident. You can copy one thing to another (in this case, the function's return value to the variable called `result`) only if they match in type. And here, they do — they're both integers.

Notice one more thing about the function header: It has no semicolon after it. This is one of the places you do *not* put a semicolon. If you do, the compiler gets horribly confused. The Code::Blocks compiler shows an error that says, "`error: expected unqualified-id before '{' token.`"

Here's a recap of some of the rules we just mentioned regarding functions:

+ **Header line:** The header line starts with a value for the return type, the name of the function, and the list of parameters.

+ **Parameters:** The parameters are written like variable declarations, and indeed, you can use them as variables inside the function.

+ **Return type:** Whatever you return from the function must match in type with the type you specified in the function header.

+ **More on format:** The function header does not have a semicolon after it.

+ **Even more on format:** After the function header, you use an open brace. The function ends with a closing brace. The final brace tells the compiler where the function ends.

Finally, ponder this line of code for a moment:

```
testnumber = AddOne(testnumber);
```

This line takes the value stored inside `testnumber`, passes it into `AddOne()`, and gets back a new number. It then takes that new number and stores it back into `testnumber`. Thus, `testnumber`'s value changes based on the results of the function `AddOne()`.

Multiple parameters or no parameters

You don't need to write your functions with only one parameter each. You can have several parameters, or you can have none. It may seem a little strange that you would want a function — a machine — that accepts no inputs. But you may run into lots of cases where this may be a good idea. Here are some ideas for functions:

+ **Day:** Determines the day and returns it as a string, as in `"Monday"` or `"Tuesday"`

+ **Number-of-users:** Figures out the current number of users logged in to a web-server computer

✦ **Current font:** In a text editor application (such as Notepad), returns a string containing the current font name, such as `"Arial"`

✦ **Editing time:** Returns the amount of time you have been using the word processor application

✦ **Username:** If you are logged on to a computer, gives back your username as a string, such as "Elisha"

All functions in this list have something in common: They look up information. Because no parameters are in the code, for the functions to process some information, they have to go out and get it themselves. It's like sending people out into the woods to find food but not giving them any tools: It's totally up to them to perform the required tasks, and all you can do is sit back and watch and wait for your yummy surprise.

If a function takes no parameters, you write the function header as you would for one that takes parameters, and you include the parentheses; you just don't put anything *in* the parentheses, as the `UserName` example in Listing 5-6 shows. So if nothing good is going in, there really can be something good coming back out, at least in the case of a function with no parameters.

Listing 5-6:   Taking No Parameters

```
#include <iostream>

using namespace std;

string Username()
{
    return "Elisha";
}

int main()
{
  cout << Username() << endl;
  return 0;
}
```

When you run Listing 5-6, you see the following output:

```
Elisha
```

Your function can also take multiple parameters. The `ConnectNames` example shown in Listing 5-7 demonstrates the use of multiple parameters. Notice that the function, `ConnectNames()`, takes the two strings as parameters and combines them, along with a space in the middle. Notice also that the function uses the two strings as variables.

Listing 5-7: Taking Multiple Parameters

```
#include <iostream>

using namespace std;

string ConnectNames(string first, string last)
{
  return first + " " + last;
}

int main()
{
  cout << ConnectNames("Richard", "Nixon") << endl;
  return 0;
}
```

In the function header in Listing 5-7, we had to put the type name `string` for each parameter. If we listed it only for the first, we would get a compile error. (Okay, we admit it — we did forget it, and that's how we remembered to tell you. But that shows that even experienced programmers can make mistakes. Occasionally.)

Here are some points about this code:

✦ **We didn't create variables for the two names in** `main()`. Instead, we just typed them as string constants (that is, as actual strings surrounded by quotes).

✦ **You can do calculations and figuring right inside the** `return` **statement.** That saves the extra work of creating a variable. In the function, we could have created a return variable of type `string`, set it to `first + " " + last`, and then returned that variable, as in the following code:

```
string result = first + " " + last;
return result;
```

But instead, we chose to do it all on one line, as in this line:

```
return first + " " + last;
```

Although you can save yourself the work of creating an extra variable and just put the whole expression in the `return` statement, sometimes that's is a bad thing. If the expression is really long, like the following:

```
return (mynumber * 100 + somethingelse / 200) *
  (yetanother + 400 / mynumber) / (mynumber + evenmore);
```

it can get just a tad complicated. Breaking it into variables, such as in this example, is best:

```
double a = mynumber * 100 + somethingelse / 200;
double b = yetanother + 400 / mynumber;
double c = mynumber + evenmore;
return a * b / c;
```

Returning nothing

In the earlier section "Multiple parameters or no parameters," we present a list of functions that take no parameters; these functions go and bring back something, whether it's a number, a string, or some other type of food.

One such example gets the username of the computer you're logged in to. But what if you are the great computer guru, and *you* are writing the application that actually logs somebody in? In that case, your application doesn't ask the computer what the username is — your application *tells* the computer what the username is, by golly!

In that case, your application would call a function, like SetUsername(), and pass the new username. And would this function return anything? It could; it could return the name, or it could return a message saying that the username is not valid or something like that. Or, it may not return anything at all.

Take a look at the case where a function doesn't return anything. In C++, the way you state that the function doesn't return anything is by using the word *void* as the return type in the function header. The SetUserName example shown in Listing 5-8 demonstrates this.

Listing 5-8:   Returning Nothing at All

```
#include <iostream>

using namespace std;

void SetUsername(string newname)
{
    cout << "New user is " << newname << endl;
}

int main()
{
    SetUsername("Harold");
    return 0;
}
```

When you run the application, you see

```
New user is Harold
```

Notice the `SetUsername()` function header: It starts with the word `void`, which means that it returns nothing at all. It's like outer space: There's just a big void with nothing there, and nothing is returned, except for static from the alien airwaves, but we won't go there. Also notice that, because this function does not return anything, there is no `return` statement.

Now, of course, this function really doesn't do a whole lot other than print the new username to the console, but that's okay; it shows you how you can write a function that does not return anything.

A function of return type `void` returns nothing at all.

Do not try to return something in a function that has a return type of `void`. *Void* means that the function returns nothing at all. If you try to put a `return` statement in your function, you get a compile error.

Keeping your variables local

Everybody likes to have their own stuff, and functions are no exception. When you create a variable inside the code for a function, that variable will be known only to that particular function. When you create such variables, they are called *local variables*, and people say that they are local to that particular function. (Well, *computer* people say that, anyway.)

To see a local variable at work, consider the code in the `PrintName` example:

```
#include <iostream>

using namespace std;

void PrintName(string first, string last)
{
    string fullname = first + " " + last;
    cout << fullname << endl;
}

int main()
{
    PrintName("Thomas", "Jefferson");
    return 0;
}
```

Notice in the `PrintName()` function that you declare a variable called `fullname`. You then use that variable in the second line in that function, the one starting with `cout`. But you cannot use the variable inside `main()`. If you try to, as in the following code, you get a compile error:

```
int main()
{
    PrintName("Thomas", "Jefferson");
    cout << fullname << endl;
    return 0;
}
```

However, you can *declare* a variable called `fullname` inside `main()`, as in the following code. But, if you do that, this `fullname` is local only to `main()`, whereas the other variable, also called `fullname`, is local only to the `PrintName()` function. In other words, each function has its own variable; they just happen to share the same name. But they are *two separate variables:*

```
int main()
{
    string fullname = "Abraham Lincoln";
    PrintName("Thomas", "Jefferson");
    cout << fullname << endl;
    return 0;
}
```

When two functions declare variables by the same name, they are two separate variables. If you store a value inside one of them, the other function does not know about it. The other function only knows about its own variable by that name. Think of it the way two people could each have a storage bin labeled Tools in the closet. If Sally puts a hammer in her bin labeled Tools and Hal opens another bin also labeled Tools at *his* house, he won't see the very same hammer in Sally's bin, will he? We hope not, or else something is seriously awry in the universe. With variables, it works the same way.

If you use the same variable name in two different functions, forgetting that you are working with two different variables is very easy. Do this only if you are sure that no confusion can occur.

If you use the same variable name in two different functions (such as a counter variable called `index`, which you use in a `for` loop), matching the case is usually a good idea. Don't use `count` in one function and use `Count` in another. Although you can certainly do that, you may find yourself typing the name wrong when you need it. But that won't cause you to access the other one. (You can't, because it is in a different function.) Instead, you get a compile error, and you have to go back and fix it. Being consistent is a timesaver.

Forward references and function prototypes

In all examples in this chapter, we have placed the code for any function we write above the code for `main()`. The reason is that the compiler scans the code from start to finish. If it has not yet encountered a function but sees a call to it, it doesn't know what it's seeing, and it issues a good old compile error.

Such an error can be especially frustrating and can cause you to spend hours yelling at your computer (or, if you're like us, running to the refrigerator to find something sweet and fattening). Nothing is more frustrating than looking at your application and being told by the compiler that it's wrong, yet knowing that it's correct because you know that you wrote the function.

You can, however, place your functions after `main()`; or you can even use function prototypes to put your functions in other source code files (a topic we talk about in Book I, Chapter 6).

What you can do is include a function prototype. A *function prototype* is nothing more than a copy of the function header. But rather than follow it with an open brace and then the code for the function, you follow the function header with a semicolon and you are finished. A function prototype, for example, looks like this:

```
void PrintName(string first, string last);
```

Then you actually write the full function (header, code, and all) later. The full function can even be later than `main()` or later than any place that makes calls to it.

Notice that this example looks just like the first line of a function. In fact, we cheated! To write it, we simply copied the first line of the original function we wrote and added a semicolon.

So where would you use this fellow? Take a look at the `PrintName2` example, shown in Listing 5-9.

Listing 5-9: Using a Function Prototype

```
#include <iostream>

using namespace std;

void PrintName(string first, string last);

int main()
{
  PrintName("Thomas", "Jefferson");
  return 0;
}

void PrintName(string first, string last)
{
  string fullname = first + " " + last;
  cout << fullname << endl;
}
```

Notice, in this listing, that we have the function header copied above `main()` and ending with a semicolon. Then we have `main()`. Finally, we have the `PrintName()` function itself (again, with the header but no semicolon this time). Thus, the function comes after `main()`.

"Whoop-de-do," we can hear you saying. "The function comes after." But why bother when now we have to type the function header twice?

Rest assured, dear readers, that this step is useful. If you have a source code file with, say, 20 functions and these functions all make various calls to each other, it could be difficult to carefully order them so that each function calls *only* functions that are above it in the source code file. Instead, most programmers put the functions in some logical order (or maybe not), and they don't worry much about the calling order. Then they have all the function prototypes toward the top of the source code file, as we did earlier, in Listing 5-9.

When you type a function prototype, many people say that you are specifying a *forward reference*: This phrase simply means that you are providing a reference to something that happens later. It's not a big deal, and it mainly comes from some of the older programming languages. But some people use the jargon, and we hope that if you hear that phrase, it will trigger happy memories of this book.

Writing two versions of the same function

There may be times when you want to write two versions of the same function, with the only difference that they take different parameter types. For example, you may want a function called Combine(). One version takes two strings and puts the two strings together, but with a space in the middle. It then prints the resulting string to the console. Another version adds two numbers and writes all three numbers — the first two and the sum — to the console.

The first version would look like this:

```
void Combine(string first, string second)
{
   cout << first << " " << second << endl;
}
```

There's nothing magical or particularly special about this function. It's called Combine(); it takes two strings as parameters; it does not return anything. The code for the function prints the two strings with a space between them.

Now the second version looks like this:

```
void Combine(int first, int second)
{
   int sum = first + second;
   cout << first << " " << second << " " << sum << endl;
}
```

Again, nothing spectacular here. The function name is Combine(), and it does not return anything. But this version takes two integers, not two strings, as parameters. The code is also different from the previous code in that it first figures the sum of the two and then prints the different numbers.

Go ahead and say it: "Well, this is all fine and dandy, but can you have two functions by the same name like this?" Yup! The `Combine` example, shown in Listing 5-10, contains the entire code. Both functions are present in the listing.

Listing 5-10: Writing Two Versions of a Function

```
#include <iostream>

using namespace std;

void Combine(string first, string second)
{
  cout << first << " " << second << endl;
}

void Combine(int first, int second)
{
  int sum = first + second;
  cout << first << " " << second << " " << sum << endl;
}

int main()
{
  Combine("David","Letterman");
  Combine(15,20);
  return 0;
}
```

Note in `main()` that we called each function. How did we specify which one we want? *By simply passing the right types*. Take a close look at the first call:

```
Combine("David","Letterman");
```

This call includes two strings. so the compiler knows to use the first version, which takes two strings. Now look at the second function call:

```
Combine(15,20);
```

This call takes two integers, so the compiler knows to use the second version of the function.

This process of writing two versions of the same function is called *overloading* the function. Normally, overloading is a bad thing, like when we go to a nice restaurant and overload our stomachs. But here it's a good thing — and even useful.

When you overload a function, the parameters must differ. For example, the functions can take the same type of information but use a different number of parameters. Of course, the previous example shows that the parameters can also vary by type. You can also have different return types, though they must differ by *more than just the return type*.

Calling All String Functions

To get the most out of strings, you need to make use of some special functions that cater to the strings. However, using these functions is a little different from the other functions used so far in this chapter. Rather than just call the function, you first type the variable name that holds the string, and then a period (or *dot*, as the netheads prefer to call it), and then the function name along with any parameters (*arguments,* if any purists are reading).

The reason you code string functions differently is because you're making use of some object-oriented programming features. Book I, Chapter 8 describes in detail how these types of functions (called *member* functions) work.

One function that you can use is `insert()`. You can use this function if you want to insert more characters into another string. For example, if you have the string `"Something interesting and bizarre"` and you insert the string `"seriously"` (with a space at the end) into the middle of it starting at index 10, you get the string `"Something seriously interesting and bizarre"`.

When you work with strings, the first character is the 0th index, and the second character is the 1st index, and so on.

The following lines of code perform an insert by using the `insert()` function:

```
string words = "Something interesting and bizarre";
words.insert(10, "seriously ");
```

The first of these lines simply creates a string called `words` and stuffs it full with the phrase `"Something interesting and bizarre"`. The second line does the insert. Notice the strange way of calling the function: You first specify the variable name, `words`, and then a dot, and then the function name, `insert`. Next, you follow it with the parameters in parentheses, as usual. For this function, the first parameter is the index where you want to insert the string. The second parameter is the actual string you are going to insert.

After these two lines run, the string variable called `words` contains the string `"Something seriously interesting and bizarre"`.

You can also erase parts of a string by using a similar function called, believe it or not, `erase()`. Although computer folks like to obfuscate through their parlance (that is, confuse people through choices of words!), they do occasionally break down and pick names that actually make sense.

The following line of code erases from the string called words 16 characters, starting with the 20th index:

```
words.erase(19,16);
```

Consequently, if the variable called words contains the string "Something seriously interesting and bizarre", after this line runs, it will contain "Something seriously bizarre".

Another useful function is replace(). This function replaces a certain part of the string with another string. To use replace, you specify where in the string you want to start the replacement and how many characters you want to replace. Then you specify the string with which you want to replace the old, worn-out parts.

For example, if your string is "Something seriously bizarre" and you want to replace the word "thing" with the string "body", you tell replace to start at index 4 and replace 5 characters with the word "body". To do this, you enter:

```
words.replace(4, 5, "body");
```

Notice that the number of characters you replace does not have to be the same as the length of the new string. If the string starts out with "Something seriously bizarre", after this replace statement runs, the string will contain "Somebody seriously bizarre". But the string will not actually contain somebody who is seriously bizarre; it contains just the string.

The OperatingOnStrings example, shown in Listing 5-11, demonstrates all these functions working together.

Listing 5-11:   Operating on Strings

```
#include <iostream>

using namespace std;

int main()
{
  string words = "Something interesting and bizarre";
  cout << words << endl;

  words.insert(10, "seriously ");
  cout << words << endl;

  words.erase(19,16);
  cout << words << endl;

  words.replace(4, 5, "body");
  cout << words << endl;

  return 0;
}
```

When you run this application, you see the following output:

```
Something interesting and bizarre
Something seriously interesting and bizarre
Something seriously bizarre
Somebody seriously bizarre
```

The first line is the original string. The second line is the result of the insert() function. The third line is the result of the erase() function. And the final line is the result of the replace() function.

Understanding main ( )

All applications so far in this chapter have had a main(). This main() is actually a function. Notice its header, which is followed by code inside braces:

```
int main()
```

You can see that this is definitely a function header: It starts out with a return type and then the function name, main(). This is just one form of the main() function — the form that Code::Blocks uses by default. However, you may decide that you want to give users the ability to provide input when they type the name of your application at the console. In this case, you use this alternative form of the main() function that includes two parameters:

```
int main(int argc, char *argv[])
```

Who, what, where, and why return?

The main() function header starts with the type int. This means that the function main() returns something. But what? And to whom? And why and when and all those *w* words?

The result of main() is sometimes used by the computer to return error messages if the application, for some reason, didn't work or didn't do what it was supposed to do. But here's the inside scoop: *Outputting a return value just doesn't work* — at least, not in the graphical environment that most people use.

It's true. For many computers, particularly Windows computers, the return value is of little use to anybody. The return type is specifically designed to work with batch files (files with a BAT extension that originally appeared as part of DOS, or Disk Operating System). Consequently, unless you plan to work with batch files (and many people still do), just return 0.

On some high-powered Unix systems, the return value of `main()` *is* used. Some of these systems running so-called *mission-critical* applications (a fancy word that means the computer programmers feel that what they're doing is important to the safety of the universe) do indeed use the return values from `main()`. These computers may run hundreds of applications. If one of these applications returns something other than 0, another application detects this and notifies somebody (usually, by sending the poor sap a page in the middle of the night). When you're still learning C++, you're not likely to need to return things other than 0, but if you're lucky enough to be working for a company that builds applications vital to the well-being of the universe, you may want to find out from your teammates if you do, in fact, need to return something other than 0.

So what about those seriously bizarre-looking parameters in `main()` shown in Listing 5-12? The first one is reasonably straightforward: It's an integer variable with the goofy name argv, which sounds like something Scooby-Doo would say. But what about that second bit of goofiness? To understand the second, you need to know that these two parameters are used as *command-line parameters*. When you run an application, especially from the command prompt, you type the name of the application and press Enter. But before pressing Enter, you can follow the application name with other words. Many of the commands you use in Unix and in the Windows command-line tool (also known as DOS) have an application name and then various parameters. For example, on Unix you could type the following command to copy the file named `myfile` to a new file named `yourfile`:

```
cp myfile yourfile
```

On Windows, you could type the following command to copy the file named `myfile` to a new file named `yourfile`:

```
copy myfile yourfile
```

When you run such a command, you are actually running an application called `copy`. The application takes two command-line parameters — in this case, `"myfile"` and `"yourfile"` — and passes these two strings into the `main()` function as parameters.

For the `main()` function, the first parameter in the header is argc (pronounced "arg-SEE"), which represents the number of command-line parameters. In the case of the `copy` or `cp` command (see the two preceding lines of code), you have two (`"myfile"` and `"yourfile"`), so argc would be 2.

The second parameter in the `main()` function is the cryptic-looking `char *argv[]`. The name of the variable is `argv`, and it is pronounced "arg-VEE." Book I, Chapter 9 deals with the topic arrays. An *array* is a sequence of variables stored under one name. The `argv` variable is one such animal. To access the individual variables stored under the single umbrella known as `argv`, you do something like this:

```
cout << argv[0] << endl;
cout << argv[1] << endl;
```

(In the preceding example, you're using brackets as you did similarly with accessing the individual characters in a string.)

In the case of the two command-line parameters `myfile` and `yourfile`, these two lines of code would print the lines

```
myfile
yourfile
```

You can access the command-line parameters using a `for` loop. The `CommandLineParameters` example, shown in Listing 5-12, demonstrates this technique.

Listing 5-12:   Accessing the Command-Line Parameters

```
#include <iostream>
#include <stdlib.h>
int main(int argc, char *argv[])
{
  for (int index=0; index < argc; index++)
  {
    cout << argv[index] << endl;
  }
  return 0;
}
```

Setting the command-line parameters in Code::Blocks

If you attempt to run the example in Code::Blocks by choosing Build⇨Run with the default settings, the example doesn't output anything other than the execution path and application name. To add command-line arguments, choose Project⇨Set Program's Arguments. You see the Select Target dialog box, where you can type the command-line arguments in the Program Arguments field. Type **CommandLineParameters Command Line Parameters** in this field and click OK. You're ready to run the example.

When you run this application from the prompt using the following command-line parameters:

```
CommandLineParameters Command Line Parameters
```

you see the following output:

```
C:\CPP_AIO\BookI\Chapter05\CommandLineParameters\bin\Debug\CommandLineParameters
.exe
CommandLineParameters
Command
Line
Parameters
```

The first item in the `argv` list is always the execution path and the name of the application.

Chapter 6: Splitting Up Source Code Files

In This Chapter

✔ **Creating multiple source code files**

✔ **Creating header files**

✔ **Sharing variables among source files**

✔ **Making use of the mysterious header wrappers**

*J*ust as you can divide your work into functions, you can also divide your work into multiple source code files. The main reason to do so is, simply, to help keep your project manageable. Also, with multiple source code files, you can have several people working on a single project, each working on a different source code file at the same time. The goal, of course, is to make sure that your coworkers work on the harder parts that are more grueling and no fun while you get all the credit.

The key to multiple source files is knowing where to break the source code into pieces. Like anything else, if you break the source code in the wrong place, it will, well, break.

In this chapter, we show you how to divide your source code into multiple files (and in all the right places). The examples we give use Code::Blocks; however, we also provide a few `Makefile` tips if you're using other tools. (*Makefiles* are special files that contain instructions the compiler uses to turn your source code into an executable file. You won't need to worry about them when using Code::Blocks and other tools tell you how to create a `Makefile` for that specific tool, but if you're still curious about `Makefiles`, check out this book's appendix for a tad more info.)

Creating Multiple Source Files

In this section, we talk about how to create multiple source code files, first for Code::Blocks and then for other compilers. This process is far simpler in Code::Blocks, and we highly recommend that approach.

When you create a second source code file, this code becomes part of your project. And when you compile, the compiler compiles all the source code files in your project, assuming that you have changed them since the last time you compiled. You can put your functions in separate source code files, and they can call each other. In this way, they all work together in the single application. In the section "Sharing with Header Files," later in this chapter, we talk about how you can have a function call another function in a different source file.

You cannot break up a single function and put it into two source files. That would be quite painful for the little fellow, and certainly not a good programming practice either, because it simply wouldn't compile. The compiler requires that your functions stay in one piece in a single source file.

Splitting a project into multiple source files in Code::Blocks

If you're using Code::Blocks, cutting your application into multiple source code files is as easy as cutting a cake. The following steps show you how to perform this task:

1. **Choose File⇨New⇨File.**

You see the New from Template dialog box, shown in Figure 6-1. Notice that you can choose from a header, source code, or an empty file (among other non-C++ possibilities). Normally, you choose either the C/C++ Header or C/C++ Source option. The Empty File option is for non-source files, such as a text file used as a ReadMe.

2. **Highlight the template you want to use, and click Go.**

You see a wizard associated with the particular file you've chosen.

Figure 6-1:
The New from Template dialog box lets you select a new file type.

3. **Click Next to get past the initial Welcome page.**

If you chose the Empty File template, skip to Step 5. When using the C/
C++ Header or C/C++ Source templates, you see a language selection
page.

4. **Highlight the language you want to use — either C or C++ — and click
Next.**

The wizard asks what you want to call the file, where you want to store
it, and which builds should use the file, as shown in Figure 6-2. (More on
these choices in Steps 5–8.)

Figure 6-2:
Provide
the file
information
required by
the wizard.

5. **Type a path and filename for the file in the Filename with Full Path
field.**

You must provide the full path, even if you want the file in the current
folder. Click the ellipses to display the Select Filename dialog box, where
you can choose the location of the file. The default path shown in the
Select Filename dialog box is the current folder.

6. **Check the individual builds that should use the file.**

As an alternative, you can click All to add the file to all builds.

A *debug* version of your application will contain special information that
you can use to find program errors. A *release* version of your application
is smaller and executes faster. Each version has a purpose, so developers usually need to create both at some point.

7. Click Finish.

The wizard adds the new file to your project. Code::Blocks automatically opens the file so that you can begin editing it. You also see the file you added in the Management window, as shown in Figure 6-3. In this case, you see both the source files and a header file. Notice that the source files appear in dark type and the header file appears in gray type. This shows that the source files are compiled to create the project and the header file isn't. The "Sharing with Header Files" section of this chapter discusses in more detail how the compiler works with header files.

Figure 6-3:
The Management window displays the files used to compile the project.

If you add a file to Code::Blocks that you really don't need, right-click the file in the Management window and choose Remove File from Project from the context menu. The file will disappear from the project but still appear in the directory in which you created it. If you later decide that you really do want that file, right-click the project entry in the Management window, choose Add Files from the context menu, and select the file you want to add back into the project using the options in the Add Files to Project dialog box.

If Code::Blocks doesn't automatically open the file you added, you can open it by double-clicking its name in the tree. When you do, an additional tab appears at the top of your source code files. These tabs represent the different files that are open. You can click a tab to have that file's code appear in the source code window. When you click another tab, the window shows the source for that file instead. And, thankfully, Code::Blocks remembers any changes you make if you switch to another tab. So you can bounce all around the screen and switch all you want, and the computer shouldn't get confused.

After you have multiple files in your project, you can put some of your source in one file and some in another. But before you do, you may want to read some of the other sections in this chapter because we explain how to properly divide your source code without it ending up like cake that got smooshed while you were trying to cut it.

Creating a project in Code::Blocks with multiple existing files

Sometimes you have a number of existing files, but no project to hold them. For example, you might be moving from another IDE to Code::Blocks. That would mean that you'd have the source files from the other IDE, but no project file that Code::Blocks would recognize. Don't worry: You can put existing files into a Code::Blocks project. The following steps tell you how to perform this process (you can see the result by opening the CopiedFiles project):

1. **Create a new project.**

Chapter 2 tells you how to perform this task.

2. **Right-click the main.cpp file found in the Sources folder of the Management window, and choose Remove File from Project from the context menu.**

You don't need this file if you're copying existing files into a new project. Code::Blocks supplies a `main.cpp` file by default so that you don't have to start the project from scratch. However, since you already have the files you need, you don't need this starter file.

3. **Right-click the CopiedFiles project entry in the Management window and choose Add Files from the context menu.**

You see the Add Files to Project window, shown in Figure 6-4. Notice that `main.cpp` still appears in the list of files for this project. You can use this dialog box to add new files or to permanently remove files you no longer need.

Figure 6-4:
Use this dialog box to add existing files to a project or to delete files you no longer need.

4. Right-click main.cpp and choose Delete from the context menu.

You may see a message asking whether you want to delete the file. If so, simply click Yes. The starter main.cpp file will be deleted at this point.

5. Locate and highlight the files you want to copy to the new project.

Use the Ctrl+click method to select multiple files from the list. Code::Blocks makes it easy to select multiple files in a single pass so that you don't have to open the Add Files to Project dialog box multiple times.

6. Click Open.

Code::Blocks displays a dialog box asking which builds to add the files to, as shown in Figure 6-5. The exact appearance of the dialog box will vary by the number of files you select.

7. Select the builds you want to use and click OK.

Code::Blocks adds the required file references to the project, as shown in Figure 6-6.

Figure 6-5:
Select
the builds
where the
files are
used.

Figure 6-6:
The new
project now
contains
references
to the
selected
files.

Notice that the references still show the original location of the files. In this case, these files come from the MultipleSourceFiles2 project. If you change the file in the original project, it also changes in the new project. To actually copy the file to a new project, you need to create a copy and paste it into the project folder — and then add it to the project as we've done here.

Multiple source files in other compilers

If you're using Code::Blocks, you don't really need to read this section, because Code::Blocks mucks around with the Makefile for you automatically. Life is good. If you want to see how Code::Blocks performs this task, look at the .depend file for your project, such as MultipleSourceFiles. depend. The .depend file is simple XML, so you can view it with any XML-capable application (including Internet Explorer or Firefox). Otherwise, you'll want to read this section.

To add source code files to other compilers, you need to modify the Makefile, and you need to understand Makefile rules and the compile process. Yuck. (Makefiles are described in more detail in Appendix A.) Many ways to modify a Makefile are available. If you use implicit rules, you probably just need to add the name of the file to the list of source files. If you use a separate rule for each file, you need to add another rule for this new file. In that case, you may still have a list of all source code files or a list of all object files (which are just the source code filenames with either an .o or .obj extension), in which case you'll have to make another entry.

For example, you may have separate rules for each source file, as in the following:

```
main.o: main.cpp
    $(CC) -c main.cpp -o main.o $(CFLAGS)
```

In this case, you need to add another line similar to this one for your new file. If your new file is orangegoo.cpp, your new rule will look like this:

```
orangegoo.o: orangegoo.cpp
    $(CC) -c orangegoo.cpp -o orangegoo.o $(CFLAGS)
```

Note that you must indent the second line by using a tab. If you use spaces, it may not work properly.

You probably also have a rule listing the object files. Remember that it will likely be the object files and not the source files, because the object files are the temporary things that the compiler generates — or *makes*. Thus, you may have a macro such as this:

```
OBJ  = main.o orangegoo.o
```

This macro would be listed in the rule for the final executable file. That way, when you make the executable file, the `make` utility first sees whether these two `.o` files are up-to-date. If not, `make` first makes these two `.o` files, based on the rules you supplied earlier. Nice and simple; it's too bad that `Makefiles` are so ugly.

Creating multiple files

Before two source files can work together, they must somehow find out about each other. Just because they're both sitting on the computer doesn't mean that they know about each other. Computers are kind of goofy about that sort of thing. To get two source files to finally open up and get to know each other, you need to tell each of them about what's in the other file.

When you write a function, normally the function must appear before any calls to it appear within the same source file. That's because of the way the compiler parses the code: If the compiler encounters a call to a function but has not yet heard of that function, it issues an error. But the way around this is to use a function prototype. A *function prototype* is simply the header line from a function, ending with a semicolon, as in the following:

```
void BigDog(int KibblesCount);
```

Later in the source file is the actual function, with this header line duplicated. But instead of a semicolon, the function would have an open brace, the function code, and a closing brace, as in the following:

```
void BigDog(int KibblesCount)
{
    cout << "I'm a lucky dog" << endl;
    cout << "I have " << KibblesCount << " pieces of food" << endl;
}
```

So, after the function prototype, you can call the function whether the function code itself is before or after the call.

For the compiler to understand a function call, all it needs at the point that the code makes the call is a function *prototype*. It's up to the linker to determine whether that function really exists.

Because the function call needs only a function prototype, you can put the function *itself* in another source code file. You could, therefore, have two separate source code files, as in the `MultipleSourceFiles` example, shown in Listings 6-1 and 6-2. (The first source code file — `main.cpp` — is shown in Listing 6-1, and the second source code file — `mystuff.cpp` — is shown in Listing 6-2.)

Listing 6-1: Calling a Function with Only a Prototype

```
#include <iostream>

using namespace std;

void BigDog(int KibblesCount);

int main()
{
  BigDog(3);
  return 0;
}
```

Listing 6-2: Using a Function from a Separate File

```
#include <iostream>

using namespace std;

void BigDog(int KibblesCount)
{
    cout << "I'm a lucky dog" << endl;
    cout << "I have " << KibblesCount << " pieces of food" << endl;
}
```

In Listings 6-1 and 6-2, we broke the function away from the prototype. When you compile these two files together as a single application (either by pressing F9 in Code::Blocks or by using the methods described in the "Multiple source files in other compilers" section, earlier in this chapter), they all fit together nicely. You can then run the application, and you see this somewhat interesting output:

```
I'm a lucky dog
I have 3 pieces of food
```

Notice also that we had to put the same #include lines at the start of the mystuff.cpp file. That's because mystuff.cpp uses cout, and to use cout, it needs the #include <iostream> line.

A quick overview of namespaces

The using namespace std; line in Listings 6-1 and 6-2 tells the compiler to use a specific namespace, std. A *namespace* is a grouping of classes and functions. The std, or standard, namespace contains a host of useful classes and functions, such as string. If you don't include this declaration, you need to preface every use of the classes or functions found in std by typing std::<class or function>. For example, to use a string, you need to type std::string. Because this is a painful way to write code, you add the using namespace std; line.

Sharing with Header Files

Breaking apart source code into multiple files is easy, but soon you may run into a problem. If you have a function — say, SafeCracker() — and this function is extremely useful and is likely to be called many times from within several other source code files, you would need a prototype for SafeCracker() in every file that calls it. The prototype may look like this:

```
string SafeCracker(int SafeID);
```

But instead of putting this line in every file that uses the function, we know of an easier way. (We computer people are always looking for the easier way so that we can finally retire.) Simply put this line inside its own file, called a *header file,* and give the filename an .h or .hpp extension. (It's your choice which extension you use, because it really doesn't matter; we usually just go with .h.) For example, we might save the line string SafeCracker (int SafeID); in a file called safestuff.h.

Then, instead of typing the header line at the start of each file that needs the function, you type

```
#include "safestuff.h"
```

You would then have the three source code files used for the Multiple SourceFiles2 example, which we have shown in Listings 6-3, 6-4, and 6-5. The first is main.cpp, which calls the function. The second is safestuff.h, which contains the function prototype. The third is safestuff.cpp, which contains the actual code for the function whose prototype appears in the header file. Lots of files, but now the code is broken into manageable pieces. Also, make sure that you save all three of these files in the same directory.

Listing 6-3:   Including the Header File in the main File

```
#include <iostream>
#include "safestuff.h"

using namespace std;

int main()
{
  cout << "Surprise, surprise!" << endl;
  cout << "The combination is (once again)" << endl;
  cout << SafeCracker(12) << endl;
  return 0;
}
```

Listing 6-4:   Containing the Function Prototype in the Header File

```
using namespace std;

#ifndef SAFESTUFF_H_INCLUDED
#define SAFESTUFF_H_INCLUDED

string SafeCracker(int SafeID);

#endif // SAFESTUFF_H_INCLUDED
```

Listing 6-5:   Containing the Actual Function Code

```
#include <iostream>

using namespace std;

string SafeCracker(int SafeID)
{
    return "13-26-16";
}
```

Before you compile this application, however, we need to give you a couple of pointers. First, the compiler *does not* compile the header file into a separate .o or .obj file. With the application in Listings 6-3 through 6-5, the compiler compiles only two files: main.cpp and mystuff.cpp. Instead of compiling the header file, when the compiler reads the main.cpp file and reaches the #include line for the header file, it temporarily switches over and reads that file, pretending that it's still reading the same main.cpp file. As it continues, it compiles everything as if it's all part of the main.cpp file. And if you include this header file in other source code files, it does the same thing again for those source files.

To get this code to compile, remember the following rules:

✦ **Makefiles:** If you are using a compiler where you have to handle your own Makefiles, do not add a rule for compiling the header files, which usually start with .hpp or .h. Only compile the source files, which usually start with .cpp or .cc.

✦ **Visual C++:** Although we've said very little so far about Microsoft Visual C++ (VC++), if you use VC++, do not add header files to your project. Only add source files. VC++ will keep a listing of the header files in a tree called dependencies, but you don't add them yourself.

✦ **Code::Blocks:** What could be easier? You just make the files, and Code::Blocks handles all the file connectivity for you — nothing to worry about. The header and source files all show in the project list, and Code::Blocks also handles the details of which ones need to be compiled.

After you follow these rules, you can go ahead and compile and run the code in Listings 6-3 through 6-5. When you run the application, you see the following output:

```
Surprise, surprise!
The combination is (once again)
13-26-16
```

If you have a source file containing some functions, creating a header file that contains the associated function prototypes is generally a good practice. Then you can name the header file the same as the source file, except with a different extension. We did this in Listings 6-4 and 6-5: We named the header file `safestuff.h`, and the source file `safestuff.cpp`.

Instead of saying *header file,* some people prefer to say *include file.* We usually say *header file* because, to us, *include* is usually a verb, and it gets kind of awkward to say something like this: "We're pretty sure that we included the include file, but if we didn't include the correct include file, would you please include us in your meeting; and in the discussion, we will be sure to include a few questions about how to include the proper include file. Then you can include an answer to our inclusions about the inclusions of an include file." It's just difficult to say, you know? So we say *header file.*

Adding the header only once

Code::Blocks includes several lines in the header file by default. These lines create a symbol that tells the compiler whether a header file is already included in the source file so that the compiler doesn't add it twice. Adding a header twice is an error because then you'd define the forward reference for a function twice. Here is what you see when you initially create a header file with Code::Blocks:

```
#ifndef SAFESTUFF_H_INCLUDED
#define SAFESTUFF_H_INCLUDED

#endif // SAFESTUFF_H_INCLUDED
```

When you type the header code into Code::Blocks, type it between the `#define SAFESTUFF_H_INCLUDED` and `#endif // SAFESTUFF_H_INCLUDED` lines. The section "Using the Mysterious Header Wrappers," later in this chapter, describes these automatic entries in detail.

Using brackets or quotes

You may have noticed something about the code in Listing 6-3. When we included the `safestuff.h` file, we did not put it inside brackets, as we did in the other `#include` lines. Instead, we put it inside quotes:

```
#include "safestuff.h"
```

That's because programmers for years have been fighting over the rules of *where* exactly on the hard drive to put the header files. Do you put them in the same directory or folder as your project? Or do you put them in a special directory all by themselves? Or do you just put them out in the back yard to dry out?

Regardless of where you put your header files, here is the rule for when to use quotes and when to use brackets: The compiler looks in several directories to find header files. And it can, possibly, look in the same directory as the source file. If you use angle brackets (that is, less-than and greater-than signs), as in `#include <string>`, the compiler does not look in the same directory as the source file. But if you use double quotes, as in `#include "safestuff.h"`, the compiler *first* looks in the same directory as the source file. And if the compiler doesn't find the header file there, it looks in the remaining directories, as it would with angle brackets.

Some people always like to use double quotes. That way, whether the header file is in the same file as the source file or not, the compiler should find it.

Most professional programmers today *always* use angle brackets. This forces programmers to put their header files in a common area. With really big projects, programmers like to have a directory dedicated to source files and another directory dedicated to header files. No header file is ever in the same directory as the source file.

For small projects, some people like to lump all the source and header files into a single directory. These people typically use angle brackets around system header files (such as `#include <string>`) and use double quotes around their own header files. In the projects in this book, we generally follow this rule. The header files that we write are in the same directory as the source files, and we use double quotes for `#include` lines of our own files and use angle brackets for the `#include` lines of system headers.

If you follow the same approach that we use here, you immediately know whether the `#include` line refers to one of your own header files or another header file. If it refers to your own, it has double quotes.

If you start working on a large C++ project, you will probably find that project managers use the rule of always using angle brackets. For large projects, this is typically the best policy.

If you try to compile and you get a `No such file or directory` error on the `#include` line, it's probably because you put the header file in a source file directory but used angle brackets instead of double quotes. Try switching that line to double quotes.

Sharing Variables among Source Files

When you declare a variable inside a function, it remains local to the function. But you may want functions to share a single variable: One function may store something, and another may read its contents and write it to the console. To do this, declare the variable outside a function. That works until you try to share a variable between multiple source files. If you're not careful, the source files end up with a separate copy of the variable. Within a single source file, the variable can be shared between functions but not between source files. That could be confusing.

There's a trick to making this work. Declare the variable inside one and only one of the source files. Then you declare it *again* inside one (and only one) header file, but you precede it with the word *extern*, as in `extern int DoubleCheeseburgers;`.

The `GlobalVariable` example shown in Listings 6-6, 6-7, and 6-8 demonstrates the use of a single variable that is shared between multiple source files.

Listing 6-6:   Making Use of a Global Variable

```
#include <iostream>
#include "sharealike.h"

using namespace std;

int main()
{
  DoubleCheeseburgers = 20;
  EatAtJoes();
  return 0;
}
```

Listing 6-7:   Using a Header File to Declare a Global Variable

```
#ifndef SHAREALIKE_H_INCLUDED
#define SHAREALIKE_H_INCLUDED

extern int DoubleCheeseburgers;
void EatAtJoes();

#endif // SHAREALIKE_H_INCLUDED
```

Listing 6-8: Declaring the Actual Storage for the Global Variable

```
#include <iostream>
#include "sharealike.h"

using namespace std;

int DoubleCheeseburgers;

void EatAtJoes() {
  cout << "How many cheeseburgers today?" << endl;
  cout << DoubleCheeseburgers << endl;
}
```

Be careful when you do this; getting it exactly right is very tricky. You declare the variable once inside the header file, but you must remember the word `extern`. That tells the various files, "This variable is declared elsewhere, but here's its name and type so that you can use it." Then you declare the variable in one of the source files, *without* the word `extern`; this creates the actual storage bin for the variable. Finally, you include the header file in each of your source files that uses the global variable.

When you share a variable among multiple source files, it is a *global variable*. A variable used by a single function is a *local variable*. If you share a variable between functions within a single source file but not between multiple source files, people call this a *global variable that is local to the source file*.

Use the word `extern` in your header file when using a global variable. If you forget to do that, you give each source file its own variable that happens to have the same name.

Using the Mysterious Header Wrappers

When you include a header file, you usually want to include it only *once* per source file. But that can create a problem: Suppose that you have a huge software project, and several header files include another of your header files, called `superheader.h`. If you include all these other header files, how can you be sure to pick up the `superheader.h` file only once?

The answer looks strange but does the trick. You start each header file with these lines:

```
#ifndef SHAREALIKE_H
#define SHAREALIKE_H
#endif
```

Depending on which C++ IDE you use, your editor may add these lines automatically, just as Code::Blocks does. In this case, you type the header file content between the `#define SHAREALIKE_H` and `#endif` lines. However, if your IDE doesn't add the lines automatically, be sure to add them so that your code looks like the code in Listing 6-7. Otherwise, the compiler may spout errors that you may not recognize immediately.

These *header wrappers,* as they are often called, ensure that the code in the header gets processed only once per source code file each time you compile. The wrappers use special lines called *preprocessor directives.* Basically, the *second* line defines something that is sort of like a variable but is used only during compilation; this something is called a *symbol.* In our case, the symbol is called `SHAREALIKE_H`; we picked it by taking the filename, making it all caps, and replacing the dot with an underscore.

The first line checks to see whether this symbol has been defined. If *not,* it proceeds with the lines of code that follow. The next line goes ahead and defines the symbol, so now it's actually defined for later. Then the compiler does all the rest of the lines in the file. Finally, the last line, `#endif`, simply finishes the very first line.

Now consider what could happen if you include this same file twice, as in

```
#include "sharealike.h"
#include "sharealike.h"
```

(That can happen indirectly if you include two different files that each include `sharealike.h`.) The *second* time the compiler goes through `sharealike.h`, it sees the first line, which checks to see whether the `SHAREALIKE_H` symbol is defined. But this time it is! So instead of going through all the lines again, the compiler skips to the #endif line at the very end of the file. Thus, your header file gets processed only once per source code file. Tricky, no? And confusing? Yes, a bit. So remember the following rule:

When you create a header file, be sure to put the header wrappers around it. You can use any symbol name you like, as long as it uses only letters, numbers, and underscores and doesn't start with a number and isn't already a variable name in your source or a C++ word. But most people base their choice on some variation of the filename itself, such as `MYFILE_H` or `MYFILE_H_` or even `_MYFILE_H_`.

Chapter 7: Referring to Your Data Through Pointers

In This Chapter

↳ Using two types of memory: the stack and the heap

↳ Accessing variable addresses through pointers

↳ Creating variables on the heap by using the new keyword

↳ Taking pointers as parameters and returning pointers

↳ Modifying variables the easy way

Where do you live? Don't say it out loud, because thousands of people are reading this book and you don't want them all to know. So just think about your address. Most places have some sort of address so that the mail service knows where to deliver your packages and the cable guy can show up sometime between now and 5:00 next Thursday. (So make sure that you're there.)

Other things have addresses, too. For example, a big corporation in an office building likely has all its cubes numbered. And offices in buildings usually have numbers; and apartments normally have numbers, too.

Now suppose that someone named Sam works in office number 180. Last week, however, Sam got booted out the door for spending too much time surfing the web. Now Sally gets first dibs on office number 180, even though she's not taking over Sam's position. Sam moved out; Sally moved in. Same office — different person staying there.

The computer's memory works similarly. Every little part of the computer's memory is associated with a number that represents its location, or *address*. In this chapter, we show you that after you determine the address of a variable stored in memory, you can do powerful things with it, which gives you the tools to create powerful applications.

If any single topic in C++ programming is most important, it is the notion of pointers. Therefore, if you want to become a millionaire, read this chapter. Okay, so it may not make you a millionaire, but suggesting it *could* give you the incentive to master this chapter. Then you can become an ace programmer and make lots of money.

Heaping and Stacking the Variables

C++ applications use two kinds of memory: heap and stack. The *heap* is a common area of memory that your application *allocates* — that is, sets aside — for the different functions in your application to use. Global variables go in this heap.

Whenever your application calls a function, however, the function gets its own little private area of memory storage in an area of memory known as a *stack*. It is called a stack because it's treated like a stack of papers: You can put something on the top of the stack, and you can take something off the top of the stack, but you can't put anything in the middle or take anything from the middle. The computer uses this stack to keep track of all your function calls.

Suppose that you have a function called GoFishing(). The function GoFishing() calls StopAndBuyBait(), which then calls PayForBait(), which calls GetOutCreditCard(), which calls UseFakeCreditCard(). How can the computer keep track of all this mess? It uses the *stack* metaphor. First it saves the original function, GoFishing(). Then when that function calls StopAndBuyBait(), the computer remembers that function by putting it *on top of* GoFishing() — not in the same storage bin, but in one on top of the preceding item so that the preceding item is still there. Then, when that function calls PayForBait(), the computer once again remembers that function by putting it on top of StopAndBuyBait(), and so on, until it has all the items piled one on top of the other, with UseFakeCreditCard() on the top and GoFishing() on the bottom. This process *pushes* items onto the top of the stack.

Next, when the computer is finished with UseFakeCreditCard(), it *pops* off the top of the stack. What it picks up is the place it left off before calling UseFakeCreditCard(), which happens to be GetOutCreditCard(). And when that function is finished, once again the computer pops the top off the stack to find PayForBait(). And, as before, that's where it left off last. It continues this process until it gets all the way back to the beginning, which was GoFishing().

Every position in memory has a number associated with it. When your application starts, the computer sets aside a large chunk of memory and then works closely with the microprocessor itself to assign a bunch of numbers to the memory. Your application's variables and your application's code go in this memory. And consider this: If your application sits in memory, each function sits in a particular place in memory, a place with a number or an address associated with it. In other words, each function has an address.

Each function and each variable in your application has a place where it resides in memory. That place has a number associated with it. Therefore, each function and each variable has an *address*.

Placing a hex on C++

Sooner or later in your computer programming, you will encounter a strange way of notating numbers on the computer. This strange way is called *hexadecimal,* or sometimes just *hex.* In C++, you can recognize a hex number because it starts with the characters 0x. These characters aren't actually part of the number; they just notate it in the same way as double quotes denote a string. Whereas the usual decimal numbers consist of the digits 0, 1, 2, 3, 4, 5, 6, 7, 8, and 9, a hex number consists of these digits plus six more: A, B, C, D, E, and F. That makes a total of 16 digits. (Yes, we know, the letters *A* through *F* are not digits. But in hex, they are considered digits.) A good way to picture counting with regular decimal numbers is to use the odometer in a car, which (if you're honest) only goes forward, not backward. It starts out with 00000000 (assuming eight digits, which is a lot). The rightmost digit runs from 0 through 9, over and over. When any digit reaches 9 and all digits to the right of that are

9, the next digit to the left goes up by 1. For example, when you reach 00000999, the next digit to the left goes up by 1 as each 9 goes back to 0, to get 00001000.

With hex numbers, you count this same way, except that instead of stopping at 9 to loop back, you then go to A, and then B, and then up to F. And then you loop back. So the first 17 hex numbers are, using eight digits, 00000000, 00000001, 00000002, 00000003, 00000004, 00000005, 00000006, 00000007, 00000008, 00000009, 0000000A, 0000000B, 0000000C, 0000000D, 0000000E, 0000000F, 00000010. Notice that when we hit F toward the end there, we wrapped around again, adding 1 to the next digit to the left. When working with hex numbers, you may see such numbers as 0xAAAA0000 and 0X0000A3FF. (We included the 0x for C++ notation.) And incidentally, 1 more than each of these is 0xAAAA0001 and 0x0000A400.

The stack where the computer keeps track of the function calls is just a bunch of memory, too. What the computer considers the *top* of the stack is really the next position in memory. And the way the computer puts a function on the stack is by putting on the stack the *address* of where the computer left off in the preceding function.

When the computer calls one of your functions, it not only saves the address of the return location on the stack but also reserves some space on the stack for your local variables.

This means that your variables can live in two places:

✦ **Heap:** The *heap* is a common area in memory where you can store global variables.

✦ **Stack:** The *stack* is the area where the computer stores both the information about the functions being called and the local variables for those functions.

A stack is an example of all sorts of wonderful things called *data structures*. Computer programmers have a tendency to try to model things from real life on the computer. A stack of papers apparently wasn't good enough for the computer folk; they wanted to be able to do the same type of thing with their data in the computer, and they called this thing a stack. They have come up with many types of data structures, including a similar one called a queue: With a *queue,* you put data in one end and take it out the other. It's like putting sheets of paper on top but taking them only from the bottom. You experience a queue when you wait in line at a store. The people are forming a queue, and some even call a line of people a queue.

Every hex number has a decimal equivalent. When you make a list showing decimal numbers side by side with hex numbers, you see, for example, that 0x0000001F is next to the decimal number 31. Thus, these two numbers represent the same quantity of items, such as apples. Remember that when you want to buy some apples: "I would like to buy one-ef apples."

Looks can be deceiving. The hex number 10 represents the same number of apples as the decimal number 16. That's why it's a good idea to use the 0x notation. Thus, instead of hex 10, we would write 0x10, making it clear that we're not talking about a decimal number.

Converting between hexadecimal and decimal

If you want to convert between hex and decimal, you can use the Hex to Decimal Converter application at http://www.binaryhexconverter.com/hex-to-decimal-converter or the Decimal to Hex Converter application at http://www.binaryhexconverter.com/decimal-to-hex-converter. These two applications make it easy to convert between the two numbering systems, and you can use them on any device that supports a browser.

To convert a hex number to decimal, select the Hex to Decimal Converter application and type the hex number into the Type Hex Number Here field by using the number keys and the letters *A* through *F,* such as FB1263. (You don't need to type the zeroes at the beginning, such as 00FB1263 — they don't show up — nor do you type the 0x used in C++.) After you finish typing it all, click Convert. The application instantly transforms this beautiful hex thing into an equally beautiful thing — a decimal number! In this case, you see 16454243. You can go the other way, too: If you have a decimal number, such as 16454243, you can select the Decimal to Hex Converter application, type its value into the Type Decimal Value Here field and click Convert to convert it to hex. If you convert 16454243 to hex, you get back FB1263, which is what you started with.

You can convert words, too (if you're bored). The hex number and disco group ABBA is 43962 in decimal. And the hex number FADE is 64222. And John's house, which he calls hex number FACADE, is 16435934. Have fun!

You can represent hex numbers by using either uppercase or lowercase letters. However, do not mix cases within a single number. Don't use 0xABab0000. Instead, use either 0xabab0000 or 0xABAB0000.

Getting a variable's address

Because every variable lives somewhere in memory, every variable has an address. If you have a function that declares an integer variable called `NumberOfPotholes`, then when your application calls this function, the computer will allocate space for `NumberOfPotholes` somewhere in memory.

If you want to take the address of (which is computerspeak for *find the address of*) the variable `NumberOfPotholes`, you simply throw an ampersand (&) in front of it.

Listing 7-1 shows the `VariableAddress` example, which obtains the address of a variable and prints it.

Listing 7-1:   Using the & Character to Obtain the Address of a Variable

```
#include <iostream>

using namespace std;

int main()
{
    int NumberOfPotholes = 532587;
    cout << &NumberOfPotholes << endl;
    return 0;
}
```

When you run this application, a hexadecimal number appears on the console. This number may or may not match ours, and it may or may not be the same each time you run the application. The result depends on exactly how the computer allocated your variable for you and the order in which it did things. This could be very different between versions of compilers. When you run Listing 7-1, you see

```
0x22ff74
```

The output you see from this application is the address of the variable called `NumberOfPotholes`. In other words, that number is the hex version of the place where the `NumberOfPotholes` variable is stored in memory. The output is not the *content* of the variable or the content of the variable converted to hex; rather, it's the address of the variable converted to hex.

That output is not useful, unless you want to sound like a computer techie. You could walk around announcing that the variable lives at 0x22ff74, but that won't get you very far in life. (It may get you some interesting looks, though, which may be worth it.) But when you obtain that address, you can use it for other purposes. For example, you can use the address to modify the variable itself by using what are called pointer variables. A *pointer variable* is just like any other variable except that it stores the *address of* another variable.

To declare a pointer variable, you need to specify the type of variable it will point to. Then you precede the variable's name with an asterisk, as in the following:

```
int *ptr;
```

This line declares a variable that *points to* an integer. In other words, it can contain *the address* of an integer variable. And how do you grab the address of an integer variable? Easy! By using the & notation! Thus, you can do something like this:

```
ptr = &NumberOfPotholes;
```

This line puts the address of the variable NumberOfPotholes in the ptr variable. Remember that ptr doesn't hold the number of potholes; rather, it holds the address of the variable called NumberofPotholes.

You specify the type of pointer by the type of item it points to. If a pointer variable points to an integer, its type is *pointer to integer.* In C++ notation, its type is int * (with a space between them) or int* (no space); you are allowed to enter it with or without a space. If a pointer variable points to a string, its type is *pointer to string*, and notation for this type is string *.

The ptr variable holds an address, but what's at that address? That address is the location in memory of the storage bin known as NumberOfPotholes. Right at that spot in memory is the data stored in NumberOfPotholes.

Think this pointer concept through carefully. If you have to, reread this section a few times until it's locked in your head. Then meditate on it. Wake up in the night thinking about it. Call strangers on the telephone and chitchat about it. The more you understand pointers, the better off your programming career will be — and the more likely you will make a million dollars.

A pointer example

Suppose that NumberOfPotholes contains the number 5000. That means the computer stores the number 5000 somewhere in memory. When you obtain the address of NumberOf Potholes, you are taking the address of the memory where you can find the number 5000.

And so, when you set

```
ptr = &NumberOfPotholes;
```

ptr points to a memory location that contains the number 5000.

Changing a variable by using a pointer

After you have a pointer variable holding another variable's address, you can use the pointer to access the information in the other variable. That means you have two ways to get to the information in a variable: Use the variable name itself (such as NumberOfPotholes), or use the pointer variable that points to it.

If you want to store the number 6087 in NumberOfPotholes, you can do this:

```
NumberOfPotholes = 6087;
```

Or you can use the pointer. To use the pointer, you first declare it as follows:

```
ptr = &NumberOfPotholes;
```

Then, to change NumberOfPotholes, you don't just assign a value to it. Instead, you throw an asterisk in front of it, like so:

```
*ptr = 6087;
```

If ptr points to NumberOfPotholes, these two lines of code will have the same effect: Both will change the value to 6087. This process of sticking the asterisk before a pointer variable is called *dereferencing* the pointer. By the time you're finished with this book, you will know gobs of words that nobody else does. (And your newly enriched vocabulary makes talking on the telephone difficult at first.)

Take a look at the DereferencePointer example, shown in Listing 7-2, which demonstrates all this.

Listing 7-2:   Modifying the Original Variable with a Pointer Variable

```
#include <iostream>

using namespace std;

int main()
{
    int NumberOfPotholes;
    int *ptr;
    ptr = &NumberOfPotholes;
    *ptr = 6087;
    cout << NumberOfPotholes << endl;
    return 0;
}
```

In Listing 7-2, the first line of main() declares an integer variable, and the second line declares a pointer to an integer. The next line takes the address of the integer variable and stores it in the pointer. Then the fourth line modifies the original integer by dereferencing the pointer. And just to make sure that the process worked, the next line prints the value of `NumberOfPotholes`. When you run the application, you see the following output:

```
6087
```

This is correct; it is the value that the application stored in the original variable by using the pointer variable.

You can also read the value of the original variable through the pointer. Take a look at the `ReadPointer` example, shown in Listing 7-3. This code accesses the value of `NumberOfPotholes` through the pointer variable, `ptr`. When the code gets the value, it saves it in another variable called `SaveForLater`.

Listing 7-3:   Accessing a Value through a Pointer

```
#include <iostream>

using namespace std;

int main()
{
  int NumberOfPotholes;
  int *ptr = &NumberOfPotholes;
  int SaveForLater;
  *ptr = 6087;
  SaveForLater = *ptr;
  cout << SaveForLater << endl;
  *ptr = 7000;
  cout << *ptr << endl;
  cout << SaveForLater << endl;
  return 0;
}
```

When you run this application, you see the following output:

```
6087
7000
6087
```

Notice also in this listing that we changed the value through `ptr` again — this time, to 7000. When you run the application, you can see that the value did indeed change, but the value in `SaveForLater` remained the same. That's because `SaveForLater` is a separate variable and is not connected to the other two. The other two, however, are connected to each other.

Pointing at a string

Pointer variables enjoy pointing. Pointer variables can point to any type, including strings. However, after you say that a variable points to a certain type, it can point to only that type. That is, as with any variable, you cannot change its type out from underneath it. The compiler won't let you do it.

To create a pointer to a string, you simply make the type of the variable `string *`. You can then set it equal to the address of a string variable. The `StringPointer` example, shown in Listing 7-4, demonstrates.

Listing 7-4:   Pointing to a String with Pointers

```
#include <iostream>

using namespace std;

int main()
{
  string GoodMovie;
  string *ptrToString;
  GoodMovie = "Best in Show";
  ptrToString = &GoodMovie;
  cout << *ptrToString << endl;
  return 0;
}
```

In Listing 7-4, you can see that the pointer variable named `ptrToString` points to the variable named `GoodMovie`. But when you want to use the pointer to access the string itself, you need to dereference the pointer by putting an asterisk (*) in front of it.

When you run this code, you see the results of the dereferenced pointer, which is the value of the `GoodMovie` variable:

```
Best in Show
```

You can change the value of the string through the pointer, again by dereferencing it, as in the following code:

```
*ptrToString = "Galaxy Quest";
cout << GoodMovie << endl;
```

Here, we dereferenced the pointer to set it equal to the string `"Galaxy Quest"` (a fine movie, we might add). Then, to show that it truly changed, we printed the variable itself: `GoodMovie`. The result of this code, when added at the end of Listing 7-4 (but prior to the `return 0`), is

```
Galaxy Quest
```

You can also use the pointer to access the individual parts of the string, as we did in the `StringPointer2` example, shown in Listing 7-5.

Listing 7-5:   Using Pointers to Point to a String

```
#include <iostream>

using namespace std;

int main()
{
  string HorribleMovie;
  string *ptrToString;

  HorribleMovie = "L.A. Confidential";
  ptrToString = &HorribleMovie;

  for (unsigned i = 0; i < HorribleMovie.length(); i++)
  {
    cout << (*ptrToString)[i] << " ";
  }

  cout << endl;
  return 0;
}
```

When you run this application, you see the letters of the terrible movie appear with spaces between them, as in

```
L . A .   C o n f i d e n t i a l
```

Okay, so we didn't like *L.A. Confidential*. But it won two Oscars and was nominated for seven more, and it won a boatload of other awards, so we don't feel so bad saying so.

When you access the characters of the string through a pointer, you need to put parentheses around the asterisk and the pointer variable. Otherwise, the compiler gets confused and first tries to access the index in brackets with the variable name and afterward applies the asterisk. That's backward, and it doesn't make sense to the computer, so the compiler gives you an error message. But you can make it all better by using parentheses, as we did in Listing 7-5.

This application loops through the entire string, character by character. We used the `length` function for the string to find out how many characters are in the string. And inside the loop, we grabbed the individual characters of the string, printing them with a space after each.

Notice that `i` is of type `unsigned` rather than `int`. The `length()` function returns an `unsigned` value rather than an `int` value. If you try to use an `int` for `i`, the compiler displays the following warning:

```
warning: comparison between signed and unsigned integer
```

It's important to use the correct data types for loop variables. Otherwise, when the loop value increases over the amount that the loop variable can support, the application will fail. Trying to find such an error can prove frustrating even for the best developers.

You can also change the individual characters in a string through a pointer. You can do this by using a line like `(*ptrToString)[5] = 'X';`. Notice, as before, that we had to put parentheses around the variable name along with the dereferencing (that is, the asterisk) character.

The length of a string is also available through the pointer. You can call the `length()` function by dereferencing the pointer, again with the carefully placed parentheses, such as in the following:

```
for (unsigned i = 0; i < (*ptrToString).length(); i++)
{
    cout << (*ptrToString)[i] << " ";
}
```

Pointing to something else

When you create a pointer variable, you must specify the type of data it points to. After that, you cannot change the type of data it points to, but you can change *what* it points to. For example, if you have a pointer to an integer, you can make it point to the integer variable called `ExpensiveComputer`. Then, later, in the same application, you can make it point to the integer variable called `CheapComputer`. We demonstrate this using the `ChangePointer` example, shown in Listing 7-6.

Listing 7-6: Using Pointers to Point to Something Else and Back Again

```
#include <iostream>

using namespace std;

int main()
{
    int ExpensiveComputer;
    int CheapComputer;
    int *ptrToComp;

    ptrToComp = &ExpensiveComputer;
    *ptrToComp = 2000;
    cout << *ptrToComp << endl;

    ptrToComp = &CheapComputer;
    *ptrToComp = 500;
    cout << *ptrToComp << endl;

    ptrToComp = &ExpensiveComputer;
    cout << *ptrToComp << endl;
    return 0;
}
```

This code starts out by initializing all the goodies involved — two integers and a pointer to an integer.

Next, the code points the pointer to `ExpensiveComputer` and uses the pointer to put something inside `ExpensiveComputer`. It then writes the contents of `ExpensiveComputer`, again by using the pointer.

Then the code changes what the pointer points to. To do this, you set the pointer to the address of a different variable, `&CheapComputers`. Pretty simple. And the next line stores 500 in whatever the pointer points to. But that's `CheapComputers`. And, again, you print it.

Now, just to drive home the point, in case the computer isn't listening, you then point the pointer back to the original variable, `ExpensiveComputer`. But you don't store anything in it. This time, you simply print what's already inside this high-powered supermachine. You do this again by dereferencing the pointer. And when you run the application, you see that `ExpensiveComputer` still has 2000 in it, which is what was originally put in it. This means that after you point the pointer to something else and do some finagling, the original variable remains unchanged. That's a good thing, considering that nobody was pointing at it and it was just being left alone, totally ignored in a world all by itself, feeling neglected.

Be careful if you use one pointer to bounce around several different variables. It's easy to lose track of which variable the pointer is pointing to.

Tips on pointer variables

Here are some pretty good tips on using pointer variables.

You can declare two pointer variables of the same type by putting them together in a single statement, as you can with regular variables. However, you must precede *each one* with an asterisk, as in the following line:

```
int *ptrOne, *ptrTwo;
```

If you try to declare multiple pointers on a single line but put an asterisk only before the first pointer, only that one will be a pointer. The rest will not be. This can cause serious headaches and muscle spasms later because this line will compile fine. The following line is just such an example:

```
int *ptrOne, Confused;
```

Here, `Confused` is not a pointer to an integer; rather, it's just an integer. Beware!

Some people like to put the asterisk immediately after the type, as in the following example, to emphasize the fact that the type is *pointer to integer:*

```
int* ptrOne;
```

However, we prefer not to do that simply because it makes it easy for forgetful persons like ourselves to not remember that any variables that follow, separated by a comma, need their own asterisks if they are to be pointers.

When we declare a pointer variable, we usually start its name with the letters `ptr`, which is an abbreviation for *pointer*. That way, we immediately know (when we're looking at our code) that it's a pointer variable. That makes life a little easier sometimes, at least in the sanity areas of life.

Dynamically Allocating with new

The *heap* is a special place where you can declare storage. However, to use this storage, you take a different approach from simply declaring a variable.

When you create a variable, you go through the process of actually typing a variable and giving it a type, a name, and (sooner or later) a value. When you write the code, that's when you decide that you want a variable. However, you can also write code that can cause the computer to allocate space only after it's running. The computer allocates this space on the heap. This process is called *dynamic allocation*.

Using new

To declare a storage bin on the heap, first you need to set up a variable that will help you keep track of the storage bin. This variable must be a pointer variable.

Suppose that you already have an integer declared out on the heap somewhere. (We show you how to do that in the next paragraph.) You don't give it a name, because such variables don't have names. Just think of it as an integer on the heap. Then, with the integer variable, you could have a *second* variable. This second variable is not on the heap, and it's a pointer holding the address of the integer variable. So if you want to access the integer variable, you do so by dereferencing the pointer variable.

To allocate memory on the heap, you need to do two things: First, declare a pointer variable. Second, call a function named `new`. The `new` function is a little different from other functions in that you don't put parentheses around its parameter. For this reason, it's actually considered to be an *operator*. Other operators are + and − for adding and subtracting integers. These other operators behave similarly to functions, but you don't use parentheses.

To use the `new` function, you specify the type of variable you want to create. For example, the following line creates a new integer variable:

```
int *somewhere = new int;
```

After the computer creates the new integer variable on the heap, it stores the address of the integer variable in the `somewhere` variable. And that makes sense: The `somewhere` variable is a pointer to an integer. Thus, it holds the address of an integer variable. The `UseNew` example, shown in Listing 7-7, demonstrates.

Listing 7-7:   Allocating Memory by Using new

```
#include <iostream>

using namespace std;

int main()
{
  int *ptr = new int;
  *ptr = 10;
  cout << *ptr << endl;
  return 0;
}
```

When you run this application, you see this sweet and simple output:

```
10
```

In this application, you first allocate a pointer variable, which you call `ptr`. Then you call `new` with an `int` type, which returns a pointer to an integer. You save that return value in the `ptr` variable.

Then you start doing your magic on it. Okay, so it's not all that magical, but you save a 10 *in the thing that `ptr` points to*. And then you print the value stored in *the thing that `ptr` points to*.

But what exactly is *the thing that `ptr` points to*, and why does it fancy itself so important as to justify italics? It's the memory that was allocated by the `new` operator. Think of it as a variable `out there somewhere`. But unlike regular variables, this variable doesn't have a name. And because it doesn't have a name, the only way you can access it is through the pointer. It's kind of like an anonymous author with a publicist. If you want to send fan mail to the author, you have to go through the publicist. Here, the only way to reach this unnamed but famous variable is through the pointer.

But this doesn't mean that the variable has a secret name such as `BlueCheese` and that, if you dig deep enough, you might discover it; it just means that the variable has no name. Sorry.

When you call `new`, you get back a pointer. This pointer is of the type that you specify in your call to `new`. You can then store the pointer only in a pointer variable of the same type.

When you use the `new` operator, the usual terminology is that you are *allocating memory on the heap.*

At this point, you may be asking the all-important question: Why? Why would I go through the trouble of creating an integer variable somewhere out on the heap, a variable that has no name, if I just have to create a second variable to point to it? Doesn't that seem counterproductive?

The answer is this: You can take advantage of many features if you allocate your variables on the heap. You can use pointers along with something called an *array*. An *array* is simply a large storage bin that has multiple slots, each of which holds one item. And if you set up an array that holds pointers, you can store away all these pointers without having to name them individually. And these pointers can point to complex things, called objects. (We cover objects in Book I, Chapter 8, and we cover arrays in Book I, Chapter 9.) And then if you want to, for example, pass all these variables (which could be quite large, if they're strings) to a function, you need to pass only the array, not the strings themselves. That step saves memory on the stack.

In addition to objects and arrays, you can have a function create and return a variable. Then, when you get the variable back from the function, you can use it, and when you finish with the variable, delete it. Finally, you can pass a pointer into a function. When you do so, the function can actually modify the pointer for you. See "Passing Pointer Variables to Functions" and "Returning Pointer Variables from Functions," later in this chapter.

Using an initializer

When you call `new`, you can provide an initial value for the memory you are allocating. For example, if you are allocating a new integer, you can, in one swoop, also store the number 10 in the integer.

The `Initializer` example shown in Listing 7-8 demonstrates.

Listing 7-8:   Putting a Value in Parentheses to Initialize Memory That You Allocate

```
#include <iostream>

using namespace std;

int main()
{
  int *ptr = new int(10);
  cout << *ptr << endl;
  return 0;
}
```

In this code, we called new, but we also put a number in parentheses. That number will get put in the memory initially. This line of code is equivalent to the following two lines of code:

```
int *ptr = new int;
*ptr = 10;
```

When you initialize a value in the new operator, the technical phrase for what you are doing is *invoking a constructor*. The reason is that the compiler adds a bunch of code to your application — code that operates behind the scenes. This code is the *runtime library*. The library includes a function that initializes an integer variable if you pass an initial value. The function that does this is known as a *constructor*. When you run it, you are *invoking* it. Thus, you are invoking the constructor. For more information on constructors, see Book I, Chapter 8.

Making new strings

You can use new to allocate almost any type, including strings. You simply type new followed by string.

You cannot allocate one special type with new. If a function has no return, you specify the return type as void. You cannot use new to allocate a void type. For that matter, neither can you create a variable of type void. The compiler won't let you do it.

The UseNew2 example, shown in Listing 7-9, is an example of calling new for a string. As usual, remember the include line for <iostream>.

Listing 7-9:   Using the new Operator with Strings

```
#include <iostream>

using namespace std;

int main()
{
  string *Password = new string;
  *Password = "The egg salad is not fresh.";
  cout << *Password << endl;
  return 0;
}
```

This code allocates a new string by using the new keyword and saves the results in the Password variable. Next, it stores an interesting commentary in the newly allocated string by dereferencing the pointer. Finally, it prints the commentary, again by dereferencing the pointer. Remember that the string variable itself is off in the heap somewhere and has no name. And if it's going to make comments like those heard at a fine restaurant, it's probably best that it remain nameless.

When you store a string of characters in a string variable that you allocated by using new, you are storing the string in the allocated memory, *not* in the pointer variable. The pointer variable still holds the address of the allocated memory. The pointer is simply the publicist for the memory, handling all its deals and transactions for it, whether ethical or not.

When you are working with strings, you can use a shortcut to the somewhat cumbersome method of putting parentheses around the name, preceded by an asterisk, in order to call the various string functions. (That was even hard to type!) Instead of typing (*Password).length(), for example, you can use a shortcut notation that looks like the following line of code (the characters after Password are a minus sign and then a greater-than sign, which together resemble an arrow):

```
cout << Password->length() << endl;
```

You can initialize a string by using parentheses when you call new for a string type. To do this, simply put the string in quotes and then in parentheses after the word string, as in the following line of code:

```
string *Password = new string("The egg salad is still not fresh.");
```

This line is equivalent to the first two lines of code inside main in Listing 7-9.

Even though the pointer points to a string, the pointer itself still holds a number (in particular, the address of the string it's pointing to). This is a number, but do not confuse it with an integer. However, you can do some basic arithmetic with pointers, as detailed in Book I, Chapter 9.

Freeing Pointers

When you allocate memory on the heap by calling the new function and you're finished using the memory, you need to let the computer know, whether it's just a little bit of memory or a lot. The computer doesn't look ahead into your code to find out whether you're still going to use the memory. So in your code, when you are finished with the memory, you *free* the memory.

The way you free the memory is by calling the delete function and passing the name of the pointer:

```
delete MyPointer;
```

This line would appear after you're finished using a pointer that you allocated by using new. (Like the new operator, delete is also an operator and does not require parentheses around the parameter.)

The FreePointer example, shown in Listing 7-10, provides a complete demonstration of allocating a pointer, using it, and then freeing it.

Listing 7-10:   Using delete to Clean Up Your Pointers

```
#include <iostream>

using namespace std;

int main()
{
  string *phrase = new string("All presidents are cool!!!");
  cout << *phrase << endl;

  (*phrase)[20] = 'r';
  phrase->replace(22, 4, "oked");
  cout << *phrase << endl;

  delete phrase;
  return 0;
}
```

When you run this application, you see the following output:

```
All presidents are cool!!!
All presidents are crooked
```

In this code, we first allocated a new string and initialized it, saving its address in the pointer variable called phrase. Then we wrote the phrase, manipulated it (providing some editorial content), and then wrote it again. Finally, we freed the memory used by the phrase.

Although people usually say that you're *deleting the pointer* or *freeing the pointer,* really you're freeing the *memory* that the pointer points to. The pointer can still be used for subsequent new operations. Nevertheless, we will abide by tradition and use these phrases.

You can actually get away with not freeing your pointers because the computer frees all the memory used by your application when it ends. That way, your memory is available to all the other cool applications you want to run. However, getting into the habit of freeing your pointers when you are finished using them is a good practice; otherwise, you may use all the memory allotted for the heap while your application is running. And some big software systems at big companies run on and on, shutting down maybe once a week or every two weeks. If one part of the application continues to refuse to free its data, eventually the heap probably fills and the whole application shuts down.

If you free a pointer, the memory it points to is now free. However, immediately after the call to delete, the pointer still points to that particular memory location, even though it's no longer being used. Therefore, do not try to use the pointer after that until you set it to point to something else through a call to new or by setting it to another variable.

Whenever you free a pointer, a good habit is to set the pointer to the value 0. (Some people set it to the value *null*, but that's the same thing, and 0 is guaranteed to work on all compilers.) Then, whenever you use a pointer, first check whether it's equal to 0 and use it only if it's not 0. This strategy always works because the computer will never allocate memory for you at address 0. So the number 0 can be reserved to mean *I point to nothing at all.*

The following code sample shows this. First, this code frees the pointer and then clears it by setting it to 0:

```
delete ptrToSomething;
ptrToSomething = 0;
```

This code checks whether the pointer is not 0 before using it:

```
ptrToComp = new int;
*ptrToComp = 10;
if (ptrToComp != 0)
{
    cout << *ptrToComp << endl;
}
```

Call delete only on memory that you allocated by using new. Although the Code::Blocks compiler doesn't seem to complain when you delete a pointer that points to a regular variable, it serves no purpose to do so. You can free only memory on the heap, not local variables on the stack.

Passing Pointer Variables to Functions

One of the most important uses for pointers is this: If a pointer points to a variable, you can pass the pointer to a function, and the function can modify the original variable. This lets you write functions that can actually modify the variables passed to them.

Changing variable values with pointers

Normally, when you call a function and you pass a few variables to the function, the computer just grabs the values out of the variables and passes those values. Take a close look at the VariablePointer example, shown in Listing 7-11.

Listing 7-11:   A Function Cannot Change the Original Variables Passed into It

```
#include <iostream>

using namespace std;

void ChangesAreGood(int myparam)
{
    myparam += 10;
    cout << "Inside the function:" << endl;
    cout << myparam << endl;
}

int main()
{
    int mynumber = 30;
    cout << "Before the function:" << endl;
    cout << mynumber << endl;

    ChangesAreGood(mynumber);
    cout << "After the function:" << endl;
    cout << mynumber << endl;

    return 0;
}
```

Listing 7-11 includes a function called `ChangesAreGood()` that modifies the parameter it receives. (It adds `10` to its parameter called `myparam`.) It then prints the new value of the parameter.

The `main()` function initializes an integer variable, `mynumber`, to `30` and prints its value. It then calls the `ChangesAreGood()` function, which changes its parameter. After coming back from the `ChangesAreGood()` function, `main()` prints the value again.

When you run this application, you see the following output:

```
Before the function:
30
Inside the function:
40
After the function:
30
```

Before the function call, `mynumber` is `30`. And after the function call, it's still `30`. But the function added `10` to its parameter. This means that when the function modified its parameter, *the original variable remained untouched.* The two are separate entities. Only the value `30` went into the function. The actual variable did not. It stayed in `main()`.

That keeps mean and nasty functions from messing things up in the outside world. But what if you write a function that you *want* to modify the original variable?

A pointer contains a number, which represents the address of a variable. If you pass this address into a function and the function stores that address into one of its own variables, its own variable also points to the same variable that the original pointer did. Make sense? The pointer variable in `main()` and the pointer variable in the function *both point to the same variable* because *both pointers hold the same address.*

That's how you let a function modify data in a variable: You pass a pointer. But when you call a function, the process is easy because you don't need to make a pointer variable. Instead, you can just call the function, putting an `&` in front of the variable. Then you are not passing the variable or its value — instead, you are passing the address of the variable.

The `VariablePointer2` example, shown in Listing 7-12, is a modified form of Listing 7-11; this time, the function actually manages to modify the original variable.

Listing 7-12:   Using Pointers to Modify a Variable Passed into a Function

```
#include <iostream>

using namespace std;

void ChangesAreGood(int *myparam)
{
    (*myparam) += 10;
    cout << "Inside the function:" << endl;
    cout << (*myparam) << endl;
}

int main()
{
    int mynumber = 30;
    cout << "Before the function:" << endl;
    cout << mynumber << endl;

    ChangesAreGood(&mynumber);
    cout << "After the function:" << endl;
    cout << mynumber << endl;

    return 0;
}
```

When you run this application, you see the following output:

```
Before the function:
30
Inside the function:
40
After the function:
40
```

Notice the important difference between this and the output from Listing 7-11: The final line of output is `40`, not `30`. The variable was modified by the function!

To understand how this happened, first look at `main()`. The only difference we had to make to `main()` was a little one: We threw an ampersand (`&`) in front of the `mynumber` argument in the call to `ChangesAreGood()`. That's it: Instead of passing the value stored in `mynumber`, we passed the address of `mynumber`.

Now the function has some major changes. We rewrote the function header so that it takes a pointer rather than a number. We did this by adding an asterisk (`*`) so that the parameter is a pointer variable. This pointer receives the address being passed into it. Thus, it points to the variable `mynumber`. Therefore, any modifications we make by dereferencing the pointer will attack the original variable. And attack it, it does: It changes it! The following line changes the original variable. Excellent!

```
(*myparam) += 10;
```

When you pass a pointer to a function, you are still passing a number. In Listing 7-11, you are passing to the function the value stored in `mynumber`. In Listing 7-12, you aren't somehow passing the variable itself. Instead, you are passing the *value* of `mynumber`'s address. The value is still a number either way. However, in Listing 7-12, because the number is an address now, we had to modify the function header so that it expects an address, not just a number. To do that, we used a pointer variable because it is a storage bin *that holds an address*. Then we had to modify the remainder of the function to make use of the pointer, instead of a number.

The `ChangesAreGood()` function in Listing 7-12 no longer modifies its own parameter. The parameter starts holding the address of the original `mynumber` variable, and that never changes. Throughout the function, the pointer variable `myparam` holds the `mynumber` address. And any changes the function performs are on the dereferenced variable, which is `mynumber`. *The pointer variable does not change.*

Passing by value versus by reference

If you work with other languages, you'll come across the terms *passing by value* and *passing by reference*. The first term, *passing by value*, means sending the actual value of a variable to a function when you call it. When working with C++, you accomplish this task by calling the function with the variable, as shown in Listing 7-11. The second term, *passing by reference*, means sending the address of the variable to the function so that the function can modify the original content of that variable. When working with C++, you accomplish this task by calling the function with a pointer, as shown in Listing 7-12. Different languages use different terminology to mean the same thing, which can be really confusing at times. C++ uses the terminology it does because C++ can work with pointers directly rather than hide the underlying mechanics of what is happening using special techniques or keywords.

Modifying string parameters

Modifying a string parameter is just as easy as modifying an integer variable. But with string variables, you have the added benefit that if you're working with pointers, you can use the shortcut `->` notation.

The `VariablePointer3` example, shown in Listing 7-13, contains a function that modifies the original `string` variable that is passed into it. The function expects a pointer to a `string`. Inside, the function uses the `->` notation to access the `string` functions. Then the function returns. The `main()` function creates a `string`, initializes it, prints the `string`'s value, calls the function, and prints the value again. As you see when you run the application, the value of the `string` has changed.

Listing 7-13:   Using a Function to Modify a String Passed into It by Using Pointers

```
#include <iostream>

using namespace std;

void Paranoid(string *realmessage)
{
  (*realmessage)[6] = 'i';
  realmessage->replace(9, 1, "");
  realmessage->insert(18, "ad");
  realmessage->replace(15, 2, "in");
  realmessage->replace(23, 7, "!");
  realmessage->replace(4, 3, "ali");
}

int main()
{
  string message = "The friends are having dinner";
  cout << message << endl;

  Paranoid(&message);
  cout << message << endl;

  return 0;
}
```

In Listing 7-13, we chose to not make the `message` variable a pointer. It's just a `string` variable. We then put a `string` into it and called the `Paranoid()` function. But instead of passing the value stored in `message`, we passed the address of `message`. The function then receives a pointer as a parameter. Because it's a `string` pointer, we made extensive use of the shortcut notation, `->`. Remember that `(*realmessage)` equals the pointer.

When you run this application, you see the original value stored in `message` and then the revised value after the function has its way with it:

```
The friends are having dinner
The aliens are invading!
```

Returning Pointer Variables from Functions

Functions can return values, including pointers. To set up a function to return a pointer, specify the type followed by an asterisk at the beginning of the function header. The `ReturnPointer` example, shown in Listing 7-14, demonstrates this. The function returns a pointer that is the result of a `new` operation.

Listing 7-14: Returning a Pointer from a String Involves Using an Asterisk in the Return Type

```
#include <iostream>
#include <sstream>
#include <stdlib.h>

using namespace std;

string *GetSecretCode()
{
  string *code = new string;
  code->append("CR");

  int randomnumber = rand();
  ostringstream converter;
  converter << randomnumber;

  code->append(converter.str());
  code->append("NQ");

  return code;
}

int main()
{
  string *newcode;
  int index;

  for (index = 0; index < 10; index++)
  {
    newcode = GetSecretCode();
    cout << *newcode << endl;
  }

  return 0;
}
```

In this code, we wedged the asterisk against the function name in the function header. This is a common way of doing it. If you prefer, you can use any of the following lines:

```
string *GetSecretCode() {
string* GetSecretCode() {
string * GetSecretCode() {
```

In the `main()` function, we created a pointer to a `string`, not just a `string`. My function is returning a pointer to a `string`, and we needed the pointer and the string to match. When we used the `string`, we had to dereference it.

Random numbers and strings

Some special code appears smack-dab in the middle of the function in Listing 7-14, and we need to explain that. It's a little trick we used for generating a random number and putting it into the middle of the string. First, we had to add two additional `include` lines:

```
#include <stdlib.h>
#include <sstream>
```

The first line provides access to the rand() function. The second line provides access to some of the special features we're about to talk about — specifically, the `ostringstream` type. Here are the three lines that perform the magic:

```
int randomnumber = rand();
ostringstream converter;
converter << randomnumber;
```

The first of these creates a random number by calling a function named `rand()`. You get back from this function an integer, which is random. The next one creates a variable of the type called `ostringstream`, which is a type

that's handy for converting numbers to strings. A variable of this type has features similar to that of a console. You can use the `insertion` operator (`<<`), except that instead of going to the console, anything you write goes into the string itself. But this isn't just any old string — it's a special string of type `ostringstream` (which comes from the words *output, string,* and *stream;* usually, things that allow the insertion operator `<<` or the extraction operator `>>` to perform input and output are called *streams*). After we do this, we can add the resulting string onto our string variable named `code`. To do that, we use the line

```
code->append(converter.str());
```

The part inside parentheses — `converter.str()` — returns an actual `string` version of the `converter` variable. And that, we can easily append to the `code` variable by using the `append` function. It's kind of tricky, but it works quite nicely.

When you run this application, you see something like the following output:

```
CR41NQ
CR18467NQ
CR6334NQ
CR26500NQ
CR19169NQ
CR15724NQ
CR11478NQ
CR29358NQ
CR26962NQ
CR24464NQ
```

Never return from a function the address of a local variable in the function. The local variables live in the stack space allocated for the function, not in the heap. When the function is finished, the computer frees the stack space used for the function, making room for the *next* function call. If you try this, the variables will be okay for a while, but after enough function calls that follow, the variable's data will get overwritten. (Wiped out. Gone to the great variable home in the sky!)

Just as the parameters to a function are normally values, a function normally *returns* a value. In the case of returning a pointer, the function is still returning just a value — it is returning the value of the pointer, which is a number representing an address.

Returning a Pointer as a Nonpointer

You may find it annoying to dereference a pointer returned from a function every time you want to use it. Listing 7-14, in the preceding section, is an example of how you need to dereference a pointer each time. But you can avoid this issue by dereferencing the pointer as soon as it comes cranking out of the machine. The `ReturnPointer2` example, shown in Listing 7-15, demonstrates: You preceded the call to the function with an asterisk, which dereferences the result immediately. You then place the result in a local non-pointer variable. After that, you have the value in the variable, and you don't need to dereference the pointer when you want to use the value. Thus, when you call `cout`, you just use the variable directly without the use of asterisks and other pointer paraphernalia.

Listing 7-15:   **Dereferencing Your Return Value Immediately So You Don't Need to Use It as a Pointer**

```
#include <iostream>

using namespace std;

string *GetNotSoSecretCode()
{
  string *code = new string("ABCDEF");
  return code;
}

int main()
{
  string newcode;
  int index;

  for (index = 0; index < 10; index++)
  {
    newcode = *GetNotSoSecretCode();
    cout << newcode << endl;
  }

  return 0;
}
```

When you run this application, you see the following secret but highly entic-ing output:

```
ABCDEF
ABCDEF
ABCDEF
ABCDEF
ABCDEF
ABCDEF
ABCDEF
ABCDEF
ABCDEF
ABCDEF
```

Passing by Reference

C++ is based on the old C language, which was a simple language. C++ has some features to make it "cushier." One feature is references. A *reference* is another way of specifying a parameter in a function whereby the function can modify the original variable. Instead of following the parameter type with an asterisk (*) to denote a pointer, you follow it with an ampersand (&). Then, throughout your function, you can use the parameter just as you nor-mally would, not as a pointer. But every change you make to the parameter affects the original variable! It's a concept that's ahead of its time (or behind its time, considering that other languages have had this feature for years).

Take a look at the `PassByReference` example, shown in Listing 7-16, and notice that we didn't use any pointers.

Listing 7-16:   With References, You Don't Need Pointers!

```
#include <iostream>

using namespace std;

void MessMeUp(int &myparam)
{
  myparam = myparam * 2 + 10;
}

int main()
{
  int mynumber = 30;
  MessMeUp(mynumber);
  cout << mynumber << endl;
  return 0;
}
```

Look at that code! No more pointers! In `main()`, you don't need to take the address of anything, and you don't need to use that *dereference* word, which the spelling checker insists is wrong. And the function itself has no pointers, either. You just throw the old ampersand-thing in front of the parameter name in the function header.

If you have `string` parameters, and you use the `&` to pass them by reference, skip the shortcut `->` notation to call the string functions. And don't dereference anything. There are no pointers. Just type the dot (or period) and the function. No asterisks needed.

If you write a function that uses a reference and somebody else uses your function in code (see Book I, Chapter 6, for information on how to do this), you could end up making that other person angry. The other person may not realize that, "Hey, man — this thing just messed up my variable!" WHAM! The variable gets changed. How do you avoid this? Warn the other person. Make it clear to anybody using your function that it uses references and will modify variables, even the unsuspecting little ones.

Passing By const Reference

In Listing 7-13, you see how to modify a string by passing it to a function by reference. Let's say that you still want to pass the string by reference, but you don't want to allow anyone to modify it. Maybe you intend to use the string later for some other purpose. Of course, you could just pass the string by value, and the caller couldn't modify it. The problem is that strings can get rather large, and moving all that data to a function is really time consuming — passing a reference is simpler and faster. Using a `const` reference makes it possible to get the speed benefits of using a reference, with the unchangeable nature of passing by value. The `VariablePointer4` example, shown in Listing 7-17, demonstrates how to perform this task.

Listing 7-17:   Using a `const` Reference to Get Speed and Unchangeable Data

```
#include <iostream>

using namespace std;

string Paranoid(const string *realmessage)
{
  string NewString = *realmessage;
  NewString[6] = 'i';
  NewString.replace(9, 1, "");
  NewString.insert(18, "ad");
  NewString.replace(15, 2, "in");
  NewString.replace(23, 7, "!");
  NewString.replace(4, 3, "ali");

  return NewString;
}
```

```
int main()
{
  string message = "The friends are having dinner";
  cout << message << endl;

  string NewMessage = Paranoid(&message);
  cout << NewMessage << endl;

  return 0;
}
```

The output of this example is precisely the same as in Listing 7-13. However, if you try to make modifications to `realmessage` in `Paranoid()`, the compiler complains. The difference is the use of the `const` keyword in the calling arguments for `Paranoid()`. You can look at the data and copy it to another variable — `NewString`, in this case — but you can't change it directly. The `Paranoid()` function makes the same changes to the string as before, but it makes those changes to `NewString`.

`Paranoid()` passes the value of `NewString` back to the caller, `main()`, so that it can display the modified string onscreen. In this case, `main()` creates a new variable, `NewMessage`, to hold the output of `Paranoid()` and display it onscreen.

Remembering the Rules

When you use pointers and references, make your life easier by following these tips:

✦ **Understand pointers and references:** Your C++ programming ventures will be much happier.

✦ **Free your pointers:** Whenever you call `new`, you should (sooner or later) call `delete`. Don't leave memory in the heap when you're finished with it.

✦ **Know your references:** If you write a function that has references, make sure that everybody knows it. And if you *use* a function that somebody else wrote, make sure that you check both the person's references and the function's references.

Chapter 8: Working with Classes

In This Chapter

✔ Understanding objects and classes and the difference between the two

✔ Becoming familiar with member functions and variables in a class

✔ Making parts of a class public, private, and protected

✔ Using constructors and destructors

✔ Building hierarchies of classes

*B*ack in the early 1990s, the big buzzword in the computer world was *object-oriented*. For anything to sell, it had to be *object-oriented,* whatever *that* meant. Programming languages were object-oriented. Software applications were object-oriented. Computers were object-oriented. Refrigerators were object-oriented. What did that all mean? *Nothing*. It was simply a catchphrase that was cool at the time.

Those days are gone, and now we can explore what object-oriented *really* means and how you can use it to organize your C++ applications. In this chapter, we introduce object-oriented programming and show how you can do it in C++. Although people disagree on the strict definition of object-oriented, in this book it means programming with objects and classes.

Understanding Objects and Classes

Consider a pen, a regular, old pen. One of us actually has a pen on our desk. Here's what we can say about it:

✦ **Ink Color:** Black

✦ **Shell Color:** Light gray

✦ **Cap Color:** Black

✦ **Style:** Ballpoint

✦ **Length:** Six inches

✦ **Brand:** Office Depot

✦ **Ink Level:** 50 percent full

- ✦ **Capability #1:** Write on paper
- ✦ **Capability #2:** Break in half
- ✦ **Capability #3:** Run out of ink

Now, look around for other things. We see a printer. Let us describe that:

- ✦ **Kind:** Laser
- ✦ **Brand:** Lexmark
- ✦ **Model:** X790
- ✦ **Ink Color:** Black
- ✦ **Case Color:** Cream
- ✦ **Input trays:** Two
- ✦ **Output trays:** Two
- ✦ **Connection:** Ethernet
- ✦ **Capability #1:** Reads print job requests from the computer
- ✦ **Capability #2:** Prints on sheets of paper
- ✦ **Capability #3:** Prints a test page
- ✦ **Capability #4:** Needs the toner cartridge replaced when empty

We're just describing the things we see. We're giving dimensions, color, model, brand. And we're also describing what the things can do. The pen can break in half and run out of ink. The printer can take print jobs, print pages, and have its cartridge replaced.

When we describe what the things can do, we're carefully writing it from the perspective of the thing itself, not from the perspective of the person using the thing. A good way to name the capability is to test it by preceding it with the words "I can" and see if it makes sense. Thus, because "I can *write on paper*" works from the perspective of a pen, we chose *write on paper* for one of the pen's capabilities.

Instead of saying the word *thing,* we will say the word *object.* The two meanings are the same: An object is just a thing. Anything, really. A book. A dirty plate. A stack of writeable CD-ROMs. These are all objects.

But is seeing all the objects in the universe possible, or are some of those objects hidden? Certainly some objects are physical, like atoms or the dark side of the moon, and we can't see them. But other objects are abstract. For example, we have a checking account. What is a checking account, exactly?

Can you point to it? Can you drop it, throw it? You can throw your checkbook across the room and, if you're brave, can even try to get into the room where the main computer is holding your checking account. But is the checking account something physical you can touch? No. It's abstract.

Using enumerations

We think that the number 12 is a good representation of the color blue, and the number 86 is a good representation of the color red. Purple? That's 182. Beige? That's getting up there — it's 1047. Yes, this sounds kind of silly. But let's suppose you want to create a variable that holds the color blue. Using the standard types of integers, floating-point numbers, characters, and letters, you don't have a lot of choices. In the old days, people would just pick a number to represent each color and store that number in a variable. Or, you could have saved a string, as in `blue`. But C++ presents a better alternative. It's called an *enumeration*. Remember that for each type, there's a whole list of possible values. An integer, for example, can be a whole number within a particular range. (This range varies between computers, but it's usually pretty big.) Strings can be any characters, all strung together. But what if you want a value called `blue`? Or `red`? Or even `beige`? Then you need enumerations. (Hurray!) This line creates an enumeration type:

```
enum MyColor {blue, red, green, yellow,
        black, beige};
```

You now have a new *type* called `MyColor`, which you can use the same way you can use other types, such as `int` or `double` or `string`. For example, you can create a variable of type `MyColor` and set its value to one of the values in the curly braces:

```
MyColor inkcolor = blue;
MyColor shellcolor = black;
```

The variable `inkcolor` is of type `MyColor`, and its value is `blue`. The variable `shellcolor` is also of type `MyColor`, and its value is `black`.

Classifying classes and objects

When we pick up a pen, we can ask somebody, "What type of thing is this an instance of?" Most people would probably say, "a pen." In computer programming, instead of using *type of thing*, we say *class*. This thing in my hand belongs to the pen class.

Now if we point to the thing parked out in the driveway, and ask you, "What class does that belong to?," you will answer, "class Car." Of course, you could be more specific. You may say that the thing belongs to class 1999 Ford Taurus.

When we show you the pen, we are asking you what class this object belongs to. If we then pick up another pen, we're showing you another example of the same class. One class, several examples. If we stand next to a busy street, we see many examples of the class called car. Or we may see many examples of the class Ford Explorer, a few instances of the class Volkswagen Beetle, and so on. It depends on how you *classify* those things roaring down the road. But regardless, we likely see several examples of any given class.

So when you organize things, you specify a *class,* which is the type of object. And when you're ready, you can start picking out examples (or *instances*) of the class. Each class may have several instances. Some classes have only one instance. That's a *singleton class*. For example, at any given time, the class United States President would have one instance.

Class names and class files

In Listings 8-3 and 8-4, nearby in this chapter, we chose filenames that match the name of our class. That's usually the way we like to do it: When we create a class, we put the class definition in a header file of the same name as the class but with an .h extension. And we put the class member function code in a source code file of the same name as the class but this time with a .cpp extension. We usually like our filenames capitalized the same as the class name; thus, we called the files Pen.h and Pen.cpp. Naming the files the same as classes has lots of advantages that can help you in your quest to become a millionaire. First, you automatically know the name of the header file you need to include if you want to use a certain class. Second, it provides a general consistency, which is always good in life, whether dealing with programming or pancake syrup. And finally, if we see a header file, we know what class is probably inside it.

Describing member functions and data

If we choose a class, we can describe some characteristics. However, because we're only describing the class characteristics, we don't actually specify them. We may say the pen has an ink color, but we don't actually say *what* color. That's because we don't yet have an example of the class pen. We have only the class itself. When we finally find an example, it may be one color, or it may be another. So, if we're describing a class called pen, we may list the following characteristics:

+ **Ink Color**

+ **Shell Color**

+ **Cap Color**

+ **Style**

+ **Length**

+ **Brand**

+ **Ink Level**

We don't specify ink color, shell color, length, or any of these. We're listing only general characteristics for all instances of the class pen. That is, every pen has these characteristics. But the actual values for these characteristics might vary from instance to instance. One pen may have a different ink color from another, but both might have the same brand. Nevertheless, they are both separate instances of the class pen.

After we actually have an instance of class pen, we can give the specifics for the characteristics. For example, Table 8-1 lists the characteristics of three actual pens.

Table 8-1	Specifying Characteristics of Instances of Class Pen		
Characteristic	*First Pen*	*Second Pen*	*Third Pen*
Ink Color	Blue	Red	Black
Shell Color	Grey	Red	Grey
Cap Color	Blue	Black	Black
Style	Ballpoint	Fountain	Felt-tip
Length	5.5 inches	5 inches	6 inches
Brand	Office Depot	Parker	Paper Mate
Ink Level	30%	60%	90%

In Table 8-1, the first column holds the names of the characteristics. The second column holds values for those characteristics for the first pen. The third column holds the values of characteristics for the second pen, and the final column holds the values for the third pen.

All the pens in the class share characteristics. But the values for these characteristics may differ from pen to pen. When we build a new pen (assuming that we could do such a thing), we would follow the list of characteristics, giving the new pen its own values. We may make the shell purple with yellow speckles, or we may make it transparent. But we would give it a shell that has some color, even if that color is *transparent*.

In Table 8-1, we didn't list capabilities. But all these pens have the same capabilities:

✦ **Capability #1:** Write on paper

✦ **Capability #2:** Break in half

✦ **Capability #3:** Run out of ink

Unlike characteristics, these capabilities don't change from instance to instance. They are the same for each class.

In computer programming, capabilities are *member functions.* That's because you'll be writing functions to perform these, and they are part of a class. The characteristics are *member variables,* because they are variables that are part of the class.

When you describe classes to build a computer application using a class, you are modeling. In the preceding examples, we modeled a class called Pen. In the following section, we implement this model by writing an application that mimics a pen.

If you work with enums (the code form of enumerations), you need to decide what to name your new type. For example, you can choose MyColor or MyColors. Many people, when they write a line such as enum MyColor {blue, red, green, yellow, black, beige};, make the name plural (MyColors) because this is a list of colors. We make it singular, as in MyColor. When you declare a variable, it makes more sense: MyColor inkcolor; would mean that inkcolor is a *color* — not a group of *colors*.

Implementing a class

To implement a class in C++, you use the keyword class. We know, it's profound. And then you add the name of the class, such as Pen. You then add an open brace, list your member variables and member functions, and end with a closing brace.

Most people capitalize the first letter of a class name in C++, and if their class name is a word, they don't capitalize the remaining letters. Although you don't have to follow this rule, many people do. You can choose any name for a C++ class provided it is not a C++ keyword; it consists only of letters, digits, and underscores; and it does not start with a number.

The PenClass example shown in Listing 8-1 contains a C++ class description, which we put inside a header file called Pen.h. (See Book I, Chapter 6, for information on how to put code in a header file.) Take a look at the header file, and you can see how we implemented the different characteristics. The characteristics of a header file are just like variables: They have a type and a name. And we implemented the capabilities simply as functions. But all this stuff goes inside curly brackets and is preceded by a class header. The header gives the name of the class. And, oh yes, the word *public* is stuck in there, and it has a colon after it. We explain the word *public* in "Accessing members," later in this chapter. By itself, this code isn't very useful, but we put it to use in Listing 8-2, an application that you can actually compile and run.

Listing 8-1:   Pen.h Contains the Class Description for Pen

```
#ifndef PEN_H_INCLUDED
#define PEN_H_INCLUDED

using namespace std;

enum Color
{
    blue,
    red,
    black,
    clear,
    grey
};
```

```
enum PenStyle
{
    ballpoint,
    felt_tip,
    fountain_pen
};

class Pen
{
public:
    Color InkColor;
    Color ShellColor;
    Color CapColor;
    PenStyle Style;
    float Length;
    string Brand;
    int InkLevelPercent;

    void write_on_paper(string words)
    {
        if (InkLevelPercent <= 0)
        {
            cout << "Oops! Out of ink!" << endl;
        }
        else
        {
            cout << words << endl;
            InkLevelPercent = InkLevelPercent - words.length();
        }
    }

    void break_in_half()
    {
        InkLevelPercent = InkLevelPercent / 2;
        Length = Length / 2.0;
    }

    void run_out_of_ink()
    {
        InkLevelPercent = 0;
    }
};

#endif // PEN_H_INCLUDED
```

When you write a class, you always end it with a semicolon. Write that down on a sticky note and hang it on the refrigerator. The effort spent in doing this will be well worth avoiding the frustration of wondering why your code won't compile.

In a class definition, you describe the characteristics and capabilities (that is, supply the member variables and member functions, respectively).

Note in Listing 8-1, earlier in this chapter, that the member functions access the member variables. However, we said that these variables don't have values yet, because this is just a class, not an *instance* of a class. How can that be? When you create an instance of this class, you can give values to these member variables. Then you can call the member functions. And here's the really great part: You can make a *second instance* of this class and give it its own values for the member variables. Yes, the two instances will each have their own sets of member variables. And when you run the member functions for the second instance, these functions operate on the member variables for the second instance. Isn't C++ smart?

Now take a look at Listing 8-2. This is a source file that uses the header file in Listing 8-1. In this code, we make use of the Pen class.

Listing 8-2: main.cpp Contains Code That Uses the Class Pen

```
#include <iostream>
#include "Pen.h"

using namespace std;

int main()
{
  Pen FavoritePen;

  FavoritePen.InkColor = blue;
  FavoritePen.ShellColor = grey;
  FavoritePen.CapColor = blue;
  FavoritePen.Style = ballpoint;
  FavoritePen.Length = 5.5;
  FavoritePen.Brand = "Office Depot";
  FavoritePen.InkLevelPercent = 30;

  Pen WorstPen;

  WorstPen.InkColor = red;
  WorstPen.ShellColor = red;
  WorstPen.CapColor = black;
  WorstPen.Style = fountain_pen;
  WorstPen.Length = 5.0;
  WorstPen.Brand = "Parker";
  WorstPen.InkLevelPercent = 60;

  cout << "This is my favorite pen" << endl;
  cout << "Color: " << FavoritePen.InkColor << endl;
  cout << "Brand: " << FavoritePen.Brand << endl;
  cout << "Ink Level: " << FavoritePen.InkLevelPercent << "%" << endl;

  FavoritePen.write_on_paper("Hello I am a pen");
  cout << "Ink Level: " << FavoritePen.InkLevelPercent << "%" << endl;

  return 0;
}
```

There are two variables of class Pen: FavoritePen and WorstPen. To access the member variables of these objects, we type the name of the variable, a dot (or period), and then the member variable name. For example, to access the InkLevelPercent member of WorstPen, we type:

```
WorstPen.InkLevelPercent = 60;
```

The string class

If you've been reading the previous chapters of Book I and trying the applications, you have seen the string type. Now for the big secret: string is actually a class. When you create a variable of type string, you are creating an object of class string. That's why, to use the string functions, you first type the variable name, a dot, and then the function name: You are really calling a member function for the string object that you created. Similarly, when you work with pointers to strings, instead of a dot you can use the – > notation to access the member functions. (See "Using classes and pointers," later in this chapter, for more information.) When working with newer versions of C++, the string class is part of the std namespace, which is why you add using namespace std; to the beginning of your code. If you use an older version of C++, the string class appears as part of the string file. In this case, you include <string> to provide the necessary header files to declare the string class.

Remember, WorstPen is the variable name, and this variable is an *object*. It is an object or instance of class Pen. This object has various member variables, including InkLevelPercent.

You can also run some of the member functions that are in these objects. In the code, we called

```
FavoritePen.write_on_paper("Hello I am a pen");
```

This called the function write_on_paper() for the object FavoritePen. Take a look at the code for this function, which is in the header file, Listing 8-1:

```
void write_on_paper(string words)
{
    if (InkLevelPercent <= 0)
    {
        cout << "Oops! Out of ink!" << endl;
    }
    else
    {
        cout << words << endl;
        InkLevelPercent = InkLevelPercent - words.length();
    }
}
```

This function uses the variable called InkLevelPercent. But InkLevel Percent is not declared in this function. The reason is that InkLevel Percent is part of the object and is declared in the class. Suppose you call this method for two different objects, as in the following:

```
FavoritePen.write_on_paper("Hello I am a pen");
WorstPen.write_on_paper("Hello I am another pen");
```

The first of these lines calls `write_on_paper()` for the `FavoritePen` object; thus, inside the code for `write_on_paper()`, the `InkLevelPercent` refers to `InkLevelPercent` for the `FavoritePen` object. It looks at and possibly decreases the variable for that object only. But `WorstPen` has its *own* `InkLevelPercent` member variable, separate from that of `FavoritePen`. So in the second of these two lines, `write_on_paper()` accesses and possibly decreases the `InkLevelPercent` that lives inside `WorstPen`.

In other words, each object has its own `InkLevelPercent`. When you call `write_on_paper()`, the function modifies the member variable based on which object you are calling it with. The first line calls it with `FavoritePen`. The second calls it with `WorstPen`. When you run this application, you see the following output:

```
This is my favorite pen
Color: 0
Brand: Pilot
Ink Level: 90%
Hello I am a pen
Ink Level: 74%
```

Now notice something about the color line. Here's the line of code that writes it:

```
cout << "Color: " << FavoritePen.InkColor << endl;
```

We're writing the `InkColor` member for `FavoritePen`. But what type is `InkColor`? It's the new enumerated type we created called `Color`. But something is wrong. It printed 0. Yet here's the line where we set it:

```
FavoritePen.InkColor = blue;
```

We set it to `blue`, not 0. Unfortunately, that's the breaks with using enum. You can use it in your code, but *under the hood,* it just stores numbers. And when we print it, we get a number. Well, that stinks. The compiler chooses the numbers for you, and it starts the first in the enum list as 0, the second as 1, then 2, then 3, and so on. Thus, `blue` is stored as 0, `red` as 1, `black` as 2, `clear` as 3, and `grey` as 4. But, as we always say (because we're forever the optimists), fear not! People have found a way to create a new class that handles the enum for you (that is, it *wraps* around the enum), and then you can print what you really want: `blue`, `red`, `black`, `clear`, and `grey`. Take a look at Book I, Chapter 9 for tips on how to do this astounding feat.

Remember that you can create several *objects* (also called *instances*) of a single class. Each object gets its own member variables, which you declare in the class. To access the members of an object, you use a period, or dot.

Separating member function code

When you work with functions, you can either make sure that the code to your function is positioned before any calls to the function, or you can use a *forward reference,* also called a *function prototype.* We talk about this handy little feature in Book I, Chapter 5.

When you work with classes and member functions, you have a similar option. Most C++ programmers prefer to keep the code for their member functions outside the class definition. The class definition contains only function prototypes, or, at least, mostly function prototypes. If the function is one or two lines of code, people may leave it in the class definition.

When you use a function prototype in a class definition, you write the prototype by ending the function header with a semicolon where you would normally have the open brace and code. If your member function looks like

```
void break_in_half()
{
    InkLevelPercent = InkLevelPercent / 2;
    Length = Length / 2.0;
}
```

a function prototype would look like

```
void break_in_half();
```

Yes, it's true: To type this, we just copied the first line of the function, put the cursor at the end, pressed backspace a couple times, and typed a semicolon. We're telling you that not to brag about our prowess with the keyboard when writing books but rather because that's how we do it when we actually write code. That way, we can be assured that the two lines *match.* Ah, the beauty of computers. Imagine how hard it would be to write a computer application without the help of computers.

Now after you have the function prototype in the class, you write the function again *outside* the class definition. However, you need to doctor it up just a bit. In particular, you need to throw in the name of the class, so that the compiler knows which class this function goes with.

The following is the same function we described earlier but souped-up with the class information:

```
void Pen::break_in_half()
{
    InkLevelPercent = InkLevelPercent / 2;
    Length = Length / 2.0;
}
```

You would put this after your class definition. And you would want to put this inside one of your source code files if your class definition is in a header file.

You can use the same function name in different classes. Like variables in different functions, function names are totally separate things. Although you don't want to go overboard on duplicating your function names, if you feel a need to, you can certainly do it without a problem.

The `PenClass2` example shown in Listings 8-3 and 8-4 contains the modified version of the `Pen` class, which originally appeared earlier in this chapter in Listing 8-1. You can use these two files together with Listing 8-2, which did not change.

Listing 8-3: Using Member Function Prototypes with the Modified Pen.h file

```
#ifndef PEN_H_INCLUDED
#define PEN_H_INCLUDED

using namespace std;

enum Color
{
    blue,
    red,
    black,
    clear,
    grey
};

enum PenStyle
{
    ballpoint,
    felt_tip,
    fountain_pen
};

class Pen
{
public:
    Color InkColor;
    Color ShellColor;
    Color CapColor;
    PenStyle Style;
    float Length;
    string Brand;
    int InkLevelPercent;

    void write_on_paper(string words);
    void break_in_half();
    void run_out_of_ink();
};

#endif // PEN_H_INCLUDED
```

Listing 8-4:   Containing the Member Functions for Class Pen in the New Pen.cpp File

```
#include <iostream>
#include "Pen.h"

using namespace std;

void Pen::write_on_paper(string words)
{
    if (InkLevelPercent <= 0)
    {
        cout << "Oops! Out of ink!" << endl;
    }
    else
    {
        cout << words << endl;
        InkLevelPercent = InkLevelPercent - words.length();
    }
}

void Pen::break_in_half()
{
    InkLevelPercent = InkLevelPercent / 2;
    Length = Length / 2.0;
}

void Pen::run_out_of_ink()
{
    InkLevelPercent = 0;
}
```

All the functions from the class are now in a separate source (.cpp) file. The header file now just lists prototypes and is a little easier for us humans to scan through. And for the source file, we included the header file at the top. That's required; otherwise, the compiler won't know that Pen is a class name, and it will get confused (as it so easily can).

The parts of a class

Here is a summary of the parts of a class and the different ways classes can work together.

✦ **Class:** A class is a type. It includes *characteristics* and *capabilities*. Characteristics describe the class, and capabilities describe its behavior.

✦ **Object (or instance):** An object is an example of a class. Or, to put it another way, an object's type is the class. If you like analogies, the object Fred is to the Human class as 17 is to int.

✦ **Class definition:** The class definition describes the class. It starts with the word *class*, then has the name of the class, and then an open brace and closing brace. Inside the braces are the members of the class.

✦ **Member variable:** A member variable is the C++ version of a characteristic in a class. You list the member variables inside the class. Each instance of the class gets its own copy of each member variable.

✦ **Member function:** A member function is the C++ version of a capability of a class. Like member variables, you list the member functions inside the class. When you call a member function for a particular instance, the function accesses the member variables for the instance.

When you divide the class, you put part in the header file and part in the source code file. The following list describes what goes where:

✦ **Header file:** Put the class definition in the header file. You can include the function code inside the class definition itself if it's a short function. Most people prefer not to put any function code longer than a line or two in the header — in fact, many don't put any function code at all in the header. You may want to name the header file the same as the class but with an .h or .hpp extension. Thus, the class Pen, for instance, might be in the file Pen.h.

✦ **Source file:** If your class has member functions, and you did not put the code in the class definition, you need to put the code in a source file. When you do, precede the function name with the class name and two colons. (Do not put any spaces between the two colons, but you can put spaces on either side of the pair of colons.) If you named the header file the same as the class, you probably want to name the source file the same as the class as well but with a .cpp or .cc extension.

Working with a Class

Many handy tricks are available for working with classes. In this section, we explore several clever ways of working with classes, starting with the way you can hide certain parts of your class from other functions that are accessing them.

Accessing members

When you work with an object in real life, there are often parts of the object that you interact with and other parts that you don't. For example, when we use the computer, we type on the keyboard but don't open the box and poke around with a wire attached to a battery. For the most part, the stuff inside is off-limits except when we're upgrading it.

In object terminology, we use the words *public* and *private* to refer to characteristics and capabilities. When you design a class, you might want to make some member variables and functions freely accessible by users of the class. You may want to keep other classes tucked away.

First, let us explain what we mean by *users of the class*. When the main() function of your application creates an instance of a class and calls one of its member functions, main() is a *user* of the class. If you have a function called FlippityFlop(), and it creates an instance of your class and does a few things to the instance, like change some its member variables, `FlippityFlop()` is a *user* of your class. In short, a user is any function that accesses your class.

If you're designing a class, it's possible that you want only these users calling certain member functions. Other member functions you may want to keep hidden away, to be called only by other member functions within the class. Suppose you're writing a class called `Oven`. This class includes a method called `Bake()`, which takes a number as a parameter representing the desired oven temperature. Now you may also have a member function called `TurnOnHeatingElement()` and one called `TurnOffHeatingElement()`.

Here's how it would work. The `Bake` method starts out calling `TurnOn HeatingElement`. Then it keeps track of the temperature, and when the temperature is correct, it calls `TurnOffHeatingElement`.

Now would you want somebody walking in the kitchen and calling the `TurnOnHeatingElement()` function without touching any of the dials, only to leave the room as the oven gets hotter and hotter with nobody watching it? No. You allow the users of the class to call only `Bake()`. The other two member functions, `TurnOnHeatingElement()` and `TurnOffHeatingElement()`, are reserved for use only by the `Bake()` function.

You bar users from calling functions by making specific functions *private*. Functions that you want to allow access to you make *public*.

After you have such a class designed, if you write a function (not a member function) that has an object and you try to call one of an object's private member functions, you get a compiler error when you try to compile it. The compiler won't allow you to call it.

The `OvenClass` example shown in Listing 8-5 defines a sample `Oven` class and a `main()` that uses it. Take a look at the class definition. It has two sections: one private and the other public. After the class definition, we put the code for the functions. The two private functions don't do much other than print a message. (Although they're also free to call other private functions in the class.) The public function, `Bake()`, calls each of the private functions, because it's allowed to.

Listing 8-5: Using the Public and Private Words to Hide Parts of Your Class

```
#include <iostream>

using namespace std;

class Oven
```

(continued)

Listing 8-5 *(continued)*

```
{
private:
    void TurnOnHeatingElement();
    void TurnOffHeatingElement();

public:
    void Bake(int Temperature);
};

void Oven::TurnOnHeatingElement()
{
    cout << "Heating element is now ON! Be careful!" << endl;
}

void Oven::TurnOffHeatingElement()
{
    cout << "Heating element is now off. Relax!" << endl;
}

void Oven::Bake(int Temperature)
{
    TurnOnHeatingElement();
    cout << "Baking!" << endl;
    TurnOffHeatingElement();
}

int main()
{
    Oven fred;
    fred.Bake(875);
    return 0;

}
```

When you run this application, you see some messages:

```
Heating element is now ON! Be careful!
Baking!
Heating element is now off. Relax!
```

Nothing too fancy here. Now if you tried to include a line in your `main()` such as the one in the following code, where you call a private function

```
fred.TurnOnHeatingElement();
```

you see an error message telling you that you can't do it because the function is private. In Code::Blocks, we see this message:

```
error: 'void Oven::TurnOnHeatingElement()' is private
```

When you design your classes, consider making all the functions private by default, and then only make those public that you want users to have access to. Some people, however, prefer to go the other way around: Make them all public, and only make those private that you are sure you don't want users to access. There are good arguments for either way; however, we prefer to make public only what must be public. That way, we minimize the risk of some other application, that's using your class, messing things up by calling things the programmer doesn't really understand.

You don't necessarily need to list the private members first followed by the public members. You can put the public members first if you prefer. Some people put the public members at the top so they see them first. That makes sense. Also, you can have more than one private section and more than one public section. For example, you can have a public section, a private section, and then another public section, as in the following code:

```
class Oven
{
public:
    void Bake(int Temperature);

private:
    void TurnOnHeatingElement();
    void TurnOffHeatingElement();

public:
    void Broil();
};
```

But we recommend having only one public section and only one private section (or no private sections). This minimalism keeps your code neater.

Using classes and pointers

As with any variable, you can have a pointer variable that points to an object. As usual, the pointer variable's type must match the type of the class. This creates a pointer variable that points to a Pen instance:

```
Pen *ptrMyPen;
```

The variable ptrMyPen is a pointer, and it can point to an object of type Pen. The variable's own type is *pointer to* Pen, or in C++ notation, Pen *.

A line of code like Pen *ptrMyPen; creates a variable that serves as a pointer to an object. But this line, by itself, does not actually create an instance. By itself, it points to nothing. To create an instance, you have to call new. This is a common mistake among C++ programmers; sometimes people forget to call new and wonder why their applications crash.

After you create the variable ptrMyPen, you can create an instance of class Pen, and point ptrMyPen to it using the new keyword like so:

```
ptrMyPen = new Pen;
```

Or you can combine both Pen *ptrMyPen; and the preceding line:

```
Pen *ptrMyPen = new Pen;
```

Now you have two variables: You have the actual object, which is unnamed and sitting on the heap. (See Book I, Chapter 7, for more information on pointers and heaps.) You also have the pointer variable, which points to the object: two variables working together.

Because the object is out on the heap, the only way to access it is through the pointer. To access the members through the pointer, you use a special notation — a minus sign followed by a greater-than sign. It bears a passing resemblance to an arrow, as the following line makes clear:

```
ptrMyPen->InkColor = red;
```

This goes through the pointer to set the InkColor of the object to red.

Get used to working with pointers and using the pointer notation for accessing the members of an object. It's not just a programming language; it's a way of life!

Although we like to begin a pointer variable's name with ptr, we sometimes forgo that when we're working with objects. Most object work involves objects on the heap, so you are always accessing objects through pointers. In our minds, we connect the two into one, and we feel like the pointer variable is the object, so we don't use the ptr prefix.

If we decide not to start our pointer variable names with ptr, the previous lines of code would look like this instead:

```
Pen *MyPen = new Pen;
MyPen->InkColor = red;
```

As with other variables you created with new, after you are finished using an object, you should call delete. To do so, start with the word delete and then the name of the object, as in this:

```
delete MyPen;
```

Store a 0 in the pointer after you *delete* it (which really means *delete the object it's pointing to*). When you call delete on a pointer to an object, you are deleting the object itself, not the pointer. If you don't store a 0 in the pointer, it still points to where the object *used to be*.

The PenClass3 example shown in Listing 8-6 demonstrates the process of declaring a pointer, creating an object and pointing to it, accessing the object's members through the pointer, deleting the object, and clearing the pointer back to 0.

Listing 8-6:   Managing an Object's Life

```
#include <iostream>
#include "Pen.h"

using namespace std;
```

```
int main()
{
    Pen *MyPen;
    MyPen = new Pen;

    MyPen->InkColor = red;
    cout << MyPen->InkColor << endl;

    delete MyPen;
    MyPen = 0;

    return 0;
}
```

Table 8-2 reiterates the process (steps) shown in Listing 8-6 in a more formal way. We call Table 8-2 "Steps to Using Objects," rather than something more specific such as "Using Objects with Pointers," because the majority of your work with objects will be through pointers. Therefore, this is the most common way of using pointers.

Table 8-2   **Steps to Using Objects**

Step	Sample Code	Action
1	`Pen *MyPen;`	Declares the pointer
2	`MyPen = new Pen;`	Calls `new` to create the object
3	`MyPen->InkColor = red;`	Accesses the members of the object through the pointer
4	`delete MyPen;`	Deletes the object
5	`MyPen = 0;`	Clears the pointer

Now that you have an overview of the process through Listing 8-6 and understand the basics through Table 8-2, let's formalize the procedure. The following steps describe precisely how to work with pointers and objects:

1. **Declare the pointer.**

The pointer must match the type of object you are going to work with, except the pointer's type name in C++ is followed by an asterisk, *.

2. **Call new, passing the class name, and store the results of new in the pointer.**

You can combine Steps 1 and 2 into a single step.

3. **Access the object's members through the pointer with the shorthand notation ->.**

You could dereference the pointer and put parentheses around it, but everyone uses the shorthand notation.

4. **When you are finished with the pointer, call `delete`.**

   This step frees the object from the heap. Remember that this does not delete the pointer itself, although programmers usually say that they're *deleting the pointer.*

5. **Clear the pointer by setting it to 0.**

   If your `delete` statement is at the end of the application, you don't need to clear the pointer to 0.

Passing objects to functions

When you write a function, normally you base your decision about using pointers on whether or not you want to change the original variables passed into the function. Suppose you have a function called `AddOne()`, and it takes an integer as a parameter. If you want to modify the original variable, you can use a pointer (or you can use a reference). If you don't want to modify the variable, just pass the variable *by value,* as it's called.

The following prototype represents a function that can modify the variable passed into it:

```
void AddOne(int *number);
```

And this prototype represents a function that cannot modify the variable passed into it:

```
void AddOne(int number);
```

With objects, you can do something similar. For example, this function takes a pointer to an object and can, therefore, modify the object:

```
void FixFlatTire(Car *mycar);
```

But what do you suppose this would do:

```
void FixFlatTire(Car mycar);
```

Based on what we said previously, most likely the function gets its own `Car` instance that cannot be modified. That's correct, but consider that for a moment: The function gets its own instance. In other words, every time you call this function, it creates an entirely new instance of class `Car`. This instance would be a duplicate of class `Car` — except that it wouldn't be the same instance. Just a copy of it.

When you work with objects, a *copy* is not always a sure thing. What if the object has member variables that are pointers to other objects? Will the copy get copies of those pointers, which in turn point to those same other objects? Or does this object's members point to its own *other objects*? Are those objects copies or the originals?

Always pass objects as pointers. Don't pass objects directly into functions. Yes, it risks bad code changing the object, but careful C++ programmers want the actual object, not a copy. That outweighs the risk of an accidental change. This chapter explains how to prevent accidental changes by using the `const` parameters.

So just do this:

```
void FixFlatTire(Car *mycar);
```

If you like references, you are welcome to do this:

```
void FixFlatTire(Car &mycar);
```

But don't just pass the object. It's messy and not nice.

Because your function receives its objects as pointers, you continue accessing them by using the `->` notation. For example, the function `FixFlatTire` may do this:

```
void FixFlatTire(Car *mycar)
{
    mycar->RemoveTire();
    mycar->AddNewTire();
}
```

Or, if you prefer references, you would do this:

```
void FixFlatTire2(Car &mycar)
{
    mycar.RemoveTire();
    mycar.AddNewTire();
}
```

In this code, because you're dealing with a reference, you access the object's members using the dot rather than the `->` notation.

Another reason to use only pointers and references as parameters for objects is that a function that takes an object as a parameter usually wants to change the function. Such changes require pointers or references. When you don't want the function to modify the object, use `const`, which is covered in the following section.

Using const parameters in functions

The "Passing By const Reference" section of Book I Chapter 7 explains how to use constant parameters with standard variable types. The `const` keyword is useful when working with objects because you generally don't want to pass an object directly. That involves copying the object, which is messy. Instead, you normally pass by using a pointer or reference, which would allow you to change the object. If you put the word `const` before the parameter, the compiler will not allow you to change the parameter. The `PenClass4` example appears in Listing 8-7. In this case, we have inserted `const` before the parameter. The function can look at the object but can't change it.

Listing 8-7: The Inspect Function Is Not Allowed to Modify Its Parameter

```
#include <iostream>
#include "Pen.h"

using namespace std;

void Inspect(const Pen *Checkitout)
{
    cout << Checkitout->Brand << endl;
}

int main()
{
    Pen *MyPen = new Pen();
    MyPen->Brand = "Spy Plus Camera";

    Inspect(MyPen);

    return 0;
}
```

Now suppose that you tried to change the object in the `Inspect` function. You may have put a line in that function like this:

```
Checkitout->Length = 10.0;
```

If you try this, the compiler issues an error. In Code::Blocks, we get

```
error: assignment of member 'Pen::Length' in read-only object
```

If you have multiple parameters, you can mix `const` and `non-const`. If you go overboard, this can be confusing. The following line shows two parameters that are `const` and another that is not. The function can modify only the members of the object called `one`.

```
void Inspect(const Pen *Checkitout, Spy *one, const Spy *two);
```

Using the this pointer

Consider a function called `OneMoreCheeseGone()`. It's not a member function, but it takes an object of instance `Cheese` as a parameter. Its prototype looks like this:

```
void OneMoreCheeseGone(Cheese *Block);
```

This is just a simple function with no return type. It takes an object pointer as a parameter. For example, after you eat a block of cheese, you can call:

```
OneMoreCheeseGone(MyBlock);
```

Now consider this: If you have an object on the heap, it has no name. You access it through a pointer variable that points to it. But what if the code is currently executing inside a member function of an object? How do you refer to the object itself?

C++ has a secret variable that exists inside every member function: `this`. It's a pointer variable. The `this` variable always points to the current object. So if code execution is occurring inside a member function and you want to call `OneMoreCheeseGone()`, passing in the current object (or block of cheese), you would pass `this`.

The `CheeseClass` example shown in Listing 8-8 demonstrates `this`. The `this` listing has four main parts. First is the definition for the class called `Cheese`. The class contains a couple of member functions.

Next is the function `OneMoreCheeseGone()` along with a global variable that it modifies. This function subtracts one from the global variable and stores a string in a member variable, `status`, of the object passed to it.

Next come the actual member functions for class `Cheese`. (We put these functions after the `OneMoreCheeseGone()` function because they call it. If we used a function prototype as a forward reference for `OneMoreCheeseGone()`, the order wouldn't matter.)

Finally we have `main()`, which creates two new instances of `Cheese`. Then it sets the global variable to 2, which keeps track of the number of blocks left. Next, it calls the `eat` function for the `asiago` cheese and `rot` for the `limburger` cheese. And then it prints the results of everything that happened: It displays the `Cheese` count, and it displays the `status` variable of each object.

Listing 8-8: Passing an Object from Inside Its Member Functions by Using the this Variable

```cpp
#include <iostream>

using namespace std;

class Cheese
{
public:
    string status;
    void eat();
    void rot();
};

int CheeseCount;
```

(continued)

Listing 8-8 *(continued)*

```
void OneMoreCheeseGone(Cheese *Block)
{
    CheeseCount--;
    Block->status = "Gone";
};

void Cheese::eat()
{
    cout << "Eaten up! Yummy" << endl;
    OneMoreCheeseGone(this);
}

void Cheese::rot()
{
    cout << "Rotted away! Yuck" << endl;
    OneMoreCheeseGone(this);
}

int main()
{
    Cheese *asiago = new Cheese();
    Cheese *limburger = new Cheese();

    CheeseCount = 2;

    asiago->eat();
    limburger->rot();

    cout << endl;
    cout << "Cheese count: " << CheeseCount << endl;
    cout << "asiago: " << asiago->status << endl;
    cout << "limburger: " << limburger->status << endl;

    return 0;
}
```

When you run the application in Listing 8-8, you see this output:

```
Eaten up! Yummy
Rotted away! Yuck

Cheese count: 0
asiago: Gone
limburger: Gone
```

The first line is the result of calling asiago->eat(), which prints one message. The second line is the result of calling limburger->rot(), which prints another message.

The third line is simply the value in the variable CheeseCount. This variable was *decremented* once each time the computer called the OneMoreCheeseGone() function. Because the function was called twice, CheeseCount went from 2 to 1 to 0.

The final two lines show the contents of the status variable in the two objects. (The OneMoreCheeseGone() function had stored the string Gone in these variables.)

Take a careful look at the OneMoreCheeseGone() function. It operated on the current object that came in as a parameter by setting its status variable to the string Gone. Where did the parameter come from? The member function eat called it, passing the object itself by using the this pointer. The member function rot also called it, again passing the object itself via the this pointer.

Overloading member functions

You may want a member function in a class to handle different types of parameters. For example, you might have a class called Door and a member function called GoThrough(). You might want the GoThrough() function to take as parameters an object of class Dog, an object of class Human, or an object of class Cat. Depending on which class is entering, you might want to change the GoThrough function's behavior.

A way to handle this is by *overloading* the GoThrough() function. C++ lets you design a class that has multiple member functions that are all named the same. However, the parameters must differ between these functions. With the GoThrough() function, one version will take a Human, another a Dog, and another a Cat.

Go through the code for the DoorClass example in Listing 8-9 and notice the GoThrough() functions. There are three of them. Now look at main(). It creates four different objects — a cat, a dog, a human, and a door. It then sends each creature through the door.

Listing 8-9:   Overloading Functions in a Class

```
#include <iostream>

using namespace std;

class Cat
{
public:
    string name;
};

class Dog
{
public:
    string name;
};

class Human
{
public:
    string name;
};
```

(continued)

Listing 8-9 *(continued)*

```cpp
class Door
{
private:
    int HowManyInside;

public:
    void Start();
    void GoThrough(Cat *acat);
    void GoThrough(Dog *adog);
    void GoThrough(Human *ahuman);
};

void Door::Start()
{
    HowManyInside = 0;
}

void Door::GoThrough(Cat *somebody)
{
    cout << "Welcome, " << somebody->name << endl;
    cout << "A cat just entered!" << endl;
    HowManyInside++;
}

void Door::GoThrough(Dog *somebody)
{
    cout << "Welcome, " << somebody->name << endl;
    cout << "A dog just entered!" << endl;
    HowManyInside++;
}

void Door::GoThrough(Human *somebody)
{
    cout << "Welcome, " << somebody->name << endl;
    cout << "A human just entered!" << endl;
    HowManyInside++;
}

int main()
{
    Door entrance;
    entrance.Start();

    Cat *SneekyGirl = new Cat;
    SneekyGirl->name = "Sneeky Girl";

    Dog *LittleGeorge = new Dog;
    LittleGeorge->name = "Little George";

    Human *me = new Human;
    me->name = "Jeff";

    entrance.GoThrough(SneekyGirl);
    entrance.GoThrough(LittleGeorge);
    entrance.GoThrough(me);

    delete SneekyGirl;
    delete LittleGeorge;
    delete me;

    return 0;
}
```

The application allows them to enter like humans. The beginning of this application declares three classes, Cat, Dog, and Human, each with a name member. Next is the Door class. A private member, HowManyInside, tracks how many beings have entered. Then we have a public function called Start(), which activates the door. Finally, the class contains the overloaded functions. They all have the same name and the same return type. You can have different return types, but they must differ by parameters. These do; one takes a Cat pointer; one takes a Dog pointer; and one takes a Human pointer.

Next is the code for the member functions. The first function, Start(), is easy to activate. It sets HowManyInside to 0. The next three functions are overloaded. They do similar things, but they write slightly different messages. Each takes a different type.

Then we have main(), which creates a Door instance. We didn't make this a pointer (just to show that you can mix pointers with stack variables in an application). After creating the Door instance, we called its Start() function. Next, we created three creature instances: one Cat, one Dog, and one Human. We also set the name member variables for each.

Then we call the entrance.GoThrough() function. The first time we pass a Cat, then we pass a Dog, and then we pass a Human. (Sounds painful.) Because you can see the Door class, you know that we're calling three different functions that happened to be all named the same. But when we're *using* the class, we consider them all one function that happens to accept a Cat, a Dog, or a Human. That's the goal of overloading: to create what feels like *versions* of the one function.

Starting and Ending with Constructors and Destructors

You can add two special functions to your class that let you provide special startup and shutdown functionality. These are called a *constructor* and a *destructor*. The following sections provide the secret details about these nifty functions.

Starting with constructors

When you create a new instance of a class, you may want to do some basic setup on the object. Suppose you have a class called Apartment, with a private member variable called NumberOfOccupants and a member function called ComeOnIn(). The code for ComeOnIn() adds 1 to NumberOfOccupants.

When you create a new instance of `Apartment`, you probably want to start `NumberOfOccupants` at `0`. The best way to do this is by adding a special member function, a *constructor,* to your class. This member function has a line of code such as

```
NumberOfOccupants = 0;
```

Whenever you create a new instance of the class `Apartment`, the computer first calls this constructor for your new object, thereby setting `NumberOfOccupants` to `0`.

Think of the constructor as an *initialization function:* The computer calls it when you create a new object.

To write a constructor, you add it as another member function to your class, and you make it public. You name the constructor the same as your class. For the class `Apartment`, we would name our constructor `Apartment()`. The constructor has no return type, not even `void`. You can have parameters in a constructor; see "Adding parameters to constructors," later in this chapter.

Listing 8-10, later in this section, shows a sample constructor along with a *destructor,* which we cover in the next section.

Ending with destructors

When you delete an instance of a class, you might want some *cleanup* code to straighten things out before the object goes off to the classroom in the sky. For example, your object may have member variables that are pointers to other objects. You may want to delete those other objects.

You put cleanup code in a special function called a destructor. A *destructor* is a finalization function that the computer calls before it deletes your object.

The destructor function gets the same name as the class, except it has a tilde, ~, at the beginning of it. (The tilde is usually in the upper-left corner of the keyboard.) For a class called `Squirrel`, the destructor would be `~Squirrel()`. The destructor does not have a return type, not even `void`, because you can't return anything from a destructor (the object is gone, after all). You just start with the function name and no parameters.

The next section, "Sampling constructors and destructors," shows an example that uses both constructors and destructors.

Constructors and destructors are a way of life for C++ programmers. Nearly every class has a constructor, and many also have a destructor.

Sampling constructors and destructors

The `WalnutClass` example shown in Listing 8-10 uses a constructor and destructor. This application involves two classes, the main one called `Squirrel` that demonstrates the constructor and destructor, and one called `Walnut`, which is used by the `Squirrel` class.

The `Squirrel` class has a member variable called `MyDinner` that is a pointer to a `Walnut` instance. The `Squirrel` constructor creates an instance of `Walnut` and stores it in the `MyDinner` variable. The destructor deletes the instance of `Walnut`.

In `main()`, we create two instances of `Squirrel`. Each instance gets its own `Walnut` to eat. Each `Squirrel` creates its `Walnut` when it starts and deletes the `Walnut` when the `Squirrel` is deleted.

Listing 8-10: Initializing and Finalizing with Constructors and Destructors

```
#include <iostream>

using namespace std;

class Walnut
{
public:
    int Size;
};

class Squirrel
{
private:
    Walnut *MyDinner;

public:
    Squirrel();
    ~Squirrel();
};

Squirrel::Squirrel()
{
    cout << "Starting!" << endl;
    MyDinner = new Walnut;
    MyDinner->Size = 30;
}

Squirrel::~Squirrel()
{
    cout << "Cleaning up my mess!" << endl;
    delete MyDinner;
}
```

(continued)

Listing 8-10 *(continued)*

```
int main()
{
    Squirrel *Sam = new Squirrel;
    Squirrel *Sally = new Squirrel;

    delete Sam;
    delete Sally;

    return 0;
}
```

Notice in this code that the constructor has the same name as the class, Squirrel(). The destructor also has the same name, but with a tilde, ~, tacked on to the beginning of it. Thus, the constructor is Squirrel() and the destructor is ~Squirrel().

When you run this application, you can see the following lines, which were spit up by the Squirrel in its constructor and destructor. (You see two lines of each because we created two squirrels.)

```
Starting!
Starting!
Cleaning up my mess!
Cleaning up my mess!
```

If our Walnut class also had a constructor and destructor, and we made the MyDinner member an actual variable in the Squirrel class rather than a pointer, the computer would create the Walnut instance after it creates the Squirrel instance but before it calls the Squirrel() constructor. It then deletes the Walnut instances when it is deleting the Squirrel instance, after it finishes calling the ~Squirrel() destructor. It would do this for each instance of Squirrel, so that each Squirrel gets its own Walnut, as before.

Constructors and destructors with stack variables

In Listing 8-10, we created the two Squirrels on the heap by using pointers and calling

```
Squirrel *Sam = new Squirrel;
Squirrel *Sally = new Squirrel;
```

But we could have made them on the stack by just declaring them without pointers:

```
Squirrel Sam;
Squirrel Sally;
```

You can do this, and the application will run fine, provided you remove the delete lines. You do not delete stack variables. The computer calls the destructor when the main() function *ends*. That's the general rule with objects on the stack: They are created when you declare them, and they stay until the function ends.

Adding parameters to constructors

Like other functions, constructors allow you to include parameters. When you do, you can use these parameters in constructors in your initialization process. To use them, you list the arguments inside parentheses when you create the object.

Although int has a constructor, it is not actually a class. However, the *runtime library* (that big mass of code that gets put in with your application by the linker) includes a constructor and destructor that you can use when calling new for an integer.

Suppose that you want the Squirrel class to have a member variable called name. Although you could create an instance of Squirrel and then set its name variable, you can specify the name directly by using a constructor.

The constructor's prototype would look like this:

```
Squirrel(string StartName);
```

Then, you would create a new instance like so:

```
Squirrel *Sam = new Squirrel("Sam");
```

The constructor is expecting a string, so you pass a string when you create the object.

The SquirrelClass example shown in Listing 8-11 presents an application that includes all the basic elements of a class with a constructor that accepts parameters.

Listing 8-11:   Placing Parameters in Constructors

```
#include <iostream>

using namespace std;

class Squirrel
{
private:
    string Name;

public:
    Squirrel(string StartName);
    void WhatIsMyName();
};

Squirrel::Squirrel(string StartName)
{
    cout << "Starting!" << endl;
    Name = StartName;
}
```

(continued)

Listing 8-11 *(continued)*

```
void Squirrel::WhatIsMyName()
{
    cout << "My name is " << Name << endl;
}

int main()
{
    Squirrel *Sam = new Squirrel("Sam");
    Squirrel *Sally = new Squirrel("Sally");

    Sam->WhatIsMyName();
    Sally->WhatIsMyName();

    delete Sam;
    delete Sally;

    return 0;
}
```

In `main()`, we passed a string into the constructors. In the code for the constructor, we're taking the string parameter called `StartName` and copying
it to the member variable called `Name`. In the `WhatIsMyName` function, we
write it to the console.

You cannot include parameters in a destructor. The C++ language does not
allow it.

Building Hierarchies of Classes

When you start going crazy describing classes, you usually discover *hierarchies* of classes. For example, you might say you have a class `Vehicle`. But
we might say, we can divide your class `Vehicle` into classes `Car`, `Pickup
Truck`, `Tractor Trailer`, and `SUV`.

Then you might say that you can take the `Car` class and divide it into
such classes as `Station Wagon`, `Four-door Sedan`, and `Two-door
Hatchback`.

Or we could divide `Vehicle` into car brands, such as `Ford`, `Honda`, and
`Toyota`. Then we could divide the class `Toyota` into models, such as
`Prius`, `Avalon`, `Camry`, and `Corolla`.

You can create similar groupings of objects for the other class hierarchies;
your decision depends on how you categorize things and how the hierarchy
is used.

In the hierarchy, class `Vehicle` is at the top. This class has characteristics
that you find in every brand or model of vehicles. For example, all vehicles
have wheels. How many they have varies, but it doesn't matter at this point
because classes don't have specific values for the characteristics.

Each brand has certain characteristics that might be unique to it, but each has all the characteristics of class `Vehicle`. That's called *inheritance*. The class `Toyota`, for example, has all the characteristics found in `Vehicle`. And the class `Prius` has all the characteristics found in `Toyota`, which includes those inherited from `Vehicle`.

Creating a hierarchy in C++

In C++, you can create a hierarchy of classes. When you take one class and create a new one under it, such as creating `Toyota` from `Vehicle`, you are *deriving* a new class.

To derive a class from an existing class, you write the new class as you would any other class, but you extend the header after the class name with a colon, `:`, the word `public`, and then the class you're deriving from, as in the following class header line:

```
class Toyota : public Vehicle {
```

When you do so, the class you create (`Toyota`) *inherits* the member variables and functions from the previous class (`Vehicle`). For example, if `Vehicle` has a public member variable called `NumberOfWheels` and a public member function called `Drive`, the class `Toyota` has these members, although you didn't write the members in `Toyota`.

The `VehicleClass` example shown in Listing 8-12 demonstrates class inheritance. We started with a class called `Vehicle`, and we derived a class called `Toyota`. In `main()`, we create an instance of `Toyota`, and we call two member functions for the instance, `MeAndMyToyota()` and `Drive()`. The definition of the `Toyota` class does not show a `Drive()` function. The `Drive()` function is inherited from the `Vehicle` class. You can call this function like a member of the `Toyota` class because in many ways it *is*.

Listing 8-12:   Deriving One Class from Another

```
#include <iostream>

using namespace std;

class Vehicle
{
public:
    int NumberOfWheels;

    void Drive()
    {
        cout << "Driving, driving, driving..." << endl;
    }
};
```

(continued)

Listing 8-12 *(continued)*

```
class Toyota : public Vehicle
{
public:
    void MeAndMyToyota()
    {
        cout << "Just me and my Toyota!" << endl;
    }
};

int main()
{
    Toyota MyCar;
    MyCar.MeAndMyToyota();
    MyCar.Drive();

    return 0;
}
```

When you run this application, you see the output from two functions:

```
Just me and my Toyota!
Driving, driving, driving...
```

Some people use the term *parent* class for the first class in a hierarchy and *child* for the one that is derived. However, these are not the best terms because some people use them to mean that one class has an instance of another class as a member variable. In that case, the parent class has as a member the child class. A better term is *base* class and *derived* class. You derive a class from the base class. The result is a derived class.

Understanding types of inheritance

When you create a class, member functions can access both public and private member variables and functions. Users of the class can access only the public member variables and functions. But when you derive a new class, the picture changes. The derived class *cannot* access the private members in its own class. Private members are reserved for a class itself and not for any derived class.

When members need to be accessible by derived classes, there's a specification you can use beyond public and private: *protected*.

Protected members and private members work the same way, but derived classes can access only protected members, not private members. Users can't access either class.

We avoid private members unless we know that we won't derive classes from a member. When we've derived classes from other people's classes with private unprotected members, we couldn't add all the cool features we wanted. My derived class required access to those private members, so we had to mess up the original code to modify the original class. If the original programmer had used *protected* members, our derived class could access the members without changing the original code!

Creating and Using Object Aliases

An alias is another name for something. If your name if Robert, someone could use an alias of Bob when calling your name. Both Robert and Bob point to the same person — you. However, the names are actually different. One is your real name, Robert, and the other is your alias, Bob. In real life, using aliases can make things easier — saying Bob is definitely easier than saying Robert (although, not by much). Using aliases in C++ applications can make things easier too.

One of the most common reasons to use an alias in C++ is to change the manner in which an object is accessed. Moving a pointer to an object is always going to be easier than moving the object itself because a pointer is simply a number that specifies the address of the object. The object could contain complex data and pointers to yet other objects. Moving objects is complicated and messy, so developers try to avoid it at all cost.

However, sending a pointer to someone gives them access to the original data. The recipient could modify the data in ways that you don't want. So, you could create an alias of the original object that is a constant. No one can modify a constant. The `ObjectAlias` example shown in Listing 8-13 demonstrates how to create a constant alias of a string object. The same technique works with any other sort of object you might want to work with.

Listing 8-13:   Creating an Object Alias

```
#include <iostream>

using namespace std;

int main()
{
    string OriginalString = "Hello";
    const string &StringCopy(OriginalString);

    OriginalString = "Goodbye";

    cout << OriginalString << endl;
    cout << StringCopy << endl;

    return 0;
}
```

The code begins by creating a `string` named `OriginalString` that contains a value of `Hello`. It then creates a `const string` alias of `OriginalString` named `StringCopy`. When the code changes the value of `OriginalString`, the value of `StringCopy` is also changed because `StringCopy` points to the same location in memory. So, when you run this example you see output of:

```
Goodbye
Goodbye
```

It may not seem like you've accomplished anything, but if you try to modify the value of StringCopy Code::Blocks outputs an error message like this:

```
error: passing 'const string {aka const std::basic_string<char>}' as
'this' argument of 'std::basic_string<_CharT, _Traits, _Alloc>&
std::basic_string<_CharT, _Traits, _Alloc>::operator=(const _CharT*)
[with _CharT = char; _Traits = std::char_traits<char>; _Alloc =
std::allocator<char>; std::basic_string<_CharT, _Traits, _Alloc> =
std::basic_string<char>]' discards qualifiers [-fpermissive]|
```

Wow, isn't that easy to read! The point is that you can't modify the value of StringCopy, but you can modify the value of OriginalString. Sending StringCopy to someone who needs access to the value is safe. Just to ensure you understand what is happening, try making StringCopy a standard string, rather than a const string. You'll be able to modify the value and the modification will now affect OriginalString as well. StringCopy truly is an alias of OriginalString, but as a const string, it's an alias that prevents modification of the underlying string value.

Chapter 9: Using Advanced C++ Features

In This Chapter

- ✓ Using comments
- ✓ Working with conversions, consoles, and preprocessor directives
- ✓ Manipulating constants, enums, and random numbers
- ✓ Structuring your code with switch statements
- ✓ Managing arrays of data

C++ has so much to offer that we thought we'd give you a mixture of advanced topics you can explore in C++. For starters, we talk a bit about some issues that are an essential part of C++ and are sure to become increasingly important as you advance in your programming career.

Filling Your Code with Comments

We have a task for a friend of ours. We want him to turn our refrigerator around and repair its compressor. We won't give him any details about how to do this, and we don't want him to look in a manual. Just grab the tools, go at it, and try to fix the thing. Now, doesn't that sound like fun?

Unless he happens to be an expert on refrigeration devices, it's doubtful that he'd get far, especially without hurting himself.

In computer programming, the risk of hurting yourself is pretty low, barring things like monitors falling on you or keyboards jumping up and attacking you. Nevertheless, other people occasionally have to fix your applications, so it's a good idea for you to provide adequate explanations of what your applications do.

How do you explain your applications? You put what are called comments into your code. A *comment* is simply some words in the code that the compiler ignores and that you put in for the benefit of the humans reading the code.

For example, you may have some code like this:

```
total = 10;
for (i = 0; i < 10; i++)
{
    total = (total + i) * 3;
}
```

But this code may not be clear to your coworkers (or to you, if you put it away for six months and come back later to look at it). So instead, you can add some comments. You denote a comment in C++ by starting a line with two slashes, like this:

```
// Initialize total to the number
// of items involved.
total = 10;

// Calculate total for the
// first ten sets.
for (i = 0; i < 10; i++)
{
    total = (total + i) * 3;
}
```

Now the people working on the project can understand what the code does. Note the white space between the groups of code. Using white space helps someone looking at the code see where one "thought" ends and another begins. You should always include white space in your code so that other developers can read the code more easily.

Of course, you could put comments like this:

```
// My salary is too low
// I want a raise
total = 10;

// Someday they'll recognize
// my superior talents!
for (i = 0; i < 10; i++)
{
    total = (total + i) * 3;
}
```

However, comments like this don't have much use in the code; besides, they may have the reverse effect from the one you're hoping for!

A comment is ignored by a compiler (but not always by other humans). You can write whatever you want as comments, and the compiler pretends that it's not even there. (Your boss, however, may notice, so use discretion.)

A comment begins with //, and it can begin anywhere on the line. In fact, contrary to what you might think, you can even put comments at the end of a line containing C++ code, instead of on a separate line. Using comments on a code line lets you focus a comment on just that line, as follows:

```
int subtotal = 10;   // Initialize the subtotal value to 10.
```

This comment gives a little more explanation of what the line does. You usually use line comments like this when you want to tell others what kind of information a variable holds or explain a complex task. Normally, you explain blocks of code as shown earlier in this section.

You can use two kinds of comments in C++. One is the double slash (as we've already described). When the compiler sees two slashes, it treats the rest of that line as a comment. That is, the comment runs from the two slashes to the end of the line. The other kind of comment begins with a slash-asterisk, /*, and ends with an asterisk-slash, */. The comments go between these *delimiters* and can span several lines, as in the following example:

```
/* This application separates the parts of the
   sandwich into its separate parts. This
   process is often called "separation of
   parts".
   (c) 1964 Sandwich Parts Separators, Inc.
*/
```

This is all one comment, and it spans multiple lines. You normally use this kind of comment to provide an overview of a task or describe the purpose of a function. This kind of comment also works well for the informational headings that some large company applications require. As with other comments, you can put these anywhere in your code, as long as you don't break a string or word in two by putting a comment in the middle. Nobody likes to be broken in two, and C++ words are no different.

Much of the code in the remainder of this chapter has comments in it so that you can see how we use comments and so that you can get a few more ideas about how the code works.

Some beginning programmers get the mistaken idea that comments appear in the application window when the application runs. That is not the case. A comment does not write anything to the console. To write things to the console, use cout.

Converting Types

Sometimes, you just don't have the type of things you want. You might want to trade in your 1999 Ford Taurus for that brand-new Porsche. But, needless to say, unless you have plenty of money, that might be difficult.

But converting between different types in C++ — now, *that's* a lot easier. For example, you may have a string variable called digits, and it holds the string "123". Further, you want to somehow get the numbers inside that string into an integer variable called amount. Thus, you want amount to hold the value 123; that is, you want to *convert the string to a number.*

In Listing 9-1, later in this chapter, we show you how you can convert between numbers and strings. Book I, Chapter 7 shows some sample code for converting a number to a string. Here we employ that same technique along with a similar technique for converting a string back to a number.

Converting strings is an interesting concept in C++ because an outstanding feature lets you *write to* and *read from* a string just as you would to and from a console. For example, although you can write a number 12 out to a console by using code like this:

```
cout << 12;
```

you can actually do the same thing with strings: You can write a number 12 to a string, as in

```
mystring << 12;
```

After this line runs, the string contains the value `"12"`. However, to do this, you need to use a special form of string called a `stringstream`. In the never-ending world of computer terminology, a *stream* is something that you can write to and read from in a flowing fashion (think about bits flowing through a wire — much as a stream flows along a waterbed). For example, you might write the word `"hello"` to a `stringstream`, and then the number 87, and then the word `"goodbye"`. After those three operations, the string contains the value `"hello87goodbye"`.

And you can similarly read from a stream. In the section "Reading from the Console," later in this chapter, we show you how you can read from a console by using the > notation. When you read from the console, although your application stops and waits for the user to enter something, the real stream technology takes place *after* the user types something: After the console has a series of characters, your application reads in the characters as a stream, one data type after other. You can read a string, and then a series of numbers, and another string, and so on.

With `stringstream`, you can do something similar. You would fill the string with something, rather than having the user fill it, as in the case of a console. From there, you can begin to read from the string, placing the values into variables of different types. One of these types is integer. But because the `stringstream` is, at heart, just a string, that's how you convert a string of digits to an integer: You put the digit characters in the string and read the string as a stream into your integer. Snazzy!

The only catch to using these is that you need to know in advance which kind of streaming you want to do. If you want to write to the `stringstream`, you create an instance of a class called `ostringstream`. (The o is for *o*utput.) If you want to read from a `stringstream`, you create an instance of a class called `istringstream`. (The i is for *i*nput.)

The `TypeConvert` example, shown in Listing 9-1, includes two handy functions that you may want to save for your own programming experience later. One is called `StringToNumber()`, and the other is called `NumberToString()`.

Listing 9-1:   Converting Between Types Is Easy

```cpp
#include <iostream>
#include <sstream>    // for istringstream, ostringstream

using namespace std;

int StringToNumber(string MyString)
{
    istringstream converter(MyString); // Converts from string to number.
    int result;                        // Contains the operation results.

    // Perform the conversion and return the results.
    converter >> result;
    return result;
}

string NumberToString(int Number)
{
    ostringstream converter; // Converts from number to string.

    // Perform the conversion and return the results.
    converter << Number;
    return converter.str();
}

int main()
{
    float NumberOfKids; // Contains the theoretical number of kids.
    int ActualKids;     // Contains an actual number of kids.

    /* You can theoretically have 2.5 kids, but in the real world,
       you can't. Convert the theoretical number of kids to a real
       number by truncating NumberOfKids and display the results. */
    cout << "Float to Integer" << endl;
    cout << "(Truncated)" << endl;
    NumberOfKids = 2.5;
    ActualKids = (int)NumberOfKids;
    cout << NumberOfKids << " " << ActualKids << endl;

    // Perform the same task as before, but use a theoretical 2.1
    // kids this time.
    NumberOfKids = 2.1;
    ActualKids = (int)NumberOfKids;
    cout << NumberOfKids << " " << ActualKids << endl;

    // This time we'll use 2.9 kids.
    NumberOfKids = 2.9;
    ActualKids = (int)NumberOfKids;
    cout << NumberOfKids << " " << ActualKids << endl;
    cout << "Float to Integer" << endl;

    // This process rounds the number, instead of truncating it.
    // We do it using the same three numbers as before.
    cout << "(Rounded)" << endl;
```

(continued)

Listing 9-1 *(continued)*

```
NumberOfKids = 2.5;
ActualKids = (int)(NumberOfKids + .5);
cout << NumberOfKids << " " << ActualKids << endl;

// Do it again using 2.1 kids.
NumberOfKids = 2.1;
ActualKids = (int)(NumberOfKids + .5);
cout << NumberOfKids << " " << ActualKids << endl;

// Do it yet again using 2.9 kids.
NumberOfKids = 2.9;
ActualKids = (int)(NumberOfKids + .5);
cout << NumberOfKids << " " << ActualKids << endl;
cout << endl << "Integer to Float" << endl;

// In this case, use the StringToNumber() function to perform the
// conversion.
ActualKids = 3;
NumberOfKids = ActualKids;
cout << NumberOfKids << endl << endl;
cout << "String to number" << endl;
int x = StringToNumber("12345") * 50;
cout << x << endl << endl;

// In this case, use the NumberToString() function to perform the
// conversion.
cout << "Number to string" << endl;
string mystring = NumberToString(80525323);
cout << mystring << endl;

return 0;
}
```

`StringToNumber()` takes a string, copies it into an `istringstream`, and then reads it into an integer. `NumberToString()` takes an integer, writes it to an `ostringstream`, and then copies it to a string.

Feel free to use the `StringToNumber()` and `NumberToString()` functions in your own code. Sooner or later, you are likely to need to convert between integers and strings, and these functions can help you out without having to go search for the answers yourself.

Another kind of conversion that's useful is converting floating-point numbers (that is, numbers with a decimal point) and integers and vice versa. In C++, this conversion is easy: You just copy one to the other, and C++ takes care of the rest. The only catch is that when C++ converts from a float to an integer, it always *truncates*. That is, it doesn't round up: When it converts 5.99 to an integer, it doesn't go up to 6; it goes *down* to 5. But there's an easy trick around that: Add 0.5 to the number before you convert it. If the number in the upper half (that is, from .5 to .9999 and so on), that 0.5 first takes the number above or equal to the upper whole number. Then, when the function rounds the number, the number rounds *down* to the *upper* whole number.

For example, if you start with 4.6, just converting it gets you a 4. But if you add .5, you first get 5.1, and then when you convert that, you get 5. It works!

Going in the other direction is even easier: To convert an integer to a float, you just copy it. If i is an integer and f is a float, you just set it as follows to convert it:

```
f = i;
```

Whenever you convert from a float to an int or from an int to float, you must tell the compiler that you know what you're doing by adding (int) or (float) in front of the variable. Adding these keywords is called *coercion* or *type conversion*. The act of coercing one type to another is called *casting*. For example, the following line tells the compiler that you know you're converting from a float to an int:

```
ActualKids = (int)NumberOfKids;
```

If you leave out the (int) part, the compiler normally displays a warning like this one:

```
warning: converting to 'int' from 'float'
```

Using the proper coercion code is important because it also tells other developers that you really do intend to perform the type conversion. Otherwise, other developers will point to that area of your code and deem it the source of an error, when it might not be the true source. Using proper coding techniques saves everyone time.

When you run the application spelled out in Listing 9-1, you see the results of all these conversions. The first big batch inside main() puts different floating-point values into NumberOfKids (starting with the usual 2.5 number of kids, of course) and then converts these two integers. In the first batch, we didn't add 0.5, so it just truncates the value. You can see in the output for this section that all the numbers were truncated (always rounded down). The first number in each pair is the original floating-point value, and the second number is the number converted to an integer. Notice that the application always rounded down:

```
Float to Integer
(Truncated)
2.5 2
2.1 2
2.9 2
```

In the next block of code, we do the same conversions as before, except this time we add 0.5 to each float. The result is an actual round to the nearest whole number. Note that the higher decimal numbers rounded up, and the lower ones rounded down:

```
Float to Integer
(Rounded)
2.5 3
2.1 2
2.9 3
```

Next is a quick one. We simply converted the integer to a float. It doesn't print with a decimal point, but it is a float:

```
Integer to Float
3
```

Then we convert between numbers and strings. The first block of these converts a string to a number. Just to prove that it really *is* a number, we go ahead and work some mathematical arithmetic on it — something you can't do with a string:

```
String to number
617250
```

And finally, we convert a number to a string:

```
Number to string
80525323
```

The output of these digits, of course, would look the same whether we print them as a string or a number, but you can see in the code that what we printed is indeed a string, not a number.

Tips for making numeric conversions more precise

If you are doing some sophisticated arithmetic by using a mixture of floats and integers, the suggestions in the following list will ensure that your answers come out right:

✔ **Don't be afraid to use temporary variables:** If you have an integer and need a float version of it, don't be afraid to create a temporary variable that's a `float` that holds the value. The following lines do this for you:

```
float MyFloat = MyInt;
```

✔ **Convert everything to floating point:** Make sure that you convert all your integers to floating points before you use them in the operations. For example, in the following two lines of code, `MyFloat` will not get `2.5`, the answer of 5 divided by 2. Instead, it gets the integer (that is, rounded) value

of `2`. To fix this, first convert `MyInt` to a `float` before doing this operation. Then you will get `2.5` for `MyFloat`:

```
int MyInt = 5;
float MyFloat = MyInt / 2;
```

✔ **Try casting:** If you want to use an integer in an arithmetic operation that involves floats and you don't want to create a special `float` variable for it, you can just throw the word `float` in parentheses before the integer in the operation. This is called a *cast*, and the C++ compiler temporarily converts the variable to the type in parentheses. The following lines do this, and this time `MyFloat` gets the value `2.5`, as you want.

```
int MyInt = 5;
float MyFloat = (float)MyInt / 2;
```

Reading from the Console

Throughout this book, we have used the console to demonstrate several topics. Many of the applications write some sort of output to the console. You can also use the console to *get* information from the user — a topic we briefly mention in Book I, Chapter 3.

To do this, instead of using the usual << with cout to write to the console, you use the >> operator along with cin (pronounced "see-in").

In the old days of the C programming language, reading data from the console and placing its variables was somewhat nightmarish because it required you to use pointers. In C++, that's no longer the case. If you want to read a set of characters into a string called MyName, you just type

```
cin >> MyName;
```

That's it! The application pauses, and the user can type something at the console. When the user presses Enter, the string that was typed will go into the string called MyName.

Reading from the console has some catches. First, the console uses spaces as delimiters. That means that if you put spaces in what you type, only the letters up to the space are put into the string. Anything after the space, the console saves for the next time your application calls cin. That situation can be confusing. Second, if you want to read into a number, the user can type any characters, not just numbers. The computer then goes through a bizarre process that converts any letters into a meaningless number. Not good.

Fear not: As usual, we have found ways around such problems! The ReadConsoleData example, shown in Listing 9-2, shows you how to read a string and then a number from the console. Next, it shows you how you can force the user to type only numbers. And finally, it shows how you can ask for a password with only asterisks appearing when the user types.

To make these last two tasks work correctly, we had to use a library called conio. This library gives you more direct access to the console, bypassing cin. But that's okay. We also used a special function called StringToNumber(), which is described in "Converting Types," earlier in this chapter.

Listing 9-2:   Having the User Type Something

```
#include <iostream>
#include <sstream>
#include <conio.h>

using namespace std;
```

(continued)

Listing 9-2 *(continued)*

```cpp
int StringToNumber(string MyString)
{
    istringstream converter(MyString); // Holds the string.
    int result;                        // Holds the integer result.

    // Perform the conversion.
    converter >> result;
    return result;
}

string EnterOnlyNumbers()
{
    string numAsString = ""; // Holds the numeric string.
    char ch = getch();        // Obtains a single character from the user.

    // Keep requesting characters until the user presses Enter.
    while (ch != '\r')  // \r is the enter key
    {
        // Add characters only if they are numbers.
        if (ch >= '0' && ch <= '9')
        {
            cout << ch;
            numAsString += ch;
        }

        // Get the next character from the user.
        ch = getch();
    }
    return numAsString;
}

string EnterPassword()
{
    string numAsString = ""; // Holds the password string.
    char ch = getch();        // Obtains a single character from the user.

    // Keep requesting characters until the user presses Enter.
    while (ch != '\r')  // \r is the enter key
    {
        // Display an asterisk instead of the input character.
        cout << '*';

        // Add the character to the password string.
        numAsString += ch;

        // Get the next character from the user.
        ch = getch();
    }

    return numAsString;
}

int main()
{
    // Just a basic name-entering
    string name;
    cout << "What is your name? ";
    cin >> name;
    cout << "Hello " << name << endl;
```

```
// Now you are asked to enter a number,
// but the computer allows you to enter anything!
int x;
cout << endl;
cout << "Enter a number, any number! ";
cin >> x;
cout << "You chose " << x << endl;

// This time you can only enter a number.
cout << endl;
cout << "This time you'll only be able to enter a number!" << endl;
cout << "Enter a number, any number! ";
string entered = EnterOnlyNumbers();
int num = StringToNumber(entered);
cout << endl << "You entered " << num << endl;

// Now enter a password!
cout << endl;
cout << "Enter your password! ";
string password = EnterPassword();
cout << endl << "Shhhh, it's " << password << endl;
return 0;
}
```

The first parts of `main()` are straightforward. You can see that we called `cin >> name;` to read a string from the console; then we printed it. Then we called `cin >> x;` to read an integer from the console, and we again printed it.

Next, we made sure that the user could enter only digits by calling the `EnterOnlyNumbers()` function. Take a close look at that function. The first thing it does is declare a string called `numAsString`. When the user types things, they come in as characters, so we save them one by one in a string variable (because a string is really a *character string*). To find out what the user types, we call the `getch()` function. That function returns a single character. (For example, if the user presses Shift-A to produce a capital *A*, the `getch()` function returns the character A.)

After retrieving a single character, we start a loop, watching for the `'\r'` character. (Remember that the backslash in a character or string means that the character is special.) The loop continues processing characters until the user presses the Enter key. At that point, the character we get from `getch()` is `\r`, so we exit the loop and return the number as a string.

Inside the loop, we test the *value* of the character, seeing whether it's in the range `'0'` through `'9'`. Yes, characters are associated with a sequence, and fortunately, the digits are all grouped together. So we can determine whether we have a digit character by checking to see whether it's in the range `'0'` through `'9'`:

```
if (ch >= '0' && ch <= '9')
```

Avoiding getch() function problems

Some compilers complain if you use the getch() function. If you want to use it, try the _getch() function instead. Both functions perform the same task. Some vendors claim that _getch() is compliant with the International Standards Organization (ISO), but

it isn't. The getch() and _getch() functions are useful, low-level library functions that you can use without hesitation, but they don't appear as part of any standard. The GNU GCC compiler, provided with Code::Blocks, can use either form of the function.

If the user presses a number key, we wind up inside this if statement, or at least the computer does. Because the user pressed a number key, we go ahead and write that out to the console and add the digit character to the end of our string. We have to write it to the console because, when you call getch(), the computer doesn't automatically print anything. But that's a good thing here, because after we're out of the if statement, we go ahead and call getch() again for another round. Thus, if the user pressed something other than the Enter key, the character the user pressed doesn't even appear on the console, and it doesn't get added to the string, either. Nifty, huh?

The EnterPassword() routine is similar to the EnterOnlyNumbers() routine, except that it allows the user to enter any character (including spaces). So no if statement is *filtering out* certain letters. And further, instead of printing only the character that the user types, it prints an asterisk: *. That gives the feeling of a password entry, which is a good feeling. People want to feel good when they're entering their passwords.

When you run this application, you get output like the following:

```
What is your name? Hank
Hello Hank

Enter a number, any number! abc123
You chose 2293728

This time you'll only be able to enter a number!
Enter a number, any number! 5001
You entered 5001

Enter your password! *****
Shhhh, it's hello
```

The first line went well; we didn't type any spaces, and the name Hank made it into our variable. But then when we were asked to enter a number, we got sneaky and typed something we weren't supposed to — abc123. And boy, the computer got confused! But the next section didn't allow us to type anything but numbers because it called our `EnterOnlyNumbers()` routine. And finally, we entered a password, and you can see that the computer displayed asterisks when we pressed each key. Then the application kept the secret password and wrote it on the screen anyway.

Understanding Preprocessor Directives

When you compile an application, the first thing the compiler does is run your code through something called a preprocessor. The *preprocessor* simply looks for certain statements in your code that start with the # symbol. You have already seen one such statement in every one of your applications: `#include`. These preprocessor statements are known as *directives* because they tell the preprocessor to do something; they direct it.

Think of the preprocessor as just a machine that transforms your code into a temporary, fixed-up version that's all ready to be compiled. For example, take a look at this preprocessor directive:

```
#include <iostream>
```

If the preprocessor sees this line, it inserts the entire text from the file called `iostream` (yes, that's a filename; it has no extension) into the fixed-up version of the source code.

Suppose that the file called `iostream` looks like this:

```
int hello = 10;
int goodbye = 20;
```

Just two lines are all that's in it. (Of course, the real `iostream` file is much more sophisticated.) And suppose that your own source file, `MyProgram.cpp`, has this in it (as found in the `Preprocessor` example):

```
#include <iostream>
int main()
{
    cout << "Hello" << endl;
}
```

Then, after the preprocessor finishes its preprocessing, it creates a temporary fixed-up file (which has the lines from the string file inserted into the `MyProgram.cpp` file where the `#include` line had been) to look like this:

```
int hello = 10;
int goodbye = 20;
int main()
{
    cout << "Hello" << endl;
}
```

In other words, the preprocessor replaced the #include line with the contents of that file. Now, the string file itself could have #include lines, and those lines would be replaced by the contents of the files *they* refer to. As you may imagine, what started out as a simple application with just a few lines could actually have hundreds of lines after the preprocessor gets through with it. (In fact, that's a conservative estimate: We ran the default Code::Blocks code through the preprocessor, and it contained *25,613 lines!* You can see the output in Main.txt, which is included in the Preprocessor folder of the downloadable source code. Many of those are blank lines, for various reasons, but nevertheless, it's a very big file!)

Don't worry: Your original source code file doesn't change when the preprocessor goes at it. The preprocessor builds a temporary file, and *that's* what the compiler compiles. Also, you don't have to run the preprocessor manually; the compiler runs it for you.

Although you don't have to run the preprocessor yourself, you can. if you're curious to see what its output looks like. The Code::Blocks compiler actually calls on gcc.exe to perform the compilation process. However, gcc is just a small application that launches the compiler. But before it launches the compiler, it runs the preprocessor. The preprocessor command is cpp (for *C pre-processor*). If your paths are set up correctly and you want to try it out, just type **cpp**, the name of your source file, the redirection symbol (>>), and the name of an output file at the command line, such as cpp main.cpp >> main.txt. In most cases, you can set up the path correctly by typing the following line at the command line and pressing Enter:

path=C:\CodeBlocks\MinGW\bin;%path%

Prepare yourself for a *lot* of lines. But seeing the output and how your code looks when it's ready to be pushed through the compiler is interesting.

The preprocessor also provides you with a lot of other directives besides #include. One of the more useful ones is the #define directive. Here's a sample #define line:

#define MYSPECIALNUMBER 42

After the preprocessor sees this line, every time it encounters the word MYSPECIALNUMBER, it replaces it with the *word* 42 (that is, whatever sequence of letters, numbers, and other characters follow the definition). But #define also lets you create what are called *macros*. Take a look at this line:

#define oldmax(x, y) ((x)>(y)?(x):(y))

After the preprocessor learns this line, every time it sees the word oldmax followed by two things in parentheses separated by a comma, it replaces it with the form ((x)>(y)?(x):(y)), substituting the thing before the comma for x and the thing after the comma for y. For example, if you then have this line

```
q = oldmax(abc, 123);
```

the preprocessor replaces the line with

```
q = ((abc)>(123)?(abc):(123));
```

and does nothing more with the line.

Book I, Chapter 3, refers to these as conditional operators. The variable q is set to the value in abc if the abc value is greater than 123; otherwise, the q gets set to 123.

However, the preprocessor doesn't have an understanding of the conditional operator, and q doesn't get set to anything during preprocessing. All the preprocessor knows is how to replace *text* in your source code file. The preprocessor replaced the earlier line of code that contained oldmax with the next line containing the conditional operator. That's it. The preprocessor doesn't run any code, it doesn't make the comparison, and it doesn't put anything in q. The preprocessor just changes the code.

Although you can still use #define statements in C++, in general you should simply create a function instead of a macro or use a constant instead of a symbol. Using symbols and macros are older and outdated styles of programming. However, they do have their place in programming, in the form of *conditional compilation,* which we discuss next.

At times, you may want to compile one version of your application for one situation and compile another for a different situation. For example, you may want to have a *debug* version of your application that has in it some extra goodies that spit out special information for you that you can use during the development of your application. Then, after your application is ready to ship to the masses so that millions of people can use it, you no longer want that extra debug information.

To accomplish this, you can use a conditional compilation. Take a look at these lines:

```
#ifdef DEBUG
    cout << "The value of j is " << j << endl;
#else
    cout << j << endl;
#endif
```

The lines that begin with # are preprocessor directives. The preprocessor has its own version of if statements. In your code, you can have a line like the following, with nothing after it:

```
#define DEBUG
```

This simply *defines* a symbol. It works just like the symbols we described earlier, except that it's not set to be replaced by anything. It's just a symbol. You can also define such symbols in the command-line options to gcc or whichever compiler you use. (In Code::Blocks, you choose Project⇨Build Options. In the Project Build Options dialog box that opens, click the Compiler Settings tab, followed by the #defines subtab, as shown in Figure 9-1. You type your compiler options as shown in the figure.) To define the DEBUG symbol through a command-line option, you add the following line to your command

```
-D DEBUG
```

either in the gcc command or in the Project Build Options dialog box in Code::Blocks. Then, when you include this compiler option, the DEBUG symbol is defined throughout your application, just as though you had included a #define DEBUG line at the beginning.

Figure 9-1: Provide the compiler options you want to use to change the application output.

Now, when the preprocessor starts going through your application and gets to the #ifdef DEBUG line, it checks whether the DEBUG symbol is defined. If the symbol is defined, it spits out to its fixed-up file the lines that follow, up until the #else line. Then it skips any lines that follow that, up until the #endif line.

But if the DEBUG symbol is *not* defined, the preprocessor skips over the lines up until the #else, and spits out the lines that follow, up until the #endif.

Thus, for the example we gave earlier in this section, if DEBUG is defined, the block of code starting with #ifdef DEBUG through the line #endif is replaced by the stuff in the first half of the block:

```
cout << "The value of j is " << j << endl;
```

But if `DEBUG` is not defined, it is replaced by the stuff following the `#else` line:

```
cout << j << endl;
```

When the preprocessor goes through your file, it is only creating a new source code file to be used by the compiler. That means these `#ifdef` lines affect your application only when the compiler fires off the preprocessor. When your application is compiled and you *run* it, these `#ifdef` lines are nowhere to be found. So remember that these `#ifdef` lines do not affect how your application runs — only how it compiles.

Using preprocessor directives, you can have two different versions of your application. In the example we gave, we're gearing up for two versions: a debug version and a release version. To tell the compiler which version to build, we then modify the command-line options by either removing or adding the `-D DEBUG` line.

The `-D` option works either with or without a space after the `D`. Thus, you can either use `-DDEBUG` or `-D DEBUG`. They both do the same thing.

The `Preprocessor2` example, shown in Listing 9-3, demonstrates all the topics we cover in this section.

Listing 9-3: Using Many Different Preprocessor Directives

```cpp
#include <iostream>

using namespace std;

#ifdef UNIVAC
const int total = 200;
const string compname = "UNIVAC";
#elif defined(HAL2000)
const int total = 300;
const string compname = "HAL2000";
#else
const int total = 400;
const string compname = "My Computer";
#endif
// This is outdated, but you might
// see it on occasion. Don't write
// code yourself that does this!
#define oldmax(x, y) ((x)>(y)?(x):(y))
#define MYSPECIALNUMBER 42

int main()
{
    cout << "Welcome to " << compname << endl;
    cout << "Total is:" << endl;
    cout << total << endl << endl;

    // Try out the outdated things.
    cout << "*** max ***" << endl;
    cout << oldmax(5,10) << endl;
    cout << oldmax(20,15) << endl;
    cout << MYSPECIALNUMBER << endl << endl;
```

(continued)

Listing 9-3 *(continued)*

```
        // Here are some standard
        // predefined macros.
        cout << "*** Predefined Macros ***" << endl;
        cout << "This is file " << __FILE__ << endl;
        cout << "This is line " << __LINE__ << endl;
        cout << "Compiled on " << __DATE__ << endl;
        cout << "Compiled at " << __TIME__ << endl << endl;

        // Here's how some people use #define,
        // to specify a "debug" version or
        // "release" version.
        cout << "*** total ***" << endl;
        int i;
        int j = 0;
        for (i = 0; i<total; i++)
        {
            j = j + i;
        }
#ifdef DEBUG
        cout << "The value of j is " << j << endl;
#else
        cout << j << endl;
#endif

        return 0;
}
```

When we run Listing 9-3 without any symbols (we did not set DEBUG), we see this output:

```
Welcome to My Computer
Total is:
400

*** max ***
10
20
42

*** Predefined Macros ***
This is file C:\CPP_AIO\BookI\Chapter 09<\Preprocessor2\main.cpp
This is line 37
Compiled on Dec 18 2013
Compiled at 10:23:07

*** total ***
79800
```

Note, at the beginning, we're testing for the symbol UNIVAC. But that `if` block is a bit more complex because we also have an #elif (else if) construct. The language of the preprocessor has no `elseifdef` or anything like it. Instead, you have to write it like so:

```
#elif defined(HAL2000)
```

With this block, the preprocessor checks for the symbol UNIVAC; if the pre-processor finds UNIVAC, it spits out these lines:

```
const int total = 200;
const string compname = "UNIVAC";
```

Otherwise, the preprocessor looks for HAL2000; if the preprocessor finds it, it adds these lines to the fixed-up code:

```
const int total = 300;
const string compname = "HAL2000";
```

And finally, if neither UNIVAC nor HAL2000 is set, the preprocessor adds these lines:

```
const int total = 400;
const string compname = "My Computer";
```

Remember that in each case, these two lines are sent out to the fixed-up version in place of the entire block starting with #ifdef UNIVAC and ending with #endif.

So if we include the command-line option -D UNIVAC, we see different output (use the Code::Blocks Build⇨Rebuild command to rebuild the project with the new option):

```
Welcome to UNIVAC
Total is:
200

*** max ***
10
20
42

*** Predefined Macros ***
This is file C:\CPP_AIO\BookI\Chapter09\Preprocessor2\main.cpp
This is line 37
Compiled on Dec 18 2013
Compiled at 10:26:21

*** total ***
19900
```

To see this different output, remember that these #define lines affect only the compilation of your application. Therefore, you need to recompile your application to see the changes. But a catch is involved: If the object file for your source code file is newer than your source, the compiler won't rebuild the object file, even though you changed the command-line options. You need to type **makeclean** first, if you are using a command-line compiler such as MinGW or Cygwin. In Code::Blocks, you choose Build⇨Rebuild. Then you can compile your application again and run it to see the new output.

And now, here's a different set of options:

```
-D HAL2000 -D DEBUG
```

When you again clean, compile, and run, you see this output. Notice that the final line is a bit different now that you have DEBUG defined.

```
Welcome to HAL2000
Total is:
300

*** max ***
10
20
42

*** Predefined Macros ***
This is file C:\CPP_AIO\BookI\Chapter09\Preprocessor2\main.cpp
This is line 37
Compiled on Dec 18 2013
Compiled at 10:30:23

*** total ***
The value of j is 44850
```

Using Constants

When you are programming, you may sometimes want a certain fixed value that you plan to use throughout the application. For example, you might want a string containing the name of your company, such as "Bobs Fixit Anywhere Anyhoo." And you don't want someone else working on your application to pass this string into a function as a reference and modify it by mistake, turning it into the name of your global competitor, "Jims Fixum Anyhoo Anytime." That could be bad. Or, if you're writing a scientific application, you might want a fixed number, such as pi = 3.1415926 or PeachPi=4.1415926.

You can create such *constants* in C++ by using the const keyword. When you create a constant, it works just like a variable, except that you *cannot change it* later in the application. For example, to declare your company name, you might use

```
const string CompanyName = "Bobs Fixit Anywhere Anyhoo";
```

Of course, you can always modify this particular string in your code, but later in your code, you cannot do something like this:

```
CompanyName = CompanyName + ", Inc.";
```

The compiler issues an error for that line, complaining that it's a constant and you can't change it.

After you declare the constant, then, you can use the string called `CompanyName` to refer to your company throughout your code. The `Constants` example in Listing 9-4 shows you how to do this. Note the three constants toward the top called `ParkingSpaces`, `StoreName`, and `pi`. In the rest of the application, we use these just like any other variables — except that we don't try to change them.

Listing 9-4: Using Constants for Permanent Values That Do Not Change

```
#include <iostream>

using namespace std;

const int ParkingSpaces = 80;
const string StoreName = "Joe's Food Haven";
const float pi = 3.1415926;

int main()
{
    cout << "Important Message" << endl;
    cout << "Here at " << StoreName << endl;
    cout << "we believe you should know" << endl;
    cout << "that we have " << ParkingSpaces;
    cout << " full-sized" << endl;
    cout << "parking spaces for your parking" << endl;
    cout << "pleasure." << endl;
    cout << endl;

    cout << "We do realize, however, that parking" << endl;
    cout << "is tight at " << StoreName << endl;
    cout << "and so we are going to double our" << endl;
    cout << "spaces from " << ParkingSpaces << " to ";
    cout << ParkingSpaces * 2;
    cout << ". Thank you again!" << endl << endl;

    float radius = 5;
    float area = radius * pi * pi;

    cout << "And remember, we sell " << radius;
    cout << " inch apple pies" << endl;
    cout << "for a full " << area << " square" << endl;
    cout << "inches of eating pleasure!" << endl;

    return 0;
}
```

When you run this application, you see the following:

```
Important Message
Here at Joe's Food Haven
we believe you should know
that we have 80 full-sized
parking spaces for your parking
pleasure.
```

```
We do realize, however, that parking
is tight at Joe's Food Haven
and so we are going to double our
spaces from 80 to 160. Thank you again!

And remember, we sell 5 inch apple pies
for a full 49.348 square
inches of eating pleasure!
```

The biggest advantage to using constants is this: If you need to make a change to a string or number throughout your application, you make the change only once. For example, if you have the string `"Bobs Fixit Anywhere Anyhoo"` pasted a gazillion times throughout your application, and suddenly you incorporate and need to change your application so that the string says `"Bobs Fixit Anywhere Anyhoo, LLC"`, you would need to do some serious search-and-replace work. But if you have a single constant in the header file for use by all your source code files, you need to change it only *once*. You modify the header file with the new constant definition and recompile your application, and you're ready to go.

There's a common saying in the programming world that goes like this (sing along now): "Don't use any magic numbers." The idea is that if, somewhere in your code, you need to calculate the number of cows that have crossed over the bridge to see whether the bridge will hold up and you happen to know that the average weight of a cow is 632 pounds, don't just put the number 632 in your code. Somebody else reading it may wonder where that number came from. Instead, make a constant called, perhaps, `AverageCowWeight` and set it equal to 632. Then, in your code, use `AverageCowWeight` anytime you need that number. Plus, if cows evolve into a more advanced species and their weight changes, all you need to do is make one change in your code — you change the header file containing the `const` declaration. Here's a sample line that declares `AverageCowWeight`:

```
const int AverageCowWeight = 632;
```

Before C++, the original C language did not have constants. The way to use constants was through preprocessor directives. For example, in C++, you could have a constant, such as

```
const int DuckCrossing = 500;
```

But in C, you couldn't do this. Your choice would be to use either a non-constant variable, as in

```
int DuckCrossing = 500;
```

or a preprocessor directive, as in

```
#define DuckCrossing 500
```

Then you can use DuckCrossing as a substitute for 500 in your application. The problem here is that if you try to debug your application (see Book III, Chapter 1), the debugger (yes, that's *really* the word) knows nothing of the word DuckCrossing, so it can't help you address problems that result from using it. Therefore, if you see a #define used this way, you know what it means; however, we recommend that you don't write new code that uses this. Use the const keyword instead.

Using Switch Statements

Many times in programming, you may want to compare a variable to one thing, and if it doesn't match, compare it to another and another and another. To do this with an if statement, you need to use a whole bunch of else if lines.

That works out pretty well, but you can do it in another way: You can use the switch statement.

The approach we're showing you in this section does not work for all types of variables. In fact, it works with only the various types of integers and characters. It won't even work with character strings. However, when you need to make multiple comparisons for integers and characters, using this approach is quite useful.

First, here's a complete switch statement that you can refer to as we describe the individual parts in the paragraphs that follow. This compares x to 1, and then 2, and, finally, includes a catchall section called default if x is neither 1 nor 2:

```
int x;
cin >> x;
switch (x)
{
    case 1:
        cout << "It's 1!" << endl;
        break;
    case 2:
        cout << "It's 2!" << endl;
        break;
    default:
        cout << "It's something else!" << endl;
        break;
}
```

To use the switch statement, you type the word switch and then the variable or expression that you want to test in parentheses. Suppose that x is type int and you want to compare it to several different values. You would first type

```
switch (x) {
```

The preceding item in parentheses is *not a comparison*. It's simply a variable. You can also put more complex expressions inside the parentheses, but they must *evaluate* to either an integer or a character. For example, if x is an integer, you can test

```
switch (x + 5) {
```

because x + 5 is still an integer.

After the header line for the switch statement, you list the items you want to compare the expression to. These have a rather strange format. They start with the word case, and then have the value to compare the expression against, and then a colon, as in

```
case 1:
```

Next is the code to run in the event that the expression matches this case (here, 1).

```
cout << "It's 1" << endl;
```

Finally (here's where it gets really strange), you have the word break. Every case in the switch statement usually has a break line, which means *get out of the switch statement now!* And here's the exceedingly strange part: If you forget the break statement, when the computer runs this case, it continues running the code for the *next* case! Yes, C++ can seem stupid at times. And this is one of those rare and less-than-beautiful moments.

Note something peculiar at the end of the switch block: The final case is default. It applies to the situation when none of the preceding cases applies.

The default case isn't required; you can leave it off if you don't need it. However, if you do include it, we recommend putting it at the end of the switch block because that's where most people expect to find it.

In the sample code we give at the beginning of this section, you can enter a number, which gets put in the x variable. The code then tests the value x against 1; if it matches, it performs the line after the case 1: line. But if it doesn't match, it tests it against 2 and performs its lines if it matches. But if none of those matches, it executes the code after the default line.

When the computer encounters the break line, it exits the switch statement altogether. So you may be wondering: Why did those goofball authors include a break line at the end? Our answer: Tradition. That's all. It's consistent with the other blocks of code. But you certainly don't need it. *However*, if you leave it off, you must remember that if you decide to add any other cases, you will probably want to put it back in. On the other hand, people typically put the default at the end. (You don't have to, but most people expect to see it at the end and not in the middle.)

A `switch` statement only compares a single variable or expression against several different items. If you have more complex comparisons, you can instead use a compound `if` statement.

In many other programming languages, a `switch` statement is called a *case block*. That's because in those languages, the word that starts the whole thing is *case*. Here, however, the whole shebang gets off with a bang on the word `switch`. Thus, in C and C++, we call it a `switch` statement. It's fun to be different. Sometimes.

The `SwitchStatement` example in Listing 9-5 is a complete application that demonstrates a `switch` statement. It also shows you how you can make a simple, antiquated-looking *menu* application on the console. You don't need to press Enter after you choose the menu item; you just press the key for your menu selection. That's thanks to the use of `getch()` rather than `cin`.

Listing 9-5:   Making Multiple Comparisons in One Big Block

```
#include <iostream>
#include <conio.h>

using namespace std;

int main()
{
    // Display a list of options.
    cout << "Choose your favorite:" << endl;
    cout << "1. Apples " << endl;
    cout << "2. Bananas " << endl;
    cout << "3. Fried worms " << endl;
    cout << "4. Poison Apples " << endl;
    cout << "5. Lobster " << endl;

    // Obtain the user's selection.
    char ch = getch();

    // Continue getting user selections until the user
    // enters a valid number.
    while (ch < '1' || ch > '5')
    {
        ch = getch();
    }

    // Use a switch to display the user's selection.
    cout << "You chose " << ch << endl;
    switch (ch) {
    case '1':
        cout << "Apples are good for you!" << endl;
        break;
    case '2':
        cout << "Bananas have plenty of potassium!" << endl;
        break;
    case '3':
        cout << "That's disgusting!" << endl;
        break;
```

(continued)

Listing 9-5 *(continued)*

```
case '4':
    cout << "All I wanna know is WHY?" << endl;
    break;
case '5':
    cout << "Expensive but good taste you have!" << endl;
    break;
}

return 0;
}
```

Supercharging enums with Classes

When you work with classes, you can use a technique called *wrapping*, which helps you manage a resource. In Book I, Chapter 8, we discuss the enum keyword and how you can use it to create your own types. However, when you print the enumeration, you don't see the word, such as red or blue; you see a number. The DisplayEnum example, shown in Listing 9-6, is a simple class that *wraps* an enum type — essentially, it helps you convert the number into a human readable form, which is a kind of resource management. You can use this class with enum ColorEnum, as main() demonstrates. When you run this application, you see the single word red in the console.

Listing 9-6:   Creating a Class for enums

```
#include <iostream>

using namespace std;

class Colors
{
public:
    enum ColorEnum {blue, red, green, yellow, black};
    Colors(Colors::ColorEnum value);
    string AsString();

protected:
    ColorEnum value;
};

Colors::Colors(Colors::ColorEnum initvalue)
{
    value = initvalue;
}

string Colors::AsString()
{
    switch (value)
    {
```

```
        case blue:
            return "blue";
        case red:
            return "red";
        case green:
            return "green";
        case yellow:
            return "yellow";
        case black:
            return "black";
        default:
            return "Not Found";
    }
}

int main()
{
    Colors InkColor = Colors::red;
    cout << InkColor.AsString() << endl;
    return 0;
}
```

In the preceding section, "Using Switch Statements," the switch statement did not include any break statements. Instead, you have a return statement. The return causes the computer to exit the function entirely, so you have no reason to worry about getting out of the switch statement. You may wonder why the switch statement includes a default clause. After all, it will never get called. In this case, if you don't supply a default clause, the compiler displays the following message:

```
warning: control reaches end of non-void function
```

Whenever possible, add the code required for your application to compile without warnings. Adding the default clause simply ensures that the AsString function always returns a value, no matter what happens.

The expression Colors::red may be unfamiliar to you. That means you're using the red value of the ColorEnum type. However, because ColorEnum is declared *inside* the class Color, you cannot just say red. You have to first say the class name, and then two colons, and then the value. Thus, you type Colors::red.

In main(), we created the InkColor instance and set it not to a Color object but to an enum. We just violated An Important Rule about setting things equal to something of the same type. Why? C++ has a neat little trick: You can create a constructor that takes a certain type. In this case, we have a constructor that takes a ColorEnum. Then when you create a stack variable (not a pointer), you can just set it equal to a value of that type. The computer will *implicitly* call the constructor, passing it that value.

Adding cout capabilities

It would be nice if the `Colors` class allowed you to just call `cout`, as in `cout << Ink Color << endl;` without having to call `Ink Color.AsString()` to get a string version. C++ has a capability called *operator overloading*, which is a technique for extending the functionality of an operator. When you type `something cout <<` followed by a variable, you are calling a function: `<<`. Several versions of the `<<` functions (they are overloaded) are available; each has a different type. For example, `int` handles the cases when you write out an integer, as in `int x = 5;`, and then `cout << x;`. Because the `<<` function doesn't use parentheses, it is an *operator*.

To add `cout` capabilities to your class, just write another `<<` function for your class. Here's the code. This is not a class member function; it goes *outside* your class. Add it to Listing 9-6 anywhere after the `class` declaration but before `main()`. Here goes:

```
ostream& operator << (ostream& out,
        Colors& inst)
{
  out << inst.AsString();
  return out;
}
```

Because this function is an operator, you have to throw in the word `operator`. The type of `cout` is `ostream`, incidentally; thus, you take an `ostream` as a parameter and you return the same `ostream`. The other parameter is the type you are printing: in this case, it's a `Colors` instance, and once again, it's passed by reference. After you add this code, you can change the line `cout << InkColor.As String() << endl;` to simply

```
cout << InkColor << endl;
```

Working with Random Numbers

Sometimes, you need the computer to generate random numbers for you. But computers aren't good at doing tasks at random. We humans can toss dice or flip a coin, but the computer must do things in a predetermined fashion.

The computer geniuses of the past century have come up with algorithms that generate *pseudorandom numbers*. These are numbers that are *almost* random or *seemingly* random. They're sufficiently random for many purposes.

The only catch with these random-number generators is that you need to *seed* them. But a computer scientist beheld a great idea. *The current time* is random. If we run an application and you run an application, most likely we won't start running them at *precisely the same moment in time*. Our scientist realized that would be a good starting point for a random-number generator. Using the `RandomNumber` example shown in Listing 9-7, we obtain the current time to start the random number generator. To do that, we include `time.h`. We create a variable called `now` of a special type called `time_t` (which is just a number), and then we call the `time()` function, passing the address of `now`. That gives us the number of seconds since January 1, 1970. Then we call `srand()`, (which requires that we include `stdlib.h`) passing that time. That process seeds the generator.

Then we print several random numbers by calling `rand()`, which returns a random number. But we noticed something strange when we ran this application. Each time, the first call to `rand()` got just a little bit bigger, and it seemed to be affected by the current time. With each second that passed, the supposedly random number got just a bit bigger. The rest seemed fine, so we decided to skip the first random number. Thus, right after we seed the random number, we call `rand()` and ignore the return value.

Then we go ahead and print five random numbers. But we wanted to limit the numbers in the range from 0 through 99, so we took the *modulus 100* of the number. (That's the remainder when we divide the number by 100.) You can choose a different number than 100 if you need a different range.

Listing 9-7:   Seeding the Random Number Generator

```
#include <iostream>
#include <time.h>
#include <stdlib.h>

using namespace std;

int main()
{
    // Re-seed the random-number generator
    time_t now;
    time(&now);
    srand(now);
    rand();

    // Print out a list of random numbers
    for (int i=0; i<5; i++)
    {
        cout << rand() % 100 << endl;
    }

    return 0;
}
```

The first time we ran Listing 9-7, we saw the following output:

```
19
69
85
83
47
```

The *second* time, we saw this output. It's very different than before:

```
79
67
38
72
73
```

Storing Data in Arrays

Most programming languages support a data structure called an array. An *array* is a list of variables, all stored side by side in a row. You access them through a single name. Each variable in the array must be of the same type.

When you create an array, you specify how many items the array holds. For example, you can have an array of 100 integers. Or you can have an array of 35 strings or an array of 10 pointers to the class `BrokenBottle`. If the code you're working with represents a type, you can create an array out of it.

When you create an array, you give it a name. You can access the array's *elements* (items) by using that name followed by an *index* number in brackets. The first element is always 0. Thus, if you have an array of five integers called `AppendixAttacks`, the first element is `AppendixAttacks[0]`. The second is `AppendixAttacks[1]`, and then `AppendixAttacks[2]`, `AppendixAttacks[3]`, and finally `AppendixAttacks[4]`.

Because an array starts with element number 0, the final element in the array has an index that is 1 less than the size of the array. Thus, an array of 89 elements has indexes ranging from 0 to 88.

Declaring and accessing an array

Here's how you declare an array:

```
int GrilledShrimp[10];
```

This line declares an array of 10 integers called `GrilledShrimp`. You first put the type (which is really the type of each element in the array), and then the name for the array, and then the number of elements in brackets. And because this declares 10 integers, their indexes range from 0 to 9.

To access the first element of the array, you put the number 0 in brackets after the type name, as in

```
GrilledShrimp[0] = 10;
```

Sometimes, people call the act of referring to a single element in the array as *subscripting*. But we avoid that word. Our brains prefer simpler words.

Often, people use a loop to fill in an array or access each member. People usually call this *looping through the array*. The `ArrayLoop` example, in Listing 9-8, shows how to create and use a basic array.

Listing 9-8:   Using a Loop to Loop Through the Array

```
#include <iostream>

using namespace std;

int main()
{
    int GrilledShrimp[5];

    for (int i=0; i<5; i++)
    {
        GrilledShrimp[i] = i * 2;
        cout << GrilledShrimp[i] << endl;
    }

    return 0;
}
```

If you use a `for` loop to go through all the elements in the array, start your loop at 0. You end the loop with 1 less than the size of the array. If you store the array size in the variable `size` and the loop index is `i`, the middle clause in the `for` loop can be either `i < size` or `i <= size - 1`. Do *not* use `i <= size`. That goes 1 more than you want.

When you use arrays, don't go beyond the array bounds. Due to some old rules of the early C language, the compiler does not warn you if you write a loop that goes beyond the upper boundary of an array. You may not get an error when you run your application, either.

Arrays of pointers

Arrays are particularly useful for storing *pointers* — a variable that contains the address of an item in memory — to objects. If you have lots of objects of the same type, you can store them in an array.

Although you can store the actual objects in the array, most people don't. Most people fill the array with pointers to the objects. To declare an array of pointers to objects, remember the asterisk in the type declaration, like this:

```
CrackedMusicCD *missing[10];
```

The `ArrayPointer` example, shown in Listing 9-9, declares an array of pointers. In this example, after declaring the array, you fill the elements of the array with zeroes. Remember that each element is a *pointer;* that way, you can immediately know whether the element points to something by just comparing it to 0. If it's 0, it's not being used. If it has something other than 0, it has a pointer in it.

Listing 9-9:   Using an Array to Store a List of Pointers to Your Objects

```
#include <iostream>

using namespace std;

class CrackedMusicCD
{
public:
    string FormerName;
    int FormerLength;
    int FormerProductionYear;
};

int main()
{
    CrackedMusicCD *missing[10];

    for (int i=0; i<10; i++)
    {
        missing[i] = 0;
    }

    return 0;
}
```

When you compile this example, you see this warning message:

```
warning: variable 'missing' set but not used [-Wunused-but-set-variable]
```

That's because you're not really doing anything with the `missing` array in the code.

If you want to create a whole group of objects and fill the array with pointers to these objects, you can do this kind of thing:

```
for (int i=0; i<10; i++)
{
    missing[i] = new CrackedMusicCD;
}
```

Because each element in the array is a pointer, if you want to access the member variables or member functions of one of the objects pointed to by the array, you need to *dereference* the pointer — obtain the value pointed to by the pointer — by using the shortcut `->` notation:

```
missing[0]->FormerName = "Shadow Dancing by Andy Gibb";
```

This sample line accesses the `FormerName` member variable of the object whose address is in the first position of the array.

Though the array contains pointers to objects, because of the mental connection between a pointer and the object it points to, some people simply refer to the objects *in the array*.

When you're finished with the objects in the array, you can delete the objects by calling `delete` for each member of the array, as in this example:

```
for (int i=0; i<10; i++)
{
    delete missing[i];
    missing[i] = 0;
}
```

In the preceding code, we clear each array element to 0. When you are working with arrays of pointers, we recommend that you do the same. That way, the pointer is *reset* to 0 and no longer points to anything after its object is gone.

Passing arrays to functions

Sometimes you need to pass an entire array to a function. Though passing entire objects to arrays can be unwieldy, passing an entire array can be dangerous. Arrays can be enormous, with thousands of elements. If each element is a pointer, each element could contain several bytes. If you pass a really big array onto the stack, you may *overflow* your application's stack — meaning your application would crash.

As with passing objects, your best bet is to pass an array's address. You *pass to a function a pointer to the array*. But passing an array's address to a function is confusing to code. The `ArrayPassing` example, shown in Listing 9-10, is a sample that passes an array, without directly coding any pointers and addresses.

Listing 9-10:   Passing an Array to a Function by Declaring the Array in the Function Header

```
#include <iostream>

using namespace std;

const int MyArraySize = 10;

void Crunch(int myarray[], int size)
{
    for (int i=0; i<size; i++)
    {
        cout << myarray[i] << endl;
    }
}

int main()
{
    int BigArray[MyArraySize];

    for (int i=0; i<MyArraySize; i++)
    {
        BigArray[i] = i * 2;
    }
```

(continued)

Listing 9-10 *(continued)*

```
    Crunch(BigArray, MyArraySize);

    return 0;
}
```

When you run this application, it prints the nine members of the array. We declared the parameter in the function header: We declared an array but did not specify a size. This means that you can pass an array of any size to the function. We included a `size` parameter, so the function knows the size of the array that we're passing in. Therefore, we included the `array size` when we called this function from `main()`. Also, we used a constant rather than `10` for the `array size`; then if we decide later to modify the application by changing the size of the array, we need to change only the one constant at the top of the application. Otherwise, we risk missing one of the 10s.

How do you pass a pointer to an array? There's a pointer symbol in the data type for `argv`, which is a pointer to a set of character pointers.

That's exactly what we did in Listing 9-10. *We did not actually pass the array itself. We passed the array's address.* When you pass an array this way, the *compiler* writes code to pass a pointer to the array. You don't worry about it.

The name of an array is actually a pointer to the first element in the array.

In the `main()` function of Listing 9-10, when we call the function, we pass the array name, `BigArray`. The compiler treats this name as the first array element address.

Thus, `BigArray` is the same as `&(BigArray[0])`. (We put parentheses around the `BigArray[0]` part so that the computer knows that the `&` refers to the combination of `BigArray[0]`, not just `BigArray`.) So you could have used this in the call:

```
Crunch(&(BigArray[0]), MyArraySize);
```

But there's no reason to do that. Just pass `BigArray`. It's the same thing!

The name of the array is a pointer to the array.

Adding and subtracting pointers

You can do interesting things when you add numbers to and subtract numbers from a pointer to an array element that is stored in a pointer variable as an address. If you take the address of an element in an array and store it in a variable, such as one called `cur` (for current), as in

```
cur = &(Numbers[5]);
```

where `Numbers` is an array of integers, you can access the element at `Numbers[5]` by dereferencing the pointer, as in

```
cout << *cur << endl;
```

Then you can add and subtract numbers from the pointer, like these lines:

```
cur++;
cout << *cur << endl;
```

The compiler knows how much memory space each array element takes. When you add 1 to `cur`, *it advances to the next element in the array.* And so the `cout` that follows prints the next element — in this case, `Numbers[6]`.

The `PointerArithmetic` example, shown in Listing 9-11, shows how to move about an array. Note that we declare a variable called cur, which is a pointer to an integer. The array holds integers, so this pointer can point to elements in the array.

We start out with `cur` pointing to the first element. The array name is the address of the first element; to accomplish that, we simply typed

```
cur = Numbers;
```

This line puts the address of the first element of the array in the variable `cur`.

Listing 9-11: Moving by Using Pointer Arithmetic

```
#include <iostream>

using namespace std;

int main()
{
    int Numbers[100];

    for (int i=0; i<100; i++)
    {
        Numbers[i] = i * 10;
    }

    int *cur;
    cur = Numbers;

    cout << *cur << endl;
    cur++;
    cout << *cur << endl;
    cur++;
    cout << *cur << endl;
    cur += 3;
    cout << *cur << endl;
    cur--;
    cout << *cur << endl;

    return 0;
}
```

When you run the application, here is the output you see:

```
0
10
20
50
40
```

In the code, the ++ and – operators add 1 to and subtract 1 from the pointer. We also directly added a 3 to the pointer to advance it three "notches" in the array. You can also subtract from a pointer, as in

```
cur -= 2;
```

You cannot do multiplication and division with pointers.

Book II

Understanding Objects and Classes

You can find a step-by-step slideshow that demonstrates how to create a project that includes a header file using Code::Blocks to make it easier to work with the examples in this minibook at http://www.dummies.com/extras/cplusplusaio. A lot of readers write to tell us that slideshows of this sort make their job a lot easier. Even though the slideshow relies on Windows, the process is similar for both Mac and Linux systems.

Contents at a Glance

Chapter 1: Planning and Building Objects

In This Chapter

✔ **Recognizing objects so that you can create classes**

✔ **Encapsulating classes into self-contained capsules**

✔ **Building hierarchies of classes through inheritance**

✔ **Discovering classes**

Step outside for a moment and look down. What is the thing you are standing on? (Hint: It's giant, it's made of rock and sand and stone and molten lava, and it's covered with oceans and land.) The answer? A thing! (Even a planet is a thing.) And now go back inside. What's the thing that you opened — the thing with a doorknob? It's a thing, too! It's a slightly *different* kind of thing, but a *thing* nevertheless. And what are you inside? Okay, you get the idea. Everything you can imagine is a *thing* — or, to use another term, an *object*. Remember that word: *object*.

Over the years, researchers in the world of computer programming (now, doesn't *that* sound like an exciting job?) have figured out that the best way to program computers is to divide whatever it is you're trying to *model* into a bunch of objects. These objects have capabilities and characteristics. (Eventually they have relationships, but that comes later.)

In this chapter, we show you how to make use of objects to create a software application. In the process, you get to twist some of the nuts and bolts of C++ that relate to objects and get tips on how to get the most out of them.

Recognizing Objects

Let's get to the meat of it: Think of an *object* as any *thing* that a computer can describe. (Object = thing. How's that for an obvious definition?) Just as physical things have characteristics, such as size, weight, and color, objects in an application can have *attributes* — say, a particular number of accounts, an engine, or even other objects that it contains, just as a car contains engines, doors, and other objects.

Further, just as real-world things have uses — for example, serving as containers, vehicles, or tools — an object in an application has *capabilities*. For example, it might be able to withdraw money or send a message or connect to the Internet.

Here's an example of an object: Outside, in front of your house, you might see a mailbox. That mailbox is an object. (See how easy this is?) A mailbox is a useful device. You can receive mail, and depending on the style (kind) of mail, you can send mail. (The style of mail is important — you can send a letter because you know how much postage to attach, but you can't send a package because the amount of postage is unknown.) Those are the mailbox's *capabilities*. And what about its characteristics? Different mailboxes come in different shapes, sizes, and styles. So those are three *characteristics*. Now, some mailboxes, such as the kind often found at apartment buildings, are great big metal boxes with several little boxes inside, one for each apartment. The front has doors for each individual box, and the back has a large door for the mail carrier to fill the boxes with all those wonderful ads addressed to your alternative name: Resident.

In this case, you could think of the apartment mailbox as one big mailbox with lots of little boxes, or you could think of it as a big *container* for smaller mailboxes. In a sense, each of the little boxes has a front door that a resident uses, and the back of each one has an entry that the mail carrier uses. The back opens when the big container door opens.

So think about this: The mail carrier interacts with the container, which holds mailboxes. The container has a big door, and when that door opens, it exposes the insides of the small mailboxes inside, which open, too. Meanwhile, when a resident interacts with the system, he or she interacts with only his or her own particular box.

Take a look at Figures 1-1 and 1-2. Figure 1-1 shows the general look of the back of the mailbox container, where the mail carrier can open the container and put mail in all the different boxes. Figure 1-2 shows the front of the container, with the boxes open so that residents can out take the mail.

So far, there are two kinds of objects here: the container box and the mailboxes. But wait! There are multiple mailboxes. So, really, you have one container box and multiple mailboxes. But each mailbox is pretty much the same, except for a different lock and a different apartment number, right? In Figure 1-2, each box that's open is an example of a single mailbox. The others are also examples of the type of object called *mailbox*. In Figure 1-2, you can see 16 examples of the objects classified as *mailbox*. In other words, Figure 1-2 shows 16 *instances* of the *class* called `Mailbox`. And all those mailboxes are inside an instance of the class that you would probably call `Mailboxes`.

There is no hard-and-fast rule about naming your classes. However, most developers use a singular name for objects and a plural name for collections. A single `Mailbox` object would appear as part of a `Mailboxes` collection. Using this naming convention makes it easier for other developers to understand how your code works. Of course, the most important issue is consistency — once you decide on a naming convention, use the same convention all the time.

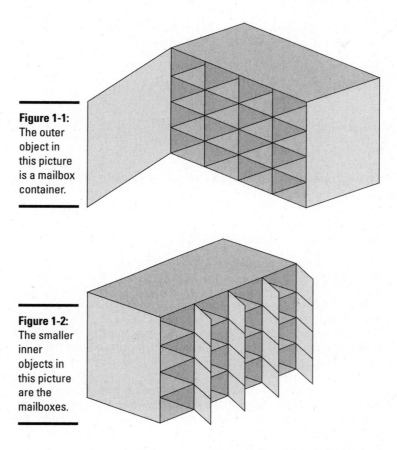

Figure 1-1:
The outer object in this picture is a mailbox container.

Figure 1-2:
The smaller inner objects in this picture are the mailboxes.

Observing the Mailboxes class

What can you say about the Mailboxes collection object?

✦ The Mailboxes collection contains 16 mailbox instances.

✦ The Mailboxes collection object is 24 inches by 24 inches in front and back, and it is 18 inches deep. (Really, it's on legs, but we don't consider those to be part of it.)

✦ When the carrier unlocks the mailboxes and pulls, its big door opens.

✦ When the mailboxes' big door opens, it *exposes the insides of each contained mailbox.*

✦ When the mail carrier pushes on the door, the door shuts and relocks. (Okay, really, the mail carrier probably has to lock it, but we don't worry about that part. We'd rather keep this example nice and simple.)

By using this list, you can discover some of the characteristics and capabilities of the `Mailboxes` collection. The following list shows its characteristics:

✦ Width: 24 inches
✦ Height: 24 inches
✦ Depth: 18 inches
✦ Mailboxes: 16 `Mailbox` objects inside

And here's a list of some of the `Mailboxes` collection capabilities:

✦ Open its door. (Well, some external thing — such as a human — opens the door, but we'll get to that shortly.)
✦ Give the mail carrier access to the mailboxes.
✦ Close its door. (And yes, again, some external force, such as a push, causes the door to close, but again, we'll get to that . . . right now!)

Think about the process of the carrier opening or closing the door. Here we seem to have a bizarre thing: *The mail carrier asks the* `Mailboxes` *collection to close its door, and the door closes.* That's the way you need to look at modeling objects: Nobody does anything to an object. Rather, someone asks the object to do something, and the object *does* it *itself.*

For example, when you reach up to shove a slice of pizza into your mouth, your brain sends signals to the muscles in your arm. Your brain sends out the signals, and your arms move up, and so does the pizza. The point is that you make the command; then the arms carry it out, even though you feel like you're causing your arms to do it.

Objects are the same way: They have their capabilities, and we tell them to do their job. We don't do it for them. At least, that's the way computer scientists view it. We know: It's a stretch sometimes. But the more you think in this manner, the better you understand object-oriented programming.

The `Mailboxes` collection contains 16 `Mailbox` objects. In C++, that means the `Mailboxes` collection would have as member variables 16 different `Mailbox` instances. These `Mailbox` instances could be an array or some other collection, and most likely the array would hold pointers to `Mail` instances.

Observing the `Mailbox` class

Consider the characteristics and capabilities of the `Mailbox` class. Each `Mailbox` has these characteristics:

✦ Width: 6 inches
✦ Height: 6 inches

✦ Depth: 18 inches

✦ Address: A unique integer. But what number exactly? That depends on *which* `Mailbox` you're talking about.

And each `Mailbox` has these capabilities:

✦ Open its door.

✦ Close its door.

Notice that we wrote the capabilities from the perspective of the `Mailbox`, not the person opening the `Mailbox`.

Now think about the question regarding the address printed on the `Mailbox`. What number goes on it? There are 16 different `Mailbox` objects, and each one gets a different number. So we can say this: The `Mailbox` *class* includes an address, which is an integer. Each *instance* of the `Mailbox` class gets its own number. The first may get 1, the second may get 2, and so on.

And so you have two concepts here for representing the mailboxes in code:

✦ **`Mailbox` class:** This is the general description of a mailbox. It includes no specifics, such as the actual address. It simply states that each mailbox *has* an address.

✦ **`Mailbox` instance:** This is the actual object. The `Mailbox` instance belongs to the class `Mailbox`. There can be several instances of the `Mailbox` class.

Think of the `Mailbox` class as a cookie cutter — or, in C++ terminology, the *type*. The `Mailbox` instance is an actual example of the class. In C++, you can create a variable of class `Mailbox` and set its `Address` integer to 1. Then you can create another variable of class `Mailbox` and set its `Address` integer to 2. Thus, you've created two distinct `Mailbox` objects, each of class `Mailbox`.

But all these have a width of 6, a height of 6, and a depth of 18. These are the same throughout the `Mailboxes` collection. Thus, you would probably not set those manually; instead, you would probably set them in the constructor for the class `Mailbox`. Nevertheless, the values of width, height, and depth go with each instance, not with the class; and the instances could, conceivably, each have their own width, height, and depth. However, when you design the class, you would probably put some stipulation in the class that these member variables cannot be changed. (You would do that by making them private and including a single function for each of them that retrieves their values.)

Finding other objects

If you are dealing with a `Mailboxes` instance and an instance of `Mailbox`, you can probably come up with some other classes. When you start considering the *parts* involved, you can think of the following objects:

✦ `Lock`: Each `Mailbox` instance would have a `Lock`, and so would the `Mailboxes` instance.

✦ `Key`: Each lock would require a `Key`.

✦ `Mail`: Each `Mailbox` instance can hold several `Mail` instances. The carrier puts these in the `Mailbox` instances, and the residents take them out.

✦ `LetterOpener`: Some residents would use these to open the `Mail`.

So you now have four more types of objects (`Lock`, `Key`, `Mail`, and `LetterOpener`). But are these classes necessary? Their need depends on the application you're building. In this case, we're modeling the mailbox system simply as an exercise. Therefore, we can pretty much choose which classes we need. But if this were an actual application for a post office, for example, you would have to determine whether the classes are necessary for the people using the software. If the application is a training exercise for people learning to be mail carriers, the application may need more detail, such as the `Key` objects. If the application were a video game, it may need all the classes we mention and even more.

In deciding whether you need certain classes, you can follow some general rules. First, some classes are so trivial or simple that it doesn't make sense to include them. For example, a letter opener serves little purpose beyond opening mail. If you're designing a `Mail` class, you would probably have the capability *Open the envelope*. Because some people would use a letter opener and others wouldn't, you have little reason to pass into that function a `LetterOpener` instance. Therefore, you would probably not include a class as trivial as `LetterOpener`. But then again, if the application teaches residents how to use the mailbox (a strange idea, we know), it might include the section *How to use your letter opener*. Yes, that's kind of silly, but you get the idea: Whether you include the class depends on the situation.

Encapsulating Objects

People have come up with various definitions for what exactly *object-oriented* means. And the phrase *various definitions* in the preceding sentence means that there aren't simple discussions around a table at a coffeehouse about what the term means. Rather, there are outright arguments! Believe it or not, one of the central points of contention is whether C++ is object-oriented.

And in such arguments (sorry — *discussions*), one of the words that usually pops up is *encapsulation*. People who defend C++ as being object-oriented point out that it supports encapsulation.

Instead of arguing, let's just all agree that yes, C++ lets you program objects and classes. Now that we've put that argument to rest and can all live peacefully, what exactly does *encapsulation* mean?

First, think about the word itself. A big part of it is *capsule*. A capsule is a small container. In the bigger picture, it's, well, a self-contained container that contains things. In the world of computer programming, *encapsulation* refers to the process of creating a stand-alone object that can take care of itself and do what it must do while holding on to information.

For example, to model a cash register, it would likely be a class. We'd *encapsulate* the cash register by putting everything about the register (its capabilities and characteristics) into a single class. In C++, the capabilities would be *member functions* and the characteristics would be *member variables*.

When we create the class, we would make some of the member variables and member functions *public;* we would make others *private*. (Some members can be *protected,* so derived classes could access them, but they still would not be public.) What exactly would private and protected member variables and member functions be? The parts that you don't want other functions modifying, that's what. For example, the cash register would probably have a value inside it representing the total dollar amount that the register contains. But the functions that use the class would not directly modify that value. Instead, they would call various member functions to perform transactions. One transaction might be `Sale()`. Another transaction might be `Refund()`; another might be `Void()`. These would be the capabilities of the register in the form of public methods, and they would modify the cash value inside the register, making sure that it balances with the sales and returns. If a function could just modify the cash value directly, the balance would get out of whack.

Accessing read-only member variables

Suppose that you have a class that contains a member variable, and you want to allow users to retrieve the value of the variable but not change it. For example, in the `Dog` class, you might set the weight in the constructor, and that's it — after that, users can get the weight but can't change it. The way to do that is to simply not have a method that sets the value. Instead, you have a method that only retrieves the value. Thus, the `Dog` class would have the `GetWeight()` method, but you would not have the `SetWeight()` method. Then users can only read the value, not set it.

The cash amount, therefore, would be a *private* or *protected member variable*. It would be hidden from the other functions and classes. As for which it would be, private or protected, that depends on whether we expect to derive new classes from the cash register class and whether we want these new classes to have access to the members. In the situation of a cash register, we would probably not want other parts of the application to access the cash register if we're worried about security. But on the other hand, if we think that we'll be creating derived classes that have added features involving the cash (such as automatically sending the money to a bank via an electronic transaction), we would want the members to be protected. (In general, we choose protected, rather than private, because we have been bitten too many times by using classes that have a gazillion private members. In those cases, we're unable to derive useful classes because everything is private!)

Encapsulation, then, is this: You combine the methods and member variables into a single entity, hiding some of them and making some accessible. The accessible ones together make up the *interface* of the object. And finally (this is important!), when you create an object, you create one that can perform on its own. In other words, the users of the class tell it what to do (such as perform a sales transaction) by calling its member functions and supplying parameters, and the object does the work. *The calling function doesn't care how the object does its thing, just that it can do it.* For example, a cash register class knows how to perform a sales transaction. As the designer of the class, don't force users to first call `Sale` and then call separate functions to manually modify the amount of cash in the register and modify the running total. Rather, the `Sale` function does all the hard work, and users of the class don't have to worry about how that work takes place.

And now the fundamental question: Why do you need to know the word *encapsulation*? Because it's a common term that computer scientists like to throw around. If they use it, however, they are likely to use it as a verb: "Look at me! I am going to encapsulate this information into an object!"

But the process matters more than the word itself. When you design objects and classes, you encapsulate your information into individual objects. If you keep the process in mind, you will be better off. Here are the things you need to do every time you design a class:

✦ **Encapsulate the information.** Combine the information into a single entity that becomes the class. This single entity has member variables representing its characteristics and member functions representing its capabilities.

✦ **Clearly define the public interface of the class.** Provide a set of functions that are public (and, possibly, member variables that are public, although it's best to keep them protected or private), and make the rest of the members either protected or private.

✦ **Write the class so that it knows how to do its own work.** The class's users should need only to call the functions in the public interface, and these public functions should be simple to use.

✦ **Think of your class as a *black box*.** The object has an interface that provides a means so that others can use it. The class includes details of how it does its thing; users only care that it does it. In other words, the users don't see into the class.

✦ **Never change the class interface after you publish the class.** Many application errors occur when a developer changes how methods, events, or access methods in the class work after publishing the class. If application developers rely on one behavior and the class developer introduces a new behavior, all applications that rely on the original behavior will break. You can always add to a class interface but never subtract from it or modify it. If you find that you must introduce a new behavior to Sale(), add the new behavior to a new method, Sale2().

A common saying in object-oriented programming is that you should never make your member variables public. The idea is that if users of the object can easily make changes to the object's member variables, a big mess could result. (For example, making the cash member variable public in a CashRegister class is asking for functions that just modify it directly, screwing up the balance.) By allowing users to call only member functions, you can put *checking code* inside to handle bad situations. For example, if you have a class called Dog that contains a member variable called Weight, you wouldn't want a user of the class to take a Dog object and set the Weight to a negative number. But if you make the Weight member public, that's exactly what any user can do.

So instead, you make the Weight member either private or protected and then give the class *access methods* (a method of implementing checking code — note that other languages use the term *properties* instead of access methods, as spelled out in the later sidebar "Access methods versus properties.") For example, you might have a method called SetWeight(). It would take an integer parameter and then check the parameter to make sure that it's greater than 0. If it is, only then would it save the number in the Weight member variable. For example, the class might look like this:

```
class Dog
{
protected:
    int Weight;

public:
    void SetWeight(int NewWeight);
};
```

And the code for the function that sets the weight might look like this:

```
void Dog::SetWeight(int NewWeight)
{
    if (NewWeight > 0)
    {
        Weight = NewWeight;
    }
}
```

Note that the `Weight` member is protected and `SetWeight()` is public. Thus, the users of the class can't modify the `Weight` member directly; they can only call `SetWeight()` to set it, which provides built-in checking. Now, this works all fine and dandy, except when the users of the class need to find Fido's weight to make sure that he's not rapidly shrinking. The only problem is that `Weight` is protected, so the user can't read it. So you need to add a function that retrieves the value of `Weight`, as in the following:

```
int Dog::GetWeight()
{
    return Weight;
}
```

You must modify the class to accommodate this function:

```
class Dog
{
protected:
    int Weight;

public:
    void SetWeight(int NewWeight);
    int GetWeight();
};
```

Now when you use this class, instead of accessing the `Weight` variable directly, you use the access methods, as in the following sample lines:

```
int main()
{
    Dog fido;
    fido.SetWeight(10);
    cout << fido.GetWeight() << endl;
    fido.SetWeight(-5);
    cout << fido.GetWeight() << endl;
    return 0;
}
```

To set the weight, you call `SetWeight()`. Note that in the first call to `SetWeight()`, we're passing a legitimate value, 10. And when the next line runs, we see the number 10 appear on the console. But in the second call to `SetWeight`, we're passing an invalid weight, –5. The `SetWeight()` function rejects this value and doesn't change the weight. So the second time we write the weight by calling `GetWeight()`, we still see 10. The number did not change. The –5 value was rejected, and the weight remained the same.

When you use access functions, you can do much more than just guard against invalid values and return the current value. The `Set()` function, for example, can process the value and make calculations or modify it. For example, the `Dog` class might have a maximum weight. If the user passes a larger weight to the `SetWeight()` function, the function could change it to the maximum weight. For example, the following function limits the weight to an upper level of 100 and a lower level of 1:

```
void Dog::SetWeight(int NewWeight)
{
    if (NewWeight < 0)
    {
        Weight = 0;
    }
    else if (NewWeight > 100)
    {
        Weight = 100;
    }
    else
    {
        Weight = NewWeight;
    }
}
```

You can use a `Get()` function to send a modified form of a member variable. For example, if you have a `SalesTransaction` class that contains a `CreditCardNumber()` variable, which is a string containing the digits and the spaces, you may not want to reveal only the last four digits instead of the entire number. A `Get()` function, then, might retrieve the `CreditCardNumber`, extract only the final four digits, and build a string of the form "XXXX XXXX XXXX 1234." It would then return that string rather than the actual `CreditCardNumber` value.

Access methods versus properties

Many modern languages support a third aspect to classes, called properties, in addition to the usual member methods and member variables. C++ doesn't support a named entity called properties, but it does support the equivalent methodality. In your programming career, you're likely to move between lots of different languages. And so we want to take a moment to introduce you to properties, which are found in languages such as C#, VB.NET, and Object Pascal. Properties are essentially a combination of member variables and methods. Think of a public member variable in C++. Anyone using an object can freely modify a member variable. But sometimes when you're creating a class, you want to place restrictions on what people can do with the member variables. For example, you might want to limit the access to reading the member variable but not changing it. Or you might want to restrict what values the variable can take on, such as limiting the

variable to integers between 1 and 100 and not allowing it to contain any other integers.

In C++, the way to impose such limitations is to make the member variable private and then write two member methods: one for reading the value of the variable and one for setting the value. The method that sets the value would impose the limits; if the caller tries to set the value to 101, for example, the method might automatically knock the value down to 100, if that's the limit you're imposing. And similarly, if you want people to be able to read the value but not change it, you might provide only a method that returns the value, and not a method for modifying the variable.

These two methods — one for setting a member variable and one for "getting" (that is, reading) a member variable — are *accessor* methods. Some languages other than C++ let you combine these member methods into what

(continued)

**Book II
Chapter 1**

**Planning and
Building Objects**

(continued)

are called properties. Because C++ doesn't support properties, we can't really show you sample code, but the idea would be like this:

```
mydog.weight = 10
cout << mydog.weight << endl;
```

Although the first line looks like we're just storing a 10 in the weight variable, if this were a property-based language, such code would instead cause your "property setter" method to get called. In that method, you'd write code that tests the value and makes sure it's a valid value before storing it. Similarly, the second line, which appears to just read the weight variable, would indirectly call the method that retrieves the value of weight. So the code would perform just like this code:

```
mydog.SetWeight(10);
cout << mydog.GetWeight() <<
    endl;
```

See how we're calling two methods — one that sets the weight and one that gets the weight? That's the idea behind properties. They let you write code that appears to read and write member variables, but in fact the code calls "getter" and "setter" methods, respectively. (When working with other languages, you can write properties such that they let the user read values, write values, or read and write values, so that the background functionality still relies on what amounts to two methods: one for setting the value and one for getting the value.) C++ doesn't have properties, but many modern languages do. Learning about them now while studying objects will help you understand properties should you end up using other languages that support them.

Building Hierarchies

One of the great powers in C++ is the capability to take a class and build new classes from it. When you use any of the available C++ libraries, such as the Standard C++ Library, you will probably encounter many classes — sometimes dozens of classes — that are all related to each other. Some classes are derived from other classes, although some classes are stand-alone. This gives programmers great flexibility. And it's good to be flexible. The blood flows more easily through your system, and you will be more relaxed. And for programming, it's good for a class library to be flexible, too, because when you are using a flexible library, you have many choices in the different classes you want to use.

Establishing a hierarchy

When you design a class, you have the option of deriving the class you're creating from an original *base* class — creating a child/parent relationship. The new class inherits the capabilities and characteristics of the base class. Normally, the members that are public in the base class will remain public in the derived class. The members that are protected in the base class will remain protected in the derived class; thus, if you derive even further, those final classes will also inherit the protected members. Private members, however, live only in the base class.

Suppose you have a base class called `FrozenFood`, and from there you derive a class called `FrozenPizza`. From `FrozenPizza`, you then derive a class called `DeepDishPizza`. `FrozenPizza` is at the top of the hierarchy. It includes various members common to all classes.

Now suppose that the `FrozenFood` class has the following member variables:

✦ `intPrice` (private): This is a private variable that represents the price of the product.

✦ `intWeight` (protected): This is a protected variable that represents the weight of the product.

The `FrozenFood` class also has these member functions:

✦ constructor: The constructor is public and takes a price and a weight as parameters. It saves them in the `Price` and `Weight` member variables, respectively.

✦ `GetPrice()`: This is a public access method that returns the value in the private `Price` member variable.

✦ `GetWeight()`: This is a public access method that returns the value in the protected `Weight` member variable.

Book II Chapter 1

Planning and Building Objects

To make this concept a little more clear to ourselves, we list these items in a box, putting the name of the class (`FrozenFood`) at the top of the box. Then the box has a horizontal line through it, and under that we list the member variables. Under the member variables, we have another line, and then we list the member functions. We show this to you in Figure 1-3.

Figure 1-3:
You can draw a class by using a box divided into three horizontal sections.

FrozenFood
−int Price
#int Weight
+FrozenFood(int APrice, int AWeight);
+int GetPrice();
+int GetWeight();

Note that in this figure, we did one other thing: Before each member variable and function, we place either a plus sign (+), a minus sign (−), or a pound sign (#). This is shorthand notation: The + means the item is public, the − means it's private, and the # means it's protected.

In Figure 1-3, note that we wrote the lines for the member variables and functions in C++ form. Normally, you don't do this; you use a special notation called Unified Modeling Language (UML) in place of the C++, which we introduce (briefly) a little later in this chapter and then examine in greater detail over the course of the rest of this book.

Protecting members when inheriting

In C++, you have options for how you derive a class. To understand this, remember that when you derive a class, the derived class inherits the members from the base class. With the different ways to derive a class, you can specify whether those inherited members will be public, protected, or private in the derived class. Here are the options:

+ **Public:** When you derive a new class as *public,* all members that were public in the base class will remain public in this derived class.

+ **Protected:** When you derive a new class as *protected,* all members that were public in the base class will now be protected in this new class. This means the members that were public in the base class will not be accessible by users of this new class.

+ **Private:** When you derive a new class as *private,* all members in the base class that this new class can access will be private. This means that these members will not be accessible by any classes that you later derive from this new class — they are private, after all.

Think of it as an order of diminishing accessibility: The highest access is public. When a member is public, users can access the member. The middle access is protected. Users cannot access protected members, but derived classes will have access to the protected members. The lowest access is private. Users cannot access private members, and derived classes can't, either.

We're talking about inheritance here: Thus, if we have a base class called FrozenFood and a derived class called FrozenPizza, the derived class is a combination of the members in FrozenFood and additional FrozenPizza members. However, only the methods in the FrozenFood portion of FrozenPizza can access the private members of the FrozenFood portion. Nevertheless, the methods in the FrozenFood portion of FrozenPizza and the private members of FrozenFood are part of the derived class.

When you derive a class as public, the base class portion of the derived class remains unchanged: Those items that were private remain in the base class portion; therefore, the derived class does not have access to them. Those that were protected are still protected, and those that were public are still public.

But when you derive a class as protected, the base class portion is different from the original base class: Its public members are now protected members of this derived class. (But remember: The actual base class itself did not change. We're talking only about the base class *portion* of the derived class.) Thus, the members that were public in the base class but are now protected in the derived class are not accessible to other functions and classes: They are now protected.

And finally, if you derive a class as private, the base class portion is again different from the original base class: All its members are now private. Because its members are private, any classes you derive from this newly derived class can't access these members: They're private. However, as before, the original base class itself didn't change; we're still talking about the base class portion of the derived class.

All these derivation approaches can be complicated. Remember that when you derive a class, you are specifying what level the inherited public and protected members will have in the derived class.

In C++, you specify the type of inheritance you want in the header line for the derived class. Take a look at the `InheritedMembers` example, shown in Listing 1-1. Notice the three classes at the top of the listing: `FrozenFood`, `FrozenPizza`, and `DeepDishPizza`. `FrozenFood` is the base class of `FrozenPizza`, and `FrozenPizza` is the base class of `DeepDishPizza`. Figure 1-4 shows this by using the special notation called UML (refer to the preceding section), where the arrows point toward the *base* class.

**Book II
Chapter 1**

Planning and Building Objects

Listing 1-1: Specifying the Access Levels of the Inherited Members

```
#include <iostream>

using namespace std;

class FrozenFood
{
private:
    int Price;

protected:
    int Weight;

public:
    FrozenFood(int APrice, int AWeight);
    int GetPrice();
    int GetWeight();
};

class FrozenPizza : public FrozenFood
{
protected:
    int Diameter;

public:
    FrozenPizza(int APrice, int AWeight, int ADiameter);
    void DumpInfo();
};
```

(continued)

Listing 1-1 *(continued)*

```
class DeepDishPizza : public FrozenPizza
{
private:
    int Height;

public:
    DeepDishPizza(int APrice, int AWeight, int ADiameter, int AHeight);
    void DumpDensity();
};

FrozenFood::FrozenFood(int APrice, int AWeight)
{
    Price = APrice;
    Weight = AWeight;
}

int FrozenFood::GetPrice()
{
    return Price;
}

int FrozenFood::GetWeight()
{
    return Weight;
}

FrozenPizza::FrozenPizza(int APrice, int AWeight, int ADiameter) :
FrozenFood(APrice, AWeight)
{
    Diameter = ADiameter;
}

void FrozenPizza::DumpInfo()
{
    cout << "\tFrozen pizza info:" << endl;
    cout << "\t\tWeight: " << Weight << " ounces" << endl;
    cout << "\t\tDiameter: " << Diameter << " inches" << endl;
}

DeepDishPizza::DeepDishPizza(int APrice, int AWeight,
int ADiameter, int AHeight) :
FrozenPizza(APrice, AWeight, ADiameter)
{
    Height = AHeight;
}

void DeepDishPizza::DumpDensity()
{
    // Calculate pounds per cubic foot of deep-dish pizza
    cout << "\tDensity: ";
    cout << Weight * 12 * 12 * 12 * 14 / (Height * Diameter * 22 * 16);
    cout << " pounds per cubic foot" << endl;
}

int main(int argc, char *argv[])
{
    cout << "Thin crust pepperoni" << endl;
    FrozenPizza pepperoni(450, 12, 14);
    pepperoni.DumpInfo();
    cout << "\tPrice: " << pepperoni.GetPrice() << " cents" << endl;
```

```
        cout << "Deep dish extra-cheese" << endl;
        DeepDishPizza extracheese(650, 21592, 14, 3);
        extracheese.DumpInfo();
        extracheese.DumpDensity();
        cout << "\tPrice: " << extracheese.GetPrice() << " cents" << endl;
        return 0;
}
```

Figure 1-4:
The arrows
in this UML
diagram
point toward
the base
class.

When you run Listing 1-1, you see the following output:

```
Thin crust pepperoni
        Frozen pizza info:
                Weight: 12 ounces
                Diameter: 14 inches
        Price: 450 cents
Deep dish extra-cheese
        Frozen pizza info:
                Weight: 21592 ounces
                Diameter: 14 inches
        Density: 35332 pounds per cubic foot
        Price: 650 cents
```

The first five lines show information about the object of class
`FrozenPizza`. The remaining lines show information about the object
of class `DeepDishPizza`, including the fact that it weighs 21,592 ounces
(which happens to be 1349.5 pounds) and has a density of 35,332 pounds
per cubic foot (35,332 pounds per cubic foot — a bit more than 17 tons per
cubic foot, which is still nowhere near that of a neutron star, which measures about 3 trillion tons per cubic foot). That's one serious pizza.

The derivations are all public. Thus, the items that were public in `FrozenFood`
are still public in `FrozenPizza` and `DeepDishPizza`. Note where the different
information in the output comes from. The line `Frozen pizza info:` and the
two lines that follow (`Weight:` and `Diameter:`) come from the public function `DumpInfo()`, which is a member of `FrozenPizza`. `DumpInfo()` is public
in the `FrozenPizza` class. Since `DeepDishPizza` derives from `FrozenPizza`
as *public,* `DumpInfo()` is also a public member of `DeepDishPizza`.

Now try changing the header for `DeepDishPizza` from

```
class DeepDishPizza : public FrozenPizza
```

to

```
class DeepDishPizza : protected FrozenPizza
```

You're changing the word `public` to `protected`. Make sure that you change the correct line, or else it will spoil the effect of this nifty thing we're showing you.

Now try compiling the application. You will get an error. We got this:

```
In function 'int main(int, char**)':
error: 'void FrozenPizza::DumpInfo()' is inaccessible
error: within this context
error: 'FrozenPizza' is not an accessible base of 'DeepDishPizza'
error: 'int FrozenFood::GetPrice()' is inaccessible
error: within this context
error: 'FrozenFood' is not an accessible base of 'DeepDishPizza'
```

This refers to the line in `main()`:

```
  extracheese.DumpInfo();
```

Why is that an error now? Because `DumpInfo()` is now a `protected` member of `DeepDishPizza`, thanks to the word `protected` in the class header. By putting the word `protected` in the class definition, you are saying that inherited members that are currently public will instead be protected. Because the `DumpInfo()` member is protected, you can't call it from `main()`. However, `DumpInfo()` is still public in the `FrozenPizza` class, so this call is fine:

```
pepperoni.DumpInfo();
```

Go ahead and change the line back to a public inheritance, as it was in Listing 1-1:

```
class DeepDishPizza : public FrozenPizza
```

And now change the header of `FrozenPizza` so that it looks like this:

```
class FrozenPizza : private FrozenFood
```

Again, make sure to change the correct lines. Now try compiling the application. When we do so in Code::Blocks, we get the following error:

```
In function 'int main(int, char**)':|
error: 'void FrozenPizza::DumpInfo()' is inaccessible|
error: within this context|
error: 'FrozenPizza' is not an accessible base of 'DeepDishPizza'|
error: 'int FrozenFood::GetPrice()' is inaccessible|
error: within this context|
error: 'FrozenFood' is not an accessible base of 'DeepDishPizza'|
```

This error refers to the line inside `DeepDishPizza::DumpDensity()` where the code is trying to access the `Weight` member. Why doesn't the compiler let us access the member now? Because the member, which was public in the original `FrozenFood` class, became private when it became a part of `FrozenPizza`. And because it's private in `FrozenPizza`, the derived class `DeepDishPizza` cannot access it from *within its own member functions.*

The rule with private members is that derived classes will not have access to them. And that's the case in this example. Make sure to change back the header of `FrozenPizza` so that it looks like this:

```
class FrozenPizza : public FrozenFood
```

Overriding member functions

One of the cool things about classes is that you can declare a member function in one class, and then when you derive a new class, you can give that class a different version of the same function. This is called *overriding* the function. For example, if you have a class `FrozenFood` and a derived class `FrozenPizza`, you may want to include a member function in `FrozenFood` called `BakeChemistry()`, which modifies the food when it's baked. Because all foods are different, the `BakeChemistry()` function would be different for each class derived from `FrozenFood`.

In C++, you can provide a different *version* of the function for the different derived classes by dropping the word `virtual` before the function name in the base class declaration, as in this line of code:

```
virtual void BakeChemistry();
```

This line is the prototype inside the class definition. Later, you would provide the code for this function.

In the class for your derived class, you would then just put the function prototype, without the word `virtual`:

```
void BakeChemistry();
```

And as before, you would include the code for the function later on. For example, you might have something like the following example. First, here are the classes:

```
class FrozenFood
{
private:
    int Price;

protected:
    int Weight;
```

```
public:
    FrozenFood(int APrice, int AWeight);
    int GetPrice();
    int GetWeight();
    virtual void BakeChemistry();
};

class FrozenPizza : public FrozenFood
{
protected:
    int Diameter;

public:
    FrozenPizza(int APrice, int AWeight, int ADiameter);
    void DumpInfo();
    void BakeChemistry();
};
```

You can see that we put the word `virtual` in the `FrozenFood` class, and then we put the function declaration again in the `FrozenPizza` class. Now, here are the `BakeChemistry()` functions:

```
void FrozenFood::BakeChemistry()
{
    cout << "Baking, baking, baking!" << endl;
}

void FrozenPizza::BakeChemistry()
{
    cout << "I'm getting crispy!" << endl;
}
```

Note that we did not put the word `virtual` in front of the functions; that only goes in the class declaration. Now, whenever you make an instance of each class and call `BakeChemistry()` for each instance, you call the one for the given class. Consider the following two lines of code:

```
FrozenPizza pepperoni(450, 12, 14);
pepperoni.BakeChemistry();
```

Because `pepperoni` is an instance of `FrozenPizza`, this code calls the `BakeChemistry()` for the `FrozenPizza` class, not for the `FrozenFood` class.

You may not want any code in your base class for the `BakeChemistry()` function. If so, you can do this:

```
virtual void BakeChemistry() {}
```

Wait! Why would you want a function that has no code? Well, we're not as goofy as we look. Okay, we are goofy. But regardless, you may not want any code here, but you do want code in the derived classes, and you want them to be different versions of the same code. The idea then is to provide a basic, default set of code that the classes inherit if they don't override the function. And sometimes, that basic, default set of code is simply *nothing*. And so you would only put an open brace and a closing brace, and you can do that inside the class itself:

```
class FrozenFood
{
private:
    int Price;

protected:
    int Weight;

public:
    FrozenFood(int APrice, int AWeight);
    int GetPrice();
    int GetWeight();
    virtual void BakeChemistry() {}
};
```

Some people prefer to put the word `virtual` in the overridden function's prototype in the derived class. Technically speaking, this step is not required, although many people who have been programming in C++ for a long time do this. You can, if you want, if you think that it looks cool. We do it for one reason (other than looking cool): It reminds us that the function *is* `virtual`. Thus, in the `FrozenPizza` class definition, your function prototype would look like this, just as it did in the `FrozenFood` class:

```
virtual void BakeChemistry();
```

Specializing with polymorphism

Suppose you have a function called `Bake()` and you want it to take as a parameter a `FrozenFood` instance. If you derive `FrozenPizza` from `FrozenFood` and then derive `DeepDishPizza` from `FrozenPizza`, by the "is a" rule, objects of the class `FrozenPizza` and `DeepDishPizza` are both examples of `FrozenFood` objects. This is true in general: If you have a class called `Base` and you derive from that a class called `Derived`, instances of class `Derived` are *also* instances of class `Base`. Think of it like a family name: If your last name is Swaddlebug and your child grows up, marries, and takes the name Higglequack, then although the child bears the name Higglequack, at heart she is and always will be a Swaddlebug.

And so it is with frozen foods and C++, too. You can treat an object of any class derived from `FrozenFood` as though it *is* a `FrozenFood` instance. Therefore, if you have a function called `Bake()` and you declare it as follows, you are free to pass to this function a `FrozenFood` instance or to pass an instance of any class derived from `FrozenFood`, such as `FrozenPizza` or `DeepDishPizza`:

```
void Bake(FrozenFood *)
{
    cout << "Baking" << endl;
}
```

Here's where the fun begins: Suppose that in this `Bake()` function you'll set the oven temperature to a fixed amount, turn on the oven, and then cook the food. Every food behaves differently in the oven. For example, a deep-dish frozen pizza might rise and become thicker, but a regular frozen pizza will become crispier but not get any thicker.

You don't really want to put all the different food types inside the Bake() function, with a million if statements: if it's this type of food, have it rise; if it's that type of food, have it brown; and if it's another type of food, have it scream and yell. Instead (and this is where things start to get *seriously* cool), you can put the actual baking chemistry in the class for the food itself! Yes! The FrozenPizza would have its own BakeChemistry() member function, and the DeepDishPizza would also have its own BakeChemistry() function. Then the Bake() function would simply call BakeChemistry() for whatever object it receives as a parameter. And how does C++ know how to do this? By virtue of the virtual functions! The Bake() function itself doesn't even know or care what type of FrozenFood it receives. It just calls BakeChemistry() for whatever object it receives. And thanks to the miraculous beauty of C++, it automatically calls the correct BakeChemistry() function, whether it's the one for FrozenPizza or the one for DeepDishPizza or even a class that you add later when you modify the application. And when you modify the application, if you write a new class and derive it from Frozen Food and give it its own BakeChemistry() function, you can pass an instance of this class to Bake(), without even having to modify Bake()! In other words, you don't need to tell Bake() about this class! Isn't that great?! Can you tell we're excited?

In short, what this means is that the Bake() function can take an object of class FrozenFood (or any class derived from FrozenFood) and call its BakeChemistry() function. Each class can have its own version of BakeChemistry(), and the computer will call the appropriate BakeChemistry() function. This whole process is called *polymorphism*.

Polymorphism is one of the most powerful aspects of object-oriented programming. The idea is that you can expand and enhance your application by simply adding new classes derived from a common base class. Then you have to make very few (if any) modifications to the rest of your application. Because you used virtual functions and polymorphism, the rest of your application automatically understands the new class you created. In essence, you are able to *snap* in the new class, and the application will run just fine.

Getting abstract about things

When you create a base class with a virtual function and then derive other classes, you may want to override the virtual function in all the derived classes. Furthermore, you may want to make sure that nobody — and we mean *nobody* — ever creates an instance of the base class.

Now, why would you do that? Because the base class might contain basic things that are common to all the other classes, but the class itself doesn't make much sense as an instance. For example, we want you to go to the store and pick up a frozen food. We hear they're on sale at the grocery store down the street. We like the purple kind. See, it doesn't make much sense to have an instance of a class called `FrozenFood`. What kind of frozen food? Well, it could be a (you guessed it!) `FrozenPizza`, or even better, a `DeepDishPizza`. But by itself, a `FrozenFood` item isn't realistic.

Philosophers have a word to describe such things: *abstract*. The class `FrozenFood` is abstract; it doesn't make sense to create an instance of it. In C++, you can make a class abstract, but when you do, the compiler will not allow you to make any instances of the class.

This is where things get a little strange: In C++, you don't actually specify that the class itself is abstract. The word *abstract* does not appear in the language. Instead, you have to be, well, more abstract about it. To specify that the class is abstract, you must have at least one virtual function that has no code. But instead of just putting an empty code block, as in { }, you follow the function prototype in the class definition with = 0, as in

**Book II
Chapter 1**

**Planning and
Building Objects**

```
class FrozenFood
{
private:
    int Price;

protected:
    int Weight;

public:
    FrozenFood(int APrice, int AWeight);
    int GetPrice();
    int GetWeight();
    virtual void BakeChemistry() = 0;
};
```

In this class definition, the function `BakeChemistry()` has = 0 after it (but before the semicolon — *don't forget the semicolon*). The = 0 magically transforms the virtual function into an *abstract virtual function*. And if you have an abstract virtual function inside you, face it: You are an abstract class. No ifs, ands, or buts. You're abstract.

This is the rule for creating an abstract class: You must have at least one abstract virtual function in your class. If you don't, the class will not be abstract, and users of the class will be able to create instances of it. But if you do have at least one abstract virtual function, the compiler will issue an error message when you and other users try to create an instance of the class.

In your extensive travels throughout the virtual world of C++, you are likely to encounter a slightly different term for *abstract virtual function*. That term is *pure virtual function*. Although the name sounds all pristine and pure, it means the same thing. You can use either term.

So now that you have your abstract class and can't make an instance of it, are you home free? Nope. Now in your derived classes, you *must* override the abstract virtual function. Otherwise, the derived classes will also be *abstract*. And when your class is abstract, you can't create instances of it.

To override the abstract virtual function, you override as you would with any virtual function. This class includes a function that overrides the `BakeChemistry()` function:

```
class FrozenPizza : public FrozenFood
{
protected:
    int Diameter;

public:
    FrozenPizza(int APrice, int AWeight, int ADiameter);
    void DumpInfo();
    void BakeChemistry();
};
```

Then you provide the code for the `BakeChemistry()` function, as in

```
void FrozenPizza::BakeChemistry()
{
    cout << "I'm getting crispy under this heat!" << endl;
}
```

There's nothing magical about defining the override function, but you are *required* to override it if you want to create an instance of this class.

Discovering Classes

In your studies of object-oriented programming, you could spend weeks and weeks searching for the answer to this question: How do you know what classes to put in your application? Oddly, many of the books on object-oriented programming don't even tackle this question. Too many people, even self-proclaimed experts, simply don't know the answer to this question.

In this section, we show you how to discover the classes you need for your project, and we put the concepts in the context of the bigger picture of software engineering.

Engineering your software

Ready to write your application? Okay, sit down and start coding. And call us in six months. Oh, and in case we forgot to mention, this software that you build has to do exactly what we, your customers, need. And please, please, don't let it mess up, okay?

Well now, isn't that nice? How are you supposed to know what we need, and much less, how are you supposed to get it perfect the first time? Yet, believe it or not, many young programmers build their software this way. The shoot-from-the-hip approach goes something like this:

1. "Hey! I have a *really* great idea!"

2. Open up the compiler.

3. Write the code.

4. Sell it.

And people wonder why so many applications crash and screw up. Have you ever seen an application mess up? Who hasn't? But fortunately, your software doesn't have to be in this group. You have, in your hands, an instruction guide for building software.

When you have a great idea, the first thing to ask yourself is this: Who will be using your software? You? Your friends? Businesspeople? Children? People at home? Teachers? Nonprofit agencies? Airline pilots? Doctors in the middle of surgery? Hackers? The dog?

Ask yourself this question, and be honest. The truth is this: No software package will be used by *everyone*. Yes, certain applications are used by a *lot* of people. Examples are the software that runs the telephone system or the software in your cable TV box. But even then, we could probably find a couple dozen people on some island somewhere who will never use your software. So when you answer this question, be realistic. And be as detailed as possible. For example, one answer might be the following: This software will be used by VPs and CEOs at Fortune 500 companies who need to divide time between surfing the web and playing Solitaire.

Once upon a time, people believed that, to create software, you should create a complete model that duplicates the real world. But people designing software quickly realized a slight, shall we say, *difficulty* in this approach: What if the real-world process you're modeling is, frankly, screwed up and a total joke? Want to find out for sure? Ask the workers who actually *use* the process you're trying to computerize. And this spawned an interesting profession that a lot of computer programmers took up: Business process reengineering. Sounds pretty cool. "What do you do?" "I'm a business process reengineer." "Cool. We bet you have a big house."

Business process reengineering simply means helping a company fix its internal processes so that they function correctly. And we're talking about the actual processes, not just the computer software they use. One of the creators of the software modeling language we advocate in this book (UML), a guy named Ivar Jacobson, even wrote one of the early great books on business process reengineering. (And we suppose that he probably *does* have a big house, although we've never seen it.)

It boils down to this: When you model a process, you may find inefficiencies in the process. So you probably won't want to model the process exactly. Besides, if the process were exactly the same, why bother? The computer should make the process better. So think of ways that the people who use your software will find that it not only automates what they do but makes their life easier, too. Here are the steps, then, to engineering your software.

The following are the general steps in building good software. Each step is a *workflow*. As you gain experience, you get better at actually following these steps. Like anything else in the real world, building software that *works* and that is *good* requires practice and patience.

1. Determine who will be using the software, and gather the requirements. In other words, find out what the people who will be using it need the software to do. This is called the *requirements workflow*. In doing so, build a glossary of terms. That's important! The *glossary* contains all the words involved in the process you are modeling. For instance, if you are writing the software that will automate a beach, you will probably encounter terms such as *surfboard, sand castle, high tide, undertow, shark, broken glass, foot, swimsuit, umbrella, volleyball, net,* and *volleyball court.* These are all nouns. But your glossary can also have verbs (possibly with a noun tacked on to the end — that's called a *direct object,* by the way), as in *dive, swim, ward off shark, avoid broken glass, rent umbrella,* and *throw volleyball.*

2. Begin the *analysis workflow.* To do this, determine your analysis classes. For more information on this topic, see "Finding those pesky classes," later in this chapter. Note that while doing this, you may realize that some things were missing or were not quite right in Step 1. That's okay — you can go back to Step 1 and fix them. Then, after you fix things in Step 1, you can return to Step 2. Remember that in this workflow, you are not worrying about the details of *how* you'll be writing the code. In fact, you *won't* be writing any code here, nor will you be worrying about things like how you will store your files, how you'll sort a list of numbers, and so on. Save all that for the implementation workflow described in Step 4. Here, you're only designing some classes. After you have your analysis classes, have the people who will be using the software (or at least some of them, if there are millions) review your classes and see whether these are the general *parts* of the software they imagined.

   During this second step, you can do one thing related to programming: Design some screens. Although many of the textbooks on object-oriented analysis and design do not put that step here, doing so has many benefits. First, it allows you to show the potential users of the application what the application might look like when it's finished. And this allows them to begin analyzing whether or not what you're building will be useful. (And if they don't find it useful, don't quit and don't yell at them. They are, after all, using this thing and paying you mondo-big bucks, so do what they want and laugh all the way to the bank.) And second, doing this lets you show them that, yes, you really are building software and not just surfing the Web.

3. Now comes the *design workflow.* This is where you take the analysis classes and begin building the classes you will use in your application. For this stage, you use UML notation and describe the classes in your application, how they all interact, and the steps that various processes in your application take. You can start thinking about the code now, but

you still won't actually write any code. And by the way, it's very possible (or even likely) that you'll discover that something you did in Step 1 or 2 is wrong, or at least not *quite* right. If so . . . that's right — go ahead and return to those steps and fix the things. But if you go back to Step 1, please revisit Step 2 before coming back to Step 3. You may end up having to change some things there, too.

4. And finally the *implementation workflow* has arrived! That's just a fancy term for *coding time*. Now that you've made it this far, you will realize that much of your work is already completed. The first several steps took care of much of the hard work, and now you can do the fun part of focusing on the coding part. And once again, you may have to backtrack a few steps if you find some things that aren't quite right.

5. But you're not finished yet. Nope. Can anyone guess what comes next? That's right: the *testing workflow*. During this workflow, you try to use your application in all the possible ways you intended it to be used. And you can also choose a few other people who you trust to use it. We say *trust* because this is a vital stage of your software. You want to make sure that the people who test it really know what they're doing and are going to seriously put the application through the wringer. And further, you want these people to give you honest, objective comments, not things like, "You messed up! You're fired!" Rather, you want them to report actual problems and difficulties they found in the software so that you, the programmer, can fix them. But remember: Having others help you test your application is to your benefit. Just like editing your own papers; you are likely to miss certain things, and having at least one more set of eyes and fingers trying it out is a good thing.

Our experience in the testing world tells us that most of the bugs you and the other testers find result in you going back to Step 4 and working on the coding to fix problems. However, occasionally you find you have to backtrack to Step 3, or even once in a while to Step 2. But that's okay: Your goal is to build the software and build it correctly.

Finding those pesky classes

When you set out to determine the classes to use in your application as part of the *analysis workflow,* the first thing you end up with is a set of analysis classes. These are not classes in a final form that you would type into an editor and compile as a C++ application. Rather, they are more of a descriptive style that depict what you are modeling. Then, after you have these classes, you move to the design workflow of your development: That's when you refine the class descriptions you can easily transform into C++ code.

People use three general ways to determine the classes. None of these approaches are perfect; if they were, a computer could program itself automatically. (Assuming that somebody programmed the computer to program, but that's a separate philosophy altogether, something we won't get into here.) Here are the three general ways people discover classes:

◆ Look at the glossary you developed during the requirements workflow, searching out the nouns and the verbs.

◆ Use CRC cards, which stands for Class, Responsibilities, and Collaborators (as described in "Using CRC cards," later in this chapter).

◆ Look for hidden or missing classes.

We recommend doing all three; or do either of the first two along with the final one. The final item on the list is important in case you missed anything.

Searching for nouns and verbs

As much as it sounds like a drag, searching for nouns and verbs is actually a fun process. Not all computer programmers are known for their love of human language grammar (such as English or Spanish), but you don't have to be a grammar whiz to make it through this stage. (There are exceptions, and we tend to write books!)

First, go through the glossary and any other documents you accumulated during the requirements workflow, and begin making two lists: all the important nouns and all the important verbs.

After you have compiled your list, think about which of the nouns are particularly important; for instance, some nouns may be major aspects of the application. If you're writing an application that models a grocery store, for example, *cash register* is probably a pretty important noun. If you're writing an application to control an intergalactic space ship, everybody knows that the antigravity booster is vital. These, then, are good candidates for classes. You will make most of the remaining nouns characteristics in your classes. (Remember that, ultimately, characteristics and capabilities will be member variables and functions, but you're not thinking about programming at this point.) If, however, you find a characteristic that just doesn't seem to work with any class, you probably want to make it a class as well. Finally, the verbs will become the capabilities of the classes. You should not have any capabilities that are without a class: Either you don't need the capability, or you are probably missing a class. Go ahead and add it.

Using CRC cards

People love CRC (Class, Responsibilities, and Collaborators) cards because they find that creating them is fun. Big corporations like to do this type of thing during team-building exercises to help employees get along. In addition to climbing ropes and such, they design software with CRC cards.

People often use sticky notes for CRC cards, although we usually just draw them on a whiteboard. (But we're not supposed to admit that because our fellow object-oriented people will be angry with us.)

A CRC card consists of three parts. The top part is the name of the class. The left side shows the responsibilities (what we call *capabilities*) of the class. The right side features the collaborations, which means you just list other classes that this class works together with. For example, an antigravity booster class certainly works together with a high-energy proton accelerator class, as everybody knows. You list the names of these classes on the right side of the card because they are collaborations.

Some people prefer to put their CRC cards as sticky notes right on a whiteboard; then instead of writing the names of the related classes on the right side of the card, they just draw a line between the cards. You can either list the classes or draw lines, whichever you like best.

By coming up with collaborations, you will spot missing classes. For example, because you know that the antigravity booster works with a high-energy proton accelerator, when you fill in the collaborators for the antigravity booster class, you will know whether you forgot about the high-energy proton accelerator class.

Look for hidden or missing classes

It's possible that when you do a class analysis, you will have left out some classes. Some of these missing classes may not be obvious, and to find them, you will probably have to get back with the people who helped suggest requirements. This is a good time to have them review the classes. Remember, the classes that you are building right now are not final classes ready for C++. Instead, these are less technical classes that are understandable by people who don't program. Therefore, the people who offered the requirements and the people who will be using the application can probably look over the classes and help you determine if you are missing anything. After you determine that you have missing classes, go ahead and add them by making another CRC card.

Completing the analysis with the design workflow

After you have your classes, you can move to the *design workflow* and write the classes in UML form. This is a simple form in that you will have a box with the class name at the top followed by the characteristics of the class and finally followed by the capabilities of the class. (Refer to Figure 1-3 for an example of a class in this form.) These are the classes you will use in the coding phase (*implementation workflow*), where you actually transform them into real, breathing C++ classes. The remaining chapters in this book show you how to do all this.

Chapter 2: Describing Your Program with UML

The ancient people knew something that we don't know. Instead of wasting their time writing these big, long sentences and descriptions, they used hieroglyphics, pictures that just got right to the point. One picture = one statement. It wasn't until the twentieth century that people in the computer world started getting back to their ancient roots and realized that maybe there was something to be said for all those drawings and pictures. One day, while working late, a small group of researchers realized that a nifty way to describe software is through drawings. And thus they came up with the Unified Modeling Language, or UML for short (pronounced, well, just *You-Em-Ell*).

In this chapter, we talk about what UML is and how you can use it to model your applications. We give a brief overview of the types of diagrams it includes, and we talk about the difference between a *methodology* and a *modeling language*.

Moving Up to UML

The Unified Modeling Language has an interesting history. When object-oriented programming was just getting off the ground in the late 1980s, several people came up with different ways to draw various diagrams to help people design their classes. This, of course, was nothing new. In addition to ancient people who used drawings in their hieroglyphics, people have always had a tendency to draw diagrams to describe something. For example, people might draw a chart listing the different parts of their applications. Or they might draw a chart that shows the steps that an application goes through, using a form called a flowchart.

A *flowchart* is simply a diagram that shows the step-by-step nature of a process, complete with the decision making that the process might involve. For example, we might have a step-by-step process (or *algorithm*) we use that helps us decide what to do on Mondays. This might look like Figure 2-1.

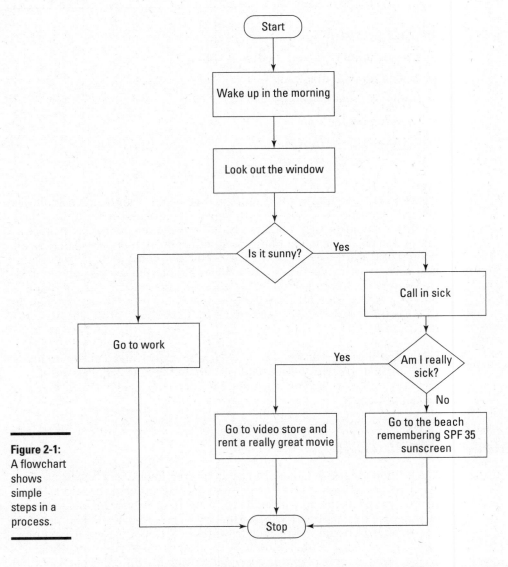

Figure 2-1:
A flowchart
shows
simple
steps in a
process.

In Figure 2-1, we start at the top in the spot called *Start,* and then we follow the arrow down to the first box. The first box is a command or statement — something that we *do.* Then after we do that, we follow the arrow down to the next box. After that we follow the arrow again, but this time we encounter a diamond. A diamond contains a decision. We answer the question, and if our answer is *yes,* we go one way, but if our answer is *no,* we go the other way. In this case, if it's *yes,* we go to the right, and begin the boxes on the right, following the arrows, responding to any decisions we find. If the first decision was *no,* we follow the arrows on the left, again doing what the boxes tell us and answering any questions we see in the diamonds.

Well, this whole flowcharting business works great for small, simple tasks. But over the years, software has become far more complex. For one thing, people now build their applications around objects and classes, which simply don't fit to the flowchart idea. And second, software has become *big.* Just a quick look at some of the software you use on a daily basis, such as the word processors, and you can see that these applications were written by lots and lots of people who seemed like they wanted to add every bell and whistle — whether you even use it or not! And the flowcharts are more suited to small portions of a software package, such as a single function or an algorithm.

And so, over the years, people have pretty much ditched the flowcharting and left it in a time capsule somewhere to be found hundreds of years from now. (Although, a portion of UML — called an *activity diagram* — is similar to a flowchart.) And during the years since programmers have started ditching flowcharts, a few well-respected researchers in the field of computer science have come up with new ways to draw pretty pictures that will describe a computer application. Several different attempts have been made, but it seems like programmers have finally come up with one that everyone can live with: UML.

UML takes the concept of flowcharting to a whole new level. Yes, that sounds like it came from a marketing brochure, but it's true. UML is much *more* than just flowcharting. UML uses symbols that show how all the classes and objects fit together in your application, and it shows how they interact and *collaborate.* You then use UML as you design and build your entire software systems. Figure 2-2 is an example of a UML diagram.

Figure 2-2:
A class diagram shows classes in UML form.

The three amigos

In your explorations of UML, sooner or later you're going to come across the term *Three Amigos*. Although that was a goofy movie back in the Greatest Decade (why, the 1980s of course), in the context of UML, it refers to the three guys who developed UML. Why are they called that? Because after about seven years or so, they finally became *friends*. It's true.

For several years, there were three guys who wrote books on object-oriented programming, and they each had their own way of doing things. But worse, the *rumor* is that these guys couldn't stand each other. (Who knows if that's even true.) "My way is better, and I don't like you, anyway." Come on guys, can't we all just get along? Well, in fact, they did end up getting along.

One day, it dawned on them: "Hey! You know what? Like Superman, Batman, and Spiderman, we can all just join forces in one great big Hall of Justice and make it a better world for all!" That and, "Hey, you know what? Our ideas really aren't all *that* different. Let's combine them into a new, better way of doing object-oriented programming." Like any time three greats join and put their heads together, the result was something pretty nifty: UML.

By the way, movieland's *Three Amigos* are Chevy Chase, Steve Martin, and Martin Short. In UML circles, the three amigos are Grady Booch, Ivar Jacobson, and James Rumbaugh.

This shows two classes, one called `Discombobulator` and another called `Perturborator`. Each is inside a box divided into three rows, with the class name at the top, the member variables in the middle, and the member functions at the bottom. The format is slightly different from regular C++ format; the types go at the end, after a colon. (Remember that in C++ you put the types first, as in `int Height;`).

The first class, `Discombobulator`, has two member variables, `Width` and `Depth`. (Everybody knows that an actual discombobulator has no height; thus, we didn't include one in this class.) The two member variables are private; therefore, they start with a minus sign, (–), and each is an integer type. The `Befuddle()` member function is public, and therefore starts with a plus sign, +. In the `Perturborator` class, the `plethora` member variable is protected, and therefore it starts with a # sign.

Notice the arrow. The arrow shows inheritance, but it goes in the opposite direction of what a lot of people might expect. *It points toward the base class*. Thus, in this diagram, `Pertuborator` is derived from `Discombobulator`.

The Unified Modeling Language has been accepted by millions of engineers as the standard way for modeling software. The Object Management Group (or OMG, found at www.omg.org) has adopted UML as its official modeling language. The OMG is a consortium of hundreds of software companies that have all joined to oversee the big sea of software development standards.

Modeling a methodology

A lot of people will start reading a book on UML and become a bit disoriented at the beginning because they quickly realize that an important question sometimes goes unanswered: How do you use UML to actually design a complete software package from start to finish? How do you use UML to go through the process of determining what classes you need, building those classes, writing your software, testing it, and all that good stuff? Some books on UML seem to avoid this question for a good reason:

UML is *not* a methodology. It's not a set of rules and steps for building software. Rather, UML is simply a set of diagrams that you can use while modeling your software. That's actually a point that many software engineers don't realize. "What methodology do you use?" "We use UML." If that's their answer, it proves they don't really know what UML is. You use UML *with* a methodology, and then you have a powerful set of tools for building software.

Modeling with UML

The idea behind UML is that it can be used for modeling pretty much any type of information — not just object-oriented systems — even information not computer-related. As such, UML has many parts. But the great thing about UML is that you don't need to *learn* all the parts to use it. You need to learn only the parts useful to your projects. (UML had become so complicated, in fact, that the latest UML 2.5 specification focuses on making things simpler.)

UML covers all the aspects of the usual software development process. Now we have said that UML itself is not a step-by-step process or methodology for building software. However, the designers of UML have provided enough diagram types and symbols that it can be used with all the different steps of software development. Therefore, to learn UML, learning a methodology along with it is a good idea. In fact, the people who designed UML, *The Three Amigos* (see the nearby sidebar by that name), have also designed a methodology. Theirs is called the Rational Unified Process (RUP, pronounced rup— like up with an R added). That's the methodology we use. (And to be quite frank, most methodologies are more or less the same.)

Diagramming and designing with UML

The diagrams in UML are simple enough that they can be drawn by hand on a sheet of paper. Of course, this is the age of computers, and using a computer makes sense, so why resort to the old-fashioned method of pencil and paper? But beyond that, there's a slight technicality as to why paper drawings are not suited to a software design.

When you use UML to design a system, you typically use a computer application called a Computer-Aided Software Engineering (CASE) tool. When you use the CASE tool, you specify all your objects; and as you do, you create your diagrams that describe the classes and how they interact. However, the model itself is the collection of classes — *not the diagrams*. You can change the diagrams and create new diagrams, but underneath it all is the collection of classes. The collection of classes itself is known as the *model*. When you draw a diagram, you are simply providing a visual representation of the model. Most of the better CASE tools (such as Rational Rose or Paradigm Plus) include a way to create and modify the model itself. You can usually do so directly or by using the drawing tools included in the CASE application.

When you build a software system by using UML, you work out your classes by using the drawings. In the process, you are creating and modifying the model and the drawings simultaneously. But the model itself is still a separate entity from the diagrams.

A good CASE tool has two ways of looking at your system: The first is through the model itself, which is often depicted as an Explorer-style tree, with the classes and their members listed. The second is through the diagrams. You can use the diagrams to add information to the model; for example, you can use a class diagram to add classes and modify the member variables and functions.

Most CASE tools have a slight catch: If you remove a class from a diagram, you don't actually remove it from the model. The class is still in the model, just in case you still want to continue working on it and add it to more diagrams. If you *really* want to remove a class, you have to go to the model itself and remove the class. Fortunately, this applies only to removing classes. You can modify and add classes from the diagrams.

In UML, you can use sixteen types of diagrams that are part of the actual specification and eight types of diagrams that are commonly used, but not part of the specification. (You can see a listing of these diagrams and how they relate to each other at `http://www.uml-diagrams.org/uml-25-diagrams.html`.) As you work on these diagrams, your model will evolve. You can make changes to the diagrams, and thereby make changes to the underlying model.

This book simplifies things by working with only nine of the available diagram types. In fact, most software projects will never use more than these nine types. Tables 2-1 and 2-2 show you the nine diagram types. We grouped them into two kinds: *static* and *dynamic*. The static diagrams (also called structure diagrams) represent the parts of the software system you are building. The dynamic diagrams (also called behavior diagrams) show how the parts work together and how things take place over time.

The words *static* and *dynamic* come up again and again in the computer world. *Static* refers to something fixed and unchanging, while *dynamic* refers to something that changes:

✦ In your application, a class is static because you describe it in your code; and after you have described your class, it does not change while the application is running. A class has a certain set of member variables and member functions that you specify in the code. Although the application is running, the members of a class do not change.

✦ The objects, however, are considered to be dynamic, because they can come to life while the application is running, their member variables can change, and they can be deleted.

Table 2-1	Static Diagrams of UML
Diagram Type	*What It Shows*
Class diagram	The different classes
Component diagram	The different parts of the system; each part contains classes related to each other
Deployment diagram	The different computers and hardware involved

The following list describes the items in Table 2-1 in a bit more detail:

✦ **Class diagram:** The class diagram shows the different classes and their relationships to each other. For example, a class diagram might show that the class called Skiddle is derived from the class Skaddle, and it might show that the class Skaddle contains as a member a list of Ruddle instances. Typically as you work on a class diagram, you will also be adding and modifying the classes from the model itself.

✦ **Component diagram:** The component diagram shows the major parts of your software system. For example, all the parts dealing with Discombobulation, including the Discombobulator class and the Perturburator class as well as other related classes, might all be grouped into a single component called SuperSystem.

✦ **Deployment diagram:** The deployment diagram shows a hardware view of your system. This might include specific computers (such as a Compaq Presario with a gigabyte of RAM), or it might include more abstract hardware components, such as *Internet connection*. Or it might show hardware components even more generic, such as *network node* or *database server*. Nevertheless, these are all hardware components.

In Windows, a single component often lives in the form of a Dynamic Link Library, or DLL for short. (Other operation systems use a DLL-like component called a function library or simply a library.) Most DLLs that you find on your computer were built as components. When you use multiple DLLs that other people built, you are building with various software components. You can show these components on a component diagram.

Table 2-2	Dynamic Diagrams of UML
Diagram Type	*What It Shows*
Use case diagram	The different functions of the software system
Object diagram	Instances of the classes and their relationships to each other
Collaboration diagram	How instances work together with other instances
Sequence diagram	The time sequence of objects working together with other objects
Statechart diagram	The lifecycle of a single object in terms of states
Activity diagram	A sequence of steps; much like a flowchart

The following list describes the dynamic diagrams in a bit more detail:

✦ **Use case diagram:** The use case diagram shows the different individual functions that the software package can perform. Here we mean *function* in a generic sense, like a process, not like a C++ function consisting of a set of code. A word processor might have a use case called *Set italic.* This use case represents the function of setting the italic style for the highlighted text. A Web browser might have a use case called *Go,* which takes a Web address and pulls down and displays the appropriate Web page.

✦ **Object diagram:** The object diagram describes the instances of the classes. This is in contrast to the class diagram, which shows the classes but not the actual instances. The reason that the object diagram is considered a dynamic diagram rather than a static diagram is because objects themselves are considered dynamic. Objects can change while the application is running. Classes, on the other hand, do not change while the application is running.

✦ **Collaboration diagram:** As your application runs, the code for an object's member function might call a member function in another object. In this sense, the two objects are working together, or *collaborating*, just as two people might collaborate to rob a bank. A collaboration diagram shows how the different objects collaborate.

✦ **Sequence diagram:** A sequence shows the collaborations of the objects over time. So if your application is a model of two bank robbers failing because they get into a severe argument over which door to leave the bank through, and you have two objects that represent the two bank robbers, this diagram would show them calling each other's member functions over time. These functions might be things like `Insult()` and `Criticize()` and `PolitelyDisagree()`.

✦ **Statechart diagram:** A statechart diagram is like a sequence diagram, but it shows only one object. It shows how an object changes over time, from the time it is created until it is deleted.

✦ **Activity diagram:** An activity diagram shows the step-by-step nature of a single member function. It is actually a type of statechart:

- A *statechart diagram* shows how an *object* changes from state to state.

- An *activity diagram* shows how a *member function* moves from one activity to the next. In that sense, each state in the activity diagram is an activity.

**Book II
Chapter 2**

**Describing Your
Program with UML**

In the world of UML, when an object's member function calls a member function of a second object, the process is called *sending a message*. The first object sends a message to the second object. This terminology is not new to UML; the original object-oriented language, Smalltalk, used the same terminology. In Smalltalk, objects sent messages to other objects. You use a collaboration diagram to show how one object *sends a message to* another object. Or you can say that the collaboration diagram shows member functions calling the member functions of other objects. They both mean the same thing.

A popular word among software engineers is *lifecycle*. Really, the word basically means life. A software development process has a lifecycle: You start building the software, go until it's all built, update the software as needed, and then retire the software when you're finished using it; that's the lifecycle of the project. However, in many senses, it does cycle back: You get bug reports from customers, and you fix the bugs, and you eventually release another version of the software. Objects have lifecycles, too: When you create an instance, you are beginning the life of the object. Then, during the object's lifecycle, you do things to the object like call its member functions and modify its member variables. Then, when you're finished, you delete the object. That finishes the lifecycle.

Software engineers like to think in terms of states. A *state* is simply the current situation in which something exists, like the state of the nation or the state of affairs. These represent the current situation for the nation or the affairs. Or somebody could be in a state of all-out confusion. That represents the current state the person is in. An object also has a particular state: The `Caboodle` class might have member variables `PenCount` and `NotebookCount`, which represent the number of pens and the number of notebooks inside an instance of the `Caboodle` class. A particular instance of the `Caboodle` class might have the value 7 for `PenCount` and the value 3 for `NotebookCount`. Thus, the current state of this particular instance is `PenCount=7, NotebookCount=3`. The `Caboodle` class might also include a member function called `AddPen()`, which takes no parameters and simply adds 1 to `PenCount`. When you call `AddPen()`, you are *changing the state of the object.*

When you consider the state of an object, you need to look at only the member variables. The values of the member variables together represent the state. The member functions may modify the state, but because the functions themselves do not change during the life of the application, they do not represent part of the object's state. Also, remember that one object can contain as a member another object. The current state of the outer object would include the state of the object that it contains.

In the world of UML, the concept of a *metadescription* comes up again and again. *Meta* is a prefix to a word, and it usually means *the next level up.* For example, with metadescription, we could first describe a tree by writing information about the tree. Then we could describe the description: "It was a beautiful paragraph with flowing words that brought the tree to life." Now that previous sentence itself is what we are referring to right now in this sentence. Do you see what is happening here? We're describing something, and then we describe the description, and then we describe *that* description. Each time we move up "one level of abstraction." The term *metadescription,* then, means a description of a description.

In UML, you encounter meta terminology all the time. For example, a class represents a type of object. But the word *class* is a kind of classifier. Another kind of classifier is *type.* So consider this somewhat philosophical concept: A class is a kind of classifier, at least from the perspective of the UML diagrams. But a particular class itself has certain attributes about it, such as the class name and the names and types of the members. That information is a *metaclass.* If you're not totally confused and you find this fascinating, we highly recommend reading *Gödel, Escher, Bach: An Eternal Golden Braid*, by Douglass R. Hofstadter (Basic Books, 1999) or, for a slightly easier read, *Metamagical Themas: Questing for the Essence of Mind and Pattern*, also by Hofstadter (Basic Books, 1996).

Building with UML and the Rational Unified Process

UML is not a methodology. That means that UML, by itself, is not a step-by-step process for building software. Rather, you can think of UML as a language you use for describing your software as you are building it. The language, however, is not a verbal talking language with a bunch of engineers in a room yelling and arguing. Yes, that sometimes happens, but fortunately it's neither a part of UML nor required. UML is a visual language. There's that adage about a picture being worth a whole bunch of words, or something like that, and it holds up here, too. You describe your software with diagrams. These diagrams provide a full description of your software.

But you create the diagrams as you move through a process. The process *is* a methodology that you use; the one that we use and describe in this book is known as the Rational Unified Process, or RUP. There are five main steps (which tend to be the same for most methodologies). These main steps, which are called *workflows,* are as follows:

1. Requirements
2. Analysis
3. Design
4. Implementation
5. Testing

When you think of the steps you would do to accomplish pretty much anything that's not computer-related, you can probably see that you often use these steps.

For example, suppose that you're going to build a time warp device so you can skip that dentist appointment next week. First, you decide what you need to build; this is called the *requirement collection.* In this case, you need a device that takes you forward into time, probably a specified amount of time. So you'll want a display on the device and a keypad so you can enter the amount of time to move forward. And you'll probably need a button to start the time warp. Those are the requirements for the project.

Then you think about how you're going to do the time warp and what you'll need, and you analyze the project. In this case, you'll need the actual time warping portion consisting of the relativistic universe bender as well as the main interface portion, where you get to control the thing. This step is called the *analysis.*

Next, you begin carefully designing the invention but not actually building it. This is the meat of your work, where you draw diagrams of what you'll be building and how the different parts work out. You draw how your particular version of the relativistic universe bender works and the parts involved in it as well as all the other major components of the system. This is the *design* step.

Then you build, or *implement,* the thing. This is the fun part, where you go into the shop and start hammering and pounding and defying gravity to build the device! And of course, this step is called the *implementation.*

But you're not finished yet; finally, you have to *test* it. For this, you pay off the guy next door to take a ride in your time machine to see whether it works. If not, he can report back to you and let you know what went wrong. (Assuming that he makes it back.)

Now this is all good, but some issues can come up that these basic five steps don't handle. For example, many people who try building a large software system quickly discover the chicken-and-egg syndrome. The problem is this: If we're in the middle of the analysis workflow and we're supposed to be getting our rough classes down, how can we possibly know all the classes we're going to need until we get down into the code and start writing the thing?

For this reason, many people have the attitude *skip engineering and just code the stupid thing!* But just imagine what your time warp device would be like if you tried to build it without planning it. After you get the thing completely built (more or less), do you really *trust* it? Would you take a ride in it, rather than just pay the unsuspecting neighbor? Well the same is true for software. If you just dive in and start grinding out code, racing for the finish line, how can you be sure that you covered everything? Did you miss anything? Most likely. And does what you wrote run perfectly? Doubtful.

Fortunately, there's a way to fit everything together. It uses steps called *iterations*.

Speaking iteratively

Suppose we want to build a new kind of Web browser. This Web browser will be super-smart and will just automatically know what Web site you want to go to by tapping into your brain waves. When you wake up in the morning, you will hear your ears ringing with the message of a faint distant phrase, "Where do you want to go?" You think, "Wouldn't it be fun to see the Smithsonian?" Then you walk to your computer, sit down, and first the browser brings up the site for the Smithsonian, and then it brings up a site that shows flights, hotels, rental car information, and maps to get there. Now wouldn't that be a seriously cool Web browser?

So, being a good engineer, you follow the formal steps of building it. You draw your requirements, and you even interview your friends to see what ideas they have about such an amazing work of software. Then you analyze the different parts and come up with the functionality of the software, and you even draw some sample screens. Next, you move into the design workflow, fleshing out the basic classes you built in the analysis workflow. And finally, you begin coding. You code for weeks, when suddenly — WHAM! — you discover that something is *seriously* wrong: You completely forgot that you need to write a portion of the software that does the grunt work of connecting to the Internet, then to a specific site, and downloading the appropriate Web page. In effect, you failed to consider the low-level *communications portion* of your super-cool application. And while ruminating over this problem, you also start to think of some other things you failed to consider earlier: After you receive the Web page, are you going to draw it on the screen, or are you going to buy some C++ library that will display it in a window for you? The latter would make your life easier, but regardless, you had not considered this.

That's when you get frustrated and start considering that position your cousin offered you to be a mime out in front of City Hall downtown, drawing customers in to buy hotdogs from your cousin's hotdog stand in front of the Hall of Justice.

What exactly happened? Here's what happened:

1. You didn't realize until coding time that the display part of the browser, the part that shows the Web page on the screen, would be extremely complicated and might require the purchase of a library that displays the browser pages for you.

2. You didn't even consider that you would need a low-level communications system. Or did you? Maybe your operating system already provides it. But either way, you hadn't thought of that during the analysis or design workflow.

As you dwell on these problems, you notice more *bad things*. For starters, if you decide to do the low-level communications system, do you make it its own library that you could potentially use in other applications? Or do you buy a library? Or is one already available on the computer? You've heard that your operating system has such things built-in, but you're not sure.

So you know *what* happened, but *why* did it happen? Finally, you put your finger on it: It's another chicken-and-egg syndrome, and it goes like this: How could you have known you needed a low-level communications system until you finally started coding the thing? Yet, you needed that information while you were in the analysis and design workflows, before you started coding it! In effect, which comes first, the chicken (the analysis and design) or the egg (the realization that you need a low-level communications system)?

Although this might sound horribly apocryphal, it happens all the time in the software world. If you want to see tempers flare, visit some software engineers when such an abysmal situation arises.

Well, we think we've made our point, but before you rush off to the psychiatrist for a nice, big supply of antidepressants, fear not: RUP is here to save the day!

The designers of RUP knew well that these problems occur. And thus, they made a set of higher-level processes called *phases,* and put the five workflows inside these higher levels. During each phase, you cycle through several of the five workflows. Then when you're finished, you can cycle through them again, or you can move on to the next phase. And you once again cycle through several of the five workflows.

The idea is that each time you cycle through several of the workflows, you finish an *iteration.*

Phasing in and out

RUP consists of four main phases. In each phase, you focus on various workflows, such as analysis or design, but you are free to move forward to later workflows. The only catch is that, although you can start and stop at any workflow, you must complete all the workflows in between for a single iteration. For example, you can't jump from analysis to test; you must first do analysis, then design, then implementation, and finally test. Here are the phases of RUP:

- ✦ **Inception:** During this phase, you determine the objectives of your software.

- ✦ **Elaboration:** In this phase, you analyze and design your software.

- ✦ **Construction:** This is when you focus primarily on coding the software.

- ✦ **Transition:** This final phase is when you deliver the software. For retail software, this means sending it to the disc duplicators and packagers; for in-house software, it means shipping it to the groups who will be using it.

And here's the really great part: Each of these four phases can be a whole set of workflows: Requirements, analysis, design, implementation, and testing. *But how can that be, my dear friend*, you ask? It goes like this: In the inception phase, you gather requirements and go through the process of getting some basic analysis and design down. And if need be, you even do some rough prototypes of the software, where you basically play around and try out some things. In effect, you do a basic coding (implementation). And yes, you might even spend a little time testing it. But you're not building a full-scale software system, by any means! You're just doing pieces and parts and parts and pieces. But more so, you're doing a *proof of concept* just to see if you think, as a professional engineer, this idea is going to fly. And undoubtedly, you will run into some issues that the original requirements failed to take into account.

For example, suppose that you're going to build a word processor application that beats Microsoft Word hands down. Now, if you have used Microsoft Word and opened up a really big document (like several hundred pages), you may have noticed something happens on occasion. Sometimes when you make a substantial change that will drastically affect the page count, such as changing the margins, Microsoft Word *repaginates*. And as it repaginates, you might find that some vital paragraphs get split, with maybe one line of text at the end of one page and the rest of the paragraph on the next page. That can create an ugly document, and thus, Microsoft Word includes a feature called *Keep paragraphs together* as an option in a dialog box.

Now if you're building a word processor, it's possible that you won't think of this hair-splitting, paragraph-splitting issue until well into the coding. So what do you do? Most likely, during one of the first two phases, after you have a basic prototype, you might notice that sometimes paragraphs are getting broken up at inconvenient places. The solution? Include an option to keep paragraphs together. And so you go back to the requirements and add a piece to the required functionality: an option for keeping paragraphs together.

Now if you're building a super-cool Web browser that specializes in mind-reading, during the inception phase you might do a basic prototype that has all the major features, even if they don't work well. But during that time, you spot something you left out: the communications system. But now you know that you need it! So you return to the analysis phase, where you can actually add it, perhaps as a component. Cool, no?

Now each time you backtrack through your workflows and change some-thing, you begin a new iteration. Therefore, you can see that the phases are broken up into iterations, each with several of the five workflows. And you may go through several iterations within a single phase.

You don't have to get all the way to the end, to the testing workflow, before you back up. Thus, each iteration might consist of only one or two workflows.

If all this sounds a little strange, look at it this way: If you discover that you don't have something quite right, what do you do? You go back and fix it! But software engineers like to sound a bit more technical than that, so instead they say that they *begin a new iteration*.

The inception phase

The *inception phase* is the first phase, where you start getting things off the ground. During this phase, you may not make it to the point where you're coding a prototype and finding problems. But if you're building a big project, you just may make it to the point of coding a prototype. However, if you are, you will probably be writing small prototypes of only various portions of the project.

Book II
Chapter 2

Describing Your
Program with UML

And during the inception phase, you try to do the following:

✦ **Determine whether the project is feasible.** The term *feasibility* is a word that comes up again and again, and it's primarily the result of people having great ideas but later determining that, well, frankly, those ideas are not practical or reasonable. But instead, businesses prefer the kinder, gentler term, *feasible*.

✦ **Determine the primary requirements.**

Requirements gathering is a particularly touchy issue because, during that time, people are going to want to include everything. Not only will they want the software to browse the Web, but they will also want it to inject the Web page back into your brain and also give you the ability to download it straight from your brain to your friends' brains and print a copy by just laying your finger on the printer. They want the software to do *everything*.

But thankfully, during this time, you start to map out the project, probably build some prototypes, and determine what it really *should* do. Is it feasible to transfer the pages back into the brain, or is that technology not going to come for another year or two? If not, it probably isn't feasible.

The goal in this phase is to solidify the requirements and do some basic analysis. During this time, you will get people to agree to what it is you're going to build. (These people are called *stakeholders* because they hold a big stake — like their *jobs* — in the success of this software. And when you finish writing it for them and they become millionaires, they will treat themselves to a nice, big steak.) You will also get them to agree on things such as what computers the software will run on and the software's limits. For example, can the browser read multiple people's brains or just one person's brain at a time? (That's a *limit*.) And will it run on Windows, or will it also run on Macintosh, Unix, and Linux?

And, of course, the business folks will want a bit of say in all this, too. So the goals of this phase will also include things such as a schedule and cost for the project: How soon will you have it completed, and how much will it cost the business? Will you need to hire more engineers to work on the project? And will you need to buy more computers and tools, such as compilers?

And finally at the end of this phase, you will want to have a basic architecture of the system, consisting of UML diagrams. Now these diagrams may be rough and basic, but they will provide an overall outline of the system.

The elaboration phase

During the *elaboration phase,* you solidify the functionality of your software. You use tools called *use cases* — descriptions of individual pieces of the software functionality. For example, a word processor would have use cases such as *set italic on, set italic off, print, set left-align,* and *delete a page.* The use cases are all the things you can do with the software.

Also during the elaboration phase, you develop a plan for when you build the thing. This means elaborating on the basic designs you created in the inception phase by going through more analysis and design.

Some of the major goals of the elaboration phase are to finalize the scope of the software and to incorporate any changes to the software (for example, after further inspection, you may have determined that more things were not feasible and that other parts were); to finalize the project plan, including the number of people you need and how long it will take; and to make sure the stakeholders are all happy and hunky-dory with the project.

And during the elaboration phase, you also create a first, rough-draft version of the software. Yes, you may have built some code in the inception phase, but that was just prototyping for determining feasibility. You don't use that rough code from the inception phase in the real coding. Here, however, you make a first run of coding the real application. To get there, you continue with your analysis and design, and get into coding (implementation). Of course, the software is just a rough draft, but it is more than a prototype; unlike the preceding phase, in the elaboration phase you'll be saving much of the code and reusing it for the next phase. Thus, you once again move through iterations, cycling through workflows, such as analysis, design, and implementation.

The construction phase

During the *construction phase,* you continue with the implementation. But by now, all your analysis and design should be pretty much finished. Everybody (including the famous stakeholders) agrees by now on what the software will and won't do, how much it will cost, how long it will take to build it, and how many people will work on it. But further, you have drawn up your groups of classes that you will be designing and have decided how the classes fit together and how they communicate with each other. The analysis and design is ready for prime time, and now you can focus on actually making the system work. Here you look for parts that don't quite fit together, and you fix problems to make them fit together. You make sure that your system has no major holes whereby the entire thing could come to a crashing halt under a strange, unexpected situation. In a word, you make your software *stable.*

If you were involved with computers in the early 1990s, when things were finally settling down and we were starting to see practical, real software, you probably also saw something else: little error messages that popped up called *general protection faults (GPFs)*. GPFs appeared when the application *really screwed up bad,* and the only way to fix the application was to attempt to click the Ignore button to *ignore* the error (an option that, trust us, never worked) or *abort* the application. We remember those days well because they made us start to consider job offers from distant cousins who rented beach umbrellas on the Gulf of Mexico.

Now why did these errors happen? Because the software wasn't *stable*. You managed to put the software into a situation that the programmers didn't expect, and the thing choked, coughing up a general protection fault. And why did the programmers create software that allowed this situation to occur? Because they didn't thoroughly go through the construction phase!

The construction phase includes *implementation* and *testing* workflows. You may have some analysis and design flaws, but they will be little; the main time you'll see these flaws is if you find you forgot something or need to change something in the classes. By now, you will be going through iterations of writing code, testing, testing, testing, and finally more testing. When the testers encounter errors, you go back and fix the code. Then, eventually, the testers determine that they can't find any more bugs. The day is done! You are ready to ship.

Thus, if you follow the construction phase properly, you will limit the number of operating system errors that pop up when your application goes haywire — because if you did everything correctly, it shouldn't go haywire.

If you are heading up a project where you will be using RUP to design a large-scale software system, you will want to give your testers a certain amount of authority. Think of the testers as the quality assurance people. And in fact, some companies call them *Q/A engineers* instead of testers. Your testers shouldn't allow your company to put its name on the software until they say it *works*. This has multiple benefits because it allows the Q/A engineers to feel a certain amount of authority, and it also puts a heavy responsibility on them, which will help ensure that they do a *thorough* job. And that will help ensure that your software is both good and stable. Sounds like a good plan to us!

The transition phase

The *transition phase* is both the happiest time and the scariest. As a software engineer, we know that this can be a frightening time because the final moment of truth has arrived: Did you and the rest of the team build a product that is actually going to work? Or is it going to get out on the customer's computer and crash and burn?

Most likely, because you did everything correctly in the first three phases, the software will run on the customer's computers. However, just because you did it right doesn't mean that you won't be anxious. But relax: If you are shipping a piece of software to one specific customer, you and the other engineers will probably be on hand that day for the big installation. It may not go perfectly at first, but in our experience most of the problems will not involve faulty software. Rather, the customer's computers will not be set up quite right. Fortunately, such problems are pretty easy to track down and fix.

But if you're shipping software that will be sold through the retail chains to potentially millions of people, the transition phase has an important step that many companies don't think of. In this final step, you choose a workday and invite all the employees who want to come in for a giant beat-up-the-software party. Yeah! They all come in, and you pass out CD-ROMs containing your software. These are copies of the CD-ROM you intend to ship, assuming that all goes well today. The employees get free pizza and soft drinks (beer isn't allowed on company property; besides, you want them thinking clearly!), and they get to beat the stuffing out of your software. They install it, play with it, manipulate it, use it, fiddle with it, and do everything they can with it; and in the process, give it a pounding it will never forget. And if they encounter a problem, they let you know (politely, of course). But your personal job, on this day, is not to join them in testing the software. Your job is to get to work fixing any problems they find. Generally, they will be minor problems, and you'll be able to crank out the fixes in no time.

If you actually have a big test day like this, try to make it as exciting as possible. Free pizza, free soft drinks, maybe loud, fun music blasting, and maybe a relaxation room where people can go and goof off for a few minutes and forget about the project. Believe us, these folks will enjoy this special day if you make it exciting for them. And the result, of course, is a successful software package.

Moving Forward with UML

Although you spend much of the time on the construction phase, a lot of the brainwork is in the analysis and design phases. That's where UML comes into play. You use UML to map your classes, draw them, work with them, and design them. Therefore, for the rest of Minibook II, you find various discussions about UML and processes that usually take place during analysis and design. However, some take place during the requirements phase.

The next two chapters focus on the nine types of diagrams you use during your requirements gathering, analysis, and design. The first chapter focuses on the static diagrams, and the next chapter focuses on the dynamic diagrams.

Chapter 3: Structuring Your Classes with UML

In This Chapter

✔ Drawing classes in UML

✔ Drawing inheritance and other relationships

✔ Building components with UML

✔ Deploying the software

*W*hen you use the Unified Modeling Language (UML) to design software, your diagrams have two aspects: One is *static*, and the other is *dynamic*. The static diagrams represent the things that do not change while your application is running. For example, a class does not change while the application is running. When you write the code, you write the class name, member variables, and member functions, and you notate what is private, protected, and public. After you compile the application, this information does not change; it remains static. This is in contrast to the information you represent in the dynamic diagrams, where the information can change. Dynamic diagrams include things like object creation and deletion as well as object collaborations (objects working together, or collaborating, conspiring, plotting, and scheming, like good little classes).

In this chapter, we discuss the three types of static diagrams:

✦ **Class diagram:** A class diagram represents the different classes in your application.

✦ **Component diagram:** A component diagram represents the major parts, or components, of your application.

✦ **Deployment diagram:** A deployment diagram represents the different computers and hardware that your application will ultimately run on.

In this chapter, we talk about the UML diagrams. And although you'll rarely hear us say this, one thing we don't talk much about (at least, not in this chapter) is the methodology. (We cover that topic in Book II, Chapter 2.) UML is a *language* you use to design software. A *methodology* is the process you use to design software. The process we recommend is the Rational Unified Process (RUP). In this chapter, we discuss the diagrams, and we mention the parts of the process where you might use the diagrams, so you get to make lots of pretty pictures.

Drawing Classes

Like so many things around us, objects can hold other objects inside of them. For instance, an alligator may have inside it . . . well, that's probably not the best example. Rather, a printer object would have a toner cartridge inside it. These could be separate objects, each belonging to its own class. One might be the `LaserPrinter` class, and the other might be the `TonerCartridge` class.

In this sense, the two classes are connected. The connection is not by inheritance; nevertheless, they have a *relationship*.

You can take this relationship a step further. We have a container of blank, writeable CD-ROMs (or CD-Rs). The container can be an instance of class `CDROMHolder`. The items inside the container might each be an instance of class `CDR`. In this case, a single instance of `CDROMHolder` might contain several instances of `CDR`. So whereas the `LaserPrinter` instance contains a single `TonerCartridge` instance, the `CDROMHolder` contains several `CDR` instances. Another example is the class `Porsche` that's parked in our driveways. It contains exactly four instances of `GoodyearTire`. (Yes, we're dreaming.) And so you can see several possibilities here:

+ **Exactly one instance:** An instance of a class might contain exactly one instance of another class.

+ **Fixed amount of instances, greater than 1:** Each instance of a class might contain an exact number of instances of another class. This number does not change between instances.

+ **Varying number of instances:** Each instance of a class might have a different number of instances of another class. This amount might vary from instance to instance, and it might even change over time for a single instance.

As for the final item, you can see that when we remove a `CDR` instance from the `CDROMHolder` instance, the number of instances the holder contains decreases by 1. Or if we put a `CDR` instance back, the holder goes up by 1. If we buy more and refill the holder, it goes up by more than 1. But with the `Porsche` that we truly believe is parked outside, the number of tires stays the same.

As you analyze the classes to build your application, you might find some disagreement here: When we go to buy new tires, the car is raised off the ground, and mechanics remove the old tires, one by one, until no tires are on the car. Then they install new tires, one by one. Thus, the number of tires isn't fixed throughout the life of the instance. But how you build your class depends on the needs of the people using the application. You need to consider that aspect, and you can therefore treat the number of tires as fixed. Or you may need to include the tire's replacements, in which case you would not treat the number as fixed.

And here's another example: If you're writing an application for a racing game or simulator, you may want to have the ability for wrecks to occur and tires to come off the car. Then you would need to vary the tire count.

How you design your classes depends on the situation. Always assuming the same thing for a similarly named class as it appears in different applications is not practical. Some applications may require a class to be different from a class in another application, even though both classes happen to have a similar name.

Another kind of relationship is inheritance. The `LaserPrinter` class might be derived from the `Printer` class.

Inheritance can also be complex. You may have a class and also have two classes derived from it. One of these two classes might have two classes derived from it, and another might have only one. And from there, you might have no more classes derived. C++ offers great flexibility.

You can look at design issues in another way. A class is a kind of *classifier*. In this regard, you can imagine an inheritance showing different words for *kind*. One would be *class,* and one would be *classifier.* Then *class* is derived from *classifier.* Another classifier is *type*, and therefore *type* would be derived from *classifier* as well. (Remember that integers are types, for example.) From this perspective of the *metainformation* or *metadata,* you can think of `int` as an instance of the classifier *type.* And you can think of `LaserPrinter` as an instance of the classifier *class.* And the particular printer on our desks, then, is an instance of `LaserPrinter`. This requires an abstract way of looking at things, but if you can keep up with this system, you're ready for some serious class designs. That's because you'll understand how classes all fit together in the greater scheme of things.

Mapping classes with UML

You can create a UML diagram that shows several classes and their various relationships. Take a look at Figure 3-1. This figure shows three classes: `Printer`, `LaserPrinter`, and `TonerCartridge`. Pay close attention to the lines connecting these three classes. The lines are different because these classes relate to each other in different ways.

Figure 3-1:
The lines
pointing
between
the classes
show
different
kinds of
relationships.

First, the line connecting `Printer` and `LaserPrinter` shows inheritance. The fat, hollow arrow points to the base class. Thus, `LaserPrinter` is derived from `Printer`.

Although you won't hear us use this term much, an opposite to the term *derived from* is *generalize*. Thus, if `LaserPrinter` is derived from `Printer`, another way to say this is that `Printer` generalizes `LaserPrinter`. The idea is that `Printer` is a general form of `LaserPrinter`, and `LaserPrinter` is a specific form of `Printer`. The reason we prefer not to use the term *generalize* is that when you create a hierarchy of classes, you typically create the base class first. Then you derive a new class. So to us, the term *generalize* is counterintuitive. And our brains don't do well with counterintuitive ideas. (However, we should add, in all fairness, that a common way to come up with classes is by noticing similarities between two classes and then coming up with a single class to serve as a base class. So, in this sense, generalization makes sense.)

Now look at the line connecting `LaserPrinter` to `TonerCartridge`. This is called a *composition,* and this word means that the two classes are *associated.* (Think of composition as a strong bond between two objects.) Therefore, each `LaserPrinter` instance will contain exactly one `TonerCartridge` instance. How you implement this later is your choice, but most likely you will include in the `LaserPrinter` class a pointer to a `TonerCartridge` instance.

In this second line, the end with the filled diamond refers to the *whole* that *contains* the *part.* Thus, `LaserPrinter` is the whole, and it contains the part `TonerCartridge`. Notice also that two numbers are below the composition line. The one on the left means that one `LaserPrinter` instance is in the association, and the one on the right means that one `TonerCartridge` instance is in the association.

Now look at Figure 3-2. Here, you have a diamond and a line, which again mean *composition*. But this time the Porsche class has a 1 by it, and the GoodyearTire class has a 4 by it. This combination means that exactly one instance of Porsche will have exactly four instances of GoodyearTire. In other words, one car has four tires.

**Book II
Chapter 3**

**Structuring Your
Classes with UML**

Figure 3-2:
The diamond and the line combined mean composition.

Next, look at Figure 3-3. Again, you see an association, but this time it is between the Pasture class and the Cow class. But in this case, the Pasture class has a 1 by it, and the Cow class has an asterisk (*) by it. The asterisk indicates that any number of Cow instances can be associated with any single Pasture instance. In other words, a single pasture can have multiple cows running around on it. When you put an asterisk in the UML diagram, it indicates that any number of instances can be in the association, including 0. Therefore, a Pasture might have no cows in it (they're all in the barn being milked), or just 1 might be in the pasture, or 100 cows may be out in the pasture, lounging around.

Figure 3-3:
Many instances of the class with the * nearby can be associated with the class with the 1 nearby.

Other possibilities for denoting the number of items in a relationship are also available. These possibilities are called *multiplicities*. Table 3-1 lists them.

Attributes and methods

In the object-oriented world, you're likely to hear two words many times over: attribute and method. An *attribute* is simply a member variable, and a *method* is just another name for *member function.* These two terms are the official UML terms. However, most people in C++ usually don't use them, except perhaps when drawing UML diagrams. Instead, most C++ programmers prefer the terms *member variables* and *member functions.* You can use whichever terms you prefer, and whichever terms you hear other people saying. In this book, we use *attribute* and *method* when talking specifically about UML diagrams and not referring to C++ code.

Table 3-1	Multiplicities
Symbols	*What They Mean*
1	Exactly one instance
n	Exactly *n* instances (where *n* is any number)
m..n	Anywhere from *m* to *n* instances allowed; 0..1 or 1..10, for example
*	Any number of instances, including 0
0..*	Any number of instances, including 0 (same as *)

For example, if you have two classes, one called `Vacuum` and another called `ExtensionTube`, and you see a 1 on the side with `Vacuum` and a 1..4 on the side of `ExtensionTube`, that means for each (1) instance of `Vacuum`, you can have anywhere from one to four (`1..4`) instances of `ExtensionTube`.

But wait. We thought these class diagrams were supposed to be static, not dynamic! And that's true: They are still static diagrams, although the line between static and dynamic is blurred. We could go into a big philosophical explanation about why class diagrams are indeed static (for example, you write a class that contains a single array, and that does not change), but instead, let us say this: Just consider a class diagram to be static, and recognize that some blurry distinctions exist. It's not a big deal.

Inheriting in UML

If you want to specify inheritance in UML, you simply draw an arrow from the derived class up to the base class and don't fill in the arrow. But you can show other types of inheritance with UML.

If you want to specify that a base class has abstract virtual functions, you specify those in the class by using italics. For example, Figure 3-4 shows a base class called `Person`. This is an abstract class because it contains an abstract virtual function: `work()`. The function is *abstract virtual* because it is in italics. (And thus the class itself is virtual. Remember that a class that has at least one abstract virtual function is therefore itself abstract.)

Figure 3-4:
You can show abstract classes in UML by putting a method in italics.

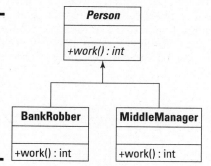

**Book II
Chapter 3**

**Structuring Your
Classes with UML**

The two classes derived from `Person`, `BankRobber` and `MiddleManager` (we just thought those made for an interesting combination) each override the `work()` function. Therefore, they are *not* abstract. And thus you can create instances of `BankRobber` and `MiddleManager`.

You may have noticed that, so far, we have not mentioned a way to specify a virtual function in UML. You can specify a member function as abstract, but what about plain old virtual? You can't. The `virtual` keyword is unique to C++, and the word simply means that you can override a function. So how do you specify virtual? Many CASE tools include an option in the model that lets you specify a member function as virtual.

Aggregating and composing classes

When you associate two classes but not by inheritance, you can do it in two common ways: composition and aggregation. Consider the `LaserPrinter` class and its association with the `TonerCartridge` class. A toner cartridge is a fundamental part of a laser printer, but a toner cartridge can't be inside more than one laser printer at a time. This is composition.

Aggregation, on the other hand, refers to two objects that are more loosely connected. In an office, you may find hundreds of computers and a dozen or so laser printers. The laser printers can function on their own, and they interact with many different computers. Meanwhile, the computers can each interact with many different laser printers. This is a much looser connection; this is aggregation.

But this does *not* imply that composition is only for one-to-one relationships and that aggregation is for many-to-many. Instead, composition simply means a much stronger, tighter relationship. A toner cartridge is an intimate *part* of a printer and therefore is in a composition relationship. But a printer is not such a tightly integrated, important part of a computer. The computer can live without the printer, and vice versa, which suggests an aggregation.

In UML, you can distinguish the two based on the quality of the diamond. Doesn't that sound nice? However, in this case, we're talking about the diamond shape on the diagram, not an actual diagram. For composition, the diamond is filled in solid black. For aggregation, it's not filled in; it's just an outline. Figures 3-1 through 3-3 show composition. Figure 3-5 shows aggregation.

Figure 3-5:
When the diamond is not filled in, you have an aggregation.

Notice that Figure 3-5 has the same classes that we put in Figure 3-3. But this time the diamond is not filled in. This means that we modified the diagram to make it an aggregation rather than a composition.

Composition and attributes

A close similarity exists between a composition and an attribute. When each `LaserPrinter` instance has its own `TonerCartridge` instance, you have a choice: Draw a composition line between `LaserPrinter` and `TonerCartridge`, with the diamond on the side of `TonerCartridge`, or simply give the `LaserPrinter` class a member variable *(attribute)* of type `TonerCartridge`. After all, when you take the composition and write the code for the class, the composition manifests itself in the form of a member variable.

So which do you do? Really, it's up to you (but don't do both at once), though you must follow one rule. (And as we would like it with most rules and laws, this is not strict.) If you have a common class that you use throughout your application (one that you might think of as a utility class) and it appears as a member variable in many classes, you probably should make it an attribute rather than show it through a composition line, simply because it will prevent your diagrams from getting cluttered.

When you use UML, you can't have two diagrams showing two conflicting associations; thus, we can't have both Figure 3-3 and Figure 3-5 in a single UML model. A UML model must provide a consistent representation of all associations within that model, even when the association would be of a different type in another model.

Another way to look at composition is through ownership. If it makes sense for one object to own another object, this is composition. For example, one `LaserPrinter` instance would have its own `TonerCartridge` instance. Another `LaserPrinter` would have a *different* `TonerCartridge` instance. That is, the two `LaserPrinters` cannot share a single `TonerCartridge`. Thus, you can think of each `LaserPrinter` instance as owning a `TonerCartridge` instance. In that case, you can use composition.

Building Components

When you are building software, grouping various classes into *components* is often convenient. This means creating a library of classes. Most operating systems refer to these collections of classes as libraries, but Windows calls them Dynamic Link Libraries, or DLLs, for short. (It's unpronounceable, so we just say "Dee-El-El.") A *library* is simply a file that contains a bunch of code that other programs can use. The other programs load the library and then call its functions. But nothing particularly magical surrounds the library. It's just a bunch of compiled classes and functions stuffed into a single file. (And it's compiled; it's not source code.)

Or a component might end up in the form of something called a static library. A *static library* is much like any other library in that it contains a bunch of code for your application to use. However, when you build your application, the *linker* (which is the tool that performs the link process) combines the code in the static library directly into your final executable file. This means that your executable file will be bigger than it would be if you link it to a dynamic library; but when you link to a dynamic library, you need to either ship the dynamic library with your application or make sure it's already installed in the user's application. With a static library, you don't need to worry about it. (Incidentally, if you're using a Unix system, a static library gets the `.a` extension, which stands for *a*rchive, and a dynamic library gets the `.so` extension, which stands for *s*hared *o*bject.)

If you're doing some sophisticated programming, you can also group classes into a component that you will ultimately put into an ActiveX control or a Component Object Model (COM) object. (These are special kinds of libraries that run on Windows.)

Therefore, you can think of a *component* as a generic way to group classes. Figure 3-6 shows a component. It's a box with a couple of additional little boxes to its left. Inside this component called `MyLibrary`, you can see that we put two classes — one called `Safe` and one called `Lock`.

Figure 3-6:
A compo-
nent is a
box with
two smaller
boxes
added to its
left.

UML provides another way to notate components, as shown in Figure 3-7. Notice here that we have drawn the classes outside the component and have instead pointed dotted arrows at them from the component. We've also enclosed the word *reside* in double angle brackets. (The French use these *guillemets* in place of double quotes. Write it down in case somebody quizzes you on it.)

Figure 3-7:
Another
way to
notate
components
is to use
dotted
arrows that
point
from the
component
to the
classes.

Stereotyping

Most people accept that stereotyping is a bad thing, but in UML it's actually a good thing. In UML, you can take an existing symbol, such as the component symbol, and slightly modify it to make your own, customized version of the symbol. This modification process is called *stereotyping*. When you do so, you add a word inside the top of the component symbol. You put the word in double angle brackets, like this: << and >>. (Guillemets again — one for everybody!) In fact, in UML, anytime you see a word enclosed in guillemets, you're seeing a stereotype. Just think of a *stereotype* as a modified form of the symbol, or as your own version of the symbol.

When you create a component diagram, you can use stereotypes in your components. Think of it this way: Suppose you have several components that you'll build into a Windows DLL. (The same principle applies to other platforms and component container types.) Because the component symbol itself doesn't have anywhere to notate that it's a DLL, you can create your own *DLL component* symbol. You do this by putting a stereotype inside the component symbol. Figure 3-8 shows three components all working together. Two will ultimately be DLLs, and one will be the final executable file that calls into the DLLs. To show these, we stereotyped them all. Notice that because we're creating our own symbol, we can *reuse* the symbol. In this case, we used the DLL component symbol twice. If we have more executables, we can also reuse the executable component symbol.

Figure 3-8:
You can use
stereotypes
and show
different
components
working
together.

CASE tools differ on how you add stereotypes. With many tools, you use a menu item; and in a dialog box that opens, you add a name for the stereotype. Then you choose the base class. Now, don't confuse that with what you normally think of as a base class. We're talking about metainformation here. Look at it this way: You have a symbol, such as component. You're making your own, specialized symbol based on a component, called, for example, DLL component. This DLL component is, in a sense, derived from the component symbol. Thus, the base class in this hierarchy is the component symbol. And so, when you create a stereotype for a component, the base class is a component.

Before you make your own stereotype, first check to see if the stereotype already exists, perhaps by reviewing the documentation that comes with your CASE tool and any stereotypes already available at your organization. Many stereotypes are already available in UML. For example, in the CASE tool we're using, *executable* already exists for the component symbol.

In Figure 3-8, you can see how we used stereotypes to create a special DLL component symbol and a special executable component symbol. Notice also that we drew an arrow from the executable called `SpyProgram` to the two DLLs, called `AccountingLibrary` and `MathLibrary`. These arrows are dashed and have no stereotype associated with them. The dashed arrows indicate that they depend on the two libraries. Meanwhile, the two libraries each have two classes in them. To show that the classes reside in the libraries, we used a dependency arrow (again, a dashed line), but we used stereotypes to show that these are *residual* forms of the dependencies. So again, this is a special version of the symbol, which we denote through stereotypes.

Deploying the Software

During the design process, you can create a diagram that shows how your software will run and will be configured on the final computer system. In UML, the diagram you use is called a *deployment diagram.* This is a static diagram because the information in it does not change while the application is running.

Figure 3-9 shows an example of a deployment diagram. In this figure, we've included two nodes. In a hardware system, a *node* is any computer component. In this case, one node is a PC and the other node is a shared drive on the network. You can see in the diagram that the shared drive contains the two DLLs. The executable itself, however, resides on the user's PC. Note also that the components have connections between them because we used the same CASE model that we used in Figure 3-8. When we added the components to the two nodes, the CASE tool automatically drew the lines to connect them.

One particularly fun aspect of designing deployment diagrams is that the UML standard lets you make your own versions of the symbols. However, this creative capability goes beyond just stereotyping, where you add a word inside those funny-looking angle brackets. Instead, you can actually use clip art. (Yes, clip art!) Take a peek at Figure 3-10 to see an example.

Figure 3-9:
This
deployment
diagram has
two modes.

Figure 3-10:
You can be
creative
when
designing
your
deployment
diagrams.

Mac Pro

Dell XPS 8700

HP Officejet Pro 8600

Chapter 4: Demonstrating Behavior with UML

In This Chapter

✔ Drawing out objects in UML

✔ Expanding use cases into use case diagrams

✔ Ordering steps with sequence diagrams

✔ Showing how objects collaborate

✔ Noting the flow of activities

✔ Stating the different states of an object

*I*n this chapter, we walk you through the five dynamic diagrams in UML. These are the diagrams that show how objects work together and change over time. Some of them you may find more useful than others, and that's fine — you don't have to use all the diagrams you see in this chapter. You are free to use those that you find the most useful.

Drawing Objects

In UML, you can draw class diagrams that show the classes in your system, or you can get right down to it and draw an *object diagram,* which contains actual instances or objects. Because you are drawing instances, you might have multiple objects of a single class on a single object diagram.

When you draw objects on a UML diagram, they look pretty much the same as class diagrams, but with one important difference: For an object, the name at the top of the rectangle is <u>underlined</u>. With classes, the name is not underlined. Be sure to remember this difference so that your diagrams don't confuse other people. The best way to explore an object diagram is to see it compared to a class diagram. Take a peek at Figure 4-1 — you can see a class diagram at the top and an object diagram at the bottom.

Two classes are in the diagram. The names are not underlined, and the two classes are related by composition. The composition is *one-to-many* — one Pasture instance to multiple Cow instances, for example. In effect, instances of the Pasture class contain 0 or more instances of Cow. We've included some attributes for each class.

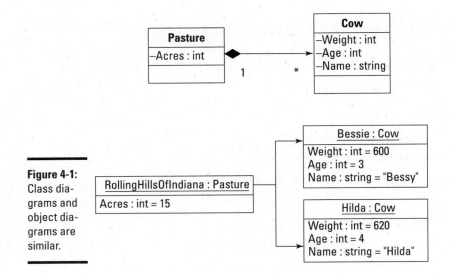

Figure 4-1:
Class diagrams and object diagrams are similar.

The lower half of the diagram shows instances of the classes. When you program, you sometimes give a name to an instance in the way of a variable name. Or you may be using a language that allows its objects to be named. (C++ does not allow this; you have to use a variable name.) In the object diagram, we named the instances. At the top of each rectangle is an underlined name, a colon, and the class type. Thus, RollingHillsOfIndiana is an instance of type Pasture. Bessie is an instance of type Cow, and Hilda is also an instance of type Cow. Inside the object boxes, we also gave values to the member variables (or attributes). For these, the name goes first, and then a colon, and then the type, just as in the class symbols. But then you see an equal sign and a value. (Because these are actual instances of the class, they can have values for the member variables.)

Look carefully at the line connecting the RollingHillsOfIndiana object to the Bessie and Hilda objects (as well as the line connecting the two classes). You can see an arrow pointing to each of the Cow instances but not to the Pasture instance. Thus, the Pasture instance contains a pointer to each Cow instance but not vice versa. That means the Cow instances don't know about the Pasture instances. That is, the Cow instance does not contain a member variable that points to the Pasture instance. You can see this is the case also with the class diagram, because an arrow is pointing to the Cow class.

If you want both instances to *know about* each other, you simply remove the arrows and use only lines. This change is called a *bidirectional association*. When you have an arrow, it indicates that the relationship is unidirectional. In the case of Pasture and Cow, the arrow indicates that the Pasture instance can call methods in the Cow instance but not vice versa. The Cow instances are not aware of the Pasture instance.

Sometimes, people really like to show that the objects are instances of the class by drawing a dashed arrow from the instance to the class and adding the <<instantiate>> stereotype. When you have lots of instances, this technique can make for a messy diagram, but if you have only one instance per class, you can easily show it in the diagram. We did just that in Figure 4-2. Notice that the word <<instantiate>> is present and that the arrow points to the class. To us, this setup seems a little backward, but lots of stuff seems backward in the world of computers, so we're not surprised.

**Book II
Chapter 4**

**Demonstrating
Behavior with UML**

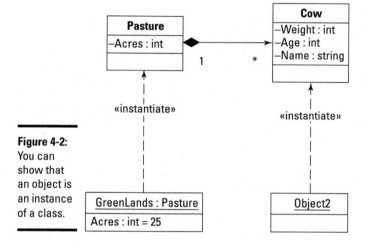

Figure 4-2:
You can show that an object is an instance of a class.

Casing Out the Use Cases

Talk about disagreement. People have argued and bickered about use cases for years. The term *use case* (pronounced with a soft *s*, as in *use,* because *use* is a noun here) refers to one single case or instance of functionality in your application. Most applications have many, many things you can do with them; for example, a web browser enables you to click the Go button to go to a web address that you've typed into a box; or it enables you to click a link to go to a page. Each of these two things is a single use case.

Use cases have become an important aspect of modeling software. So why the contention? Because use cases focus on the functions (that is, verbs!) of a software package, and objects focus on the things, or nouns. So it would make sense by that argument that use cases have no big place in object-oriented analysis and design. However, the flaw in this argument is in saying that the term *object-oriented* means that you focus only on the nouns. It's true that it's oriented to the objects, but that doesn't mean you ignore verbs, or have a disdain for them. (Personally, we like verbs. Life without verbs boring. Talking difficult with no verbs. Me car grocery store.)

And the same is true with object-oriented programming. Although we focus our building around the objects, we still have functions, which are verbs. And we still have functionality. And we can organize and group the functionality, such as through menus or through dialog boxes.

And so, when we design software, one thing we do is review the usage environment and list all the use cases we can think of for the software. This often takes place in the analysis phase.

Figure 4-3 shows an example of a use case diagram. The actual use cases are the oval shapes. And you've certainly noticed the other goofy symbol: the stickman figure! The stickman figure is called an *actor* because it represents the user interacting with the application, similar to the way an actor interacts with the audience. Yes, this is one time when we, the software engineers of the world, get to revert to our childhood roots and draw pretty pictures. In this case, we get to draw stick figures. (Now, just to be crystal-clear, please realize that this a unisex stick figure. It is neither a man nor a woman, nor *both* a man and a woman. Thus, we don't need to draw a skirt to show a woman, as so many other fields do. Here, we believe that all people are, at heart, all the same. Thus, we draw our stick figures all the same.)

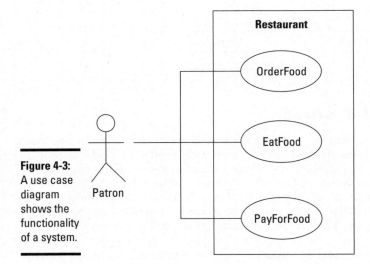

Figure 4-3:
A use case diagram shows the functionality of a system.

Now, if you look at Figure 4-3, you can see that the use cases each have names. These are the things that the user can do with the system. (We use the word *system* to mean a collection of software that you're building.) The system in this example is called Restaurant.

The actor represents the *user* of the system. In the case of a word processor, that could be you sitting there using it, or it could be another human. Either way, it represents a user, a human being. The lines point to the different use cases the user has access to.

Use case: Order food

Ordering food is a handy and tasty example of how events flow in a use case:

ID: UC1000

Actors: Patron

Preconditions: Patron must be seated at the table with a napkin covering clothing. Hands must be clean.

Flow of events:

1. The patron waits for the server to arrive.

2. When the server arrives, the patron orders the food.

3. The server takes the order to the kitchen.

4. The cook prepares the food.

5. The server delivers the food to the table.

6. The patron eats the food.

Postconditions: The patron has a full stomach and is ready to pay for the food.

For some steps, you may have what amounts to an `if-then-else` block in your code. You can notate this in different ways, but here's a handy one: The flow of events goes beyond Step 6, like this:

7. The server asks the patron whether dessert will close out the evening meal.

8. If the patron wants dessert:

   8.1. The patron looks at the dessert menu.

   8.2. The patron chooses a dessert.

   8.3. The server fetches the dessert.

   8.4. The patron eats the dessert.

9. else

   9.1 The server relaxes for a moment, dreaming about what life could have been like if dessert had in fact been part of the evening meal.

Steps 1 through 9 can easily be a function or an algorithm. You can also use `for` loops and `while` loops by putting the `for` or `while` condition and following it with steps:

9.2 For each dessert on the menu, the patron imagines:

   9.2.1 Eating a single bite.

   9.2.2 Contemplating the flavor.

   9.2.3 Devouring the rest.

Expanding use cases

After you draw your use cases on the diagrams, you can define what they do on paper. The way you do this is to write the information in a single-column table, with each row specifying different information about the use case. This information includes

✦ **Name:** The name of the use case as you described it in the diagram

✦ **Unique Identifier:** A special code that some people like to include, such as UC (which stands for use case), followed by a number, as in UC1000

✦ **Actors:** The actors involved with the use case

✦ **Preconditions:** The situation that must exist before the use case can begin to operate

✦ **Flow of events:** A step-by-step flow of the events that take place when the use case *runs*

✦ **Postconditions:** The situation that will exist after the use case runs

A sample use case makes an exclusive guest appearance in the earlier sidebar "Use case: Order food."

Matching use cases and requirements

When you are designing software, make sure that every requirement has at least one use case associated with it.

The requirements describe what the software does.

Table 4-1 shows an example of how to ensure that each requirement has at least one associated use case. Remember that you normally give each use case an identifier. (The need for the identifier increases as project complexity increases.) You can do the same with the requirements.

Table 4-1	Sample Requirements			
	UC1	*UC2*	*UC3*	*UC4*
REQ1	✓	✓		
REQ2	✓			
REQ3			✓	
REQ4			✓	✓

In this grid, each requirement has at least one use case associated with it. Further, each use case satisfies at least one requirement. If a requirement were missing, you would need to add a use case. If you have a use case that does not satisfy a requirement, you must make a decision: Either you discovered a new use case, and therefore a new requirement, and you need to add that requirement; or you went overboard and added an unnecessary feature, in which case you can eliminate the use case.

Sequence Diagrams

When you are working with objects, showing a time sequence of how objects interact with each other is helpful. You can do this by using a sequence diagram. A sequence diagram can be mind-boggling when you first look at it (at least it was for us), but after you understand the layout, a sequence diagram makes more sense. In a *sequence diagram:*

✦ Time moves from top to bottom. In effect, things positioned higher on the diagram happen earlier; things positioned lower happen later.

✦ Objects are drawn side by side, from left to right.

✦ When one object *sends a message to* (calls a member function of) another object, you show this as a solid arrow with a filled-in arrowhead. Above the arrow, you put the name of the function (or the name of the message, if you prefer that jargon).

Refer to Figure 4-3 for a moment, and you can see how this sequencing business works. We took the use case shown in the figure and built a sequence diagram from it. Note, however, that we did not include the added part about the dessert. We will add that shortly, because the process of adding it is a bit more complex. Also, note that to build this sequence diagram, we first had to come up with some classes:

✦ Server: This is a class whose instances receive an order, send it to a Cook instance for preparation, and then take the order and deliver it to the patron.

✦ Cook: This is a class that can receive an order and prepare it.

✦ Food: This is a class that represents, well, food!

Notice that we did not create a class for the Patron. That's because the Patron is outside the system and not a part of it. The Patron, instead, *uses* the system.

Figure 4-4 is an example of a sequence diagram. Remember that the stuff at the top takes place earlier in time, and as you move your eyes down the diagram, you are advancing forward in time. And even though you can move your eyes upward on the diagram, be careful: You don't want to go back in time and relive your past!

Here's how this diagram works. The objects are listed at the top, along with the user who initiates the use case. Below the objects are dashed lines that represent the lifeline of the object. The top of the lifeline represents the time the object is created. For example, if you create an object in the middle of a use case, you would begin the object at that time position (that is, vertical position) on the use case. Here, most of our objects existed before the use case (because they're at the top of the diagram) and their lifeline stretches to the bottom of the diagram; it does not end. That means the objects are around for the full duration of the use case. However, one object, the Food instance, comes to life in the middle of the use case.

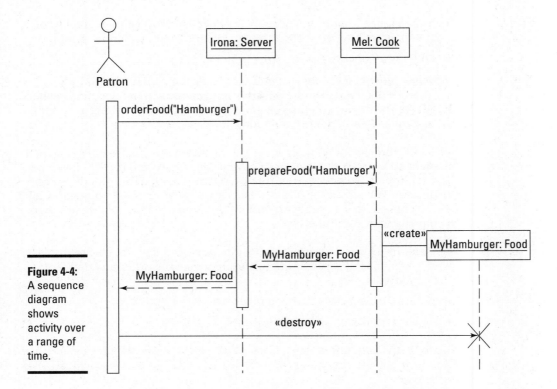

Figure 4-4:
A sequence
diagram
shows
activity over
a range of
time.

Now, notice that a *bar* (a tall, thin rectangle) replaces the lifeline in some places. This is where the object has *focus* in the use case. Or you can say that the object is *active*. Before and after, the object is sitting there, but this use case isn't actually using the object. Although the bar is present, the use case is using the object.

Finally, look at the horizontal arrows. This is where an object to the left calls a member function in an object to the right. The first arrow has a label orderFood("Hamburger"). This arrow starts on the bar for the user (called Patron) and points to the Server object called Irona. In effect, the user calls the orderFood member function in the Server object. Then right under that, the Server lifeline becomes a bar, which means it's active. The Server then calls prepareFood("Hamburger") for the Cook object called Mel.

When the Mel object receives the prepareFood("Hamburger") message, it creates a new instance of Food. Notice that the arrow to the right of the Mel lifeline calls a function in the Food object, but this is not a typical function. Instead, it's a stereotype with the word create in double angle brackets. This means that the Mel object creates a new instance of Food and calls it MyHamburger. Because the object was just created, its lifeline begins midway down the diagram.

Then the returns follow: The Cook object returns an object called MyHamburger (which is of class Food). The Server object receives this and returns it to the user.

Think about this: How can the user call a function? A user can do it through a *user interface,* such as a window on the screen with buttons on it or, perhaps, a menu item. That is, the user interface is the part that you see on the screen! And the name makes sense: It's the interface to the application for the user. Thus, you have a deeply philosophical concept here: By using the screen, keyboard, and mouse, you are interfacing with the computer application, calling member functions. Pretty good!

And finally, notice that the user deletes the object. How can this be? Remember that this use case has a function that the user called. That function then calls destroy. The object's lifeline ends with the deletion, and you see a big X to show that the line ends.

When an object on a sequence diagram calls a member function of an object to the right, a common term for this process is that the first object is *sending a message* to the second object. If you are using a tool to help you draw UML diagrams, the arrows might be called something like *message* arrows.

Notating sequence diagrams

When you create a sequence diagram, you are free to put some notes to the left of the sequence diagram. These notes on the left describe what the thing does. Figure 4-5 shows an example of this.

**Book II
Chapter 4**

**Demonstrating
Behavior with UML**

Figure 4-5: You can notate a sequence diagram by putting text along the left side.

The MySquid object creates a new Kladdbuggle object

«create»

The MySquid object sends the skidaddle message to the Kladdy object

skidaddle()

MySquid::Squuddle

Kladdy: Kladdbuggle

Looping and comparing in sequence diagrams

To show a loop (such as a for loop or a while loop) in a sequence diagram, you enclose part of the sequence diagram in a rectangle and put the loop condition immediately below the rectangle. You can see this in Figure 4-6, where we put the rectangle around the point when the Server object calls the payBill() method on the CashRegister object.

Believe it or not, UML does not have a standard syntax for specifying a loop condition beyond the fact that you must start it with an asterisk. However, a common approach is to use notation, such as i := 1..5, which means that the loop counter i increases from 1 to 5. Thus, there are five iterations: In the first, i is 1; in the second, i is 2; and so on; and in the final i is 5. So you can see in Figure 4-6 that Patron sends a message to Server to pay for all the meals in the restaurant. (Apparently, this Patron has just won the lottery.) The Server then goes to the CashRegister object and processes all the orders.

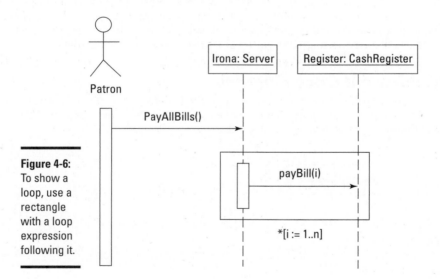

Figure 4-6:
To show a loop, use a rectangle with a loop expression following it.

Now suppose in our little restaurant model that the restaurant serves a particular food, such as French fries. In that case, the Server object might go back and ask the cook whether any French fries are still available. If they are, the Server requests that they be included in the order. The Server then returns the order of fries to the Patron; otherwise, the Server sends a message back to the Patron (that is, *returns* a message, in computerese) that there are no more fries. You can show this as we did in Figure 4-7.

Look at how this works. First, the Server object sends the message doWeHave("French fries") to the Cook object. (We simplified this part of the diagram by not showing how the Cook object does this.) The result of this comes back as either true or false, which we store in the h symbol. Then, in the next step, the Server calls prepareFood("French fries") only if h is true. That's what the brackets with the h in them mean.

Finally, if h is true, the Server object returns the order of fries in the form of a new Food object. This is the return line that starts with [h], which means that h is true. (We don't show the process of the Cook creating the Food object; you can see that kind of thing in Figure 4-3.) But if h is not true, the Server object returns a symbol indicating that there are no more French fries. (You will probably make this symbol an enum in C++, or perhaps a 0.)

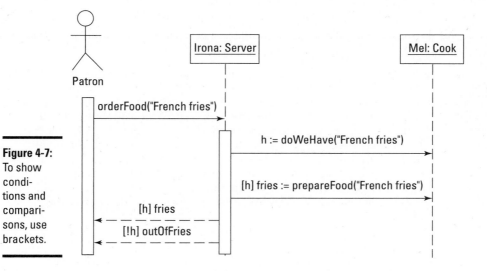

Figure 4-7:
To show conditions and comparisons, use brackets.

At this point, we're actually getting into some local variable names, such as the value of whether there are French fries. However, most CASE tools aren't sophisticated enough to take a sequence diagram such as this and generate C++ code that works. Most can generate some basic code, and some let you type the code by using the CASE tool. You will most likely use this diagram as a guide to write your own code. Designing it through the diagram is a lot easier than with the code. And other people — those who *don't program* — can get a basic idea of the flow of events by looking at the sequence diagram. It's less likely that they would understand code. That way, the *stakeholders* (anyone who has a vested interest in the application, which includes both management and users) can look at the diagram and tell you whether you're building what they want you to build. Often, the level and type of stakeholder participation affects the viability of your application and determines whether people actually use it, so getting stakeholder feedback is essential to the success of your programming efforts.

Colons in assignment statements?

In UML, you often see an assignment statement with a colon rather than just an equals sign. For example, you might see `index := 10`. Why the colon? Well, it turns out that this syntax is borrowed from some languages *other than* C and C++. Lucky us. C++ is probably the single most popular language on the planet, and the designers of UML used another language for some of its syntax. In the two languages, Pascal (which is the underlying language for a programming tool called Delphi) and Ada (which the military *supposedly* uses), the colon always precedes the equals sign in an assignment statement. And, to make matters more complicated, these two languages also use a single equals sign for comparison. C++, of course, uses two equals signs for comparison. Maybe someday we'll have a standard computer programming language. Until then, life is messy in the programming world. But we'll survive.

As you refine your sequence diagrams, you may discover member functions that you didn't include in a class, or you might even discover new classes. As we built the sequence diagrams in this section, we discovered that we didn't have methods for paying the bills. And so we ended up adding a `CashRegister` object and some methods in various objects for paying the bills. We also discovered that we needed some methods for finding out whether a certain food item existed. As you can see, we *refined* the software system as we worked on these diagrams. And that's the goal of UML: to refine it and get it all right! If you're curious, check out Figure 4-8, which is the updated class diagram we created as we were working on these sequence diagrams.

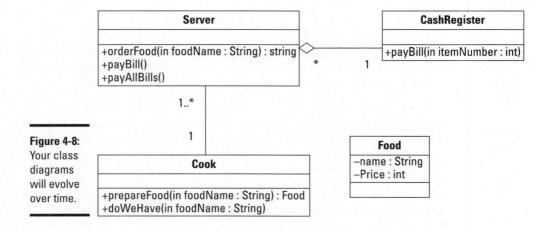

Figure 4-8: Your class diagrams will evolve over time.

Collaboration Diagrams

Collaboration diagrams are similar to sequence diagrams, but they don't show the time ordering. The idea is that they give an overview of the interactions between the diagrams. Frankly, we always opt for sequence diagrams and tend to skip the collaboration diagram; in many ways, a sequence diagram is a type of collaboration diagram that has the benefit of showing a time sequence. However, if you don't want to show time sequence and you want instead to focus on interactions between the objects, you can use a collaboration diagram.

If you look back at Figure 4-7, earlier in this chapter, you can see an example of a sequence diagram. Now, in Figure 4-9 we have the same information, but it is in the form of a collaboration diagram.

**Book II
Chapter 4**

**Demonstrating
Behavior with UML**

Figure 4-9:
A collaboration diagram shows information similar to that in a sequence diagram but focuses on object interactions.

In Figure 4-9, no time sequence is given. The diagram focuses on the interactions between the objects and between the user and the objects. However, we did give the basic notion of steps by numbering the messages (1, 1.1, and 1.2). First, the user sends a message to the Server object; second, the Server asks the Cook whether there are more fries. And third, if there are, the Server puts in the order for the fries.

We didn't just number these things 1, 2, 3. We started with 1, and then 1.1, and then 1.2. The reason is that we imagine the second and third steps as being *substeps* to Step 1. Ultimately, these will be inside a single function, such as this *pseudocode* (simplified code that illustrates the basic point):

```
orderFood() {
    h = doWeHave("French fries")
    if (h) {
        fries = prepareFood("French fries")
        return fries
```

```
    }
    else {
        return outOfFries
    }
}
```

This is almost C++ code, and it would be easy to change it to real C++ code (such as declaring the variables and making this an actual member function with a return type and a parameter list). This is partly how we envision the collaboration diagram looking in C++ code; the calls to doWeHave() and prepareFood() are inside the code for orderFood(). And thus they get substep numbers 1.1 and 1.2 (like an outline) rather than their own Steps 2 and 3.

Activity Diagrams

An *activity diagram* is essentially a flowchart. It shows a sequence of steps. Yes, so does a sequence diagram and, in some senses, a collaboration diagram. However, there's a slight difference: You normally use a sequence diagram to show the steps in a use case. You can use an activity diagram to show individual parts of a sequence diagram, such as a single member function.

The idea behind an activity diagram is that it shows the *lowest possible level* of steps. In effect, the steps (activities) in an activity diagram can't be divided into substeps. The word that computer people like is that the activities are *atomic* and cannot be divided, as people once believed atoms could not be divided. (But this time the theory will stick.)

Figure 4-10 shows an example of an activity diagram. The diagram shows the starting point with a filled-in circle (in this case, at the top of the diagram). Then an arrow points to the first activity (Eat first bite), which is inside an oval. Next comes a decision. Unlike in traditional flowcharting, you do not put any text inside the decision. Instead, you show arrows extending away from the diamond; beside them, you put a Boolean condition inside brackets. Or you can put the word *else* for all other cases. Thus, in this diagram, if the food is yummy, you can move down to the oval on the lower right (Eat another bite). Otherwise, you move down to the oval on the lower left (Throw food away).

We followed the Eat another bite activity with a decision. If the condition [more food] is true, you go back to Eat another bite. Otherwise, you move to the final diamond.

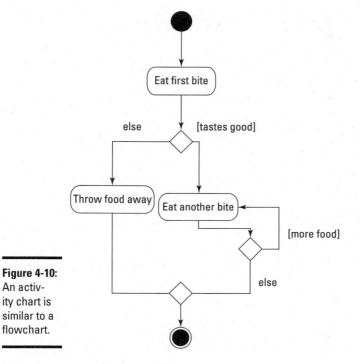

Figure 4-10:
An activity chart is similar to a flowchart.

The final diamond shows all the steps coming together. A diamond represents a return from a decision, where the different paths come back together. We did not put any conditions around it. We show two arrows going in but only one coming out.

And then the final thing is a filled circle with a border around it. That represents the *final state* or, more simply, the end of the activity diagram.

Sometimes, you might want your activity diagram to include a step that is not atomic; you might want to show that you perform a complex step next, but you just give the name of the step without showing all the steps. Such a step is called a *subactivity*. A subactivity is not atomic, and it can be broken up into further subactivities. In Figure 4-11, we created a subactivity called Eat Food. We don't show the detailed steps for eating the food; we simply point out that the computer must perform the function called Eat Food. To make this clear, we used a slightly different diagram. It's an oval with two ovals inside, with one pointing up to the other.

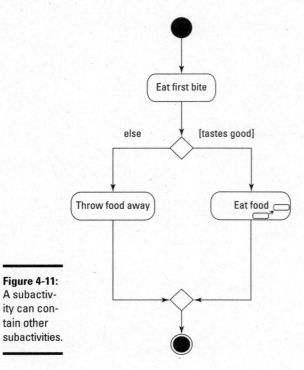

Figure 4-11:
A subactivity can contain other subactivities.

State Diagrams

A *state diagram* shows the different states in which an object can live. We don't mean Nebraska or California, but rather a state such as this collection:

+ The food name is `Hamburger`.

+ The burger's top bun is present (or `true`).

+ The burger's meat is present (or `true`).

+ The burger's bottom bun is present (or `true`).

+ The food is accompanied by ketchup and mustard.

+ There are ten remaining bites.

These items together all show the current state of an object. An object's *state* is represented by the values in the member variables, what function the object is presently running (if any), and how it is currently associated with other objects. For example, this `Hamburger` object might be in the hands of the `Server` and not the `Patron`. That is one part of the object's current state.

A state diagram is similar to an activity diagram. A state diagram shows flow from state to state. But it also shows how to get from one state to the next.

States on a diagram are rounded rectangles (rectangles with rounded corners).

We show a basic state diagram in Figure 4-12. The burger has two states: `Hamburger present` (meaning it's all there) and `Bottom-only Burger` (meaning the top bun has been removed because the diner didn't want it). These two states are shown in rounded rectangles, and their names are present.

Book II
Chapter 4

Demonstrating
Behavior with UML

Figure 4-12:
A state diagram shows the different states an object can be in.

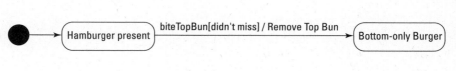

How does the burger transform from one state to the next? In the diagram, you can see an arrow pointing from one state, `Hamburger present`, to the next, `Bottom-only Burger`. That arrow is the only one in the diagram, which means that it's the only possible *state transition*. That is, the burger can be in the `Hamburger present` state and, next, it can move to the `Bottom-only Burger` state, but not back. And the burger gets there when the situation written above the arrow takes place. Here's what that means:

1. The first portion of the text is `biteTopBun`. This is a process or activity or step that takes place. The diner took a bite of the burger with the top bun in place.

2. The next portion is `[didn't miss]`. That's a condition. The diner decided that there is too much bun and really wouldn't miss the presence of the top bun.

3. To go on to the new state, you do what follows: `removeTopBun`. Of course, the biting and the removing really are one step. But in computers, you can break it up. The biting is the process of starting to remove the bun. When the diner decides that there is too much bun (in other words, the diner wouldn't miss the presence of the bun), the computer must perform the activity called `removeTopBun`.

Finally, notice how this is all divided. First is the process that takes place. Next is the condition in brackets. Then there's a slash, and, finally, the activity that puts the object in the next state appears. Thus the state diagram shows an entire transition between two states.

Chapter 5: Modeling Your Applications with UML

In This Chapter

✔ Using some UML extras, such as packages, notes, and tags

✔ Taking advantage of the freedom UML gives you

✔ Creating C++ enumerations in UML

✔ Using static members in UML

✔ Notating templates with UML

*I*n this chapter, we list some miscellaneous details about using UML. After you understand how to use the diagrams and you have a feel for a methodology or process, read this chapter for interesting details about UML. For example, you can use several symbols in any of your diagrams to make them more descriptive; we discuss them here. We also talk about how to show various C++ features in UML.

Using UML Goodies

The UML specification is huge. We're talking *big*. You can see the currently released versions at `http://www.omg.org/spec/UML/` or the UML 2.5 specification at `http://www.omg.org/spec/UML/2.5/`. In this section, we give you some additional information that you can use when creating UML diagrams.

Packaging your symbols

In computer programming, a common term is *namespace*. When you have functions and classes and variables, you can put them into their own namespace, which is nothing more than a grouping. When you do so, the names of the functions, classes, and variables must be unique within the namespace. But if you create another namespace, you can reuse any of the names from the other namespace. In technical terms, *identifiers* must be unique *within a namespace*.

To make this concept clear, let us show you a C++ example. In C++, you can create a namespace by using none other than the `namespace` keyword. Have a gander at the `Namespace01` example, shown in Listing 5-1 — and bear in mind the `using namespace std;` line you see in each of these applications, too.

Listing 5-1:   Using the Namespace Keyword to Create a Namespace in C++

```cpp
#include <iostream>

using namespace std;

namespace Work
{
    int FavoriteNumber;

    class Info
    {
    public:
        string CompanyName;
        string Position;
    };

    void DoStuff()
    {
        cout << "Doing some work!" << endl;
    }
}

namespace Play
{
    int FavoriteNumber;

    class Info
    {
    public:
        string FullName;
        string Hobby;
    };

    void DoStuff()
    {
        cout << "Having fun!" << endl;
    }
}

int main()
{
    // Work stuff
    Work::FavoriteNumber = 7;
    Work::Info WorkInformation;
    WorkInformation.CompanyName = "Spaceley Sprockets";
    WorkInformation.Position = "Worker";
    Work::DoStuff();
```

```
// Play stuff
Play::FavoriteNumber = 13;
Play::Info PlayInformation;
PlayInformation.FullName = "George Jetson";
PlayInformation.Hobby = "Playing with the dog";
Play::DoStuff();

return 0;
}
```

In Listing 5-1, we created two different namespaces — one called `Work` and one called `Play`. Just to prove the point, we created a global variable, a class name, and a function inside each namespace, and they are each named the same as in the other namespace. To make use of these items, down in `main` we precede them with the namespace name and two colons. So you can see that we have two separate global variables:

```
Work::FavoriteNumber = 7;
Play::FavoriteNumber = 13;
```

and that we created instances of two separate classes:

```
Work::Info WorkInformation;
Play::Info PlayInformation;
```

These are completely separate classes and variables; they just happen to have the same name. But they're inside their own namespaces, so this is perfectly legal. And you can see that we also called the function in each namespace. Again, we put the namespace name, two colons, and then the function name. As before, these are each separate functions; they just happen to share the same name.

Think of a namespace as a grouping mechanism. You can group related items, and it frees you from having to worry about whether the name you came up with is unique.

To keep everything neat and tidy, the designers of C++ have put all their own features, such as `cout`, in their own namespace. This namespace is called `std`, which is short for *standard*. To make use of `cout` and other standard features, you need to use the `std` namespace. This means you would normally type `std::cout` to access `cout`. However, having a lot of `cout` entries in your code can be cumbersome. To simplify access to the `std` namespace, then, you can just put `using namespace std;` near the start of your code. Then every time the compiler comes across an identifier it doesn't recognize, it follows up by checking the `std` namespace. Thus, you can have `cout` without the `std::cout` before it. The compiler at first won't recognize `cout`, but then the compiler will check the `std` namespace, thus locating `cout`.

And now, on to UML. In UML, you can show namespaces in your diagrams by using packages. In UML, a *package* is equivalent to a namespace in C++ and other languages. A package looks like a file folder (not the kind in your computer, but the kind in those wondrous and archaic things that past generations of the late 20th century called *file cabinets*).

Figure 5-1 shows an example of a package. You can see that it's a file-folder-looking thing, and the classes are inside it. We put two packages in this diagram — one called Work and one called Play — to match the classes in Listing 5-1.

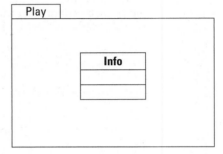

Figure 5-1:
A package looks like a file folder.

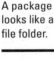

Different Computer-Aided Software Engineering (CASE) tools and diagramming software do packages differently. If you are using Microsoft Visio to create diagrams, for example, its built-in UML tool does not let you draw your classes inside the package symbol. Instead, when you create a package symbol, you get a new, blank page on which to put your symbols.

Fortunately, there are a number of free CASE tools listed at http://sourceforge.net/directory/development/case-tools/freshness:recently-updated/ that you can try in order to find a tool that meets your needs. (Despite what you might see online, there doesn't appear to be a Code::Blocks CASE plugin as of this writing — please write me at John@JohnMuellerBooks.com if you find one.)

In UML, by default, a namespace already exists. It's called topLevel. If you don't explicitly put your data inside a namespace, it automatically goes in the topLevel package.

Notating your diagrams

UML has a handy little symbol called a *note* whose only purpose is to provide comments on a UML diagram. A note is much like a comment in C++ code: It has no bearing on the actual diagrams but is there for the benefit of us humans and other creatures with highly evolved brains to read.

Figure 5-2 shows an example of a note. The note symbol is a sheet of paper with a folded corner, like an actual note.

Figure 5-2:
A note
contains a
comment.

> When the discombobulator itself becomes discombobulated, the users will want to run the disDiscombobulate member function followed by the recombobulate member function.

Tagging your symbols

Sometimes, you want to add some extra information, such as a class diagram, directly to a symbol. Although you could put a note symbol on the page, another possibility is to put the information right into the symbol itself through a *tag* (sometimes called a *tagged property*). A tag gets a name and a value. For example, you might want to put a date on a symbol, such as `Date = January 1, 2014`. You can notate this through a tag. Figure 5-3 shows two tags added to a class symbol and a single tag added to a component symbol.

MyComponent
{designer = Gwyneth}

Figure 5-3:
You can add
tags to your
symbols.

Discombobulator
{Date = January 1, 2014,
Owner = Discombs, Inc.}
+size[1] : int

The tags shown in Figure 5-3 are of the format `name = value`, and they are surrounded by *curly brackets*.

To have tags show up in some CASE tools, you have to make them visible for the symbol. For example, some CASE tools have an option called `ShowProperties`. Using this option allows the tags to show up in the symbol.

Free to Be UML

One of the great things about UML is that it gives you a great deal of free-dom. For example, if you find a diagram that you don't care to use, you don't have to use it; you can still move though an entire software development process or methodology. For example, some people prefer to use sequence diagrams while staying away from collaboration diagrams. And some people don't use state diagrams and activity diagrams. Now some purists might complain about this, but as a software engineer, you need to do what works best for you and your team.

Further, UML is not intended to be used only for software engineering. The creators of UML designed it to be a general-purpose language for modeling, and it can be used for all sorts of projects. For example, in one book, every chapter started out with a UML activity diagram showing the flow of sec-tions in the book.

Of course, most people will use UML for software engineering, primarily because many people outside the software field have simply never heard of UML.

Another area where UML allows freedom is in the methodology you choose. Although this book focuses on the Rational Unified Process (RUP), UML contains a rich set of diagrams and symbols that work with nearly any methodology.

Thanks to *stereotypes* (a method of creating a new symbol), you can even add symbols to UML; so if you're using a methodology with its own sym-bols, you are not trapped with those built into UML. Normally, you take an existing symbol and from it *derive* a new symbol that has similar, but more specialized features. You put the name in the funny-looking angle brackets, as in <<MyStereotype>>. However, there's an alternative: Rather than put the name inside those brackets (called *guillemets*), you can use your own, custom icon. In Figure 5-4, for example, we used the scroll symbol.

Figure 5-4:
You can use custom icons for stereotypes.

Discombobulator

+size[1] : int

In Figure 5-4, the scroll symbol is a stereotype based on a class diagram. Because a stereotype creates a new type of symbol derived from another symbol, this is still a class, but a class used for certain purposes. In our case, we defined this as a class that's stored as a document. From now on, every time we create a new class, we use this symbol to indicate a type of class that can be stored. When we finally implement this class, we will probably derive it from a base class called something like `Storable`. That means, then, that instead of creating a stereotype, we could recognize how this stereotype will be used when we ultimately code it in C++, and instead just draw our diagram as a base class, `Storable`, and then derive a new class, `Discombobulator`, as shown in Figure 5-5. Either is fine.

**Book II
Chapter 5**

Modeling Your
Applications with
UML

Figure 5-5:
You can
get around
using
stereotyped
classes
by using
abstract
classes.

However, stereotypes go beyond just classes. Remember that stereotypes in UML give you the opportunity to *extend UML*. That is, stereotypes let you add new symbols with their own new meanings. In the case of our scroll symbol, we extended the class symbol and still ultimately have a class. But we can stereotype other symbols, and that gives them a totally different (or slightly related) meaning from the original symbol.

For example, we may have a special association in our application that specifically means that one class (the composite) holds instances of the other class (the parts) in the form of a sorted list. We can do this in one of two ways: Stereotype it, or create a tagged property. Figure 5-6 shows the relationship as a stereotype.

Figure 5-6:
You can use
a stereotype
to specify
a type of
association.

Figure 5-7, in turn, shows the relationship with a tagged property. Notice that, with the tagged property, the tag is in curly brackets.

Figure 5-7:
You can also use tagged properties to specify a type of association.

Not all CASE tools support all the features of UML. (However, UML 2.5 seeks to reduce complexity and also ensure that CASE tools provide a more consistent level of support, so going with a product that's compliant with UML 2.5 is the best bet if you want a consistent UML implementation.) If you find that a feature is missing, you can typically work around it by using related features. Most UML tools, however, support both stereotypes and tagged properties.

C++ *and UML*

When you study UML, you may come across various items that you know are present but that you can't find in UML. Here we direct you toward some smaller parts of UML that have a direct connection to something in C++. Specifically, we talk about enumerated types, static members, and templates.

Drawing enumerations

If you want to show an enumeration in UML, you can use a symbol similar to a class symbol. Remember that in C++, an enumeration is a type. In UML, symbols for types are called *classifiers*. Thus, in UML you use a special classifier to show an enumeration. (However, note that this classifier is really a class diagram that has been stereotyped. This is a good example of how you can use stereotypes.)

Figure 5-8 shows an example of an enumeration in UML. At the top is the stereotype name: <<enumeration>>. Under the name is the type — in this case, Color. In the compartment following are the enumerations themselves.

Figure 5-8:
UML
includes
a special
classifier for
enumera-
tions.

«enumeration»
Color
–red
–green
–yellow
–blue
–orange
–violet

«enumeration»
Color2
–red2 = 10
–green2 = 20
–yellow2 = 30
–blue2 = 40
–orange2 = 50
–violet2 = 60

In Figure 5-8, we give two enumerations. The first one, called Color, simply lists the symbols for the enumeration. The second one, called Color2, includes values for each enumeration. In C++, these two enumerations would look like this:

```
enum Color {red, green, yellow, blue, orange, violet};
enum Color2 {red2 = 10, green2 = 20, yellow2 = 30, blue2 = 40,
    orange2 = 50, violet2 = 60};
```

Including static members

In C++, you can include static members in a class. *Static members* are those members that are part of the class but shared among all instances of the class. Normally, all instances of a class get their own member variables. But if a member variable is static, there is only one copy of the variable for all the instances to share. For this reason, people associate such variables as being part of the class itself, not part of the instances. In UML language, these variables have a *class scope*. Regular member variables have an *instance scope*.

Member functions can also have a class scope. Such functions do not oper-ate on an individual instance (and therefore can't access the member vari-ables that are of the instance scope).

A common use of class-scoped members is to maintain a count of the number of instances. Here, you would have a class-scoped member variable called, for example, instanceCount. This would be an integer. In the constructor, you would increment instanceCount, and in the destructor, you would decrement it. Because there's only one copy of the instanceCount member, each time you create an instance, you would increment this single copy. Thus, you would have a count of the number of instances.

Figure 5-9 shows an example in UML of a class with two class-scoped members. The class-scoped members are underlined. In this case, the class is called MessedUpWebSite. We suppose that the idea is that every time you visit a poorly designed and unappealing website, you would create a new instance of

Modeling Your
Applications with
UML

this class and save its web address in the instance. This has two class-scoped members, siteCount, which is a private integer, and getSiteCount, which is a public function that returns the value of siteCount. (We made siteCount private so that other objects can't change it.) And although we didn't show it, you would increment and decrement siteCount in the constructor and destructor, respectively.

Figure 5-9:
You can show static members in UML by using a class scope.

MessedUpWebSite
−siteCount : int
+getSiteCount() : int
+webAddress() : string

In C++, the class in Figure 5-9 looks like the following lines of code:

```
class MessedUpWebSite
{
private:
    static int siteCount;

public:
    static int getSiteCount();
    string webAddress();
    MessedUpWebSite() { siteCount++; }
    ~MessedUpWebSite() { siteCount--; }
};

int MessedUpWebSite::getSiteCount()
{
    return siteCount;
}

int MessedUpWebSite::siteCount = 0;
```

Parameterizing classes with templates

UML includes a notation that you can use along with C++ templates. (We discuss templates in Book IV, Chapter 5.) In UML terms, a *template* is a *parameterized class*. If you think about how a template works in C++, you can see that this makes sense because a template takes several parameters that are used by the compiler to build the class.

When you add the template parameters, the UML standard states that if the parameter is of type class, you can leave the parameter type blank. That's what we did in Figure 5-10. Note that the parameter called MyType has no type after it; thus, its type is class.

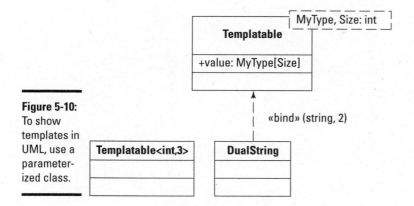

Figure 5-10:
To show
templates in
UML, use a
parameter-
ized class.

Figure 5-10 shows a UML parameterized class. It looks just like a regular old class symbol, except that it has a nifty little dashed rectangle in the upper-right corner. This dashed rectangle contains the template parameters.

Note in Figure 5-10 that we then declared two classes that use the template type. The first one is unnamed and simply specifies the parameters. The second is named DualString and shows an association back to the template class. A stereotype name called <<bind>> appears next to the association arrow. After the stereotype name come the two parameters for the template.

Here is the C++ equivalent of this UML diagram. Notice that the MyType parameter is of type class:

```
template <class MyType, int Size> class Templatable
{
public:
    MyType value[Size];
};
```

And here is some sample code that uses this template. In this code, we also use the two classes based on the template. Note that in order to get the named template instantiation, we use a typedef:

```
Templatable<int,3> inst;
inst.value[0] = 10;
inst.value[1] = 20;
inst.value[2] = 30;
cout << inst.value[2] << endl;
typedef Templatable<string,2> DualString;
DualString inst2;
inst2.value[0] = "abc";
inst2.value[1] = "def";
cout << inst2.value[1] << endl;
```

Chapter 6: Building with Design Patterns

In This Chapter

✔ Understanding what design patterns are and how you can use them

✔ Implementing an Observer pattern

✔ Building a Mediator pattern

*W*hen you work as a software designer, eventually you start to notice that you do certain things over and over. For example, you may get into a pattern of getting mad and shutting off the computer. But that's not directly related to software design.

For an example related to software design, whenever we need to keep track of how many instances of a certain class get created, we always create a static member variable called something like `int InstanceCount`; and in the constructor, we include a line that increments `InstanceCount`; and in the destructor, we put a line that decrements `InstanceCount`. Further, we typically make `InstanceCount` private and include a static method that retrieves the value, such as `int GetInstanceCount()`.

We have used this design so many times that we know it works. The first time we used it, we had to think about it and how we would design and implement it. Now, we barely have to think about it; we just do it, sometimes even when we're driving down the road. Well, maybe not then, but we do use it when we're designing software. Thus, it's a *design pattern* that we use.

Way back in 1995, a book came became an instant best seller in the computer programming world: *Design Patterns: Elements of Reusable Object-Oriented Software*, by Erich Gamma, Richard Helm, Ralph Johnson, and John Vlissides. The four authors of this groundbreaking book would become known in the field of programming as The Gang of Four. They drew on a body of knowledge in the field of architecture — not software architecture, but rather the field of those people who build tall buildings, brick-and-mortar style, for Superman to leap over and see through. That kind of architecture has been around for at least two-and-a-half centuries, so the field is a wee bit more mature than the field of software engineering. And, in the field of building design, people have come up with common ways to design and build buildings and towns, without having to start over from scratch every time with a new set of designs. Some guy (apparently famous in that field) named Christopher Alexander wrote a book in 1977 that teaches the major concepts of building architecture by using patterns. The Gang of Four drew on this knowledge and applied it to software engineering principles. They then wrote *Design Patterns*.

In it, they point out something that seems obvious in hindsight (but then again, great discoveries are often deceptively simple): The best software engineers reuse techniques in the sense of patterns. Our description of the class that keeps an instance count is an example of a technique that can be used over and over.

Now, if you heavily explore the field of object-oriented programming (and computer science in general, really), you will often see the term *reusable*. One of the goals of object-oriented programming is to make code reusable by putting it in classes. You then derive your own classes from these classes, thereby reusing the code in the base classes.

That's all fine and dandy, but it doesn't always work. Yes, we could probably put our instance-counting class in a base class and always derive from it. But for some other designs, this doesn't always work. Instead, software engineers simply apply the same design to a new set of classes. Yes, they reused the design by pulling it from the back dusty caverns of their brains (isn't that pleasant), but they didn't actually reuse any code. That's okay! They drew on experience. And that's the idea behind design patterns. You don't just write up your design patterns and stuff them into a bunch of base classes. Instead, you simply know the patterns. Or you keep a list or catalog of them. So in this chapter, we present you with some of the more common design patterns.

Introducing a Simple Pattern: the Singleton

In this section, we walk you step-by-step through creating a design pattern so that you can see what it is and, more important, how you can use it.

Here's the situation: You are designing a truly great piece of software — so great that everybody from the North Pole to the South Pole will not only buy a copy but will invest in your company as well. And while designing the software, you discover many situations where you need a class such that *only one instance can exist at any given time*.

You've come across this many times. For example, you may have a class that represents the computer itself. You want only one instance of it. You also may have a class that represents the planet Earth. Again, you need only one instance. And you might want a class that models the great leader of the universe (you). Again, only one instance. If people try to create a second instance of the class in their code, they will receive a compiler error. How do you do this?

You could spend a couple hours coming up with an approach. Or you could look at a pattern that already exists somewhere, such as what we're about to show you.

To understand how to create a pattern, you need to first understand an unusual concept that a lot of C++ programmers don't usually consider: You can make a constructor of a class *private or protected!* Now, why would you do that? It turns out that making a constructor private prevents you from directly creating an instance of a class. We can hear you now: "Oh, boy! Doesn't that sound like a useful class, if you can't make an instance of it? These guys are nut jobs!" But you *can* make an instance of the class. There's a trick: You include a static member function that creates the instance for you.

Static member functions do not have an instance associated with them. You call them directly by giving the class name, two colons, and the function name.

But as it happens, the static member function is itself a member of the class, so it can call the constructor and create an instance for you.

One of the more popular examples of basic pattern creation is a *singleton* class — a class that lets you instantiate only one object. A singleton class is useful because it ensures that only one object is available across an application. Developers often use a singleton to coordinate the activities of other parts of the application.

Here's how you make a singleton class: First, make the constructor private. Next, add a public static member function that does the following:

1. Checks to see whether a single instance of the class already exists. If so, it returns the instance's pointer.

2. Creates a new instance and returns its pointer if an instance doesn't already exist.

Finally, where do you store this single instance? You store its pointer in a static member of the class. Because it's static, only one member variable is shared throughout the class, rather than a separate variable for each class instance. Also, make the variable private so that users can't just modify it at will.

And, voilà — you have a singleton class! Here's how it works: Whenever you need the single instance of the class, you don't try to create it. (You'll get a *compile* error! Yes, the *compiler itself* won't let you do it.) Instead, you call the static member function.

The following lines of code from the `Singleton` example show how to create such a class:

```
class Planet
{
private:
    static Planet *inst;
    Planet() {}

public:
    static Planet *GetInstance();
};

Planet *Planet::inst = 0;

Planet *Planet::GetInstance()
{
    if (inst == 0)
    {
        inst = new Planet();
    }
    return inst;
}
```

To use this class, you do not just create an instance directly. Instead, you call the `GetInstance()` member function:

```
Planet *MyPlanet = Planet::GetInstance();
```

You call this any time you want to get a copy of the single instance.

Every time you call `GetInstance()`, you always get a pointer to the same instance.

Now take a look at the constructor: It's private. Therefore, if you attempt something like this somewhere outside the class (such as in `main()`)

```
Planet MyPlanet;
```

you get a compiler error. In Code::Blocks, we get this error:

```
error: 'Planet::Planet()' is private
error: within this context
```

Or if you try to create a pointer, you get the same error when you call `new`:

```
Planet *MyPlanet = new Planet();
```

When you have a class such as this, you probably also want to ensure that nobody attempts to delete the single instance. Just as you would make the constructor private, you would also make the destructor private, as in this example:

```
class Planet
{
private:
```

```
    static Planet *inst;
    Planet() {}
    ~Planet() {}

public:
    static Planet *GetInstance();
};
```

If you try to delete an instance after you obtain it, as in

```
Planet *MyPlanet = Planet::GetInstance();
delete MyPlanet;
```

then once again you receive an error message — this time, for the destructor:

```
error: 'Planet::~Planet()' is private
error: within this context
```

Book II
Chapter 6

Building with Design Patterns

You may be tempted to make a constructor that takes a parameter. You could pass parameters into the `GetInstance()` member function, which would in turn pass them to the constructor. This would work the first time, but there's a catch: Remember that after the `GetInstance()` function creates the instance, it never does so again. That means it won't call the constructor again. Therefore, if you have a class that looks like this:

```
class Planet
{
private:
    static Planet *inst;
    Planet(string name)
    {
        cout << "Welcome to " << name << endl;
    }
    ~Planet() {}

public:
    static Planet *GetInstance(string name);
};
```

and your `GetInstance` method has this code in it:

```
Planet *Planet::GetInstance(string name)
{
    if (inst == 0)
    {
        inst = new Planet(name);
    }
    return inst;
}
```

and you make two calls like this:

```
Planet *MyPlanet = Planet::GetInstance("Earth");
Planet *MyPlanet2 = Planet::GetInstance("Venus");
```

the results may not be as you expect. You end up with only one instance, which gets created with the first line — the one with `"Earth"` passed in. In your second call to the `GetInstance()` function, `GetInstance()` sees that an instance already exists and does not even use the `"Venus"` parameter. So be careful if you're using parameters in constructors.

Watching an Instance with an Observer

A common task in computer programming is when one or more instances of a class (or different classes) need to keep an eye on a certain object and perform various actions when that object changes. For example, you may be writing an application that monitors various activities around your house when you're away. Your application could be configurable; you could set it up so that the user can choose various actions to take if something goes awry. You might have the following options:

✦ The application saves a note in a file so that you can later review it.

✦ The application sends an e-mail to you.

✦ If the computer is linked to a telephone security system, it can notify the police.

✦ The robotic dog can receive a signal to go on high alert.

. . . and so on. Each of these different actions can exist in a different class, each with its own code for handling the situation. The one about saving a note to a file is easy: You would open a file, write to it, and close the file. The e-mail example might involve obtaining a Simple Mail Transfer Protocol (SMTP) library, using it to create a message object, and then sending the message. To notify the police, your computer would have to be hooked up to an online security system that's accessible via the phone lines or perhaps via the Internet, and the police would need a similar system at their end. The class for this would send a signal over the lines to the police, much like the way a secret button that notifies the police of a robbery at a gas station works. Finally, you might have a similar contraption hooked up to the brain of your little robotic watchdog, Fido; after receiving a high-voltage jolt, Fido can go on high alert and ward off the intruders. Sounds like fun, no? We call all these classes `Observer` classes (and by this we mean that each class will be derived from a base class called `Observer`).

Now, you would also have a class whose object detects the problem in the house. This object might be hooked up to an elaborate security system, and when the change takes place, the computer calls a method inside this object. We call this class the `Subject` class.

So think about what is happening here:

1. When a security issue happens, the computer calls a method inside the single `Subject` instance.

2. The `Observer` classes have objects that watch the `Subject` instance. The method in the `Subject` class then calls methods in each of the `Observer` objects. These methods take the appropriate action, whether it's write to a file, notify the police, zap the robotic dog, or whatever.

Here's the catch: The people using your computer application can determine which `Observer` classes they want to respond to the event (possibly, via an Options dialog box). But just to be difficult and to make sure that we design this with great flexibility, we add the following requirement: Over the next year, you might add new `Observer` classes as they come up. One might signal a helicopter to fly in and chase a robber who's making a getaway. But you can't be sure what you'll come up with over the next year. All you know is that you may add `Observer` subclasses and instances of these subclasses. So the point is this: You want to make the `Subject` class as flexible as possible.

Here are the issues that come up when designing such a set of classes. First, you could just keep a long list of instances inside the `Subject` class, and whenever an event takes place, the event handler calls a routine in all the `Observer` instances. The `Observer` instances then decide whether they want to use the information. The problem with this situation is that you have to call a method *within* the `Observer` classes (call *into* the class), even if the individual instances don't want the information. The robotic dog might be sleeping and not want to be bothered by the break-in. Or the police might be on break themselves. (Because this is a serious book, we'll avoid any jokes about doughnut shops.)

But on the other hand, you could have each `Observer` instance constantly check the `Subject` instance, looking for an event. (This process is called *polling*.) The problem here is that this process can push the computer to its limits, believe it or not: If every single `Observer` instance is constantly calling into the `Subject` class, you'll have a lot of activity going on for possibly hours on end, keeping the CPU nice and toasty. That's not a good idea, either.

The way you can perform polling without overextending the CPU is by using the *Observer pattern*. In this pattern, the `Observer` class contains a method called `Respond()`. Meanwhile, the `Subject` class includes a list of `Observer` instances. Further, the `Subject` class includes a method called `Event`, which the computer calls whenever something happens, such as a break-in.

Now, here's the twist that makes it work: Your application will add and remove `Observer` instances to and from the `Subject`'s list of `Observer` instances, based on the options the people choose when using your application.

As you can imagine, this is a recurring pattern that a lot of applications use. Although zapping a robotic dog might not be commonplace, other applications use this general model. For example, in some C++ editors, we can open the same document in multiple windows, all under one instance of the editor application. When we change the code in one window, we can immediately see the change in the other windows. Each class probably has a window, and these windows are the `Observer` classes. The `Subject` represents the underlying document. Or, for another example, you can open multiple browser windows, all looking at the same web page. As the page comes down from the Internet, it gradually appears in all windows. Again, the windows are associated with the `Observer` classes, and the actual web document is associated with a `Subject` class.

So, on to the code already! First, the `Observer` class contains a member function called `Respond()`. In the `Observer` class itself, this is a purely *abstract* function — meaning the derived classes must create their own version of the Respond function. It's up to the derived classes to respond to the event in their own ways.

The following lines from our `AddRemoveItems` example (look ahead to Listing 6-1) show how to create the `Observer` class:

```
class Observer
{
public:
    virtual void Respond() = 0;
};
```

As you can see, there's not much here, so we'll add some derived classes. Here are a couple:

```
class Dog : public Observer
{
public:
    void Respond();
};

class Police : public Observer
{
protected:
    string name;

public:
    Police(string myname) { name = myname; }
    void Respond();
};
```

And here are the `Respond()` member functions for these two classes. For now, to keep it simple, we're just writing something to the console:

```
void Dog::Respond()
{
    cout << "Bark bark" << endl;
}

void Police::Respond()
{
    cout << name << ": 'Drop the weapon! Now!'" << endl;
}
```

Again, so far, there's nothing particularly interesting about this. These lines of code represent just a couple member functions that do their thing, really. When the next step rolls around, though, things get exciting. Here we make the `Subject` class:

```
class Subject
{
protected:
    int Count;
    Observer *List[100];

public:
    Subject() { Count = 0; }
    void AddObserver(Observer *Item);
    void RemoveObserver(Observer *Item);
    void Event();
};
```

This class has a list of `Observer` instances in its `List` member. The `Count` member is the number of items in the list. Two methods for adding and removing `Observer` instances are available: `AddObserver` and `RemoveObserver`. A constructor initializes the list (by just setting its count to 0, really), and there's the famous `Event` member function.

Here's the code for the `AddObserver()` and `RemoveObserver()` methods. These functions simply manipulate the arrays:

```
void Subject::AddObserver(Observer *Item)
{
    List[Count] = Item;
    Count++;
}

void Subject::RemoveObserver(Observer *Item)
{
    int i;
    bool found = false;
    for (i=0; i < Count; i++)
    {
        if (found)
        {
        }
        else if (List[i] == Item)
```

```
        {
            found = true;
            List[i] = List[i+1];
        }
    }
    if (found)
    {
        Count--;
    }
}
```

The `RemoveObserver()` function uses some little tricks (again, a pattern!) to remove the item. It searches through the list until it finds the item; after that, it continues through the list, pulling items back one slot in the array. And finally, if it finds the item, it decreases `Count` by 1.

And now, here's the fun part! The `Event()` method looks like this:

```
void Subject::Event()
{
    int i;
    for (i=0; i < Count; i++)
    {
        List[i]->Respond();
    }
}
```

This code just climbs through the list, calling `Respond()` for each item in the list. When you put this all together, you can have a `main()` that sets up these items. Here's one possibility:

```
Dog Fido;
Police TJHooker("TJ");
Police JoeFriday("Joe");
Subject Alarm;
Alarm.AddObserver(&Fido);
Alarm.AddObserver(&TJHooker);
Alarm.AddObserver(&JoeFriday);
Alarm.RemoveObserver(&TJHooker);
Alarm.Event();
```

We make three `Observer` instances (one dog and two cops) and a `Subject` instance called `Alarm`. We then add all three instances to the list; but then TJ Hooker backs out, so we remove him from the list.

Then we call `Event()`. (If this were an actual system, we wouldn't call `Event()` right now; we would call `Event()` when an actual break-in event occurs.) And when we run this code, we get the responses of each of the *registered* observers:

```
Bark bark
Joe: 'Drop the weapon! Now!'
```

Notice that TJHooker didn't respond, because he was no longer interested. And so he didn't receive a notification. He is, however, still an instance.

In this example, the three observers (Fido, TJ Hooker, and Joe Friday) are *watching* the alarm, ready to respond to it. They are observers, ready for action. The alarm is their subject of observation. That's why we use the metaphor of Observer and Subject.

Observers and the Standard C++ Library

If you're interested in using templates and the Standard C++ Library, you can make the Subject class a bit more sophisticated by using a list rather than an array. You can do this by using the standard list class. The only catch is that the list class doesn't seem to do well with abstract classes. So you need to "de-abstractify" your Observer class, by setting it up like this:

```
class Observer
{
public:
    virtual void Respond() {}
};
```

Then, you can modify the Subject class and its methods like so:

```
class Subject
{
protected:
    list<Observer *> OList;

public:
    void AddObserver(Observer *Item);
    void RemoveObserver(Observer *Item);
    void Event();
};

void Subject::AddObserver(Observer *Item)
{
    OList.push_back(Item);
}

void Subject::RemoveObserver(Observer *Item)
{
    OList.remove(Item);
}

void Subject::Event()
{
    list<Observer *>::iterator iter;
    for (iter = OList.begin(); iter != OList.end(); iter++)
    {
        Observer *item = (*iter);
        item->Respond();
    }
}
```

Note that, in the list, we're saving pointers to `Observer`; we're not saving the `Observer` instances themselves. That's because, by default, the `list` class makes a copy of whatever you put in the array. If you put in an actual instance, the `list` class will make a copy (which creates problems with derived classes because the `list` copies only the object being stored as an `Observer` instance, not a class derived from `Observer`). With pointers, a copy of a pointer still points to the original object, and therefore the items in the list are the originals (at least their addresses are in the list).

Automatically adding an observer

When you have an application that lets its users configure various observers, you may want to create and delete observers based on the configurations. In that case, it's possible to add an `Observer` to a `Subject`'s list automatically when you create the `Observer`, and to remove the `Observer` from the list when you delete the `Observer`. To do this, you can call the `AddObserver()` method from within the constructor and call the `RemoveObserver()` method from within the destructor. But to make this work, you need to tell the object who the `Subject` is. That's easy: Just pass the name as a parameter to the constructor. The following code does this. Note that we had to move the `Subject` class above the `Observer` class because the `Observer`'s constructor and destructor call into `Subject`. Also, note that we made the `AddObserver()` and `RemoveObserver()` functions protected. But because we want the `Observer` class to use these functions, we used a little trick called a *friend*: We put the word `friend` followed by the word `Observer` in the `Subject` class; now the `Observer` member functions can call the protected and private member functions of `Subject`. The code for the complete AddRemoveItems application is in Listing 6-1.

Listing 6-1: Using the Add and Remove Items in the Constructor and Destructor

```
#include <iostream>

using namespace std;

class Observer;

class Subject
{
    friend class Observer;

protected:
    int Count;
    Observer *List[100];
    void AddObserver(Observer *Item);
    void RemoveObserver(Observer *Item);
```

```
public:
    Subject() { Count = 0; }
    void Event();
};

class Observer
{
protected:
    Subject *subj;

public:
    virtual void Respond() = 0;

    Observer(Subject *asubj)
    {
        subj = asubj;
        subj->AddObserver(this);
    }

    virtual ~Observer() { subj->RemoveObserver(this); }
};

class Dog : public Observer
{
public:
    void Respond();
    Dog(Subject *asubj) : Observer(asubj) {}
};

class Police : public Observer
{
protected:
    string name;

public:
    Police(Subject *asubj, string myname) : Observer(asubj) {
        name = myname; }
    void Respond();
};

void Dog::Respond()
{
    cout << "Bark bark" << endl;
}

void Police::Respond()
{
    cout << name << ": 'Drop the weapon! Now!'" << endl;
}

void Subject::AddObserver(Observer *Item)
{
    List[Count] = Item;
    Count++;
}
```

Book II
Chapter 6

Building with
Design Patterns

(continued)

Listing 6-1 *(continued)*

```cpp
void Subject::RemoveObserver(Observer *Item)
{
    int i;
    bool found = false;
    for (i=0; i < Count; i++)
    {
        if (found)
        {
        }
        else if (List[i] == Item)
        {
            found = true;
            List[i] = List[i+1];
        }
    }

    if (found)
    {
        Count--;
    }
}

void Subject::Event()
{
    int i;
    for (i=0; i < Count; i++)
    {
        List[i]->Respond();
    }
}

int main()
{
    Subject Alarm;

    Police *TJHooker = new Police(&Alarm, "TJ");

    cout << "TJ on the beat" << endl;
    Alarm.Event();
    cout << endl;
    cout << "TJ off for the day" << endl;
    delete TJHooker;
    Alarm.Event();

    return 0;
}
```

Mediating with a Pattern

Suppose that you're designing a sophisticated, complex model of a car. You're going to include the following parts, each of which will have its own class:

+ The engine

+ The electrical supply (for technically minded folks, the battery and alternator combined)

+ The radio
+ The wheels
+ The brakes
+ The headlights
+ The air conditioner
+ The road

Now see whether you can keep up (read this as fast as you possibly can): When the amount of electricity produced increases, the headlights get brighter. When the engine speeds up, the amount of electricity produced increases. When the amount of electricity produced decreases, the radio volume decreases. When the air conditioner turns on, the amount of electricity available decreases. When the air conditioner turns off, the amount of electricity available increases. When the engine speed increases, the wheels accelerate. When the amount of electricity produced increases, the radio volume increases. When the road angle increases due to going uphill, the speed of the wheels decreases. When the brakes come on, the speed of the wheels decreases. When the amount of electricity produced decreases, the headlights get dimmer. When the engine slows down, the amount of electricity produced decreases. When the road angle decreases due to going downhill, the speed of the wheels increases.

Your job is to model all this behavior. Sound like fun? Not particularly. In fact, it's a total mess! How can you model this?

Here's the problem: You have a million objects (well, eight), all interacting with each other in different ways. You could try to make all the objects communicate. In the code, making them communicate would mean that most of the classes would have to contain references to objects of the other classes. That technique could get pretty confusing.

If you followed all this, the UML diagram in Figure 6-1 shows the interactions. As you can see, it's kind of messy. It's a *little* cleaner now in UML form than in the long-winded paragraph earlier, but it's still messy, and the code itself will be complicated.

When you have this kind of a mess, first try to rearrange things visually to see whether there's a way to simplify it. Figure 6-2 shows our cleaned-up version. Looking at this figure, we still get a little confused, but the figure does help us see the connections a bit more clearly.

So now we introduce the theme of this pattern. The idea is that when you have a set of classes that interact in a complex way, a *mediator* class through which the classes all communicate is often easiest to create. That way, only the mediator class needs to know about all the instances. The instances themselves communicate only with the mediator.

In the example, when there's a hill, the road angle either increases or decreases, depending on the side of the hill you're on (uphill or downhill). The road does not need to know about all the other car parts. Instead, it just informs the mediator of the change. The mediator then informs the necessary car parts.

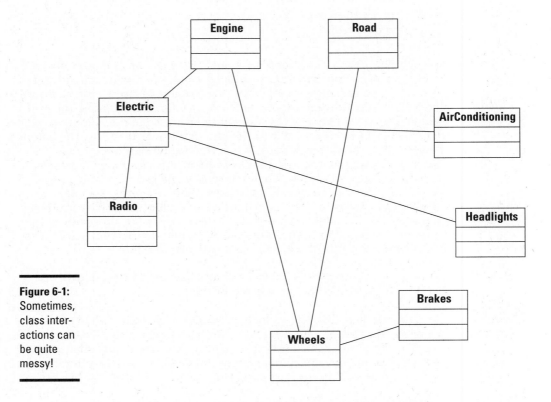

Figure 6-1: Sometimes, class interactions can be quite messy!

This may seem like overkill: Why can't the road just talk directly to the car parts? The idea is that if you enhance this application later, you may want to add more car parts. Rather than have to go through and hook up connections to all the necessary car parts, you just make a connection with the mediator object. Suppose that you add a new part called an automatic transmission. When the car begins to climb a hill, the automatic transmission might detect this and automatically shift to a lower gear, resulting in an increase to the engine speed. To add this class, you only need to define its behavior and how it responds to various events, and then hook it up to the mediator. You will also modify the mediator so that it knows something about the automatic transmission's behavior. Thus, you don't need to hook it up to all the other instances.

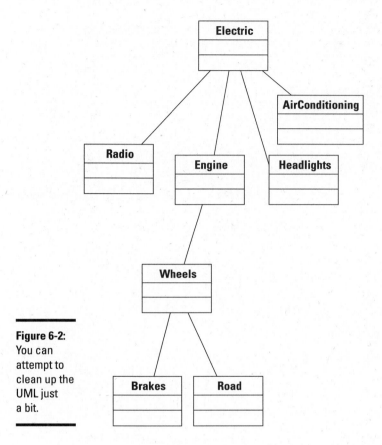

Figure 6-2:
You can
attempt to
clean up the
UML just
a bit.

Figure 6-3 is the revised UML with the addition of a mediator. Now it looks a bit cleaner!

One thing we're not showing in Figure 6-3 (for the purpose of avoiding clutter) is that we're going to derive all the various car parts (including the road!) from a base class called CarPart. This class will have a single member: a pointer to a Mediator instance. Each of the car parts, then, will inherit a pointer to the Mediator instance.

The Mediator class has a member function called PartChanged(). This is the key function: Anytime any of the car parts experiences a change, it calls PartChanged(). But remember that a car part can experience a change in only one of two ways: through an outside force unrelated to the existing classes (such as the driver pushing the gas pedal or turning the steering wheel) or through the Mediator instance. If the change comes from the Mediator instance, it was triggered through one of the other objects.

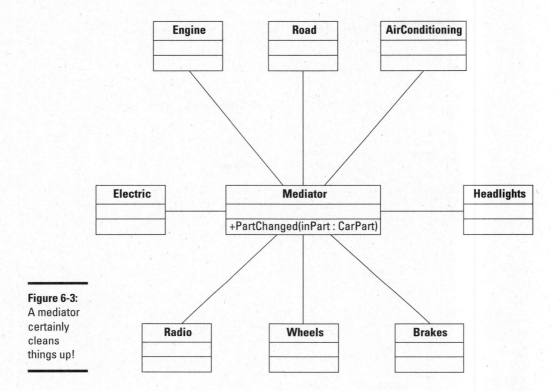

Figure 6-3:
A mediator
certainly
cleans
things up!

For example, look at the following steps:

1. The driver pushes the gas pedal by calling a method in the `Engine` instance.

2. The `Engine` instance changes its speed and then tells the `Mediator` of the change.

3. The `Mediator` instance knows which objects to notify of the change. For this change, it notifies the wheels to spin faster and the amount of electricity produced to increase.

Here's another possible sequence:

1. The road has a hill. To tell the car about the hill, the main routine calls a member function in the `Road` instance. The hill has a 10 degree incline.

2. The `Road` instance notifies `Mediator` of the change.

3. The `Mediator` instance handles this by figuring out how much to decelerate; it then notifies the wheels to slow down.

So you can see that most of the *smarts* are in the `Mediator` class.

Putting up a façade (pattern)

In the CarParts example, we felt as though it would be cumbersome to have to manipulate the car system by paying separate attention to all the different parts, such as the engine and the wheels, simultaneously. Imagine what life would be like if you had to drive a car while constantly worrying about every little thing. Instead, we created a class called CarControls through which you can interact with the system. The CarControls class is a pattern itself, called a Façade pattern. (A *façade* is the front of something — it's a French word.) This pattern is also a front: It's the interface into the system through which you interact. That way, you don't have to keep track of the individual classes. When you add a class through which users can interact with the system, you are using a Façade pattern.

You may have noticed what seems like a contradiction in things we have told you and what other OOP (object-oriented people) have told you. Here, we're saying to put the smarts in the Mediator class. Elsewhere, you may hear that objects must be able to do their own work. But that's not really a contradiction. In fact, the Mediator class is handling all the smarts dealing with *collaborations* between objects. After the Mediator instance figures out, for example, that the wheels must spin faster, it notifies the wheels and tells them to spin faster. That's when the wheels take over and do their thing. At that point, they know how to spin faster without outside help from other classes and objects. So it's not a contradiction, after all.

Take a look at the CarParts example, shown in Listing 6-2. This is a header file that contains the class declarations for the car parts.

Listing 6-2:   Using the carparts.h File

```
#ifndef CARPARTS_H_INCLUDED
#define CARPARTS_H_INCLUDED

#include "mediator.h"

class CarControls; // forward reference

class CarPart
{
protected:
    Mediator *mediator;
    CarPart(Mediator *med) : mediator(med) {}
    void Changed();
};

class Engine : public CarPart
{
protected:
    friend class Mediator; friend class CarControls;
```

(continued)

Listing 6-2 *(continued)*

```cpp
    int RPM;
    int Revamount;

public:
    Engine(Mediator *med) : CarPart(med),
        RPM(0), Revamount(0) {}
    void Start();
    void PushGasPedal(int amount);
    void ReleaseGasPedal(int amount);
    void Stop();
};

class Electric : public CarPart
{
protected:
    friend class Mediator; friend class CarControls;
    int Output;
    int ChangedBy;

public:
    Electric(Mediator *med) : CarPart(med),
        Output(0), ChangedBy(0) {}
    void ChangeOutputBy(int amount);
};

class Radio : public CarPart
{
protected:
    friend class Mediator; friend class CarControls;
    int Volume;

public:
    Radio(Mediator *med) : CarPart(med),
        Volume(0) {}
    void AdjustVolume(int amount) { Volume += amount; }
    void SetVolume(int amount) { Volume = amount; }
    int GetVolume() { return Volume; }
};

class Wheels : public CarPart
{
protected:
    friend class Mediator; friend class CarControls;
    int Speed;

public:
    Wheels(Mediator *med) : CarPart(med),
        Speed(0) {}
    int GetSpeed() { return Speed; }
    void Accelerate(int amount);
    void Decelerate(int amount);
};

class Brakes : public CarPart
{
protected:
    friend class Mediator; friend class CarControls;
    int Pressure;
```

```
public:
    Brakes(Mediator *med) : CarPart(med),
        Pressure(0) {}
    void Apply(int amount);
};

class Headlights : public CarPart
{
protected:
    friend class Mediator; friend class CarControls;
    int Brightness;

public:
    Headlights(Mediator *med) : CarPart(med),
        Brightness(0) {}
    void TurnOn() { Brightness = 100; }
    void TurnOff() { Brightness = 0; }
    void Adjust(int Amount);
    int GetBrightness() { return Brightness; }
};

class AirConditioner : public CarPart
{
protected:
    friend class Mediator; friend class CarControls;
    int Level;
    int ChangedBy;

public:
    AirConditioner(Mediator *med) : CarPart(med),
        Level(0), ChangedBy(0) {}
    void TurnOn();
    void TurnOff();
    bool GetLevel() { return Level; }
    void SetLevel(int level);
};

class Road : public CarPart
{
protected:
    friend class Mediator; friend class CarControls;
    int ClimbAngle;
    int BumpHeight;
    int BumpWhichTire;

public:
    Road(Mediator *med) : CarPart(med) {}
    void ClimbDescend(int angle);
    void Bump(int height, int which);
};

#endif
```

These classes know little of each other. That's a good thing. However, they do know all about the mediator, which is fine. In this example, we used an important small feature of the American National Standards Institute (ANSI) version of C++. Notice the constructor line in the Engine class definition:

```
Engine(Mediator *med) : CarPart(med),
    RPM(0), Revamount(0) {}
```

After the constructor definition, you see a colon and the name of the base class, `CarPart`. This calls the base class constructor. Then there's a comma and the name of a member variable (`RPM`) and a value in parentheses, which together form an *initializer*. When you create an instance of `Engine`, the `RPM` variable will get set to the value `0`. Further, the `Revamount` variable will also get set to the value `0`. Using the constructor with an initializer causes the constructor to behave just like this code:

```
Engine(Mediator *med)
{
    RPM = 0;
    Revamount = 0;
}
```

Next, in Listing 6-3, is the header file for the mediator along with a special class called `CarControls`, which provides a central place through which you can control the car. You may have noticed that we gave the `CarControls` class friend access to the car parts in the `carparts.h` file. We also included in this file several forward declarations. Remember: This class knows about the various `CarParts` classes. This file also includes a class, derived from `Mediator`, that provides a general interface to the whole system.

Listing 6-3:   Using the mediator.h File

```
#ifndef MEDIATOR_H_INCLUDED
#define MEDIATOR_H_INCLUDED

// Define all of the required forward references.
class CarPart;
class Engine;
class Electric;
class Radio;
class SteeringWheel;
class Wheels;
class Brakes;
class Headlights;
class AirConditioner;
class Road;

class Mediator
{
public:
    Engine *MyEngine;
    Electric *MyElectric;
    Radio *MyRadio;
    SteeringWheel *MySteeringWheel;
    Wheels *MyWheels;
    Brakes *MyBrakes;
    Headlights *MyHeadlights;
```

```
        AirConditioner *MyAirConditioner;
        Road *MyRoad;
        Mediator();
        void PartChanged(CarPart *part);
};

class CarControls : public Mediator {
public:
        void StartCar();
        void StopCar();
        void PushGasPedal(int amount);
        void ReleaseGasPedal(int amount);
        void PressBrake(int amount);
        void Turn(int amount);
        void TurnOnRadio();
        void TurnOffRadio();
        void AdjustRadioVolume(int amount);
        void TurnOnHeadlights();
        void TurnOffHeadlights();
        void ClimbHill(int angle);
        void DescendHill(int angle);
        void TurnOnAC();
        void TurnOffAC();
        void AdjustAC(int amount);
        int GetSpeed();
        CarControls() : Mediator() {}
};

#endif
```

Book II
Chapter 6

Building with
Design Patterns

Next is the code for the member functions for all the car parts, shown in
Listing 6-4. Note in these functions that we never, ever call the functions in
other car parts. We do, however, call a general Changed method that's in the
car parts base class, CarParts. This calls into the Mediator to let it know
that a change has taken place.

Listing 6-4:   Presenting the carparts.cpp File

```
#include <iostream>
#include "carparts.h"

using namespace std;

void CarPart::Changed()
{
    mediator->PartChanged(this);
}

void Engine::Start()
{
    RPM = 1000;
    Changed();
}
```

(continued)

Listing 6-4 *(continued)*

```
void Engine::PushGasPedal(int amount)
{
    Revamount = amount;
    RPM += Revamount;
    Changed();
}

void Engine::ReleaseGasPedal(int amount)
{
    Revamount = amount;
    RPM -= Revamount;
    Changed();
}

void Engine::Stop()
{
    RPM = 0;
    Revamount = 0;
    Changed();
}

void Electric::ChangeOutputBy(int amount)
{
    Output += amount;
    ChangedBy = amount;
    Changed();
}

void Wheels::Accelerate(int amount)
{
    Speed += amount;
    Changed();
}

void Wheels::Decelerate(int amount)
{
    Speed -= amount;
    Changed();
}

void Brakes::Apply(int amount)
{
    Pressure = amount;
    Changed();
}

void Headlights::Adjust(int Amount)
{
    Brightness += Amount;
}
```

```
void AirConditioner::TurnOn()
{
    ChangedBy = 100 - Level;
    Level = 100;
    Changed();
}

void AirConditioner::TurnOff()
{
    ChangedBy = 0 - Level;
    Level = 0;
    Changed();
}

void AirConditioner::SetLevel(int newlevel)
{
    Level = newlevel;
    ChangedBy = newlevel - Level;
    Changed();
}

void Road::ClimbDescend(int angle)
{
    ClimbAngle = angle;
    Changed();
}

void Road::Bump(int height, int which)
{
    BumpHeight = height;
    BumpWhichTire = which;
    Changed();
}
```

And now, in Listing 6-5, you can see the mediator source code and the source code for the `CarControls` class.

**Book II
Chapter 6**

**Building with
Design Patterns**

The magic words: high cohesion, low coupling

In the world of software engineering, two buzzwords are *cohesion* and *coupling*.

Cohesion refers to the process of grouping similarly minded functions together. If you create good classes, this shouldn't be a problem. Functions involving the wheels should go in the `Wheels` class — not, for example, the `Engine` class.

Coupling is a bit more complex. It refers to the process of tying together classes so that they can't function independently. In effect, the classes are coupled. In good object-oriented programming, having lots of coupling is not good. You want your classes to be as independent as possible; you want *low coupling*. The `Mediator` pattern helps a great deal toward the low-coupling goal. In the `CarParts` example, if we had instead given the `Electric` class pointers to an `Engine` instance and a `Radio` instance, and so on, we would be forcing all these classes to work dependently. In effect, we would have coupled them. But by using the `Mediator` instance, each class works only with the `Mediator`. We have low coupling. You should, therefore, try to design for *high cohesion and low coupling*. It's a good thing!

Listing 6-5: Using the carparts.cpp File

```cpp
#include <iostream>
#include "mediator.h"
#include "carparts.h"

using namespace std;

Mediator::Mediator()
{
    MyEngine = new Engine(this);
    MyElectric = new Electric(this);
    MyRadio = new Radio(this);
    MyWheels = new Wheels(this);
    MyBrakes = new Brakes(this);
    MyHeadlights = new Headlights(this);
    MyAirConditioner = new AirConditioner(this);
    MyRoad = new Road(this);
}

void Mediator::PartChanged(CarPart *part)
{
    if (part == MyEngine)
    {
        if (MyEngine->RPM == 0)
        {
            MyWheels->Speed = 0;
            return;
        }

        if (MyEngine->Revamount == 0)
        {
            return;
        }

        // If engine increases, increase the electric output
        MyElectric->ChangeOutputBy
            (MyEngine->Revamount / 10);

        if (MyEngine->Revamount > 0)
        {
            MyWheels->Accelerate(
                MyEngine->Revamount / 50);
        }
    }

    else if (part == MyElectric)
    {
        // Dim or brighten the headlights
        if (MyHeadlights->Brightness > 0)
          MyHeadlights->Adjust(MyElectric->ChangedBy / 20);

        if (MyRadio->Volume > 0)
            MyRadio->AdjustVolume(MyElectric->ChangedBy / 30);
    }

    else if (part == MyBrakes)
    {
        MyWheels->Decelerate(MyBrakes->Pressure / 5);
    }
```

```
    else if (part == MyAirConditioner)
    {
        MyElectric->ChangeOutputBy(
            0 - MyAirConditioner->ChangedBy * 2);
    }

    else if (part == MyRoad)
    {
        if (MyRoad->ClimbAngle > 0)
        {
            MyWheels->Decelerate(MyRoad->ClimbAngle * 2);
            MyRoad->ClimbAngle = 0;
        }

        else if (MyRoad->ClimbAngle < 0)
        {
            MyWheels->Accelerate(MyRoad->ClimbAngle * -4);
            MyRoad->ClimbAngle = 0;
        }
    }
}

void CarControls::StartCar()
{
    MyEngine->Start();
}

void CarControls::StopCar()
{
    MyEngine->Stop();
}

void CarControls::PushGasPedal(int amount)
{
    MyEngine->PushGasPedal(amount);
}

void CarControls::ReleaseGasPedal(int amount)
{
    MyEngine->ReleaseGasPedal(amount);
}

void CarControls::PressBrake(int amount)
{
    MyBrakes->Apply(amount);
}

void CarControls::TurnOnRadio()
{
    MyRadio->SetVolume(100);
}

void CarControls::TurnOffRadio()
{
    MyRadio->SetVolume(0);
}

void CarControls::AdjustRadioVolume(int amount)
{
    MyRadio->AdjustVolume(amount);
}
```

**Book II
Chapter 6**

**Building with
Design Patterns**

(continued)

Listing 6-5 *(continued)*

```cpp
void CarControls::TurnOnHeadlights()
{
    MyHeadlights->TurnOn();
}

void CarControls::TurnOffHeadlights()
{
    MyHeadlights->TurnOff();
}

void CarControls::ClimbHill(int angle)
{
    MyRoad->ClimbDescend(angle);
}

void CarControls::DescendHill(int angle)
{
    MyRoad->ClimbDescend( 0 - angle );
}

int CarControls::GetSpeed()
{
    return MyWheels->Speed;
}

void CarControls::TurnOnAC()
{
    MyAirConditioner->TurnOn();
}

void CarControls::TurnOffAC()
{
    MyAirConditioner->TurnOff();
}

void CarControls::AdjustAC(int amount)
{
    MyAirConditioner->SetLevel(amount);
}

int main()
{
    // Create a new car.
    Mediator *MyCar = new Mediator();

    // Start the engine.
    MyCar->MyEngine->Start();
    cout << "Engine Started!" << endl;

    // Accelerate.
    MyCar->MyWheels->Accelerate(20);
    cout << "The car is going: " << MyCar->MyWheels->GetSpeed() << endl;

    // Apply the brakes.
    MyCar->MyBrakes->Apply(20);
    cout << "Applying the brakes." << endl;
    cout << "The car is going: " << MyCar->MyWheels->GetSpeed() << endl;
```

```
// Stop the car.
MyCar->MyBrakes->Apply(80);
cout << "Applying the brakes." << endl;
cout << "The car is going: " << MyCar->MyWheels->GetSpeed() << endl;

// Shut off the engine.
MyCar->MyEngine->Stop();
cout << "Engine Stopped" << endl;

return 0;
}
```

The `CarControls` part runs a bit long, but it's handy because it provides a central interface through which you can operate the car. The workhorse of the pattern, however, is in the `Mediator` class. This is a bunch of `if` statements that look at the change that took place and then call into other classes to modify the objects of the other classes. That's the whole goal with the `Mediator` pattern: *It has a `Mediator` class containing a general function that looks for changes and then changes other classes.*

If you look back at Listing 6-4, you can see that, after each change, we call the `Changed()` function. This function is in the base class, and it calls into the Mediator's `PartChanged()` function, which does all the hard work. Also note that in some of the car parts classes, the `Mediator` doesn't respond to their changes (such as the `Wheel` class); however, we still call `Change()` in the member functions for the class. The reason is that we may add features whereby the `Mediator` would respond to these changes. Then we wouldn't have to check to see whether we included a `Change()` method; it's already there. This helps avoid the problem of wondering why `Mediator` isn't doing what it's supposed to do when the code forgets to call `Change()`.

Book II
Chapter 6

Building with Design Patterns

Documenting your work

Imagine that somebody else will use your set of car classes. You have saved your header files and your source files, along with a static library containing the compiled code, on a network drive. Your coworker begins looking at your header files and sees a big collection of classes. How does that person know how to use the classes? Does the coworker know to use the main Façade class called `CarControls`? Or will that person have to buckle down and dig through the code to figure out which classes to use and which ones not to?

The answer is no. Instead, clearly document your classes. Somewhere, put together a simple document (no more than a page or two) that explains how to use your class library. Write this document for other programmers to use (make it readable, please!), and explicitly state that programmers are to interact with the system through the `CarControls` class. You should then describe the public member functions (the *interface*) to the `CarControls` class and provide concrete examples. You might also include a reference section for advanced programmers who want to understand how the whole thing works. Whatever you do, don't just hand over the classes and expect other people to understand them without sufficient documentation!

At some point, you'll want to test the new class. The `main()` function in this example does precisely that. The code doesn't provide a complete test, but it does demonstrate some of what you can do. In this case, the code turns the engine on, accelerates the car, applies the brake a little, applies the brake more to come to a stop, and then stops the engine.

Book III
Fixing Problems

```
main.cpp  ✕   carparts.h  ✕   carparts.cpp  ✕   mediator.h  ✕

  1    #ifndef CARPARTS_H_INCLUDED
  2    #define CARPARTS_H_INCLUDED
  3
  4    #include "mediator.h"
  5
  6    class CarControls; // forward reference
  7
  8    class CarPart
  9    {
 10    protected:
 11        Mediator *mediator;
 12        CarPart(Mediator *med) : mediator(med) {}
 13        void Changed();
 14    };
 15
 16    class Engine : public CarPart
 17    {
 18    protected:
 19        friend class Mediator; friend class CarControls;
 20        int RPM;
```
```
Logs & others                                                    ✕

  ◄  🔺 Code::Blocks  ✕  🔍 Search results  ✕  🔺 Cccc  ✕  🔵 Build log  ✕  🔻 Build messa ►
```

Contents at a Glance

Chapter 1: Dealing with Bugs

*W*ho knows whether it's true, but as the story goes, back when the first computer was built over a half-century ago, it filled an entire room with circuitry (yet was about as powerful as one of those inexpensive calculators — the kind that perform only basic math). One day, the thing was misbehaving, and some brave engineers climbed deep into the thing. (The version we're thinking of has them wearing white radiation suits, of course.) Deep in *The Bowels of the Machine* (sounds like a movie title), they found none other than . . . an insect! A bug! It was a great *big* bug that had gotten messed up in the circuitry, causing the computer to malfunction. So the story goes, anyway. Today, we use the term *bug* to mean something that is wrong with an application. In this minibook, we show you how to track down bugs and fix them in your software. In this chapter, we talk about what exactly a bug is (and is not!), how bugs occur, and how you can try to avoid them.

It's Not a Bug. It's a Feature!

So we're using a word processor, and all of a sudden, the application freaks out and saves our file automatically. We didn't tell it to do that; we didn't ask for it. Then we're using the same copy of the word processor, and we try to do a copy-and-paste procedure (that's called a *use case,* by the way), and suddenly the Font dialog box pops up. And then later, we're sitting with our laptops at Starbucks, and it automatically begins the shutdown procedure. We didn't tell it to do that.

Bugs! Bugs! They're all bugs! Or are they? Seems that these pesky little incidents might be considered *features* by some programmers.

Some word processors have an optional *autosave* feature that causes the application to automatically save *recovery* information in case the computer goes dead. And that Font dialog box that popped up was a mistake of ours: we meant to press Ctrl+V, but our fingers slipped and caught the *D* key instead. As it happens, by default Ctrl+D opens the Font dialog box in some word processors. (Why *D?* We have no idea.) And newer versions of most operating systems understand laptop computers: When the battery is just about to be completely drained, the operating system saves the entire state of the machine to a giant file on the hard drive and shuts down. This is called *hibernation.* So these aren't bugs, after all. We guess we can close up that bug report we just sent to the vendor.

Now consider this: Suppose that you're using an application that we won't name here, and in the middle of it, you get a message box that says something like `Exception Error`, and the application simply closes. All your work is lost. So you call tech support, and the helpful friend on the other end says, "You must have typed something it didn't like. This application has a built-in protection scheme whereby if you type something you're not supposed to, it shuts down."

Oh, yeah. We get it. That's when the guy says, "It's a *feature*, not a bug!" Tell me another one. But sometimes situations walk the fine line between bug and feature. We don't think that an application crashing could be considered a feature, but consider this instead: When your browser messes up, a message asks whether you want it to send the vendor a trouble report. *That's* a feature that handles bugs.

But the unnamed application that shut down definitely has a bug. And other applications have bugs. For example, we have been quickly switching between browser windows, typing, resizing, doing things quickly as we go back and forth between the windows (too much caffeine, perhaps), when suddenly the thing crashes and we see the trouble-report message. That really was a bug: The application choked when we, the user, *did something that the programmers did not anticipate.*

Now, why did the application choke? Well, in addition to what we did that the programmers hadn't expected, it's possible that the programmers simply messed up. Either they didn't include code to handle a rough situation (rapidly switching, resizing — that sort of thing), or perhaps they wrote code that did something wrong, such as free a pointer but then continue to use the memory address.

Here's an example of programmers not expecting something. Suppose that we're writing an application that reads a number from the console. You should type a single character for your first choice and then type another character for your second choice. The code might look like this:

```
char x, y;
cout << "Enter your first choice" << endl;
cin >> x;
cout << "Enter your second choice" << endl;
cout << x << endl;
cin >> y;
cout << y << endl;
```

It's a simple little code, but suppose that you respond to the first request by typing an entire word for what you want, such as *Read* rather than a single letter, such as *R*. Our application would then take the letters *e, a,* and *d* and use them for the subsequent `cin` calls — something we might not have anticipated. The *e* would go into the `cin > y` line and get put in `y`. That's the bug of not anticipating something: You, the programmer, must make sure that your application can handle all situations. All of them. Every single one. But fortunately, there are ways around such problems, and we share these with you in this chapter.

You can group these situations into the following categories:

✦ Real features, not bugs at all

✦ A situation that the programmers didn't anticipate

✦ A mistake, plain and simple

Make Your Application Features Look Like Features

The last thing you want is to get calls from users complaining about *a bug* in your application that was, in fact, *a feature.* This can happen, and it does. But the technical-support people are embarrassed when they have to explain, "No, sir/ma'am. That really is the way it's supposed to work." And it's also not fun for the technical-support people to be subjected to name-calling after this, especially when they didn't write the software — *you did*.

But, as programmers, we want to make everybody's lives easier (starting with our own, of course!), so building our software so that it's easy to use and *makes sense* is best. The key, then, in creating software where the features actually look like features is to make it all sensible. Don't have your software start the Zapper automatically unless the user explicitly asks for the Zapper to come on:

> Smiling technical-support representative: "It's a feature! The Zapper comes on after the computer has been sitting idle for ten minutes."

> Angry customer: "Yes, but I would kind of like to be at least ten feet away from the thing when the Zapper starts up!"

> Smiling technical-support representative: "But why would you be sitting there for ten minutes and not using the computer if you're not away from it?"

> Angry customer: "I was reading the manual on how to configure the Zapper!"

You know the rest: Lawsuits follow and people get fired. Not a pretty sight, and that says nothing for the poor customer who was in the vicinity of the computer when the Zapper kicked in at full force.

With features, the rules are simple: Let the user choose which features they want to happen and when. If they don't want autosave, for example, let them turn it off. Let them configure the software, and don't let it do anything surprising.

Anticipating (Almost) Everything

When you write an application, try to anticipate the different things that users can do to your application — much of which may not exactly be associated with the proper use of your application. Most of this kind of protection — that is, ensuring that your application doesn't choke when the users do something you don't anticipate — that you build into your software centers around the *user interface,* the area where the users interact with your application.

If your application is a console-based application or if users can enter characters into text boxes in a windowing application, you must guard against invalid input. Take a look at this output from a hypothetical application:

```
What would you like to do?
    A. Add random information to the system.
    B. Boil information.
    C. Compress information.
    D. Delete the information.
    Your choice:
```

Now suppose that the user chooses *D* for Delete, and the following menu appears:

```
What would you like to delete?
    A. None of the data — forget it!
    B. Some of the data.
    C. Most of the data.
    D. All the data! Get rid of it all!
```

Now imagine that a user starts this application and sees the first menu. The user doesn't know whether to type **A** for the first choice or **Add** for the first choice. The user types **Add** and presses Enter. Oops. The *A* went to the first choice, and the system added the random information and printed the same first menu again. The *d* (the second character the user typed) then went to the choice `Delete the information`. That caused the second menu, the Delete menu, to appear. The third character that the user typed, *d*, caused the second menu's *D* selection to take place — `All the data! Get rid of it all` — all in one shot, without the user realizing what happened.

Oops! What was supposed to be `Add` turned into `Add`, `Delete`, `Delete all the data`. Not good! How can you avoid this kind of thing?

✦ Restrict the user's choices.

✦ Clearly state what the user should do.

✦ Support multiple options.

✦ Anticipate what could go wrong.

For example, you might tell the user to type only a single character, with a message such as this:

```
Please enter a single character for your choice:
```

But now, does the user have to press Enter afterward? This message suggests so. But maybe not. So you must be more specific. Maybe one of these examples would work better:

```
Type a single character and do not press Enter:
```

```
Type a single character and then press Enter:
```

But even these aren't good enough. First, you should generally allow the user to press Enter. Doing something automatically with a single keystroke may surprise the user. Further, you may want to support multiple options. If the user wants to choose option A in the menu, you might support any of the following for input:

✦ A

✦ a

✦ Add

✦ ADD

✦ add

This can all be wrapped up into some short code that looks like this:

```
string choice;
cin >> choice;
char ch = choice[0];
ch = toupper(ch);
switch (ch)
{
    case 'A':
        cout << "Adding random data..." << endl;
        break;
    case 'B':
        cout << "Boiling it down!" << endl;
        break;
    case 'C':
        cout << "Compressing!" << endl;
        break;
    case 'D':
        cout << "Deleting..." << endl;
        break;
}
```

Now the user can type any word, and the only thing that the application checks is the first letter. But if you don't like the idea that *aompress* can be taken as *add* and not *compress* (who knows what they meant to type?), you can do something like this:

```
string choice;
cin >> choice;
choice = MyUppercase(choice);
if (choice == "A" || choice == "ADD")
{
    cout << "Adding random data..." << endl;
}
else if (choice == "B" || choice == "BOIL")
{
    cout << "Boiling it down!" << endl;
}
else if (choice == "C" || choice == "COMPRESS")
{
    cout << "Compressing!" << endl;
}
else if (choice == "D" || choice == "DELETE")
{
    cout << "Deleting..." << endl;
}
else
{
    cout << "I don't know that word" << endl;
}
```

Now this code looks for only the first letter, or the exact word, and the letter or word can be in either uppercase or lowercase. This choice is probably the best one. However, you may notice that we used a function called MyUppercase. That's our own function because support in C++ for converting an entire string to uppercase leaves a bit to be desired. So we wrote our own function. Here it is:

```
string MyUppercase(string str)
{
    char *buf = new char[str.length() + 1];
    strcpy(buf, str.c_str());
    strupr(buf);
    return string(buf);
}
```

Be careful if you're dealing with a sophisticated application. Suppose that you are writing an application that looks up information in a database for a particular customer name. You could run into the following situations:

✦ The names in the database are in all uppercase letters (for example, *GEORGE WASHINGTON*), and the user can enter names in mixed case (for example, *George Washington*).

✦ The first and last names are stored separately, so your application must look in the database for the situation where the last name is Washington and the first name is George. The user, who doesn't know to enter just the last name, may enter both names into a single text box. Or you might allow the user to enter both names at one time, but the user doesn't realize that the last name was supposed to come first, or perhaps it was last name, and then a comma, and then the first name.

✦ The user can type some spaces at the beginning or end of the name. The application then looks for an entry like " George Washington " and does not find it, because it's stored as "George Washington" (with no spaces before or after).

✦ The user might include middle initials when the name is not stored in the database with middle initials.

All these problems are easy to avoid. Here are some tips:

✦ You must know how the names are stored in the database before you go looking for them. If they are stored in all caps, you shouldn't require the user to enter them in all caps. Instead, accept words in any case and *convert them* to all uppercase.

✦ You must know whether the names are stored with the first name separated from the last. Then allow any format. If the user types **George Washington** (no comma), you can split the string at the space and pull out the first name and last name. But if the user types the name with a comma between the first and last names, you can split it at the comma and extract the last name and then the first name.

✦ Spaces should not be a problem. You can strip the spaces off a string after a user types it in.

✦ Are middle initials required? Document things well. Your application should clearly tell the user whether to enter a middle name, a middle initial, or neither. If you are using text controls, don't even include a middle name field if you don't want a middle name. Or if you do, specify right on the window whether the user should type a middle initial or an entire middle name. If the entry is just an initial, you can remove a trailing period, or add it, depending on what's stored in the database.

All these steps will help make your application bulletproof. The idea is to encourage users to do things the way they prefer, but to prevent them from doing things in ways that your application doesn't like. If your application doesn't want middle initials, don't give users the opportunity to enter them.

Listing 1-1 shows you how you can strip spaces, strip a possible period off the end of a middle initial, and split a string based on either spaces or commas. In this listing, we used a special class called `vector`. The `vector` class is much like an array, except that the `vector` class is a bit more powerful: `vector` is a class, and you can add things to it and remove things from it easily by using member functions. `vector` is also a *template,* so when you declare it, you must state what type of variables you want it to hold. You put the variable types in angle brackets. We're putting strings in it, so we declared it as `vector<string>`. But to make our lives simpler, we used a `typedef` to make an easier name for this type: `StringList`.

Listing 1-1:   Processing Strings to Reduce Bugs

```
#include <iostream>
#include <vector>
#include <string.h>

using namespace std;

typedef vector<string> StringList;

StringList Split(string orig, string delims)
{
    StringList list;
    int pos;

    while((pos = orig.find_first_of(delims)) != -1)
    {
        list.push_back(orig.substr(0, pos));
        orig = orig.substr(pos + 1);
    }

    list.push_back(orig);

    return list;
}

string MyUppercase(string str)
{
    char *buf = new char[str.length() + 1];

    strcpy(buf, str.c_str());
    strupr(buf);

    return string(buf);
}

string stripspaces(string orig)
{
    int left;
    int right;

    // If string is empty, just return it.
    if (orig.length() == 0)
        return orig;

    // Strip right
    right = orig.find_last_not_of(" \t");
    if (right > -1)
        orig.resize(right + 1);

    // Strip left
    left = orig.find_first_not_of(" \t");
    if (left > -1)
        orig.erase(0, left);

    // If left still has a space, it
    // means the whole string is whitespace.
    // So just remove it all.
    if (orig[0] == ' ' || orig[0] == '\t')
    {
        orig = "";
    }
```

```
        return orig;
}
void ProcessName(string name)
{
    StringList list;
    string first, middle, last;
    int size, commapos;
    name = stripspaces(name);
    commapos = name.find(",");

    if (commapos > 0)
    {
        // Name has a comma, so start with last name.
        name.erase(commapos, 1);
        list = Split(name, " ");
        size = list.size();

        if (size > 0)
            last = list[0];
        if (size > 1)
            first = list[1];
        if (size > 2)
            middle = list[2];
    }
    else
    {
        // Name has no comma, so start with first name.
        list = Split(name, " ");
        size = list.size();

        if (size > 0)
            first = list[0];
        if (size > 2)
        {
            middle = list[1];
            last = list[2];
        }
        if (size == 2)
        {
            last = list[1];
        }
    }

    // If middle name is just initial and period,
    // then remove the initial.
    if (middle.length() == 2)
    {
        if (middle[1] == '.')
        {
            middle.erase(1,1);
        }
    }

    // Convert all to uppercase
    first = MyUppercase(first);
    middle = MyUppercase(middle);
    last = MyUppercase(last);
```

(continued)

Listing 1-1 *(continued)*

```
    cout << "first: " << first << endl;
    cout << "middle: " << middle << endl;
    cout << "last: " << last << endl;
    cout << endl;
}

int main()
{
    string name;

    name = "   Washington, George Zeus   ";
    ProcessName(name);

    name = "Washington, George Z.";
    ProcessName(name);

    name = "George Z. Washington";
    ProcessName(name);

    name = "George Zeus Washington";
    ProcessName(name);

    name = "George Washington";
    ProcessName(name);

    return 0;
}
```

Listing 1-1 is rather bug-proof, but it still does not handle some situations properly. For example, if somebody tries to process a string with a middle name, such as *Zeus.* (notice the period after the name), the application does not remove the period. But is that correct? Who knows, but people don't normally format names that way. And so here are some improvements you might make to this application:

✦ **Eliminate improper characters:** You might make sure that no improper characters appear in the names. We would probably do this after we found the first, middle, and last names; that way, we wouldn't kill the attempt to find the data based on the presence of a single comma that might be needed to specify the name order. You can use various `if` statements to do this kind of thing.

✦ **Handle more names than three:** We would probably add a special precaution for the case of more than three names. Some people have lots of names (like 10 or 11, especially if they're members of British royalty). But if this application is to be used, for example, in an oil change operation, we don't think you'll see Charles Philip Arthur George, Prince of Wales coming through (although it's possible). And so, as usual, how you handle the names depends on your particular situation.

✦ **Perform initial processing:** We would also do some initial processing. Right after the user enters the names, we would make sure that the names are not empty strings — that is, "" (one pair of quotation marks with no space between them).

The myth of the bulletproof application

Anyone who has spent time reviewing the trade press knows that many applications have recurring problem with bugs. Just as soon as the vendor fixes one bug, another bug turns up. Some developers may think that the developers at these companies are morons and are giving us all a black eye. However, these developers, more often than not, are just like us. Because they're human, and humans make mistakes — at both the developer and user ends of the application — applications will never become bug-free. Sure, you may be able to create a simple, nearly bulletproof application, but as application complexity increases, so do the number of interactions and the number of potential bugs. At some point, the number of interactions between application parts increases to

the point that a bug-free application becomes impossible.

Over the years, we have read any number of articles and books that purport to supply the magic that's required to create an application that not only lacks bugs but also prevents unanticipated user actions. The bulletproof application is a myth. If you buy into this myth, you may be tempted to stop looking for bugs the moment the development staff can't find any more of them. Unfortunately, this attitude leads to headlines proclaiming your application as the next significant Windows security hole. Don't buy into the myth of the bulletproof application — always be alert for potential errors.

Avoiding Mistakes, Plain and Simple

Even though many programmers take measures to prevent bugs, programmers still sometimes let problems slip through. However, if you're careful, you can avoid a lot of these problems. When you create software, you should be in the right frame of mind to watch for potential problems *as you're writing the code.* (Getting into the right frame of mind includes ensuring that you have enough sleep, avoiding distractions, and doing other things that help you concentrate on your work, but this section also describes some specifics that you should consider.)

The list of potential problems that we give you here could probably go on and on for thousands of pages. However, the point is not to have a big checklist, but rather for you to review this list and start to recognize the things you need to do to write good code. Writing code is conscious and deliberate. It's similar to walking down a sidewalk and being vaguely aware of such things as whether cars are coming or whether you need to step over any holes. These hazards are always in the back of your mind as you carefully walk along. Writing code is the same way: Certain *gotchas* should stay in the back of your mind, too:

✦ **Indexes:** Strings and arrays run from index 0 to 1 less than the length. Using a loop, such as for (i=0; i<=size; i++), is a common mistake. The less-than-or-equal-to symbol is incorrect, yet people make this mistake a lot. The scary thing is that sometimes the code will still function, and you'll end up simply overwriting something else. And worse, you might not immediately catch this coding error, so it will manifest itself as a bug in the application later.

✦ **For every new, there's a delete:** Whenever you allocate an object using new, remember to free it. But forgetting the delete doesn't usually create noticeable bugs in your application; read the next item to see what's more likely to cause a noticeable bug.

✦ **Remember what you deleted:** Worse than forgetting to delete an object is forgetting *that* you deleted it and continuing to use it. When you delete a pointer, make sure that you didn't pass it to some other object that stored it away and plans to use it again.

✦ **Don't forget to create an object:** You may have seen this one: An error message pops up that says:

```
The instruction at 0x00402119 referenced memory at 0x00000000. The
    memory could not
be written.
```

This means that someone had a pointer variable and forgot to call new. We generated this message easily on purpose with the following code:

```
int *x = 0;

*x = 10;
```

We created a pointer variable and initialized it to 0, meaning that it's not being used. But before calling new or setting the variable equal to some object's address, we tried to stuff something into the memory it points to (which is address 0, something that the operating system doesn't like). And the operating system responded with the error message. This is a bug that we see far more than we would expect in commercial software.

These are just a few items to think about, but you can see that they deal mostly with memory issues, such as allocating memory and using it incorrectly. Most important, you can avoid them if you're conscientious about your programming. As you code, bear in mind the repercussions of what you're doing. And as crazy as this sounds, remember what you might be forgetting! Ask yourself whether you're forgetting to delete some pointers or whether someone else has a copy of the pointer you're about to delete. If you keep these things in mind, you should avoid some of the most common bugs.

Chapter 2: Debugging an Application

In This Chapter

✔ Working with debuggers

✔ Using the Code::Blocks debugger

✔ Tracing code flow through an application and in and out of functions

✔ Using other debuggers

✔ Getting seriously advanced debuggers

✔ Adding command line arguments to Code::Blocks debugging

In this chapter, we talk about how you can use a debugger to track down problems and bugs in your application. Sooner or later, things don't work the way you planned them. In this case, you have several plans of attack. One plan involves a hammer and the computer, but we don't recommend that one. Instead, we suggest using a debugger to try to *fix* the application.

Programming with Debuggers

A *debugger* is a special tool that you use for tracing line by line through your application. (*Tracing* is the act of viewing the code execution flow in an application.) Take a look at the BuggyProgram example, shown in Listing 2-1. This is just a basic application with a main() and a couple of functions that we use to demonstrate the debugger.

Listing 2-1: Tracing a Simple Application

```
#include <iostream>
#include <cstdlib>

using namespace std;

int CountRabbits(int original)
{
    int result = original * 2;
    result = result + 10;
    result = result * 4;
    cout << "Calculating " << result << endl;
    return result * 10;
}
```

(continued)

Listing 2-1 *(continued)*

```
int CountAntelopes(int original)
{
    int result = original + 10;
    result = result - 2;
    cout << "Calculating " << result << endl;
    return result;
}

int main()
{
    int rabbits = 5;
    int antelopes = 5;
    rabbits = CountRabbits(rabbits);
    cout << "Rabbits now at " << rabbits << endl;
    antelopes = CountAntelopes(antelopes);
    cout << "Antelopes now at " << antelopes << endl;
    //system("PAUSE"); // add this for Windows
    return 0;
}
```

When you type and run this application, you see the following output:

```
Calculating 80
Rabbits now at 800
Calculating 13
Antelopes now at 13
```

Now look closely at main() and follow it through, line by line. The first thing main() does is declare a couple of integers. Then main() calls the CountRabbits() function. The CountRabbits() function declares an integer and completes a few lines of calculations. Then the CountRabbits() function prints a message. Finally, it returns. Once back in main(), the application prints another message and then calls the CountAntelopes() function. This function also declares an integer, completes some calculations, prints a message, and then returns. Back in main(), the application prints another message, and, finally, the application finishes.

What we just gave you is a linear description of the entire process of this application. You can see these same steps by using a debugger. With a debugger, you see the computer moving line by line through your code. A debugger performs the first line of your application and then waits for you to tell it to perform the next line — then the next, and the next, and so on, until the end of the application.

In this example, we use the debugger that comes with the Code::Blocks application. If you prefer to use another debugger, we recommend that, for most of this chapter, you at least try the Code::Blocks debugger. It is a nice tool, and we think that you'll be happy with it. But besides that, it allows you to follow through the examples we give. Then you can return to whatever other tool you're using.

Adding debug and symbol information

When you compile with debug information, you are adding debug and symbol information to the final executable file. This information includes data about the source code files, including the line numbers and the variable names. This is the primary difference between a *debug* version and a *release* version of your product: People typically don't include debug and symbol information in a version of the product that they release to the general public. One reason is that including it makes it too easy for competitors and hackers to reverse-engineer the product. (Another reason is that including the debug and symbol information makes the application run slower and consume more system resources.) However, the actual source code is not in the debug and symbol information; that stays in the source code file. The debug information, instead, just contains line numbers, which serve as references (pointers, if you will!) into the source code file. So hackers and competitors won't have the complete source to your application, but they will have variable names and other information that could make their job easier (and yours harder).

You must know one important aspect before using a debugger: For the debugger to understand your code, you must compile it with debugging information. The compiler adds extra information into the final executable so that the debugger can locate your source code and variable information. Here's how you turn on debug information:

- ✦ **Code::Blocks:** Choose Debug in the Build Target drop-down list box.
- ✦ **Dev-C++ 5.0:** Open the project and choose Tools⇨Compiler Options. In the Linker tab, make sure that Generate Debugging Information is turned on.
- ✦ **gcc under MinGW and Cygwin:** Add the -g option to the compiler. You will probably do this inside a `Makefile`.

After you change the compiler options to generate debug information, you must rebuild your project. The reason is that the compiler and linker must regenerate object files and executable files with the debug information.

Running the debugger

After you have rebuilt your project, you can run the debugger. To start the debugger, click Debug/Continue, choose Debug⇨Start, or press F8. (If you click Run, the application runs as normal without entering debug mode.) When you start the debugger, you should see a screen like the one shown in Figure 2-1. (You also get a console window behind that screen. This console window contains the output for the application you are debugging.)

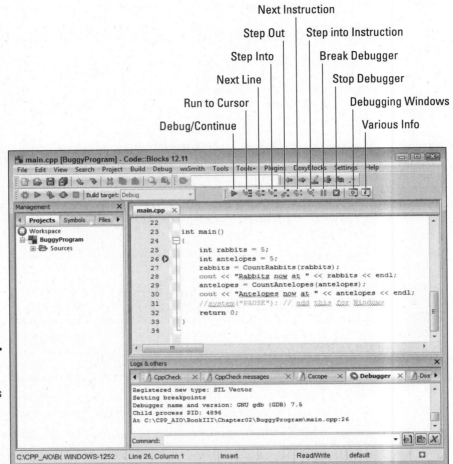

Figure 2-1:
The main
Code::Blocks
window
shows your
source
code.

Figure 2-1 shows two special features you need to know in order to (successfully) debug applications. The first is the red octagon (like a stop sign), and the second is the yellow triangle. The red octagon is a *breakpoint* — a place where you want the debugger to stop. You add breakpoints to the Editing window by clicking the left side next to the instruction where you want to stop. When you click that spot again, the red octagon goes away, showing that you have cleared the breakpoint. You can place as many breakpoints as you want in the application, but you can place breakpoints only on instructions.

The yellow triangle is the *instruction pointer,* which shows the instruction that the debugger will execute next. As you tell the debugger to execute instructions, the yellow triangle moves. Whenever you start the application in debug mode, the yellow pointer automatically stops at each breakpoint. Figure 2-1 shows how the debugger looks when the yellow triangle stops at a breakpoint.

When you start the debugger again by clicking Debug/Continue, execution begins as if the application is in normal run mode until the debugger encounters another breakpoint. If the debugger doesn't encounter a breakpoint, the dialog box closes, and the application returns to the source screen.

If you don't set any breakpoints and try to debug your application, it will run without letting you trace through the code. That is, the application will run as if you're not running it in the debugger.

Look at the Debugger tab of the Logs and Others window, shown in Figure 2-1. This tab contains debugging messages from your application. Whenever you see the At message, you know that the debugger has stopped at a particular location. The remainder of the message tells you where the debugger has stopped. In Figure 2-1, the debugger has stopped at line 26 of this file:

```
C:\CPP_AIO\BookIII\Chapter02\BuggyProgram\main.cpp file
```

So go ahead and run the application. Begin by setting a breakpoint at line 23, the `int main()` entry. Click Debug/Continue, choose Debug⇨Start, or press F8 to start the debugger. You'll see a number of messages appear on the Debugger tab, and then you'll see the At message when the debugger stops at line 23. (If you spaced your application slightly differently from the way we did in Listing 2-1, you may see a slightly different line number.) The yellow triangle should appear on line 23, which contains a curly bracket, meaning that the application is stopped at that line. The instruction pointer stopped at the curly bracket because it is the first instruction after the `main()` entry.

Click Next Line, which is the third button on the Debugger toolbar. The button you want is the one with an icon with two squares and an arrow pointing from the first square to the second square. (You can also press F7.) The yellow triangle (instruction pointer) moves to the first assignment statement on line 25, which is

```
int rabbits = 5;
```

Click Next Line. When you click the button, the instruction pointer advances to the next line. The computer just performed the first line in `main()`, and next the computer will perform the second line in `main()`, which is this:

```
int antelopes = 5;
```

Click Next Line again. Now the instruction pointer is on the third line of `main()`, which looks like this:

```
rabbits = CountRabbits(rabbits);
```

This third line of `main()` is a function call, and now you have a choice. (*Don't* click Next Line!) You can either tell the computer to perform only what's inside this function without stopping on each line for you to see, or you can "step into it" and see the individual lines.

Click the fourth button from the left, the one called Step Into, which shows two squares and an arrow going from the left between them. (Or press Shift+F7.) When you do, the instruction pointer moves into the `CountRabbits()` function. The highlight will be on the first line in that function:

```
int result = original * 2;
```

When the highlight moved into the function, the computer *stepped into* the function. Now think about the symbol for the icon that caused this to happen: The icon has squares and an arrow pointing between them. The two squares represent lines of code in the current function and you go between them, or *step into* the called function. That's the idea behind the odd symbols. The one you've been clicking before, the Next Line icon that has an arrow going over, means *stepping over* the function.

Now, before stepping into this function — because you were clicking lines that were not functions but just individual lines — you used the Next Line (that is, the step over) button. But you could have used either the Next Line button or the Step Into button, because *stepping into a function* doesn't bear much meaning on statements that are not functions.

Normally, we use the Next Line button by default and choose the Step Into button only when we specifically want to go into a function. The reason is that some lines of code that may not appear to be functions really are. For example, `cout << "a";` is, in fact, a function, and you might not want to step into that code, because either the source code for it might not be present or you simply might not be interested in the details of the function.

It's time to see how these debugging features work. The following procedure takes you through the debugging process so that you can see the Code::Blocks debugger in action:

1. **Click Next Line three times until the instruction pointer appears on the `cout` line:**

```
cout << "Calculating " << result << endl;
```

This line writes output to the console. Remember, in addition to the main Code::Blocks window, you have a console window. That's where the output from this line goes.

2. **Click Next Line.**

3. **Click the console window.**

You see the results of the cout statement:

```
Calculating 80.
```

Then the instruction pointer lands on the return statement.

4. **Click Next Line again.**

The instruction pointer is on the closing brace of the function. Note that Code::Blocks highlights both the opening brace and the closing brace in blue. This feature helps you see where a function begins and ends in the Integrated Development Environment (IDE).

5. **Click Next Line yet again.**

The instruction pointer returns to main(), on the line following the call to the CountRabbits() function:

```
cout << "Rabbits now at " << rabbits << endl;
```

6. **Click Next Line again.**

The instruction pointer is on the second function call:

```
antelopes = CountAntelopes(antelopes);
```

7. **But this time, instead of stepping into the function, just press Next Line to step over it.**

The instruction pointer advances to the next line, which is this:

```
cout << "Antelopes now at " << antelopes << endl;
```

Take a look at the console. The CountAntelopes() function itself contained a call to cout. You can see on the console that this cout line did its stuff:

```
Calculating 13
```

You saw the output from the CountAntelopes() function because, although you stepped over the function, you didn't actually skip it: The function ran in its entirety during that one click of the Next button. The debugger just didn't go through it line by line, that's all.

8. **Click Next Line to do the final cout line.**

Your entire output now looks like this:

```
Calculating 80
Rabbits now at 800
Calculating 13
Antelopes now at 13
```

and the instruction pointer ends on the final return statement:

```
return 0;
```

9. **Click Next Line one more time and the highlight is on the closing brace of** `main()`.

   Now things get just a little strange. Unbeknownst to us, there's really more code than we see. When you compile and link your application, the linker includes some special start-up code that calls your `main()` function.

10. **Click Next Line one more time and you are time-warped out of your source file and into some assembly language code. The Debugger window shows the following message:**

    ```
    In __mingw_CRTStartup () ()
    ```

11. **Click a new button, Next Instruction (six buttons from the left on the Debugger toolbar), to advance to the next instruction. The Debugger window shows the following message again:**

    ```
    In __mingw_CRTStartup () ()
    ```

12. **To see what this all means, click Debugging Windows (ten buttons from the left on the Debugger toolbar) and choose Disassembly from the drop-down list box.**

    Code::Blocks displays a new window called Disassembly, as shown in Figure 2-2. The numbers in your figure may differ from ours, but the code is the same.

Figure 2-2:
The Disassembly window displays the assembly language version of your code.

Yuck. This is assembly, a human-readable form of the language that the computer understands. You don't have to know what all this means, but you can probably figure out that the line

```
(hexadecimal number) call    (another hexadecimal number) <__main>
```

is where this code stuff calls into your `main()`.

13. **To get out of this, just click the first button (called Debug/Continue) or the fifth button (called Step Out), the one with an arrow pointing to the left of the squares. (Or just press Ctrl+F7 or Ctrl+Shift+F7, respectively.)**

    Clicking Debug/Continue causes the application to run to the real end of your application (or to the next breakpoint) and then finish. Clicking Step Out tells the debugger to step out of the current function, which in this case is the same as running to the end of the application.

14. **If you want to avoid going into the crazy assembly-code stuff, you can avoid it by clicking Debug/Continue when you get to the final `return` line of your application.**

And that's how you step through your application line by line. But you can do a lot more with the application when you're stepping through it. You can look at the values in your variables, you can change the values of the variables, and you can get a list of all the function calls that led up to the current position in your application. You can do plenty, and we explain all this in the remainder of this minibook.

**Book III
Chapter 2**

Debugging an
Application

Recognizing the parts of the Code::Blocks debugger

The Code::Blocks debugger displays the Debugger toolbar whenever you debug an application. The previous sections of this chapter discuss many of the buttons on the Debugger toolbar: Debug/Continue, Next Line, Next Instruction, Step Into, and Step Out. However, the toolbar contains a number of other interesting buttons you should know about.

Sometimes you examine a piece of code in the editor and want to see what the variables look like when you get to that point. To see what happens, place the text cursor at the place you want to stop (hovering the mouse cursor over the place you want to stop isn't enough) and click Run to Cursor (the second button on the Debugger toolbar). The debugger stops at the line where the cursor is resting. In this case, the text cursor acts as a kind of breakpoint for the debugger.

After you debug your application for a while and locate problems you want to fix, you may not want to run the rest of the application. When this situation occurs, simply click Stop Debugger (the button that looks like a box with an X in the middle). The debugger stops immediately. You can make any required changes and restart the debugger as normal.

Code::Blocks provides access to a number of debugging windows. In fact, you can see one of these windows previously in this chapter — the Disassembly window. You access these windows by clicking the Debugging Windows button (the one that looks like a window, to the right of the Stop Debugger button). Later chapters in this minibook describe these windows in detail. Here is a quick summary of the windows for now:

✦ **Breakpoints:** Presents all the breakpoints you've set in your application. Double-clicking a breakpoint entry takes you to that breakpoint in the editor. You can use this window also to remove one or more breakpoints.

✦ **CPU Registers:** Shows the contents of the hardware registers in the processor. You won't normally need to view these registers unless you're performing low-level programming tasks (such as writing a device driver).

✦ **Call Stack:** Displays the function calls used to get to the current point in the code.

✦ **Disassembly:** Lets you see the underlying machine code used to make your code work. You won't normally need to view this information unless you're performing low-level programming tasks.

✦ **Memory Dump:** Displays the precise way that the application stores data in memory, which may not look very much like the C++ view. This window is a useful one because it helps you better understand how memory works and how your application uses memory. In some cases, knowing how a variable stores memory can help you locate problems with your code.

✦ **Running Threads:** Shows a list of threads, other than the main thread, associated with the current application. You use this window for debugging multithreaded applications.

✦ **Watches:** Displays a list of local variables and function arguments. You can also add other variables to monitor as a watch. The Watches window is probably the most useful debugger window because it illustrates the C++ view of your data and shows how the application code manipulates that data.

The debugger also provides access to a number of information windows. You access these windows by clicking the Various Info button (the one with an *i* in italics far down on the left). Here is a quick summary of the information windows:

✦ **Current Stack Frame:** Shows the current stack frame information. C++ creates something called a *stack frame* when certain events occur, such as calling a function. This stack frame contains the data and data references for the current function. You won't normally need to view this information unless you're performing low-level programming tasks.

✦ **Loaded Libraries:** Contains a list of all of the libraries loaded to run your application. It's important to know which libraries your application uses when you deploy (load) it on other machines. In many cases, you may not even know that C++ requires certain libraries to run your application, so this window is exceptionally useful.

✦ **Targets and Files:** Provides a detailed view of how the loaded libraries are used in your application. You won't normally need to view this information unless you're performing low-level programming tasks.

✦ **FPU Status:** Displays the register information for the Floating-Point Unit (FPU) in your processor. At one time, the FPU was a separate chip, but now it appears as part of your main processor. The FPU is exceptionally adept at performing real number (versus integer) math. You won't normally need to view this information unless you're performing low-level programming tasks.

✦ **Signal Handling:** Shows how Code::Blocks handles signals between the hardware and your application, such as an arithmetic exception or a segmentation fault. You won't normally need to view this information unless you're performing low-level programming tasks.

Debugging with Different Tools

You can use several tools for debugging your code. However, which compiler you usually use dictates which debugging tools you can use. For example, Microsoft Visual C++ has a really good debugger. But getting it to debug an application compiled with Dev-C++, for example, is difficult because different compilers use different forms of debugging and symbol information. The type used by the various breeds of gcc compilers is different from the type used by Microsoft Visual C++.

Standard debuggers

Here's a quick rundown of some of the debuggers that are available:

✦ **Visual C++:** This debugger works similarly to the Code::Blocks debugger. It's primarily for debugging applications that were built by using Visual C++. However, if you are brave and need to debug something for which you have no code or symbol information, its support for assembly-code debugging is good.

✦ **gdb:** This is the standard debugger that ships with MinGW and Cygwin. It's a command-line tool, but we don't recommend using it as such. Instead, we suggest using the Insight debugger with it so that you can use a graphical *front end*. This makes life a lot easier. But if you insist on using the command-line version, you can learn about it by typing **gdb** at the command prompt and then typing **help**.

✦ **Dev-C++ 5:** Starting with Version 5, Dev-C++ has an integrated debugger that works similarly to the Insight debugger. You may want to give this a try. (If you're using a version of Dev-C++ prior to 5.0, you have to use the Insight debugger.)

Debugging a Code::Blocks Application with Command Line Arguments

A *command line argument* is something you type along with the command for an application at the command prompt. For example, when you type the `Dir` (directory listing command) at the command prompt, you can include additional information such as `*.DOC`, which will list all files with a `.DOC` extension. (If you use `Dir *.DOC?` instead, you also see any files with a .DOCX extension.) The full command `Dir *.DOC` consists of a command (`Dir`) and a command line argument (`*.DOC`). The addition of command line arguments allows you to extend the functionality of an application and make it do more. In order to test such an application, you need to be able to specify command line arguments as part of the debugger environment.

Code::Blocks, like most other capable IDEs, provides the means for specifying command line arguments. The "Setting the command line parameters in Code::Blocks" sidebar in Book I, Chapter 5 provides you with the basics of setting command line arguments. However, a number of readers of previous editions of this book wanted more information. With this in mind, I wrote a more detailed description of how command line arguments work as part of the post "Debugging a CodeBlocks Application with Command Line Arguments" for this book on my blog at `http://blog.johnmuellerbooks.com/2011/11/01/debugging-a-codeblocks-application-with-command-line-arguments.aspx`. Please be sure to check out this blog post if you want additional information about precisely what is going on.

Chapter 3: Stopping and Inspecting Your Code

In This Chapter

✔ Setting, enabling, and disabling breakpoints

✔ Temporarily setting or disabling a breakpoint

✔ Inspecting a variable

✔ Watching all the local variables

✔ Watching any variable

Sometimes, things break. But what we're talking about here is the code. Now this is one of those instances when a word or phrase has lots of different meanings. Programmers talk about *breaking the code*. This phrase usually means one of two things. It may mean that the programmer made a mistake and the code no longer *works*. But in this chapter, we're using a different definition for the term. When you're debugging an application, you can have the application run until it gets to a certain line in the code. The debugger then stops at that line, and you can look at the values of variables, inspect the code, or even change the variables. When the application stops, that's called *breaking*. The reason it stops on that particular line is because you put a *breakpoint* on that line.

In this chapter, we talk about setting and manipulating breakpoints in your code (if nothing else in your code is broken) and inspecting and modifying various aspects of your code, such as variables, after your code stops at a breakpoint.

In the examples in this chapter, we use the debugger supplied with the Code::Blocks IDE. If you use a different product, the debugger will probably work about the same but not precisely the same. For example, everything we show you how to do here you can do in Microsoft Visual C++. The keystrokes and mouse clicks may be different, but the features are present. Make sure you check the vendor documentation for precise details on using your debugger.

To work through the examples in this chapter, make sure that you compile with debug information turned on. (In Code::Blocks, you can compile with debug information by choosing Debug in the Build Target field of the Compiler toolbar. If you can't see the Compiler toolbar, choose View➪Toolbars➪Compiler to place a check mark next to the Compiler entry.)

When you are developing software, you should always have debug information on. That way, you're always ready to debug your code and fix things. Only when you're ready to release the product formally should you recompile it without debug information. (We do recommend doing a full test of the software again without debug information, just to make sure that it still functions correctly.)

Setting and Disabling Breakpoints

A *breakpoint* is a place in your code where you tell the debugger to stop.

In the sections that follow, we talk about breakpoints. Please use the `Breakpoints` sample code, shown in Listing 3-1, for these sections. Remember what you're supposed to do? Make sure that you compile it with debug information on.

Listing 3-1:   Using an Application for Breakpoints and Inspections

```
#include <iostream>

using namespace std;

class BrokenMirror
{
private:
    int NumberOfPieces;

public:
    int GetNumberOfPieces();
    void SetNumberOfPieces(int newamount);
    BrokenMirror() : NumberOfPieces(100) {}
};

int BrokenMirror::GetNumberOfPieces()
{
    return NumberOfPieces;
}

void BrokenMirror::SetNumberOfPieces(int newamount)
{
    newamount = newamount * 20;
    NumberOfPieces = newamount;
}

int main()
{
    BrokenMirror mirror;
    mirror.SetNumberOfPieces(10);
    cout << mirror.GetNumberOfPieces() << endl;

    return 0;
}
```

Setting a breakpoint in Code::Blocks

Go ahead and compile the application in Listing 3-1 (with debug information turned on). Look at the left margin of the window, to the right of the line numbers. Figure 3-1 shows a small octagon on line 16. When you view the IDE, this octagon is red. The red octagon is a breakpoint that we set. To set this breakpoint in your own code, click in the area between the left margin and the code (or right-click the line of code and choose Toggle Breakpoint from the context menu), as shown in the figure on line 16. (It's line 16 on our screens, but if you formatted your code differently, you may see it on a different line number.) If you haven't done so, go ahead and click the mouse in the left margin of the `int BrokenMirror::GetNumberOfPieces()` line. You see a red octagon appear in the left margin. You just placed a breakpoint on that line! Hurray!

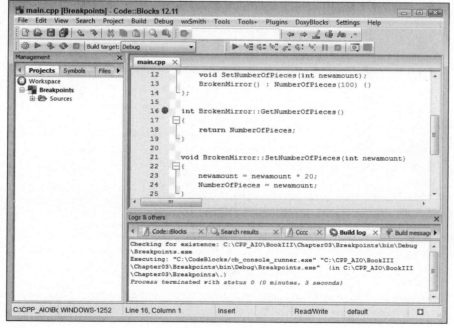

Figure 3-1: Code::Blocks displays any breakpoints you set using a red octagon.

Book III Chapter 3

Stopping and Inspecting Your Code

Click again in the left margin of the same line. The red octagon disappears. When the octagon disappears, the breakpoint is gone.

Finally, click a third time, because for now you do want a breakpoint there.

Now, run the application by clicking the Debug/Continue button (the icon with the red right-pointing arrow on it) on the Debugger toolbar. If you don't see the Debugger toolbar, choose View➪Toolbars➪Debugger to place a check mark next to the Debugger entry. (Don't click the Run button, the green right-pointing triangle, on the Compiler toolbar, because choosing this option simply runs the application without debugging it.) When you click

Debug/Continue, the console window may pop in front, so just click the Code::Blocks window to bring it back to the front.

The application runs until it gets to the breakpoint you chose for the `int BrokenMirror::GetNumberOfPieces()` line, as shown in Figure 3-2. Note that execution actually ends with the opening curly brace because this is the beginning of execution for this function. The yellow right-pointing triangle tells you the current instruction that the Code::Blocks debugger will execute. You can now click the Next Line button (it's the button with two squares and an arrow pointing from the upper square to the lower square) to move to the next line, or you can click Debug/Continue to run the rest of the application.

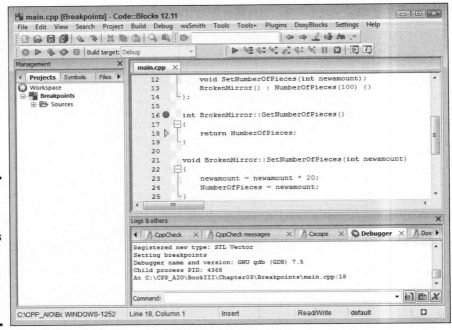

Figure 3-2:
Debug mode tells Code::Blocks to stop execution when it reaches the breakpoint.

Enabling and disabling breakpoints

You may have times when you have several breakpoints set and you want to turn them off momentarily but you don't want to lose them, because you may want to turn them back on later. You can do this by *disabling* the breakpoints. Disabling the breakpoint is faster than removing the breakpoints and then going back and finding them again to turn them back on. Use the following steps to disable a breakpoint:

1. **Right-click the red circle and choose Edit Breakpoint from the context menu.**

You see the Edit Breakpoint dialog box, as shown in Figure 3-3.

Figure 3-3:
Use the Edit
Breakpoint
dialog box
to enable
and disable
breakpoints.

2. **Clear the Enabled option and click OK.**

Code::Blocks disables the breakpoint so that it no longer stops application execution.

Many debuggers show a disabled breakpoint using a hollow red circle (or sometimes an octagon). Code::Blocks turns the red octagon gray instead. However, you'll still want to see that disabling the breakpoint actually does work. Set a new breakpoint at the line that reads `return NumberOfPieces;`. Click Debug/Continue and you'll see that the debugger bypasses the first breakpoint and stops at the second, as shown in Figure 3-4.

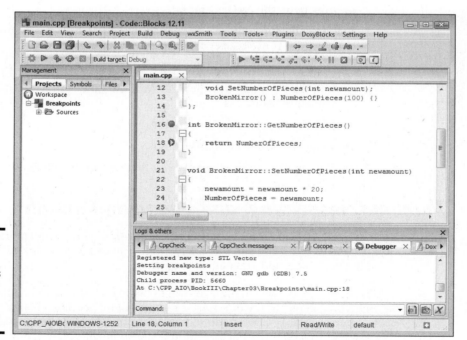

Figure 3-4:
Disabled
breakpoints
don't stop
application
execution.

In some cases, you want to enable or disable a number of breakpoints. Use the following steps to perform this task:

1. **Choose Debug⟡Debugging Windows⟡Breakpoints.**

   You see the Breakpoints window, shown in Figure 3-5. The window shows the kind of breakpoint (with a red or gray octagon to tell you whether it's enabled or disabled), the breakpoint location, the line in the code file where the breakpoint appears, and the name of the debugger being used.

Figure 3-5:
Use the
Breakpoints
window to
access a
number of
breakpoints
at one time.

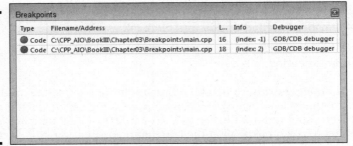

2. **Right-click the breakpoint entry and choose one of the management options from the context menu.**

   The management options help you control one or more breakpoints. You can perform these tasks using the management options:

   • Open the breakpoint in the editor so that you can see where it's located.

   • Edit the breakpoint, which displays the Edit Breakpoint dialog box, shown in Figure 3-3.

   • Disable the selected breakpoint.

   • Remove the selected breakpoint.

   • Remove all the breakpoints you have set in the application.

Watching, Inspecting, and Changing Variables

When you stop at a breakpoint in an application, you can do more than just look at the code. You can have fun with it! You can look at the current values of the variables, and you can change them.

The Breakpoints2 example shown in Listing 3-2 is a sample application that you can use to try out these examples of inspecting, changing, and watching variables. Please note that this application is similar to Listing 3-1, earlier in this chapter, but you should see some differences. Specifically, we added a line to the SetNumberOfPieces() member function

```
newamount = newamount * 20;
```

We added a new function called `SpecialMath()`, and we added an `i` variable to `main()` that is initialized to `10`; then we doubled it, and we passed it into the `SetNumberOfPieces()` function.

Listing 3-2: Using an Application for Breakpoints and Inspections

```cpp
#include <iostream>
#include <cstdlib>

using namespace std;

class BrokenMirror
{
private:
    int NumberOfPieces;

public:
    int GetNumberOfPieces();
    void SetNumberOfPieces(int newamount);
    BrokenMirror() : NumberOfPieces(100) {}
};

int BrokenMirror::GetNumberOfPieces()
{
    return NumberOfPieces;
}

void BrokenMirror::SetNumberOfPieces(int newamount)
{
    newamount = newamount * 20;
    NumberOfPieces = newamount;
}

int SpecialMath(int x)
{
    return x * 10 - 5;
}

int main()
{
    int i = 10;
    BrokenMirror mirror;

    i = i + SpecialMath(i);

    mirror.SetNumberOfPieces(i);
    cout << mirror.GetNumberOfPieces() << endl;

    // Clear this comment if you want the application to stop to
    // display the results.
    // system("PAUSE");

    return 0;
}
```

Watching the variables

To watch the variables in your application, follow these steps:

1. **Compile this application with debug information on.**

2. **Set a breakpoint at the `int i = 10;` line in `main()`.**

3. **Click Debug/Continue.**

4. **When the debugger stops at the breakpoint, choose Debug⇨Debugging Windows⇨Watches.**

   You see the Watches window, as shown in Figure 3-6.

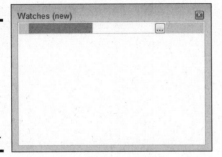

Figure 3-6: The Watches window shows the value of variables and objects.

5. **Type i in the first column (the highlighted cell in Figure 3-6) of the Watches window and press Enter.**

   You see the current value of `i`, which is some very odd number — 1981092194 in Figure 3-7 — but the value you see is probably different. The third column shows the variable type, which is `int`. In this case, the variable is shown in red because C++ has just created it.

Figure 3-7: Providing the name of a variable shows you its value.

When C++ creates a new variable, it simply creates the variable and doesn't assign a value to it. The variable contains a junk value — you have no idea of what the variable might contain. This is the reason you never want to use a variable until after you assign a value to it.

6. **Click the Next Line button on the Debugger toolbar so that you are one line beyond the following line:**

```
int i = 10;
```

The application changes the value of i to 10, as shown in Figure 3-8. The variable is still shown in red because its value has just changed.

Figure 3-8: Assigning a value to *i* changes its value in the Watches window.

7. **Click Next Line on the Debugger toolbar.**

The entry for i turns black to show that it has remained stable during the execution of this command. The use of red for changed variables and black for unchanged variables makes it easy to determine which variables have changed.

8. **Click Debug/Continue.**

The application ends.

Watching objects

Objects are just a little bit more complex than variables when you use the Watches window. When you type the name of an object in the Watches window, such as mirror, what you see is the name of the object with a plus sign next to it. Click the plus sign and the view expands to show the content of the object, such as NumberOfPieces, as shown in Figure 3-9.

Figure 3-9:
Objects
can contain
variables
and other
objects.

Objects contain not only variables but also other objects. When an object contains a child object, the child object will also have a plus sign next to it. To see the contents of this child object, simply click the plus sign next to it. You can keep drilling down until you reach the end of the object list.

Changing values

Sometimes you need to verify that the application works as intended by simulating changes that might occur in the code. In many cases, this means changing a value from its default to the value you want to test. Fortunately, the Watches window provides the means to perform this task. Follow these steps to see how you can change variable values. (We assume that you have already compiled the application with debug information.)

1. **Set a breakpoint at the** `i = i + SpecialMath(i);` **line in** `main()`.

2. **Click Debug/Continue.**

3. **When the debugger stops at the breakpoint, choose Debug➪Debugging Windows➪Watches.**

   You see the Watches window, as shown in Figure 3-6.

4. **Type** i **in the first column of the Watches window and press Enter.**

   You see the current value of i, which is 10.

5. **Select the value, 10, in the second column of the Watches window, type** 100, **and click on the next line of the Watches window.**

   Code::Blocks changes the value of i to 100. The i variable entry used to be black, and now it has turned red because you changed the value.

6. **Click Next Line three times so that the instruction pointer is on the line that reads:**

   ```
   return 0;
   ```

   Notice that the output of the application has changed to 21900. Normally the output is 2100. The difference occurs because the value of i was changed.

7. **Click Debug/Continue.**

   The application ends.

Chapter 4: Traveling About the Stack

In This Chapter

- ✓ Moving about the stack
- ✓ How local variables are stored
- ✓ Viewing threads
- ✓ Tracing through assembly code
- ✓ Viewing memory

Debuggers can be powerful things. They can leap tall computer applications in a single bound and see through them to find all their flaws. The more you know about these little debuggers, the more you can put them to use. In this chapter, we show you how to move about the stack and make use of advanced debugger features.

Stacking Your Data

A stack is a common thing in the computer world. We have stacks of bills and stacks of paychecks and stacks of data. The stacks of data are interesting because, unlike bills and paychecks, they live inside the computer's memory. But the stack metaphor is appropriate. When the operating system runs an application, it gives that application a *stack,* which is simply a big chunk of memory. But the data is stored just like a stack of cards: With a stack of real cards, you can put a card on the top, and then another, and do that six times over; then you can take a card off and take another card off. You can put cards on the top and take them off the top. And if you follow these rules, you can't insert them into the middle or bottom of the stack. You can only look at what's on the top. A stack *data structure* works the same way: You can store data in it by *pushing* the data *onto* the stack, and you can take data off by *popping* it *off* the stack. And yes, because the stack is just a bunch of computer memory, sneaking around and accessing memory in the middle of the stack is possible. But under normal circumstances, you don't do that: You put data on and take data off.

What's interesting about the stack is that it works closely with the main CPU, such as the Intel Pentium or AMD Athlon 64 or whatever is inside your computer. The CPU has its own little storage bin right on the chip itself. (It isn't in the system memory, or RAM; it's inside the CPU itself.)

This storage bin holds what are called *registers*. One such register is the *stack pointer*, called the ESP. (It stands for extended stack pointer, consisting of 32 bits or 64 bits, because the earlier Intel processors had only a 16-bit stack pointer, or SP. When the folks at Intel replaced the earlier chips with newer, more powerful chips, they made the registers bigger and stuck on the letter *E,* for *e*xtended, to denote the bigger registers.)

The stack is useful in many situations and is used extensively behind the scenes in the applications you write. The compiler generates code that uses the stack to store:

✦ Local variables

✦ Function parameters

✦ Function calling order

It's all stacked onto the stack and stuck in place, ready to be unstacked.

Moving about the stack

The Code::Blocks debugger, like most debuggers, lets you look at the stack. But really, you're not looking directly at the stack. When a debugger shows you the *stack,* it is showing you the list of function calls that led up to the application's current position in the application code. However, that information is stored in the stack, and the debugger uses the stack to get that information. So that's why programmers always call the list of function calls the *stack,* even though you're not actually looking at the stack.

Figure 4-1 shows an example of the Call Stack window in Code::Blocks. To see the Call Stack window, simply choose Debug⇨Debugging Windows⇨Call Stack. You can see the Call Stack window in front of the main Code::Blocks window. No information appears in the Call Stack window until you start running an application.

Figure 4-1:
The Call Stack window shows the function calls that led up to the current position.

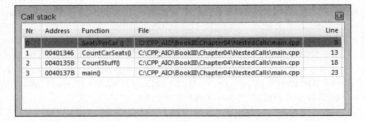

Nr	Address	Function	File	Line
0		SeatsPerCar ()	C:\CPP_AIO\BookIII\Chapter04\NestedCalls\main.cpp	8
1	00401346	CountCarSeats()	C:\CPP_AIO\BookIII\Chapter04\NestedCalls\main.cpp	13
2	0040135B	CountStuff()	C:\CPP_AIO\BookIII\Chapter04\NestedCalls\main.cpp	18
3	0040137B	main()	C:\CPP_AIO\BookIII\Chapter04\NestedCalls\main.cpp	23

You can try viewing the stack yourself. Take a look at the `NestedCalls` example, shown in Listing 4-1. This listing shows a simple application that makes several nested function calls.

Listing 4-1:   Making Nested Function Calls

```
#include <iostream>
#include <cstdlib>

using namespace std;

int SeatsPerCar()
{
    return 4;
}

int CountCarSeats()
{
    return 10 * SeatsPerCar();
}

int CountStuff()
{
    return CountCarSeats() + 25;
}

int main()
{
    cout << CountStuff() << endl;
    // Remove the following comment to see the code
    // execute in the debugger.
    //system("PAUSE");
    return 0;
}
```

To try out the Call Stack window, follow these steps:

1. **Compile this application (set the Build Target field to Debug).**

2. **Set a breakpoint at the `int main()` line.**

3. **Run the application in the Code::Blocks debugger by pressing F8.**

4. **Step into the `CountStuff` function, and then into the `CountCarSeats` function, and then into the `SeatsPerCar` function.**

   (Or, just put a breakpoint in the `SeatsPerCar` function and run the application until it stops at the breakpoint.)

5. **Choose Debug⇨Debugging Windows⇨Call Stack.**

   A window like the one in Figure 4-1 appears. Note the order of function calls in the Call Stack window:

   ```
   SeatsPerCall()
   CountCarSeats()
   CountStuff()
   main()
   ```

This information in the Call Stack window means that your application started out with `main()`, which called `CountStuff()`. That function then called `CountCarSeats()`, which in turn called `SeatsPerCall()`. And that's where you are now. Code::Blocks places a red highlight on the current stack location — the block of code that the application is currently executing.

This window is handy if you want to know what path the application took to get to a particular routine. For example, you might see a routine that is called from many places in your application and you're not sure which part is calling the routine when you perform a certain task. To find out which part calls the routine, set a breakpoint in the function. When you run the application and the debugger stops at that line, the Call Stack window shows you the path the computer took to get there, including the name of the function that called the function in question.

In the Call Stack window, you can double-click any function name, and the Debugger moves the cursor to the function's body in the source code. This feature makes it easy for you to locate any function within the call stack and see why the code followed the path it did. When you switch to a new location in the call stack, the red bar moves to that location in the Call Stack window so that you can always keep track of where you are in the call stack.

Stack features are common to almost all debuggers. We won't say *all,* because we're sure that some truly bad debuggers that don't have stack features are out there. But the good debuggers, including those built into Code::Blocks and Microsoft Visual C++, include features for moving about the stack.

Debuggers use different terminology for the window that shows stack information. Borland C++ Builder and Borland Delphi (a Pascal tool) both use the term *call stack,* just like Code::Blocks. To open the Call Stack window in C++ Builder, choose View⇨Debug Windows⇨Call Stack. The Insight debugger uses the term *Stack window;* you access it by choosing View⇨Stack. No matter what a particular product calls the window that contains stack information, the essential functionality is the same — to show how you arrived at a particular point in the code.

Storing local variables

As you get heavily into debugging, it always helps to fully understand what goes on under the hood of your application. At this point, we'll speak on two levels: One level is your C++ code, and the other is the resulting assembly code that the compiler generates based on your C++ code. (*Assembly* is the human-readable form of machine code that the processor on your machine understands.) Throughout this chapter, we clearly state which level we're referring to.

Suppose that you write a function in C++ and you call the function in another part of your application. When the compiler generates the assembly code for the function, it inserts some special code at the beginning and at the end of the function. At the start of the function, this special code allocates space for the local variables. At the end of the function, the special code de-allocates the space. This space for the variables is called the *stack frame* for the function.

This space for the local variables lives on the stack. The storage process works as follows: When you call your function, the computer pushes the return address onto the stack. After the computer is running inside the function, the special code that the compiler inserted saves some more of the stack space — just enough for the variables. This extra space becomes the local storage for the variables; and just before the function returns, the special code removes this local space. Thus, the top of the stack is now the return address. The return then functions correctly.

This process with the stack frame takes place with the help of the internal registers in the CPU. Before a function call, the assembly code pushes the arguments to the function onto the stack. Then it calls the function by using the CPU's built-in `call` statement. (That's an assembly-code statement.) This `call` statement pushes the return address onto the stack and then moves the instruction pointer to the function address. After the execution is inside the function, the stack contains the function arguments and then the return address. The special function start-up code (called a *prolog*) saves the value in one of the CPU registers, called the Extended Base Pointer (or EBP) register.

Where does the prolog save the value? On the stack! The prolog code first pushes the EBP value onto the stack. Then the prolog code takes the current stack pointer (which points to the top of the stack in memory) and saves it back in the EBP register for later use. Then the prolog code adjusts the stack pointer to make room for the local variable storage. The code inside the function then accesses the local variables as offsets above the position of EBP on the stack and the arguments as offsets below the position of EBP on the stack.

Finally, at the end of the function, the special code (now called an *epilog*) undoes the work: The epilog copies the value in EBP back into the stack pointer; this de-allocates the local variable storage. Then it *pops* the top of the stack off (as opposed to *blow* the top of the stack off) and restores this value back into EBP. (That was, after all, the original value in EBP when the function started.) Now the top of the stack contains the function return address, which is back to the way it was when the function began. The next assembly statement is a `return`, which *pulls* the top of the stack off and goes back to the address that the epilog code pulled off the stack. Just think: Every single time a function call takes place in your computer, this process takes place. (Kinda gives you newfound respect for that big pile of bits and bytes, doesn't it?)

Inside the computer, the stack actually runs upside down. When you push something onto the stack, the stack pointer goes *down* in memory — it gets *decremented.* When you pop something off the stack, the stack pointer gets *incremented.* Therefore, in the stack frame, the local variables are actually *below* EBP in memory, and you access their addresses by subtracting from the value stored in the EBP register. The function arguments, in turn, are *above* the EBP in memory, and you get their addresses by adding to the value stored in EBP.

The one topic we didn't discuss in the preceding Technical Stuff paragraph is the return value of a function. In C++, the standard way to return a value from a function is for the function's assembly code to move the value into the Extended Accumulator, or EAX, register. Then the calling code can simply inspect the EAX register after the function is finished. However, if you are returning something complex, such as a class instance, things get a bit more complex. Suppose that you have a function that returns an object, but not as a pointer, as in the function header `MyClass MyFunction();`. Different compilers handle this differently, but when the gcc compiler that's a part of Code::Blocks, Dev-C++, MinGW, or Cygwin encounters something such as `MyClass inst = MyFunction();`, it takes the address of `inst` and puts it in EAX. Then, in the function, it allocates space for a local variable, and in the `return` line it copies the object in the local variable into the object whose address is in EAX. So when you return a nonpointer object, you are, in a sense, passing your object into the function as a pointer!

Debugging with Advanced Features

Most debuggers, including Code::Blocks, have some advanced features that are handy when tracing through your application. These features include the capability to look at threads and assembly code.

Viewing threads

If you are writing an application that uses multiple threads and you stop at a breakpoint, you can get a list of all current threads by using the Running Threads window. To open the Running Threads window, in the main Code::Blocks window choose Debug⇨Debugging Windows⇨Running Threads. A window showing the currently running threads opens. Each line looks something like this:

```
2 thread 2340.0x6cc  test() at main.cpp:7
```

The first number indicates which thread this is in the application; for example, this is the second thread. The two numbers after the word `thread` are the process ID and the thread ID, separated by a dot. Then you see the name of the function where the thread is stopped, along with the line number where the thread is stopped.

Tracing through assembly code

If you feel the urge, you can view the actual assembly code. The only time we ever do this is when we absolutely must get down to the hard-core nitty-gritty. Code::Blocks lets you do this. Choose Debug⇨Debugging Windows⇨Disassembly to see the Disassembly window. We strongly suggest checking the Mixed Mode option so that you can see a mix of C++ and assembly code, as shown in Figure 4-2. This approach makes it a lot easier to understand how Code::Blocks turns your C++ code into assembly language. Notice that the top of the window tells you the name of the function you're viewing and which file contains the function, and the C++ code includes line numbers so that you know precisely where you are in the source code.

Figure 4-2:
The Disassembly window shows the assembly code that results from the C++ code you write.

Some readers have noted that Code::Blocks will sometimes freeze when displaying the Disassembly window. The IDE will report that the disassembly is being loaded, but the process never completes. In this case, close the sample code and restart the IDE. In most cases, the disassembly will load on the second try.

The window shown in Figure 4-2 is the disassembly of the `SeatsPerCar()` function, shown in Listing 4-1. Here's the function again so that you can compare it to Figure 4-2:

```
int SeatsPerCar()
{
    return 4;
}
```

The following lines create the stack frame:

```
004013EE    push    %ebp
004013EF    mov     %esp,%ebp
```

After the code creates a stack frame, it moves a value of 4 (the return 4; part of the code) into EAX, as shown here:

```
004013F1    mov     $0x4,%eax
```

The code then pops EBP and returns to the caller (the CountCarSeats() function) using this code:

```
004013F6    pop     %ebp
004013F7    ret
```

Now, if you move into the CountCarSeats() function, you see assembly like that shown in Figure 4-3.

Figure 4-3:
This Disassembly window shows the CountCarSeats() function code.

As before, the assembly code begins by creating a stack frame. It then issues a call to the SeatsPerCar() function. When the function returns, the assembly performs the multiplication part of the task. Finally, the code performs the usual task of placing the return value in EAX, popping EBP, and returning to the caller. Notice that what appears to be simple multiplication to you may not be as simple in assembly language. Let's say that you change the code to read

```
int CountCarSeats()
{
    return 4 * SeatsPerCar();
}
```

The math is simpler now because you're using 4, which is easily converted into a binary value. Figure 4-4 shows the assembly that results from this simple change.

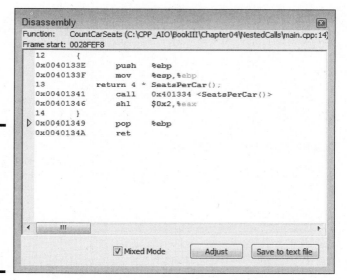

Figure 4-4: Small C++ code changes can result in large assembly-code changes.

Now all the code does is perform a shift-left (SHL) instruction. Shifting the value in EAX left by 2 is the same as multiplying it by 4. The reason the assembler uses the SHL instruction is that shifting takes far fewer clock cycles than multiplication, which makes the code run faster. The result is the same, even if the assembly code doesn't quite match your C++ code.

If you want to see the values in the registers so that you can more easily follow the assembly code, choose Debug➪Debugging Windows➪CPU Registers. You see the CPU Registers window, shown in Figure 4-5. This window reflects the state of the registers at the current stopping point in the code. Consequently, you can't see each step of the assembly code shown in the Disassembly window reflected in these registers unless you step through the code, one instruction at a time.

CPU Registers			
Register	Hex	Integer	
eax	0x10	16	
ecx	0x1	1	
edx	0x8e3c8	582600	
ebx	0x7efde000	2130567168	
esp	0x28fef0	2686704	
ebp	0x28fef0	2686704	
esi	0x0	0	
edi	0x0	0	
eip	0x401349	4199241	
eflags	0x202	514	
cs	0x23	35	
ss	0x2b	43	
ds	0x2b	43	
es	0x2b	43	
fs	0x53	83	
gs	0x2b	43	

Figure 4-5:
Viewing
the CPU
registers
can give you
insight into
how code
interacts
with the
processor.

Book IV
Advanced Programming

This edition of the book looks at some new features of C++, including dynamic arrays. You can find an example of how to use a dynamic array with a structure at http://www.dummies.com/extras/cplusplusaio. Dynamic arrays make it possible to create extremely flexible data containers that rely on the heap to store information.

Contents at a Glance

Chapter 1: Working with Arrays, Pointers, and References

In This Chapter

✔ Working with arrays and multidimensional arrays

✔ Understanding the connection between arrays and pointers

✔ Dealing with pointers in all their forms

✔ Using reference variables

When the C programming language, predecessor to C++, came out in the early 1970s, it was a breakthrough because it was *small*. C had only a few keywords. Tasks like printing to the console were handled not by built-in keywords but by functions.

Technically, C++ is still small. So what makes C++ big?

✦ The language itself is small, but its libraries are huge.

✦ The language is small, but it's extremely sophisticated, resulting in millions of things you can do with the language.

In this chapter, we give you the full rundown of topics that lay the foundation for C++: arrays, pointers, and references. In C++, these items come up again and again.

We assume that you have a basic understanding of C++ — that is, that you understand the material in Book I and Book II, Chapter 1. You know the basics of pointers and arrays (and maybe just a teeny bit about references) and you're ready to grasp them thoroughly.

Building Up Arrays

As you work with arrays, it seems like you can do a million things with them. This section provides the complete details on arrays. The more you know about arrays, the less likely you are to use them incorrectly, which would result in a bug.

Know how to get the most out of arrays when necessary — not just because they're there. Avoid using arrays in the most complex way imaginable.

Declaring arrays

The usual way of declaring an array is to simply line up the type name, followed by a variable name, followed by a size in brackets, as in this line of code:

```
int Numbers[10];
```

This code declares an array of 10 integers. The first element gets index 0, and the final element gets index 9. Always remember that in C++ arrays start at 0, and the highest index is one less than the size. (Remember, *index* refers to the position within the array, and *size* refers to the number of elements in the array.)

A common question that the usual programming student asks is, "Can I just declare an array without specifying a size?" The line would look like this:

```
int Numbers[]
```

In certain situations, you can declare an array without putting a number in the brackets. For example, you can initialize an array without specifying the number of elements:

```
    int MyNumbers[] = {1,2,3,4,5,6,7,8,9,10};
```

The compiler is smart enough to count how many elements you put inside the braces, and then the compiler makes that count the array size.

Specifying the array size helps decrease your chances of having bugs, bugs, everywhere bugs. Plus, it has the added benefit that, in the actual declaration, if the number in brackets does not match the number of elements inside braces, the compiler issues an error, at least if the number is smaller anyway. The following

```
int MyNumbers[5] = {1,2,3,4,5,6,7,8,9,10};
```

yields this compiler error:

```
error: too many initializers for 'int [5]'
```

But if the number in brackets is greater than the number of elements, as in the following code, you will not get an error. So be careful!

```
int MyNumbers[15] = {1,2,3,4,5,6,7,8,9,10};
```

You also can skip specifying the array size when you pass an array into a function, like this:

```
int AddUp(int Numbers[], int Count) {
    int loop;
    int sum = 0;
    for (loop = 0; loop < Count; loop++) {
        sum += Numbers[loop];
    }
    return sum;
}
```

This technique is particularly powerful because the AddUp function can work for any size array. You can call the function like this:

```
cout << AddUp(MyNumbers, 10) << endl;
```

But this way to do it is kind of annoying because you have to specify the size each time you call in to the function. However, you can get around this problem. Look at this line of code:

```
cout << AddUp(MyNumbers, sizeof(MyNumbers) / 4) << endl;
```

With the array, the sizeof operator tells you how many bytes it uses. But the size of the array is usually the number of elements, not the number of bytes. So you divide the result of sizeof by 4 (the size of each element).

But now you have that magic number, 4, sitting there. (By *magic number*, we mean a seemingly arbitrary number that's stuffed somewhere into your code.) So a slightly better approach would be to enter this line:

```
cout << AddUp(MyNumbers, sizeof(MyNumbers) / sizeof(int)) << endl;
```

Now this line of code works, and here's why: The sizeof the array divided by the sizeof each element in the array gives the number of elements in the array.

Arrays and pointers

The name of the array is a pointer to the array itself. The *array* is a sequence of variables stored in memory. The *array name* points to the first item.

This is an interesting question about pointers: Can we have a function header, such as the following line, and just use sizeof to determine how many elements are in the array? If so, this function wouldn't need to have the caller specify the size of the array.

```
int AddUp(int Numbers[]) {
```

Consider this function found in the `Array01` example and a `main()` that calls it:

```
void ProcessArray(int Numbers[]) {
    cout << "Inside function: Size in bytes is "
      << sizeof(Numbers) << endl;
}
int main(int argc, char *argv[])
{
    int MyNumbers[] = {1,2,3,4,5,6,7,8,9,10};
    cout << "Outside function: Size in bytes is ";
    cout << sizeof(MyNumbers) << endl;
    ProcessArray(MyNumbers);
    return 0;
}
```

When you run this application, here's what you see:

```
Outside function: Size in bytes is 40
Inside function: Size in bytes is 4
```

Outside the function, the code knows that the size of the array is 40 bytes. But why does the code think that the size is 4 after it is inside the array? The reason is that even though it appears that you're passing an array, you're really passing a *pointer* to an array. The size of the pointer is just 4, and so that's what the final `cout` line prints.

Declaring arrays has a slight idiosyncrasy. When you declare an array by giving a definite number of elements, such as

```
int MyNumbers[5];
```

the compiler knows that you have an array, and the `sizeof` operator gives you the size of the entire array. The array name, then, is *both* a pointer and an array! But if you declare a function header without an array size, such as

```
void ProcessArray(int Numbers[]) {
```

the compiler treats this as simply a *pointer* and nothing more. This last line is, in fact, equivalent to the following line:

```
void ProcessArray(int *Numbers) {
```

Thus, inside the functions that either line declares, the following two lines of code are *equivalent*:

```
Numbers[3] = 10;
*(Numbers + 3) = 10;
```

This equivalence means that if you use an `extern` declaration on an array, such as

```
extern int MyNumbers[];
```

and then take the size of this array, the compiler will get confused. Here's an example: If you have two files, `numbers.cpp` and `main.cpp`, where `numbers.cpp` declares an array and `main.cpp` externally declares it (as shown in the Array02 example), you will get a compiler error if you call `sizeof`:

```
#include <iostream>

using namespace std;

extern int MyNumbers[];
int main(int argc, char *argv[])
{
    cout << sizeof(MyNumbers) << endl;
    return 0;
}
```

In Code::Blocks (which is the compiler we're using for most of this book; see Appendix B for more information), the gcc compiler gives us this error:

```
error: invalid application of 'sizeof' to incomplete type 'int []'
```

The solution is to put the size of the array inside brackets. Just make sure that the size is the same as in the other source code file! You can fake out the compiler by changing the number, and you *won't get an error*. But that's bad programming style and just asking for errors.

Although an *array* is simply a sequence of variables all adjacent to each other in memory, the *name* of an array is really just a pointer to the first element in the array. You can use the name as a pointer. However, do that only when you really need to work with a pointer. After all, you really have no reason to write code that is cryptic, such as `*(Numbers + 3) = 10;`.

The converse is also true. Look at this function:

```
void ProcessArray(int *Numbers) {
    cout << Numbers[1] << endl;
}
```

This function takes a pointer as a parameter, yet we access it as an array. Again, we do not recommend writing code like this; instead, we recommend that you understand *why code like this works*. That way, you gain a deeper knowledge of arrays and how they live inside the computer, and this knowledge, in turn, can help you write code that works properly.

Book IV Chapter 1

Working with Arrays, Pointers, and References

Even though, throughout this chapter, we're telling you that the array name is just a pointer, the name of an array of integers isn't the exact same thing as a pointer to an integer. Check out these lines of code (found in the Array03 example):

```
int LotsONumbers[50];
int x;
LotsONumbers = &x;
```

We're trying to point the LotsONumbers *pointer* to something different: something declared as an integer. The compiler doesn't let you do this; you get an error. That wouldn't be the case if LotsONumbers were declared as int *LotsONumbers; then this code would work. But as written, this code gives you a compiler error. And believe it or not, here's the compiler error we get in Code::Blocks:

```
error: incompatible types in assignment of 'int*' to 'int [50]'
```

This error implies the compiler does see a definite distinction between the two types, int * and int[]. Nevertheless, the array name is indeed a pointer, and you can use it as one; you just can't do everything with it that you can with a normal pointer, such as reassign it. (If we were philosophers, we might argue that an array name's type is not equivalent to its equivalent. But we're not philosophers, so when we suggest something like that, we're only being equivalent to philosophers.)

When using arrays, then, we suggest the following tips. These will help you keep your arrays bug-free:

✦ Keep your code consistent. If you declare, for example, a pointer to an integer, do not treat it as an array.

✦ Keep your code clear and understandable. If you pass pointers, it's okay to take the address of the first element, as in &(MyNumbers[0]) if this makes the code clearer — though it's equivalent to just MyNumbers.

✦ When you declare an array, always try to put a number inside the brackets, unless you are writing a function that takes an array.

✦ When you use the extern keyword to declare an array, go ahead and also put the array size inside brackets. But be consistent! Don't use one number one time and a different number another time. The easiest way to be consistent is to use a constant, such as const int ArraySize = 10; in a common header file and then use that in your array declaration: int MyArray[ArraySize];.

Using multidimensional arrays

Arrays do not have to be just one-dimensional. You can declare a multidimensional array, as shown in the `Array04` example in Listing 1-1.

Listing 1-1:   Using a Multidimensional Array

```
#include <iostream>
#include <cstdlib>

using namespace std;

int MemorizeThis[10][20];

int main(int argc, char *argv[])
{
    int x,y;
    for (x = 0; x < 10; x++) {
        for (y = 0; y < 20; y++ ) {
            MemorizeThis[x][y] = x * y;
        }
    }
    cout << MemorizeThis[9][13] << endl;
    cout << sizeof(MemorizeThis) / sizeof(int) << endl;
    return 0;
}
```

When you run this, `MemorizeThis` gets filled with the multiplication tables (thus the clever name!). Here's the output for the application, which is the contents of `MemorizeThis[9][13]`, and then the size of the entire two-dimensional array:

```
117
200
```

And indeed, 9 times 13 is 117. The size of the array is 200 elements. Because each element, being an integer, is 4 bytes, that means that the size in bytes is 800.

You can have many, many dimensions, but be *careful*. Every time you add a dimension, the size multiplies by the size of that dimension. Thus an array declared like the following line has 48,600 elements, for a total of 194,400 bytes:

```
int BigStuff[4][3][5][3][5][6][9];
```

And the following array has 4,838,400 elements, for a total of 19,353,600 bytes. That's about 19 megabytes!

```
int ReallyBigStuff[8][6][10][6][5][7][12][4];
```

Book IV
Chapter 1

Working with
Arrays, Pointers,
and References

If you really have this kind of a data structure, consider redesigning it. Any data stored like this would be downright confusing. And fortunately, the compiler will stop you from going totally overboard. Just for fun we tried this giant monster:

```
int GiantMonster[18][16][10][16][15][17][12][14];
```

This is the error we got:

```
error: size of array 'GiantMonster' is too large
```

(That would be 1,974,067,200 bytes: more than a gigabyte!)

Initializing multidimensional arrays

Just as you can initialize a single-dimensional array by using braces and separating the elements by commas, you can initialize a multidimensional array with braces and commas and all that jazz, too. But to do this, you combine arrays inside arrays, as in this code:

```
int Numbers[5][6] = {
    {1,2,3,4,5,6},
    {7,8,9,10,12},
    {13,14,15,16,17,18},
    {19,20,21,22,23,24},
    {25,26,27,28,29,30}
};
```

The hard part is remembering whether you put in five batches of six or six batches of five. Think of it like this: Each time you add another dimension, it goes *inside* the previous dimension. That is, you can write a single-dimensional array like this:

```
int MoreNumbers[5] = {
    100,
    200,
    300,
    400,
    500,
};
```

Then, if you add a dimension to this array, each number in the initialization is replaced by an array initializer of the form {1,2,3,4,5,6}. Then you end up with a properly formatted multidimensional array.

Passing multidimensional arrays

If you have to pass a multidimensional array to a function, things can get just a bit hairy. That's because you don't have as much freedom in leaving off the array sizes as you do with single-dimensional arrays. Suppose you have this function:

```
int AddAll(int MyGrid[5][6]) {
    int x,y;
    int sum = 0;
    for (x = 0; x < 5; x++) {
        for (y = 0; y < 6; y++) {
            sum += MyGrid[x][y];
        }
    }
    return sum;
}
```

So far, the function header is fine because we're explicitly stating the size of each dimension. But you may want to do this:

```
int AddAll(int MyGrid[][]) {
```

or maybe pass the sizes as well:

```
int AddAll(int MyGrid[][], int rows, int columns) {
```

But unfortunately, when we compile either of these two lines, we get this error:

```
declaration of 'MyGrid' as multidimensional array
must have bounds for all dimensions except the first
```

That's strange: The compiler is telling us that we must explicitly list all the dimensions, but it's okay if we leave the first one blank, as with one-dimensional arrays.

So that means this crazy thing will compile:

```
int AddAll(int MyGrid[][6]) {
```

How about that? The reason is that the compiler treats multidimensional arrays in a special way. A multidimensional array is not really a two-dimensional array, for example; rather, it's an array of an array. Thus, deep down inside C++, the compiler treats the statement MyGrid[5][6] as if it were MyGrid[5] *where each item in the array is itself an array of size 6.* And you're free not to specify the size of a one-dimensional array. Well, the first brackets represent the one-dimensional portion of the array. So you can leave that space blank, as you can with other one-dimensional arrays. But then, after that, you have to give the array *bounds.* Sounds strange, we know. And perhaps just a bit contrived. But it's C++, and it's the rule: You can leave the first dimension blank in a function header, but you must specify the remaining dimension sizes.

When using multidimensional arrays, it's often easier on our brains if we think of them as an *array of arrays*. Then we use a `typedef` so that, instead of it being an array of arrays, it's an array of some user-defined type, such as `GridRow`. Either of the following function headers, for example, is confusing:

```
int AddAll(int MyGrid[][6]) {

int AddAll(int MyGrid[][6], int count) {
```

Here's our recommendation: Use a `typedef`. So here's a cleaner way:

```
typedef int GridRow[6];
int AddAll(GridRow MyGrid[], int Size) {
    int x,y;
    int sum = 0;
    for (x = 0; x < Size; x++) {
        for (y = 0; y < 6; y++) {
            sum += MyGrid[x][y];
        }
    }
    return sum;
}
```

The `typedef` line defines a new type called `GridRow`. This type is an array of six integers. Then, in the function, you're passing an array of `GridRow`s.

Using this `typedef` is the same as simply using two brackets, except it emphasizes that you're passing an *array of an array* — that is, an array in which each member is itself an array of type `GridRow`.

Arrays and command-line parameters

In a typical C++ application, the `main()` function receives an array and a count as *command line parameters* — parameters provided as part of the command to execute that application at the command line. However, to beginning programmers, the parameters can look intimidating. But they're not: Think of the two parameters as an array of strings and a size of the array. However, each string in this array of strings is actually a character array. In the old days of C, and earlier breeds of C++, no `string` class was available. Thus strings were always character arrays, usually denoted as `char *MyString`. (Remember, an array and a pointer can be used interchangeably for the most part). Thus you could take this thing and turn it into an array — either by throwing brackets at the end, as in `char *MyString[ ]`, or by making use of the fact that an array is a pointer and adding a second pointer symbol, as in `char **MyString`. The following code from the `CommandLineParams` example shows how you can get the command-line parameters:

```
#include <iostream>

using namespace std;

int main(int argc, char *argv[])
{
    int loop;
    for (loop = 0; loop < argc; loop++) {
        cout << argv[loop] << endl;
    }
    return 0;
}
```

When you compile this application, name the executable CommandLineParams, and then run it from the command prompt, using the following command:

```
CommandLineParams abc def "abc 123"
```

You see the following output. (Note that the application name comes in as the first parameter and the quoted items come in as a single parameter.)

```
CommandLineParams
abc
def
abc 123
```

You can also specify command-line arguments using the IDE for debugging purposes when working with the Code::Blocks compiler. Choose Project↪Set Program's Arguments. Code::Blocks displays the Select Target dialog box, where you choose a target in the first field and type the arguments in the Program Arguments field. Click OK and then click Run. CommandLineParams displays the command-line arguments in the command window as it did when you typed the command at the command prompt.

Allocating an array on the heap

Arrays are useful, but it would be a bummer if the only way you could use them were as stack variables. If you could allocate an array on the heap by using the new keyword, that would be nice. (If you can't quite remember the difference between the stack and the heap, check out the "Heaping and Stacking the Variables" section in Book I, Chapter 7.) Well, good news! You can! But you need to know about a couple of little tricks to make it work.

First, you can easily declare an array on the heap by using new int[50], for example. But think about what this is doing: It declares 50 integers on the heap, and the new word returns a pointer to the allocated array. But, unfortunately, the makers of C++ didn't see it that way. For some reason, they based the array pointer type on the first element of the array (which is, of course, the same as all the elements in the array).

Thus the call

```
new int[50]
```

returns a pointer of type `int *`, not something that explicitly points to an array, just as this call does:

```
new int;
```

Nice, huh? But that's okay. We can deal with it. So if you want to save the results of new `int [50]` in a variable, you have to have a variable of type `int *`, as in the following:

```
int *MyArray = new int[50];
```

But here's the bizarre part: An array name is a pointer and vice versa. So now that you have a pointer to an integer, you can treat it like an array:

```
MyArray[0] = 25;
```

And now for the *really* bizarre part. When you're all finished with the array, you can call `delete`. But you can't just call `delete MyArray;`. The reason is that the compiler knows only that `MyArray` is a pointer to an integer; it doesn't know that it's an array! Thus `delete MyArray` will only delete the first item in the array, leaving the rest of the elements sitting around on the heap, wondering when their time will come. So the makers of C++ gave us a special form of `delete` to handle this situation. It looks like this:

```
delete[] MyArray;
```

Whenever you allocate an array by using the `new` keyword, remember to delete the array by using `delete[]` rather than just plain old `delete`.

If you're really curious about the need for `delete[]` and `delete`, know first off that there's a distinction between allocating an array and allocating a single element on the stack. Look closely at these two lines:

```
int *MyArray = new int[50];
int *somenumber = new int;
```

The first allocates an array of 50 integers, while the second allocates a single array. But look at the types of the pointer variables: They are both the same! How about that? They are both pointers; each one points to an integer. And so the statement

```
delete something;
```

is ambiguous if `something` is a pointer to an integer: Is it an array, or is it a single number? The designers of C++ knew this was a problem, so they *unambiguated* it. They declared and proclaimed that `delete` shall only delete a single member. Then they invented a little extra that must have given the compiler writers a headache: They said that if you want to delete an array instead, just throw on an opening and closing bracket after the word `delete`. And all will be good.

All this stuff about pointers and arrays raises an interesting question: How do you specify a pointer to an array? Well, remember that if you have a line like this

```
int LotsONumbers[50];
```

`LotsONumbers` is really a pointer to an integer — it points to the first position in the array. So, in that regard, you already have a pointer to an array. In fact, if you were to write a function declared with a header like this

```
int AddUp(int Numbers[], int Count) {
```

and look at the generated assembly code, you would see that the `Numbers` array really does get passed in as a pointer. To view the disassembly in Code::Blocks, create a breakpoint, start the debugger by pressing F8, and choose Debug⇨Debugging Windows⇨Disassembly. Code::Blocks displays the Disassembly window, which contains an assembler view of the code.

So the real question is this: When you have an array, how do you *not* use a pointer with it? The answer? You don't! C++ simply does not have a fundamental array type. Other languages do (Pascal, for example), but C and C++ don't. Yet, even though that's the case, the compiler does have a basic feel for the brackets and does seem to understand arrays. Strange but true.

Storing arrays of pointers and arrays of arrays

Because of the similarities between arrays and pointers, you are likely to encounter some strange notation. For example, in `main()` itself, we have seen both of these at different times:

```
char **argc
char *argc[]
```

If you work with arrays of arrays and arrays of pointers, the best bet is to make sure that you completely understand what these kinds of statements mean. Remember that although you can treat an array name as a pointer, you're in for some technical differences. The following lines of code show these differences. First, think about what happens if you initialize a two-dimensional array of characters like this:

```
char NameArray[][6] = {
    {'T', 'o', 'm', '\0', '\0', '\0'},
    {'S', 'u', 'z', 'y' , '\0', '\0'},
    {'H', 'a', 'r', 'r' , 'y', '\0'}
};
```

This is an array of an array. Each *inner* array is an array of six characters. The *outer* array stores the three inner arrays. (The individual content of an array is sometimes called a *member* — the inner array has six members and the outer array has three members.) Inside memory, the 18 characters are stored in one consecutive row, starting with T, then o, and ending with y and finally \0, which is the null character.

But now take a look at this:

```
char* NamePointers[] = {
    "Tom",
    "Suzy",
    "Harry"
};
```

This is an array of character arrays as well, except that it's not the same as the code that came just before it. This is actually an array holding three pointers: The first points to a character string in memory containing Tom (which is followed by a null-terminator, \0); the second points to a string in memory containing Suzy ending with a null-terminator; and so on. Thus, if you look at the memory in the array, you won't see a bunch of characters; instead, you see three numbers, each being a pointer.

It's often helpful to see the content of memory as you work with arrays. To see memory in Code::Blocks, choose Debug⇨Debugging Windows⇨Memory Dump. You see the Memory window. Type & (ampersand) plus the name of the variable you want to view in the Address field and click Go. (You can also see the content of a specific memory address by typing its address, such as **0x28ff08**, or the memory pointed to by a register by typing **$** plus the register name, such as **$sp**.)

So where on earth (or in the memory, anyway) are the three strings, Tom, Suzy, and Harry when you have an array of three pointers to these strings? When the compiler sees string constants such as these, it puts them in a special area where it stores all the constants. These constants then get added to the executable file at link time, along with the compiled code for the source module. (For information on linking, see Appendix A.) And that's where they reside in memory. The array, therefore, contains pointers to these three constant strings in memory.

Now, if you try to do the following (notice the type of `PointerToPointer`)

```
char **PointerToPointer = {
    "Tom",
    "Suzy",
    "Harry"
};
```

you will get an error:

```
error: initializer for scalar variable requires one element
```

A *scalar* is just another name for a regular variable that is not an array. In other words, the `PointerToPointer` variable is a regular variable (that is, a scalar), *not* an array.

Yet, inside the function header for `main()`, you can use `char **`, and you can access this as an array. What's going on? As usual, there's a slight but definite difference between an array and a pointer. You cannot always just treat a pointer as an array; for example, you can't initialize a pointer as an array. But you can go the other way: You can take an array and treat it as a pointer *most of the time*. Thus you can do this:

```
char* NamePointers[] = {
    "Tom",
    "Harry",
    "Suzy"
};
char **AnotherArray = NamePointers;
```

This code compiles, and you can access the strings through `AnotherArray[0]`, for example. Yet you're not allowed to skip a step and just start out initializing the `AnotherArray` variable like so:

```
char** AnotherArray = {
    "Tom",
    "Harry",
    "Suzy"
};
```

If you write the code that way, it's the same as the code shown just before this example — and it yields a compiler error! This is one (perhaps obscure) example where the slight differences between arrays and pointers become obvious, but it does help explain why you can see something like this

```
int main(int argc, char **argv)
```

and you are free to use the `argv` variable to access an array of pointers — specifically, in this case, an array of character pointers, also called *strings*.

Building constant arrays

If you have an array and you don't want its contents to change, you can make it a constant array. The following lines of code, found in the Array05 example, demonstrate this approach:

```
const int Permanent[5] = { 1, 2, 3, 4, 5 };
cout << Permanent[1] << endl;
```

This array works like any other array, except you cannot change the numbers inside it. If you add a line like the following line, you get a compiler error, because the compiler is aware of constants:

```
Permanent[2] = 5;
```

Here's the error we got when we tried this in Code::Blocks:

```
error: assignment of read-only location 'Permanent[2]'
```

Being the inquisitive sorts, we asked ourselves this question: What about a constant array of nonconstants? Can we do that? Well, sometimes — depending on the compiler. As horrible as the following code (found in the Array06 example) looks — and it's not ANSI-standard! — you are allowed to do this with older versions of the gcc compilers. (Microsoft Visual C++ and Borland C++ Builder don't allow it, and the Code::Blocks compiler presents you with an error: invalid array assignment error message.)

```
int NonConstant[5] = { 1, 2, 3, 4, 5 };
int OtherList[5] = { 10, 11, 12, 13, 14 };
OtherList = NonConstant;
```

In other words, that third line is saying, "Forget what OtherList points to; instead, make it point to the first array, {1,2,3,4,5}!" Now, we *really* don't recommend writing code like this (remember, keep things simple and understandable), so if you want to prevent this kind of thing, you can make the array constant:

```
const int NonConstant[5] = { 1, 2, 3, 4, 5 };
const int OtherList[5] = { 10, 11, 12, 13, 14 };
OtherList = NonConstant;
```

Now, when the compiler gets to the third line, it gives us an error:

```
error: assignment of read-only variable 'OtherList'
```

But you may notice that the way we made the array constant was the same way that we made its elements constant in the code that came just before this example. Oops! What's that all about? Turns out there are some rules.

The following list describes the rules, in detail, for making arrays constant:

✦ If you want to make an array constant, you can precede its type with the word `const`. When you do so, the array name is constant, and the elements inside the array are *also* constant. Thus you cannot have a constant array with nonconstant elements, nor can you have a nonconstant array with constant elements.

✦ The notion of a *nonconstant array* exists only in gcc and is not ANSI-standard.

If you really want to get technical, the C++ ANSI standard says that when you put the word `const` in front of an array declaration, you're not making the array constant; you're saying that the array holds only constants. Yet, when you use `const` this way, most compilers also make the array itself constant. But that's fine; people shouldn't be taking an array name and copying it to something else. That's not good programming style, and it's just asking for bugs — or, at the very least, confusion — later.

Pointing with Pointers

To fully understand C++ and all its strangeness and wonders, you need to become an expert in pointers. One of the biggest sources of bugs is when programmers who have a so-so understanding of C++ work with pointers and mess them up. But what's bad in such cases is that the application may run properly for a while, and then suddenly not work. Those bugs are the hardest bugs to catch, because the user may see the problem occur and then report it; but when the programmer tries to reproduce the problem, he or she can't make the bug happen! (It's just like when you take your car in to be fixed and suddenly it doesn't misbehave.) Both the car-repair person and the programmer would say, "Worked fine when I tried it!" How frustrating is that?

In this section, we show you how you can get the most out of pointers and use them correctly in your applications, so you won't have these strange problems.

Becoming horribly complex

We're not making this up, we have seen a function header like this:

```
void MyFunction(char ***a) {
```

Yikes! What are all those asterisks for? Looks like a pointer to a pointer to a pointer to . . . something! How confusing. Now, we suppose that some humans have brains that are more like computers, and they can look at that code and understand it just fine. Not us. So don't worry if you don't either.

So to understand the code, think about this: Suppose you have a pointer variable, and you want a function to change *what the pointer variable points to*. Now be careful: We're not saying that the function wants to change the contents of the thing that it points to. Rather, we're saying that the function wants to make the pointer *point to something else*. There's a big difference. So how do you do that? Well, any time you want a function to change a variable, you have to either pass it by reference or pass its address. And this process can get confusing with a pointer. So what we like to do is take a detour. First, we define a new type — using our friend, the typedef word. It goes like this (as shown in the Pointer01 example):

```
typedef char *PChar;
```

This is a new type called PChar that is equivalent to char *. That is, PChar is a pointer to a character.

Now look at this function:

```
void MyFunction(PChar &x)
{
    x = new char('B');
}
```

This function takes a pointer variable and points it to the result of new char('B'). That is, it points it to a newly allocated character variable containing the letter B. Now, think this through carefully: A PChar simply contains a memory address, really. We pass it by reference into the function, and the function modifies the PChar so that the PChar contains a different address. That is, the PChar now points to something different from what it previously did.

To try out this function, here's some code you can put in main() that tests MyFunction:

```
char *ptr = new char('A');
char *copy = ptr;
MyFunction(ptr);
cout << "ptr points to " << *ptr << endl;
cout << "copy points to " << *copy << endl;
```

Think it through carefully: The first line declares a variable called ptr that is a pointer to a character. (Notice that we're just using char * this time, but that's okay — char * is the same as PChar because of our typedef.) The first line also allocates a new character A on the heap and stores its address in the ptr variable.

The second line allocates a second variable that's also a pointer to a character. The variable is called copy, and it gets the same value stored in ptr; thus it also points to that character A that's floating around out in the heap.

Next, we call `MyFunction()`. That function is supposed to change what the pointer points to. Then we come back from the function and print two characters: the character that `ptr` points to and the character that `copy` points to. Here's what we get when we run it:

```
ptr points to B
copy points to A
```

This means that it worked! The `ptr` variable now points to the character allocated in `MyFunction` (a B), while the `copy` variable still points to the original A. In other words, they no longer point to the same thing: `MyFunction()` managed to change what the variable points to.

Now consider the same function, but instead of using references, try it with pointers. Here's a modified form (as found in the `Pointer02` example):

```
void AnotherFunction(PChar *x)
{
    *x = new char('C');
}
```

Now because the parameter is a pointer, we have to dereference it to modify its value. Thus we have an asterisk, `*`, at the beginning of the middle line.

And here's a modified `main()` that calls this function:

```
char *ptr = new char('A');
char *copy = ptr;
AnotherFunction(&ptr);
cout << "ptr points to " << *ptr << endl;
cout << "copy points to " << *copy << endl;
```

Because our function uses a pointer rather than a reference, we have to pass the address of the `ptr` variable, not the `ptr` variable directly. So notice the call to `AnotherFunction()` has an ampersand, `&`, in front of the `ptr`. And this code works as expected. When we run it, we see this output:

```
ptr points to C
copy points to A
```

This version of the function, called `AnotherFunction()`, made a new character called C. And indeed it's working correctly: `ptr` now points to a C character, while `copy` hasn't changed. Again, the function pointed `ptr` to something else.

Now we can unravel things. We created a `typedef`, and honestly, we would prefer to keep it in our code because we think that using `typedef`s makes it much easier to understand what the functions are doing. However, not everybody does it that way; therefore we have to understand what other people are doing when we have to go in and fix their code. You may have to, too. So here are the same two functions, `MyFunction()` and `AnotherFunction()`, but without `typedef`. Instead of using the new `PChar` type, they directly use the equivalent `char *` type:

```
void MyFunction(char *&x)
{
    x = new char('B');
}

void AnotherFunction(char **x)
{
    *x = new char('C');
}
```

To remove the use of the `typedef`s, all we did was replace the `PChar` in the two function headers with its equivalent `char *`. You can see that the headers now look goofier. But they mean exactly the same as before: The first is a reference to a pointer, and the second is a pointer to a pointer.

But think about `char ** x` for a moment. Because `char *` is also the same as a character array in many regards, `char **x` is a pointer to a character array. In fact, sometimes you may see the header for `main()` written like this

```
int main(int argc, char **argv)
```

instead of

```
int main(int argc, char *argv[])
```

Notice the `argv` parameter in the first of these two is the same type as we've been talking about: a pointer to a pointer (or, in a more easily understood manner, the address of a `PChar`). But you know that the argument for `main()` is an array of strings.

So bear with us and follow this somewhat convoluted thought (go slowly if you have to): What if you have a pointer that points to an array of strings, and you have a function that is going to make it point to a different array of strings?

Better `typedef` this one; it's going to get ugly. And just as a reminder, we're still using the previous `typedef`, `PChar`, too (as shown in the `Pointer03` example):

```
typedef char **StringArray;
typedef char *PChar;
```

Make sure that you believe us when we tell you that `StringArray` is a type equivalent to an array of strings. In fact, if you put these two lines of code before your `main()`, you can actually change your `main()` header into the following and it will compile.

```
int main(int argc, StringArray argv)
```

Now here's a function that will take as a parameter an array of strings, create a new array of strings, and set the original array of strings to point to this new array of strings. (Whew!)

```
void ChangeAsReference(StringArray &array)
{
    StringArray NameArray = new PChar[3];
    NameArray[0] = "Tom";
    NameArray[1] = "Suzy";
    NameArray[2] = "Harry";
    array = NameArray;
}
```

Just to make sure that it works, here's something you can put in `main()`:

```
StringArray OrigList = new PChar[3];
OrigList[0] = "John";
OrigList[1] = "Paul";
OrigList[2] = "George";
StringArray CopyList = OrigList;
ChangeAsReference(OrigList);
cout << OrigList[0] << endl;
cout << OrigList[1] << endl;
cout << OrigList[2] << endl << endl;
cout << CopyList[0] << endl;
cout << CopyList[1] << endl;
cout << CopyList[2] << endl;
```

This time, in `main()`, we're using the `typedef` types — because, frankly, the code is getting a bit confusing, and that helps keep what we're doing clear. Note that we first create a pointer to an array of three strings. Then we store three strings in the array. Next, we save a copy of the pointer in the variable called `CopyList`, and we print all the values.

Now, when you run this `main()`, you see the following:

```
Tom
Suzy
Harry

John
Paul
George
```

The first three are the elements in `OrigList`, which we passed into the function: But they no longer have the values `John`, `Paul`, and `George`. The three original Beatles names have been replaced by three new names: `Tom`, `Harry`, and `Suzy`. However, the `Copy` variable still points to the original string list. Thus, once again, it worked.

We managed this change from `John`, `Paul`, and `George` to `Tom`, `Suzy`, and `Harry` by reference, but you can also do it with pointers. Here's the modified version of the function, this time using said pointers (as shown in the `Pointer04` example):

```
void ChangeAsPointer(StringArray *array)
{
    StringArray NameArray = new PChar[3];
    NameArray[0] = "Tom";
    NameArray[1] = "Harry";
    NameArray[2] = "Suzy";
    *array = NameArray;
}
```

As before, here's the slightly modified sample code that tests the function:

```
StringArray OrigList = new PChar[3];
OrigList[0] = "John";
OrigList[1] = "Paul";
OrigList[2] = "George";
StringArray CopyList = OrigList;
ChangeAsPointer(&OrigList);
cout << OrigList[0] << endl;
cout << OrigList[1] << endl;
cout << OrigList[2] << endl << endl;
cout << CopyList[0] << endl;
cout << CopyList[1] << endl;
cout << CopyList[2] << endl;
```

You can see that when we call `ChangeAsPointer()`, we're passing the address of `OrigList`. The *output of this version is the same as that of the previous version.*

And now, as before, we unravel all this. Here are the two function headers without using the `typedef`s:

```
int ChangeAsReference(char **&array) {
```

and

```
int ChangeAsPointer(char ***array) {
```

We have seen code like these two lines from time to time. Such code isn't the easiest to understand, but after you know what these lines mean, you can interpret them.

Our preference is to go ahead and use a `typedef`, even if it's just before the function in question. That way, it's much more clear to other people what the function does. You are welcome to follow suit. But if you do, make sure that you're familiar with the non-`typedef` version so you understand that version when somebody else writes it without using `typedef` — or if that person says to you, "This function takes a pointer to a pointer to a pointer." (Yes, we've heard people say that!)

Pointers to functions

When an application is running, the functions in the application exist in the memory; so just like anything else in memory, they have an address. And having an address is good, because that way, people can find you.

You can take the address of a function by taking the name of it and putting the `address-of` operator (`&`) in front of the function name, like this:

```
address = &MyFunction;
```

But to make this work, you need to know what type to declare `address`. The `address` variable is a pointer to a function, and the cleanest way to assign a type is to use a `typedef` (as shown in the `FunctionPointer01` example). (Fortunately, this is one time when most people are willing to use a `typedef`.)

Here's the `typedef`, believe it or not:

```
typedef int(*FunctionPtr)(int);
```

It's hard to follow, but the name of the new type is `FunctionPtr`. This defines a type called `FunctionPtr` that returns an integer (the leftmost `int`) and takes an integer as a parameter (the rightmost `int`, which must be in parentheses). The middle part of this statement is the name of the new type, and you must precede it by an asterisk, which means that it's a pointer to all the rest of the expression. Also, you must put the type name and its preceding asterisk inside parentheses.

And then you're ready to declare some variables! Here goes:

```
FunctionPtr address = &MyFunction;
```

This line declares `address` as a pointer to a function and initializes it to `MyFunction()`. Now, for this to work, the code for `MyFunction()` must have the same prototype declared in the `typedef`: In this case, it must take an integer as a parameter and return an integer.

So, for example, you may have a function like this:

```
int TheSecretNumber(int x) {
    return x + 1;
}
```

Then you could have a `main()` that stores the address of this function in a variable — and then calls the function by using the variable:

```
int main(int argc, char *argv[])
{
    typedef int (*FunctionPtr)(int);
    int MyPasscode = 20;
    FunctionPtr address = &TheSecretNumber;
    cout << address(MyPasscode) << endl;
}
```

Now, just so you can say that you've seen it, here's what the `address` declaration would look like *without* using a `typedef`:

```
int (*address)(int) = &TheSecretNumber;
```

The giveaway should be that you have two things in parentheses side by side, and the set on the right has only types inside it. The one on the left has a variable name. So this line is not declaring a type; rather, it's declaring a variable.

Pointing a variable to a member function

It's surprising to find out that most C++ programmers have no idea that a pointer called `this` exists. So `this` is a big secret! Revel in it! What is the secret? The secret is that you can take the address of an object's member function so that you can access the member function instance data directly. Ooh-wee!

Now, remember that each instance of a class gets its own copy of the member variables, unless the variables are static. But functions are shared throughout the class. Yes, you can distinguish static functions from nonstatic functions. But that just refers to what types of variables they access: Static functions can access only static member variables, and you don't need to refer to them with an instance. Nonstatic (that is, *normal, regular*) member functions work with a particular instance. However, inside the memory, really only one copy of the function exists.

So how does the member function know which instance to work with? A secret parameter gets passed into the member function: the `this` pointer. Suppose you have a class called `Gobstopper` that has a member function called `Chew()`. Next, you have an instance called `MyGum`, and you call the `Chew()` function like so:

```
MyGum.Chew();
```

When the compiler generates assembly code for this, it actually passes a parameter into the function — the address of the `MyGum` instance, also known as the *this pointer*. Therefore only one `Chew()` function is in the code, but to call it you must use a particular instance of the class.

Because only one copy of the `Chew()` function is in memory, you can take its address. But to do so requires some sort of cryptic-looking code. Here it is, quick and to the point. Suppose your class looks like this:

```
class Gobstopper {
public:
    int WhichGobstopper;
    int Chew(string name) {
        cout << WhichGobstopper << endl;
        cout << name << endl;
        return WhichGobstopper;
    }
};
```

The `Chew()` function takes a string and returns an integer. Here's a `typedef` for a pointer to the `Chew()` function:

```
typedef int (Gobstopper::*GobMember)(string);
```

And here's a variable of the type `GobMember`:

```
GobMember func = &Gobstopper::Chew;
```

If you look closely at the `typedef`, it looks similar to a regular function pointer. The only difference is that the classname and two colons precede the asterisk. Other than that, it's a regular old function pointer.

But whereas a regular function pointer is limited to pointing to functions of a particular set of parameter types and a return type, this function pointer shares those restrictions but has a further limitation: It can only point to member functions within the class `Gobstopper`.

To call the function stored in the pointer, you need to have a particular instance. Notice that in the assignment of `func` in the earlier code there was no instance, just the classname and function, `&Gobstopper::Chew`. So to call the function, grab an instance, add func, and go! The FunctionPointer02 example as shown in Listing 1-2 contains a complete example with the class, the member function address, and two separate instances.

Listing 1-2: Taking the Address of a Member Function

```
#include <iostream>
#include <string>

using namespace std;

class Gobstopper
{
public:
    int WhichGobstopper;
    int Chew(string name) {
        cout << WhichGobstopper << endl;
        cout << name << endl;
        return WhichGobstopper;
    }
};

int main()
{
    typedef int (Gobstopper::*GobMember)(string);
    GobMember func = &Gobstopper::Chew;
    Gobstopper inst;
    inst.WhichGobstopper = 10;
    Gobstopper another;
    another.WhichGobstopper = 20;
    (inst.*func)("Greg W.");
    (another.*func)("Jennifer W.");
    return 0;
}
```

You can see in main that first we create the type for the function, which we call GobMember, and then we create a variable, func, of that type. Then we create two instances of the Gobstopper class, and we give them each a different WhichGobstopper value.

Finally, we call the member function, first for the first instance and then for the second instance. Just to show that you can take the addresses of functions with parameters, we pass in a string with some names.

When you run the code, you can see from the output that it is indeed calling the correct member function for each instance:

```
10
Greg W.
20
Jennifer W.
```

Now, when we say "the correct member function for each instance," what we *really* mean is that the code is calling the same member function each time but using a different instance. If you're thinking in object-oriented terms, consider each instance as having its own copy of the member function. Therefore it's okay to say "the correct member function for each instance."

Pointing to static member functions

A *static member function* is, in many senses, just a plain old function. The difference is that you have to use a class name to call a static function. But remember that a static member function does not go with any particular instance of a class; therefore you don't need to specify an instance when you call the static function.

Here's an example class (as shown in the `FunctionPointer03` example) with a static function:

```
public:
    static string MyClassName() {
        return "Gobstopper!";
    }
    int WhichGobstopper;
    int Chew(string name) {
        cout << WhichGobstopper << endl;
        cout << name << endl;
        return WhichGobstopper;
    }
};
```

And here's some code that takes the address of the static function and calls it by using the address:

```
typedef string (*StaticMember)();
StaticMember staticfunc = &Gobstopper::MyClassName;
cout << staticfunc() << endl;
```

Note that in the final line, we didn't have to refer to a specific instance to call `staticfunc()` — and we didn't need to refer to the class, either. We just called it. Because the truth is that deep down inside, the static function is just a plain old function.

Referring to References

In this section, we reveal all the ins, outs, upsides, and downsides of using references. And we tell you a few things about them, too.

We're assuming in this section that you already know how to pass a parameter by reference when you're writing a function. (For more information about passing parameters by reference, see Book I, Chapter 7.) But you can

**Book IV
Chapter 1**

**Working with
Arrays, Pointers,
and References**

use references for more than just parameter lists. You can declare a variable as a reference type. And just like job references, this use of references can be both good and devastating. So be careful when you use them.

Reference variables

Declaring a variable that is a reference is easy. Whereas the pointer uses an asterisk, *, the reference uses an ampersand, &. But there's a twist to it. You cannot just declare it like this:

```
int &BestReference; // Nope! This won't work!
```

If you try this, you see an error that says `BestReference declared as reference but not initialized`. That sounds like a hint: Looks like you need to initialize it.

Yes, references need to be initialized. As the name implies, *reference* refers to another variable. Therefore, you need to initialize the reference so it refers to some other variable, like so (as shown in the `Reference01` example):

```
int ImSomebody;
int &BestReference = ImSomebody;
```

Now, from this point on, forever until the end of eternity (or at least as long as the function containing these two lines runs), the variable `BestReference` will refer to — that is, be an *alias* for — `ImSomebody`.

And so, if you type

```
BestReference = 10;
```

then you'll *really* be setting `ImSomebody` to 10. So take a look at this code that could go inside a `main()`:

```
int ImSomebody;
int &BestReference = ImSomebody;
BestReference = 10;
cout << ImSomebody << endl;
```

When you run this code, you see the output

```
10
```

That is, setting `BestReference` to 10 caused `ImSomebody` to change to 10, which you can see when you print out the value of `ImSomebody`.

That's what a reference does: It refers to another variable.

Because a reference refers to another variable, that implies that you cannot have a reference to just a number, as in int &x = 10. And, in fact, the offending line has been implicated: You are not allowed to do that. You can only have a reference that refers to another variable.

Returning a reference from a function

It's possible to return a reference from a function. But be careful if you try to do this: You do not want to return a reference to a local variable within a function — because when the function ends, the storage space for the local variables goes away. Not good!

But you can return a reference to a global variable. Or, if the function is a member function, you can return a reference to a member variable.

For example, here's a class found in the Reference02 example that has a function that returns a reference to one of its variables:

```
class DigInto
{
private:
    int secret;
public:
    DigInto() { secret = 150; }
    int &GetSecretVariable() { return secret; }
    void Write() { cout << secret << endl; }
};
```

Notice the constructor stores 150 in the secret variable, which is private. The GetSecretVariable() function returns a reference to the private variable called secret. And the Write() function writes out the value of the secret variable. Lots of secrets here! And some surprises too, which we tell you about shortly. You can use this class like so:

```
int main(int argc, char *argv[])
{
    DigInto inst;
    inst.Write();
    int &pry = inst.GetSecretVariable();
    pry = 30;
    inst.Write();
    return 0;
}
```

When you run this, you see the following output:

```
150
30
```

Referring to something else . . . hold on there

And now for the $1,000,000 question: After you have a reference referring to a variable, how can you change that reference so it refers to something else? Brace yourself for a wild answer. Here goes: *You can't*. Yes, it's true, and yes, you may know some people who, nevertheless, have managed to do it. Here's the whole story.

Back when C++ first came out, companies that made compilers gave their compilers some sophisticated capabilities in terms of references. Many of them let you *unseat* a reference — that is, make the reference refer to something else. But, lo and behold, when the ANSI standard came out in the late 1990s, the standard outlawed this practice. So now the rule is that you cannot unseat a reference. Further, you cannot have a pointer to a reference, nor can you have a reference

that refers to another reference. This somewhat restrictive rule actually resolves some ambiguity: Suppose you wrote a line of code asking for the address of a reference with the hope of storing it in a `pointer to reference` variable: Because a reference refers to another variable, does that mean you want the address of the other variable, or do you somehow want the address of the reference itself?

The standard clears this up: You don't have a pointer to a reference. But interestingly, older versions of the gcc compiler do let you write code that seems to take the address of a reference; however, in fact, you are taking the address of the variable the reference refers to. So, again, no pointers to references, and that means that you can't even take the address of a reference!

The first line is the value in the secret variable right after the application creates the instance. But look at the code carefully: The variable called `pry` is a reference to an integer, and it gets the results of `GetSecretVariable()`. And what is that result? It's a reference to the private variable called `secret` — which means that `pry` itself is now a reference to that variable. Yes, a variable outside the class now refers directly to a private member of the instance! After that, we set `pry` to 30. When we call `Write()` again, the private variable will indeed change.

Is it just us, or does that seem like a bad idea? We made the variable private. And now the `GetSecretVariable()` function pretty much wiped out any sense of the variable actually remaining private. The `main()` function was able to grab a reference to it and poke around and change it however it wanted, as if it were not private! Trouble in C++ land!

That's a problem with references: They can potentially leave your code wide open. Therefore think twice before returning a reference to a variable. Here's one of the biggest risks: Somebody else might be using this code, may not understand references, and may not realize that the variable called `pry` has a direct link to the private `secret` variable. Such an inexperienced programmer might then write code that uses and changes `pry` — without realizing that the member variable is changing along with it. Later on, then, a *bug* results — a pretty nasty one at that!

Because functions returning references can leave unsuspecting and less-experienced C++ programmers with just a wee bit too much power on their hands, we recommend using caution with references. No, don't you don't have to avoid them altogether; we suggest just plain being careful. Use them only if you really feel you must. But remember also that a better approach in classes is to have member access functions that can guard the private variables.

However, now that we've issued the usual warnings, references can be very powerful, provided you understand what they do. When you use a reference, you can easily modify another variable without having to go through pointers — which can make life much easier sometimes. So, please: Use your newfound powers carefully.

Chapter 2: Creating Data Structures

In This Chapter

↙ **Discovering all the different data types**

↙ **Casting and converting**

↙ **Using structures with your data**

↙ **Comparing and manipulating structures**

C++, being a computer language and all, provides you with a lot of ways to manipulate *data* — numbers, letters, strings, arrays — anything you can store inside the computer memory. To get the most out of C++, you should know as much as you can about the fundamental data types. This chapter covers them and how to use them.

In this chapter, we refer to the *ANSI standard* of C++. ANSI is the American National Standards Institute. The information we provide in this chapter deals with *the* ANSI standard (singular) of C++. Fortunately, the GNU gcc compiler that comes with Code::Blocks is ANSI-standard-compliant. (Little nuances show up, but not often.)

Working with Data

In the sections that follow, we tell you how you can manipulate your data, discuss the types of data available to you, and point out how you can change them.

The great variable roundup

The ANSI C++ standard dictates these fundamental C++ types:

✦ `char`: This is a single character. On most computers, it takes 1 byte.

✦ `int`: This is an integer. On most computers from the late 1990s until now, a single integer takes 4 bytes — which gives you a range from –2147483648 to 2147483647.

✦ `short int`: This is a half-size integer. Just a little 2-byte fellow, which leaves just enough room for –32768 to 32767.

✦ `long int`: You would expect a `long int` to be longer than, well, an `int`. But it's not with the gcc compiler. The compiler recognizes two types: `short int` (2 bytes) and `long int` (4 bytes). If you leave off the first word, the compiler considers it a `long int`. So a `long int` is an `int`.

✦ `bool`: This can take on a value of either `true` or `false`. Inside the computer, it's a single byte, stored as a number. Normally `true` is stored as 1, and `false` is stored as 0. However, you shouldn't have to convert `bool` to a number; you should only compare it to the values `true` or `false`.

✦ `float`: This is a number with a decimal point (a *floating-point* number). The ANSI standard doesn't define this, but gcc uses 4 bytes. If your compiler adheres to the IEEE 754-1985 standard (which the gcc compiler does), a `float` can store any value between $\pm 1.18 \times 10^{-38}$ to $\pm 3.4 \times 10^{38}$.

✦ `double`: This is another floating-point type, and it means *double-precision floating-point*. Again, the ANSI standard doesn't say how long it should be. The gcc compiler uses 8 bytes for a double. If your compiler adheres to the IEEE 754-1985 standard (which the gcc compiler does), a `double` can store any value between $\pm 2.23 \times 10^{-308}$ to $\pm 1.80 \times 10^{308}$.

✦ `long double`: This is a humongous size, a real space hog. In gcc (at the time of this writing), it takes up a whole 12 bytes of space. However, most compilers define a `long double` as being the same as a double. There is no IEEE standard range for the 12 byte version of the `long double`.

✦ `void`: The ANSI standard considers this an *incomplete type*. You're not allowed to declare a variable of type `void`. However, you can declare a type *pointer to* `void`.

✦ `wchar_t`: Many computers today support a *wide character* set, primarily for international and non-English characters. The characters in these sets usually are 2 bytes. `wchar_t` represents these characters. Some operating systems (such as Windows CE) require you to use `wchar_t`.

You can use some variations of these. You can have arrays of any of these. And you can also modify some of these just a bit:

✦ `signed`: You can tack the word `signed` to the beginning of `char`, `short int`, `int`, and `long int` to get `signed char`, `signed short int`, `signed int`, and `signed long int`. If you put `signed` in front, the numbers (and underlying numbers for the `char` type) can include negatives or positives.

✦ `unsigned`: You can put the word `unsigned` at the beginning of these types to get `unsigned char`, `unsigned short int`, `unsigned int`, and `unsigned long int`. Unsigned means that the numbers (and underlying numbers for the `char` type) cannot be negative.

Note that when you use `signed` and `unsigned`, the size of the variable doesn't change: It takes the same number of bytes. Instead, the range *shifts*. For example, a signed short int ranges from −32768 to 32767, so there are 65536 possibilities. An `unsigned short int` ranges from 0 to 65535; again, there are 65536 possibilities.

The easiest way to see how the signed integers are stored is to use the hexadecimal (hex) numbering system. The hex numbers line themselves up nicely with the bytes. An *unsigned* `short int` can hold any hex values from 0x0000 through 0xffff. These two numbers correspond to the decimal numbers 0 through 65535. Now, if you put these same numbers into a *signed* `short int`, you can see how they're stored. Here's how (as shown in the `SignedAndUnsigned` example):

```
short int hoopla;
hoopla = 0x0000;
cout << "0x0000: " << hoopla << endl;
hoopla = 0x0001;
cout << "0x0001: " << hoopla << endl;
hoopla = 0x7fff;
cout << "0x7fff: " << hoopla << endl;
hoopla = 0x8000;
cout << "0x8000: " << hoopla << endl;
hoopla = 0xffff;
cout << "0xffff: " << hoopla << endl;
```

When you run this code, here's what you see:

```
0x0000: 0
0x0001: 1
0x7fff: 32767
0x8000: -32768
0xffff: -1
```

These numbers in the output are out of order. Here they are in the correct order:

+ Negative numbers from −32768 to −1 are stored from 0x8000 to 0xffff.

+ The number 0 is stored as 0x0000, as you would expect.

+ Positive numbers from 1 to 32767 are stored from 0x0001 to 0x7fff.

The larger integers behave similarly. For `signed long int`, the negatives are stored from 0x800000000 to 0xffffffff. The number 0 is 0x00000000. Positives go from 0x00000001 to 0x7fffffff.

When you are working with the different floating-point types, remember this rule: It's not about *range*, it's about *precision*. The `double` doesn't just hold a bigger range of numbers than the `float` type; it holds more decimal places.

void * is just a generic type pointer. If you want a pointer and don't want to specify what type it points to, you can make it a void * . If you're writing a C++ application that uses structures from an older C application, you may see void * crop up. When you use a void * pointer, normally you must cast it to another pointer type (such as MyStruct *).

Expressing variables from either side

Occasionally, when you look at error messages (or if you read the ANSI standard!) you see the terms lvalue and rvalue. The l and r refer to *left* and *right,* respectively. In an assignment statement, an lvalue is any expression that can be on the left side of the equals sign, and an rvalue is an expression that can be on the right side of an equals sign.

The terms lvalue and rvalue do *not* refer to what happens to be on the left side and right side of an assignment statement. They refer to what is *allowed* or *not allowed* on the left side of an assignment statement. You can only have lvalues on the left side of an assignment statement and rvalues on the right side of an assignment statement.

Here are some examples, where ploggle is an int type. This is allowed, because ploggle is an lvalue:

```
ploggle = 3;
```

On the left side, you cannot have items that are strictly an rvalue. The following is not allowed, because 2 is strictly an rvalue:

```
2 = ploggle;
```

Now how do we know ploggle is an lvalue? Because it's allowed to appear on the left side of an assignment statement. The number 2 can't appear on the left (setting it equal to something else makes no sense!), therefore it isn't an lvalue. In fact, *anything you can set equal to something else is an lvalue.*

The main reason you need to know these terms is their tendency to show up in error messages. If you try to compile the line 2 = ploggle, here are some error messages that appear (one for each of three compilers):

✦ Borland C++ Builder: Lvalue required

✦ gcc (whether Code::Blocks, MinGW, or Cygwin): non-lvalue in assignment

✦ Visual C++: left operand must be l-value

If you don't know what the term `lvalue` means, these messages can be confusing. And while seeing the problem with `2 = ploggle` is pretty easy, sometimes the problem is not that obvious. Look at this:

```
ChangeMe() = 10;
DontKnow() = 20;
```

Do these even make sense? Putting a function call on the left side? In other words: Are the expressions `ChangeMe()` and `DontKnow()` lvalues?

It depends. Take a look at this code from the `LValueAndRValue` example:

```
int uggle;

int &ChangeMe()
{
    return uggle;
}

int DontKnow()
{
    return uggle;
}
```

The *function* `ChangeMe` returns a reference to an integer; this line is valid:

```
ChangeMe() = 10;
```

The *expression* `ChangeMe()` refers to the variable `uggle`, and thus this line of code stores 10 in `uggle`. But the second function, `DontKnow`, returns just an integer *value* (a number, not a variable). Therefore this line is not valid:

```
DontKnow() = 20;
```

The left side, `DontKnow()` is not an `lvalue` — it's an `rvalue` — therefore it cannot appear on the left side of an equation, and that line is an error.

Indeed, when we try to compile these lines, the compiler is happy with the `ChangeMe() = 10;` line. But for the `DontKnow() = 20;` line, it gives us the following error message.

```
error: non-lvalue in assignment
```

The words `lvalue` and `rvalue` are *not* C++ words. You do not type these into an application. (Well, yeah, we suppose you *could* use them as variable names, but we'd really rather not — and we suggest you don't, either.)

Casting a spell on your data

Although C++ has all these great data types, such as integer and char, the fact is this: Underneath they are just stored as numbers. And sometimes you may have a character and need to use its underlying number. To do this, you can *cast* the data.

The way you cast is to take a variable of one type and type the variable's name, preceded by the other type you would like it to be. You put that other type in parentheses, as shown in the SimpleCast example.

```
char buddy = 'A';
int underneath = (int)buddy;
cout << underneath << endl;
```

When you run this code, you obtain an output value of 65. If you substituted a lowercase a, the output would be 97 because uppercase and lowercase letters have different numeric values.

Comparing casting and converting

The idea behind casting is to take some data and, without changing it (and with nothing up our sleeves), use it in another way. For example, we could have an array containing the characters Applecrisp. But inside the memory, each letter is stored as a number. For example, the A is stored as 65, p is stored as 112, and l as 108. Therefore, if we wanted to, we could cast each character to an integer, using such code as

```
cout << (int)(str[loop]) << endl;
```

where str is the string (Applecrisp) and loop is a loop counter that cycles through the string. This would print out the numerical equivalents of each letter. In other words, we cast the characters to integers — but we did not actually change any data. Now we can copy the data like this:

```
int num = str[0];
```

This code would copy the data, but again, it wouldn't change it. We'd just have two copies of the same data. That's what casting is all about: using data as a different data type from what it was originally.

Converting, however, is different. If we want to take the number 123, casting it to a string will not create a string 123. The string 123 is made up of three underlying byte-sized snacks of numbers. The numbers for the string 123 are 49, 50, and 51, respectively. Casting the number 123 just won't give us that. Instead, you would need to convert the number to a string.

But, like most rules, this one has an exception — and that exception comes into play when converting between floats and integers. Instead of using a conversion function, the C++ compiler automatically converts from float to integer and vice versa if you try to cast one to the other. Ugh. That goes against the rest of the rules, so be careful. Here's an example of converting a float to an integer:

```
float f = 6.3;
int i = (int)f;
```

But the crazy part is that you can also do the same thing without even using the cast, although you will get a compiler warning:

```
float f = 6.3;
int i = f;
```

Back in the old days of the C programming language, casting was a common way of converting data — *but it's actually somewhat dangerous.* In C, you could take any data type and directly cast it to any other data type. The idea was that if you wanted to burrow into the system and manipulate something (just about anything), you could. But over the years, people started to figure out that maybe, just *maybe*, this wasn't such a good idea. (As in, "Hey, bugs, welcome to my computer!") So although we're showing you how to cast, you should *try to avoid casting.* Instead, focus on converting (which sometimes uses castlike syntax) or using what are referred to as *safe casts.* See Chapter 9 in Book 1, as well as the next section ("Casting safely with C++") in this chapter, for details.

Casting safely with C++

With the ANSI standard of C++ came all kinds of new goodies that make life easier than it used to be. Casting is one example. Originally, you could just cast all you wanted and change from one data type to another, possibly causing a mess, especially if you take existing code and compile it under a different operating system or perhaps even under a different compiler on the same operating system. One type may have a different underlying representation, and then, when you convert it on one system, you get one thing; take it to a different system and you get something else. That's bad. It creates bugs!

So the ANSI standard for C++ gives some newer and better ways of casting between items of data. These include `dynamic_cast` and `static_cast`.

Dynamically casting with dynamic_cast

When the makers of C++ came up with these new ways of casting, their motivation was this: Think in terms of *conversions*. A cast simply takes one data type and tells the compiler to treat it as another data type. So first ask yourself if one of the conversions will work for you. If not, you can consider one of the new ways of casting.

But remember, a *cast* tells the compiler to treat some data as another type of data. But the new ways of casting prevent you from doing a cast that doesn't make sense. For example, you may have a class hierarchy, and you have a pointer to a base class. But because an instance of a derived class can be treated as an instance of a base class, it's possible that this instance that you're looking at could actually be an instance of a derived class.

In the old style of C and C++ programming, you could just cast the instance and have at it:

```
DoSomethingCool( (derivedclass *) someptr);
```

In this case, we're assuming that `someptr` is of type pointer-to-base-class, but we're *hoping* that, in fact, it points to a `derivedclass` instance. Does it? It may, depending on how we wrote the rest of the application. But maybe not. And when the word *hope* meets the word *application*, the word *disaster* tends to show up. Tempers fly and people lose their jobs. It's not a pretty sight.

But have no fear: ANSI is here! With the new ways of casting, you can be sure. The DynamicCast example shown in Listing 2-1 is a complete application that demonstrates a proper *down-cast*, where we take a pointer to a base class and cast it down to a pointer of a derived class.

Listing 2-1: Casting Instances Dynamically for Safety

```cpp
#include <iostream>
#include <string>

using namespace std;

class King
{
protected:
    string CrownName;
public:
    virtual string &MyName() { return CrownName; }
    virtual ~King(){}
};

class Prince : public King
{
public:
    string School;
};

void KingInfo(King *inst)
{
    cout << "=========" << endl;
    cout << inst->MyName() << endl;
    Prince *asPrince = dynamic_cast<Prince *>(inst);
    if (asPrince != 0)
    {
        cout << asPrince->School << endl;
    }
}

int main()
{
    Prince George;
    George.MyName() = "George I";
    George.School = "School of the Kings";
    KingInfo(&George);
    King Henry;
    Henry.MyName() = "Henry II";
    KingInfo(&Henry);
    return 0;
}
```

Go ahead and run this code. You'll see output that looks something like this:

```
=========
George I
School of the Kings
=========
Henry II

Process returned 0 (0x0)    execution time : 0.062 s
Press any key to continue.
```

Some strange things are going on in this code. But first, we want to point out the main thing that this code demonstrates: In `main()`, we call the `KingInfo()` function, first passing it the address of `George` (a `Prince` instance, derived from `King`) and then the address of `Henry` (a `King` instance).

The `KingInfo()` function first prints the information that is common to both due to inheritance; it calls the `MyName()` function and prints the resulting name. Then comes the important part, the dynamic cast. To do this, we call `dynamic_cast` and save it in a pointer variable called `asPrince`. Notice the syntax of `dynamic_cast`. It looks like a template in that you include a type in angled brackets. Then you put the thing you want to cast in parentheses (in this case, the instance that was passed into the function).

If the dynamic cast worked, it returns a pointer that you can save as the type inside angled brackets. Otherwise the dynamic cast will return 0. You can see that after we called `dynamic_cast`, we tested it against 0. If the result is not 0, the dynamic cast worked, which means that we successfully cast the data to the desired type. And then, in the `if` block, we retrieve the `School` member, which is part of `Prince`, not `King`.

You may notice the unique design of the `King` class. Take a look at just the `King` class:

```
class King
{
protected:
    string CrownName;
public:
    virtual string &MyName() { return CrownName; }
    virtual ~King(){}
};
```

For `dynamic_cast` to work, the base class involved must have *at least one virtual function*. Thus the base class — and each of its derived classes — has a virtual table (also needed for `dynamic_cast` to work). In addition, the Code::Blocks compiler raises a warning message when you don't provide a virtual destructor:

```
warning: 'class King' has virtual functions but non-virtual destructor
```

Consequently, the example includes a virtual destructor as well.

Originally, we wanted `CrownName` to be public. But because we needed to add a virtual function to class `King`, we decided to make the function useful, rather than just add a function that does nothing at all. So we made it access the `CrownName` member. And for that, we wanted to give the function a reason for its existence, so we made the `CrownName` protected. Then we had the `MyName()` function return a reference to it. The end result is that it's like `CrownName` is public, which is the way we wanted the class in the beginning.

You don't need to use references in a class as we did here just to make `dynamic_cast` work. But you do need at least one virtual function.

Some compilers (including Microsoft Visual C++) do not, by default, handle `dynamic_cast`. To use a dynamic cast in Visual C++, you have to go into the project settings and select Enable Run-time Type Information (RTTI) found in C++ Language Settings. Then you need to recompile your application for the change to take effect. Note that if you don't select this setting, you get a warning (not an error) that says, `dynamic_cast used on polymorphic type 'class King' with /GR-; unpredictable behavior may result`. The application will still compile and link, but when you run it, a runtime error message pops up.

Remember, here's the fundamental difference between an old-style direct cast and the new `dynamic_cast`: The compiler generates code that automatically does an old-style cast, regardless of whether the cast is valid. That is, the cast is *hardcoded*. But `dynamic_cast`, on the other hand, tests the types *at runtime*. The dynamic cast may or may not work depending on the type of the object.

When you use a dynamic cast, you can cast either a pointer or a reference. The `KingInfo()` function back in Listing 2-1 uses a pointer. Here's a modified form that uses a reference:

```
void KingInfoAsReference(King &inst)
{
    cout << "=========" << endl;
    cout << inst.MyName() << endl;
    try
    {
        Prince &asPrince = dynamic_cast<Prince &>(inst);
        cout << asPrince.School << endl;
    }
    catch (...)
    {
    }
}
```

To make this work, we had to use an *exception handler* (which is a way to deal with unusual situations; see Chapter 3 in this minibook for more information on exception handlers). The reason for using an exception handler is that with a pointer, you can simply test the result against 0. But with references, you have no such thing as a *null reference* or *0 reference*. The reference *must* work, or you get a runtime error. And in C++, the way you can catch a situation that didn't work is by typing the word `try`, followed by your code that attempts to do the job, in braces. Follow that with the word `catch` and a set of parentheses containing three periods. Following that, you put braces — and possibly any code you want to run — just in case the earlier code didn't work

In this code, you can see that we didn't do anything inside the `catch` block. We want to do something only if the code works. We would just leave off the `catch` block because we didn't have it do anything, but alas, C++ doesn't allow that: If you have a `try` block, you must have a `catch` block. Them's the rules.

Statically casting with static_cast

The ANSI C++ standard includes a special type of cast that does no type checking. If you have to cast directly without the help of `dynamic_cast`, you should opt for `static_cast` instead of the old C-style cast.

When you want to do a static cast, call `static_cast` and follow it with angled brackets containing the type you want to cast to. Then put the item being cast inside parentheses, as in the following:

```
FinalType *f = static_cast<FinalType *>(orig);
```

The advantage of using `static_cast` is that it does some type checking at compile time, whereas old C-style casts do not. The compiler allows you to do `static_cast` only between related objects. For example, you can do a `static_cast` from an instance of one class to an instance of a derived or base class. But if two classes are not related, you will get a compiler error.

For example, suppose that you have these two lines of code:

```
class FinalType {};
class AnotherType {};
```

They are unrelated classes. Then, if you have these lines of code

```
AnotherType *orig = new AnotherType;
FinalType *f = static_cast<FinalType *>(orig);
```

and you try to compile the code, you get an error:

```
static_cast from 'AnotherType *' to 'FinalType *'
```

**Book IV
Chapter 2**

**Creating Data
Structures**

But if, instead, you make the classes related (as shown in the `StaticCast` example)

```
class FinalType {};
class AnotherType : public FinalType {};
```

then the following two lines of code will compile:

```
AnotherType *orig = new AnotherType;
FinalType *f = static_cast<FinalType *>(orig);
```

However, if you're using the Code::Blocks compiler, you will receive a warning message:

```
warning: unused variable 'f' [-Wunused-variable]
```

 A lot of people think that `static_cast` is useless and is essentially identical to old-style C casts. It's not true. Tell them they're wrong! (But be nice, now. Friends come before software, after all.) The mistaken notion is that `static_cast` does no type checking, when in fact it *does*. The difference between `static_cast` and `dynamic_cast` is that `static_cast` does its type checking at compile time; the compiler makes sure the cast is okay. `dynamic_cast`, however, also does the same type checking at compile time, but when it runs, it does more checking to make sure that the instance is precisely what you're converting to. Old C-style casts do none of this type checking.

If you're just doing a conversion between floating-point numbers and integers, you can do an old-style cast. (That's because an old-style cast is really a conversion, not a cast.) Alternatively, of course, you're welcome to use `static_cast` to get the same job done:

```
float f = static_cast<float>(x);
```

Structuring Your Data

Before C++ came to life, C had something that was similar to classes, called *structures*. The difference was that structures had only member variables — no member functions. Here's an example of a structure:

```
struct Dimensions
{
    int height;
    int width;
    int depth;
    int weight;
    int price;
};
```

This block of code is similar to a class; as you can see, it has some member variables but no member functions. Nor does it have any access control (such as public, private, or protected).

But not only did the designers of C++ add classes to C++, they also enhanced the structures in C++. So now you can use structures more powerfully in C++ than you could in C. The main change to structures in C++ is that they can have member functions and access control. Thus we can add to the `Dimensions` structure like so:

```
struct Dimensions
{
private:
    int price;
public:
    int height;
    int width;
    int depth;
    int weight;
    int GetPrice() { return price; }
};
```

Then we can create an instance of `Dimensions` in our code like this:

```
Dimensions FirstIem;
Dimensions *SecondItem = new Dimensions;
```

Well, now, isn't that interesting? This `struct` business is looking *suspiciously* like a class, wouldn't you say? Hmmm. As it happens, the `struct` code *is* a `class`. It's the *same* thing.

When the great founder of the C++ language (Bjarne Stroustrup) created C++, he enhanced structures to the point that classes and structures are *identical*, with one exception. Members of a structure are public by default. Members of a class, however, are private by default.

That's nice. But why would you use a structure? Really, it doesn't matter. Most C++ programmers today never even touch a structure.

However, some C++ programmers use a special convention concerning structures. If a class has only public member variables and no member functions, then make it a structure.

In other words, programmers use structure for simple data types that are themselves a collection of smaller data types. (That is, they use structures in the same way C originally had it.) That's actually a pretty good idea. In the sections that follow, we tell you about some of these data-structure issues. (And for what it's worth, keeping structures around in C++ was a good idea because a lot of people originally took C applications and recompiled them with a C++ compiler. It was good that the C++ compiler handled the structures.)

If you're familiar with C and just learning C++, you may be interested to know that when you declare a variable that is a structure type, in C++ you need to give only the name of the structure. You no longer need the word `struct` in the declaration. Thus the following line will still compile in C++

```
struct Dimensions another;
```

but all you really need is

```
Dimensions another;
```

Structures as component data types

A common use of structures is as an advanced data type made up of underlying data types. For example, a lot of operating systems that deal with graphics include some libraries that require a `Point` structure. Typically, a `Point` structure is simply a grouping of an X-coordinate and a Y-coordinate, all in one package.

You might declare such a structure like this:

```
struct Point
{
    int x;
    int y;
};
```

Then, when you need to call a function that requires such a structure — such as one we made up for this example called `DrawDot` — you would simply declare a `Point` and call the function, as in the following:

```
Point onedot;
onedot.x = 10;
onedot.y = 15;
DrawDot(onedot);
```

The `DrawDot` function would have a prototype that looks like this:

```
void DrawDot(Point pt);
```

Note that the function doesn't take a pointer to a `Point`, nor does it take a reference to a `Point`. It just gets right to the `Point` directly.

TIP

If you want, you can initialize the members of a structure the same way you would an array:

```
Point seconddot = { 30, 50 };
DrawDot(seconddot);
```

Equating structures

Setting simple structures that are equal to another structure is easy. The C++ compiler automatically handles this by copying the members one by one. The `EquateStruct` example shown in Listing 2-2 is an example of this process in action.

Listing 2-2: Copying Structures Easily

```
#include <iostream>

using namespace std;

struct Point3D
{
    double x;
    double y;
    double z;
};

int main()
{
    Point3D FirstPoint = { 10.5, 22.25, 30.8 };
    Point3D SecondPoint = FirstPoint;
    cout << SecondPoint.x << endl;
    cout << SecondPoint.y << endl;
    cout << SecondPoint.z << endl;
    return 0;
}
```

TIP

Because structures are almost identical to classes, you can take Listing 2-2 and change the structure definition to the following class definition, and the application will continue to function the same:

```
class Point3D
{
public:
    double x;
    double y;
    double z;
};
```

**Book IV
Chapter 2**

**Creating Data
Structures**

No matter which form of the application you use, the output is simple. When you run this application, you see output similar to this:

```
10.5
22.25
30.8

Process returned 0 (0x0)    execution time : 0.015 s
Press any key to continue.
```

Returning compound data types

Because simple structures are just a grouping of smaller data items, you can treat them as one chunk of data. For that reason, you can easily return them from functions without having to use pointers.

The following function (found in the `CompoundData` example) shows how to return a structure:

```
Point3D StartingPoint(float x)
{
    Point3D start;
    start.x = x;
    start.y = x * 2;
    start.z = x * 3;
    return start;
}
```

This function relies on the `Point3D` `struct` defined in the "Equating structures" section of the chapter. You can easily call this guy, then, by using code like this:

```
Point3D MyPoint = StartingPoint(5.2);
Point3D OtherPoint = StartingPoint(6.5);
cout << MyPoint.x << endl;
cout << MyPoint.y << endl;
cout << MyPoint.z << endl;
cout << endl;
cout << OtherPoint.x << endl;
cout << OtherPoint.y << endl;
cout << OtherPoint.z << endl;
```

These `cout` statements produce the following output:

```
5.2
10.4
15.6

6.5
13
19.5

Process returned 0 (0x0)    execution time : 0.125 s
Press any key to continue.
```

Note that in the function, we simply created a local variable of type Point3D. This variable is not a pointer, nor is it a reference. And at the end of the function, we just returned it. When we called it, we copied the value of the returned structure into our own variables, first MyPoint and then OtherPoint.

You may start to see some trouble in paradise when returning structures (or class instances, because they're the same thing). Does returning a structure work? Why yes, it does, but what happens is sophisticated. When you create an instance of the structure in the function, you're just creating a local variable. That's definitely *not* something you want to return; it would sit on the stack as a local variable. But consider this call:

```
Point3D MyPoint = StartingPoint(5.2);
```

At the assembly level, the StartingPoint() function receives the address of MyPoint. Then at the end of the function, again at the assembly level, the compiled code copies the contents of the local variable (called start in this case) into the MyPoint structure by using the pointer to MyPoint. So nothing is actually *returned*, per se; instead, the data is copied. Thus, if your structure includes a pointer variable (for example), you will get a copy of the pointer variable as well — that is, your pointer variable will point to the same thing as the pointer in the function. That may be what you want, or it may not be, depending on your situation. So be careful and make sure you fully understand what you're doing when you return a structure from a function!

Naming Your Space

It's often nice to be able to use a common name for a variable or other item without fear that the name will clash with a pre-existing identifier. For example, somewhere in a header file you may have a global variable called Count, and somebody else may want to make a variable called Count in one of his or her functions that uses your global header file. Or you may want to name a function GetData() — but how can you be sure the people who use your function won't include a header file somebody else wrote that already has a GetData() function? Is it the great Battle of the GetData() functions, where only one will survive? Not good! What can you do to avoid the clash?

You can use namespaces. A *namespace* is simply a way to group identifiers, such as all your classes. If you called this group Menagerie, for example, Menagerie would be your namespace. You would then put your classes inside it, as shown in the SimpleNamespace example:

```
namespace Menagerie
{
    class Oxen {
    public:
```

```
    int Weight;
    int NumberOfTeeth;
};
class Cattle {
public:
    int Weight;
    int NumberOfChildren;
};
}
```

The names `Oxen` and `Cattle` are unique within the `Menagerie` namespace. You are free to reuse these names in other namespaces without worrying about a clash. Then, if you want to use either of the two classes inside the `Menagerie` namespace, you would *fully qualify* the names of the classes, like so (notice the use of the double colons between `Menagerie` and `Cattle`):

```
Menagerie::Cattle bessie;
bessie.Weight = 643;
```

Unlike class and structure declarations, a namespace declaration *doesn't* have to end with a semicolon.

If you plan to use the names in the `Menagerie` namespace without having to retype the namespace name each time, just put a line after the namespace declaration (but somewhere preceding the use of the names `Cattle` and `Oxen` in your code), like this:

```
using namespace Menagerie;
```

Then you can access the names as if they're not in a namespace:

```
Cattle bessie;
bessie.Weight = 643;
```

When you include a line that has `using namespace`, the compiler knows the namespace is only for lines that follow the `using namespace` declaration. Consider the following code:

```
void cattleranch()
{
    Cattle x;
}

using namespace Menagerie;

void dairy()
{
    Cattle x;
}
```

Here the first function won't compile because the compiler won't know the name `Cattle`. To get it to work, you have to replace `Cattle` with `Menagerie::Cattle`. But the second function *will* compile, thanks to some help from our buddy `using namespace`.

The `using namespace` line is good only for lines that follow it. If you put `using namespace` inside a code block — inside curly braces { and }, as you would inside a function — the line applies only to lines that follow it *within the same code block*. Thus, in this case

```
void cattleranch()
{
    using namespace Menagerie;
    Cattle x;
}

void dairy() {
    Cattle x;
}
```

the compiler will be happy with the first function, `cattleranch()` but not with the second function, `dairy()`. The `using namespace` line is good only for the length of the `cattleranch()` function; it's inside that function's code block.

When you have a `using namespace` line, any variables or identifiers you create after that line don't become *part* of the namespace you're using. The `using namespace` line simply tells the compiler that if it finds an identifier it doesn't recognize, it should check next inside the namespaces you're using.

When you have a `using namespace` line, you can follow it with more `using namespace` lines for other namespaces — and doing so won't cause the compiler to forget the previous `using namespace` line. Thus, if you have

```
using namespace Menagerie;
using namespace Ocean;
```

you can successfully refer to identifiers in both the `Menagerie` and the `Ocean` namespaces.

Creating one namespace in many places

After you create a namespace, you can add to it later in your code if necessary. All you have to do is start the first block of code with (for example) `namespace Menagerie {` and then finish it with a closing brace. Then later in your code, do the same line again — starting the block again with `namespace Menagerie {` and ending it with a closing brace. The identifiers in both blocks become part of the `namespace Menagerie`.

Using variables and part of a namespace

You can put variables in a namespace and then later refer to them through the namespace, as in the following:

```
namespace Menagerie
{
    int CattleCount;
}
```

And do it again later — for example, in your `main()` — like this:

```
Menagerie::CattleCount = 10;
```

But remember: *A namespace is not a class!* Only one instance of the `CattleCount` variable exists; it just happens to have a full name of `Menagerie::CattleCount`. This doesn't mean you can get away with creating multiple instances of `Menagerie`: You can't. It's a namespace. (Think of it like a surname: There could be multiple people named John, and to distinguish between them in a meeting at work, you might tack on their last names: John Squibbledash and John Poltzerbuckin.) Although the namespace name comes first in `Menagerie::CattleCount`, it's analogous to the last name. Two variables can be called `CattleCount`: one in the `Menagerie` namespace and one in the `Farm` namespace. Thus their full names would be `Menagerie::CattleCount` and `Farm::CattleCount`.

If you want to use only a portion of a namespace, you are free to do that, too. With the `Menagerie` namespace that we declared earlier in this section, you could do something like this outside the namespace:

```
using Menagerie::Oxen;
Oxen ollie;
```

(Notice that no `namespace` word appears after `using`.) The first line tells the compiler about the name `Oxen`, and the second line creates an instance of `Oxen`. Of course, if you have `using namespace Menagerie`, the `using Menagerie::Oxen` isn't very useful because the `Oxen` name is already available from the `using namespace Menagerie` line.

Think of a `using` declaration as pulling a name into the current namespace. Therefore a declaration such as `using Menagerie::Oxen` pulls the name `Oxen` into the current namespace. The single name then lives in both namespaces.

The standard namespace

Sooner or later, you're going to encounter something like this:

```
std::cout << "Hi" << std::endl;
```

You see this because normally `cout`, `cin`, `endl`, and everything else that comes from `#include<iostream>` is in a namespace called `std` (which is short for *standard*). But we find that line of code ugly. We don't want to write a namespace name and two colons every time we want to write a `cout` or `endl` (or anything else from `iostream`, for that matter). So what do you do to avoid it? You simply put

```
using namespace std;
```

at the beginning of your application, after the `include` lines. Fortunately, the gcc compiler automatically recognizes the `std` namespace, and you don't need the `using namespace std;` line. But if you're using other compilers (notably Borland C++Builder or Microsoft Visual C++), you need to add `std::` before each `cout` and `cin` and `endl` words or take the easier way out and use the `using namespace std;` line. We prefer the `using namespace std;` line. So if you look at the downloadable code, you see that line at the beginning of every application.

To understand how one name becomes a part of two namespaces, take a look at the `Namespace` example shown in Listing 2-3.

Listing 2-3: Pulling Names into Other Namespaces with the using Declaration

```
#include <iostream>

using namespace std;

namespace A
{
    int X;
}

namespace B
{
    using A::X;
}

int main()
{
    A::X = 2;
    cout << B::X << endl;
    return 0;
}
```

This code has two namespaces, A and B. The first namespace, A, has a variable called X. The second namespace, B, has a `using` statement that pulls the name X into that namespace. The single variable that lives inside A is now part of both namespaces, A and B. `main()` verifies this: It saves a value in the X variable of A and prints the value in the X variable of B. And lo and behold, the result on the screen is this:

```
2
```

Yes, indeed, `A::X` and `B::X` *refer to the same variable*, thanks to the `using` declaration!

Chapter 3: Constructors, Destructors, and Exceptions

In This Chapter

✓ Writing constructors

✓ Using different kinds of constructors

✓ Writing destructors

✓ Understanding the order that takes place in construction and destruction

✓ Throwing and catching exceptions

Now's the time to seriously master C++. In this chapter, we talk about three vital topics: constructors, destructors, and exceptions. Fully understanding what goes on with constructors and destructors is very important. The better you understand how constructors and destructors work, the less likely you are to write code that doesn't function the way that you expected and the more likely you are to avoid bugs.

Exceptions are important also in that they let you handle error situations — that is, you can handle problems when they do come up.

Many developers feel that constructors, destructors, and exceptions are extremely simple. In fact, many developers would doubt that these three topics could fill an entire chapter, but they can. After you read this chapter, you should have a good mastery of constructors, destructors, and exceptions.

So without further ado, you can begin to construct your reading as you destruct any old ways of programming, without exception.

Constructing and Destructing Objects

Classes are goofy little things. They like to have some say in how their instances get started. But that's okay. We're programmers, and we like to do what the computer wants us to do (as opposed to the other way around). And so the great founders of the C++ language gave us constructors. *Constructors* are member functions that the application calls when it creates an instance. *Destructors,* on the other hand, are member functions that the application calls when it deletes an instance.

A single class can have multiple constructors. In fact, several kinds of constructors are available. There aren't as many kinds of destructors. (In fact, there's really only one.) In the sections that follow, we give you all the necessary information so that, when your classes want constructors, you can happily add them.

If you see some older C++ code, you're more than likely to see the word `virtual` before a constructor in a class definition. The idea was that you can override a constructor when you derive a new class, so you should make it `virtual`. However, in ANSI C++, this construction is not supported. You cannot make a constructor `virtual`. If you put the word `virtual` before a constructor, you get a compiler error. If you see an older class that has a virtual constructor, create constructors as you normally would in the derived classes, and all will be fine. (Unfortunately, all is not fine for those million or so C++ programmers who spent years writing code that had the word `virtual` before a constructor. They get to practice using that Backspace key.)

Overloading constructors

You're allowed to put multiple constructors in your class. The way the user of your class chooses a constructor is by setting up the parameters in the variable declaration. Suppose you have a class called `Clutter`, and suppose you see the following two lines of code:

```
Clutter inst1("Jim");
Clutter inst2(123, "Sally");
```

These two lines have different types of parameters in the list. Each one is making use of a different constructor for the single class.

You can put multiple constructors in your class. The process of putting multiple constructors is called *overloading* the constructors. The `Constructor01` example demonstrates how to create a `Clutter` class that has two constructors, as shown here:

```
class Clutter
{
protected:
    string ChildName;
    int Toys;

public:
    Clutter(int count, string name)
    {
        ChildName = name;
        Toys = count;
    }
```

```
Clutter(string name)
{
    ChildName = name;
    Toys = 0;
}
};
```

The compiler will figure out which overloaded constructor to use, based on the parameters. Therefore the overloaded constructors must differ in their parameter lists — specifically, this means the *types* of parameters; just changing the names doesn't count! If the parameter lists don't differ, the compiler won't be able to distinguish them, and you will get an error when it tries to compile the class definition.

If your constructor doesn't have a parameter provided by other constructors, you should initialize the associated variable within the constructor code. For example, the second constructor doesn't include a parameter for Toys, so the constructor code initializes this variable to 0. As an alternative, you can use an initializer as described in the "Initializing members" section of the chapter.

Having multiple constructors makes your class much more flexible and easy to use. Multiple constructors give the users of your class more ways to use the class, allowing them to configure the instances differently, depending on their situations. Further, the constructors force the user to configure the instances only in the ways your constructors allow.

Initializing members

When C++ originally came out, any time you wanted to initialize a member variable, you had to put it inside a constructor. This created some interesting problems. The main problem had to do with references: You can put reference variables in a class, but normally reference variables must be initialized. You can't just have a reference variable floating around that doesn't refer to anything. But if you put a reference variable inside a class and create an instance of the class, the application will first create the instance and then call the constructor. Even if you initialize the reference in the first line of the constructor, there's still a moment when you have an uninitialized reference! Oh, what to do, what to do?

The ANSI standard uses a single approach for setting up member variables: initializers. An *initializer* goes on the same line as the constructor in the class definition; or, if the constructor isn't *inline* — defined within the class code block — the initializer goes with the constructor in the code outside the class definition.

The `Constructor02` example demonstrates how to add initializers right inside the class definition, as shown here:

```
class MySharona
{
protected:
    int OneHitWonders;
    int NumberRecordings;
public:
    MySharona() : OneHitWonders(1), NumberRecordings(10) {}
};
```

When you create an instance of this class, the `OneHitWonders` member gets the value `1` and the `NumberRecordings` member gets the value `10`. Note the syntax: The constructor name and parameter list (which is empty in this case) is followed by a single colon. The member variables appear after that, each followed by an initial value in parentheses. Commas separate the member variables.

After the member variables is the open brace for any code you would want in the constructor. In this case, we had no code, so we immediately put a closing brace.

You can put any of the class member variables in the initializer list, but you don't have to include them all. If you don't care to initialize some, you don't have to. Note also that you cannot put inherited members in the initializer list; you can include only members that are in the class itself.

You can also pass these initial values in through the constructor. Here's a slightly modified version of this same class. This time the constructor has a parameter that we save in the `NumberRecordings` member:

```
class MySharona
{
protected:
    int OneHitWonders;
    int NumberRecordings;
public:
    MySharona(int Records) : OneHitWonders(1),
        NumberRecordings(Records) {}
};
```

By associating an initializer list with a constructor, you can have different initializers with different constructors. You're not limited to initializing the data the same way for all your constructors.

You may have noticed that the member initialization follows a format similar to the way you initialize an inherited constructor. Take a look at how we're calling the base class constructor in this code:

```
class MusicInfo
{
public:
    int PhoneNumber;
    MusicInfo(int Phone) : PhoneNumber(Phone) {}
};

class MySharona : public MusicInfo
{
protected:
    int OneHitWonders;
    int NumberRecordings;
public:
    MySharona(int Records) : OneHitWonders(1),
        NumberRecordings(Records),
        MusicInfo(8675309) {}
};
```

In the MySharona class, the member variables get initialized, and the base class constructor gets called, all in the initialization. The call to the base class constructor is this portion:

```
MusicInfo(8675309)
```

But note that we're passing a number into the constructor. The MusicInfo constructor takes a single number for a parameter, and it uses the number it receives to initialize the Phone member:

```
MusicInfo(int Phone) : PhoneNumber(Phone) {}
```

Therefore, every time someone creates an instance of the class MySharona, the inherited PhoneNumber member is automatically initialized to 8675309.

Thus you can create an instance of MySharona like this:

```
MySharona CD(20);
```

This instance starts out having the member values OneHitWonders = 1, NumberRecordings = 20, and Phone = 8675309. The only thing that the user can specify here for a default value is the NumberRecordings member. The other two members are set automatically by the class.

However, you don't have to do it this way. Perhaps you want the users of this class to be able to specify the PhoneNumber when they create an instance. Here's a modified form that does it for you:

```
class MusicInfo
{
public:
    int PhoneNumber;
    MusicInfo(int Phone) : PhoneNumber(Phone) {}
};
```

```
class MySharona : public MusicInfo
{
protected:
    int OneHitWonders;
    int NumberRecordings;
public:
    MySharona(int Records, int Phone) : OneHitWonders(1),
        NumberRecordings(Records), MusicInfo(Phone) {}
};
```

Look carefully at the difference: The `MySharona` class now has two parameters. The second is an integer, and we pass that one into the base class through the portion:

```
MusicInfo(Phone)
```

So to use this class, you might do something like this:

```
MySharona CD(20, 5551212);
```

This code snippet creates an instance of `MySharona`, with the members initialized to `OneHitWonders = 1`, `NumberRecordings = 20`, and `PhoneNumber = 5551212`.

If you have overloaded constructors, you can have different sets of initializations. For example, take a look at yet one more modification to this final version of the `Constructor02` example:

```
class MusicInfo
{
public:
    int PhoneNumber;
    MusicInfo(int Phone) : PhoneNumber(Phone) {}
};

class MySharona : public MusicInfo
{
protected:
    int OneHitWonders;
    int NumberRecordings;
public:
    MySharona(int Records, int Phone) : MusicInfo(Phone),
        OneHitWonders(1), NumberRecordings(Records) {}

    MySharona(int Records) : MusicInfo(8675309),
        OneHitWonders(1), NumberRecordings(Records) {}
};
```

Now this class has two constructors. We combined the previous two versions, so now you can use either constructor. You can, then, have the following two variables, for example, each using a different constructor:

```
MySharona CD(20, 5551212);
MySharona OldCD(30);
cout << CD.PhoneNumber << endl;
cout << OldCD.PhoneNumber << endl;
```

When you run the `cout` lines, they have different values for the `PhoneNumber` member. The first passes a specific value; the second accepts a default value:

```
5551212
8675309
```

You should initialize the base class values first. Otherwise the compiler is likely to display warning messages when you compile the application.

If the only real difference in the different constructors is whether or not the user supplies a value (as was the case in the previous example), you can use a slightly better approach. Constructors (and any function in C++, really) can have default values. The `Constructor03` example shortens the previous examples by using default values. The result is the same:

```
class MusicInfo
{
public:
    int PhoneNumber;
    MusicInfo(int Phone) : PhoneNumber(Phone) {}
};

class MySharona : public MusicInfo
{
protected:
    int OneHitWonders;
    int NumberRecordings;
public:
    MySharona(int Records, int Phone=8675309) :
        MusicInfo(Phone), OneHitWonders(1),
        NumberRecordings(Records) {}
    };
```

In the preceding code, the second parameter to the constructor has an equals sign and a number after it. That means the user of the class doesn't have to specify this parameter. If the parameter is not present, it automatically gets the value 8675309.

You can have as many default parameters as you want in a constructor or any other function, but the rule is that the default parameters must come at the end. After you have a default parameter, all the parameters that follow must have a default value. Therefore the following type of code is not allowed:

```
MySharona(int Records = 6, int Phone) :
    MusicInfo(Phone), OneHitWonders(1),
        NumberRecordings(Records) {}
```

There's a practical reason for this prohibition: When the user calls the constructor (by creating a variable of type `MySharona`, there is no way to leave out just a first parameter and have only a second one. It's not possible, unless C++ were to allow an empty parameter followed by a comma, as in `MySharona(,8675309)`. But that's not allowed.

Adding a default constructor

A *default constructor* is a constructor that takes no parameters. You can have a default constructor in a class in either of two ways: by coding it or by letting the compiler *implicitly* build one for you. By *implicitly build one for you,* we mean that you don't actually have a constructor in your code, but the compiler gives you one when it compiles the code for you.

You've probably seen a default constructor before. This class has no constructor, so the compiler generates an implicit one for you. It works like this:

```
class Simple
{
public:
    int x,y;
    void Write()
    {
        cout << x << " " << y << endl;
    }
};
```

Of course, the preceding class doesn't do much. It's the same as this:

```
class Simple
{
public:
    int x,y;
    void Write()
    {
        cout << x << " " << y << endl;
    }
    Simple() {}
};
```

Recognizing that the default constructor is there, however, is important. And you need to realize when the compiler *doesn't* create a constructor automatically because you may run into some problems. Take a look at this modified version of the class (found in the `Constructor04` example):

```
class Simple
{
public:
    int x,y;
    void Write()
    {
        cout << x << " " << y << endl;
    }
    Simple(int startx) { x = startx; }
};
```

We included in this code our own constructor that takes a parameter. After we do this, the class no longer gets an implicit default constructor. If we have a line later like this:

```
Simple inst;
```

the compiler will give us an error message like this:

```
In function 'int main()'
error: no matching function for call to 'Simple::Simple()'
note: candidates are: Simple::Simple(const Simple&)
note:                  Simple::Simple(int)
```

Yet, if we take out the constructor we added (so it goes back to an earlier example), this error goes away! Therefore, if you provide no constructors, the compiler gives you an implicit default constructor.

If you're using the Code::Blocks compiler, you obtain some helpful additional information. In this case, you see two note lines that tell you about the available constructor candidates. You can use this information as part of your troubleshooting efforts.

Now here's where you could run into trouble: Suppose you build a class and provide no constructors for it. You give the class to other people to use. They're using it in their code, all happy, making use of the default constructor. Then one day somebody else (not you — you don't make mistakes) decides that he wants to enhance the class by adding a special constructor with several parameters. The rogue programmer adds the constructor and then makes use of it. Mr. Rogue thinks all is fine, because he's using only his new constructor. But little does he know: All the other people who were using the implicit default constructor suddenly start getting compiler errors!

Believe it or not, we have seen this happen. One day, all of a sudden, your code won't compile. Any time you try to create an instance of a class, you start getting errors stating that the compiler can't find `Simple::Simple()`. Oops. Somebody changed it.

But you can avoid this problem by making sure that you explicitly include a default constructor, even if it does nothing:

```
class Simple
{
public:
    int x,y;
    void Write()
    {
        cout << x << " " << y << endl;
    }
    Simple() {}
};
```

Then when Mr. Rogue adds his own constructor, the default constructor will still be there (assuming, of course, that *he* doesn't *remove* it. But if he does, move him to that nice secluded inner office that has no windows and no doors). When he adds his extra constructor, he will be overloading it:

```
class Simple
{
public:
    int x,y;
    void Write()
    {
        cout << x << " " << y << endl;
    }
    Simple() {}
    Simple(int startx) { x = startx; }
};
```

Note that now this class has two constructors! And all will be happy, because everybody's code will still compile.

Functional constructors

Every once in a while, you may come across something that looks like this:

```
Simple inst = Simple(5);
```

What *is* that? It looks like a function call. Or it looks like the way you would declare a pointer variable, except there's no asterisk and no `new` word. So what is it? It's a functional syntax for calling a default constructor. The right side creates a new instance of `Simple`, passing 5 into the constructor. Then this new instance gets copied into the variable called `inst`.

This approach can be handy if you're creating an array of objects, where the array contains actual objects, not pointers to objects:

```
Simple MyList[] = { Simple(1), Simple(50), Simple(80),
  Simple(100), Simple(150) };
```

The approach seems a little strange because the variable `MyList` is not a pointer, yet you're setting it equal to something on the right. But this approach is handy because every once in a while you need a temporary variable. The `Constructor05` example, shown in Listing 3-1, demonstrates how you can use the functional syntax to create a temporary instance of the class `string`.

Listing 3-1: Creating Temporary Instances with Functional Constructors

```
#include <iostream>
#include <string>

using namespace std;

void WriteMe(string str)
{
    cout << "Here I am: " << str << endl;
}

int main()
{
    WriteMe(string("Sam"));
    return 0;
}
```

When you compile and run this, you see this output:

```
Here I am: Sam
```

In `main()`, we created a temporary instance of the `string` class. (Remember, `string` is a class!) But as it turns out, an even shorter version of this is available. If we had called `WriteMe()`, we could have just done this:

```
WriteMe("Sam");
```

This code works out well because you don't even feel like you're working with a class called `string`. The parameter just seems like a basic type, and you're passing a character array, `Sam`. However, the parameter is an instance of a class. Here's how the code works. Suppose you have a class like the one found in the `Constructor06` example and a function to go with it:

```
class MyNumber
{
public:
    int First;
    MyNumber(int TheFirst) : First(TheFirst) {}
};

void WriteNumber(MyNumber num)
{
    cout << num.First << endl;
}
```

(`WriteNumber()` is *not* a member of `MyNumber`.) You can do any of the following calls to `WriteNumber()`.

```
MyNumber prime = 17;
WriteNumber(prime);
WriteNumber(MyNumber(23));
WriteNumber(29);
```

The first call uses a previously declared variable of type `MyNumber`. The second call creates a temporary instance, passing the value 23 into the constructor. The third one also creates a temporary instance, but it does so implicitly! The output from this example is

```
17
23
29
```

You may wonder when your temporary variables get destroyed. For instance, if you call `WriteNumber(MyNumber(23));`, how long does the temporary `MyNumber` instance live on? The ANSI standard proudly proclaims that the instance will get deleted at the end of the *full expression*. In other words, after the line is *done,* the temporary instance will be *done for*.

Be careful when using implicit temporary objects. Consider the following class and function found in the `Constructor07` example:

```
class MyName
{
public:
    string First;
    MyName(string TheFirst) : First(TheFirst) {}
};

void WriteName(MyName name)
{
    cout << "Hi I am " << name.First << endl;
}
```

Seems straightforward. The `MyName` constructor takes a string, so it seems like we should be able to do this when we call the `WriteName()` function:

```
WriteName("George");
```

Except we can't. The compiler gives us an error message:

```
In function 'int main()':
error: could not convert '(const char*)"George"' from 'const char*'
    to 'MyName'
```

Here's the problem: The compiler got shortsighted. The compiler considers the type of the string constant a `const char *` (that is, a pointer to a `const` character, or really a constant character array). Although we don't have any constructors that take a `const char *` parameter, we do have one that takes a `string`, and it has a constructor that takes a `const char *` parameter. Unfortunately, the compiler doesn't fall for that, and it complains. So we have to adjust our function call just a tad, like so:

```
WriteName(string("George"));
```

And this time it works. Now we *explicitly* create a temporary string instance. And by using that, we *implicitly* create a temporary instance of our own class, `MyName`. It would be nice if the compiler could wade through this and implicitly create the `string` instance for us, but it doesn't seem to want to. Oh well. Calling `WriteName(string("George"));` works well enough for us.

Calling one constructor from another

If you have some initialization code and you want several constructors to call it, you might try putting the code in one constructor and then having the other constructors call the constructor that has the initialization code.

Unfortunately, that won't work. Some things in life we just can't have, and this is one of them. If you have a constructor and write code to call another constructor, such as this

```
CallOne::CallOne(int ax)
{
    y = 20;
    CallOne();
}
```

where `CallOne` is your class, then this will compile but won't behave the way you may expect. The line `CallOne();` is not calling a constructor for the same instance! The compiler treats this line as a *functional* constructor. Thus the line creates a *separate, temporary instance*. And then at the end of the line `CallOne()`, the application deletes the instance.

You can see this behavior with the following class:

```
class CallOne
{
public:
    int x,y;
    CallOne();
    CallOne(int ax);
};

CallOne::CallOne()
{
    x = 10;
    y = 10;
}

CallOne::CallOne(int ax)
{
    y = 20;
    CallOne();
}
```

When you create an instance by using the second constructor like this, the value of the y member of the instance will be 20, not 10:

```
CallOne Mine(10);
```

To people who don't know any different, it may look like the y would first get set to 20 in the second constructor, and then the call to the default constructor would cause it to get changed to 10. But that's not the case: The second constructor is not calling the default constructor for the same object; it's creating a separate, temporary instance.

If you have common initialization code that you want in multiple constructors, put the code in its own private or protected function (called, for example, Init()), and have each constructor call the Init() function. If you have one constructor call another constructor, it won't work. The second constructor will be operating on a separate instance.

Copying instances with copy constructors

One nice thing about C++ is that it lets you copy instances of classes. For example, if you have a class called Copyable, you can write code like this:

```
Copyable first;
Copyable second = first;
```

This will create two instances, and second will be a duplicate of first. The application will accomplish this by simply copying all the member variables from first to second.

That works pretty well, except sometimes you want to customize the behavior just a bit. For example, you may have a member variable that contains a unique ID for each instance. In your constructor, you may have code that generates a unique ID. The problem is that the previous sample will not call your constructor: It will just make a duplicate of the object. Thus your two objects will have the same number for their supposedly "unique" IDs. So much for diversity.

So if you want to have control over the copying, you can create a copy constructor. A *copy constructor* is just a constructor that takes as a parameter a reference to another instance of the same class, as in this example:

```
Copyable(const Copyable& source);
```

When you copy an instance, your application will call this constructor. The parameter to this constructor will be the instance you're copying. Thus, in the case of Copyable second = first;, the source parameter will be first. And because it's a reference (which is required for copy constructors), you can access its members by using the dot notation (.) rather than the pointer notation (->).

The `Constructor08` example shown in Listing 3-2 is a complete application that demonstrates copy constructors.

Listing 3-2: Customizing the Copying of Instances

```
#include <iostream>

using namespace std;

class Copyable
{
protected:
    static int NextAvailableID;
    int UniqueID;
public:
    int SomeNumber;
    int GetID() { return UniqueID; }
    Copyable();
    Copyable(int x);
    Copyable(const Copyable& source);
};

Copyable::Copyable()
{
    UniqueID = NextAvailableID;
    NextAvailableID++;
}

Copyable::Copyable(int x)
{
    UniqueID = NextAvailableID;
    NextAvailableID++;
    SomeNumber = x;
}

Copyable::Copyable(const Copyable& source)
{
    UniqueID = NextAvailableID;
    NextAvailableID++;
    SomeNumber = source.SomeNumber;
}

int Copyable::NextAvailableID;

int main()
{
    Copyable take1 = 100;
    Copyable take2;
    take2.SomeNumber = 200;
    Copyable take3 = take1;

    cout << take1.GetID() << " "
        << take1.SomeNumber << endl;
```

(continued)

```
    cout << take2.GetID() << " "
        << take2.SomeNumber << endl;
    cout << take3.GetID() << " "
        << take3.SomeNumber << endl;
    return 0;
}
```

Go ahead and run this application to see how it works. The output from this example is

```
0 100
1 200
2 100
```

We need to tell you two things about the copy constructor in this code. First, *we included* `const` *in the parameter of the copy constructor*. That's because of a small rule in C++ where, if you have a constant instance, you won't be able to copy it otherwise. If we left off `const`, this line would not compile properly.

The second thing we need to tell you is that, in the code for the copy constructor, we had to copy the member variables manually from one instance to the other. That's because now that we're supplying our own copy constructor, the computer will not copy the members as it would when we supply no copy constructor at all.

Listing 3-2 uses a *static* member to keep track of what the next available `UniqueID` is. Remember that a class shares a single static member among all instances of the class. Therefore you have only one instance of `NextAvailableID`, and it's shared by all the instances of class `Copyable`.

For a long, happy life

✦ Put a `const` in your copy constructor.

✦ Copy the items manually.

When constructors go bad: Failable constructors?

Suppose that you're writing a class that will connect to the Internet and automatically download the latest weather report for the country of Upper Zamboni. The question is this: Do you put the code to connect to the Internet in the constructor or not?

People are often faced with this common design issue. Putting the initialization code in the constructor provides many advantages. For one, you can just create the instance without having to first create it and then call a separate member function that does the initialization. And in general, that works fine.

But what if that initialization code can result in an error? For example, suppose that the constructor is unable to connect to the Internet. Then what? Remember: A constructor doesn't return a value. So you can't have it return, for example, a `bool` that would state whether it successfully did its work.

You have many choices for this, and different people seem to have rather strong opinions about which choice is best. (Programmers with strong opinions? Now there's an unlikely concept.) Here are the ones we've seen:

✦ **Just don't do it:** Write your constructors so they create the object but don't do any work. Instead, put the work code in a separate member function, which can return a `bool` representing whether it was successful.

✦ **Let the constructor do the work:** If the work fails (such as it can't connect to the Internet), have the constructor save an error code in a member variable. When you create an instance, you can check the member variable to see whether it works.

✦ **Let the constructor do some more of the work:** If the work fails, throw an exception. In your code, then, you would wrap the creation of the instance with a try block and include an exception handler. (See "Programming the Exceptions to the Rule," later in this chapter, for more information on `try` blocks and exception handlers.)

We don't like this choice. If other people are using the class that we wrote, we don't want them to have to go through the motions of wrapping it in a `try` block and an exception handler. But other than being a nice guy, there's a practical reason for avoiding this choice: If we have teammates who are beginners at programming, they may just skip that part. "Oh shoot. It'll never fail," might be their attitude. And when it does fail on a customer's computer — if it can, then it will, Mr. Murphy! — the customer will be very unhappy that his or her application couldn't connect to the Internet and crashed.

Destroying your instances

Although constructors are versatile and it seems like people could write entire books on them (good for family story time reading), destructors are simple, and there's not a whole lot to say about them. But you do need to know some information to make them work properly.

First, destructors don't get parameters, and (like constructors) they do not have return types. So not much more to say about that.

Suppose you have a class that contains, as members, instances of other classes. When you delete an instance of the main class, will the contained instances be deleted automatically? That depends. If your class contains actual instances (as opposed to pointers), they will get deleted. Look at this code from the `Destructor01` example:

```
class LittleInst
{
public:
    int MyNumber;
    ~LittleInst() { cout << MyNumber << endl; }
};

class Container
{
public:
    LittleInst first;
    LittleInst *second;
    Container();
};

Container::Container()
{
    first.MyNumber = 1;
    second = new LittleInst;
    second->MyNumber = 2;
}
```

We have two classes, `LittleInst` and `Container`. The `Container` class holds an instance of `LittleInst` (the member variable called `first`) and a pointer to `LittleInst`. In the constructor we set up the two `LittleInst` instances. For `first`, it already exists, and all we have to do is set up its `MyNumber` member. But `second` is just a pointer, so we have to create the instance before we can set up its `MyNumber` member. Thus we have two instances, one a pointer and one a regular instance.

Now suppose you use these classes like so:

```
Container *inst = new Container;
delete inst;
```

We gave `Container` no destructor. So will its members, `first` and `second`, get destroyed? Here's what we see after these two lines run:

```
1
```

That's the output from the `LittleInst` destructor. The number 1 goes with the `first` member. So you can see that `first` was deleted, but `second` wasn't.

Here's the rule: When you delete an instance of a class, the members that are direct (that is, not pointers) are deleted as well. Any pointers, however, you must manually delete in your destructor (or elsewhere).

Sometimes you may want an object to hold an instance of another class but want to keep the instance around after you delete the containing object. In that case, you wouldn't delete the other instance in the destructor.

Here's a modification to the `Container` class (found in the `Destructor02` example) that deletes the `second` instance:

```
class Container
{
public:
    LittleInst first;
    LittleInst *second;
    Container();
    ~Container() { delete second; }
};
```

Then, when you run these two lines again

```
Container *inst = new Container;
delete inst;
```

you see this output, which deletes both instances:

```
2
1
```

In the preceding output, you can see that it deleted the second instance first. The reason is that the application calls the destructor before it destroys the direct members. In this case, when we deleted our `Container` instance, the application first called our destructor before deleting our `first` member. That's actually a good idea, because in the code for our destructor, we may want to do some work on our member variables before they get wiped out.

Virtually inheriting destructors

You can (and should) make destructors virtual — unlike constructors. The reason is that you can pass an instance of a derived class into a function that takes a base class, like this:

```
void ProcessAndDelete(DeleteMe *inst)
{
    cout << inst->Number << endl;
    delete inst;
}
```

This function takes an instance of class `DeleteMe`, does some work on it, and deletes it. Now, suppose you have a class derived from `DeleteMe`, say class `Derived`. Because of the rules of inheritance, you're allowed to pass the instance of `Derived` into this function. But by the rules of *polymorphism* (as described in the "Specializing with polymorphism" section of

Book II Chapter 1), if you want the `ProcessAndDelete()` function to call an overloaded member function of `Derived`, you need to make the member function virtual. And that's the case with all destructors as well. The `Destructor03` example shown in Listing 3-3 demonstrates this.

Listing 3-3:   Making the Destructors Virtual

```
#include <iostream>

using namespace std;

class DeleteMe
{
public:
    int Number;
    virtual ~DeleteMe();
};

class Derived : public DeleteMe
{
public:
    virtual ~Derived();
};

DeleteMe::~DeleteMe()
{
    cout << "DeleteMe::~DeleteMe()" << endl;
}

Derived::~Derived()
{
    cout << "Derived::~Derived()" << endl;
}

void ProcessAndDelete(DeleteMe *inst)
{
    cout << inst->Number << endl;
    delete inst;
}

int main()
{
    DeleteMe *MyObject = new(Derived);
    MyObject->Number = 10;
    ProcessAndDelete(MyObject);
    return 0;
}
```

When you run this application, thanks to the `cout` calls in the destructors, `delete` is calling the destructor for `Derived` (which in turn calls the base class destructor). Here's the output:

```
10
Derived::~Derived()
DeleteMe::~DeleteMe()
```

Ordering your constructors and destructors

When you have constructors and destructors in a base and derived class and you create an instance of the derived class, remember the ordering: The computer first creates the members for the base class, and then the computer calls the constructor for the base class. Next, the computer creates the members of the derived class, and then the computer calls the constructor for the derived class.

The order for destruction is opposite. When you destroy an instance of a base class, first the computer calls the destructor for the derived class and then deletes the members of the derived class. Next the computer calls the destructor for the base class and then deletes the members of the base class.

The first line is the output from the `ProcessAndDelete` function. The middle line is the output from the `Derived` destructor, and the third line is the output from the `DeleteMe` destructor. We passed in a `Derived` instance, and the application called the `Derived` destructor.

Now try this: Remove `virtual` from the `DeleteMe` destructor:

```
class DeleteMe
{
public:
    int Number;
    ~DeleteMe();
};
```

Now, when you compile and run the application, the application calls the base class destructor. Because the `ProcessAndDelete()` function takes a `DeleteMe` instance, you see this output:

```
10
DeleteMe::~DeleteMe()
```

In the preceding example, the destructor isn't virtual; it's not able to find the proper destructor when you pass in a `Derived` instance. So it just calls the destructor for whatever type is listed in the parameter.

 Getting into the habit of always making your destructors virtual is a good idea. That way, if somebody else writes a function, such as `ProcessAndDelete()`, you can be assured that his or her function will automatically call the correct destructor.

Programming the Exceptions to the Rule

An *exception* is a bad situation that occurs in your software, causing your application to have to handle the bad situation. For example, if you try to write to a file but somehow that file got corrupted and you can't, the operating system might *throw* an exception. Or you might have a function that processes some data, and if the function encounters corrupted data, it might throw an exception.

Exceptions were new to C++; they did not exist in C. People were a little suspicious of them when they first came out, and some people even consider them to be Bad (that's with a capital *B*). The reason is this: People who oppose exceptions feel that writing code that relies too heavily on exceptions is too easy. But you should use them because they help you handle situations that you might not otherwise anticipate.

The Exception01 example shown in Listing 3-4 is an sample of a function that we wrote that throws an exception and an entire application that uses the function.

Listing 3-4: Throwing and Catching Exceptions

```
#include <iostream>
#include <string>

using namespace std;

void ProcessData()
{
    throw new string("Oops, I found some bad data!");
}

int main()
{
    try
    {
        ProcessData();
        cout << "No problems!" << endl;
    }
    catch (string *excep)
    {
        cout << "Found an error. Here's the message.";
        cout << endl;
        cout << *excep;
        cout << endl;
    }
    cout << "All finished." << endl;

    return 0;
}
```

Go ahead and run this application. You see the following text as output:

```
Found an error. Here's the message.
Oops, I found some bad data!
All finished.
```

Look closely at what this application does. In `main()`, there's a call to `ProcessData()`, which we put inside a `try` block. Because the call is inside a `try` block, the computer calls the function; and if the function throws an exception, the application automatically comes back out of the function and goes into the `catch` block. The `catch` block receives the item that was thrown as a parameter, much like a parameter to a function.

But if the `ProcessData()` function didn't encounter any problems and therefore didn't throw an exception, the function will complete its work and the application will continue with the code after the function call. In this case, one more line is inside the `try` block. If there was no exception, then upon completion of the `ProcessData()` function, the computer does the `cout` line after the `ProcessData()` call.

Think of an exception handler as a way to catch errors: If an exception gets thrown, your application can catch the error by including a `catch` block.

After the `try`/`catch` block is complete, the application will run any lines that follow, regardless of whether or not an exception was present. Thus, in all cases, Listing 3-4 will execute the line

```
cout << "All finished." << endl;
```

Now, in the listing, note that our `ProcessData()` function calls `throw`, meaning that it generates an exception. Normally, you probably wouldn't just have a function throw an exception for no reason, as this function does (unless you're trying to have fun with your users), but we do that just to demonstrate how the exceptions work. And besides, this is fun!

This particular `throw` looks like this:

```
throw new string("Oops, I found some bad data!");
```

We create a new `string` instance, and *that's* what we throw. You can create an instance of any class you want, and it can be either a pointer or a direct instance, depending on whether you prefer to work with pointers or references (it's your choice).

Now look at the `catch` block in Listing 3-4. Notice that it starts with this:

```
catch (string *excep)
```

Because in the function we threw a pointer to a string instance, here we catch a pointer to a string instance. Everything must match.

You can have more than one catch block. Suppose different types of exceptions could get thrown. For example, you might have another function like this:

```
void ProcessMore()
{
    throw new int(10);
}
```

The other function threw a pointer to a string, but this one throws a pointer to an integer. Watch out! Lots of things getting thrown around!

Then, when you call the two functions, your try/catch block can look like this:

```
try
{
    ProcessData();
    ProcessMore();
    cout << "No problems!" << endl;
}
catch (string *excep)
{
    cout << "Found an error. Here's the message.";
    cout << endl;
    cout << *excep;
    cout << endl;
}
catch (int *num)
{
    cout << "Found a numerical error. Here it is.";
    cout << endl;
    cout << *num;
    cout << endl;
}
cout << "All finished." << endl;
```

If you add this code and the ProcessMore() function to Listing 3-4, you probably want to comment out the throw line from the ProcessData() function if you want to see this application handle the integer exception. That's because the execution of the lines in the try block will cease as soon as a throw statement occurs, and *control will be transferred* to the appropriate catch block. Which catch block gets the honor depends on the type of the object thrown.

Throwing direct instances

You can throw a direct instance that is not a pointer. In your throw line, you would do this:

```
void ProcessData()
{
    throw string("Oops, I found some bad data!");
}
```

or this:

```
void ProcessMore()
{
    throw 10;
}
```

Instead of throwing pointers, we're throwing the object or value itself. In the `catch` block, then, you can catch the type itself without a pointer:

```
try
{
    ProcessData();
    ProcessMore();
}
catch (string excep)
{
    cout << excep;
}
catch (int num)
{
    cout << num;
}
```

Or, if you prefer, you can use references in the `catch` block. (The `throw` line does not change.) It looks like this:

```
try
{
    ProcessData();
    ProcessMore();
}
catch (string &excep)
{
    cout << excep;
}
catch (int &num)
{
    cout << num;
}
```

You may notice something just a little strange. For the integer version, the `throw` statement looks like this:

```
throw 10;
```

That is, the line of code is throwing a value, not an object. But the `catch` line looks like this:

```
catch (int &num) {
```

The `catch` statement is catching a reference. Normally you can have references only to variables, not to values! But it works here because inside the computer, the application makes a temporary variable, and that's what you're referring to in the `catch` block. So all is fine.

Catching any exception

If you want to write a general `catch` handler that will catch any exception and you don't care to actually catch the object that was thrown, you can write your handler like this:

```
try
{
    ProcessData();
    ProcessMore();
    cout << "No problems!" << endl;
}
catch (...)
{
    cout << "An unknown exception occurred." << endl;
}
```

That is, instead of putting what is effectively a `function` parameter in the `catch` header, you just put three dots, called an ellipsis.

Some word processors (Microsoft Word being one) can transform three typed periods into a single ellipses character. Don't paste that character into the code editor because the compiler won't know what to do with it. Instead, type three periods.

You can use the ellipses also as a general exception catcher in addition to your other handlers. Here's an example:

```
try
{
    ProcessData();
    ProcessMore();
    cout << "No problems!" << endl;
}
catch (string excep)
{
    cout << "Found an error. Here's the message.";
    cout << endl;
    cout << excep;
    cout << endl;
}
catch (int num)
{
    cout << "Found a numerical error. Here it is.";
    cout << endl;
    cout << num;
    cout << endl;
}
```

```
catch (...)
{
    cout << "An unknown exception occurred." << endl;
}
```

If your function calls throw an exception and you don't have any exception handler for it (because your `catch` blocks don't handle the type of exception being thrown or you don't have any `try`/`catch` blocks), your application will *stop*. The gcc compiler that comes with Code::Blocks, Dev-C++, MinGW, and Cygwin prints the following message on the console and then immediately terminates the application:

```
abnormal program termination
```

That's not good at all! Imagine the looks on your users' faces if they saw this. We know that we wouldn't want to be standing there with them, knowing that we're the ones who wrote the application.

Visual C++ also prints this same message but shows it in a message box. Borland C++ Builder shows the same message, too, and writes it to the console.

Two programming rules keep your users happily ignorant of exceptions:

✦ Know when you're calling a function that could throw an exception.

✦ When you're calling a function that could throw an exception, include an exception handler.

  It doesn't matter how *deep* the exception is when it's thrown; somewhere, *somebody* needs to catch it. A function could call a function that calls a function that calls a function that calls a function that throws an exception. If no intermediate function has an exception handler, put one in your outer function.

Rethrowing an exception

When inside a `catch` block, a `throw` statement without anything after it will simply rethrow the same exception. Although this may seem a bit convoluted (and indeed it can be), you may have a function that contains a `try`/`catch` block. But this function might also be called by another function that has a `try`/`catch` block. In other words, you might have something like the code found in the `Exception02` example:

```
#include <iostream>

using namespace std;

void Inner()
{
    throw string("Error!");
}
```

**Book IV
Chapter 3**

**Constructors,
Destructors, and
Exceptions**

```
void Outer()
{
    try
    {
        Inner();
    }
    catch (string excep)
    {
        cout << "Outer caught an exception: ";
        cout << excep << endl;
        throw;
    }
}

int main()
{
    try
    {
        Outer();
    }
    catch (string excep)
    {
        cout << "main caught an exception: ";
        cout << excep << endl;
    }

    return 0;
}
```

In the preceding code, main() calls Outer(). Outer(), in turn, calls Inner(). Inner() throws an exception, and Outer() catches it. But main() also wants to catch the exception. So we had Outer() *rethrow* the exception. You do that by calling throw without anything after it, like this:

```
throw;
```

When you run this application, you see the following output.

```
Outer caught an exception: Error!
main caught an exception: Error!
```

Chapter 4: Advanced Class Usage

In This Chapter

✔ Using polymorphism effectively

✔ Adjusting member access between private, protected, and public when deriving new classes

✔ Multiple-inheriting new classes

✔ Making virtual inheritance work correctly

✔ Keeping your friends straight, especially in class

✔ Putting one class or type inside another

Classes are amazingly powerful. You can do so much with them. In this chapter, we talk about many of the extra features you can use in your classes. But these aren't just little extras that you may want to use on occasion. If you follow the instructions in this chapter, you should find that your understanding of classes in C++ will greatly improve, and you'll want to use many of these topics throughout your programming.

We also talk about many issues that come up when you're deriving new classes and inheriting members. This discussion includes virtual inheritance and multiple inheritance, topics that people mess up a lot. We also describe the ways you can put classes and types inside other classes.

Inherently Inheriting Correctly

Without inheritance, doing object-oriented programming would be nearly impossible. Yes, you could divide your work into objects, but the real power comes from inheritance. However, you have to be careful when using inheritance, or you can really mess things up. In the sections that follow, we talk about different ways to use inheritance — and how to keep it all straight.

Morphing your inheritance

Polymorphism refers to using one object as an instance of a base class. For example, if you have the class `Creature` and from that you derive the class `Platypus`, you can treat the instances of class `Platypus` as if they're instances of class `Creature`. This concept is useful if you have a function that takes as a parameter a pointer to `Creature`. You can pass a pointer to `Platypus`.

However, you can't go further than that. You can't take a pointer to a pointer to Creature. (***Remember:*** When you say a "pointer to a pointer," the first pointer really means "the address of the second pointer variable." We need to phrase things like that, or our brains might explode in certain situations.)

So if you have a function such as this:

```
void Feed(Creature *c)
{
    cout << "Feed me!" << endl;
}
```

you're free to pass the address of a Platypus object, as in the following:

```
Platypus *plato = new Platypus;
Feed(plato);
```

with a function that takes the address of a pointer variable (note the two asterisks in the parameter), like this:

```
void Eat(Creature **c)
{
    cout << "Feed me!" << endl;
}
```

You *cannot* pass the address of a pointer to a Platypus instance, as in this example:

```
Platypus *plato = new Platypus;
Eat(&plato);
```

If you try to compile this code, you get a compiler error.

You don't always use polymorphism when you declare a variable. If you do, you would be declaring variables like this:

```
Creature *plato = new Platypus;
```

The type plato is a pointer to Creature. But the object is a Platypus. You can do this because a pointer to a base class can point to an object of a derived class. But now the compiler thinks that plato is a pointer to a Creature instance, so you can't use plato to call a member function of Platypus — you can use plato to call only members of Creature. For example, if your two classes look like this:

```
class Creature
{
public:
    void EatFood()
    {
        cout << "I'm eating!" << endl;
    }
};
```

```
class Platypus : public Creature
{
public:
    void SingLikeABird()
    {
        cout << "I'm siiiiiinging in the rain!" << endl;
    }
};
```

the following would not work:

```
Creature *plato = new Platypus;
plato->SingLikeABird();
```

Although the first line would compile, the second wouldn't. When the compiler gets to the second line, it thinks that plato is only an object of class type Creature. And Creature does not have a member called SingLikeABird(), so the compiler gets upset. You can fix the situation by casting like this:

```
Creature *plato = new Platypus;
static_cast <Platypus *>(plato)->SingLikeABird();
```

If you want to save some work, start by declaring plato as type Platypus as shown here:

```
Platypus *plato = new Platypus;
plato->SingLikeABird();
```

You may need to do perform a cast at times. For example, you may have a variable that can hold an instance of an object or its derived object. Then you would have to use polymorphism, as in the following code:

```
Creature *plato;
if (HasABeak == true)
{
    plato = new Platypus;
}
else
{
    plato = new Creature;
}
```

In this code, we have a pointer to Creature. In that pointer, we store the address of either a Platypus instance or a Creature instance, depending on what's in the HasABeak variable.

But if you use an if statement like that, you shouldn't follow it with a call to SingLikeABird(), even if you cast it:

```
static_cast <Platypus *>(plato)->SingLikeABird();
```

The reason is that if the `else` clause took place and `plato` holds an instance of `Creature`, not `Platypus`, then the `Creature` instance won't have a `SingLikeABird()` member function. Either you get some type of error message when you run the application or you don't, but the application will mess up later. And those messing-up-later errors are the worst kind to try to fix.

Adjusting access

You may have a class that has protected members; and in a derived class, you may want to make these members public. You do this by adjusting the access. You have two ways to do this: One is the older way, and the other is the newer American National Standards Institute (ANSI) way, which is the method supported by the current version of the GNU Compiler Collection (GCC). If your compiler supports the newer way, the creators of the ANSI standard ask that you use the ANSI way.

In the following classes, `Secret` has a member, `X`, that is protected. The derived class, `Revealed`, makes the member `X` public. Here's the older way:

```
class Secret
{
protected:
    int X;
};

class Revealed : public Secret
{
public:
    Secret::X;
};
```

We declared the member `X`: We used the base classname, two colons, and then the member name. We didn't include any type information; that was implied. So in the class `Secret`, the member `X` is protected. But in `Revealed`, it is public.

Here's the ANSI way. We've thrown in the word `using`. Otherwise it's the same:

```
class Secret
{
public:
    int X;
};

class Revealed : public Secret
{
public:
    using Secret::X;
};
```

And now, when you use the `Revealed` class, the inherited member `X` is public (but `X` is still protected in the base class, `Secret`).

If you want to make a protected member public in a derived class, don't just redeclare the member. If you do, you end up with *two member variables of the same name* within the class; and needless to say, that can be confusing! Take a look at the following two classes:

```
class Secret
{
protected:
    int X;

public:
    void SetX()
    {
        X = 10;
    }

    void GetX()
    {
        cout << "Secret X is " << X << endl;
    }
};

class Revealed : public Secret
{
public:
    int X;
};
```

The `Revealed` class has two `int X` members! Suppose you try this code with it:

```
Revealed me;
me.SetX();
me.X = 30;
me.GetX();
```

The first line declares the variable. The second line calls `SetX()`, which stores `10` in . . . which variable? The inherited `X`, because `SetX()` is part of the base class! The third line stores `10` in . . . which one? The new `X` declared in the derived class! So then `GetX()` is again part of the base class, but will it print `10` or `30`? It will print `10`!

Personally, having two member variables of the same name is downright confusing. (Fortunately, our brains didn't quite explode because we're still here, writing away.) We think that it would be best if the compiler didn't allow you to have two variables of the same name. But even though the compiler allows it, that doesn't mean you should do it; having two variables of the same name is a perfect way to increase the chances of bugs creeping into your application.

Now think about this: Suppose you have a class that has several public members, and when you derive a new class, you want all the public members to become *protected*, except for one. You can do this task in a couple of ways. You could adjust the access of all the members except for the one you want left public. Or if you have lots of members, you can take the opposite approach. Look at this code:

```
class Secret
{
public:
    int Code, Number, SkeletonKey, System, Magic;
};

class AddedSecurity : protected Secret
{
public:
    using Secret::Magic;
};
```

Notice what we did: We derived the class as protected, as you can see in the header line for the `AddedSecurity` class. That means all the inherited public members of `Secret` will be protected in the derived class. But then we promoted `Magic` back to public by adjusting its member access. Thus, after all is said and done, `Magic` is the only public member of `AddedSecurity`. All the rest are protected.

If you have a member that is private and you try to adjust its access to protected or public in a derived class, you quickly discover that the compiler won't let you do it. The reason is that the derived class *doesn't even know about the member* because the member is public. And because the derived class doesn't know about the member, you can't adjust its access.

Returning something different, virtually speaking

Two words that sound similar and have similar meanings but are, nevertheless, different are *overload* and *override*. Although both words appear in movies ("Danger, danger! The system is overloaded, so we need to override the built-in security!"), they're less glamorous in computer programming. But the real danger that results in an overloading of your brain is in confusing the two words where one meaning overrides the other. Whew!

So first, let us clarify: To *override* means to take an existing function in a base class and give the function new code in a derived class. The function in the derived class has the same prototype as the base class: It takes the same parameters and returns the same type.

To *overload* means to take a function and write another function of the same name that takes a different set of parameters. An overloaded function can optionally return a different type, but the parameters must be different, whether in number or type or both. The overloaded function can live in the same class or in a derived class. The idea here is to create what appears to be a single function that can take several types of parameters. For example, you may have a function called Append() that works on strings. By using Append(), you would be able to append a string to the end of the string represented by the instance, or you could append a single character to the end of the string represented by the instance. Now, although it feels like one function called Append(), really you would implement it as two separate functions: one that takes a string parameter and one that takes a character parameter.

In this section, we talk about one particular issue dealing with *overriding* functions (that is, replacing a function in a derived class). We said something a few paragraphs back that many others have said: We mentioned that the function must have the same parameter types and must return the same type.

A situation exists under which you can violate this rule, although only slightly. You can violate the rule of an overridden function returning the same type as the original function if *all three* of the following are true:

✦ The overridden function returns an instance of a class derived from the type returned by the original function.

✦ You return either a pointer or a reference, not an object.

✦ If you return a pointer, the pointer doesn't refer to yet another pointer.

Typically, you want to use this approach when you have a *container* class that holds multiple instances of another class. For example, you may have a class called Peripheral. You may also have a container class called PeripheralList, which holds instances of Peripheral. You may later derive a new class from Peripheral, called Printer, and a new class from PeripheralList, called PrinterList. If PeripheralList has a function that returns an instance of Peripheral, you would override that function in PrinterList. But instead of having it return an instance of Peripheral, you would have it return an instance of Printer. The OverridingDerived example shown in Listing 4-1 shows how to perform this task.

**Book IV
Chapter 4**

**Advanced Class
Usage**

Listing 4-1:   Overriding and Returning a Derived Class

```
#include <iostream>
#include <string>
#include <map>

using namespace std;

class Peripheral {
public:
    string Name;
    int Price;
    int SerialNumber;
```

(continued)

Listing 4-1 *(continued)*

```cpp
        Peripheral(string aname, int aprice, int aserial) :
            Name(aname), Price(aprice),
            SerialNumber(aserial) {}
};
class Printer : public Peripheral {
public:
    enum PrinterType {laser, inkjet};
    PrinterType Type;
    Printer(string aname, PrinterType atype, int aprice,
        int aserial) :
            Peripheral(aname, aprice, aserial), Type(atype) {}
};
typedef map<string, Peripheral *> PeripheralMap;
class PeripheralList {
public:
    PeripheralMap list;
    virtual Peripheral *GetPeripheralByName(string name);
    void AddPeripheral(string name, Peripheral *per);
};
class PrinterList : public PeripheralList {
public:
    Printer *GetPeripheralByName(string name);
};
Peripheral *PeripheralList::GetPeripheralByName
 (string name){
    return list[name];
}
void PeripheralList::AddPeripheral(
string name, Peripheral *per) {
    list[name] = per;
}
Printer *PrinterList::GetPeripheralByName(string name) {
    return static_cast<Printer *>(
        PeripheralList::GetPeripheralByName(name));
}
int main(int argc, char *argv[])
{
    PrinterList list;
    list.AddPeripheral(string("Koala"),
        new Printer("Koala", Printer::laser,
        150, 105483932)
    );
    list.AddPeripheral(string("Bear"),
        new Printer("Bear", Printer::inkjet,
        80, 5427892)
    );
    Printer *myprinter = list.GetPeripheralByName("Bear");
    if (myprinter != 0) {
        cout << myprinter->Price << endl;
    }
    return 0;
}
```

We used a special type called map, which is simply a container or list that holds items in pairs. The first item in the pair is called a *key*, and the second item is called a *value*. You can then retrieve items from the map based on the key. In this example, we're storing peripherals (the value) based on a name, which is a string (the key). To create the `map`, we use a `typedef` and specify the two types involved: first the key and then the value. The key is a string, and the value is a pointer to `Peripheral`. The `typedef`, then, looks like this:

```
typedef map<string, Peripheral *> PeripheralMap;
```

This line creates a type of a `map` that enables us to store a set of `Peripheral` instances, and we can look them up based on a name. To put an item in the `map`, we use a notation similar to that of an array, where `list` is the `map`, `name` is a `string`, and `per` is a pointer to `Peripheral`. The key goes inside square brackets, like this:

```
list[name] = per;
```

To retrieve the item, we simply refer to the `map` using brackets again, as in this line from the listing:

```
return list[name];
```

In Listing 4-1, we have a `Peripheral` class, and from that we derive a `Printer` class. We then have a `container` class that we created called `PeripheralList`, and from that we derived a class called `PrinterList`. The idea is that the `PrinterList` holds only instances of the class called `Printer`. So in the code, we overrode the `GetPeripheralByName()` function. The version inside `PrinterList` casts the item to a `Printer`. We did this because the items in the list are instances of `PeripheralList`. But if we were to leave this function as is, then every time we wanted to retrieve a `Printer`, we'd get back a pointer to a `Peripheral` instance, and we'd have to cast it to a `(Printer *)` type. But that's annoying. We don't want to have to do that every time because we're lazy. Instead, we overrode the `GetPeripheralByName()` function and did the cast right in there.

Even though we overrode it, we're allowed to return from the function a slightly different (but related) type. And it works!

The code in Listing 4-1 has a small bug: Nothing is stopping you from putting an instance of `Peripheral` in the `PrinterList` container. Or, for that matter, you could put an instance of any other class derived from `Peripheral` if there were more. But when we retrieve the instance in the `GetPeripheralByName()`, we automatically cast it to a `Printer`. That would be a problem if somebody had stuffed something else in there other than a `Printer` instance. To prevent that, create a special `AddPeripheral()` function for the `PrinterList` class that takes, specifically, a `Printer`. To do that, you would make the `AddPeripheral()` function in `PrinterList` virtual and then override it, modifying the parameter to take a `Printer` rather than a `Peripheral`. When you do so, you'll *hide* the function in the base class. But that's okay: You don't want people calling that one because that can take any `Peripheral`, not just a `Printer` instance. When you run this application, you should get an output value of 80 (the price of the printer named Bear).

Multiple inheritance

In C++, having a single base class from which your class inherits is generally best. However, it is possible to inherit from multiple base classes, a process called *multiple inheritance*.

One class may have some features that you want in a derived class, and another class may have other features you want in the same derived class. If that's the case, you can inherit from both through multiple inheritance.

Multiple inheritance is messy and difficult to pull off properly. But when you use it with care, you can make it work. The `DerivingTwoDiff` example shown in Listing 4-2 shows how to perform this task.

Listing 4-2:   Deriving from Two Different Classes

```
#include <iostream>
using namespace std;

class Mom {
public:
    void Brains() {
        cout << "I'm smart!" << endl;
    }
};
class Dad {
public:
    void Beauty() {
        cout << "I'm beautiful!" << endl;
    }
};
class Derived : public Mom, public Dad {
};
int main(int argc, char *argv[])
{
    Derived child;
    child.Brains();
    child.Beauty();
    return 0;
}
```

When you run this code, you see the following output:

```
I'm smart!
I'm beautiful!
```

In the preceding code, the class `Derived` inherited the functions of both classes `Mom` and `Dad`. Because it did, the compiler allowed us to call both functions for the instance `child`. Also notice how we caused that to happen:

```
class Derived : public Mom, public Dad
```

We put the base classes to the right of the single colon as with a single inheritance, and we separated the classes with a comma. We also preceded each class with the type of inheritance, in this case public.

As with single inheritance, you can use inheritance other than public. But you don't have to use the same access for all the classes. For example, the following, although a bit confusing, is acceptable:

```
class Derived : public Mom, protected Dad
```

What this means is that public members derived from `Dad` are now protected in the class called `Derived`. This means users cannot call the `member` functions inherited from `Dad`, nor can they access any `member` variables inherited from `Dad`. If you used this type of inheritance in Listing 4-2, this line would no longer be allowed:

```
child.Beauty();
```

If you try to compile it, you'll see the following error, because the `Beauty()` member is protected now:

```
'void Dad::Beauty()' is inaccessible
```

When you're working with multiple inheritance, be careful that you understand what your code is doing. Although it may compile correctly, it still may not function correctly. That leads to the famous creepy-crawling thing called a *bug*.

Strange, bizarre, freaky things can happen with multiple inheritance. What if both base classes have a member variable called `Bagel`. What happens if you derive a class from both of these classes? The answer is this: The compiler gets confused. Suppose you enhance the two base classes with a `Bagel` effect:

```
class Mom
{
public:
    int Bagel;
    void Brains()
    {
        cout << "I'm smart!" << endl;
    }
};
```

Book IV
Chapter 4

Advanced Class
Usage

```
class Dad
{
public:
    int Bagel;
    void Beauty()
    {
        cout << "I'm beautiful!" << endl;
    }
};

class Derived : public Mom, public Dad
{
};
```

In the preceding code, each of the two base classes, Mom and Dad, has a Bagel member. The compiler will let you do this. But if you try to access the member as in the following code, you get an error:

```
Derived child;
child.Bagel = 42;
```

Here's the error message we see in Code::Blocks:

```
error: request for member 'Bagel' is ambiguous
```

Aha! We're being *ambiguous!* It means the compiler isn't sure which Bagel we're referring to: The one inherited from Mom or the one inherited from Dad. If you write code like this, make sure you know which inherited member you're referring to. Now this is going to look bizarre, but we promise that it's correct. Suppose we're referring to the Bagel inherited from Mom. Then we can put the name Mom before the word Bagel, separated by two colons:

```
child.Mom::Bagel = 42;
```

Yes, that really is correct, even though it seems a little strange. And if we want to refer to the one by Dad, we do this:

```
child.Dad::Bagel = 17;
```

Both lines compile properly because we're removing any ambiguities.

When you use multiple inheritance, remove any ambiguities by specifying the name of the base class. But don't worry if you forget: The compiler will give you an error message because it won't know which item you're referring to.

Virtual inheritance

At times, you may see the word *virtual* thrown in when deriving a new class, as in the following:

```
class Diamond : virtual public Rock
```

This inclusion of `virtual` is to fix a strange problem that can arise. When you use multiple inheritance, you can run into a crazy situation where you have a diamond-shaped inheritance, as in Figure 4-1.

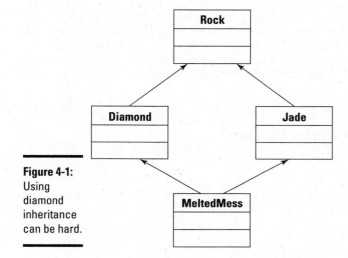

Figure 4-1:
Using diamond inheritance can be hard.

In Figure 4-1, you can see the base class is `Rock`. From that we derived two classes, `Diamond` and `Jade`. So far, so good. But then something strange happened: We used multiple inheritance to derive a class `MeltedMess` from `Diamond` and `Jade`. Yes, you can do this. But you have to be *careful*.

Think about this: Suppose `Rock` has a public member called `Weight`. Then both `Diamond` and `Jade` inherit that member. Now when you derive `MeltedMess` and try to access its `Weight` member, you get an ambiguously melted mess: The compiler claims that it doesn't know which `Weight` you're referring to — the one inherited from `Diamond` or the one inherited from `Jade`. Now, you know and we know that there should only be one instance of `Weight`, because it came from a single base class, `Rock`. But the compiler sees the situation differently and has trouble with it.

To understand how to fix the problem, recognize what happens when you create an instance of a class derived from another class: Deep down inside the computer, the instance has a portion that is itself an instance of the base class. Now, when you derive a class from multiple base classes, instances of the derived class have one portion for each base class. Thus an instance of `MeltedMess` has a portion that is a `Diamond` and a portion that is a `Jade`, as well as a portion for anything `MeltedMess` added that wasn't inherited.

But remember, Diamond is derived from Rock. Therefore Diamond has a portion inside it that is a Rock. Similarly, Jade is derived from Rock. That means Jade has a portion inside it that is a Rock.

And melting all these thoughts together, if an instance of MeltedMess has both a Diamond in it and a Jade in it, and each of *those* in turn has a Rock in it, then by the powers of logic vested in us, we declare that MeltedMess must have *two* Rocks in it! And with each Rock comes a separate Weight instance. The CrackingDiamonds example shown in Listing 4-3 demonstrates the problem. In this listing, we declare the classes Rock, Diamond, Jade, and MeltedMess.

Listing 4-3:   Cracking up Diamonds

```
#include <iostream>
using namespace std;

class Rock {
public:
    int Weight;
};
class Diamond : public Rock {
public:
    void SetDiamondWeight(int newweight) {
        Weight = newweight;
    }
    int GetDiamondWeight() {
        return Weight;
    }
};
class Jade : public Rock {
public:
    void SetJadeWeight(int newweight) {
        Weight = newweight;
    }
    int GetJadeWeight() {
        return Weight;
    }
};
class MeltedMess : public Diamond, public Jade {
};
int main(int argc, char *argv[])
{
    MeltedMess mymess;
    mymess.SetDiamondWeight(10);
    mymess.SetJadeWeight(20);
    cout << mymess.GetDiamondWeight() << endl;
    cout << mymess.GetJadeWeight() << endl;
    return 0;
}
```

There is one member called Weight, and it's part of Rock. In the Diamond class, we included two accessor methods, one to set the value of Weight and one to get it. We did the same thing in the Jade class.

We derived the class `MeltedMess` from both `Diamond` and `Jade`. We created an instance of it and called the four member functions that access the `Weight` member. First, we called the one for `Diamond`, setting `Weight` to 10. Then we called the one for `Jade`, setting the `Weight` to 20.

In a perfect world where each object only has one `Weight`, this would have first set the `Weight` to 10 and then to 20. When we print it, we should see 20 both times. But we don't. Here's the output:

```
10
20
```

When we asked the `Diamond` portion to cough up its `Weight`, we saw 10. But when we asked the `Jade` portion to do the same, we saw 20. They're different! Therefore we have two different `Weight` members. That's not a good thing.

To fix it, add the word `virtual` when you inherit it. According to the ANSI standard, you put `virtual` in the two middle classes. In our case, that means `Diamond` and `Jade`. Thus you need to modify the class headers in Listing 4-3 in order for `Diamond` and `Jade` to look like this:

```
class Diamond : virtual public Rock {

class Jade : virtual public Rock {
```

When you do that and then run the application, you find that you have only one instance of `Weight` in the final class `MeltedMess`. It's not such a mess after all! Here's the output after we made the change:

```
20
20
```

Polymorphism with multiple inheritances

If you have multiple inheritance, you can safely treat your object as any of the base classes. In the case of the diamond example, you can treat an instance of `MeltedMess` as a `Diamond` instance or as a `Jade` instance. For example, if you have a function that takes as a parameter a pointer to a `Diamond` instance, you can safely pass a pointer to a `MeltedMess` instance. Casting also works: You can cast a `MeltedMess` instance to a `Diamond` instance or to a `Jade` instance. However, if you do, we suggest using the new style `static_cast` keyword, rather than the old C-style casts where you simply put the type name in parentheses before the variable you're casting.

Now this makes sense: Only one instance of `Weight` is in the `MeltedClass` object, so the following line changes the `Weight` to 10:

```
mymess.SetDiamondWeight(10);
```

Then the following line changes the *same* `Weight` to 20:

```
mymess.SetJadeWeight(20);
```

Then the following line prints the value of the one `Weight` instance, 20:

```
cout << mymess.GetDiamondWeight() << endl;
```

The following line again prints the value of the one `Weight` instance.

```
cout << mymess.GetJadeWeight() << endl;
```

With a diamond inheritance, use *virtual inheritance* in the middle classes to *clean* them — ensure they point to the correct type. Although you *can* also add the word `virtual` to the final class (in the example's case, that's `MeltedClass`), you don't need to.

Friend classes and functions

You may encounter a situation where you want one class to access the private and protected members of another class.

Normally, this isn't allowed. But it is if you make the two classes best friends. Okay, that sounds corny, but C++ gives us that word: `friend`. Only use `friend` when you really need to. If you have a class, say `Square`, that needs access to the private and protected members of a class called `DrawingBoard`, you can add a line inside the class `DrawingBoard` that looks like this:

```
friend class Square;
```

Friends of a same class

Can an instance of a class access the private and protected members of other instances of the *same class*? Yes, the compiler allows you to do it. Should you? That depends on your situation. Now think about how you would do that: Inside a member function for a class you would have a pointer to another instance of the same class, perhaps passed in as a parameter. The member function is free to modify any of its members or the object passed in. For your situation, you may need to use `friend` classes, but always be careful.

This will allow the member functions in Square to access the private and protected members of any instance of type DrawingBoard. (Remember that ultimately we're talking about instances here.)

The friend word is powerful because it allows object two to access the functionality provided by object three, possibly against the will of object one (the object that created object three). And that can create bugs! As Grandma always warned us, "Please use discretion when picking your friends, especially when writing object-oriented programming code in C++."

Some compilers will let you declare a friend without the word class, like so:

```
friend Square;
```

However, the GNU compiler under Code::Blocks doesn't allow this. Instead, you must use the class keyword:

```
friend class Square;
```

Using Classes and Types within Classes

Sometimes an application needs a fairly complex internal structure to get its work done. Three ways to accomplish this goal with relatively few headaches are nesting classes, embedding classes, and declaring types within classes. The following sections discuss the two most common goals: nesting classes and declaring types within classes. The "Nesting a class" section also discusses protection for embedded classes.

Nesting a class

You may have times when you create a set of classes where one class acts as the primary class while all the other classes function as supporting classes. For example, you may be a member of a team of programmers, and your job is to write a set of classes that log on to a competitor's computer at night and lower all the prices on the products. Other members of your team will use your classes in their applications. You're just writing a set of classes; the teammates are writing the rest of the application.

In the classes you're creating, you want to make the task easy on your coworkers. In doing so, you may make a primary class, such as EthicalCompetition, that they will instantiate to use your set of classes. This primary class will include the methods for using the system. In other words, it serves as an *interface* to the set of classes.

In addition to the main EthicalCompetition class, you might create additional auxiliary classes that the EthicalCompetition class will use, but your coworkers will not directly create instances of. One might be a class called Connection that handles the tasks of connecting to the competitor's computer.

Here's the first problem: The class Connection may be something you write, but *another* class somewhere may be called Connection, and your coworkers might need to use that class. And here's the second problem: If you have that Connection class, you may not want your coworkers using it. You just want them using the main interface, the EthicalCompetition class.

To solve the unique name problem, you have several choices. For one, you can just rename the class something a bit more unique, such as EthicalCompetitionConnection. But that's a bit long. And why go through all that trouble if it's not even going to be used except internally in the code for EthicalCompetition? However, you could shorten the classname and call it something that's likely to be unique, such as ECConnection.

Yet at the same time, if the users of your classes look at the header file and see a whole set of classes, which classes they should be using may not be clear. (Of course, you would write some documentation to clear this up, but you do want the code to be at least somewhat self-explanatory.)

One solution is to use *nested* classes. With a nested class, you write the declaration for the main class, EthicalCompetition, and then, inside the class, you write the supporting classes, as in the following:

```
class EthicalCompetition
{
private:
    class Connection
    {
    public:
        void Connect();
    };

public:
    void HardWork();
};
```

Note that we wrote a class inside a class. We did not provide the code for the functions themselves, so here they are:

```
void EthicalCompetition::HardWork()
{
    Connection c;
    c.Connect();
    cout << "Connected" << endl;
```

```
}
void EthicalCompetition::Connection::Connect()
{
    cout << "Connecting..." << endl;
}
```

The header for the `Connect` function in the `ConnectionClass` requires first the outer classname, then two colons, then the inner classname, then two colons again, and finally the function name. This follows the pattern you normally use where you put the classname first, then two colons, and then the function name. But in this case, you have two classnames separated with a colon.

If you want to declare an instance of the `Connection` class, you do it differently, depending on where you are when you declare it. By that we don't mean whether you're in an office cube or sitting on the beach with a laptop; rather, we mean where in the code you're trying to declare an instance.

If you're inside a member function of the outer class, `EthicalCompetition`, you simply refer to the class by its name, `Connection`. You can see we did that in the member function `HardWork`, with this line:

```
Connection c;
```

If you're outside the member functions, you can declare an instance of the inner class, `Connection`, without an instance of the outer class, `EthicalCompetition`. To do this, you *fully qualify* the classname, like this:

```
EthicalCompetition::Connection myconnect;
```

This line would go, for instance, in the `main` of your application if you want to create an instance of the inner class, `Connection`.

However, you may recall that one of the reasons for putting the class inside the other was to shield it from the outside world, to keep your nosy coworkers from creating an instance of it. But so far, what you've done doesn't really stop them from using the class. They can just use it by referring to its fully qualified name, `EthicalCompetition::Connection`.

 In a sense, so far, you've created a handy grouping of the class, and you also set your grouping up so you can use a simpler name that won't conflict with other classes. If you just want to group your classes, you can use a nested class. If you want to add higher security to a class so that others will be prevented from using your inner class, however, you'll have to work with something called an *inner class definition*.

Here's a series of tricks devoted to showing you how you create that inner class definition. For the first trick, we need to show you how you can declare the class with a forward definition but put the class definition outside the outer class. (***Note:*** Never put the inner class definition *inside* a private or protected section of the outer class definition; it doesn't work.) The following code takes care of that declaration for you:

```
class EthicalCompetition
{
private:
    class Connection;

public:
    void HardWork();
};

class EthicalCompetition::Connection
{
public:
    void Connect();
};
```

Here, inside the outer class, we wrote a header for the inner class and a semicolon instead of writing the whole inner class; that's a *forward declaration*. Then we wrote the rest of the inner class after the outer class. To make this work, we had to again fully qualify the name of the class, like this:

```
class EthicalCompetition::Connection
```

If we skipped the word `EthicalCompetition` and two colons, the compiler compiles this class like a different class. Later, the compiler would complain that it couldn't find the rest of the declaration for the `ConnectionClass`. The error is

```
error: aggregate 'EthicalCompetition::Connection c' has incomplete type and
    cannot be defined
```

Remember that message, so you know how to correct it when you forget the outer classname.

By declaring the inner class after the outer class, you can now employ another trick. The idea is to write it so that only the outer class can access the members. To accomplish this, you can make all the members of the inner class either private or protected and then make the outer class, `EthicalCompetition`, a friend of the inner class, `Connection`.

Here's the modified version of the `Connection` class:

```
class EthicalCompetition::Connection
{
protected:
    friend class EthicalCompetition;
    void Connect();
};
```

Only the outer class can access most of its members. But we say *most* because we left something out. Although the members are protected, nothing stops users outside EthicalConnection from creating an instance of the class. To add this security, you need a constructor for the class that is either *private or protected*. And when you do that with a constructor, following suit with a destructor is a good idea. Make the destructor private or protected, too. Even if the constructor and destructor don't do anything, by making them private or protected you prevent others from creating an instance of the class — others, that is, except any friends to the class.

So here's yet one more version of the class:

```
class EthicalCompetition::Connection
{
protected:
    friend class EthicalCompetition;
    void Connect();
    Connection() {}
    ~Connection() {}
};
```

This does the trick. When we try to make an instance of the class outside EthicalCompetition (such as in main()), as in this:

```
EthicalCompetition::Connection myconnect;
```

we see the following message:

```
EthicalCompetition::Connection::~Connection()' is protected
```

Yet we can still make an instance from within the member functions of EthicalCompetition. It worked! The ProtectingEmbedded example shown in Listing 4-4 contains the final application.

Listing 4-4: Protecting Embedded Classes

```
#include <iostream>
using namespace std;

class EthicalCompetition {
private:
    class Connection;
public:
    void HardWork();
};
class EthicalCompetition::Connection {
protected:
    friend class EthicalCompetition;
    void Connect();
    Connection() {}
    ~Connection() {}
};
```

**Book IV
Chapter 4**

**Advanced Class
Usage**

(continued)

Listing 4-4 *(continued)*

```
void EthicalCompetition::HardWork() {
    Connection c;
    c.Connect();
    cout << "Connected" << endl;
}
void EthicalCompetition::Connection::Connect() {
    cout << "Connecting..." << endl;
}
int main(int argc, char *argv[])
{
    // EthicalCompetition::Connection myconnect;
    EthicalCompetition comp;
    comp.HardWork();
    return 0;
}
```

We purposely left in a commented-out line where we attempted to make an instance of the inner class, `Connection`. Previously, we had the line there, but it wasn't commented out; that way we could see which error message it would print and then tell you about it. If you want to see the error message, you can remove the two slashes so the compiler will try to compile the line.

Types within classes

When you declare a type, such as an `enum`, associating it with a class can be convenient. For example, you may have a class called `Cheesecake`. In this class, you may have the member variable `SelectedFlavor`. The `SelectedFlavor` member can be your own enumerated type, such as `Flavor`, like this:

```
enum Flavor
{
    ChocolateSuicide,
    SquishyStrawberry,
    BrokenBanana,
    PrettyPlainVanilla,
    CoolLuah,
    BizarrePurple
};
```

To associate these with a class, you can put them in a class, like this:

```
class Cheesecake
{
public:
    enum Flavor
    {
        ChocolateSuicide, SquishyStrawberry, BrokenBanana,
        PrettyPlainVanilla, CoolLuah, BizarrePurple
    };

    Flavor SelectedFlavor;
    int AmountLeft;
```

```
    void Eat()
    {
        AmountLeft = 0;
    }
};
```

The type `Flavor` now can be used anywhere in your application, but to use it outside the member functions of the `Cheesecake` class, you must fully qualify its name by lining up the classname, two colons, then the type name like this:

```
Cheesecake::Flavor myflavor = Cheesecake::CoolLuah;
```

As you can see, for an `enum`, we also had to fully qualify the enumeration itself. If we had just put `CoolLuah` on the right side of the equals sign, the compiler would complain and say that `CoolLuah` is undeclared.

The `Cheesecake` example shown in Listing 4-5 demonstrates how we can use the `Cheesecake` class.

Listing 4-5:   Using Types within a Class

```
#include <iostream>

using namespace std;

class Cheesecake {
public:
    enum Flavor {
        ChocolateSuicide, SquishyStrawberry, BrokenBanana,
        PrettyPlainVanilla, CoolLuah, BizarrePurple
    };
    Flavor SelectedFlavor;
    int AmountLeft;
    void Eat() {
        AmountLeft = 0;
    }
};


int main()
{
    Cheesecake yum;
    yum.SelectedFlavor = Cheesecake::SquishyStrawberry;
    yum.AmountLeft = 100;
    yum.Eat();
    cout << yum.AmountLeft << endl;
    return 0;
}
```

Notice in Listing 4-5 that we had to fully qualify the name `SquishyStrawberry`.

When you declare a type (using a `typedef` or an `enum`) inside a class, you do not need an instance of the class present to use the type. But you must fully qualify the name. Thus, you can set up a variable of type `Cheesecake::Flavor` and use it in your application without creating an instance of `Cheesecake`.

Do you have types that you want used only within the class? Make them protected or private. That way you cannot use them outside the class.

Unlike what you can do with nested classes, you can make a type within a class private or protected. If you do so, you can use the type only within the member functions of the class. If you try to use the type outside the class (including setting a member variable, as in `yum.SelectedFlavor = Cheesecake::SquishyStrawberry;`), you get a compiler error.

You can also put a `typedef` inside your class in the same way you'd put an `enum` inside the class, as in the following example:

```
class Spongecake
{
public:
    typedef int SpongeNumber;
    SpongeNumber weight;
    SpongeNumber diameter;
};

int main(int argc, char *argv[])
{
    Spongecake::SpongeNumber myweight = 30;
    Spongecake fluff;
    fluff.weight = myweight;
    return 0;
}
```

Chapter 5: Creating Classes with Templates

In This Chapter

✓ Creating class templates

✓ Using parameters in templates

✓ Deriving with templates

✓ Creating function templates

*I*f C++ programming has any *big secret,* it would have to be templates. Templates seem to be the topic that beginning programmers strive to understand because they've heard about them and seem to think that templates are the big wall over which they must climb to ultimately become The C++ Guru.

We can't say whether understanding templates will make you a C++ guru (we like to think that it will!), but we can say that it will open your abilities to a whole world out there, primarily because the entire Standard C++ Library is built around templates. Further, understanding templates can help you understand all that cryptic code that you see other people posting on the Internet. (And it will help you realize that it didn't have to be so cryptic! Simplify, simplify, we always say!)

So, in this chapter, we show you how to use application templates in C++.

 Templates have an interesting history. Back when people started building C++ compilers, no standard for how to do templates existed. As a result, different compilers supported different ways of doing templates. The whole template thing was a mess and very confusing. So if you're using a compiler that's older than around 1999 or 2000 and you're interested in using templates, you should seriously consider upgrading to a newer compiler (such as the GNU GCC compiler included with Code::Blocks).

Templatizing a Class

"Templates are complicated and difficult to understand." That was a lie. We don't know why people think templates are so hard to create and use, but they're really not. In this section, we show you just how simple templates are to understand.

First, think of a class. Pick one, any class. We'll pick `OldGasStation`. That's a class, and it has some members. Remember, a class is a *type*. You can declare variables of the type. Thus we can declare a variable of type `OldGasStation` called, for example `HanksGetGas`. We can also create another variable of type `OldGasStation`; maybe this one would be called `FillerUp`. And, of course, we could create a third one; this one might be called `GotGasWeCanFillIt`.

Each of these variables, `HanksGetGas`, `FillerUp`, and `GotGasWeCanFillIt`, are each instances of the type (or class) `OldGasStation`.

In the same way, we can take an existing type, say `int`, and make some instances of it. We can name one `CheckingAccountBalance`, and we can name another `BuriedTreasuresFound`. Each of these is an instance of the type called `int`. Although `int` isn't a class, it is a type.

Now, think about this so far: You have the two different types available to you that we mentioned; one is called `OldGasStation`, and the other is called `int`. One of these is a type you make; the other is built into C++.

We want to focus on the one you create, `OldGasStation`. This is a type that you create by declaring it in your application when you write the code. The compiler takes your declaration and builds some data inside the resulting application that represents this type. After the application runs, the type is created, and it does not change throughout the course of the application.

The variables in your application may change at run time; you can create new instances of a type and delete them and change their contents. But the *type* itself *is created at compile time* and *does not change at run time*. Remember this as one property of types in general. You will need to keep this in mind when dealing with templates.

Suppose that you have a class called `MyHolder`. This class is going to hold some integers. Nothing special, but it looks like this:

```
class MyHolder
{
public:
    int first;
    int second;
    int third;
    int sum()
    {
        return first + second + third;
    }
};
```

This class is easy to use; you just create an instance of it and set the values of its members. But remember: After the application is running, the class is a done deal. But at run time, you're free to create new instances of this class.

For example, the following creates ten instances of the class, calls `sum()`, and prints the return value of `sum()`:

```
MyHolder *hold;
int loop;
for (loop = 0; loop < 10; loop++)
{
    hold = new MyHolder;
    hold->first = loop * 100;
    hold->second = loop * 110;
    hold->third = loop * 120;
    cout << hold->sum() << endl;
    delete hold;
}
```

This creates an instance at run time, does some work with it, and then deletes the instance. It then repeats this process over and over for a total of ten times. Instances (or variables) are created, changed, and deleted — all at run time. But the class, which we'll say one more time, is created at compile time.

Suppose you're coding away, and you discover that this class `MyHolder` is pretty handy, except it would be nice if you had a version of it that holds `float`s instead of `int`s. You could create a second class just like the first that uses the word `float` instead of `int`, like this:

```
class AnotherHolder
{
public:
    float first;
    float second;
    float third;
    float sum()
    {
        return first + second + third;
    }
};
```

This works the same way as the previous class, but it stores three `float` types instead of `int` types. But you can see, if you have a really big class, this method would essentially require a lot of copying and pasting followed by some search-and-replacing — in other words, busywork. But you can minimize this busywork by using templates. Instead of typing two different versions of the class, type one version of the class that you can, effectively, modify when you need different versions of the class.

Take a look at this code:

```
template <typename T>
class CoolHolder
{
public:
    T first;
    T second;
    T third;
    T sum()
```

```
    {
        return first + second + third;
    }
};
```

Think of this as a rule for a class that does exactly what the previous two classes did. (Ignore the template declaration, `template <typename T>`, for now, it's explained a little later in the chapter.) In this rule is a place-holder called `T` that is a placeholder for a type. Imagine, in your mind, this set of code; then remove the first line and replace all the remaining `T`s with the word `int`. If you did that, you would end up with this:

```
class CoolHolder
{
public:
    int first;
    int second;
    int third;
    int sum()
    {
        return first + second + third;
    }
};
```

This is, of course, the same as the earlier class called `MyHolder`, just with a different name. Now imagine doing the same thing but replacing each `T` with the word `float`. You can probably see where we're going with this. Here it is:

```
class CoolHolder
{
public:
    float first;
    float second;
    float third;
    float sum()
    {
        return first + second + third;
    }
};
```

And once again, this is, of course, the same as the earlier class called `AnotherHolder`, but with a different name.

That's what a template does: It specifies a placeholder for a class. But it doesn't actually *create* a class . . . yet. You have to do one more thing to tell the compiler to take this template and create a class. The way you do this is by writing code to create a variable or by using the class somehow. Look at this code:

```
CoolHolder<int> IntHolder;
IntHolder.first = 10;
IntHolder.second = 20;
IntHolder.third = 30;
```

Do you see what's happening? This code is telling the compiler to take the CoolHolder template and make a version of it where T is replaced by the word int. In other words, the compiler creates a class. What is the class called? It's called CoolHolder<int>. And then these four lines of code first create an instance of CoolHolder<int> called IntHolder; then they set the members of IntHolder.

And when does the computer create this class? (That is, not the instance, but the class itself?) At *compile time*. Remember, types are created at compile time, and this is no exception to this rule.

Here's an easy way to look at a template. When you see a line like CoolHolder<int> IntHolder; you can think of it like CoolHolderint IntHolder. Although that's not really what the template is called, you are telling the compiler to create a new class. In your mind, you may think of the class as being called CoolHolderint, that is, a name without the angle brackets. (But remember that the name really isn't CoolHolderint. It's CoolHolder<int>.)

The CoolHolder example shown in Listing 5-1 contains a complete application that uses the CoolHolder template.

Listing 5-1:   Using Templates to Create Several Versions of a Class

```
#include <iostream>

using namespace std;

template <typename T>
class CoolHolder
{
public:
    T first;
    T second;
    T third;
    T sum()
    {
        return first + second + third;
    }
};

int main()
{
    CoolHolder<int> IntHolder;
    IntHolder.first = 10;
    IntHolder.second = 20;
    IntHolder.third = 30;

    CoolHolder<int> AnotherIntHolder;
    AnotherIntHolder.first = 100;
    AnotherIntHolder.second = 200;
    AnotherIntHolder.third = 300;
```

**Book IV
Chapter 5**

**Creating Classes
with Templates**

```
CoolHolder<float> FloatHolder;
FloatHolder.first = 3.1415;
FloatHolder.second = 4.1415;
FloatHolder.third = 5.1415;

cout << IntHolder.first << endl;
cout << AnotherIntHolder.first << endl;
cout << FloatHolder.first << endl;

CoolHolder<int> *hold;
for (int loop = 0; loop < 10; loop++)
{
    hold = new CoolHolder<int>;
    hold->first = loop * 100;
    hold->second = loop * 110;
    hold->third = loop * 120;
    cout << hold->sum() << endl;
    delete hold;
}

return 0;
}
```

When you run this application, you see a bunch of results from calls to sum():

```
10
100
3.1415
0
330
660
990
1320
1650
1980
2310
2640
2970
```

Look closely at the code. Near the beginning is the same template that we showed you earlier. Remember that the compiler doesn't create a type for this template. Instead, the compiler uses it as a rule to follow to create additional types. That is, the code indeed serves as a template for other types, thus its name.

Here's the first line of the template:

```
template <typename T>
```

All this means is that a template class is going to follow, and that it has a type with a placeholder called T. That means that inside the class anywhere a T appears, it will be replaced by the typename. (The T is standalone; if you have it as part of a word, it won't be replaced.) The standard practice is for people to use T for the placeholder, but you can use any identifier (starting with a letter or underscore, followed by any combination of letters, numbers, or underscores).

Down inside the `main()` for this class, we then declare several variables of types based on this template. Here's one such line:

```
CoolHolder<int> IntHolder;
```

This line declares a variable called `IntHolder`. For this variable, the compiler creates a type called `CoolHolder<int>`, which is a type based on the `CoolHolder` template, where `T` is replaced by `int`.

Here's another line where we declare a variable:

```
CoolHolder<int> AnotherIntHolder;
```

This time, the compiler doesn't have to create another type because it just created the `CoolHolder<int>` type earlier. But again, this line uses the same type based on the template, where `T` is replaced by `int`.

Here we create another class based on the template, and we declare a variable of this new type:

```
CoolHolder<float> FloatHolder;
```

When the compiler sees this line, it creates another type by using the template, and it replaces `T` with the word `float`. So in this case, the three members of the instance `FloatHolder`, called `first`, `second`, and `third`, each hold a floating-point number. And the member function called `sum()` returns a floating-point number.

The following line uses the type created earlier called `CoolHolder<int>`, and it declares a pointer to `CoolHolder<int>`. Yes, you can do that; pointers are allowed:

```
CoolHolder<int> *hold;
```

Then the code that follows cycles through a loop where we call `new` to create instances of type `CoolHolder<int>` by using the line

```
hold = new CoolHolder<int>;
```

We access the members using the pointer notation, `->`, like so:

```
hold->first = loop * 100;
```

And those are the basics of templates. They're really not as bad as people make them out to be. Just remember that when you see an identifier followed by angle brackets containing a type or class, it's a template. So see what you think of this line of code:

```
vector<string> MyList;
```

Any idea what this code does? It uses some template called `vector` and tells `vector` to use the string type inside it. In fact, `vector` is part of the Standard C++ Library, and it works similar to an array. Its *template parameter* (the thing in angle brackets) represents the type of the items the `vector` holds. So this declares a variable called `MyList`, which is a `vector` that holds `string` instances.

Separating a template from the function code

In the earlier days of templates and C++, the rule was that you had to put the member function code for a class template inside the template itself; you couldn't put a forward declaration in the template and then put the function code outside the template, as you could do with classes. However, the ANSI standard changed this situation and made putting the code outside the template legal. If you are using an ANSI-compliant compiler, you can put the function code outside the template. The GNU GCC compiler is, for the most part, ANSI-compliant; with it, you can put the code outside the template. However, you have to place the code carefully to get it to compile correctly. The `ImFree` example in Listing 5-2 shows you how to do this.

Listing 5-2:   Separating a Template from Function Code

```
#include <iostream>

using namespace std;

template <typename T>
class ImFree
{
protected:
    T x;

public:
    T& getx();
    void setx(T);
};

template <typename T>
T &ImFree<T>::getx()
{
    return x;
}

template <typename T>
void ImFree<T>::setx(T newx)
{
    x = newx;
}

int main()
{
    ImFree<int> separate;
    separate.setx(10);
    cout << separate.getx() << endl;
    return 0;
}
```

As you can see, the format is ugly. To be honest, whenever we do this, we have to look up the format; it's hard to memorize. (Maybe you can memorize it, but our brains are too prone to explosions.)

Look closely at one of the member functions:

```
template <typename T>
T &ImFree<T>::getx()
{
    return x;
}
```

The first line is the same as the first line of the template definition. It's just the word `template` followed by the parameter in angle brackets.

The next line looks almost like you might expect it to. With classes you put the function prototype, adding the classname and two colons before the function name itself, but after the return type. Here you do that too; the sticky part is how you write the template name. You don't just give the name; instead, you follow the name by two angle brackets, with the parameter inside, like this: `T &ImFree<T>::getx()`. Note the `<T>` part.

Earlier compilers didn't allow you to separate the function code the way we did in Listing 5-2. Instead, you would have to put the function code inside the template itself, as in the following:

```
template <typename T>
class ImFree
{
protected:
    T x;
public:
    T& getx()
    {
        return x;
    }
    void setx(T newx)
    {
        x = newx;
    }
};
```

Note one little thing that we did in both Listing 5-2 and in the old type of code: For the `getx()` member function, instead of just returning a variable of type `T`, we returned a reference. That is, instead of this:

```
T getx()
```

we declared the function as

```
T& getx()
```

(We added the ampersand.) Although that has the potential of upsetting some people, there's a good reason for doing it. In the `main()` of Listing 5-2, we created the class based on the template with an integer parameter:

```
ImFree<int> separate;
```

However, we could instead create the class with some other class:

```
ImFree<SomeOtherClass> separate;
```

If we do that, we don't really want to return just an instance from the function, as in

```
T& getx()
{
    return x;
}
```

Returning just an instance copies the instance rather than just returning the instance itself. The solution might be to use a pointer, as in

```
T* getx()
{
    return &x;
}
```

And, in fact, we tried that when we first wrote the code. But then the code gets annoying because we would have to dereference the result when we use the function, even if the result is just an integer. Our `cout` statement ended up looking like this when we used a pointer:

```
cout << *(separate.getx()) << endl;
```

And frankly, we found that code, shall we say, yucky. So, as in a presidential election, we picked the lesser of the evils by making it a reference. We figured a reference was less evil because the user of the class wouldn't have to do any bizarre coding. Instead, the `cout` is rather straightforward:

```
cout << separate.getx() << endl;
```

Including static members in a template

You can include static members in a template, but you need to be careful when you do so. Remember that all instances of a class share a single static member of the class. You can think of the static member as being a member of the class itself, whereas the nonstatic members are members of the instances.

Now, from a single template, you can potentially create multiple classes. This means that to maintain the notion of static members, you need to either get creative with your rules or make life easy by just assuming that each class based on the template gets its own static members. And the easy way is exactly how this process works.

When you include a static member in a template, each class that you create based on the template gets its own static member. Further, you need to tell the compiler how to store the static member just as you do with static members of classes that aren't created from templates.

The StaticMembers example shown in Listing 5-3 contains an example of static members in a template.

Listing 5-3:   Using Static Members in a Template

```
#include <iostream>

using namespace std;

template <typename T>
class Electricity
{
public:
    static T charge;
};

template <typename T>
T Electricity<T>::charge;

int main()
{
    Electricity<int>::charge = 10;
    Electricity<float>::charge = 98.6;
    Electricity<int> inst;
    inst.charge = 22;

    cout << Electricity<int>::charge << endl;
    cout << Electricity<float>::charge << endl;
    cout << inst.charge << endl;

    return 0;
}
```

First, see how we declared the storage for the static member; it's the two lines in between the template and main(). The syntax is somewhat difficult to remember: First, you supply the same template header you would for the class. (That is, notice that the line template <typename T> appears both before the class template and the storage line.) Then, you specify the type of the static member (in this case T, which is the template parameter). Next, you refer to the static member by using the usual class name::member name syntax. But remember that the class name gets the template parameter in angle brackets after it. Done deal.

In this code, you can also see that we created two classes based on the templates Electricity <int> and Electricity <float>. Each of these classes has its own instance of the static member; for the `<int>` version, we put a `10` in it, and for the `<float>` version, we put a `98.6` in it. Then, just to show that there's only a single static member per class, we created an instance of `Electricity<int>` and set its static member to `22`. Then we wrote them to the console with the `cout` statement. And, indeed, the two lines for `Electricity<int>` are the same, and the one for `Electricity<float>` is different from the two for `Electricity<int>`. Done deal!

Parameterizing a Template

A template consists of a template name followed by one or more *parameters* inside angled brackets. Then comes the class definition. When you politely ask the compiler to create a new class based on this template, the compiler happily obliges by making a substitution for whatever you supply as the parameter. At least we think that the compiler is happy. It doesn't complain much beyond the occasional error message.

Focus your eyes on this template:

```
template <typename T>
class SomethingForEveryone
{
public:
    T member;
};
```

Not much to it: It's just a simple template with one member called, conveniently enough, `member`. Life is simple sometimes.

But what we want you to notice in particular is what's inside the angled brackets. This is the parameter: `typename T`. Like parameters in a function, first is the type of the parameter (`typename`), and second is the name of the parameter (`T`).

But is `typename` an actual, um, typename? Not really; it's a special C++ word reserved for use in templates. *typename* means that what follows (in this case, `T`) is a *type*. So when you politely tell the compiler to create a new class based on this template, you specify a *type* for `T`. For example, this line tells the compiler to create the new class and make a variable named `JustForMe` that is of the new class:

```
SomethingForEveryone<int> JustForMe;
```

Now the compiler looks at what you supplied inside angle brackets and uses that as a parameter for the template. Here `int` goes with the `T` in the template. The compiler will take each instance of `T` that isn't inside a word, and replace it with the parameter, which is `int`.

Putting different types in the parameter

It turns out there's more to this parameter thing than meets the computer screen. You can put many more things inside the parameter beyond just the boring word `typename`. For example, suppose you have a class that does some comparisons to make sure that a product isn't too expensive for a person's budget. Each person would have several instances of this class, one for each product. This class would have a constant in it that represents the maximum price the person is willing to spend.

But there's a twist: Although you would have multiple instances of this class, one for each product the person wants to buy, the maximum price would be different for each person.

You can create such a situation with or without templates. Here's a way you can do it with a template:

```
template <int MaxPrice>
class PriceController
{
public:
    int Price;
    void TestPrice()
    {
        if (Price > MaxPrice)
        {
            cout << "Too expensive" << endl;
        }
    }
};
```

Before we show you an example that uses this template, we'll quickly explain what's going on with it. This time, the template parameter isn't a type at all — it's an integer value, an actual number. Then, inside the class, we use that number as a constant. As you can see in the `TestPrice` function, we compare the `Price` member to the constant, which is called `MaxPrice`. So this time, instead of using `T` for the name of the template parameter, we used something a little more sensible, `MaxPrice`. And `MaxPrice` is a value, not a type.

The `PriceController` example shown in Listing 5-4 contains a complete example that uses this template.

Listing 5-4: Using Different Types for a Template Parameter

```
#include <iostream>

using namespace std;

template <typename T>
class SomethingForEveryone
{
```

(continued)

Listing 5-4 *(continued)*

```cpp
public:
    T member;
};

template <int MaxPrice>
class PriceController
{
public:
    int Price;
    void TestPrice()
    {
        if (Price > MaxPrice)
        {
            cout << "Too expensive" << endl;
        }
    }
};

int main()
{
    SomethingForEveryone<int> JustForMe;
    JustForMe.member = 2;
    cout << JustForMe.member << endl;

    const int FredMaxPrice = 30;
    PriceController<FredMaxPrice> FredsToaster;
    FredsToaster.Price = 15;
    FredsToaster.TestPrice();

    PriceController<FredMaxPrice> FredsDrawingSet;
    FredsDrawingSet.Price = 45;
    FredsDrawingSet.TestPrice();

    const int JulieMaxPrice = 60;
    PriceController<JulieMaxPrice> JuliesCar;
    JuliesCar.Price = 80;
    JuliesCar.TestPrice();

    return 0;
}
```

Each person gets a different class. You can see that Fred gets a class called
PriceController <FredMaxPrice>. Julie, however, gets a class called
PriceController <JulieMaxPrice>. And remember, these really *are*
different classes. The compiler created two different classes, one for each
item passed in as a template parameter. And notice that the parameters are
constant integer values. FredMaxPrice is a constant integer holding 30.
JulieMaxPrice is a constant integer holding 60.

For the first one, PriceController <FredMaxPrice>, we created
two instances of that class. And for the second one, PriceController
<JulieMaxPrice>, we created one instance.

The compiler really does create two separate classes, one called `Price Controller <FredMaxPrice>` and one called `PriceController <JulieMaxPrice>`. These are as separate as they would be if you typed in two separate classes, one called `PriceControllerFredMaxPrice` and one called `PriceControllerJulieMaxPrice`. They aren't separate instances of a class — they are separate classes.

So far in this section, we've shown you that you can use a type as a template parameter or a value of a certain type. You can also use a class as a template parameter. The following list describes each type of parameter:

✦ **Value parameters:** (The ANSI standard calls these *non-type* parameters, but we like *value* better.) You can give the type and name for a value in the parameter, as in `template <int MaxPrice>`. But for some reason, the ANSI standard forbids you from using a floating-point value here, as in `template <float MaxPrice>`, or a class, as in `template <MyClass inst>`, or a `void` type, as in `template <void nothing>`. But you're free to use *pointers*, so `template <float *MaxPrice>` is allowed, and so are `template <MyClass *inst>` and `template <void *MaxPrice>`. (Although, in general, you should avoid `void *` because it's not very useful; try to be more specific with your pointers, as in `int *MaxPrice`.)

✦ **typename parameters:** You can use a type as a parameter to a class, as in `template <typename T>`. You then use a type when you ask the compiler to create the class based on the template. And when you use `typename`, you have to make sure that you actually use it as a type inside the class; don't just pass a variable for the parameter.

✦ **Class parameters:** Remember that a class is in itself a type, so you can pass a classname when your template requires a type. But remember that we're not talking about passing an instance of a class to the template; we're talking about passing a class itself by specifying its name in the template parameter.

The GNU GCC compiler that's used for Code::Blocks corrects a strange error message that other compilers sometimes provide when you use something you're not supposed to inside a template. The problem is, these older compilers don't give an error message for the line that has the word *template* in it, such as `template <float MaxPrice>`; instead, they give two error messages for the line that tries to create the class based on the template, such as `PriceController<FredMaxPrice> FredsToaster;`. Here are the two messages we saw:

```
non-constant 'FredMaxPrice' cannot be used as template argument
ANSI C++ forbids declaration 'FredsToaster' with no type
```

Parameterizing with a class

When your template is expecting a class for its parameter (remember, a class, not an instance of a class), you can use the word `typename` in the template parameter as we did in the examples in this chapter. You would then instruct the compiler to create a class based on the template by passing a classname into the template, as in `MyContainer<MyClass> inst;`. Typically, you would use a class, called a *container*, as a template parameter if you have a template that you intend to hold instances of a class. However, instead of using the word `typename`, you can instead use the word `class`, like so:

```
template <class T>
class MyContainer
{
public:
    T member;
};
```

But whichever you use, `typename` or `class`, really doesn't matter: According to the C++ ANSI standard, the word `typename` and the word `class` are interchangeable when used in a template parameter.

When working with Code::Blocks, you still see the message associated with the class creation when there is an error in your code. However, you also see the following message, which tells you precisely where the problem lies:

```
error: 'float' is not a valid type for a template non-type parameter
```

Including multiple parameters

You're not limited to only one parameter when you create a template. For example, the Standard C++ Library has a template called `map`. The `map` template works like an array, but instead of storing things based on an index as you would in an array, you store them based on an object called a *key*. In other words, you store things in an array in pairs; the first item in the pair is called a key and the second item is called a value. To retrieve an item from `map`, you specify the key, and you get back the value. When you create a class based on the `map` template, you specify the two types `map` will hold, one for the key and one for the value. Note that we said the *types* that `map` will hold, not the *objects or instances* it will hold. After you specify the types, the compiler creates a class, and inside that class you can put the instances.

To show how this works, instead of using the actual `map` template, we're going to make our own template that works similarly to a `map`. Instances of classes based on this template will hold only as many items as you specify when you create the class, whereas a real `map` doesn't have any limitations beyond the size of the computer's memory. These days that means `map` can hold just about as much as you want. So load up on `map` items! The `MultipleParameters` example shown in Listing 5-5 demonstrates our `map` template.

Listing 5-5:   Using Multiple Parameters with Templates

```
#include <iostream>

using namespace std;

template<typename K, typename V, int S>
class MyMap
{
protected:
    K key[S];
    V value[S];
    bool used[S];
    int Count;

    int Find(K akey)
    {
        int i;
        for (i=0; i<S; i++)
        {
            if (used[i] == false)
                continue;
            if (key[i] == akey)
            {
                return i;
            }
        }
        return -1;
    }

    int FindNextAvailable()
    {
        int i;
        for (i=0; i<S; i++)
        {
            if (used[i] == false)
                return i;
        }
        return -1;
    }

public:
    MyMap()
    {
        int i;
        for (i=0; i<S; i++)
        {
            used[i] = false;
        }
    }

    void Set(K akey, V avalue)
    {
        int i = Find(akey);
        if (i > -1)
        {
            value[i] = avalue;
        }
        else
        {
```

(continued)

Listing 5-5 *(continued)*

```
                i = FindNextAvailable();
                if (i > -1)
                {
                    key[i] = akey;
                    value[i] = avalue;
                    used[i] = true;
                }
                else
                    cout << "Sorry, full!" << endl;
        }
    }

    V Get(K akey)
    {
        int i = Find(akey);
        if (i == -1)
        {
            return 0;
        }
        else
        {
            return value[i];
        }
    }
};

int main()
{
    MyMap<char,int,10> mymap;

    mymap.Set('X',5);
    mymap.Set('Q',6);
    mymap.Set('X',10);

    cout << mymap.Get('X') << endl;
    cout << mymap.Get('Q') << endl;

    return 0;
}
```

When you run this application, you'll see this output:

```
10
6
```

This listing is a good exercise — not just for your fingers as you type it in, but for understanding templates. Notice the first line of the template definition:

```
template<typename K, typename V, int S>
```

This template takes not one, not two, but (count them!) three parameters. The first is a type, and we use it as the key for map, so we call it K. The second is a type, and we use it as the value for map, so we call it V. The final is S, and it's not a type. Instead, S is an integer value; it represents the maximum number of pairs that map can hold.

The member functions that follow allow the user of any class based on this map to add items to map and retrieve items from map. We didn't include any functions for removing items; you might think about ways you could add such an item. You might even take a look at the header files for the map template in the Standard C++ Library to see how the designers of the library implemented a removal system.

Typedefing a Template

If there's a template that you use with particular parameters over and over, often just using `typedef` for the thing is the easiest way to go. For example, if you have a template like this

```
template <typename T>
class Cluck
{
public:
    T Chicken;
};
```

and you find yourself using `Cluck <int>` over and over, you can `typedef` this, as in the following:

```
typedef Cluck<int> CluckNum;
```

Then, anytime you need to use `Cluck<int>`, you can use `CluckNum` instead. This `main` demonstrates the use of `CluckNum`:

```
int main()
{
    CluckNum foghorn;
    foghorn.Chicken = 1;
    return 0;
}
```

We like to `typedef` our templates, because then the classname looks like a regular old classname, rather than a template name. In the preceding example, we get to use the classname `CluckNum` instead of the somewhat cryptic `Cluck<int>`. And interestingly, if you're working as part of a team of programmers and the other programmers aren't as knowledgeable about templates as you are, they tend to be less intimidated if you `typedef` the template. That way you get to use a regular name, and they won't have a brain overload when they see your code. But don't tell them we said that.

When the compiler creates a class based on a template, people say that the compiler is *instantiating* the template. We know, we know, most people use the word *instantiate* to mean that you create an object based on a class. But if you stretch your imagination, you can see how the template itself is a type from which you can create other types. And thus, a class based on a template is actually an *instance of a template!* And the process of creating a class based on a template is called *template instantiation*.

When you use a `typedef` to give a simpler name to a specific class based on a template, the compiler instantiates the class based on the template. Or, to put it another way, the compiler *instantiates the template class*.

Deriving Templates

If you think about it, you can involve a class template in a derivation in at least three ways. You can

✦ Derive a class from a class template

✦ Derive a class template from a class

✦ Derive a class template from a class template

Or you could do none of these three items. But if you want to find out about them, read the following sections, where we show you how they work.

Deriving classes from a class template

You can derive a class from a template, and in doing so, specify the parameters for the template. In other words, think of it like this, if it's not too roundabout: From a template, you create a class, and from that created class, you derive your final class.

Suppose you have a template called `MediaHolder`, and the first two lines of its declaration look like this:

```
template <typename T>
class MediaHolder
```

Then you could derive a class from a particular case of this template, as in this header for a class:

```
class BookHolder : public MediaHolder<Book>
```

Here we created a new class (based on `MediaHolder`) called `MediaHolder<Book>`. And from that class, we derived our final class, `BookHolder`. The `ClassFromTemplate` example shown in Listing 5-6 is an example of the class `MediaHolder`, and the listing includes some good books and magazines to add to your reading list as well.

Listing 5-6:   Deriving a Class from a Class Template

```cpp
#include <iostream>

using namespace std;

class Book
{
public:
    string Name;
    string Author;
    string Publisher;
    Book(string aname, string anauthor, string apublisher) :
        Name(aname), Author(anauthor), Publisher(apublisher)
        {}
};

class Magazine
{
public:
    string Name;
    string Issue;
    string Publisher;
    Magazine(string aname, string anissue,
        string apublisher) :
        Name(aname), Issue(anissue), Publisher(apublisher)
        {}
};

template <typename T>
class MediaHolder
{
public:
    T *array[100];
    int Count;

    void Add(T *item)
    {
        array[Count] = item;
        Count++;
    }

    MediaHolder() : Count(0) {}
};

class BookHolder : public MediaHolder<Book> {
public:
    enum GenreEnum
        {childrens, scifi, romance,
         horror, mainstream, hownotto};

    GenreEnum GenreOfAllBooks;
};

class MagazineHolder : public MediaHolder<Magazine>
{
public:
    bool CompleteSet;
};

int main()
{
```

(continued)

Listing 5-6 *(continued)*

```
MagazineHolder dl;
dl.Add(new Magazine(
    "Dummies Life", "Vol 1 No 1", "Wile E."));
dl.Add(new Magazine(
    "Dummies Life", "Vol 1 No 2", "Wile E."));
dl.Add(new Magazine(
    "Dummies Life", "Vol 1 No 3", "Wile E."));
dl.CompleteSet = false;
cout << dl.Count << endl;

BookHolder bh;
bh.Add(new Book(
    "CEOing for Dumdums", "Gookie Dan", "Wile E."));
bh.Add(new Book(
    "Carsmashing for Dumdums", "Woodie and Buzz",
    "Wile E."));
bh.Add(new Book(
    "Turning off the Computer for Dumdums",
    "Wrath of Andy",
    "Wile E."));
bh.GenreOfAllBooks = BookHolder::hownotto;
cout << bh.Count << endl;

return 0;
}
```

Deriving a class template from a class

A template doesn't have to be at the absolute top of your hierarchy, the total king of the hill. No, a template can be derived from another class that's not a template. The brain acrobatics work like this: When you have a template and the compiler creates a class based on this template, the resulting class will be derived from another class.

For example, suppose you have a class called SuperMath that is *not a template*. You could derive a class template from SuperMath. The TemplateFromClass example shown in Listing 5-7 demonstrates how you can do this.

Listing 5-7:   Deriving a Class Template from a Class

```
#include <iostream>

using namespace std;

class SuperMath
{
public:
    int IQ;
};

template <typename T>
```

```
class SuperNumber : public SuperMath
{
public:
    T value;

    T &AddTo(T another)
    {
        value += another;
        return value;
    }

    T &SubtractFrom(T another)
    {
        value -= another;
        return value;
    }
};

void IncreaseIQ(SuperMath &inst)
{
    inst.IQ++;
}

int main()
{
    SuperNumber<int> First;
    First.value = 10;
    First.IQ = 206;
    cout << First.AddTo(20) << endl;

    SuperNumber<float> Second;
    Second.value = 20.5;
    Second.IQ = 201;
    cout << Second.SubtractFrom(1.3) << endl;

    IncreaseIQ(First);
    IncreaseIQ(Second);
    cout << First.IQ << endl;
    cout << Second.IQ << endl;

    return 0;
}
```

Note something really great that we did here! The base class is called
SuperMath, and it has a member called IQ. From SuperMath, we derived a
class template called SuperNumber that does some arithmetic. Later, we put
an Incredible IQ-Inflating Polymorphism to use in this function:

```
void IncreaseIQ(SuperMath &inst)
{
    inst.IQ++;
}
```

Note what this function takes: A reference to SuperMath. Because the
SuperNumber class template is derived from SuperMath, that means any
class we create based on the template is, in turn, derived from SuperMath.
And that means that if we have an instance of a class based on the template,
we can pass the instance into the IncreaseIQ() function. (Remember,

when a function takes a pointer or reference to a class, you can instead pass an instance of a derived class.)

Deriving a class template from a class template

If you have a class template and you want to derive another class template from it, first you need to think about *exactly* what you're doing. Not like what you're doing spending all your days programming when you could be out enjoying the sunshine; rather, what we mean is, "What process takes place when you attempt to derive a class template from another class template?"

Remember that a class template isn't a class: A class template is a cookie-cutter that the compiler uses to build a class. If, in a derivation, the base class and the derived classes are both templates, what you really have is the following:

1. The first class is a template from which the compiler builds classes.

2. The second class is a template from which the compiler will build classes that are derived from classes built from the first template.

Now think about this: You create a class based on the base class template. Then you create a second class based on the second template. Does this automatically mean that the second class is derived from the first class? Nope! Here's why: From the first template, you can create many classes. Now if you create a class from the second template, which of those many classes will it be derived from?

To understand what's happening here, take a look at the `TemplateFrom Template` example shown in Listing 5-8. To keep the code simple, we put the jokes aside and just gave the identifiers basic names. (And notice that we commented one of the lines out. If you're typing this, go ahead and type that line in, too, with the comment slashes, because we want you to try something in a moment.)

Listing 5-8:   Deriving a Class Template from a Class Template

```
#include <iostream>

using namespace std;

template <typename T>
class Base
{
public:
    T a;
};

template <typename T>
```

```
class Derived : public Base<T>
{
public:
    T b;
};

void TestInt(Base<int> *inst)
{
    cout << inst->a << endl;
}

void TestDouble(Base<double> *inst)
{
    cout << inst->a << endl;
}

int main()
{
    Base<int> base_int;
    Base<double> base_double;

    Derived<int> derived_int;
    Derived<double> derived_double;

    TestInt(&base_int);
    TestInt(&derived_int);

    TestDouble(&base_double);
    TestDouble(&derived_double);
    //TestDouble(&derived_int);

    return 0;
}
```

Now compile the application. The preceding example has two functions, each taking a different class — and each class based on the first template called Base. The first takes Base<int> * as a parameter, and the second takes Base<double> * as a parameter.

If a function takes a pointer to a class, we can legally pass a pointer to an instance of a derived class. Now note that we created this variable:

```
Derived<int> derived_int;
```

**Book IV
Chapter 5**

And we pass this variable to the function that takes a Base<int>. *And it compiles.* That means Derived<int> is derived from Base<int>. In the same way, Derived<double> is derived from Base<double>.

Now, just to make sure that this is correct, if you look at the commented out line, you should see that if you uncomment the line, it should not compile. Go ahead and try uncommenting the line TestDouble(&derived_int). When you do this, and you try to compile the listing, you see this message:

```
error: cannot convert 'Derived<int>*' to 'Base<double>*' for argument '1'
to 'void TestDouble(Base<double>*)'
```

**Creating Classes
with Templates**

Thus you can't pass a pointer to `Derived<int>` to a function that takes a pointer to `Base<double>`. That's because `Derived<int>` isn't derived from `Base<double>`. Yet it would appear from the code that the template is derived from the template for `Base<double>`. But that's not true. Here's why. . . .

Templates are not derived from other templates. You can't derive templates because templates are not classes. Rather, templates are cookie cutters for classes, and the class resulting from a template can be derived from a class resulting from another template.

Now that we've that cleared up, look closely at how we declared the second template class. Its header looks like this:

```
template <typename T>
class Derived : public Base<T>
```

The clue here is that the `Derived` template takes a template parameter called `T`. Then the class based on the template is derived from a class called `Base<T>`. But in this case, `T` is the parameter for the `Derived` template.

See what happens if we create a class based on `Derived`, such as this one:

```
Derived<int> x;
```

We just created a class called `Derived<int>`; then, in this case, the parameter is `int`. Thus the compiler replaces the `T`s so that `Base<T>` in this case becomes `Base<int>`. And so `Derived<int>` is derived from `Base<int>`.

And *that's* how this template derivation stuff works!

When you derive a template class from another template class, you actually make use of the template parameter, and that gets passed into the base class template as a parameter.

Templatizing a Function

A *function template* is a function that allows the user to essentially modify the types used by a function as needed. For example, take a look at these two functions:

```
int AbsoluteValueInt(int x)
{
    if (x >= 0)
        return x;
    else
        return -x;
}
```

```
float AbsoluteValueFloat(float x)
{
    if (x >= 0)
        return x;
    else
        return -x;
}
```

If the user of the functions needs to take the absolute value of an integer, he or she would use the `AbsoluteValueInt()` function. But to take the absolute value of a float, he or she would instead use the `AbsoluteValueFloat()` function. What about a `double`? Or some other numerical type?

But instead of having a separate function for double and a separate function for every other type, we would suggest using a template, as in this:

```
template <typename T> T AbsoluteValue(T x)
{
    if (x >= 0)
        return x;
    else
        return -x;
}
```

Now you need only one version of the function, which handles any numeric type, including `double`. The users of the function can, effectively, create their own versions of the function as they need them. For example, to use an integer version of this function, we just put the typename, `int`, inside angle brackets after the function name when calling the function:

```
int n = -3;
cout << AbsoluteValue<int>(n) << endl;
```

And if we want to use the function for a float, we just do this:

```
float x = -4.5;
cout << AbsoluteValue<float>(x) << endl;
```

Note how we declared the function template itself. The real difference between the function template and a regular run-of-the-mill function is in the header:

```
template <typename T> T AbsoluteValue(T x)
```

First we put the word `template`. Then we follow it with any number of optional spaces, and then an open angle bracket (that is, a less-than sign). Following the angle bracket, we put the word `typename`, a close angle bracket (that is, a greater-than sign), and then an identifier name. Most people like to use the name T (since it's the first letter in *type*), so that's what we did, being ones to follow the crowd. Then we put in the rest of the function header, which, taken by itself, looks like this:

```
T AbsoluteValue(T x)
```

Remember, T represents a type. Therefore, this portion of the function header shows a function called `AbsoluteValue` that takes T as a parameter and returns T. So if we create a function based on this template by using an integer, the function will take an integer as a parameter and return an integer. Remember, T is basically a placeholder for a typename. So when the compiler encounters a line like this:

```
cout << AbsoluteValue<float>(x) << endl;
```

it creates a function based on the template, substituting float anywhere it sees T.

However, if you have two lines that use the same type, as in this

```
cout << AbsoluteValue<float>(x) << endl;
cout << AbsoluteValue<float>(10.0) << endl;
```

the compiler only creates a single function for both lines. (And these two lines don't need to be one after the other.)

Overloading and function templates

If you really want to go out on a limb and create flexibility in your application, you can use overloading with a function template. Remember, *overloading a function* means that you create two different versions of a single function. Really, what you're doing is creating two separate functions that have different parameters (that is, either a different number of parameters or different types of parameters), but they share the same name.

Look at these two functions found in the `FunctionOverloadingAndTempl ates` example:

```
int AbsoluteValue(int x)
{
    if (x >= 0)
        return x;
    else
        return -x;
}

float AbsoluteValue(float x)
```

```
{
    if (x >= 0)
        return x;
    else
        return -x;
}
```

These functions are an example of overloading. They take different types as parameters. (One takes an int, and the other takes a float.) Of course, you could combine these functions into a template:

```
template <typename T> T AbsoluteValue(T x)
{
    if (x >= 0)
        return x;
    else
        return -x;
}
```

But is this really any different? After all, you can use the following two lines of code either after the overloaded functions or after the function template:

```
cout << AbsoluteValue<int>(n) << endl;
cout << AbsoluteValue<float>(x) << endl;
```

(We're assuming that n is an integer and x is a float.) However, the template is a better choice. First, if you use the overloaded form and then try this, you'll get a problem:

```
cout << AbsoluteValue(10.5) << endl;
```

We all know that 10.5 is a float; therefore, the compiler should just call the float version of the overloaded function. However, the GNU GCC compiler that ships with Code::Blocks gives us this error message:

```
error: call of overloaded 'AbsoluteValue(double)' is ambiguous
```

Ambiguous? But look! The message is saying AbsoluteValue(double)! Hmmm . . . apparently, the GNU GCC compiler thinks that our 10.5 is a double, not a float. And you can actually pass a double into either a function that takes an int or a function that takes a float. The compiler will just convert it to an int or a float, whichever it needs. And because the compiler thinks that 10.5 is a double, it figures it can pass it to either version of the overloaded function. So that leaves you a choice: You can either cast it to a float or create a third overloaded version of the function, one that takes a double.

Yuck. At least Code::Blocks gives you some clue as to the problem because the extended error information is

```
note: candidates are: int AbsoluteValue(int)
note:                  float AbsoluteValue(float)
```

Creating a template is easier. And that brings us to the second reason the template version is better: If you want a new type of the function, you don't need to write another version of the function.

But what if you want to *overload a function template*? That sounds kind of scary, but you can do it. The `OverloadedFunctionTemplate` example shown in Listing 5-9 contains an overloaded function template.

Listing 5-9:   Overloading a Function Template Provides Even Greater Flexibility

```
#include <iostream>

using namespace std;

template <typename T> T AbsoluteValue(T x)
{
    cout << "(using first)" << endl;
    if (x >= 0)
        return x;
    else
        return -x;
}

template <typename T> T AbsoluteValue(T *x)
{
    cout << "(using second)" << endl;
    if (*x >= 0)
        return *x;
    else
        return -(*x);
}

int main()
{
    int n = -3;
    cout << AbsoluteValue<int>(n) << endl;

    float *xptr = new float(-4.5);
    cout << AbsoluteValue<float>(xptr) << endl;
    cout << AbsoluteValue<float>(10.5) << endl;

    return 0;
}
```

When we pass a pointer (as in the second call to `AbsoluteValue()` in `main()`), the compiler figures out that it needs to use the second version of the template. And just to be sure which version gets used and at what time during application execution, we threw in a `cout` line at the beginning of each function template. When you run this code, here's what you see:

```
(using first)
3
(using second)
4.5
(using first)
10.5
```

From the middle two lines you can see that the computer did indeed call the second version of the template.

You can make life a little easier by using a little trick. Most compilers let you leave out the type in angle brackets in the function template call itself. The compiler is smart enough to figure out what type of function to build from the template, based on the types that you pass into the function call! Pretty wild. Here's an example `main()` that you can substitute for the `main()` in Listing 5-9:

```
int main()
{
    int n = -3;
    cout << AbsoluteValue(n) << endl;

    float *xptr = new float(-4.5);
    cout << AbsoluteValue(xptr) << endl;
    cout << AbsoluteValue(10.5) << endl;

    return 0;
}
```

In this code, we replaced `AbsoluteValue<int>(n)` with just `Absolute Value(n)`. When you run the modified Listing 5-9, you see the same output as when you run Listing 5-9.

Templatizing a member function

When you write a template for a class, you can put function templates inside the class template. To people who were familiar with some of the early versions of C++ where template support was minimal, this seems a little shocking. But when the electrical current wears off, we all see that putting a template function inside a template class is possible. You simply declare a function template inside a class, as in the following:

```
class MyMath
{
public:
    string name;
    MyMath(string aname) : name(aname) {}

    template <typename T> void WriteAbsoluteValue(T x)
    {
        cout << "Hello " << name << endl;
        if (x >= 0)
```

```
            cout << x << endl;
        else
            cout << -x << endl;
    }
};
```

The `WriteAbsoluteValue()` member function is a template. It's preceded by the word `template` and a `template` parameter in angle brackets. Then it has a return type, `void`, the function name, and the function parameter.

When you create an instance of the class, you can call the member function, providing a type as need be, as in the following:

```
int main()
{
    MyMath inst = (string("George"));
    inst.WriteAbsoluteValue(-50.5);
    inst.WriteAbsoluteValue(-35);
    return 0;
}
```

In the first call, the function takes a `double` (because, by default, the C++ compiler considers -50.5 a `double`). In the second call, the function takes an integer. The compiler then generates two different forms of the function, and *they both become members of the class.*

Although you can use function templates as class members, you cannot make them virtual. The compiler will not allow it, and the ANSI standard forbids ("Forbids," we say!) you from doing it. In fact, we tried it with Code::Blocks just to see what friendly message we would get. Here it is:

```
'virtual' can only be specified for functions
```

We guess by *functions* it means actual functions — not function templates.

Chapter 6: Programming with the Standard Library

In This Chapter

✔ **Architecting the Standard C++ Library**

✔ **Storing data in `vector` or `map`**

✔ **Containing data with a list or set**

✔ **Stacking and queuing**

✔ **Copying containers**

✔ **Using dynamic arrays**

✔ **Working with unordered data**

*W*hen you get around in the world of C++ programming (a fun world indeed!), you're going to encounter two different *libraries* that people use to make their lives easier. That is, after all, the ultimate point of computers — to make our lives easier, right? These two libraries are

✦ Standard C++ Library

✦ Standard Template Library (STL)

Some people say, "We use STL." Others say, "We use the Standard C++ Library." In this case, *library* means a set of classes that you can use in your applications. These libraries include handy classes, such as `string` and `vector` (which is like an array in that it's a list in which you can store objects).

The difference between the Standard C++ Library and STL is that STL came first. STL was used by so many developers that the American National Standards Institute (ANSI) decided to standardize it. The result is the similar Standard C++ Library that is part of the official ANSI standard and now part of most modern C++ compilers (including Code::Blocks, Microsoft Visual C++, Borland C++ Builder, MinGW, Cygwin, and Dev-C++). We use the Standard C++ Library in this chapter. Because we know that this is C++, we just call it the *Standard Library*.

The concepts that we present here apply to STL, so if you're using STL, you can use this chapter.

Architecting the Standard Library

When people start using the Standard Library, they often ask: Where's the source code? We see the header files, but where are the .cpp files? This question has an easy answer: There are no .cpp files! ANSI architected the Standard Library for ease of use and reliability.

The classes contain their functions inside the class definitions; there are no forward declarations. You don't add source files to your project or linking in compiled libraries. Just add an include line for the libraries you want.

Containing Your Classes

Computers need a place to store things, so the Standard Library includes containers in which you can put things. The classes for containing things are called *container classes*. These classes are templates. When you create an instance of a container class, you specify what class it holds.

When you specify the class in a container, you are saying that the container will contain instances of your specified class or of classes derived from your specified class. You must decide whether the container will hold instances of the class, pointers to the instances, or references to the instances.

Storing in a vector

The Vectors example shown in Listing 6-1 demonstrates how to use a container class. This particular container is a datatype called a vector, and it works much like an array.

Listing 6-1:   Using Vectors as Examples of Container Classes

```
#include <iostream>
#include <vector>

using namespace std;

int main()
{
    vector<string> names;

    names.push_back("Tom");
    names.push_back("Dick");
    names.push_back("Harry");
    names.push_back("April");
    names.push_back("May");
    names.push_back("June");
```

```
cout << names[0] << endl;
cout << names[5] << endl;

return 0;
}
```

Now, note how we used `vector`. First, it's a template. That means it's going to have a template parameter! And what is the template parameter? Why, you guessed it. (Or you looked at the code.) The template parameter is the type that the template will hold. Thus the following line declares a `vector` that holds strings:

```
vector<string> names;
```

Note also the header files that we included. Among them, we included `<vector>` (with no `.h` after the filename). In general, you include the header file that matches the name of the container you are using. Thus, if there were such a thing as a container called `rimbucklebock`, you would type `#include <rimbucklebock>`. Or, if there were such thing as a container called `set` (which there is), you would type `#include <set>`.

At this point, you may be wondering, "What's the advantage to using a `vector` instead of a regular, plain old, no-frills array?" The advantage is that when you declare the `vector` instance, you don't need to know up front how many items will be going in it. With an array, you need to know the size when you declare it. When you run this example you see two names as output:

```
Tom
June
```

A `vector` is the closest thing the Standard Library has to an array. In fact, a `vector` is very much like an array, except (because it's a class template) you get all the goodies that go with a class, such as member functions that operate on `vector`.

Here are some things you can do with `vector`:

✦ Add items to the end of it.

✦ Access its members by using bracket notation.

✦ Iterate through it, either from beginning to end or from end back to beginning.

The `Vectors2` example shown in Listing 6-2 demonstrates how to use multiple `vectors` in a single application. You can see that each one holds a different type, which we specified in the template parameter.

**Book IV
Chapter 6**

**Programming with
the Standard Library**

Listing 6-2: Containing the Type You Specify in Classes

```
#include <iostream>
#include <vector>

using namespace std;

class Employee
{
public:
    string Name;
    string FireDate;
    int GoofoffDays;

    Employee(string aname, string afiredate,
        int agoofdays) : Name(aname), FireDate(afiredate),
        GoofoffDays(agoofdays) {}
};

int main()
{
    // A vector that holds strings
    vector<string> MyAliases;
    MyAliases.push_back(string("Bud The Sailor"));
    MyAliases.push_back(string("Rick Fixit"));
    MyAliases.push_back(string("Bobalou Billow"));
    cout << MyAliases[0] << endl;
    cout << MyAliases[1] << endl;
    cout << MyAliases[2] << endl;

    // A vector that holds integers
    vector<int> LuckyNumbers;
    LuckyNumbers.push_back(13);
    LuckyNumbers.push_back(26);
    LuckyNumbers.push_back(52);
    cout << LuckyNumbers[0] << endl;
    cout << LuckyNumbers[1] << endl;
    cout << LuckyNumbers[2] << endl;

    // A vector that holds Employee instances
    vector<Employee> GreatWorkers;
    GreatWorkers.push_back(Employee("George Washington","123100", 50));
    GreatWorkers.push_back(Employee("Thomas Jefferson","052002", 40));
    cout << GreatWorkers[0].Name << endl;
    cout << GreatWorkers[1].Name << endl;

    return 0;
}
```

After you compile and run this application, you see the following output from the cout statements:

```
Bud The Sailor
Rick Fixit
Bobalou Billow
13
26
52
George Washington
Thomas Jefferson
```

Mapping your data

The Maps example shown in Listing 6-3 demonstrates a type of container called a map. A map works much like a vector, except for one main difference: You look up items in vector by putting a number inside brackets as in this

```
cout << names[0] << endl;
```

but with a map, you can use any class or type you want for the index, not just numbers. This feature lets you associate objects. Take a gander at Listing 6-3 to see where we're coming from.

Listing 6-3:   Associating Objects with map

```
#include <iostream>
#include <map>

using namespace std;

int main()
{
    map<string, string> marriages;

    marriages["Tom"] = "Suzy";
    marriages["Harry"] = "Harriet";

    cout << marriages["Tom"] << endl;
    cout << marriages["Harry"] << endl;

    return 0;
}
```

First, you can see that to use map, we declare a variable of class map, supplying to the template the types of first the keys (a kind of index into the map) and then the values:

```
map<string, string> marriages;
```

Then we store something in map by putting a key inside brackets and setting it equal to a value:

```
marriages["Tom"] = "Suzy";
```

And to retrieve that particular item, we grab it, basing our choice of it on the key:

```
cout << marriages["Tom"] << endl;
```

And voilà! We get back the item stored in map for that particular key. Think of map like an array, except the keys can be any object, not just a string. When you run this example, you see the following two strings as output:

```
Suzy
Harriet
```

Even though the keys can be any type or class, you must specify the type or class you're using when you set up map. And after you do that, you can use only that type for the particular map. Thus, if you say the keys will be strings, you cannot then use an integer for a key, as in marriages[3] = "Suzy";.

Containing instances, pointers, or references

One of the most common discussions you encounter when people start talking about how to use the container templates is whether to put instances in the containers, pointers, or references. For example, which of these should you type:

```
vector<MyClass>
vector<MyClass *>
vector<MyClass &>
```

In other words, do you want your container to store the actual instance (whatever that might mean), a reference to the actual instance, or a pointer to the instance?

To explore this idea, have a look at the Maps2 example in Listing 6-4. Here we're trying out the different ways of storing things in map: instances, pointers, and references.

Listing 6-4: Making Decisions: Oh, What to Store?

```
#include <iostream>
#include <map>

using namespace std;

class StoreMe
{
public:
    int Item;
};

bool operator < (const StoreMe & first,
const StoreMe & second)
{
    return first.Item < second.Item;
}

int main()
{
```

```
            // First try storing the instances
            map<StoreMe, StoreMe> instances;

            StoreMe key1 = {10}; // braces notation!
            StoreMe value1 = {20};
            StoreMe key2 = {30};
            StoreMe value2 = {40};

            instances[key1] = value1;
            instances[key2] = value2;
            value1.Item = 12345;
            cout << instances[key1].Item << endl;

            instances[key1].Item = 34567;
            cout << instances[key1].Item << endl;

            // Next try storing pointers to the instances
            map<StoreMe*, StoreMe*> pointers;

            StoreMe key10 = {10};
            StoreMe value10 = {20};
            StoreMe key11 = {30};
            StoreMe value11 = {40};

            pointers[&key10] = &value10;
            pointers[&key11] = &value11;
            value10.Item = 12345;
            cout << (*pointers[&key10]).Item << endl;

            // Finally try storing references to the instances.
            // (I commented it out because it will
            // get an error. See the text!)
    //      map<StoreMe&, StoreMe&> pointers;
            return 0;
    }
```

First, note that to create the instances of `StoreMe`, we used the braces notation. You can do that when you have no constructors. So the line

```
StoreMe key1 = {10};
```

creates an instance of `StoreMe` and puts `10` in the `Item` member variable.

Also note that we commented out the single line

```
// map<StoreMe&, StoreMe&> pointers;
```

This is where we attempt to declare a `map` that holds references. But the line gets a compiler error. When you type this listing, you can try uncommenting the commented line and see the error message. We get several error messages as a result of this line, the main two errors are as follows:

```
error: conflicting declaration 'std::map<StoreMe&, StoreMe&> pointers'
error: 'pointers' has a previous declaration as 'std::map<StoreMe*,
    StoreMe*> pointers'
```

Apparently references are out of the question. But why is that?

Here's why: It turns out `map` is making a copy of everything you put in it. How do we know this? By the output. Here's what you see when you type this application (and recomment out the line that you uncommented out so that it's a recommented-decommented line).

```
20
34567
12345
```

Aha! Tricky. Tricky indeed! But now we need to determine what this output means. For the first line, we stored a pair in `map` for `key1` and `value1`:

```
instances[key1] = value1;
```

And then we changed the `Item` member variable in `value1`:

```
value1.Item = 12345;
```

Next we retrieved the value from the pair in `map` and printed the `Item` member:

```
cout << instances[key1].Item << endl;
```

When we did, we saw `20`, *not* `12345`. That means the value stored in `map` is a copy, not the original. We changed the `Item` member of the original to `12345`, but the copy still had the previous value of `20`.

But then we did this:

```
instances[key1].Item = 34567;
```

The hope here was that this action would change the `Item` member of the value stored in `map`. And so we printed the value again:

```
cout << instances[key1].Item << endl;
```

And this time it *did* indeed change. We saw `34567`. Excellent! Where there's a will, there's a way, and where there's a value, there's a change. (Or something like that.)

And now that we've figured out that `map` is storing copies of what we put in it, the idea of storing a pointer should be pretty clear: If we have a pointer variable and then we make a copy of it, although we have a separate pointer variable now, the original and the copy both point to the same thing. And that's the idea behind the second part of Listing 6-4. We created `map` like this:

```
map<StoreMe*, StoreMe*> pointers;
```

Now this `map` stores pointer variables. Remember that a pointer variable just holds a number that represents an address. If two separate pointer variables hold the same number, it means they point to the same thing. Furthermore, because this `map` is holding pointers, *really* it's holding numbers, not instances — something to think about.

And so we next set up some instances and then made one association:

```
pointers[&key10] = &value10;
```

Note the use of the ampersand (`&`), which we used as a reference operator to help us store the addresses in `map`. Then we changed the `Item` member of one the value objects:

```
value10.Item = 12345;
```

And this time, when we print it by using this carefully parenthesized line

```
cout << (*pointers[&key10]).Item << endl;
```

we see this:

```
12345
```

And once again . . . aha! This time the change stuck. Why is that? Because even though `map` holds a copy, it's holding a copy of a pointer. And that pointer happens to point to the original `value10` object. So when we changed the `Item` member of `value10`, `map` picked up the change. `map` itself didn't change, but `map` is pointing to that value.

From all this discussion about the containers holding copies, you can come to the following conclusion. Because `map` holds copies, you can remember these two rules about deleting your original objects:

✦ **When the container holds instances:** If you're putting instances in `map`, you can delete the original instances after they're in `map`. This is okay because `map` has its own copies of the instances.

✦ **When the container holds pointers:** If you're putting pointers in `map`, you don't want to delete the original instances because the pointers in `map` still point to these instances.

So which method is best? It's up to you. But here are a couple of things to consider:

✦ **Keeping instances around:** If you don't want to keep instances lying around, you can put the instances in the container, and it will make copies.

✦ **Copyability:** Are your classes copyable? Some classes, such as classes filled with pointers to other classes or classes that are enormous, don't copy well. In that case, you may want to put pointers in the container.

Comparing instances

When you work with classes that contain other classes (such as `vector`), you need to provide the class with a way to compare two things. For us humans, having the superbrains that we do, comparing is easy. But it's not that easy for a computer. For example, suppose you have two pointers to string objects. The first points to a string containing `abc`. The second points to another string containing `abc`. Are these two pointers the same?

Well, that depends on how you look at it. If you mean do they point to the same sequence of characters, then, yes, they are the same. But if you mean do they point to the same object, then maybe or maybe not. Look at this code:

```
string *pointer1 = new string("abc");
string *pointer2 = new string("abc");
```

Are `pointer1` and `pointer2` *equal?* Again, it depends on how you look at it. If you mean do they point to strings that are equivalent, then, yes, they are equal in that sense. If you mean do they point to the same object, then, no, they are *not* equal in that sense. Now look at this code:

```
string *pointer3 = new string("abc");
string *pointer4 = pointer3;
```

These two pointers point to the same object. So in that sense, they are equal. And because they point to the same object, they also point to the same string of characters. So, again, in that sense, they are equal.

As you can see, you have two kinds of comparisons when dealing with objects:

✦ You are comparing two objects and determining whether they are identical, even though they're separate objects. If the two objects are separate but identical, you would say that they are equal.

✦ You are comparing two objects and determining if they are the same object. This can happen if you have two pointers and they both point to the same object. In that case, you say that they are equal.

So why do you need to know all this, besides having a way to drive people batty? ("You say your car and our cars are the same, but in fact, they are different: One is yours, and the others are ours!") You need to know this distinction because when you create a container class that holds instances of your object, often the class needs to know how to compare objects. This is particularly true in the case of `map`, which holds pairs of items, and you locate the items based on the first element of the pair — the key element. When you tell `map` to find an item based on a key, `map` must search through its list of pairs until it finds one such that the key in the pair is equal to the one you passed in to the search.

Well, that's all fine and dandy; but now, how can the computer know whether two objects are identical? That is, suppose you're doing your comparison based on whether two separate objects are identical. How does the computer compare the two objects to determine whether they are, in fact, identical?

And because we like to get people thinking, how about this: What if you have a list of objects, and you want to keep them in a sorted order? How does the computer determine a sort order?

Here's an example. We create a class called `Employee`. That's a standard example that you see in lots of books, but in this case it makes for a good example, for once. Now our `Employee` class contains these member variables: `FirstName`, `LastName`, and `SocialSecurityNumber`.

Next, we have a `Salary` class that contains payroll information for an employee. This class has member variables `MonthlySalary` and `Deductions`. (Yes, in real life, you would probably have more member variables, but this is good enough for now.)

Next, we have a `map` instance, where each *key,value* pair contains an `Employee` instance for the key and a `Salary` instance for the value. So the big question is this: If we want to look up an employee, we would make an instance of `Employee` and fill in the `FirstName`, `LastName`, and `SocialSecurityNumber` member variables. We would then retrieve the value based on this key. But we can think of two issues here:

✦ We would create an instance and allow `map` to find the key that matches the instance. Is `map` looking for the exact same instance or one identical to it?

✦ If `map` is looking for an instance identical to the object we filled in, what happens if the employee changed his or her name (such as during a marriage). Can you cause `map` to still find the right key if `map` has one name and the search object has another? Most likely. In such cases, you would want the value to match only on the basis of the `SocialSecurityNumber`, without worrying about the others. So in that case, can you tell `map` to treat the two objects as *identical*?

Here's how to resolve these two issues: If you're dealing with your own classes, in addition to setting up a container class, you also provide a function that compares two instances of your own class. Your comparison function can determine whether two classes are equal, if the first is *less than* the second, or if the first is *greater than* the second.

REMEMBER

At first, how *less than* and *greater than* can apply to things like an `Employee` class may not seem apparent. But the idea behind *less than* and *greater than* is to give the container class a way to determine a sort order. If you have a list class holding `Employee` instances, for example, and you tell the list to keep them in a sorted order, how does the list know how to sort them? By using the notion of *less than* and *greater than*. The list can determine if one is greater than another and can group them in a sorted order. But if you're dealing with an Employee class, *you* would choose how to sort them: Should an Employee instance with a Social Security Number of 111-11-1111 be less than 999-99-9999? Or should they be sorted based on name, so that the person with Social Security Number 111-11-1111 but the name Zoë Zusseldörf come after the person with Social Security number 999-99-9999 but the name Aaron Aackman? Well, the answer is this: It's your decision. And after you decide how you want them sorted, you would create a function that determines if one is less than, equal to, or greater than the other. If you want the list to sort by name, you would make your function look strictly at the names. (And will it look at last name, first name, or both? That's your decision.) But if you want your list to sort by Social Security Number, you would write your function to compare the Social Security Numbers.

The Maps3 example shown in Listing 6-5 contains a map class with a comparison function that determines whether two keys are equal.

Listing 6-5: Containing Instances and Needing Functions That Compare Them

```
#include <iostream>
#include <map>

using namespace std;

class Employee
{
public:
    string Nickname;
    string SocialSecurityNumber;

    Employee(string anickname, string asocial) :
        Nickname(anickname),
        SocialSecurityNumber(asocial) {}

    Employee() : Nickname(""), SocialSecurityNumber("") {}
};

class Salary
{
public:
    int AnnualRipoff;
    int IRSDeductionsCheat;

    Salary(int aannual, int adeductions) :
        AnnualRipoff(aannual),
        IRSDeductionsCheat(adeductions) {}

    Salary() : AnnualRipoff(0), IRSDeductionsCheat(0) {}
};
```

```
bool operator < (const Employee& first, const Employee& second)
{
    return first.Nickname < second.Nickname;
}

int main()
{
    map<Employee, Salary> employees;

    Employee emp1("sparky", "123-22-8572");
    Salary sal1(135000, 18);
    employees[emp1] = sal1;

    Employee emp2("buzz", "234-33-5784");
    Salary sal2(150000, 23);
    employees[emp2] = sal2;

    // Now test it out!
    Employee emptest("sparky", "");
    cout << employees[emptest].AnnualRipoff << endl;

    return 0;
}
```

When you run this application, you will see the `AnnualRipoff` member of the `Salary` value, where the key is an `Employee` with the name `sparky`:

```
135000
```

Now notice a couple things about this code. First, to locate the salary for Sparky, we didn't need the `Employee` instance for Sparky. Instead, we created an instance of `Employee` and set up the `Nickname` member without worrying about the `SocialSecurityNumber` member. Then we retrieved the value by using the bracket notation for `map`:

```
cout << employees[emptest].AnnualRipoff << endl;
```

Now why did this work? Because the `map` code uses our less-than function that we provided. And in that function, we compared only the `Nickname` members, not the `SocialSecurityNumber` member. We could, however, change things around a bit. Instead of comparing the `Nickname` members, we could compare the `SocialSecurityNumber` members. We could change the less-than function like so:

```
bool operator < (const Employee& first,
const Employee& second)
{
    return first.SocialSecurityNumber <
        second.SocialSecurityNumber;
}
```

**Book IV
Chapter 6**

**Programming with
the Standard Library**

And then we can locate Sparky's salary based on his social security number:

```
Employee emptest("", "123-22-8572");
cout << employees[emptest].AnnualRipoff << endl;
```

Wait! This can't be right! How can the computer locate the item with the matching key if all you're giving it is a less-than comparison? Good question. Here's how: Suppose you want to find out if two numbers, say 5 and 5, are equal. (We know, they are equal, but bear with us.) But suppose the only comparison you have available is *less-than*. How can you determine if they are equal? You first see if the first is less than the second: Is 5 less than 5? Nope. Then you see if the second is less than the first: Is the second 5 less than the first 5? Nope. And because neither is less than the other, they must be equal. Aha! And that's how the code for the various containers matches objects: It calls your less-than function twice, the second time flip-flopping the order of the parameters; and if your function returns false both times, the computer determines that they are equal. That approach makes life easier because you need to provide only a single comparison function. Yay!

Iterating through a container

When your house is full of things, sometimes being able to climb over it all so you can look down on it (obtaining an overview) and see what all is there is nice. Containers in the Standard Library are the same way: If you have a container filled with things you normally get an overview of what's there — but being able to climb through it (obtaining a close up view) would be nice.

To climb through a container, you use an iterator. And *iterator* works with a container to let you step one-by-one through the container, seeing what-all is in it.

Each container class contains an embedded type called `iterator`. To create an iterator instance, then, you need to use the fully qualified name. For example, if you have a `map` that holds integers and strings as in `map<int, string>`, you would create an `iterator` instance like this:

```
map<string, int>::iterator loopy
```

Although `loopy` is an instance of `iterator`, some serious `typedefing` is going on, and, in fact, `loopy` is a pointer to an item stored inside the container.

Now, you want to initialize `loopy` to point to the first item in the container. And you can do this by calling the container's `begin()` member function and storing the results in `loopy`. Then `loopy` will point to the first item in the container. You can access the item by dereferencing `loopy`; then when you're finished, you can move to the next item by incrementing `loopy` like this:

```
loopy++;
```

Less<MyClass> is more

When we create a class that we will be using in a container, we prefer to write our own overloaded less-than function. The containers in the Standard Library work as follows: When you create a class based on a container template, you provide the types that the container holds, and you also provide a class (or `struct`) that includes a *less-than* member function. However, this class doesn't have a function called `<`. Instead, it's called `()`, and it takes two parameters, one for each of the two items you're comparing. The container class then calls this function to compare instances.

Well, that's all great, but why haven't we seen this in action? The reason is the containers have *default template parameters*. If you don't supply this magical less-than class, the container supplies one *for you*. What does it supply? It supplies a class based on a template called `less`. This template is simple; it includes a single member function that returns the Boolean value

```
x < y
```

For most basic types, that's fine. The compiler can easily use that if, for example, you're working

with integers. But what if you're working with one of your own classes? The compiler doesn't understand the `<` operator unless you provide your own `<` operator function, as we did everywhere else in this chapter. However, because the container takes a class in its parameter that defaults to the class `less`, you can put together your own class and use that instead of writing your own `<` operator function. Here's a sample:

```
class MyLess
{
public:
    bool operator()(const MyClass &x,
    const MyClass &y) const
    {
        return x.Name < y.Name;
    }
};
```

Then when you create, for example, a `map`, you would pass this class as a third parameter, rather than relying on the default:

```
map<MyClass, MyClass, MyLess> mymap;
```

And, of course, then you don't need your own *less-than* function.

That's pretty easy. And you can tell whether you're finished by checking to see whether `loopy` points to the last item in the container. To do this, you call the container's `end()` member function and compare `loopy` to the results of `end()`. If it's equal, you're done.

The following few lines of code do these steps:

```
vector<string>::iterator vectorloop = Words.begin();

while (vectorloop != Words.end())
{
    cout << *vectorloop << endl;
    vectorloop++;
}
```

You can see the type we used for the iterator, in this case called `vectorloop`. And you can see that we initialized it by calling `begin()`. We dereferenced it to get to the data itself, and then incremented `vectorloop` to get to the next item. And in the `while` loop we tested `vectorloop` against the results of `end()` to see whether we were all done.

Many people seem to forget how to use iterators. We suggest keeping the `Iterators` example code in Listing 6-6 handy somewhere. (Print it and hang it on the wall, or save a copy in a directory on your hard drive where you can find it quickly, or maybe print it on really big paper and paste it to the front windshield of your car.) Then, if you forget how to put together a simple iterator, you can easily find the answer.

Listing 6-6:   Iterating

```cpp
#include <iostream>
#include <map>
#include <vector>

using namespace std;

int main()
{
    // Iterating through a map
    map<string, int> NumberWords;

    NumberWords["ten"] = 10;
    NumberWords["twenty"] = 20;
    NumberWords["thirty"] = 30;

    map<string, int>::iterator loopy = NumberWords.begin();

    while (loopy != NumberWords.end())
    {
        cout << loopy->first << " ";
        cout << loopy->second << endl;
        loopy++;
    }

    // Iterating through a vector
    vector<string> Words;

    Words.push_back("hello");
    Words.push_back("there");
    Words.push_back("ladies");
    Words.push_back("and");
    Words.push_back("aliens");

    vector<string>::iterator vectorloop = Words.begin();

    while (vectorloop != Words.end())
    {
        cout << *vectorloop << endl;
        vectorloop++;
    }

    return 0;
}
```

When you compile and run this application, you see the following output:

```
ten 10
thirty 30
twenty 20
hello
there
ladies
and
aliens
```

When you create a `vector`, it allocates some space for the data you put in it. But after all that space gets filled up and `vector` is stuffed to the brim, `vector` will resize itself, adding more space. But in doing so, it uses the old memory-shuffle trick where it first allocates a bigger chunk of memory; then it copies the existing data into the beginning of that bigger chunk of memory, and finally it frees the original chunk of memory. Now, if you use the various iterator functions to home in on a certain item in `vector` (giving you a pointer to the item) — and you save that pointer — then, after `vector` reallocates itself, that pointer will no longer be valid! It will point to somewhere in the original memory block that's no longer being used. So be careful.

For example, suppose you have the following code to set up a `vector`

```
vector<int> test;
test.push_back(1);
test.push_back(2);
test.push_back(3);
```

and then you use an iterator to get to the beginning; from there you go to the second item in `vector`; then you print the address of the second item:

```
vector<int>::iterator i1 = test.begin();
i1++;
cout << i1 << endl;
```

Then you decide to add a whole bunch of items:

```
for (int loop = 0; loop < 5000; loop++)
{
    test.push_back(loop);
}
```

Now, if you once again use an iterator to get to the second item, and then print the address like so

```
vector<int>::iterator i2 = test.begin();
i2++;
cout << i2 << endl;
```

you will likely see a different number from the one you saw previously. If so, it means `vector` reallocated itself — which means, in turn, that the original pointer is no longer valid.

A map of pairs in your hand

When you iterate through map, you get back not just the value of each item nor do you get just the key of each item. Instead, you get back a pair of things — the key and the value together. These live inside an instance of a class called Pair. (Although, really, it's a template.) This pair instance has two member variables, first and second. The first member refers to the key in the pair, and the second member refers to the value in the pair. When you iterate through map, the iterator points to an instance of Pair, so you can grab the key by looking at first and the value by looking at second. But be careful, because Pair is the internal storage bin inside map. You're not looking at copies; you're looking at the actual data in map. If you change the data as in this code

```
while (loopy != NumberWords.end())
{
    loopy->second = loopy->second * 2;
    loopy++;
}
```

you will be changing the value stored in map — not a copy of it. So use caution!

The Great Container Showdown

In the sections that follow, we give a rundown of the containers available in the Standard Library. Different containers have different places in life. Some are tall, some are short — wait a minute, that's not right. They each have a different purpose; in the following sections, we show you where you can use each of them.

Associating and storing with a set

First things first. set is not a *set*. If you have any background in mathematics, you've likely come across the notion of a set. And in math, a set doesn't have an order to it. It's a group of items stored in, well, a set.

In the Standard Library, set has an order to it. However, like a math set, set doesn't allow duplicates. If you try to put an item in set that's already there, set will ignore your attempt to do so.

The Sets example shown in Listing 6-7 demonstrates how to use set.

Listing 6-7:   Using set to Look up Items

```cpp
#include <iostream>
#include <set>

using namespace std;

class Employee
{
public:
    string Nickname;
    string SocialSecurityNumber;

    Employee(string anickname, string asocial) :
        Nickname(anickname),
        SocialSecurityNumber(asocial) {}

    Employee() : Nickname(""), SocialSecurityNumber("") {}
};

bool operator < (const Employee& first,
const Employee& second)
{
    return first.SocialSecurityNumber <
        second.SocialSecurityNumber;
}

ostream& operator << (ostream &out, const Employee &emp)
{
    cout << "(" << emp.Nickname;
    cout << "," << emp.SocialSecurityNumber;
    cout << ")";
    return out;
}

int main()
{
    set<Employee> employees;

    Employee emp1("sparky", "123-22-8572");
    employees.insert(emp1);

    Employee emp2("buzz", "234-33-5784");
    employees.insert(emp2);

    Employee emp3("coollie", "123-22-8572");
    employees.insert(emp3);

    Employee emp4("sputz", "199-19-0000");
    employees.insert(emp4);

    // List the items
    set<Employee>::iterator iter = employees.begin();
    while (iter != employees.end())
    {
        cout << *iter << endl;
        iter++;
    }
```

(continued)

Listing 6-7 *(continued)*

```
// Find an item
cout << "Finding..." << endl;
Employee findemp("", "123-22-8572");

iter = employees.find(findemp);
cout << *iter << endl;

return 0;
}
```

When you compile and run this example, you see the following output:

```
(sparky,123-22-8572)
(sputz,199-19-0000)
(buzz,234-33-5784)
Finding...
(sparky,123-22-8572)
```

In Listing 6-7, we included an `Employee` class, along with a less-than function. The less-than function compares the `SocialSecurityNumber` member of two `Employee` instances. This results in two things:

✦ **Ordering:** The items in `set` will be ordered according to Social Security Number. This is not true with all containers, but it is the way a `set` works.

✦ **Duplicates:** If we try to add two employees with matching `SocialSecurityNumber` members (but the other members can be different), the second addition won't take. The `set` will ignore it.

You can see in this listing that we tried to add two employees with the same `SocialSecurityNumber` members:

```
Employee emp1("sparky", "123-22-8572");
employees.insert(emp1);
```

and

```
Employee emp3("coollie", "123-22-8572");
employees.insert(emp3);
```

Later, when we print all the items in `set`, we see only the one for `"sparky"`, not the one for `"coollie"`. `set` ignored the second employee.

Finding an item in `set` is interesting. Look at how we did it: We created an instance of `Employee`, and we filled in only the `SocialSecurityNumber` member, because that's the only member that the less-than function looks at. Then we called `find()`. But what did we get back? If you look at the function header, you will see that the `find()` function returns an iterator. But that seems silly. Why an iterator? We're not iterating, by cracky!

The reason we get back an iterator is because the iterator type is really a typedef for a pointer to an item inside set. Oh, okay; that makes sense, then: When we call find(), we get back a pointer to an item in set, even if its typename is iterator. And so, to access the item, we dereference the pointer.

In Listing 6-7, we did something handy: We created a function that lets us use our Employee instance with cout. We did this by overloading the insertion function. This function's header looks like this:

```
ostream& operator << (ostream &out, const Employee &emp) {
```

The first parameter represents cout, and the second is the item we're couting. And so, inside this function, we write to cout the individual members of the Employee. Not a problem.

Unionizing and intersecting sets

Everybody has an opinion on unionizing, but fortunately, we're not talking about workers' unions in this section. Instead, we're talking about sets and how you can a) combine two sets to get the union, or b) find the common elements to get the intersection.

When you #include <set>, you automatically get a couple of handy functions for finding the union and intersection of some sets.

Showdown: maps versus sets

And for the first showdown, we'd like to offer you a philosophical (yet practical!) discussion on the difference between map and set. map lets you store information based on a key, through which you can retrieve a value. Elsewhere in this chapter, we use an example where the key is an Employee instance and the value is a Salary instance. But with set, you can achieve something similar: In Listing 6-7, we could have had a single class containing both Employee and Salary information. And you can see in Listing 6-7 that we were able to look up the Employee instance based on nothing but a social security number. So in this sense, we created a map where the key is a social security number and the value is the rest of the employee information. Tricky, no? The fact is, you can often accomplish associations with set, as you can with map. But the advantage to set is that you need to store only one instance for each item, whereas with map, you must have two instances, both a key and a value. But the advantage to map is that you can use the nice bracket notation. The choice is yours.

---

set does not allow duplicates. A union of two sets is a set that consists of all the elements of the two sets combined, but without any duplicates. The intersection is also itself a set, and therefore it has no duplicates.

The Sets2 example in Listing 6-8 demonstrates how you can find the intersection and union of two sets.

Listing 6-8:   Finding an Intersection and a Union Is Easy!

```
#include <iostream>
#include <set>
#include <algorithm>

using namespace std;

void DumpClass(set<string> *myset)
{
    set<string>::iterator iter = myset->begin();

    while (iter != myset->end())
    {
        cout << *iter << endl;
        iter++;
    }
}

int main()
{
    set<string> EnglishClass;
    set<string> HistoryClass;

    EnglishClass.insert("Zeus");
    EnglishClass.insert("Magellan");
    EnglishClass.insert("Vulcan");
    EnglishClass.insert("Ulysses");
    EnglishClass.insert("Columbus");

    HistoryClass.insert("Vulcan");
    HistoryClass.insert("Ulysses");
    HistoryClass.insert("Ra");
    HistoryClass.insert("Odin");

    set<string> Union;
    set<string> Intersection;

    insert_iterator<set<string> >
        IntersectIterate(Intersection, Intersection.begin());

    insert_iterator<set<string> >
        UnionIterate(Union, Union.begin());

    set_intersection(EnglishClass.begin(),
        EnglishClass.end(),
        HistoryClass.begin(), HistoryClass.end(),
        IntersectIterate);
    cout << "===Intersection===" << endl;
    DumpClass(&Intersection);
```

```
    set_union(EnglishClass.begin(),
        EnglishClass.end(),
        HistoryClass.begin(), HistoryClass.end(),
        UnionIterate);
    cout << endl << "===Union===" << endl;
    DumpClass(&Union);

    return 0;
}
```

When you run the code in Listing 6-8, you see this output:

```
===Intersection===
Ulysses
Vulcan

===Union===
Columbus
Magellan
Odin
Ra
Ulysses
Vulcan
Zeus
```

But as you can see, something a little bizarre is in the code. Specifically, this part isn't exactly simple:

```
insert_iterator<set<string> >
    IntersectIterate(Intersection, Intersection.begin());
```

This is used in the call to set_intersection. First, recognize that this crazy code is a variable declaration. The first line is the type of the variable, a template called `insert_iterator`. The template parameter is the type of set, in this case set<string>.

The next line is the instance name, `IntersectIterate`, and the constructor requires two things: the `set` that will hold the intersection (called `Intersection`) and an iterator pointing to the beginning of the `Intersection` set (even though `set` is empty).

The variable that these two lines create is an iterator, and it is basically a helper object that some function can use to insert multiple items into a list. In this case, the function is set_intersection(). Now the set_intersection() function doesn't take as parameters the sets directly; instead, it takes the beginning and ending iterators of the two sets, along with the `IntersectIterate` thingamabob declared earlier. And you can see in Listing 6-8 that those are the five items we passed to the set_intersection() function.

Then, after calling the set_intersection() function, the `Intersection` object will contain the intersection of the two sets.

Book IV
Chapter 6

Programming with
the Standard Library

The set_union() function works precisely the same way, except it figures out the union of the two sets, not the intersection.

To use the set_intersection() and set_union() functions, you need to add #include <algorithm> to the top of your listing. This is one of the header files in the Standard Library.

If you find the code in Listing 6-8 particularly ugly, a slightly easier way to call set_intersection() where you don't need to directly create an instance of insert_iterator is available. It turns out there's a function that will do it for you. To use this function, you can remove the declaration for IntersectIterate and UnionIterate, and then instead call set_intersection() like this:

```
set_intersection(EnglishClass.begin(),
    EnglishClass.end(),
    HistoryClass.begin(), HistoryClass.end(),
    inserter(Intersection, Intersection.begin()));
```

The fourth line simply calls a function called inserter(), which creates an instance of insert_iterator for you. Then you can do the same for set_union():

```
set_union(EnglishClass.begin(),
    EnglishClass.end(),
    HistoryClass.begin(), HistoryClass.end(),
    inserter(Union, Union.begin()));
```

Listing with list

A list is a simple container similar to an array, except you can't access the members of list by using a bracket notation as you can in vector or with an array. You don't use list when you only need to access one item in the list; you use it when you plan to *traverse* through the list, item by item.

To add items to a list, use the list's push_front() member function or its push_back() member function. The push_front() function inserts the item in the beginning of the list, in front of all the others that are presently in the list. If you use push_front() several times in a row, the items will be in the reverse order from which you put them in. The push_back() function adds the item to the end of the list. So if you put items in a list by using push_back(), their order will be the same as the order in which you added them.

You can also insert an item before an existing item if you've placed a pointer to the item inside the list.

For operations where you need a pointer to an item in the list, you need to use an iterator. An *iterator* is simply a `typedef` for a pointer to an item in the list; however, it points to the item *in* the list, not the original item you added to the list. Remember, the containers hold copies. Thus, if you do an `insert` into a list and point to an original item, that item won't be a member of the list, and the `insert` won't work.

Although the `list` template includes an `insert()` function, this function has only very special uses. To use `insert()`, you must have a pointer to an item in the list — that is, you need to have an iterator. But how do you get this pointer? By traversing the list. It has no `find()` function, and so really the only time you would use the `insert()` function is if you're already working your way through the list. But if you do need to do an insert and you're willing to use iterators to move through the list to find the location where you want to put the new item, `insert()` will do the job.

The `Lists` example shown in Listing 6-9 demonstrates lists by using a duck metaphor. (They're all in a row.) In this example, we create a list, add our ducks to it, and then reverse it. Next, we create a second list and *splice* its members into the first list.

Listing 6-9: Handling Items in a List Template

```
#include <iostream>
#include <list>

using namespace std;

class Duck
{
public:
    string name;
    int weight;
    int length;
};

ostream& operator << (ostream &out, const Duck &duck)
{
    cout << "(" << duck.name;
    cout << "," << duck.weight;
    cout << "," << duck.length;
    cout << ")";
    return out;
}

void DumpDucks(list<Duck> *mylist)
{
    list<Duck>::iterator iter = mylist->begin();

    while (iter != mylist->end())
    {
```

(continued)

Listing 6-9 *(continued)*

```cpp
        cout << *iter << endl;
        iter++;
    }
}

list<Duck>::iterator MoveToPosition(list<Duck> *mylist, int pos)
{
    list<Duck>::iterator res = mylist->begin();

    for (int loop = 1; loop <= pos; loop++)
    {
        res++;
    }

    return res;
}

int main()
{
    list<Duck> Inarow;

    // Push some at the beginning
    Duck d1 = {"Jim", 20, 15}; // Braces notation!
    Inarow.push_front(d1);

    Duck d2 = {"Sally", 15, 12};
    Inarow.push_front(d2);

    // Push some at the end
    Duck d3 = {"Squakie", 18, 25};
    Inarow.push_front(d3);

    Duck d4 = {"Trumpeter", 19, 26};
    Inarow.push_front(d4);

    Duck d5 = {"Sneeky", 12, 13};
    Inarow.push_front(d5);

    // Display the ducks
    cout << "===========" << endl;
    DumpDucks(&Inarow);

    // Reverse
    Inarow.reverse();
    cout << "===========" << endl;
    DumpDucks(&Inarow);

    // Splice
    // Need another list for this
    list<Duck> extras;

    Duck d6 = {"Grumpy", 8, 8};
    extras.push_back(d6);

    Duck d7 = {"Sleepy", 8, 8};
    extras.push_back(d7);
```

```
        Duck d8 = {"Ornery", 8, 8};
        extras.push_back(d8);

        Duck d9 = {"Goofy", 8, 8};
        extras.push_back(d9);

        cout << "===========" << endl;
        cout << "extras:" << endl;
        DumpDucks(&extras);

        list<Duck>::iterator first =
            MoveToPosition(&extras, 1);

        list<Duck>::iterator last =
            MoveToPosition(&extras, 3);

        list<Duck>::iterator into =
            MoveToPosition(&Inarow, 2);

        Inarow.splice(into, extras, first, last);

        cout << "===========" << endl;
        cout << "extras after splice:" << endl;
        DumpDucks(&extras);

        cout << "===========" << endl;
        cout << "Inarow after splice:" << endl;
        DumpDucks(&Inarow);

        return 0;
    }
```

We made a function, MoveToPosition(), that moves to a position in the
list. This may seem counterproductive because the list template doesn't
allow random access. But we needed three iterators to perform the splice:
Two to target the start and end position of the second list (the one we're
splicing members from) and one to target the position in the first list where
we want to put the spliced members. For that last bit of business, we needed
the third iterator, which MoveToPosition() finds for us.

The function we created, MoveToPosition(), is a template function. But
when we called the function, we didn't provide the typename in angle
brackets. The compiler can figure out which class version we need; the
compiler knows that it can look at what we pass into the function as a
parameter and use its type to decide the template parameter. (Without the
template type in the function parameter, the compiler can't figure it out.)
Here's the application output:

```
===========
(Sneeky,12,13)
(Trumpeter,19,26)
(Squakie,18,25)
(Sally,15,12)
(Jim,20,15)
```

```
===========
(Jim,20,15)
(Sally,15,12)
(Squakie,18,25)
(Trumpeter,19,26)
(Sneeky,12,13)
===========
extras:
(Grumpy,8,8)
(Sleepy,8,8)
(Ornery,8,8)
(Goofy,8,8)
===========
extras after splice:
(Grumpy,8,8)
(Goofy,8,8)
===========
Inarow after splice:
(Jim,20,15)
(Sally,15,12)
(Sleepy,8,8)
(Ornery,8,8)
(Squakie,18,25)
(Trumpeter,19,26)
(Sneeky,12,13)
```

You can see the elements that were inside the two lists before and after the splice; the ducks moved from one list to another.

When you specify the positions for the splice operation, the splice includes the start position *up to but not including* the ending position. Listing 6-9 shows this: We spliced from position 1 to 3 in the second list (`extras`). But we got the ducks from positions 1 and 2 because the code spliced position 1 up to but not including 3 — which is 2.

Showdown: lists versus vectors

With a list, you do not have *random access* to the list, which is a fancy-schmancy way of saying that you can't drop into the middle of the list and look at whatever item is stored there (as you can with a vector). If you want to look at the items in the list, you must either start at the beginning or the end and work your way through it one by one. But with a vector, you can refer to any element by using brackets, as in `MyVector[3]`. This may seem like a disadvantage for the list, but the ANSI document claims that "many algorithms only need sequential access anyway." We suppose that there are times when you don't need to drop into the middle of an array, and then a list might do. But lists have definite advantages. The list template allows you to splice together multiple lists, and it has good support for sorting the list, for splicing members out of one list and into another, and for merging multiple lists.

Stacking the deque

A deque (pronounced "deck") container is a sequential list of items like vector and list. Like vectors and unlike lists, deques allow bracket notation for *random access*. Unlike vector, deque lets you *push* (insert) items at the beginning and *pop* (remove) items off the beginning. To create a deque that holds integers, do something like this:

```
deque<int> mydek;
mydek.push_front(10);
mydek.push_front(20);
mydek.push_front(30);
mydek.push_back(40);
mydek.push_back(50);
mydek.push_back(60);
```

Then you can loop through the deque, accessing its members with a bracket, as if it's an array:

```
int loop;
for (loop = 0; loop < mydek.size(); loop++)
{
    cout << mydek[loop] << endl;
}
```

You can also grab items off the front or back of the deque. Here's an example from the front:

```
while (mydek.size() > 0)
{
    cout << mydek.front() << endl;
    mydek.pop_front();
}
```

Two functions show up here, front() and pop_front(). The front() function returns a reference to the item at the front of the deque. The pop_front() function removes the item that's at the front of the deque.

Waiting in line with stacks and queues

Two common programming data structures are in the Standard Library:

✦ **Stack:** You put items on top of a stack one by one — and you only take items off the stack one by one, and only off the top. You can add several items, one after the other, before taking an item off the top. This process is sometimes called a First In Last Out (FILO) algorithm.

✦ **Queue:** A queue is like waiting in line at the post office (some people call such a line a *queue*): The line gets longer and longer as people arrive; each new person goes to the back of the line. But people leave only by the front of the line. The queue data structure is like that: You add data at the back of the queue, and take data off one-by-one at the front of the queue. Like the stack, the queue also has an alternate name: it's a First In First Out (FIFO) algorithm.

To use the Standard Library to make a stack, you can use a `deque`, a `list`, or a `vector` as the underlying storage bin. Then you declare the stack, as in the following example:

```
stack<int, vector<int> > MyStack;
```

Or you can optionally use the default, which is queue:

```
stack<int> MyStack;
```

For a queue, you can't use `vector` because `vectors` don't include operations for dealing with a front. So, for that situation, you can use either `deque` or `list`. For example, here's a line of code that uses `list`:

```
queue<int, list<int> > MyQueue;
```

Or here's a line of code that uses `deque` by default:

```
queue<int> MyQueue;
```

You normally perform three operations with a stack and a queue:

✦ **push:** When you add an item to a stack or queue, you *push* the item. This puts the item on top of the stack or at the back of the queue.

✦ **peek:** When you look at the top item of the stack or the front of the queue, you *peek*. The peek operation doesn't remove the item, however.

✦ **pop:** When you remove an item from a stack or from the front of the queue, you pop it off. For some libraries, this gives you the item. For the Standard Library, it removes the item. To use an item off the top or front of the stack or queue, first you peek at it and then you pop it off.

Showdown: deques versus vectors

If you go online to any discussion board and use a search phrase like *C++ deque vector*, you will see a lot of discussion, arguments, and confusion between when to use `deque` and when to use `vector`. To know which to use when, you need to understand the differences between the two. Under the hood, `vector` usually stores all its data in a regular old array, making it easy to directly access the members. But that also means that, to insert items, `vector` must slide everything over to make room for the inserted items. `deque`, however, does not use the *contiguous* approach that `vector` does. Inserting is then easier for it because it doesn't need to shuffle things around. Also, `deque` doesn't have to *regrow* (add new elements) itself if it runs out of space, whereas `vector` does. And finally, `deque` includes a `push_front()` member function that allows you to easily add an item at the beginning. The `vector` template does not include this member.

In the Standard Library, for peeking at the front of a queue, you call the front() member function. For a stack, you call the top() member function.

For pushing and popping, the Standard Library uses these terms. The queue and stack each include a push() function and a pop() function. The StackAndQueue example shown in Listing 6-10 demonstrates both a stack and a queue.

Listing 6-10:   Creating a Stack and a Queue

```
#include <iostream>
#include <stack>
#include <queue>

using namespace std;

void StackDemo()
{
    cout << "===Stack Demo===" << endl;
    stack<int, vector<int> > MyStack;

    // Remember the space between the > >
    MyStack.push(5);
    MyStack.push(10);
    MyStack.push(15);
    MyStack.push(20);
    cout << MyStack.top() << endl;

    MyStack.pop();
    cout << MyStack.top() << endl;

    MyStack.pop();
    MyStack.push(40);
    cout << MyStack.top() << endl;

    MyStack.pop();
}

void QueueDemo()
{
    cout << "===Queue Demo===" << endl;
    queue<int> MyQueue;

    // No container specified in the queue, so it
    // uses deque by default. The same goes for stack.
    MyQueue.push(5);
    MyQueue.push(10);
    MyQueue.push(15);
    cout << MyQueue.front() << endl;

    MyQueue.pop();
    cout << MyQueue.front() << endl;

    MyQueue.pop();
    MyQueue.push(40);
    cout << MyQueue.front() << endl;
```

**Book IV
Chapter 6**

**Programming with
the Standard Library**

(continued)

Listing 6-10 *(continued)*

```
    MyQueue.pop();
}

int main()
{
    StackDemo();
    QueueDemo();
    return 0;
}
```

When you specify a container to use inside the stack or queue, remember to put a space between the closing angle brackets. Otherwise the compiler reads it as a single insertion operator, >>, and gets confused. Here is the output from this example:

```
===Stack Demo===
20
15
40
===Queue Demo===
5
10
15
```

Copying Containers

Structures are easy to copy when class libraries are well designed. The Standard Library is that well designed. Each container class contains both a *copy constructor* and an *equal operator.* To copy a container, you either set one equal to the other or pass the first container into the constructor of the second (which copies the first into the second). The CopyContainer example shown in Listing 6-11 demonstrates how to perform this task.

Listing 6-11:   Copying Containers Couldn't Be Easier

```
#include <iostream>
#include <map>

using namespace std;

class Scrumptious
{
public:
    string Dessert;
};

bool operator < (const Scrumptious & first,
const Scrumptious & second)
{
```

```
        return first.Dessert < second.Dessert;
}

class Nutrition
{
public:
    int VitaminC;
    int Potassium;
};

int main()
{
    map<Scrumptious, Nutrition> ItsGoodForMe;

    Scrumptious ap = {"Apple Pie"}; // Braces notation!
    Nutrition apn = {7249, 9722};

    Scrumptious ic = {"Ice Cream"};
    Nutrition icn = {2459, 19754};

    Scrumptious cc = {"Chocolate Cake"};
    Nutrition ccn = {9653, 24905};

    Scrumptious ms = {"Milk Shake"};
    Nutrition msn = {46022, 5425};

    ItsGoodForMe[ap] = apn;
    ItsGoodForMe[ic] = icn;
    ItsGoodForMe[cc] = ccn;
    ItsGoodForMe[ms] = msn;

    map<Scrumptious,Nutrition> Duplicate = ItsGoodForMe;
    map<Scrumptious,Nutrition> AnotherDuplicate(ItsGoodForMe);

    ItsGoodForMe[ap].Potassium = 20;
    cout << ItsGoodForMe[ap].Potassium << endl;
    cout << Duplicate[ap].Potassium << endl;
    cout << AnotherDuplicate[ap].Potassium << endl;

    return 0;
}
```

You can see in this listing that we created two classes, `Scrumptious` and `Nutrition`. We then created a `map` called `ItsGoodForMe` that associates `Scrumptious` instances with `Nutrition` instances.

We copied `map` twice, using both an equals sign and a copy constructor:

```
map<Scrumptious,Nutrition> Duplicate = ItsGoodForMe;
map<Scrumptious,Nutrition> AnotherDuplicate(ItsGoodForMe);
```

And that was it! We then changed one of the elements in the original `map`, to see what would happen. Then we printed that element, as well as the corresponding element in the two copies. Here's the output:

```
20
9722
9722
```

Yep, they're different: This implies that the maps each have their own copies of the instances — that there's no sharing of instances between the maps.

Containers hold copies, not originals. That's true when you copy containers, too. If you put a structure in a container and copy the container, the latter container has its own copy of the structure. To change the structure, you must change all copies of it. The way around this is to put pointers inside the containers. Then each container has its own copy of the pointer, but all these pointers point to the same one-and-only object.

Creating and Using Dynamic Arrays

Sometimes when you don't know the array size you need until run time. The default arrays provided with C++ rely on static sizes. In other words, you need to know what size array you need at the time you write the code. Unfortunately, the real world is dynamic — it changes. The earlier sections of this chapter discussed a number of array alternatives, such as stacks, queues, and deques. However, these solutions all require that you use a library. They also tend to increase the memory requirements of your application and slow it down as well. You have another alternative in the form of dynamic arrays. The following sections describe dynamic arrays and show how to use them.

Configuring the IDE

Dynamic arrays aren't usable in earlier versions of C++. You need to reconfigure Code::Blocks to provide the support required to use them effectively. This means adding support for C++ 11 extensions to the language. To do this, choose Project➪Build Options. You see the Project Build Options dialog box. Check the Have G++ Follow the C++ 11 ISO C++ Language Standard check box (as shown in Figure 6-1) and then click OK. Your IDE will now allow you to use newer language features required to work with dynamic arrays and many other new extensions.

Declaring a dynamic array

A dynamic array relies on the *heap*, the common area of memory that your application allocates for the different functions in your application to use. (See the "Heaping and Stacking the Variables" section of Book 1 Chapter 7 for more details.) You create a pointer to a variable of the correct type and then allocate memory for the resulting array. The functionality for performing this task is found in the new.h file, so you need to include it as part of your application. The DynamicArray example shown in Listing 6-12 demonstrates the use of a dynamic array.

Figure 6-1:
Configure
Code::Blocks
to allow
use of new
language
features.

Listing 6-12:   Creating and Using Dynamic Arrays

```cpp
#include <iostream>
#include <new>

using namespace std;

int main()
{
    int HowMany;
    int* DynArray;

    cout << "How many numbers would you like?" << endl;
    cin >> HowMany;

    DynArray = new (nothrow) int[HowMany];
    if (DynArray == nullptr)
        cout << "Error: Could not allocate memory!";
    else
    {
        for(int i = 0; i < HowMany; i++)
            DynArray[i] = i;

        cout << "Displaying entries:" << endl;
        for (int i = 0; i < HowMany; i++)
            cout << DynArray[i] << endl;

        delete[] DynArray;
    }
    return 0;
}
```

The example begins by creating variables to hold the number of array elements and the array itself, which is a pointer to an array of `int` elements. The application asks you how many array elements to create. It then uses the `new` operator to create the dynamic array, `DynArray`. Notice the technique used to do this. The `new` operator is followed by `(nothrow)`. What this tells the application is that if there isn't enough memory to create the array, to return a `nullptr` value, which is simply a pointer that doesn't point to anything.

Normally, the application would display an incomprehensible error message that only geeks could love if there wasn't enough memory. Using the `(nothrow)` approach gives you the opportunity to handle the error differently. The application handles the error by displaying a human-readable error message if `DynArray == nullptr`.

You work with a dynamic array just as you do any other array. The example shows how to fill the array with data and to display the data on screen. The array has the same capabilities, advantages, and disadvantages of any other array. However, when you get done using the array, you need to use the `delete[]` operator to delete the dynamic array and free the memory it uses for some other purpose. The output from this example looks like this if you request four array elements:

```
How many numbers would you like?
4
Displaying entries:
0
1
2
3
```

Working with Unordered Data

Creating data that has a particular order is appealing because it's a) easier to search and b) certain tasks, such as removing old elements, are easier. However, creating an ordered set of information is also problematic because you need to spend time keeping it in order. Newer versions of C++ provide access to an unordered set that is both searchable and easy to maintain. It has the advantage of adding the data in any order in which it comes. There is no overhead associated with trying to keep the data in a particular order. The following sections provide an overview of using unordered data.

Using std::unordered_set to create an unordered set

Like the other containers discussed in this chapter, an `unordered_set` provides a particular method for storing data in a manner that makes it easy to access later. In this case, you have access to functions that `insert()` and `erase()` elements from the container. A special function, `emplace()` makes it possible to add new elements only if the element doesn't exist. Otherwise the unordered set will allow as many duplicates as you want (and you can easily count them using `count()`). It's also possible to use the `find()` function to track down elements that you want. Special functions tell you when you're at the beginning or end of the set.

The `unordered_set` container is found in the Standard Library. However, you need to enable C++ 11 extensions in the IDE in order to use them. The "Configuring the IDE" section of this chapter describes how to configure Code::Blocks to provide the required support.

Manipulating unordered sets

The easiest way to see how an unordered set works is to create one. The `UnorderedSet` example shown in Listing 6-13 demonstrates how to use the various `unordered_set` features to maintain a listing of colors.

Listing 6-13:   Creating and Using Dynamic Arrays

```
#include <iostream>
#include <unordered_set>

using namespace std;

int main()
{
    unordered_set<string> Colors;

    Colors.insert("Red");
    Colors.insert("Green");
    Colors.insert("Blue");

    if(Colors.find("Red") != Colors.end())
        cout << "Found Red!" << endl;
    else
        cout << "Red Missing!" << endl;

    auto ReturnValue = Colors.emplace("Red");
    if(!ReturnValue.second)
        cout << "Red is Already in Set!" << endl;
    else
        cout << "Red Added to Set!" << endl;

    cout << "There are " << Colors.count("Red")
        << " Red entries." << endl;

    ReturnValue = Colors.emplace("Orange");
    if(!ReturnValue.second)
        cout << "Orange is Already in Set!" << endl;
    else
        cout << "Orange Added to Set!" << endl;

    Colors.erase("Red");
```

(continued)

Listing 6-13 *(continued)*

```
    if(Colors.find("Red") != Colors.end())
        cout << "Found Red!" << endl;
    else
        cout << "Red Missing!" << endl;

    return 0;
}
```

The example begins by creating a new `unordered_set`, `Colors`. Notice that this is a template, so you need to provide a type for the information the set will hold It uses the `insert()` function to add three colors to the set.

The `find()` function makes it possible to look for a particular value in the set. When the value is missing, the `end()` function returns `true`, which means that the current position within the set is at the end.

This example uses the `auto` data type. It's a type you can use when you don't know what type to assign to a variable. `Return` is used to detect when a value that you want to add to the set using `emplace()` already exists. If the value already exists, then `unordered_set` refuses to add it when you call `emplace()`. On the other hand, if you call `insert()`, `unordered_set` will add duplicate entries.

To remove entries from a set, you call `erase()` with the value you want to remove. In this case, the example removes the color Red. It then searches for Red using `find()`. As you might expect, Red isn't found this time. The output from this example is as follows:

```
Found Red!
Red is Already in Set!
There are 1 Red entries.
Orange Added to Set!
Red Missing!
```

Chapter 7: Working with Lambda Expressions

In This Chapter

✔ Considering the problem that lambda expressions solve

✔ Writing your first lambda expression

✔ Using lambda expressions in real-world programming

The previous chapters in this book focus on the Unified Modeling Language (UML) and how you use it to better model applications. Chapter 6 moves on to design patterns, which actually help you implement a model. This chapter takes the process one step further by looking at *lambda expressions* — an elegant method of turning a model into a math expression. Let's say that you need to calculate the number of widgets produced in an hour before you can print out the value. Adding the equation directly to the existing code might look bulky, but adding it as a separate function makes the code hard to read. Lambda expressions provide a middle ground where you can define the calculation in an easy-to-read manner without creating a separate function.

Unlike many of the odd terms you've encountered so far in the book, we programmers have nothing to do with the term *lambda expression* — you can blame it on the mathematicians, for once! It's actually a kind of calculus that was introduced by Alonzo Church in the 1930s and it's used as short-hand for complex equations. The equations are *anonymous* — that is, they aren't given a name.

For once, the programming version of something found in math is actually easier to understand and use than what Alonzo Church created. We'll show you how to use lambda expressions to define simple functions that you only need to use in one place. They don't need a name because you won't use them again. It's sort of a disposable function and they come in really handy for those times when you need to do something simple, but you want to separate it from the main function. Think of lambda expressions as a kind of function within a function (a nested function).

Lambda expressions aren't usable as part of earlier versions of C++. In order to work with most of the examples in this chapter, you must configure the project to use C++ 11. The "Configuring the IDE" section of Book IV, Chapter 6 tells you how to perform this task. If you don't perform the required configuration, you see an error message when you attempt to compile the example.

Creating More Readable and Concise C++ Code

One of the advantages of using C++ is that you can create concise code that is easy to read. Because you can see more of the code in one glance, C++ is often easier to understand as well because you don't have to scroll the editor page to see the entire solution to a particular problem. However, there are some types of C++ problems that did require a rather verbose solution in earlier versions of C++. Starting with C++ 11, developers have a new technique for solving these problems in ways that bring C++ code back to its concise roots.

You can solve a number of C++ development problems using lambda expressions, but the typical problem is one of making the code more concise and easier to read. There is absolutely nothing wrong with the `Problem` example shown in Listing 7-1 — it works just fine as shown.

Listing 7-1: Defining a Problem Solved by Lambda Expressions

```cpp
#include <iostream>
#include <algorithm>
#include <vector>

using namespace std;

class MyFunctor
{
public:
    void operator()(int x)
    {
        cout << x << endl;
    }
};

void ProcessVector(vector<int>& vect)
{
    MyFunctor Func;
    for_each(vect.begin(), vect.end(), Func);
}

int main()
{
    vector<int> MyVector;
    MyVector.push_back(1);
    MyVector.push_back(2);
    MyVector.push_back(3);
    MyVector.push_back(4);

    ProcessVector(MyVector);
}
```

In this case, the example creates a `vector`, `MyVector`, and populates it with data. It then calls `ProcessVector()` to perform a task with the data in the vector.

The call to `ProcessVector()` creates a *functor* — a special class of object that acts as if it's a function — named `Func`. This is an extremely useful kind of a class that you explore further in the "Functors" section of Book VI, Chapter 1. For now, all you need to know is that it's a special kind of a class that acts like a function.

The `for_each()` algorithm (demonstrated fully in the "Creating Improved Loops Using Foreach" section of Book VI, Chapter 5) is part of the standard library. It processes each element in `vect`, the vector passed to `ProcessVector()`, starting at the first element (defined by `vect.begin()`) and ending with the last element (defined by `vect.end()`) using `Func`.

When you look at `MyFunctor`, you see a definition for an `operator` that requires a single `int` input, `x`. All that the code does is output `x` to the console. So you see the following output from this example.

```
1
2
3
4
```

Defining the Essential Lambda Expression

The intent of a lambda expression is to make code shorter and easier to read. It creates a new method for presenting code. However, it doesn't actually create a new C++ capability. What you're doing is using the same techniques, but in a different manner than before. The following sections help you create your first lambda expressions so that you get a better idea of precisely how they work.

Defining the parts of a lambda expression

The example in the previous section is perfectly usable. However, the functor is only used one time in the example. This situation happens relatively often and it causes confusion for developers who need to work through the resulting code. A lambda expression makes it possible to incorporate the functor as part of the `for_each()` algorithm, as shown in the `Solution` example in Listing 7-2.

Listing 7-2:   Defining the Lambda Expression Solution

```
#include <iostream>
#include <algorithm>
#include <vector>

using namespace std;

void ProcessVector(vector<int>& vect)
{
    for_each(vect.begin(), vect.end(), [](int x){cout << x << endl;});
}

int main()
{
    vector<int> MyVector;
    MyVector.push_back(1);
    MyVector.push_back(2);
    MyVector.push_back(3);
    MyVector.push_back(4);

    ProcessVector(MyVector);
}
```

As you can see, using the lambda version of the example is much shorter and easier to understand because you no longer require a separate class to process the data in the `for_each()` algorithm. A lambda expression always appears like this:

```
[](int x){cout << x << endl;}
```

That pair of square brackets ([]), followed by any input arguments in parenthesis, always needs to be at the beginning of a lambda expression; the code you want to execute — set between a pair of curly braces ({}) — always takes up the rear. Like any function, a lambda expression can accept multiple input variables and provide a return value. The beginning square brackets are called the *capture clause* and you see it used later in the chapter. Lambda expressions can include other features — including the ones you see demonstrated in the "Developing with Lambda Expressions" section of the chapter — but every lambda expression includes the following three features:

✦ Capture clause in square brackets

✦ Argument list in parenthesis

✦ Executable code in curly braces

Relying on compiler detection of return type

Lambda expressions can process information and present it directly, or provide the information as part of a return type. Simple lambda expressions can return information without telling the compiler much about it because the compiler can automatically detect the return type. The ReturnType01 example in Listing 7-3 demonstrates how you would implement a lambda expression that returns data that is automatically detected by the compiler.

Listing 7-3: Using a Compiler Detected Return Type

```
#include <iostream>
#include <algorithm>
#include <vector>

using namespace std;

void ProcessVector(vector<int>& vect)
{
    vector<bool> Result;
    Result.resize(vect.size());

    transform(vect.begin(), vect.end(), Result.begin(),
              [](int x){return x > 3;});

    cout.setf(ios::boolalpha);
    for_each(Result.begin(), Result.end(),
             [](bool x){cout << x << endl;});
}

int main()
{
    vector<int> MyVector;
    MyVector.push_back(1);
    MyVector.push_back(2);
    MyVector.push_back(3);
    MyVector.push_back(4);

    ProcessVector(MyVector);
}
```

As in the previous example, this example (and most of the examples that follow) creates a vector<int> named MyVector, fill it with information, and pass it to ProcessVector(). ProcessVector() receives the data as vect and processes it one element at a time.

ProcessVector() begins by creating a vector<bool> named Result to receive the results of the data processing. In this case, the processing occurs in a transform() function that receives the beginning and ending position of vect, along with the beginning position of Result and a lambda expression. In order for the transform() to work, the lambda expression must return a value that defines precisely how the transformation process works. In this case, the process is a simple comparison of the input value, x, with the number 3.

When the `transform()` is complete, `Result` contains a list of `bool` values that indicate whether the individual numbers in `vect` are greater than 3. To see these values as true or false text output, rather than numbers, you need to call `cout.setf(ios::boolalpha)`. The code then uses a `for_each()` loop to display the individual values in `Result`. Here is the output you see when you run this example.

```
false
false
false
true
```

Given that the input values in `vect` are 1, 2, 3, and 4, it's true that the last element of `vect`, 4, is greater than the number 3. Using a `transform()` with a lambda expression, as shown here, is a great way to reduce the code required to perform various kind of bulk comparisons (among other transformation-specific tasks).

Using a specific return type

Sometimes a lambda expression is complex enough that the compiler can't figure out what return type to use. Often you see an error message during the compilation process when this occurs. Fortunately, it's easy to fix this problem by simply telling the compiler what sort of return type to expect. The `ReturnType02` example shown in Listing 7-4 demonstrates how to perform this task.

Listing 7-4:   Using a Specific Return Type

```
#include <iostream>
#include <algorithm>
#include <vector>

using namespace std;

void ProcessVector(vector<int>& vect)
{
    vector<bool> Result;
    Result.resize(vect.size());

    transform(vect.begin(), vect.end(), Result.begin(),
            [](int x)->bool{return x > 3;});

    cout.setf(ios::boolalpha);
    for_each(Result.begin(), Result.end(),
            [](bool x){cout << x << endl;});
}
```

```
int main()
{
    vector<int> MyVector;
    MyVector.push_back(1);
    MyVector.push_back(2);
    MyVector.push_back(3);
    MyVector.push_back(4);

    ProcessVector(MyVector);
}
```

The essential code, application flow, and output are the same as ReturnType01. However, notice that this example changes the lambda expression to include a return type. Whenever you want to define a return type for a lambda expression, add the arrow operator and the return type, which is `bool` in this case.

There are other reasons to use a specific return type. In some cases, providing a specific return type allows the compiler to better optimize your code so that you obtain better performance from your application. Using this approach can be quite helpful when you suspect your lambda expression is going to be processing a considerable amount of data. In this case, you won't see any difference in application speed between ReturnType01 and ReturnType02 because the data set is so small.

Using the auto keyword

The `auto` keyword is a new feature, added since C++ 11. What this keyword does is provide a shortcut method for defining the type of a variable, no matter what the variable may ultimately contain. Essentially, you use the `auto` keyword to save typing time — rather than type the full text of a lambda expression each time you need it, you simply type the name of the variable that contains the lambda expression.

When you use the `auto` keyword, you're asking the compiler to determine the type of a variable based on how that variable is used. This means that it must be possible to determine the type of the variable by examining the context in which it is used. When you use the `auto` keyword, these outcomes are possible:

✦ The compiler will determine the type automatically and assign it to the variable.

✦ The variable will receive a correct type, but not the type that you had originally envisioned (such as assigning a `long` where an `int` might serve better).

✦ Two or more types are possible, which means that the compiler will display an error message saying it can't figure out the ambiguous assignment.

✦ Determination of the variable type is impossible given the context and you must specifically assign a type to the variable.

The auto keyword is used in all sorts of situations and you see it pop up several times in the book. The ReturnType03 example shown in Listing 7-5 demonstrates how you can use the auto keyword with lambda expressions to store the associated code and make it easier to access within the application.

Listing 7-5:   Using the Auto Keyword to Automate the Return Type

```
#include <iostream>
#include <algorithm>
#include <vector>

using namespace std;

void ProcessVector(vector<int>& vect)
{
    vector<bool> Result;
    Result.resize(vect.size());

    auto Transformer = [](int x){return x > 3;};
    transform(vect.begin(), vect.end(), Result.begin(),
            Transformer);

    cout.setf(ios::boolalpha);
    auto DoPrint = [](bool x){cout << x << endl;};
    for_each(Result.begin(), Result.end(),
            DoPrint);
}

int main()
{
    vector<int> MyVector;
    MyVector.push_back(1);
    MyVector.push_back(2);
    MyVector.push_back(3);
    MyVector.push_back(4);

    ProcessVector(MyVector);
}
```

The overall effect of this application is the same as ReturnType01 shown in Listing 7-3. The code uses a transform() to determine the truth value of whether a value in vect is greater than 3. The output is precisely the same as well. The big difference is that the lambda expression is placed within a variable that you can then use as needed. As a result, the transform() code is made simpler and easier to read (albeit not quite as short).

Using the `auto` keyword with other types

The `auto` keyword can be used in any situation where you want to define the type of a variable. For example, you could use it in a `for` loop should you wish to do so, as shown in the `AutoKeyword` example:

```
for (auto i = 0; i < 8; i++)
    cout << i << endl;
```

Depending on your compiler, when you view `i` in the debugger, you find that the compiler has made it an `int` — the same type you would have used when choosing the type manually. Of course, you probably won't use the `auto` keyword in this manner because typing `int` is actually shorter than typing `auto`. Even so, you can use `auto` anywhere the compiler can determine the type of a variable based on the variable's context. Even something as simple as this following code (also part of the `AutoKeyword` example) works just fine.

```
auto Greeting = "Hello";
cout << Greeting << endl;
```

In this case, the compiler will create a `const char *` variable for you. However, there is a problem with this particular bit of code. If you were to assume that the compiler has created a `string` instead, you might write code like this:

```
auto Greeting = "Hello";
cout << Greeting.length() << endl;
```

Making the wrong assumption means the code won't compile. You receive an error message stating, `error: request for member 'length' in 'Greeting', which is of non-class type 'const char*'`. To obtain the `string` that you need, you must specifically declare the variable as type `string`.

Sometimes you also get the wrong type in situations that aren't quite so clear. For example, the following code should rely on a `long long` data type.

```
auto LargeNumber = 15;
LargeNumber += 2147483647;
cout << LargeNumber << endl;
```

When you run the code, you get an answer of `-2147483634`, which is clearly wrong. The problem here is that the compiler assumes you want an `int` variable. To obtain the `long long` variable you need, you must specifically declare the variable as type `long long`. When you run the example using a `long long` variable, you get the correct output of `2147483662`.

Developing Applications with Lambda Expressions

The previous section of the chapter acquaints you with the essentials of working with lambda expressions. There are a number of ways in which you can expand a lambda expression to meet specific needs. The following sections show how to use some of the more common methods.

Creating lambda expressions with multiple inputs

Some lambda expressions require that you provide multiple inputs. The two most common examples are checks for equality and sorting algorithms. However, any instance where you must compare one value to another in order to create the desired output will usually require two inputs as a minimum. The `MultiInput` example in Listing 7-6 performs an equality check between the content of a vector and an array.

Listing 7-6: Providing Multiple Input Values

```
#include <iostream>
#include <algorithm>
#include <vector>

using namespace std;

void CompareRanges(vector<int>& vect, int values[])
{
    auto Result =
        equal(vect.begin(), vect.end(), values,
            [](int x, int y){return x==y;});

    cout.setf(ios::boolalpha);
    cout << "The values are equal: " << Result << endl;
}

int main()
{
    vector<int> MyVector;
    MyVector.push_back(1);
    MyVector.push_back(2);
    MyVector.push_back(3);
    MyVector.push_back(4);

    int MyInts[] = {1, 2, 3, 4};

    CompareRanges(MyVector, MyInts);
}
```

The example begins by creating the vector and array. It then calls `Compare Ranges()` and supplies both items as input.

The `CompareRanges()` function relies on the `equal()` algorithm to determine whether the two objects contain the same values. The four inputs determine the beginning and ending of the vector comparison range, the list of values to compare it against, and a lambda expression to define the comparison method.

Notice that the lambda expression takes two parameters in this case, `x` and `y`, both of which are `int` values. The `equal()` algorithm acts somewhat like a `for_each()` algorithm in that it checks the values one at a time. The lambda expression must return a Boolean value that expresses whether the two inputs are equal. When you run this example, you see the following output.

```
The values are equal: true
```

Try changing one value in either the vector or the array. You see that the output now changes to `false`.

Working with the capture clause

In some cases, you can't access a value you need in a lambda expression by passing it as a parameter. The value is available as part of the function, but the lambda expression can't see it because it's essentially another function. The way to overcome this problem is to use the *capture clause* to access and use (that is, capture) the value you need. Once captured, the lambda expression can access the value as if it were passed as a parameter. The `Capture` example in Listing 7-7 shows how to capture and use a value within a lambda expression.

Listing 7-7:   Using the Capture Clause

```
#include <iostream>
#include <algorithm>
#include <vector>

using namespace std;

void ProcessVector(vector<int>& vect, int Exclude)
{
    for_each(vect.begin(), vect.end(),
            [Exclude](int x)
            {
                if ((int)x != Exclude)
                    cout << x << endl;
            });
}

int main()
{
    vector<int> MyVector;
    MyVector.push_back(1);
    MyVector.push_back(2);
    MyVector.push_back(3);
    MyVector.push_back(4);

    ProcessVector(MyVector, 3);
}
```

The caller provides both `vect` and `Exclude` as parameters to `Process Vector()`. However, only the values in `vect` are available to the lambda expression unless the lambda expression captures the value within the square brackets at the beginning of the lambda expression as shown.

Because `Exclude` appears within the square brackets, the lambda expression can use it to perform the comparison. When you run this example, you see the following output:

```
1
2
4
```

Notice that the value of 3 is excluded from the output because this is the value passed as part of the call to `ProcessVector()`. When you provide a different value, a different number is removed from the output. The main purpose of the capture clause is to provide a means of passing additional information to the lambda expression to aid in processing the data it receives.

Sorting data using a lambda expression

One of the most common tasks that applications must perform before presenting data to the user is placing it in some sort of sorted order. Although a computer can easily locate a specific value in a long list of values, even if that list isn't sorted, users are quite different. The longer the list, the more important it becomes to present the information in a particular order.

At one time, developers had to create their own sorting algorithms for every need; the topic of sorting received more than a little emphasis in computer science classes. Today, however, a developer only needs to worry about sorting algorithms when a specific kind of sort is needed. The `sort()` algorithm used by itself will perform most generic sorting tasks. However, you still need a custom sorting method to perform specialized sorts, such as when you're working with a structure or complex data.

For the sake of simplicity, it's easiest to review sorting using a simple vector. The `Sorting` example in Listing 7-8 performs both a standard sort and a custom sort on the same vector.

Listing 7-8:   Sorting Data Using a Lambda Expression

```cpp
#include <iostream>
#include <algorithm>
#include <vector>

using namespace std;

void StandardSort(vector<int>& vect)
{
    sort(vect.begin(), vect.end());
    cout << "Using the Standard Sort" << endl;
    for_each(vect.begin(), vect.end(), [](int x){cout << x << endl;});
```

```
}

void ProcessVector(vector<int>& vect)
{
    sort(vect.begin(), vect.end(), [](int S1, int S2){return S1 < S2;});
    cout << "Using a Custom Sort" << endl;
    for_each(vect.begin(), vect.end(), [](int x){cout << x << endl;});
}

int main()
{
    vector<int> MyVector;
    MyVector.push_back(11);
    MyVector.push_back(2);
    MyVector.push_back(33);
    MyVector.push_back(4);

    StandardSort(MyVector);
    ProcessVector(MyVector);
}
```

Look at the StandardSort() function first. When an application calls sort(), it places the resulting data in the same object that it received. At first, vect contains unsorted data. However, after the call to sort(), the data is sorted using a generic sorting method. Notice that you don't need a lambda expression to perform a generic sort.

The ProcessVector() function looks almost the same as StandardSort(). The difference is that this function relies on a lambda expression to perform a custom sort. Sorting is a process of comparing one value to another, so the lambda expression receives two inputs, S1 and S2. By knowing which value is greater, sort() can determine where to place the two values in the list.

The result is the same in both cases. Here is what you can expect to see from the example as written.

```
Using the Standard Sort
2
4
11
33
Using a Custom Sort
2
4
11
33
```

Of course, this might lead you to believe that vect remains sorted. As an experiment, change return S1 < S2 to read return S1 > S2. Try the example again and you see that the lambda expression approach lets you present the data in reverse order.

```
Using the Standard Sort
2
4
11
33
Using a Custom Sort
33
11
4
2
```

Specifying that the lambda expression throws exceptions

An *exception* is an indicator of an unexpected occurrence within an application. The occurrence could be due to an error, such as someone sending a function an incorrect value. However, the occurrence could just as easily be due to a loss of a network connection or a full disk drive. The important consideration here is that the occurrence is unexpected — that the application couldn't automatically check for the potential problem and proactively compensate for it.

The process of indicating the unexpected occurrence is called *throwing an exception*. Lambda expressions can throw any sort of exception required to indicate an error condition. However, there are methods of indicating the precise sort of exception that a lambda expression might throw. By indicating the kind of exception, you make it possible for the compiler to optimize the lambda expression and make it faster — more efficient.

In some cases, a lambda expression never throws an exception. Perhaps the functionality it provides is quite simple and there literally isn't anything that can go wrong in the sense of generating an exceptional condition. When this is the case, you add the throw() clause to the lambda expression as shown here.

```
auto myLambda = [] () throw() {return true;};
```

It's far more likely that your lambda expression will throw a specific exception. For example, the input may be outside the range the lambda expression expects and there isn't any good way to compensate for this condition. Even in this situation, telling the compiler specifically which exception the lambda expression will throw allows the compiler to better optimize the code — making it faster. The Exceptions example in Listing 7-9 shows just such a situation.

Listing 7-9: Throwing an Exception within a Lambda Expression

```
#include <iostream>
#include <algorithm>
#include <vector>
#include <stdexcept>
```

```
using namespace std;

void ProcessVector(vector<int>& vect)
{
    sort(vect.begin(), vect.end(),
        [](int S1, int S2) throw(out_of_range)
        {
                if (S1 > 100 || S2 > 100)
                    throw new out_of_range("Value over 100");

            return S1 < S2;
        });

    for_each(vect.begin(), vect.end(),
            [](int x) throw() {cout << x << endl;});
}

int main()
{
    vector<int> MyVector;
    MyVector.push_back(11);
    MyVector.push_back(2);
    MyVector.push_back(33);
    MyVector.push_back(4);

    // Remove comment to see the exception.
    //MyVector.push_back(101);

    ProcessVector(MyVector);
}
```

When you run this example normally, you see the same output as shown for the custom sorting portion in the previous example. However, when you remove the comments from MyVector.push_back(101); and run the example, you get the following exception message.

```
terminate called after throwing an instance of 'std::out_of_range*'

This application has requested the Runtime to terminate it in an unusual way.
Please contact the application's support team for more information.
```

Notice that the code used to display the output from the example doesn't throw any exceptions. The code is defined in a way that allows the compiler to perform additional optimization. With an example of this sort, it would be hard to actually quantify the speed difference, but there is such a difference — and it would become apparent with a larger data set.

Book V
Reading and Writing Files

One of the more common tasks with files today is writing configuration information for an application. Most applications have some kind of configuration associated with them. You can find a simple example of how to create and use a configuration file at http://www.dummies.com/extras/cplusplusaio.

Contents at a Glance

Chapter 1: Filing Information with the Streams Library

In This Chapter

✔ Seeing the need for a streams library

✔ Using the right header files

✔ Opening a file

✔ Dealing with errors

✔ Working with flags to customize your file opening

*F*irst things first. We've all heard of rivers and lakes and streams, and it's interesting just how many common words are used in computer programming. That's handy, because it lets us use words we already know with similar meaning, but it's also a bummer because it's harder to impress strangers. While we don't have gluggerbumbles and plickershops in computer programming — words most people have never even heard of, mainly because we made them up — we do have *streams!*

Most programmers think of a stream as the same thing as a file. You know — a file that's stored on your hard drive or maybe on a Universal Serial Bus (USB) flash drive or Secure Digital (SD) card. But streams go beyond just files. A *stream* is any type of data structure that you *stream* (that is, flow) your data into and out of in a sequence of bytes.

For example, if we open an Internet connection to a top-secret computer that stores all our top-secret data (ooooh), and we start putting our data on the remote computer, we might use a stream-based data structure. By that we mean we write the data in sequence, one byte after another, as the data goes over the Internet like a stream of water, reaching the remote computer. The data we wrote first gets there first and so on.

You can use the same approach for storing data into a file. Rather than just filling a huge 500MB data structure and then dropping it onto the hard drive, you write your data piece after piece; the information goes into the file.

In this chapter, we talk about different kinds of streams available to you, the C++ programmer.

Seeing a Need for Streams

When you write an application that deals with files, you must use a specific order:

1. **Open the file.**

   Before you can use a file, you must open it. In doing so, you specify a filename.

2. **Access the file.**

   After you open a file, you either store data into it (this is called *writing* data to the file) or get data out of it (this is called *reading* data from the file).

3. **Close the file.**

   After you have finished reading from and writing to a file, you must close the file.

For example, an application that tracks your stocks and writes your portfolio to a file at the end of the day might do these steps:

1. **Ask the user for a name of a file.**

2. **Open the file.**

3. **For each stock object, write the stock data to the file.**

4. **Close the file.**

The next morning, when the application starts, it might want to read the information back in. Here's what it might do:

1. **Ask the user for the name of the file.**

2. **Open the file.**

3. **While there's more data in the file, create a new Stock object, read the data from the file, and put the data into the Stock object.**

4. **Close the file.**

Here are a couple of reasons to close a file after you've finished using it:

✦ **Other applications might be waiting to use the file.** Some operating systems allow an application to *lock* a file, meaning that no other applications can open the file while the application that locked the file is using it. In such situations, another application can use the file after you close it, but not until then.

✦ **When you write to a file, the operating system decides whether to immediately write the information onto the hard drive or flash drive/ SD card or to hold on to it and gather more information, finally writing it all as a single batch.** When you close a file, the operating system puts all your remaining data into the file. This is called *flushing* the file.

You have two ways to write to a file:

✦ **Sequential access:** In sequential access, you write to a file or read from a file from beginning to end. With this approach, when you open the file, you normally specify whether you plan to read from or write to the file, but not both at the same time. After you open the file, if you're writing to the file, the data you write gets added continually to the end of the file. Or if you're reading from the file, you read the data at the beginning, then you read the data that follows, then you read the data that follows that data, and so on, up to the end.

✦ **Random access:** With random access, you can read and write to any byte in a file, regardless of which byte you previously read or wrote. In other words, you can skip around. You can read some bytes, then move to another portion of the file and write some bytes, and then move elsewhere and write some more.

Back in the days of the C programming language, several library functions let you work with files. However, they stunk. They were cumbersome and made life difficult. And so, when C++ came along, people quickly created a set of classes that made life with files much easier. These people used the stream metaphor we've been raving about.

In the sections that follow, we show you how to open files, write to them, read from them, and close them.

Programming with the Streams Library

Before we begin talking about the streams library (the actual libraries include `fstream`, `iostream`, and `sstream`, but don't worry about that now — we'll get into the specifics later), we need to tell you about some compatibility issues. The ANSI C++ standard document gives a complete library of classes that handle streams and general input/output. (There is a joint ANSI/ISO standard today, but we'll focus on the ANSI standard in this book because it's the standard that appears in the GNU GCC documentation.)

Fortunately, most of the classes in the Standard Library are available with almost all the compilers currently available. Therefore, in most of this book, we limit ourselves to the classes you can find in most compilers. That way, everyone can be happy (and that includes even us!). However, because you may have compilers that use the newer classes, we sometimes discuss them in sidebars.

Getting the right header file

The streams library includes several classes that make your life much easier. It also has several classes that can make your life more complicated, mainly because these are auxiliary classes that you'll probably rarely use. Here are two of the more common classes that you will use. (And remember: These classes are available in pretty much all C++ implementations, whether the complete Standard Library is present or not.)

✦ `ifstream`: This is a stream you instantiate if you want to read from a file.

✦ `ofstream`: This is a stream you instantiate if you want to write to a file.

Before you can use the `ifstream` and `ofstream` classes, you include the proper header file. This is where things get ugly. In the early days of C++, people used the header file `<fstream.h>`. But somewhere in the mid-1990s, people started using the Standard Template Library (and in the late 1990s, the Standard C++ Library), both of which required you to include `<fstream>` (without the `.h` extension).

Because we want to stay up to date, in this book we use the ones without the `.h`. However, the Standard Template Library and the Standard Library put all their classes and objects inside the `std` namespace. (The Standard Template Library and Standard Library are both C++ libraries but implement some functionality differently — the article at `http://en.wikipedia.org/wiki/Standard_Template_Library` describes these differences, but you won't need to worry about them when working through the examples in this book.) Thus, when you want to use an item from the streams library, you must either

✦ Prepend its name with `std`, as in this example:

```
std::ofstream outfile("MyFile.txt");
```

✦ Include a `using` directive before the lines where you use the stream classes, as in this example:

```
using namespace std;
ofstream outfile("MyFile.txt");
```

By default, the GCC compiler automatically recognizes the `std` namespace (it's as if you had a line `using namespace std;` even when you don't). We focus on the GCC compiler, we don't use either of the two preceding methods — putting `std::` before our stream class names or including a `using namespace std;` line.

In the spirit of the rest of this book, if you're using a compiler other than GCC, we recommend that you follow your `#include` lines with the line `using namespace std;`. Then you can type all the sample code as-is throughout this book, including the stream examples, without needing to put `std::` before every class or object from the Standard Library.

Opening a file

Let's see . . . what did we call the name of this file? We think it was MyGreat Chapter.doc. So we go to the word processor, choose File➪Open, and type **MyGreatChapter.doc**.

Oops. We get an error message. That file doesn't exist.

Oh, that's right; we haven't written it yet. Instead, we create a new document inside the word processor, type 800 cool pages over the course of a relaxing evening, and then (when we're all finished) we save the file. We give it the name `MyGreatChapter.doc`. Then we shut down the word processor, hang out by the pool, brag to our friends about the new novels we're writing, and go to bed.

The next morning, we open the document. This time it exists, so the word processor opens it and reads in the information.

As you can see, two issues present themselves in opening a file:

✦ Create a new file

✦ Open an existing file

Here's where life gets a little strange: Some operating systems treat these two items as a single entity. The reason is that when you create a new file, normally you want to immediately start using it, which means you want to create a new file and then open it. And so the process of creating a file is often embedded right into the process of opening a file.

And when you open an existing file that you want to write to, you have two choices:

✦ Erase the current contents; then write to the file.

✦ Keep the existing contents and write your information to the end of the file. This is called *appending* information to a file.

Separating a pathname

Everybody wants to be different and unique. The people who wrote Microsoft's MS-DOS operating system, instead of following in the tradition of using Unix's / for a pathname separator, decided to use \, thus adding the word *backslash* to the vocabularies of millions of people. So today, on Windows, you see such pathnames as C:\MyDataFolder\ MyMessyPath\DifficultToType\ LetterToEditor.doc. But on Unix, you see forward slashes, as in /usr/ something/LetterToEditor.doc. And if this difference isn't bad enough, think about what the backslash means in a string in C++. It means that a letter follows, and the compiler interprets the two characters together as something else. For example, \t means a tab, and \n means a newline character. And how do you put a backslash into a string? You put two backslashes. Ugh! That means the earlier MS-DOS-style string (the one with Windows in it, Mr. Bill Gates!) must look like this if you use it in a C++ application:

```
"C:\\MyDataFolder\\MyMessyPath\\
        DifficultToType\\
        LetterToEditor.doc"
```

Yes, you must type every backslash twice if you want the compiler to get the correct string. But instead of doing this, we'd like to propose a much better solution! Don't use backslashes at all, even if you're programming for Windows (or, we suppose, MS-DOS). Yes, it's true! Stop the presses! Call the talk radio show! Announce it to the world! When you write a C++ application on Windows, the libraries are smart enough to know that a forward slash works instead of a backslash! Therefore you can use this string:

```
"C:/MyDataFolder/MyMessyPath/
        DifficultToType/LetterToEditor.
        doc"
```

In this book, you see us using forward paths. That way, our samples work on both Unix and Windows.

The FileOutput01 example code in Listing 1-1 shows you how to open a brand-new file, write some information to it, and then close it. (But wait, there's more: This version works whether you have the newer ANSI-compliant compilers or the older ones!)

Listing 1-1:   Using Code That Opens a File and Writes to It

```cpp
#include <iostream>
#include <fstream>

using namespace std;

int main()
{
    ofstream outfile("../MyFile.txt");
    outfile << "Hi" << endl;
    outfile.close();

    return 0;
}
```

Finding your files

Whenever you open a new file, you must know where the file is, not just what the file is called. In other words, you need to supply both a *path* and a *filename*, not just a filename. You can obtain a path for your file in different ways, depending on your application. For example, you may be saving all your files in a particular directory; you would then precede your file-names with that directory (that is, *path*) name. The `string` class makes this easy, as in this code:

```
const string MyPath = "c:\\
    GreatSoftwareInc";
string Filename = MyPath + "\\" +
    "MyFile.txt";
ofstream outfile(Filename.c_str());
```

The reason we had to call `c_str` on the `string` is that the `ofstream` class doesn't have a constructor for a `string` instance, only a C-style `string`. The `c_str` function returns a pointer to a C-style `string` equivalent of the `string`. Also, remember to add `#include <string>` when you use the `string` class!

Also, when you're using a constant path as we did in this example, you may, instead, store the pathname in some initialization file that lives somewhere on your user's computer, rather than *hard-code* it in your application as we did in this example. You may also include an Options window where your users can change the value of this path.

The short application in Listing 1-1 opens a file called `MyFile.txt`. (The "../" part of the file path places the file in the parent directory for the example, which is the Chapter01 folder — see the "Finding your files" sidebar for details.) It does this by creating a new instance of `ofstream`, which is a class for writing to a file. The next line of code writes the string `"Hi"` to the file. It uses the insertion operator, `>>`, just as `cout` does. In fact, `ofstream` is derived from the very class that `cout` is an instance of, and so that means all the things you can do with `cout` you can also do with your file! Wow! We know we're excited!

When we're finished writing to the file, we close it by calling the `close` member function. This is important!

If you want to open an existing file and append to it, you can modify Listing 1-1 slightly. All you do is change the arguments passed to the con-structor as follows:

```
ofstream outfile("MyFile.txt", ios_base::app);
```

The `ios::app` item is an enumeration inside a class called `ios`, and the `ios_base::app` item is an enumeration in the class called `ios_base`.

The `ios` class is the base class from which the `ofstream` class is derived. The `ios` class also serves as a base class for `ifstream`, which is for reading files.

For newer compilers, the `ios_base` class is a base for `ofstream` and `ifstream`. (A couple of classes are in between. `ofstream` is a template class derived from a template class called `basic_ofstream`, which is derived from a template class called `basic_ios`, which is derived from the class `ios_base`. You can view a simplified diagram of these classes at `http://www.cplusplus.com/reference/iostream/`.)

You can also read from an existing file. This works just like the `cin` object. The `FileRead01` example shown in Listing 1-2 opens the file created by Listing 1-1 and reads the string back in. This example uses the parent directory again as a common place to create, update, and read files.

Listing 1-2: Using Code to Open a File and Read from It

```
#include <iostream>
#include <fstream>
#include <string>

using namespace std;

int main()
{
    string word;
    ifstream infile("../MyFile.txt");
    infile >> word;
    cout << word << endl;
    infile.close();

    return 0;
}
```

When you run this application, the string written earlier to the file in Listing 1-1 — `"Hi,"` — appears onscreen. It worked! It read the string in from the file!

Handling Errors When Opening a File

When you open a file, all kinds of things can go wrong. A file lives on a physical device — a fixed disk, for example, or perhaps on a flash drive or SD card — and you can run into problems when working with physical devices. For example, part of the disk might be damaged, causing an existing file to become corrupted. Or, less disastrous, you might run out of disk space. Or, even less disastrous, you might try to open a file in a directory that doesn't exist.

If you try to open a file for writing by specifying a full path and filename but the directory does not exist, the computer responds differently, depending on the operating system you're using. If you're unsure how your particular operating system will respond, try writing a simple test application that tries to create and open something like /abc/def/ghi/jkl/abc.txt. (Of course, you'll want to be sure to use a directory that doesn't exist; we're assuming /abc/def/ghi/jkl doesn't exist on your hard drive.) Then one of two things will happen: Either the directory and the file will get created, or nothing will happen.

For example, on a Windows system, if we attempt to create a file in a directory that doesn't exist, the system does not create the directory. That's because deep down inside, the application ultimately calls an operating system function that does the dirty work of creating the file. And this particular operating system function (it's called CreateFile(), if you even care) has a rule that it will not create a directory for you.

If you want to determine whether the ostream class was unable to create a file, you can call its fail() member function. This function returns true if the object couldn't create the file. And that's what happens when a directory doesn't exist. The DirectoryCheck01 example shown in Listing 1-3 demonstrates an example of this.

Listing 1-3:   Returning True When ostream Cannot Create a File

```
#include <iostream>
#include <fstream>

using namespace std;

int main()
{
    ofstream outfile("/abc/def/ghi/MyFile.txt");
    if (outfile.fail()) {
        cout << "Couldn't open the file!" << endl;
        return 0;
    }
    outfile << "Hi" << endl;
    outfile.close();

    return 0;
}
```

When you run this code, assuming that you don't have a directory called /abc/def/ghi on your system, you should see the message Couldn't open the file! We're assuming also that your particular operating system doesn't create a directory in this case; if it does, your computer will open the file, write Hi to it, and move on with its happy life after closing things out.

As an alternative to calling the `fail()` member function, you can use an operator available in various stream classes. This is `!`, fondly referred to as the "bang" operator, and you would use it in place of calling `fail()`, as in this code:

```
if (!outfile)
{
    cout << "Couldn't open the file!" << endl;
    return 0;
}
```

Most people prefer to use `!outfile` instead of `outfile.fail()`, although our opinion is that `!outfile` stinks. In addition to its aromatic properties, we think it makes confusing code. The reason is that `outfile` is an object, and in our brains, the notion of `!outfile`, which we would pronounce "not outfile," simply doesn't make sense. In fact, `!outfile` trips up many beginning programmers. They know that `outfile` is not a pointer in this sample code, and they wonder how you could test it against 0 as you normally can only do with a pointer. (Remember, by saying `!x`, where x is some pointer, you're testing x against 0.) And that simply doesn't make sense! And so, to avoid confusion, we prefer to just call `fail()`. It makes more sense.

Here are some reasons your file creation may choke:

✦ The directory doesn't exist.

✦ You're out of disk space and out of luck.

✦ Your application doesn't have the right permissions to create a file.

✦ The filename was invalid — that is, it contained characters the operating system doesn't allow in a filename, such as * or ?.

Like any good application, your application should do two things:

1. Check whether a file creation succeeded.

2. If the file creation failed, handle it appropriately. Don't just print a horrible message like `Oops! Aborting!`, leaving your poor users with no choice but to toss the monitor onto the floor. Instead, do something friendlier — such as presenting a message telling them there's a problem and suggesting that they might free more disk space. (There are other reasons not covered in this book, such as lack of rights to the area of disk where the file is written — you need to perform application testing to locate them all and then provide error handling for each potential issue.)

Flagging the ios Flags

When you open a file by constructing either an `ofstream` or `ifstream` instance, you can modify the way the file will open by supplying what are called flags. In computer terms, a *flag* is simply a small item whose presence or lack of presence tells a function how to do something. With the `ofstream` and `ifstream` classes, the function in question is the constructor.

A flag looks like `ios::app` if you're using a compiler that is not fully ANSI-compliant, or looks like `ios_base::app` if you're using one that is fully ANSI-compliant. This particular flag means that you want to write to a file, but you want to append to any existing data that may already be in a file. You supply this flag as an argument of the constructor for `ofstream`, as in either of the following examples:

```
ofstream outfile("AppendableFile.txt", ios::app);
```

```
ofstream outfile("AppendableFile.txt", ios_base::app);
```

You can see that we added the flag as a second parameter to the constructor. Other flags exist besides `app`, and you can combine them by using the or operator, `|`. For example, one flag is `ios::nocreate` (which isn't included in newer compilers, but we show you how to overcome this limitation later in this section). This one means "only open the file if it already exists." That is, don't create the file if it doesn't exist. (Remember, `ofstream` creates a file if it doesn't already exist.) If the file doesn't exist, the open will fail, and when you call `fail`, you will get back a `true`.

The `ios::nocreate` flag is handy with `ios::app`. Together, these mean *open an existing file and append to it.* That is, the two together will work only if the file already exists, and the call will open the file for an append operation. If the file doesn't already exist, the file won't be created. Here's a sample call:

```
ofstream outfile("../MyFile.txt", ios::app | ios::nocreate);
if (outfile.fail()) {
    cout << "Couldn't open the file!" << endl;
    return 0;
}
outfile << "Hi" << endl;
outfile.close();
```

If `MyFile.txt` doesn't exist when you run this code, you get the message `Couldn't open the file!` But if `MyFile.txt` does exist, the application opens it, appends the string `Hi` to it, and finally closes it.

It turns out that the `nocreate` flag is not available in the new Standard Library. Bummer. Therefore the code we just gave you works only if you're using an earlier version of the library. When using the Code::Blocks compiler, you see the following error message:

```
error: 'nocreate' is not a member of ';std::ios'
```

However, you'll want to test whether your particular compiler includes a library that supports `ios::nocreate`. Your compiler may support it anyway, even if it includes the new Standard Library. As an alternative to `ios::nocreate`, you can use the following code (found in the `FileOutput02` example):

```
ifstream infile("../MyFile.txt");
if (infile.fail())
{
    cout << "Couldn't open the file!" << endl;
    return 0;
}
infile.close();

ofstream outfile("../MyFile.txt", ios::app);
outfile << "Hi" << endl;
outfile.close();
```

In this case, you begin by attempting to open the file for reading. If the file doesn't exist, you can't read from it and the code exits with a failure message. If the code can read from the file, it reopens the file for writing. This is a cumbersome workaround, but it works.

Following is a list of the available flags. First, here are the ones for `ios`, in case you're using a compiler that is not completely ANSI-compliant:

✦ `ios::app`: This flag means that you want to open a file and append to it.

✦ `ios::in`: Include this flag if you want to read from a file.

✦ `ios::out`: Include this flag if you want to write to a file.

✦ `ios::trunc`: Include this flag if you want to wipe out the contents of the file before writing to it. It's the opposite of `append`, and it's also the default if you don't specifically include `ios::app`.

✦ `ios::nocreate`: Use this flag if you want to ensure that the file will not be created if it doesn't exist, resulting in the file not being opened.

✦ `ios::noreplace`: This flag is the opposite of `nocreate`. Use this flag if you only want to create a new file. If you use this flag and the file already exists, the file will not open, and that failure will return `true`.

ANSI-compliant compilers don't support the `ios::noreplace` flag either. In this case, you can use the opposite of the fix for the `ios:nocreate` flag, as shown here (and found in the `FileOutput03` example):

```
ifstream infile("../MyFile.txt");
if (!infile.fail())
{
    cout << "The file already exists!" << endl;
    return 0;
}
infile.close();

ofstream outfile("../MyFile.txt");
outfile << "Hi" << endl;
outfile.close();
```

In this case, the code attempts to open the file for reading. If the file exists, the code shows an error message and exits. Otherwise the code creates a new file and writes to it.

The following flags are available in a complier that's absolutely ANSI-compliant!

✦ `ios::ate`: Use this flag to go to the end of the file after you open it. Normally, you use this flag when you want to append data to the file.

✦ `ios_base::binary`: Use this flag to specify that the file you're opening will hold binary data — that is, data that does not represent character strings.

✦ `ios_base::in`: Specify this flag when you want to read from a file.

✦ `ios_base::out`: Include this flag when you want to write to a file.

✦ `ios_base::trunc`: Include this flag if you want to wipe out the contents of a file before writing to it.

✦ `ios_base::app`: Include this flag if you want to append to the file. It's the opposite of `trunc` — that is, the information that's already in the file when you open it will stay there.

Why do you need an `in` flag and an `out` flag? It seems that the computer should know whether you're writing to a file or reading from it, depending (respectively) on whether you use `ofstream` or `ifstream`. The answer to why you have an `in` flag and an `out` flag is that other classes are available besides `ofstream` and `ifstream`. The compilers that don't yet fully support the ANSI standard have a generic class in their libraries called `fstream`. The ANSI-compliant compilers have in their libraries a template class called `basic_filebuf` and a class called `filebuf`. If you use these classes, you can use the `in` and `out` flags.

Chapter 2: Writing with Output Streams

In This Chapter

✔ Using the insertion operator

✔ Working with manipulators

✔ Formatting your output

✔ Using flags to format your output

✔ Specifying a precision for writing numbers

✔ Setting field widths

✔ Ensuring data safety with locked streams

*Y*ears ago, one of us had an old computer that had 3,000 bytes of memory. (Yes, that's *three thousand bytes*, not 3MB.) As an option, this computer came with a floppy disk drive that sat outside it. It did not have a hard drive. Therefore, if you didn't have a hard drive but you wanted to use an application, you had to *load the application from a floppy, type its name, and press Enter!* Ah, those were the days.

Nowadays, the notion of a computer without a hard drive seems almost unthinkable. Not only do your applications sit on the hard drive in the form of files, but your applications also create files to store on the hard drive.

When you use a word processor, you save your documents to a file. Imagine if every time you needed the same document, you had to retype it. In this chapter, we show you the different ways you can write to a file.

Inserting with the << Operator

Writing to a file is easy in C++. You're probably already familiar with how you can write to the console by using the cout object, like this:

```
cout << "Hey, I'm on TV!" << endl;
```

Operating the insertion operator

The insertion operator, <<, is an overloaded operator function. For the 100 percent ANSI-compliant libraries, inside the `basic_ostream` class (or, for the non-100 percent ANSI libraries, inside the `ostream` class), you can find several overloaded forms of the << operator function. Each one provides input for a basic type as well as for some of the standard C++ classes, such as `string` or one of its base classes. (We say *or* because most libraries that ship with compilers are written by compiler vendors — who may implement their code slightly differently but get the same results.)

Well, guess what! The `cout` object is a file stream! Amazing! And so, if you want to write to a file, you can do it the same way you would with `cout`: You just use the double-less-than symbol, called the *insertion operator,* like this: <<.

If you open a file for writing by using the `ofstream` class, you can write to it by using the insertion operator. The `FileWrite01` example shown in Listing 2-1 demonstrates how to perform this task.

Listing 2-1:   Using Code to Open a File and Write to It

```
#include <iostream>
#include <fstream>

using namespace std;

int main()
{
    ofstream outfile("outfile.txt");
    outfile << "Lookit me! I'm in a file!" << endl;
    int x = 200;
    outfile << x << endl;
    outfile.close();
    return 0;
}
```

The first line inside the `main()` creates an instance of `ofstream`, passing to it the name of a file called `outfile.txt`.

We then write to the file, first giving it the string, `Lookit me! I'm in a file!`, then a newline, then the integer `200`, and finally a newline. And after that, we show the world what good programmers we are by closing our file.

Placing data in specific folders

Sometimes you want to place data in a specific common folder, such as the current working directory — the directory used by the application. C++ provides a method to obtain this information: `getcwd()`. This method appears in the `<direct.h>` header. Using the `getcwd()` method is relatively straightforward. You create a place to put the information, called a buffer, and then ask C++ to provide the information. The `GetWorkingDirectory` example demonstrates how to perform this task, as shown here:

```
#include <iostream>
#include <direct.h>
#include <stdlib.h>

using namespace std;

int main()
{
```

```
    char CurrentPath[_MAX_PATH];
    getcwd(CurrentPath, _MAX_PATH);
    cout << CurrentPath << endl;
    return 0;
}
```

As output, you should see the name of the directory that contains the application, such as `C:\CPP_AIO\BookV\Chapter02\GetWorkingDirectory`. The `_MAX_PATH` constant is the maximum size that you can make a path. So, what this code is saying is to create a char array that is the size of `_MAX_PATH`. Use the resulting buffer to hold the current working directory (which is where the name of the method `getcwd()` comes from). You can then display this directory onscreen or use it as part of the path for your output stream — amazing!

Formatting Your Output

If you're like us and are saving lists of numbers to a file, you may find that the process works better if the numbers are *formatted* in various ways. For example, you may want them all aligned on the right; or you might want your floating-point numbers to have a certain number of digits to the right of the decimal point.

There are three aspects to setting these formats. They are

+ **Format flags:** A *format flag* is a general style that you want your output to appear in. For example, you may want floating-point numbers to appear in scientific mode, or you may want to be able to print the words *true* and *false* for Boolean values, rather than their underlying numbers. To do these tasks, you specify format flags.

+ **Precision:** This refers to how many digits are on the right of the decimal point when you print floating-point numbers.

+ **Field width:** This refers to how much space the numbers take (both floating point and integer). This feature allows you to align all your numbers.

The next three sections discuss each of these in all their glory and grandeur.

You can use the format flags (detailed in the upcoming section), as well as precision and width specifiers, when writing to your files — and also when writing to `cout`. Because `cout` is a stream object in the `iostream` hierarchy, it accepts the same specifiers as output files. So have at it!

Formatting with flags

The folks who made the ISO C++ standard gave us a slew of *format flags*.

If you're using a compiler that includes a library that's not fully ANSI-compliant, you will be able to use *most* of these format flags but not all of them. Therefore, in this section, we're giving you lists for

✦ `ios_base` (for ANSI-compliant libraries)

✦ `ios` (for noncompliant libraries)

To use the following format flags, you call the `setf` member function for the file object. (This can be either your own file object or the `cout` object.) For example, to turn on scientific notation, you would do this:

```
cout.setf(ios_base::scientific);
cout << 987654.321 << endl;
```

or, if you're using a non-ANSI-compliant library:

```
cout.setf(ios::scientific);
cout << 987654.321 << endl;
```

To turn off scientific mode, you call the `unsetf` member function:

```
cout.unsetf(ios_base::scientific);
cout << 987654.321 << endl;
```

or, if you're using a non-ANSI library:

```
cout.unsetf(ios::scientific);
cout << 987654.321 << endl;
```

And if you're using your own file, you would do something like this (as found in the `FileWrite02` example):

```
ofstream myfile("numbers.txt");
myfile.setf(ios_base::scientific);
myfile << 154272.524 << endl;
myfile.close();
```

or, for the non-ANSI folks:

```
ofstream myfile("numbers.txt");
myfile.setf(ios::scientific);
myfile << 154272.524 << endl;
myfile.close();
```

When you run this code for writing to a file, the `numbers.txt` file will contain one of the following examples, depending on your particular compiler and library:

```
1.542725e+005
```

```
1.542725e+05
```

Each of the `ios_base` flags exists both as a format specifier and as a manipulator. (Don't worry about the precise differences for right now; Book V, Chapter 5 explains manipulators in detail.) Therefore you can, for example, use either of the following lines to set `boolalpha`:

```
cout.setf(ios_base::boolalpha);
```

```
cout << boolalpha;
```

We're talking only about the `ios_base` flags here. The `ios` flags do not coexist as manipulators. You can use these flags as manipulators only with an ANSI-compliant library.

If you use the manipulator form of a format specifier, don't put an `endl` at the end of the line unless you want an endline to print, as in this:

```
cout << boolalpha << endl;
```

Following is a rundown of the format flags available in both the ANSI-compliant and non-ANSI compliant libraries. As mentioned earlier, you'd set these flags by calling `setf`, and you'd turn off a flag by either calling `unsetf`, or (for some flags) by setting a different flag. For example, both of these turn off scientific mode:

```
cout.unsetf(ios_base::scientific);
```

```
cout.setf(ios_base::fixed);
```

In the following list, we point out when you can set another flag to turn off a particular flag. One of these, `boolalpha`, is available only to you ANSI-style folks. Remember, "ANSI-people" must use `ios_base::` before each of these; "non-ANSI-people" must use `ios::` before each of these.

✦ `boolalpha`: (ANSI only) Setting this flag causes Boolean variables to write with the words *true* or *false* (or the equivalent words for your particular locale). Clearing this flag causes Boolean variables to write 0 for false or 1 for true. (The default is for this flag to be cleared.)

✦ `fixed`: This flag specifies that, when possible, the output of floating-point numbers will not appear in scientific notation. (We say *when possible* because large numbers always appear as scientific notation, whether you specified `scientific` or `fixed`.)

✦ scientific: When you specify this flag, your floating-point numbers always appear in scientific notation.

✦ dec: When you set this flag, your integers will appear as decimal numbers. To turn this off, you turn on a different *base*, either hex (for hexadecimal) or oct (for octal).

✦ hex: With this flag, all your integers appear in hexadecimal format. To turn this off, choose a different base — dec or oct. Computer people like hexadecimal because it looks cool to see *letters* in your numbers.

✦ oct: When you turn on this flag, your integers will appear in *octal* format. Oh fun, fun.

✦ left: When you turn on this flag, all numbers will be left-aligned with a width field. (See "Setting the width and creating fields," later in this chapter, for information on how to set the width.)

✦ right: With this flag, all your numbers will be right-aligned with a width field.

✦ showbase: When you turn on this flag and print an integer, the integer will be preceded with a super-special character that represents none other than the base — decimal, hexadecimal, or octal. That can be good because the number 153 can represent 153 in decimal or 153 in hexadecimal (which is equivalent to 339 in decimal) or 153 in octal (which is equivalent to 107 in decimal). Yikes.

✦ showpoint: With this flag, your floating-point numbers have a decimal point, even if they happen to be whole numbers. (That is, a floating-point variable that contains 10.0 will print as *10.* with a decimal point after it. Without this flag, it will just print as *10* with no decimal point.)

✦ showpos: Normally, a negative numbers gets a minus sign before it, and a positive number gets no sign before it. But when you turn on this flag, each of your positive numbers *will* get a plus sign before it. Cool!

✦ unitbuf: This is for the advanced people. When you turn this on, your output will flush after each output operation. In other words, the library will not accumulate a certain amount of output before writing it in batches. Instead, the library will write the output all out each time you use the insertion operator, <<.

✦ uppercase: When you write hexadecimal or scientific numbers, the various letters in the number will appear as uppercase. Thus, the letters *A, B, C, D, E,* and *F* will appear in capitals in a hexadecimal number, and the *E* representing the exponent in scientific notation will print as a capital *E.* When this is not set, you will get *a, b, c, d, e,* and *f* for hexadecimal numbers and *e* for the exponent in scientific notation.

Table 2-1 shows the manipulator forms of some flags. We're providing three columns in this table: First is the flag; then the manipulator to turn on the flag. Then comes the manipulator to turn *off* the flag. Yes, you need a way to turn it off. (We coined a new word: *demanipulator*. Yeah, that sounds good.) Remember, if you're pre-ANSI, you don't have access to these manipulators. Instead, you have to call `setf`.

Table 2-1   Using ANSI-Standard Manipulators and Demanipulators

Flag	Manipulator	Demanipulator
boolalpha	boolalpha	noboolalpha
showbase	showbase	noshowbase
showpoint	showpoint	noshowpoint
showpos	showpos	noshowpos
skipws	skipws	noskipws
uppercase	uppercase	nouppercase
fixed	fixed	scientific
scientific	scientific	fixed

The `scientific` flag and `fixed` flag are opposites: `fixed` turns off `scientific`, and `scientific` turns off `fixed`. The default if you don't specify either is `fixed`.

Six manipulators aren't in Table 2-1 because they don't have a demanipulator. Instead, they are *three-way*:

✦ **Bases:** `dec`, `hex`, and `oct`. Only one base can be active at a time. Activating a base automatically switches off the other bases.

✦ **Alignments:** `internal`, `left`, and `right`. Only one alignment can be active at a time. Activating an alignment automatically switches off the other alignments.

Specifying a precision

When you are writing floating-point numbers to a file or to `cout` (that is, numbers stored in `float` or `double` variables), having all the numbers print with the same number of digits to the right of the decimal point is often handy. This feature is called the *precision*.

Do not confuse this form of the word *precision* with the idea that `double` variables have a greater precision than `float` variables. Here, we're just talking about the number of digits printed to either the file or `cout`. The value inside the variable does not change, nor does the precision of the variable's type.

To set or read the precision, call the stream's `precision` function. If you call `precision` with no parameters, you can find out the current precision. Or to set the precision, pass a number specifying how many digits you want to appear to the right of the decimal point.

For example, the following line sets the precision of an output:

```
cout.precision(4);
```

The output would take this form:

```
0.3333
```

If you don't set the precision, the stream will have a default precision, probably six, depending on your particular compiler.

Precision has an interesting effect if you use it with the `showpoint` format flag. In the scientific community, these three numbers have the same precision:

```
3.5672
8432.2259
0.55292
```

Even though the first two of the preceding numbers have the same number of digits to the right of the decimal point, scientists consider precision to mean the same number of total digits not counting leftmost 0s to the left of the decimal (as in the final of the three). Therefore a scientist would consider the three following numbers to have the same precision because they all have four digits. (Again, for the final one, you don't count the 0 because it's to the left of the decimal point.) Scientific folks call these *significant digits*. You can accomplish significant digits with an output stream by combining `precision` with the `showpoint` flag. The `PrecisionFunction` example shown in Listing 2-2 contains an example of `showpoint` and `precision` working together in perfect harmony.

```
3.567
8432.
0.1853
```

Listing 2-2: Using the Precision Function to Work with the showpoint Format Flag

```
#include <iostream>

using namespace std;

int main()
{
    int i;
    cout.setf(ios_base::showpoint);
    cout.precision(4);
    for (i=1; i<=10; i++) {
        cout << 1.0 / i << endl;
    }
    cout << 2.0 << endl;
    cout << 12.0 << endl;
    cout << 12.5 << endl;
    cout << 123.5 << endl;
    cout << 1234.9 << endl;
    cout << 12348.8 << endl;
    cout << 123411.5 << endl;
    cout << 1234111.5 << endl;
    return 0;
}
```

If you're using a non-ANSI-compliant compiler, you need to change ios_ base to ios in the third line in main. Also, because Listing 2-2 is for a fully ANSI-compliant compiler, we included the using namespace std; line. (You can always have this line, whether your compiler requires it or not.)

When you run this application, here's the output you see:

```
1.000
0.5000
0.3333
0.2500
0.2000
0.1667
0.1429
0.1250
0.1111
0.1000
2.000
12.00
12.50
123.5
1235.
1.235e+004
1.234e+005
1.234e+006
```

The preceding output has a couple of interesting cases:

✦ The last three lines of the preceding output are scientific notation to maintain four significant digits.

✦ The fourth line from the end, 1235., is rounded up from 1234.9 because of this line:

```
cout << 1234.9 << endl;
```

The precision function has an associated manipulator. Instead of calling precision as a function, you can use it as a manipulator. But the manipulator's name is slightly different: It's setprecision. To use it, you include this header:

```
#include <iomanip>
```

These two lines cause the same thing to happen:

```
cout.precision(4);
```

```
cout << setprecision(4);
```

And these two lines are available for all the recent more-or-less-ANSI-compliant compilers, even those that aren't fully compliant. Yay! Just make sure you remember to add #include <iomanip>, or you will get a compiler error.

Setting the width and creating fields

This is where you can start making the numbers and data all nice and neat by aligning them in columns. To align your data, use the width member function for the stream or cout, passing the width of the field, like this:

```
cout.width(10);
```

Then, when you print a number, think of the number as sitting inside a field 10 spaces wide, with the number wedged against the right side of these 10 spaces. For example, look at this:

```
cout.width(10);
cout << 20 << endl;
```

This code produces this output:

```
        20
```

Although seeing this in the printed text is hard, this 20 is pushed to the right of a field of spaces 10 characters wide. That is, because the 20 takes two character spaces, there are eight spaces to the left of it.

If you prefer, you can have the numbers pushed to the left of the field. To do this, set the `left` format flag by using `setf`. (Or, for absolutely perfectly ANSI-compliant libraries, you can use the `left` manipulator.)

For the width function, you can alternatively add `#include <iomanip>` and then use a manipulator:

```
cout << setw(10);
```

This works for both the newer, 100-percent ANSI-compliant compilers and the slightly older, slightly less-compliant compilers.

Due to some oddities in the libraries, when you set the width, it stays that way only for the next output operation. Call it forgetful if you will. Therefore, suppose you have code that looks like this:

```
cout.width(10);
cout << 20 << 30 << endl;
```

Only the first output, 20, will have a field width of 20. The 30 will just take as much space as it needs. Therefore these lines of code produce this output, which is probably not what most people would intend:

```
     2030
```

This is why we prefer to use the manipulator form: You precede each output item with a width specification. Try this instead:

```
cout << setw(10) << 20 << setw(10) << 30 << endl;
```

which writes this to `cout`:

```
     20        30
```

That looks a little nicer!

The `WidthFunction` example in Listing 2-3 shows the great things you can do when you set the width. This listing is for the absolute money-back-guarantee ANSI compilers. If yours is slightly less than ANSI compliant, you have to change these two lines:

```
sals << fixed;
sals << left;
```

to this:

```
sals.setf(ios::fixed);
sals.setf(ios::left);
```

Listing 2-3: Setting the Width of a Field Using the setw Manipulator or Width Function

```
#include <iostream>
#include <iomanip>
#include <fstream>

using namespace std;

int main()
{
    ofstream sals("salaries.txt");
    sals << setprecision(2);
    sals << fixed;
    sals << left;

    sals << setw(20) << "Name" << setw(10) << "Salary";
    sals << endl;

    sals << "------------------- "; // 19 hyphens, one space
    sals << "----------" << endl;   // 10 hyphens
    sals << setw(20) << "Hank Williams";
    sals << setw(10) << 28422.82 << endl;

    sals << setw(20) << "Buddy Holly";
    sals << setw(10) << 39292.22 << endl;

    sals << setw(20) << "Otis Redding";
    sals << setw(10) << 43838.55 << endl;
    sals.close();
    return 0;
}
```

When you run Listing 2-3, you get a file called `salaries.txt`, like this:

```
Name                Salary
------------------- ----------
Hank Williams       28422.82
Buddy Holly         39292.22
Otis Redding        43838.55
```

See how it's neatly lined up? That's pretty! Notice one thing we did, however: The first field, `Name`, is 20 characters wide. For the hyphens, we put only 19 to give the appearance of a space between the two fields. In fact, the two fields are wedged against each other with no space between them.

If you ran Listing 2-3 and each salary printed in a scientific format as in `2.8e+04`, you need to use `sals.setf(ios::fixed);` and `sals.setf(ios::left);`.

We used the `left` format flag so that the data in each field is aligned to the left end of the field. By default, each field is aligned to the right.

Although you can specify the field width, really you're specifying a *minimum*. If the characters in the output are less than the field width, the runtime library will pad them with spaces to make them that minimum size. If they are bigger than that width, the library will not chop them off to make them fit. If you add letters to the Hank Williams line in Listing 2-3 (like this: `sals << setw(20) << "Hank WilliamsABCDEFGHIJ";`), the output looks like the following example instead. The Hank Williams line runs beyond the 20 characters into the next field.

```
Name                Salary
------------------- ----------
Hank WilliamsABCDEFGHIJ28422.82
Buddy Holly         39292.22
Otis Redding        43838.55
```

Chapter 3: Reading with Input Streams

In This Chapter

✔ Reading with the extraction operators

✔ Dealing with the end of the file

✔ Reading various data types

✔ Reading data that is formatted with text

*W*ell, isn't this nice. You have a file that you wrote to, but you need to read from it! After all, what good is a file if it's just sitting on your hard drive collecting dust?

In this chapter, we show you how you can read from a file. Reading a file is tricky because you can run into some formatting issues. For example, you may have a line of text in a file with a sequence of 50 digits. Do those 50 digits correspond to 50 one-digit numbers, or maybe 25 two-digit numbers, or some other combination? If you created the file, you probably know; but the fun part is getting your C++ application to properly read from them. The file might contain 25 two-digit numbers, in which case you make sure that the C++ code doesn't just try to read one enormous 50-digit number. In this chapter, we give you all the dirt on getting the dust off your hard drive and the file into memory. Have at it!

Extracting with Operators

When you read from a file, you can use the *extraction* operator, >>. This operator is very easy to use, provided you recognize that the phrase, "Look mom, no caveats!" just doesn't apply to the extraction operator.

Suppose you have a file called `Numbers.txt` with the following text on one line:

```
100 50 30 25
```

What's a protocol?

Okay, we're going to give you a list of numbers: 1600 20500 1849 20240. Go ahead and use them the way we intend you to use them, and then send us back the answer, at which point we'll send you our response. What's that? You're not sure what we want you to do with them? Aha! You need a protocol. As defined in this chapter, a *protocol* is simply a rule for how data is ordered. A protocol in general defines rules for exchanging information of any sort between computers (think of it as a diplomatic role).The two systems negotiate the exchange of data based on standardized rules.

As it happens, the first number in the set of numbers we provided is the street address of the White House in Washington, DC, and the second number is the zip code for the White House. The third number is the street address of the main office for the National Park Service headquarters, and the fourth is the National Park Service zip code. Of course, you probably didn't realize that (unless you happen to work for the Park Service and recognized parts of your address!).

But now suppose you tell us, "Send me the White House street address, then its zip code, then the National Park Service street address, and then its zip code." Then we would go ahead and send the four numbers to you. At that point, we wouldn't have any need to send a bunch of extra information, such as English words describing what each number is. If we give them to you in the exact order you requested them, that will be all you need. In fact, if you're writing a computer application that receives this information and we pad it with other information, such as descriptions, your application may not be equipped to handle all that info, and you have a problem. In other words, our application and your application must agree on a protocol. A protocol dictates the order of the information and how it's formatted. Further, a protocol dictates how you'll respond: You may send back a single number 1, which means that you received the data properly, and we may send a single 0, which means that you'll be getting no further information. That's a protocol, and protocols are useful when reading data, whether it's from a file or over the Internet.

You can easily read in these numbers with the following code. First, make sure you add #include <fstream> (but *not* fstream.h, as you'll pick up an old, outdated, yucky file) as well as #include <iostream>. And you probably will need the line using namespace std; if you're using a newer compiler and library.

It's important to define some variables to hold the data you want to read. These variables (found in the FileRead01 example) will work fine:

```
string weight;
string height;
string width;
string depth;
```

The variables define the statistics for some type of widget you want to build. After you have the variables in place, this code will do the work:

```
ifstream MyFile("Numbers.txt");
MyFile >> weight;
MyFile >> height;
MyFile >> width;
MyFile >> depth;
```

In the preceding code, the input file, Numbers.txt, had its numbers separated with spaces. You can also separate them with newline characters, like this:

```
100
50
30
25
```

The application doesn't care. It looks for *white space,* which is any number of *spaces, tabs,* and *newlines.* You could format the data so it looks like the following example, and the application will still read them in correctly.

```
100        50
                30
    25
```

When you are dealing with the standard input object, cin, the same rules about white space apply: If you read in four numbers, like the following example, the cin object, like the ifstream object, will separate the numbers based on the white space.

```
cin >> weight;
cin >> height;
cin >> width;
cin >> depth;
```

If the user *accidentally* inserts a space, the computer will apply the separated values in two places — both incorrectly. Be careful!

When you are reading information from a file, make sure that you have clearly defined the order of the information. In other words, make sure that you have agreed upon a protocol for the information. Otherwise you'll likely end up with errors and mistakes, and your coworkers will want to blame somebody. That's the way computer people are, after all.

Of course, you'll want to verify that the application actually works. Adding this code will do the trick:

```
cout << "Weight = " << weight << "\r\n";
cout << "Height = " << height << "\r\n";
cout << "Width  = " << width << "\r\n";
cout << "Depth  = " << depth;
```

When you run the application, you see the result of reading the file. Here is what you should see:

```
Weight = 100
Height = 50
Width  = 30
Depth  = 25
```

Encountering the End of File

When we get to the end of a really good novel, we often feel disappointed that it's done, and we wish that we could just keep reading. But alas, we have encountered the EON (end of novel) condition.

Files have an ending as well, called the *EOF*, which stands for End of File. When you are reading from a file, you need to know when you reach the end. If you know how big the file is going to be, you can write your application so it knows exactly when to stop. So here are the cases we cover in this section: First, how you can read to the end of the file simply because you know how big the file is — and (therefore) when to stop reading; and second, how you can keep reading until you reach the EOF without having to know the file size in advance.

You, the programmer, know the format of the file you are reading. (Perhaps your application even wrote the file and now you're writing the part of the application that reads it.) And it's possible your format starts with a *size*. For example, you may be reading in a file, and you start by reading a number from the file, where the number represents how many pieces of information you are to read from the file. This requires that whoever created the file started by writing the size before the rest of the data, and that you agree to this format.

Here's an example. First, the `FileRead02` example in Listing 3-1 writes two files that you can later read in.

Listing 3-1:   Using Code to Open a File and Write to It

```cpp
#include <iostream>
#include <fstream>
#include <string>

using namespace std;

void WriteFile(string filename, int count, int start)
{
    ofstream outfile(filename.c_str());
    outfile << count << endl;
    int i;
    for (i=0; i<count; i++)
```

```
    {
        outfile << start + i  << endl;
    }
    outfile.close();
}

int main()
{
    WriteFile("../nums1.txt", 5, 100);
    WriteFile("../nums2.txt", 6, 200);
    return 0;
}
```

You can see that this application writes two files. This example places the files in your /CPP_AIO/BookV/Chapter 03 folder. The .. path refers to the parent folder of the current folder, which is /CPP_AIO/BookV/Chapter 03/FileRead02. The reason we're giving a path is that the next listing reads from the files, and we want to make sure that the application can find the files. Using the parent folder also avoids problems with newer operating systems that don't allow root directory access, such as Windows 7, OS X, and Linux.

Note that the WriteFile() function takes a filename, a count, and a start. It uses this information to write a series of numbers to the file. But before it writes those numbers, it writes the count, like this:

```
    outfile << count << endl;
```

Then it uses a loop to write count numbers to the file.

And, of course, when the WriteFile() function is all done, it closes the file. *Good application, good.*

The FileRead03 example shown in Listing 3-2 is an example of how to read this data back in.

Listing 3-2:   Using Code to Open a File and Read It Back In

```
#include <iostream>
#include <fstream>
#include <string>

using namespace std;

void ReadFile(string filename)
{
    ifstream infile(filename.c_str());
    int count;
    int i;
    int num;
```

(continued)

Listing 3-2 *(continued)*

```cpp
    cout << "File: " << filename << endl;
    infile >> count;
    cout << "This file has " << count << " items." << endl;
    for (i=0; i<count; i++)
    {
        infile >> num;
        cout << num << endl;
    }
    infile.close();
}

int main()
{
    ReadFile("../nums1.txt");
    ReadFile("../nums2.txt");
    return 0;
}
```

You can see in Listing 3-2, like Listing 3-1, `filename` includes the path names for the files the application is reading in.

Now look at the `ReadFile()` function. This function opens the file and then immediately reads in a number. This number represents the number of items to read in. It's the first number that was written by the `WriteFile()` function in the previous listing, Listing 3-1.

As the writer of both the application that writes the file and the application that reads the file, we agreed (both sides of us agreed, that is, or so we think) on the format of the file both for reading it and for writing it. And by sticking to this format, we can assure ourselves that we can read in the file that we previously wrote. When you run this application, you'll see the following output.

```
File: /MyData/nums1.txt
This file has 5 items.
100
101
102
103
104
File: /MyData/nums2.txt
This file has 6 items.
200
201
202
203
204
205

Process returned 0 (0x0)   execution time : 0.000 s
Press any key to continue.
```

Now another possibility for reading and writing a file is that you continue reading data from the file until you reach the end of the file. How do you do this? You test the istream or ifstream object for the EOF.

Listings 3-3 and 3-4 show you how you can do this. As with the earlier listings, the first writes a couple of files, and the second reads them in.

First, Listing 3-3 shows the FileRead04 example.

Listing 3-3:   Using Code to Write to a File but Not Record a Count

```
#include <iostream>
#include <fstream>
#include <string>

using namespace std;

void WriteFile(string filename, int count, int start)
{
    ofstream outfile(filename.c_str());
    int i;
    for (i=0; i<count; i++)
    {
        outfile << start + i  << endl;
    }
    outfile.close();
}

int main()
{
    WriteFile("../nums1.txt", 5, 100);
    WriteFile("../nums2.txt", 6, 200);
    return 0;
}
```

As you can probably see, Listing 3-3 is like Listing 3-1, except Listing 3-3 does not start out by writing out a count.

The FileRead05 example in Listing 3-4 reads the numbers back in.

Listing 3-4:   Reading from a File and Looking for the EOF Condition

```
#include <iostream>
#include <fstream>
#include <string>

using namespace std;

void ReadFile(string filename)
{
    ifstream infile(filename.c_str());
    int num;
```

(continued)

Listing 3-4 *(continued)*

```
    cout << "File: " << filename << endl;
    bool done = false;
    while (!done)
    {
        infile >> num;
        if (infile.eof() == true)
        {
            done = true;
        }
        else
        {
            cout << num << endl;
        }
    }
    infile.close();
}

int main()
{
    ReadFile("../nums1.txt");
    ReadFile("../nums2.txt");
    return 0;
}
```

This listing is like Listing 3-2. However, instead of first reading a count, it just dives in and starts reading. The output of this example differs a little as a result. Here's what you get as output:

```
File: ../nums1.txt
100
101
102
103
104
File: ../nums2.txt
200
201
202
203
204
205

Process returned 0 (0x0)    execution time : 0.010 s
Press any key to continue.
```

Note carefully how Listing 3-4 does its thing: The listing first *tries* to read in a number, and *then* it checks if it encountered an EOF. If you're familiar with other styles of reading in files, this approach may seem a little backwards to you. But that's the way the streams do it: First read, and if the read doesn't work, then abort.

Therefore, you have to have some strange logic in your code. Here's the general algorithm:

```
set done to false
while not done
    read a number
    if encounter an end of file
        set done to true
    else
        process the number read in
    end-if
end-while
```

Something bothers us about this approach: We need a big `if` statement, and the `process the number` part goes in an `else` block. We like having a Boolean variable called `done`, because then we can use a `while` loop that reads like this:

```
while (!done) // pronounced "while not done"
```

If lots of processing is needed, the processing will all be piled inside the `else` portion of the `if` block. And that can get ugly with a million indentations. In this case, check for EOF and then break out of the loop, like this:

```
if (infile.eof() == true)
    break;
```

But if you do that, you have no reason for the `done` variable. So what do you put in the `while` loop? A lot of people do this:

```
while (1)
{
    infile >> num;
    if (infile.eof() == true)
        break;
    cout << num << endl;
}
```

Yes, they put `while (1)`. In other words, the `while` loop spins forever until a `break` statement comes along. We're not particularly fond of the `while (1)` construct because it's a bit counterintuitive for our little tiny brains, but a lot of people do it; and we have to admit that we like the short `if` statement, just breaking if the EOF is true. You choose which method you want to use. And heck, you may even be able to dream up a couple more ways to do this.

Reading Various Types

Reading a file is fun, but it can get complicated when you want to read spaces. Suppose we have these two strings that we want to write to a file:

```
"That's the steak by the poodle that I'll have for dinner."

"I will have the Smiths for dinner, too."
```

Now suppose you wrote these to a file as one big long line to get, "That's the steak by the poodle that I'll have for dinner. I will have the Smiths for dinner, too."

Now later, you want to read back in these two strings. How can you do that? You can't just do this:

```
string first, second;
infile >> first;
infile >> second;
```

If you do this, the variable `first` will hold *That's*, and the variable `second` will hold *the*. Why? Because, when you read in strings, the `ifstream` and `istream` classes use spaces to break (or *delimit*) the strings. Bummer.

But even if you could somehow get the `ifstream` class to go past the spaces, how does the `ifstream` class know when it has reached the end of the first string? Now, in this case, you may write your application to follow this protocol: A string ends with a period.

And that protocol is fine, because ending with a period is the case with these two strings that we wrote to the file. But what if they were just sequences of words, like this:

```
"poodle steak eat puddle"

"dinner Smiths yummy"
```

And then, when you write these two strings to a file, you may end up with this inside the file:

```
poodle steak eat puddle dinner Smiths yummy
```

Or worse, you may get this, which contains no space between the two strings:

```
poodle steak eat puddledinner Smiths yummy
```

Here's what we suggest that you do: First, you must agree on a protocol. This, of course, may just mean agreeing with yourself. (Always a good idea. No, it's not! Yes, it is!) Here are some choices for your protocols:

✦ You can write each string on a separate line, and when you read the file, you will know that each line is a separate string.

✦ You can delimit each string with a particular character. Then you would split your strings based on those delimiters.

Writing a string to a separate line is very easy; you simply do this:

```
cout << mystring << endl;
```

Nothing earth-shattering there. Reading it in is pretty easy, too; you just use the `getline()` function in the `ifstream` or `istream` class. The catch is that the `getline()` function wants a character array, not a `string` object. So go ahead and read it into a character array, and then convert it to a `string` object like so:

```
char buf[1024];
infile.getline(&(buf[0]), 1024);
string str(buf);
```

You don't have to convert the array to a `string` object; if you want, you can just work with the character array. But we prefer to work with `string` objects because they're instances of classes and you get all kinds of nice member functions that can manipulate the strings. We're all about making our lives easier.

The `ReadString01` example in Listing 3-5 shows how to write the strings with a delimiter. You can see that this has nothing particularly magical about it (other than the quantum physics involved in running the microprocessor, but we don't care about that).

Listing 3-5: Writing Strings with a Delimiter Is Easy

```
#include <iostream>
#include <string>
#include <fstream>

using namespace std;

void WriteString(ofstream &file, string words)
{
    file << words;
    file << ";";
}

int main()
{
    ofstream delimfile("../delims.txt");

    WriteString(delimfile, "This is a dog");
    WriteString(delimfile, "Some dogs bite");
    WriteString(delimfile, "Some dogs don't bite");
    WriteString(delimfile, "Humans that is");
    WriteString(delimfile, "All dogs bite");
    WriteString(delimfile, "Food that is");
    WriteString(delimfile, "I say, food food food.");

    delimfile.close();
    return 0;
}
```

The `ReadString02` example in Listing 3-6 shows you how to read in the file strings. We used a trick for this. The `ifstream` class inherits from the `istream` class the `getline()` function. Most people use this to read a line of text. However, a little-known fact is that you can specify the delimiter you prefer to use instead of the end-of-line character. You pass the delimiter as the third parameter. And so we passed a semicolon character for the third character, and lo and behold, the thing worked!

Listing 3-6:   Specifying a Delimiter with the getline Function

```
#include <iostream>
#include <string>
#include <fstream>

using namespace std;

string ReadString(ifstream &file)
{
    char buf[1024]; // Make sure this is big enough!
    file.getline(&(buf[0]), 1024, ';');
    return string(buf);
}

int main()
{
    ifstream delimfile("../delims.txt");

    while (1)
    {
        string words = ReadString(delimfile);
        if (delimfile.eof() == true)
            break;
        cout << words << endl;
    }
    delimfile.close();
    return 0;
}
```

When you run Listing 3-6, you see this output:

```
This is a dog
Some dogs bite
Some dogs don't bite
Humans that is
All dogs bite
Food that is
I say, food food food.
```

Yay! That's the correct list of strings!

Reading Formatted Input

Sooner or later, you may be reading a file that has this kind of information in it:

```
Hello there my favorite number is 13. When I go to the
store I buy 52 items each week, except on dates that
start with 2, in which case I buy 53 items.

Hello there my favorite number is 18. When I go to the
store I buy 72 items each week, except on dates that
start with 1, in which case I buy 73 items.

Hello there my favorite number is 10. When I go to the
store I buy 40 items each week, except on dates that
start with 2, in which case I buy 41 items.
```

This file has a general *format* (or protocol!). The text is easy because it can only be interpreted in one way — as text. However, the numbers could be interpreted as text (the characters 1 and 3 for example) or as a value (the number 13). How can you read in the numbers? One way is to read strings for each of the words and skip them. Here's a sample piece of code that reads up to the first number, the favorite number:

```
ifstream infile("words.txt");
string skip;
for (int i=0; i<6; i++)
    infile >> skip;
int favorite;
infile >> favorite;
```

This code reads in six strings and just ignores them. You can see how we do this through a loop that counts from 0 up to but not including 6. (Ah, you gotta love computers. Most people would just count 1 to 6. We suppose we *could* have, but we're computer guys, no more, no less.)

Then, after we read the six strings that we just ignored, we finally read the favorite number as a number. Notice that the individual words use a variable of type `string` and the numeric value uses a variable of type `int`. You can then repeat the same process to get the remaining numbers.

Chapter 4: Building Directories and Contents

In This Chapter

✔ Creating and deleting directories

✔ Getting the contents of a directory

✔ Copying and moving, and why they are related

✔ Moving and renaming files and why they are similar

We're about to say something you might not believe: *C++ provides no functions for creating directories and getting the contents of a directory.*

Really! We know it's hard to believe, but we can make two points about this:

✦ There really is a (more-or-less) good reason for this lack: C++ is a general-purpose language: Issues that deal with directories are specific to individual operating systems. Thus it doesn't make sense to include such features in C++. (Supposedly. So they say. We guess. Whatever.)

✦ Some brave rebels have added some functions — and these functions exist in most C++ implementations. Whew! That's a good thing — otherwise you'd have to call in to the operating system to create or modify a directory.

C++ has a holdover from the C programming language in the header file stdio.h that includes functions for renaming and removing files and directories. (Interesting.) Oh, yes, and there's another one in there for creating a temporary file. (Even more interesting.)

In this chapter, we present you with ways to manipulate directories and files. (We have tested these routines only for the GNU GCC compiler that comes with the Code::Blocks product for OS X, Linux, and Windows. If you're working with a different compiler or operating system, try out. They probably will work.)

For the examples in this chapter, you need to add both #include <stdio.h> and #include <io.h> to the beginning of the source code file. (Please do not confuse this file with ios.h. That's *another* header file but not the right one to mess with just now.) Now again, if you're working with a compiler other than Code::Blocks, we cannot guarantee that you'll find io.h in your include directory. However, there's a good chance you will. Look for it!

Manipulating Directories

There are a couple functions you can use for creating and deleting directories. These functions are in the io.h header file.

Creating a directory

If you want to create a directory, you can call the mkdir function. If the function can create the directory for you, it returns a 0. Otherwise it returns a nonzero value. (When we ran it we got a –1, but your best bet — always — is to test it against 0.)

Here's some sample code (found in the MakeDirectory example) that uses this function:

```
#include <iostream>
#include <stdio.h>
#include <io.h>

using namespace std;

int main()
{
    if (mkdir("../abc") != 0)
    {
        cout << "I'm so sorry. I was not" << endl;
        cout << "able to create your directory" << endl;
        cout << "as you asked of me. I do hope" << endl;
        cout << "you are still able to achieve" << endl;
        cout << "your goals in life. Now go away." << endl;
    }
    return 0;
}
```

Notice (as usual) that we used a forward slash (/) in the call to mkdir. In Windows, you can use either a forward slash or a backslash. But if you use a backslash, you have to use two of them (as you normally would to get a backslash into a C++ string). For the sake of portability, we recommend always using a forward slash. After you run this example, you should see a new directory named abc added to the /CPP_AIO/BookV/Chapter04 directory on your system.

It would be nice to create an entire directory-tree structure in one fell swoop — doing a call such as mkdir("/abc/def/ghi/jkl") without having any of the abc, def, or ghi directories already existing. But alas, you can't. The function won't create a jkl directory unless the /abc/def/ghi directory exists. That means you have to break this call into multiple calls: First create /abc. Then create /abc/def, and so on.

If you do want to make all the directories at once, you can use the system() function, as we describe in "Using the quick-and-dirty method" sidebar, later in this chapter. If you execute system("mkdir \\abc\\def\\ghi\\ jkl"); , you will be able to make the directory in one fell swoop.

Deleting a directory

It's fun to go on a cleaning spree and just toss everything out. And so it makes sense that deleting a directory is easy. To do it, you just call the `rmdir` function, passing the name of the directory. If you want to find out whether it worked, test its results against 0. Here's some sample code as found in the `DeleteDirectory` example:

```cpp
#include <iostream>
#include <stdio.h>
#include <io.h>

using namespace std;

int main()
{
    if (rmdir("../abc") != 0)
    {
        cout << "Life is difficult sometimes, and" << endl;
        cout << "sometimes you just don't get what" << endl;
        cout << "you asked for. And this is one" << endl;
        cout << "such case. I just couldn't remove" << endl;
        cout << "the directory for you. Better" << endl;
        cout << "luck next time, my dear friend." << endl;
    }
    return 0;
}
```

After you run this example, the `/CPP_AIO/BookV/Chapter04/abc` directory that you created in the previous section will go away. Make sure you verify that the directory is added and removed as expected.

 This approach works only if the directory is *not empty*. If the directory has at least one file in it, the function can't remove the directory — and returns a nonzero result. Then you get to see the nice, friendly message that we're particularly proud of.

Getting the Contents of a Directory

If you want to read the contents of a directory, you're really going against what's available in the standard C++ language. However, the Kind Souls of the Great Libraries of C++ (that is, the people who wrote most of the available C++ libraries) usually built in some handy functions for getting the contents of a directory.

A directory usually contains multiple files as well as other directories. Getting a list of contents is involved. You don't just call a function and get something back — we're not sure what that something would be, other than a pretty basic list.

Of course, if the Standard C++ Library included a function for getting information, it would likely be a template class that contains the directory contents. Alas, the library doesn't support it. (Delphi, supports it, but don't get us going.) Instead, you have to climb through some functions. Here's how it works.

1. Call `_findfirst()`, passing it a pathname and a pattern for the files whose names you want to find.

   For example, pass `*.*` to get all files in the directory, or `*.txt` to get all files ending in `.txt`. Also pass it a pointer to a `_finddata_t` structure.

2. Check the results of `_findfirst()`.

   If `_findfirst()` returned –1, it didn't find any files (which means you're finished). Otherwise it fills the `_finddata_t` structure with the first file it found, and it will return a number that you use in subsequent calls to the various find functions.

3. Look at the `_finddata_t` structure to determine the name of the file, and other information such as create date, last access date, and size.

4. Call `_findnext()` and pass it the following values: the number returned from `_findfirst()` and the address of a `_finddata_t` structure

   If `_findnext()` returns –1, it found no more files; you can go to Step 5. Otherwise look at the `_finddata_t` structure to get the information for the next file found. Then repeat Step 4.

5. Call `_findclose()` and pass it the number returned from `_findfirst()`.

   You're all finished.

Youch! That's kind of bizarre, but it's the way things used to be done in the old days of programming, before the mainstream languages developed such civilized features as classes and objects. We just had structures; we had to pass a bunch of information around by hand (and walk to school, uphill both ways, in the snow).

The `GetDirectoryContents` example in Listing 4-1 shows how we implemented this elegant, old-fashioned process.

Listing 4-1: Using Code to Read the Contents of a Directory

```
#include <iostream>
#include <io.h>
#include <time.h>
#include <string>

using namespace std;

string Chop(string &str)
{
    string res = str;
```

```
    int len = str.length();
    if (str[len - 1] == '\r')
    {
        res.replace(len - 1, 1, "");
    }
    len = str.length();
    if (str[len - 1] == '\n')
    {
        res.replace(len - 1, 1, "");
    }
    return res;
}

void DumpEntry(_finddata_t &data)
{
    string createtime(ctime(&data.time_create));
    cout << Chop(createtime) << "\t";
    cout << data.size << "\t";
    if ((data.attrib & _A_SUBDIR) == _A_SUBDIR)
    {
        cout << "[" << data.name << "]" << endl;
    }
    else
    {
        cout << data.name << endl;
    }
}

int main()
{
    _finddata_t data;

    int ff = _findfirst ("../*.*", &data);

    if (ff != -1)
    {
        int res = 0;
        while (res != -1)
        {
            DumpEntry(data);
            res = _findnext(ff, &data);
        }
        _findclose(ff);
    }
    return 0;
}
```

You can see how in main() we followed the steps we just outlined. And for
each of the data structures, we used our own function called DumpEntry().
The DumpEntry() function prints out the information about the file. Here's
what you should see when you run the application (the current directory
entry, the parent directory entry, and the four directories containing the
examples for this chapter):

```
Sun Dec 15 19:40:00 2013          0        [.]
Sun Dec 15 19:40:00 2013          0        [..]
Sun Dec 15 19:40:00 2013          0        [DeleteDirectory]
Sun Dec 15 19:40:00 2013          0        [GetDirectoryContents]
Sun Dec 15 19:40:00 2013          0        [MakeDirectory]
Sun Dec 15 19:40:00 2013          0        [RenameFile]
```

Note how, in the `DumpEntry()` function, we're testing whether the item is a directory. This is another old (but reliable) way to program: We check for the presence of one particular tiny little bit in the middle of the `attrib` member of the structure, like this:

```
if (data.attrib & _A_SUBDIR == _A_SUBDIR)
{
    cout << "[" << data.name << "]" << endl;
}
```

And finally, you'll notice a strange function we included called `Chop()`. That's because when we wrote the application, we discovered that the `ctime()` function — otherwise handy for formatting the time — adds a carriage return (or *newline*) to the end of the string it creates. So we chop that off. Otherwise the information after the date has to start on the next line of text, which wasn't what we wanted.

Copying Files

Ah, copying a file — something so simple, it happens all the time. Copy this file there; copy that file here. But what exactly takes place when you copy a file? You actually create a *new* file, and fill it with the same contents as the original file. And how do you do that? Well, from what we just said, it sounds like you have to read each and every byte from the first file, and write it to the second. Big-time yuck.

Copying with windows: You're in luck

If you're programming in Windows, you're in luck! As long as you're not using the ancient Windows 3.1, you get a `CopyFile` function! To get ready to use it, you include the line `#include <windows.h>` in your application. Then here's all you have to do:

```
CopyFile("c:/dog.txt", "c:/dog2.txt",
    TRUE);
```

This copies from `c:/dog.txt` to `c:/dog2.txt`. But notice the final parameter: It's the word `TRUE` in all capitals. What's that? That's a preprocessor macro defined somewhere in the bowels of the Windows header files. You have to use either `TRUE` or `FALSE` when calling any of the Windows functions. That's because in the old days of C, when the early versions of Windows were invented, no `bool` type existed. Those resourceful people of the late 20th century had to define their own `TRUE` and `FALSE` as integers (usually either 1 and 0, respectively, or 0 and 1, respectively). And by the way, that final parameter in `CopyFile` tells the function what to do if the file you're copying to already exists: `TRUE` means don't overwrite the existing file; just abort. `FALSE` means overwrite it.

Using the quick-and-dirty method

Okay, time for a secret: There's another way you can copy a file, and you can use this to also move, delete, and rename files. However, this method we're about to show you is absolutely not portable: in effect, if you do this on Windows, for example, you won't be able to run the same application on Unix, and vice versa. That is, you have to make a version for the operating system you're using. Now, if you're familiar with DOS (remember that?) or the Unix shell, you can execute any DOS or Unix-shell commands by using the `system` function. If you use Dev-C++, you've already seen the `system` function many times:

```
system("PAUSE");
```

This runs the DOS `pause` command, which prints the message

```
Press any key to continue . . .
```

and waits for you to press the Any key (or any other key for that matter). Because the `system` function can run any DOS or shell command, you can use it to call the DOS copy command, like this:

```
system("copy c:\\abc.txt c:\\def.txt");
```

Note that we had to use the backslash, not a forward slash; DOS really doesn't like forward slashes. To make the command DOS-friendly, we had to use two backslashes inside the string.

When you use this approach, you can run into some strange situations. For example, if you write an application that calls `system` and you're planning to run it under the `Cygwin` environment in Windows, you can use the Unix-style `cp` command instead of the DOS `copy` command. The resulting weird command looks like this:

```
system("cp c:\\abc.txt c:\\def.txt");
```

But you can only use this command under the `Cygwin` environment. Otherwise it gives you a huffy error message:

```
'cp' is not recognized as an internal
      or external command, operable
      program or batch file.
```

Moral: You have to make sure that whatever command you call in the `system` function really exists in the environment from which you issue the call.

But to make matters worse, copying a file means you have to make sure that you copy it exactly the same, that you don't accidentally tack an extra 0 or two at the end of the file, or an extra carriage return or linefeed at the end of the file (which could happen when you copy a text file). When all is done, the two files should be identical — not only contain the *same information*, but also be the *same size*. (We can hear the nonconformists now: "*Super* big-time yuck!")

And on top of all that, most good copy routines do even more! They give the new file a date that matches the date of the original file, and they will set all the attributes — including, say, read-only if the original is a read-only file. (We're pointedly ignoring that if the file is read-only, then maybe we shouldn't be able to copy it in the first place. . . .)

Suddenly copying a file doesn't sound so easy after all!

Now, this is going to go against the norm for every computer book you've ever seen, but we're *not* going to give you code and tell you to use it for your file-copying operations. The reason for this heresy? Well, as simple as it may sound, we've seen too many people write code that's *supposed* to copy files but runs too slowly, or screws up the process, or both!

So we tucked a couple of sidebars into this section to give you the *best* way to copy a file. Enjoy!

Moving and Renaming Files and Directories

Think about this: We have a file called

```
dog1.txt
```

and we're going to rename it to

```
temp\dog1.txt
```

Is that a valid way to rename a file? If you notice, the file started out being called `dog1.txt`, and afterwards it was called `dog1.txt`. Did we rename it or did we just *move* it? Indeed, we moved it from the current directory to the `temp` subdirectory. Why did we call this operation a rename? Because that's *also* what we did! We're thinking of the file's real name as *the entire pathname and filename together*.

For that reason, you can move *and* rename by using the same function. If you want to move a file, rename it with a different path. Of course, the path must exist (details, details). If we try to rename `c:\dog1.txt` to `c:\temp\dog1.txt` and there's no `c:\temp` directory, the rename fails and we get an error message.

The `RenameFile` example renames a file:

```cpp
#include <iostream>
#include <stdio.h>

using namespace std;

int main()
{
    if (rename("dog1.txt","dog2.txt") == 0)
    {
        cout << "Renaming dog1.txt to dog2.txt." << endl;
    }

    if (rename("dog2.txt","dog1.txt") == 0)
    {
        cout << "Renaming dog2.txt to dog1.txt." << endl;
    }
```

```
if (rename("dog1.txt","temp/dog1.txt") != 0)
{
    cout << "Same old story. No respect at all." << endl;
}
return 0;
}
```

We used the `rename()` function, passing first the old filename and then the new filename. The first call renames the file from `dog1.txt` to `dog2.txt`. The second call renames it from `dog2.txt` to `dog1.txt`. Finally, we try to rename `dog1.txt` to `temp\dog1.text`, which (in effect) moves the file. When you run this example, you see the following output:

```
Renaming dog1.txt to dog2.txt.
Renaming dog2.dat to dog1.txt.
Same old story. No respect at all.
```

The final `rename()` call fails because the temp subdirectory doesn't exist in the example (unless you've created it).

You can also give the file a new filename when you move it, as in this code:

```
rename("dog1.txt","temp/cat.txt")
```

There are conditions under which the rename operation won't work:

+ You're renaming the file to move it to a new directory, but that directory does not exist. In this case, create the directory before you move the file.

+ You're renaming a file but some other file in the current directory already exists under that name. In this case, either delete the other file or (better yet) make your application ask its users what they want it to do: Delete the old file (that is, "overwrite it")? Abort the operation? Abort! Abort! Abort! (No, wait, that's only for the self-destruct. Never mind.)

+ You're renaming a file to move it to a new directory, but there's already a file by that name in that directory. In this case, as in the previous example, get your application to ask the users what to do — overwrite or abort?

Now for some really exciting news! Renaming also works with directories! You can move directory names around just as if they were files! But there's a catch: If any application has a file open within that directory, the `rename()` function won't work. The operating system lets you move or rename a directory only if you're not accessing any files inside the directory. That's still true if you're using a DOS window and staying inside the `C:` directory like this:

```
C:\>cd dog
C:\dog>
```

If you have a DOS window open with this sort of operation in it, you can't move the `dog` directory unless you either move out of the `dog` directory first or close the DOS window before you move the `dog` directory. (Or you can just make a new directory and move everything out of the old directory.)

Chapter 5: Streaming Your Own Classes

In This Chapter

✔ Streaming a class to a text file

✔ Getting the most out of manipulators

✔ Writing your own manipulators

The C++ stream classes can read and write all sorts of goodies, such as integers, characters, strings, floating-point numbers, and Boolean variables. But sooner or later, being able to stream one of your own classes (like the following) would be nice:

```
MyClass x;
cout << x << endl;
```

Now C++ has a good reason not to have done this already: The compiler and library can't predict on their own how you want to stream your class. What should `cout` write? The name of the class followed by the values of the public member variables? Or maybe just the private member variables? None of the above?

Therefore you should make the class streamable. In this chapter, we show you how to do it. But keep in mind that you have (at least) two separate reasons why you may want to make a class streamable:

✦ To provide a format for writing the object to a text stream.

✦ To save the information in an object so you can read it back in at a later date, thereby reconstructing the object. A class with this feature is called a *persistent* class.

We cover both topics in this chapter. We also show how you can create your own manipulators. Remember, a *manipulator* is this kind of code:

```
cout << endl;
```

That is, the `endl` is the manipulator. You can make your own manipulators that manipulate the stream in various ways, as we show you later in this chapter.

Streaming a Class for Text Formatting

When dealing with instances of one of your classes, the ability to use the insertion and extraction operators << and >> is nice.

To use these operators, you overload them to take parameters of your class. Sounds easy, doesn't it? When people first find out about overloading the insertion and extraction operators, the process often seems so much harder than it really is.

Here's the scoop: If you have a class, say `MicrowaveOven`, and you have an instance of this class, say `myoven`, all you do to accomplish the overloading of an operator is code a function that takes as a parameter a stream and an object and writes the members of the object *to* the stream. Then you will be able to code one of the following lines:

```
cout << myoven;
```

```
outfile << myoven;
```

Now what if you want to code an operator that reads from a stream? Then all you do is write a function that reads the members *from* a stream if you want to code one of the following lines:

```
cin >> myoven;
```

```
infile >> myoven;
```

Again, no biggie. The key is *what to call the function*.

Remember that `cout << myoven` actually calls a function called <<. Here's the function header:

```
ostream &operator <<(ostream &out, MicrowaveOven &oven)
```

This technique isn't as hard to remember as you may think. First, always remember that every type in this is a reference. (That makes sense when you look at `cout << myoven`. The second parameter, `myoven`, is not a pointer. And you normally don't want to pass objects around directly, so that leaves only one possibility: passing it by reference.)

Second, remember that the function must return the stream that it's working with. Returning the stream allows you to chain together operators like this:

```
cout << "hi" << myoven << 123 << endl;
```

Finally, remember that the operator function takes two parameters. You can see their order when you look at the order of cout << myoven. The first is the stream; the second is your class. Thus, when you put this all together, you get the function header we just described, that is

```
ostream &operator <<(ostream &out, MicrowaveOven &oven)
```

Now, what do you do with this function that you wrote? You just write to the stream passed into it! What do you write? Whatever you want! It's true: Because you designed the class that the function takes as a parameter, you decide how the output *looks* when you write the object to a stream. So pretend that this is your MicrowaveOven class:

```
class MicrowaveOven
{
public:
    int HighVoltageRadiation;
    int RadioactiveFoodCount;
    int LeakLevel;
    string OvenName;
};
```

Then your insertion function may look like this:

```
ostream &operator <<(ostream &out, MicrowaveOven &oven)
{
    out << "High Voltage Radiation: ";
    out << oven.HighVoltageRadiation << endl;
    out << "Radioactive Food Count: ";
    out << oven.RadioactiveFoodCount << endl;
    out << "Leak Level: ";
    out << oven.LeakLevel << endl;
    out << "Oven Name: ";
    out << oven.OvenName << endl;
    return out;
}
```

Now for some points about the preceding code:

✦ We took complete liberty with how we wanted the object to look on the stream. For each member variable, we wrote a description, a colon, a space, and then a value. We then put an endl. Would you like the output to look different? Then go for it! It's your choice how you want the output to look.

✦ We returned the same output stream that came in as the first parameter. This is important!

✦ When we wrote to the stream, we wrote to out, not to cout. If we messed up and wrote to cout, this function would not work properly when used with a file. If we tried myfile << myoven, the information would just go to cout, not into the file. Oops!

In this function, we accessed only the public member variables of the oven instance. As it stands, we can't access the private members because this function is not a member of MicrowaveOven. (Now of course, MicrowaveOven doesn't actually have any private members, but most of your classes probably do.) To access the private members, make this function a friend of MicrowaveOven by adding this inside the MicrowaveOven class:

```
friend ostream &operator <<(ostream &out,
    MicrowaveOven &oven);
```

Here's a similar function for reading from a stream:

```
istream &operator >(istream &in, MicrowaveOven &oven)
{
    in >> oven.HighVoltageRadiation;
    in >> oven.RadioactiveFoodCount;
    in >> oven.LeakLevel;
    in >> oven.OvenName;
    return in;
}
```

You can see that the format of this function is like that of the insertion operator: The function returns a reference to the stream, and for parameters, the function takes a reference to a stream and a reference to a MicrowaveOven object.

And as before, we had complete freedom on how we wanted to read this in. We chose to just read in each member separately. So, if we call this function by using cin like this

```
cin > myoven;
```

then — when we run this line — we could type the member values on one line with spaces, or on separate lines, or any combination:

```
1234 5555
1054 "Buzz"
```

And that's it! Using the insertion and extraction operators isn't really magical at all.

To use the insertion and extraction operators, remember that you simply write two functions, one for each operator. These functions write to a stream or read from it. And always remember the two most important aspects of these functions:

✦ Remember to return the stream at the end!

✦ Remember to use references!

Manipulating a Stream

A lot of people see this kind of thing:

```
cout << "Hello" << endl;
```

and wonder what on Earth endl is. Is it a variable? Is it a keyword? What is it? And how can you add your own things like it? In this section, we answer this and every other question you ever had about these strange little creatures called *manipulators*.

What's a manipulator?

What exactly is endl? Here's the answer, and it might surprise you: endl is a *function*. However, you may notice that it has no parentheses. And so you're not actually calling the function.

So what are you doing? (Seems as though we've made the story even more complicated.) In this section, we show you that a manipulator is actually the address of a function. How's that for a strange thought? Read on.

To clarify exactly what endl is, think about this:

```
cout << endl;
```

And think about the operator function, <<. By writing cout << endl, you're calling an overloaded insertion operator function and passing in two parameters, cout and endl. The first parameter, cout, is an instance of ostream. The second parameter, endl, is the *address of a function*. Yes, when you type a function name but don't include parentheses, you're giving the address of the function rather than calling the function.

And so, somewhere out there (in the standard header files, actually) is an overloaded insertion function that takes both an ostream and the address of a function. Now the thing about function addresses is that the type of a function pointer is based on the function's return type and parameter types. Thus pointers to these two functions have the same type:

```
void WriteMe(int x, char c);

void AlwaysAndForever(int y, char x);
```

Even though the names of the parameters are different, the types of the parameters are the same. That's why pointers to the two functions have the same type. But pointers to the following two functions do *not* have the same type:

```
void SomethingForNothing(int x);

int LeaveMeAlone(int y, int z);
```

The functions do not have the same type because their prototypes are different. The first takes a single integer as a parameter and returns a void. The second takes two integers as parameters and returns an integer.

Now here's the prototype for the endl function:

```
ostream& endl(ostream& outs);
```

This function takes a reference to ostream and returns a reference to ostream. And here's a sufficient typedef for a pointer to this function:

```
typedef ostream& (*omanip)(ostream&);
```

This defines a new type called omanip, which is a pointer to a function that takes as a parameter a reference to ostream and returns a reference to ostream. Perfect! Therefore, if we have a variable of type omanip, we can set it to the address of the endl function.

So now back to this:

```
cout << endl;
```

For this manipulator to work, you need an overloaded insertion operator function that takes two parameters: first a reference to ostream (for the cout) and then omanip. Yes, the second parameter must be a reference to omanip because the second item in cout << endl is omanip.

If you're not clear on why endl is omanip, think about this: There's a function called endl, and to call that function, you would type its name, an opening parenthesis, some parameters, and then a closing parenthesis. But if you leave off the parentheses, you're just taking the address of the function. And the type omanip, which we defined earlier, is exactly that: an address to a function. But on top of being an address, the endl function's prototype matches that for the omanip type. Therefore we can say that endl is of the type omanip. Whew.

Here's a possibility for the header of the overloaded insertion operator:

```
ostream& operator<<(ostream& out, omanip func);
```

You can see the parameters that this function takes: First, it takes a reference to ostream and then omanip.

But remember what we're doing. We're trying to explain how the following manipulator works:

```
cout << endl;
```

Two functions are involved. Here are their headers:

```
ostream& endl(ostream& outs);

ostream& operator<<(ostream& out, omanip func);
```

When you type `cout << endl`, you're *not* calling the `endl` function. Instead, you're calling this `operator<<` function because `endl` by itself — without parentheses — is nothing more than the *address of the* `endl` *function*. And the address is of type `omanip`.

Thus, when you type **cout << endl**, you're calling this `operator<<` function, passing in `cout` and `endl`.

Here's the `operator<<` function in its entirety:

```
ostream& operator<<(ostream &out, omanip func)
{
    return (*func)(out);
}
```

The second parameter is called `func`. When you call `cout << endl`, you're passing `endl` in as the `func` parameter. And what does this `operator<<` function do? It calls the function passed into it. Thus it calls `endl`. Huh?

Why did we go through all this rigmarole, if, ultimately, we're just calling this mysterious `endl` function? Here's why. Believe it or not, the use of `endl` is all about aesthetics. The following line is short and clear:

```
cout << "hello" << endl;
```

And to make this line work, you need an overloaded insertion operator. Fortunately, the `operator<<` function we've been talking about does the trick.

Finally, the computer eventually calls the `endl` function itself, and that function does the actual work of adding a newline character to the stream. Wow, all that just for a newline! And you thought you had it rough! Imagine being the compiler!

Now, this isn't the only way to accomplish coding a manipulator, as we explain in the following section, "Writing your own manipulator." In that section, we use a slightly different approach that works equally well. But the technique we've been describing works, too.

Time for some honesty: We did doctor the overloaded insertion operator function a bit, because, really, this function is a member of `ostream`. But the overloaded insertion operator function works equally well as a standalone function, as we've described in this section.

Writing your own manipulator

You can write your own manipulators in several ways. The goal is to allow for this type of code:

```
cout << mymanipulator;
```

and this line causes a function such as the following to get called:

```
ostream &operator << (ostream &out, somespecialtype a);
```

Now, think about the overloading that goes on here: Several `operator <<` functions are available; ultimately, they all differ in the type of the second parameter, where we wrote `somespecialtype`. And whatever `mymanipulator` is, it must be the `somespecialtype` type as well. But on top of it, this type must be unique: There cannot already be an overloaded function that has that type! Unique, unique, unique!

Although the "What's a manipulator?" section (earlier in this chapter) gives you all the gory details on how the `endl` manipulator works, we think that amount of detail is a bit too complicated. We'd rather use a slightly different approach for our own manipulators. Here's what we do in the following example: We want to make sure that we have a unique type and that the manipulator is an object of that type. As with other manipulators, function pointers work well. But for the function pointer to be unique, its return type and parameter types must be unique. That's not too hard; to guarantee that no other function has that prototype, we're going to make our own special type — a structure — and use that as the parameter for the function, like this:

```
struct FullOvenManip {};
void FullOvenInfo(FullOvenManip x) {}
```

Check this sample carefully. We created a structure called `FullOvenManip`. This structure has nothing in it; its sole purpose in life is to provide for a unique parameter experience. Yee-hah! And the function `FullOvenInfo()` takes this structure as a parameter. Considering that we just invented this structure, we can be quite certain that no other function in the C++ header files matches this prototype. More than certain, in fact. We'd be willing to bet our Hollywood Hills mansion (which we don't have, so we have nothing to lose!).

Now we can provide an overloaded `operator >>` function. That function takes a pointer to the `FullOvenInfo()` function. But to do that, we had better use `typedef`:

```
typedef void(*FullPtr)(FullOvenManip);
```

This line of code creates a type called `FullPtr`, which is a pointer to a function that takes a `FullOvenManip` parameter and returns a `void`. We can think of only one function that does that! It's the `FullOvenInfo()` function. Woo-hoo!

When writing your own manipulators, don't shy away from using `typedef`. The manipulator concept is confusing, and can be a serious struggle for many of us to keep straight. By using a `typedef`, you can simplify your life a bit.

Here's the overloaded `operator >>` function header:

```
ostream &operator << (ostream &out, FullPtr);
```

You can see the second parameter: It's a `FullPtr`. And look at this code:

```
cout << FullOvenInfo;
```

The `FullOvenInfo` item is also a `FullPtr` because it's a pointer to a function that takes a `FullOvenManip()`. Voilà. That does the trick.

The `CustomManipulator` example in Listing 5-1 is a really great example of all this!

Listing 5-1: Using Manipulators

```
#include <iostream>
#include <string>
#include <fstream>
#include <map>

using namespace std;

class MicrowaveOven
{
    friend ostream &operator <<(ostream &out,
        MicrowaveOven &oven);
public:
    typedef map<ostream *, bool> FlagMap;
    int HighVoltageRadiation;
    int RadioactiveFoodCount;
    int LeakLevel;
    string OvenName;
    static FlagMap Flags;
};

MicrowaveOven::FlagMap MicrowaveOven::Flags;
ostream &operator <<(ostream &out, MicrowaveOven &oven)
{
    bool full = true;
    MicrowaveOven::FlagMap::iterator iter =
        MicrowaveOven::Flags.find(&out);
    if (iter != MicrowaveOven::Flags.end())
    {
        full = iter->second;
    }
```

(continued)

Listing 5-1 *(continued)*

```
        if (full)
        {
            out << "High Voltage Radiation: ";
            out << oven.HighVoltageRadiation << endl;
            out << "Radioactive Food Count: ";
            out << oven.RadioactiveFoodCount << endl;
            out << "Leak Level: ";
            out << oven.LeakLevel << endl;
            out << "Oven Name: ";
            out << oven.OvenName;
        }
        else
        {
            out << oven.HighVoltageRadiation << ",";
            out << oven.RadioactiveFoodCount << ",";
            out << oven.LeakLevel << ",";
            out << oven.OvenName;
        }

        return out;
    }

istream &operator >(istream &in, MicrowaveOven &oven)
{
    in >> oven.HighVoltageRadiation;
    in >> oven.RadioactiveFoodCount;
    in >> oven.LeakLevel;
    in >> oven.OvenName;
    return in;
}

struct FullOvenManip {};

void FullOvenInfo(FullOvenManip x) {}
typedef void(*FullPtr)(FullOvenManip);

ostream &operator << (ostream &out, FullPtr)
{
    MicrowaveOven::Flags[&out] = true;
    return out;
}

struct MinOvenManip {};

void MinOvenInfo(MinOvenManip x) {}
typedef void(*MinPtr)(MinOvenManip);

ostream &operator << (ostream &out, MinPtr)
{
    MicrowaveOven::Flags[&out] = false;
    return out;
}

int main()
{
    MicrowaveOven myoven;
    myoven.HighVoltageRadiation = 9832;
    myoven.RadioactiveFoodCount = 7624;
    myoven.LeakLevel = 3793;
    myoven.OvenName = "Burnmaster";
```

```
cout << myoven << endl;
cout << "============" << endl;
cout << FullOvenInfo << myoven << endl;
cout << "============" << endl;
cout << MinOvenInfo << myoven << endl;

    return 0;
}
```

The code in Listing 5-1 creates two manipulators, one called `FullOvenInfo()` and one called `MinOvenInfo()`. When you use one of these manipulators, as in the following line, you call our overloaded `operator >>` function:

```
cout << FullOvenInfo << myoven << endl;
```

That function works with a map to keep track of which stream you're manipulating. The map lives as a static member in the `MicrowaveOven` class. So when you use the `FullOvenInfo()` manipulator on `cout`, the map's item for `cout` gets a `true`. And when you use the `MinOvenInfo()` manipulator on `cout`, the map's item for `cout` gets a `false`.

So why did we bother with the map? The idea is that you may be working with multiple streams, such as one for an `ofstream` file and one for `cout`, and you may want some streams to show the full information via the `FullOvenInfo()` manipulator — and some other streams to show the minimal information via the `MinOvenInfo()`. And so we keep a map based on the stream. And the really great thing is that the code actually works. In the overloaded `operator >>` function that prints a `MicrowaveOven` object, you can see how we check the map for a `true` or `false` for the current stream.

When you run this application, you see this output:

```
High Voltage Radiation: 9832
Radioactive Food Count: 7624
Leak Level: 3793
Oven Name: Burnmaster
============
High Voltage Radiation: 9832
Radioactive Food Count: 7624
Leak Level: 3793
Oven Name: Burnmaster
============
9832,7624,3793,Burnmaster
```

We printed the same object three times. The first one demonstrates the default: If you provide no manipulators, you get a full listing. We handled that in the overloaded `operator >>` for printing a `MicrowaveOven` object:

```
bool full = true;
MicrowaveOven::FlagMap::iterator iter =
    MicrowaveOven::Flags.find(&out);
if (iter != MicrowaveOven::Flags.end())
{
    full = iter->second;
}
```

Remember that `iterator` is really a pointer to the `map` entry. And so we call `find` to determine if the item is inside the `map` entry. If it's not, `find` returns `Flags.end()`. (That's just the way the `find` function works. If we'd written the `map` class, we would have done things differently. Can you say simplify, simplify, simplify rather than obfuscate, obfuscate, obfuscate?)

And if we don't get back `Flags.end()`, that means we found the item in the map. So in that case, we use `iter->second` to obtain the value.

But notice what happens if we do get back `Flags.end()`, meaning the stream wasn't found in the map. Then we just stick with the default value for `full`, which was `true`:

```
bool full = true;
```

And so you can see that these output lines will function properly:

```
cout << myoven << endl;
cout << "============" << endl;
cout << FullOvenInfo << myoven << endl;
cout << "============" << endl;
cout << MinOvenInfo << myoven << endl;
```

The first line with `myoven` line uses the default, which is a full listing. The second line with `myoven` says to definitely give us a full listing, using the `FullOvenInfo()` manipulator. And the third line with `myoven` gives a minimal listing, which we chose with the `MinOvenInfo()` manipulator.

Life is good.

Book VI

Advanced C++

C++ programming can encompass a huge range of topics. In fact, the number of ways in which you can use C++ is so huge that there really isn't a way to cover it in one book (or 20 or even 30). With this in mind, this part of the book discusses some advanced C++ topics, one of which is using the Standard Template Library (STL) in advanced ways. One of the advanced programming techniques you can use is the multimap — a version of the map discussed in Book IV Chapter 6 that allows you to use duplicate keys. You can see a multimap described at http://www.dummies.com/extras/cplusplusaio.

Contents at a Glance

Chapter 1: Exploring the Standard Library Further

In This Chapter

✔ Categorizing the Standard Library functions

✔ Working with container functions such as hash

✔ Performing random access with iterator functions

✔ Working with algorithms such as find

✔ Creating random numbers with functors

✔ Working with utilities such as min and max

✔ Creating temporary buffers with allocators

*T*he Standard Library is one of the most important parts of the C++ developer's toolkit because it contains a host of interesting functions that let you write great applications. The Standard Library originally started as the Standard Template Library (STL), and a number of companies, including Silicon Graphics, Inc. (SGI) and IBM, distributed it for everyone to use. The International Standards Organization (ISO) eventually took over STL, made a few minor changes to it, and renamed it the Standard Library. Consequently, when you see the STL online, don't get confused; it's merely an older version of the Standard Library.

For the purposes of this book, the differences between the Standard Library and the STL are so small that you can probably use the terms interchangeably. Just remember that the Standard Library is newer and does contain some changes to make the various versions of the STL work together. In addition, the STL won't provide support for features such as polymorphic allocators and optional inputs.

This chapter provides an overview of the Standard Library and shows you some examples of how to use it. However, if you don't see what you want here, don't worry; we discuss more examples in later chapters and you can always refer to the Standard Library documentation for additional examples. Before the chapter moves on to any examples, however, it's important to know what the Standard Library contains, so the first section of this chapter provides you with a list of Standard Library function categories.

Getting a copy of the Standard Library documentation

The Standard Library is incredibly large, so this book doesn't document it completely. The `Code::Blocks` product doesn't come with a Standard Library reference either. However, to really use the Standard Library, you really do need a copy of the documentation.

You can join ISO for a bazillion bucks and get a copy of their document free or purchase a copy of it from `http://www.iso.org/iso/home/store/catalogue_ics/catalogue_detail_ics.htm?csnumber=50372`. As an alternative, you can buy a copy of the Standard Library documentation from an ISO member such as the American National Standards Institute (ANSI) for a more reasonable sum. Check it out at `http://webstore.ansi.org/`

`FindStandards.aspx` (simply type ISO/IEC 14882:2011 in the search field).

Because the STL and the Standard Library are relatively close, you have a third alternative: use an STL resource. One of the best written and easiest to use resources is from SGI at `http://www.sgi.com/tech/stl/`. The downside to using the STL documentation is that it doesn't contain information about newer features found only in the Standard Library.

In addition to the resources mentioned so far, you'll want to check out Bjarne Stroustrup's website at `http://www.stroustrup.com/#standard`. Just in case you don't know, he's the guy who designed and originally implemented C++.

Considering the Standard Library Categories

The Standard Library documentation uses a formal approach that you're going to find difficult to read and even harder to understand; it must have been put together by lawyers more interested in the precise meaning of words rather than the usability of the document. This 1,338-page tome (in the current version) requires quite a bit of time to review. Fortunately, you don't have to wade through all that legal jargon mixed indiscriminately with computer jargon and the occasional bit of English. This chapter provides the overview you need to get going quickly.

The best way to begin is to break the Standard Library into smaller pieces. You can categorize the Standard Library functions in a number of ways. One of the most common approaches is to use the following categories:

✦ Containers

✦ Iterators

✦ Algorithms

✦ Functors

SGI color-coding

The SGI website at `http://www.sgi.com/tech/stl/stl_index_cat.html` uses color-coding to tell you about the content. Here are the categories you'll see and their associated color:

- ↙ Concept is red
- ↙ Type is yellow
- ↙ Function is green
- ↙ Overview is purple

- ✦ Utilities
- ✦ Adaptors
- ✦ Allocators
- ✦ Polymorphic allocators

The following sections provide a brief description of each of these categories and tell what you can expect to find in them. Knowing the category can help you locate the function you need quickly on websites that use these relatively standard category names.

Containers

Containers work just like the containers in your home — they hold something. You've already seen containers at work in other areas of this book. For example, both queues and deques are kinds of containers. The Containers category doesn't contain any functions, but it does contain a number of types including those in the following table:

basic_string	bit_vector	bitset
char_producer	deque	hash
list	map	multimap
multiset	priority_queue	queue
rope	set	slist
stack	vector	

Iterators

Iterators enumerate something. When you create a list of items, and then go through that list checking items off, you're enumerating the list. Using iterators helps you create lists of items and manipulate them in specific ways.

The kind of iterator you create is important because some iterators let you go forward only, some can go in either direction, and some can choose items at random. Each kind of iterator has its specific purpose.

The Iterators category includes a number of types. These types determine the kind of iterator you create in your code and the capabilities of that iterator. The following is a list of the iterator types:

back_insert_ iterator	bidirectional_ iterator	bidirectional_ iterator_tag
forward_iterator	forward_ iterator_tag	front_insert_ iterator
input_iterator	input_iterator_ tag	insert_iterator
istream_iterator	iterator_traits	ostream_iterator
output_iterator	output_iterator_ tag	random_access_ iterator
random_access_ iterator_tag	raw_storage_ iterator	reverse_ bidirectional_ iterator
reverse_iterator	sequence_buffer	

The Standard Library also includes a number of iterator-specific functions. These functions help you perform tasks such as advance (increment) the iterator by a certain number of positions. You can also measure the distance between the beginning and end of the iterator. The following is a list of iterator functions:

advance	distance	distance_type
iterator_category	value_type	

Algorithms

Algorithms perform data manipulations such as replacing, locating, or sorting information. You've already seen some algorithms used in the book because it's hard to create a substantial application without using one. There aren't any types in the Algorithms category. The following is a list of algorithm functions:

accumulate	adjacent_ difference	adjacent_find
advance	binary_search	copy

copy_backward	copy_n	count
count_if	distance	equal
equal_range	fill	fill_n
find	find_end	find_first_of
find_if	for_each	generate
generate_n	includes	inner_product
inplace_merge	iota	is_heap
is_sorted	iter_swap	lexicographical_ compare
lexicographical_ compare_3way	lower_bound	make_heap
max	max_element	merge
min	min_element	mismatch
next_permutation	nth_element	partial_sort
partial_sort_copy	partial_sum	partition
pop_heap	power	prev_permutation
push_heap	random_sample	random_sample_n
random_shuffle	remove	remove_copy
remove_copy_if	remove_if	replace
replace_copy	replace_copy_if	replace_if
reverse	reverse_copy	rotate
rotate_copy	search	search_n
set_difference	set_ intersection	set_symmetric_ difference
set_union	sort	sort_heap
stable_partition	stable_sort	swap
swap_ranges	transform	uninitialized_ copy
uninitialized_ copy_n	uninitialized_ fill	uninitialized_ fill_n
unique	unique_copy	upper_bound

Functors

Functors are a special class of object that acts as if it's a function. In most cases, you call a functor by using the same syntax you use for a function, but functors possess all the good elements of objects as well, such as the ability to instantiate them at runtime. (See Book IV Chapter 7 for an example of using a functor in this way.) Functors come in a number of forms.

For example, a binary function functor accepts two arguments as input and provides a result as output. Functors include a number of types that determine the kind of function the code creates, as shown in the following table:

binary_compose	binary_function	binary_negate
binder1st	binder2nd	divides
equal_to	greater	greater_equal
hash	identity	less
less_equal	logical_and	logical_not
logical_or	mem_fun1_ref_t	mem_fun1_t
mem_fun_ref_t	mem_fun_t	minus
modulus	multiplies	negate
not_equal_to	plus	pointer_to_binary_function
pointer_to_unary_function	project1st	project2nd
select1st	select2nd	subtractive_rng
unary_compose	unary_function	unary_negate

The Functors category contains only one function, ptr_fun. This function accepts a function pointer as input and outputs a function pointer adapter, which is a kind of function object. You use ptr_fun when you need to pass a function as input to another function such as transform. Here is an example of such code (as found in the functor_ptr_fun example):

```
#include <iostream>
#include <math.h>
#include <ext/functional>
#include <algorithm>

using namespace std;
using namespace __gnu_cxx;

int main()
{
    const int N = 10;
    double A[N];
    fill(A, A+N, 100);

    cout << A[0] << endl;
```

```
transform(A, A+N, A, compose1(negate<double>(), ptr_fun(fabs)));

cout << A[0] << endl;

return 0;
}
```

This example begins by creating a constant that determines the number of elements in the array A. The code then fills every element in A with the value 100 and displays just one of those elements onscreen.

The tricky part comes next. The transform() algorithm accepts the beginning of an input iterator, the end of an input iterator, an output iterator, and the transformation you want to perform. The transform() algorithm takes each of the values in the input iterator, performs the transformation you requested, and places the result in the output iterator.

In this case, the code uses the nonstandard SGI functor compose1(), which takes two adaptable unary functions as input. Because fabs() is a standard function, you must use ptr_fun() to change it into a function pointer adapter before you can use it with compose1(). The result is that A contains the negation of the absolute value of the original value in A or -100 when the transformation is complete. When you run this example, you see the following output:

```
100
-100
```

The GNU GCC compiler supports a number of STL features that don't appear as part of the Standard Library. In this case, compose1() appears in the ext/functional header, so you must provide the #include <ext/functional> line of code. In addition, because compose1() is nonstandard, it appears as part of a different namespace. Consequently, you must also provide the using namespace __gnu_cxx; line of code to access the functor without having to precede it with the namespace information.

Many C++ examples rely on the nonstandard parts of STL to perform tasks. If you want maximum compatibility and transportability for your code, you should avoid these nonstandard features.

Utilities

Utilities are functions and types that perform small service tasks within the Standard Library. The functions are min(), max(), and the relational operators. The types are chart_traits (the traits of characters used in other Standard Library features, such as basic_string) and pair (a pairing of two heterogeneous values).

Adaptors

Adaptors perform conversions of a sort. They make it possible to adapt one kind of data to another. In some cases, adaptors perform data conversion, such as negating numbers. The Adaptors category includes one function, `ptr_fun()`, which is explained in the "Functors" section of the chapter. In addition, the Adaptors category includes the types shown in the following table:

back_insert_ iterator	binary_compose	binary_negate
binder1st	binder2nd	front_insert_ iterator
insert_iterator	mem_fun1_ref_t	mem_fun1_t
mem_fun_ref_t	mem_fun_t	pointer_to_ binary_function
pointer_to_ unary_function	priority_queue	queue
raw_storage_ iterator	reverse_ bidirectional_ iterator	reverse_iterator
sequence_buffer	stack	unary_compose
unary_negate		

Allocators

Allocators manage resources, normally memory. In most cases, you won't ever need to use the members of the Allocators category. For example, you normally create new objects using the new operator. The new operator allocates memory for the object and then creates it by calling the object's constructor. In rare cases, such as when you want to implement a form of object pooling, you may want to separate the memory allocation process from the construction process. In this case, you call `construct()` to perform the actual task of constructing the object based on its class definition. The Allocators category has the following functions.

construct	destroy	get_temporary_ buffer
return_ temporary_buffer	uninitialized_ copy	uninitialized_ copy_n
uninitialized_ fill	uninitialized_ fill_n	

The Allocators category also includes a couple of types. These types help you manage memory, and you may find more use for them than you will the functions in this category. The types are

`raw_storage_iterator`	`temporary_buffer`

Polymorphic allocators

When working with older versions of the Standard Library, allocators used as arguments to templates create problems because they're bound by type. What this means is that a vector created using `std::vector<int>` is a completely different type from a vector created using `std::vector<int, myalloc>`, even though one is simply an extension of the other.

The `myalloc` part of the template simply defines the method used to allocate memory; it doesn't actually affect the type of data managed by the template. So, in both cases, you're created a `vector` to hold `int` data — the types are the same. The only difference is the method in which memory is allocated (the first uses standard memory allocation techniques, while the second uses a custom allocator). Using polymorphic allocators eliminates this problem by defining an abstract base memory class, `memory_resource`, to use for all memory allocators. This abstract class defines the following pure virtual methods:

`allocate`	`deallocate`	`is_equal()`

In order to use this new feature in Code::Blocks, you must enable support for C++ 11 extensions using the technique found in the "Configuring the IDE" section of Book IV, Chapter 6. In addition, you must use a version of Code::Blocks that supports C++ 14 because older versions won't include the required resources (such as header files). To add support for this feature, you must `#include <polymorphic_allocator>` and add `using namespace std::polyalloc`.

Parsing Strings Using a Hash

Hashes are an important security requirement for applications today. A *hash* creates a unique numeric equivalent of any string you feed it. Theoretically, you can't duplicate the number that the hash creates by using another string. A hash isn't reversible — it isn't the same as encryption and decryption.

A common use for hashes is to send passwords from a client to a server. The client converts the user's password into a numeric hash and sends that number to the server. The server verifies the number, not the password. Even if people are listening in, they have no way to ascertain the password from the number; therefore they can't steal the password for use with the target application.

The latest version of Code::Blocks provides excellent support for hashes. However, in order to use it, you must enable support for C++ 11 extensions using the technique found in the "Configuring the IDE" section of Book IV, Chapter 6. After you enable the required support, you can create the HashingStrings example shown here to demonstrate the use of hashes.

```
#include <iostream>
#include <unordered_map>

using namespace std;

int main()
{
    hash<const char*> MyHash;

    cout << "The hash of \"Hello World\" is:" << endl;
    cout << MyHash("Hello World") << endl;
    cout << "while the hash of \"Goodbye Cruel World\" is:" << endl;
    cout << MyHash("Goodbye Cruel World") << endl;

    return 0;
}
```

The example begins by creating a hash function object, MyHash. You use this function object to convert input text to a hash value. The function object works just like any other function, so you might provide the input text as MyHash("Hello World"). Hashes always output precisely the same value given a particular input. Consequently, you should see the following output from this example.

```
The hash of "Hello World" is:
4644931
while the hash of "Goodbye Cruel World" is:
4644988
```

Hashes have uses other than security requirements. For example, you can create a container that relies on a hash to make locating a particular value easier. In this case, you use a key/value pair in a *hash map*. The STL uses an actual hash_map<> template. However, the Standard Library replaces hash_map<> with unordered_map<>, which means you must enable C++ extension support for this example. Except for the template name, you can actually use the two templates interchangeably, but using the hash_map<> template will display a warning message in newer versions of Code::Blocks.

The `HashMap` example shown next illustrates how to create a hash map:

```
#include <iostream>
#include <unordered_map>
#include <string.h>

using namespace std;

struct eqstr
{
    bool operator()(const char* s1, const char* s2) const
    {
        return strcmp(s1, s2) == 0;
    }
};

int main()
{
    unordered_map<const char*, int, hash<const char*>, eqstr> Colors;

    Colors["Blue"] = 1;
    Colors["Green"] = 2;
    Colors["Teal"] = 3;
    Colors["Brick"] = 4;
    Colors["Purple"] = 5;
    Colors["Brown"] = 6;
    Colors["LightGray"] = 7;

    cout << "Brown = " << Colors["Brown"] << endl;
    cout << "Brick = " << Colors["Brick"] << endl;

    // This key isn't in the hash map, so it returns a
    // value of 0.
    cout << "Red = " << Colors["Red"] << endl;
}
```

An unordered (hash) map requires four inputs:

✦ Key type

✦ Data type

✦ Hashing function

✦ Equality key

The first three inputs are straightforward. In this case, the code uses a string as a key type, an integer value as a data type, and `hash<const char*>` as the hashing function. You already know how the hashing function works from the previous example in this section.

The Equality Key class is a little more complex. You must provide the hash map with a means of determining equality. In this case, the code compares the input string with the string stored as the key. The `eqstr` structure performs the task of comparing the input string to the key. The structure must return a Boolean value, so the code compares the `strcmp` function to 0. When the two are equal, meaning the strings are equal, `eqstr` returns `true`.

Standard Library versus STL headers

You'll find a wealth of STL examples on the Internet because STL was around for a long time before the Standard Library appeared. In fact, some developers continue to prefer the STL simply because they're familiar with it. Here's a little secret: The STL headers use a `.h` extension and the Standard Library headers don't have an extension. For example, the now familiar `iostream` header used in every previous example in the book is actually the Standard Library form — the STL form is `iostream.h`.

Here's another secret. The Standard Library headers often call on the STL headers, so you've also been using STL throughout the book. It's amazing to see how these things work out.

The example goes on to check for three colors, only two of which appear in the hash map `Colors`. In the first two cases, you see the expected value. In the third case, you see 0, which indicates that `Colors` doesn't contain the desired key. Always reserve 0 as an error indicator when using a hash map, because the hash map will always return a value, even if it doesn't contain the desired key. The output from this example is:

```
Brown = 6
Brick = 4
Red = 0
```

Obtaining Information Using a Random Access Iterator

Most containers let you perform random access of data they contain. For example, the `RandomAccess` example shows that you can create an `iterator` and then add to or subtract from the current offset to obtain values within the container that `iterator` supports:

```
#include <iostream>
#include <vector>

using namespace std;

int main()
{
    vector<string> Words;

    Words.push_back("Blue");
    Words.push_back("Green");
    Words.push_back("Teal");
```

```
        Words.push_back("Brick");
        Words.push_back("Purple");
        Words.push_back("Brown");
        Words.push_back("LightGray");

        // Define a random iterator.
        vector<string>::iterator Iter = Words.begin();

        // Access random points.
        Iter += 5;
        cout << *Iter << endl;

        Iter -= 2;
        cout << *Iter << endl;

        return 0;
    }
```

In this case, the `vector`, `Words`, contains a list of seven items. The code creates an `iterator` for `Words` named `Iter`. It then adds to or subtracts from the `iterator` offset and displays the output onscreen. Here is what you see when you run this example:

```
Brown
Brick
```

Sometimes you need to perform a special task using a random-access `iterator`. For example, you might want to create a special function to summate the members of `vector` or just a range of members within `vector`. In this case, you must create a specialized function to perform the task as follows because the Standard Library doesn't include any functions to do it for you, as shown in the `RandomAccess2` example:

```
#include <iostream>
#include <vector>

using namespace std;

template <class RandomAccessIterator>
float AddIt(RandomAccessIterator begin, RandomAccessIterator end)
{
    float Sum = 0;

    RandomAccessIterator Index;

    // Make sure that the values are in the correct order.
    if (begin > end)
    {
        RandomAccessIterator temp;
        temp = begin;
        begin = end;
        end = temp;
    }

    for (Index = begin; Index != end; Index++)
        Sum += *Index;

    return Sum;
}
```

```
int main()
{
    vector<float> Numbers;

    Numbers.push_back(1.0);
    Numbers.push_back(2.5);
    Numbers.push_back(3.75);
    Numbers.push_back(1.26);
    Numbers.push_back(9.101);
    Numbers.push_back(11.3);
    Numbers.push_back(1.52);

    // Sum the individual members.
    float Sum;
    Sum = AddIt(Numbers.begin(), Numbers.end());
    cout << Sum << endl;

    Sum = AddIt(Numbers.end(), Numbers.begin());
    cout << Sum << endl;

    // Sum a range.
    vector<float>::iterator Iter = Numbers.begin();
    Iter += 5;
    Sum = AddIt(Iter, Numbers.end());
    cout << Sum << endl;

    return 0;
}
```

This example builds on the previous example. You still create vector, Numbers, and fill it with data. However, in this case, you create an output variable, Sum, that contains the summation of the elements contained in Numbers.

AddIt() is a special function that accepts two RandomAccessIterator values as input. These two inputs represent a range within the vector that you want to manipulate in some way. The example simply adds them, but you can perform any task you want. The output is a float that contains the summation.

AddIt() works as you expect. You call it as you would any other function and provide a beginning point and an end point within vector. The first two calls to AddIt sum the entire vector, while the third creates an iterator, changes its offset, and then sums a range within vector. Here is the output from this example:

```
30.431
30.431
12.82
```

A random-access iterator can go in either direction. In addition, you can work with individual members within the container supplied to iterator. As a result, the functions you create for iterator must be able to work with the inputs in any order. How you handle this requirement depends on the kind of function you create.

Locating Values Using the Find Algorithm

The Standard Library contains a number of functions to find something you need within a container. Locating what you need as efficiently as possible is always a good idea. Unlike your closet, you want your applications well organized and easy to manage! The four common find() algorithms are

✦ find()

✦ find_end()

✦ find_first_of()

✦ find_if()

The algorithm you use depends on what you want to find and where you expect to find it. You'll likely use the plain find() algorithm most often. The FindString example shows how to locate a particular string within vector — you can use the same approach to locate something in any container type:

```
#include <iostream>
#include <vector>
#include <algorithm>

using namespace std;

int main()
{
    vector<string> Words;

    Words.push_back("Blue");
    Words.push_back("Green");
    Words.push_back("Teal");
    Words.push_back("Brick");
    Words.push_back("Purple");
    Words.push_back("Brown");
    Words.push_back("LightGray");

    vector<string>::iterator Result =
        find(Words.begin(), Words.end(), "LightGray");

    if (Result != Words.end())
        cout << *Result << endl;
    else
        cout << "Value not found!" << endl;

    Result = find(Words.begin(), Words.end(), "Black");

    if (Result != Words.end())
        cout << *Result << endl;
    else
        cout << "Value not found!" << endl;
}
```

The example starts with vector containing Color strings. In both cases, the code attempts to locate a particular color within vector. The first time the code is successful because LightGray is one of the colors listed in vector. However, the second attempt is thwarted because Black isn't one of the colors in vector. Here's the output from this example:

```
LightGray
Value not found!
```

Never assume that the code will find a particular value. Always assume that someone is going to provide a value that doesn't exist and then make sure you provide a means of handling the nonexistent value. In this example, you simply see a message stating the value wasn't found. However, in real-world code, you often must react to situations where the value isn't found by

✦ Indicating an error condition

✦ Adding the value to the container

✦ Substituting a standard value

✦ Defining an alternative action based on invalid input

The find() algorithm is a personal favorite because it's so flexible. You can use it for external and internal requirements. Even though the example shows how you can locate information in an internal vector, you can also use find() for external containers, such as disk drives. Have some fun with this one — experiment with all the containers you come across.

Using the Random Number Generator

Random number generators fulfill a number of purposes. Everything from games to simulations require a random number generator to work properly. Randomness finds its way into business what-if scenarios as well. In short, you need to add random output to your application in many situations.

Creating a random number isn't hard. All you need to do is call a random number function as shown in the RandomNumberGenerator example:

```cpp
#include <iostream>
#include <time.h>
#include <stdlib.h>

using namespace std;

int main()
{
    // Always set a seed value.
    srand((unsigned int)time(NULL));

    int RandomValue = rand() % 12;
    cout << "The random month number is: " << RandomValue + 1 << endl;

    return 0;
}
```

Actually, not one of the random number generators in the Standard Library works properly — imagine that! They are all *pseudorandom* number generators: The numbers are distributed such that it appears that you see a random sequence, but given enough time and patience, eventually the sequence repeats. In fact, if you don't set a seed value for your random number generator, you can obtain predictable sequences of numbers every time. How boring. Here is typical output from this example:

```
The random month number is: 7
```

The first line of code in `main()` sets the seed by using the system time. Using the system time ensures a certain level of randomness in the starting value — and therefore a level of randomness for your application as a whole. If you comment out this line of code, you see the same output every time you run the application. In our case, our system output 6 every time.

The example application uses `rand()` to create the random value. When you take the modulus of the random number, you obtain an output that is within a specific range — 12 in this case. The example ends by adding 1 to the random number because there isn't any month 0 in the calendar, and then outputs the month number for you.

The Standard Library provides access to two types of pseudorandom number generators. The first type requires that you set a seed value. The second type requires that you provide an input value with each call and doesn't require a seed value. Each generator outputs a different data type, so you can choose the kind of random number you obtain. Table 1-1 lists the random number generators and tells you what data type they output.

Book VI Chapter 1

Exploring the Standard Library Further

Table 1-1	Pseudorandom Number Generator Functions	
Function	*Output Type*	*Seed Required?*
rand	integer	yes
drand48	double	yes
erand48	double	no
lrand48	long	yes
nrand48	long	no
mrand48	signed long	yes
jrand48	signed long	no

Now that you know about the pseudorandom number generators, look at the seed functions used to prime them. Table 1-2 lists the seed functions and their associated pseudorandom number generator functions.

Table 1-2	Seed Functions
Function	*Associated Pseudorandom Number Generator Function*
srand	rand
srand48	drand48
seed48	mrand48
lcong48	lrand48

Performing Comparisons Using min and max

Computer applications perform many comparisons. In most cases, you don't know what the values are in advance or you wouldn't be interested in performing the comparison in the first place. The min() and max() functions make it possible to look at two values and determine the minimum or maximum value. The MinAndMax example demonstrates how you use these two functions:

```
#include <iostream>

using namespace std;

int main()
{
    int Number1, Number2;

    cout << "Type the first number: ";
    cin >> Number1;

    cout << "Type the second number: ";
    cin >> Number2;

    cout << "The minimum number is: " << min(Number1, Number2) << endl;
    cout << "The maximum number is: " << max(Number1, Number2) << endl;

    return 0;
}
```

In this case, the code accepts two numbers as input and then compares them using min() and max(). The output you see depends on what you provide as input, but the first output line tells you which number is smaller and the second tells you which is larger. Assuming you provide values of 5 and 6, here is the application output you see:

```
Type the first number: 5
Type the second number: 6
The minimum number is: 5
The maximum number is: 6
```

Working with Temporary Buffers

Temporary buffers are useful for all kinds of tasks. Normally, you use them when you want to preserve the original data, yet you need to manipulate the data in some way. For example, creating a sorted version of your data is a perfect use of a temporary buffer. The `TemporaryBuffer` example shows how to use a temporary buffer to sort some strings.

```
#include <iostream>
#include <vector>
#include <memory>
#include <algorithm>

using namespace std;

int main()
{
    vector<string> Words;

    Words.push_back("Blue");
    Words.push_back("Green");
    Words.push_back("Teal");
    Words.push_back("Brick");
    Words.push_back("Purple");
    Words.push_back("Brown");
    Words.push_back("LightGray");

    int Count = Words.size();
    cout << "Words contains: " << Count << " elements." << endl;

    // Create the buffer and copy the data to it.
    pair<string*, ptrdiff_t> Mem = get_temporary_buffer<string>(Count);

    uninitialized_copy(Words.begin(), Words.end(), Mem.first);

    // Perform a sort and display the results.
    sort(Mem.first, Mem.first+Mem.second);

    for (int i = 0; i < Mem.second; i++)
        cout << Mem.first[i] << endl;

    return 0;
}
```

The example starts with the now familiar list of color names. It then counts the number of entries in `vector` and displays the count onscreen.

At this point, the code creates the temporary buffer using `get_temporary_ buffer`. The output is `pair`, with the first value containing a pointer to the string values and the second value containing the count of data elements. `Mem` doesn't contain anything — you have simply allocated memory for it.

The next task is to copy the data from vector (Words) to pair (Mem) using uninitialized_copy. Now that Mem contains a copy of your data, you can organize it using the sort function. The final step is to display the Mem content onscreen. Here is what you'll see:

```
Words contains: 7 elements.
Blue
Brick
Brown
Green
LightGray
Purple
Teal
```

Chapter 2: Working with User-Defined Literals (UDLs)

In This Chapter

✔ Considering the needs and uses for UDLs

✔ Using the UDL features of the Standard Library

✔ Developing custom UDLs

*P*revious chapters have discussed literals as a kind of constant. For example, in the expression X = 5, the number 5 is a literal constant. The constant X stands in for the value 5 in application code. Using a literal makes it possible to create code that states the use of a value clearly, rather than having code that is filled with mystery values that no one can figure out. In addition, using literals makes it possible to change constant values in one place, rather than in each place they're needed in an application.

Up to this point, you have used every other kind of literal constant in the various examples except for User-Defined Literals (UDLs). Unlike other kinds of literal constants, a UDL isn't defined as part of the C++ compiler — you create UDLs as needed to make your code more readable and easier to manage. In some cases, UDLs come with the libraries you use in C++, such as the Standard Library. This chapter does discuss UDLs that come as part of the Standard Library, but it also looks at how you'd create your own UDLs as needed.

UDLs aren't part of older C++ specifications. In fact, they first made an appearance in C++ 11. What this means is that you must configure Code::Blocks to use the features provided by C++ 11 by using the technique found in the "Configuring the IDE" section of Book IV, Chapter 6. If you don't perform the configuration for each example in this chapter, you see error messages telling you that the default setup doesn't provide the desired support.

Understanding the Need for UDLs

The whole point of literals is to make code more readable and easier to maintain. However, built-in literals are limited to a few data types, summarized as follows:

✦ Integer

✦ Floating-point

+ Character
+ String
+ Boolean
+ Pointer
+ UDL

Sometimes you need a literal of a type other than these built-in types and that's where UDLs come into play. Unlike variables, the value of a UDL is always known at compile time. The compiler substitutes whatever value you define for the UDL with the actual value in the code. The purpose of the UDL is to make the code easier for the human developer to read and understand. Once that task is completed, the compiler is free to use the actual value referenced by the UDL in the compiled code so the application doesn't need to convert it during runtime. What this means is that your application runs faster and uses fewer resources, while remaining easy to read.

Built-in literals are straightforward because they're based on core types. A UDL can be as complex as you need it to be to express a real-world data type. For example, if you're involved in a field that uses imaginary numbers, you can create a UDL to fulfill that need. You can also perform data conversions and other tasks that would be time-consuming to perform in other ways. It's even possible to create side effects, such as performing some sort of output, using a UDL.

Prefixes and suffixes

Saving time and effort is part of the reason you use literals. There is a short-hand way to create literals and ensure that you obtain the correct constant type. Many of the standard literals provide you with a prefix or suffix you can use to access them. Precisely how the prefix or suffix is interpreted depends on how you use it. For example, a suffix of U could mean an `unsigned int` when used with an `int` value, while a prefix of U could mean a `char32_t const` pointer when used with a character string. Table 2-1 shows a listing of the prefixes and suffixes that most compilers support.

Table 2-1		Standard Prefixes and Suffixes	
Data Type	*Prefix*	*Suffix*	*Resultant Type*
int		U or u	unsigned int
int		L or l	long
int		UL, Ul, uL, ul, LU, Lu, lU, or lu	unsigned long
int		LL or ll	long long

Data Type	Prefix	Suffix	Resultant Type
int		ULL, Ull, uLL, ull, LLU, LLu, llU, or llu	unsigned long long
double		F or f	float
double		L or l	long double
char	L		wchar_t
char	U		char32_t
char	u		char16_t
String	L		wchar_t const*
String	U		char32_t const*
String	u		char16_t const*

Using the prefixes and suffixes can save you considerable time. The PrefixesAndSuffixes example in Listing 2-1 demonstrates how you'd employ them to create variables of various sorts.

Listing 2-1:   Creating Literals Using Prefixes and Suffixes

```
#include <typeinfo>
#include <cxxabi.h>

using namespace std;
using namespace abi;

char* Demangle(const char* Object)
{
    int Status;
    char* RealName;

    RealName = __cxa_demangle(Object, 0, 0, &Status);
    return RealName;
}

int main()
{
    auto Int1 = 23;
    auto Int2 = 23L;
    auto Int3 = 23U;
    auto Int4 = 23u;

    auto String1 = "Hello";
    auto String2 = L"Hello";
    auto String3 = U"Hello";
    auto String4 = u"Hello";

    cout << Int1 << endl << Demangle(typeid(Int1).name()) << endl;
    cout << Int2 << endl << Demangle(typeid(Int2).name()) << endl;
```

(continued)

Listing 2-1 *(continued)*

```
cout << Int3 << endl << Demangle(typeid(Int3).name()) << endl;
cout << Int4 << endl << Demangle(typeid(Int4).name()) << endl;

cout << String1 << endl << Demangle(typeid(String1).name()) << endl;
cout << String2 << endl << Demangle(typeid(String2).name()) << endl;
cout << String3 << endl << Demangle(typeid(String3).name()) << endl;
cout << String4 << endl << Demangle(typeid(String4).name()) << endl;

return 0;
}
```

The `Demangle()` function is GCC specific. Most C++ compilers *mangle* (modify the spelling of) keywords and type information to make an application harder for someone to *reverse-assemble* (convert from machine language back into C++ source code). In order to determine type information, you use the `typeid()` function to create a `typeinfo` structure. The `name()` function returns the type name found in this structure to display it onscreen. However, this name is mangled, so you must use the `Demangle()` function to change it back to its original readable form.

Most of the examples in this chapter rely on the `auto` keyword to automatically detect the variable type created by a UDL. This keyword is an important feature for newer C++ applications that make use of the new extensions that the language provides. You can read about the `auto` keyword in the "Using the auto keyword" section of Book IV, Chapter 7. In this case, the code uses the `auto` keyword to detect the output of the literal prefix or suffix so that the variable is automatically the correct type for a situation. When you run this application, you see the following output:

```
23
int
23
long
23
unsigned int
23
unsigned int
Hello
char const*
0x46e02c
wchar_t const*
0x46e038
char32_t const*
0x46e02c
char16_t const*
```

Even though the data is the same in every case, the variables used to hold the data differ because of the prefix or suffix used to create the variable. Notice that the same prefix or suffix has different effects depending on the type of the variable to which it's applied. In addition, sometimes the case of the prefix or suffix matters (as in working with a string).

Some compilers, such as GCC, include non-standard extensions for numeric data that you need to use with care. Given the popularity of GCC and the need for these number formats, you may find that you absolutely do need to use them at times. Here are some common suffix extensions provided by GCC implementations:

✦ **d:** double

✦ **df:** _Decimal32

✦ **dd:** _Decimal64

✦ **dl:** _Decimal 128

✦ **w:** __float80

✦ **q:** __float128

✦ **i:** double complex

✦ **fi:** float complex

Differentiating between raw and cooked

There are many ways to define literals. Of course, the kind of information that a literal affects is the most common method. However, literals can also be raw or cooked. A *raw* literal receives input from the application source and doesn't interpret it in any way. What this means is that the information is interpreted character by character, precisely as the sender has presented it. *Cooked* literals interpret the sender's input and automatically perform any required conversions to make the data usable to the recipient.

The easiest way to see this principle in action is through an example. The RawAndCooked example shown in Listing 2-2 demonstrates the technique used to create either raw or cooked string processing.

Listing 2-2: Using Raw and Cooked String Processing

```
#include <iostream>

using namespace std;

int main()
{
    auto Cooked = "(Hello\r\nThere)";
    auto Raw = R"(Hello\r\nThere)";

    cout << Cooked << endl;
    cout << Raw << endl;
}
```

Most of the time when you see the \r\n combination, you know that the application will output a carriage return and line feed combination. This is the cooked method of processing a string. The string is interpreted and any escape characters converted into *control characters* (characters that are normally regarded as commands, rather than data, such as the carriage return). However, notice how the Raw string is created. The R in front of the string tells the compiler to create the variable without interpreting the content. Here's the output you see from this example:

```
(Hello
There)
Hello\r\nThere
```

Notice that the cooked form does output the parenthesis, but the raw form doesn't. The parenthesis is required as part of the raw form input. As you might imagine, the cooked form outputs the \r\n combination as control characters, while the raw form outputs the actual characters.

Working with the UDLs Included in the Standard Library

Even though you can currently create UDLs for the basic types described in the "Understanding the Need for UDLs" section of the chapter, there are many situations where developers need UDLs for classes as well. In some cases, these classes are part of the Standard Library. Rather than have a number of nonstandard implementations of these UDLs, the standards committee decided to add the UDLs directly to the Standard Library. You can read about all the gritty details, if you want, in the "User-defined Literals for Standard Library Types" at http://isocpp.org/blog/2013/04/n3642-user-defined-literals-for-standard-library-types. There are now consistent and standardized UDLs attached to some classes. The following sections describe the more important classes and show how to use them.

std::basic_string

The std::basic_string class makes it possible to work with sequences of char-like objects. The class currently has templates defined for

✦ char

✦ wchar_t

✦ char16_t

✦ char32_t

However, the class could easily be extended for other kinds of characters. In addition, the templates make it possible to specify character traits and the method used to store the data in memory. The essential idea behind the basic_string is to make it possible to accommodate a variety of character types within one character class to simplify coding.

Obtaining Standard Library UDL support

Adding UDLs to the Standard Library is a new feature for C++ 14. In order to actually see this feature at work, your compiler must support all of the C++ 14 additions. Because some of these features require time to implement, your C++ compiler may not provide all of the standardized features, even if it purports to provide C++ 14 support.

The GCC 4.7.1 compiler used throughout most of this book doesn't provide the required UDL support. However, the examples show how to simulate such support if you need it immediately. The GCC 4.8.1 compiler, which is currently unstable, provides some C++ 14

support. However, in order to obtain full support, you must wait for the upcoming GCC 4.9 compiler.

Other compiler vendors are also creating the support required to fully implement C++ 14. For example, you can find the required support in the upcoming Clang 3.4 distribution. Visual C++ 2013 also includes some level of C++ 14 support, but Microsoft is currently working to implement C++ 14 fully. The bottom line is that you must ensure that your compiler actually provides the C++ 14 language support you need before these new UDL features will work.

In C++ 14, the Standard Library includes built-in literal support for `basic_string`. All you need to do is add the `s` suffix to a string to create one. However, it's important to get an idea of how all this works behind the scenes. The `BasicString` example in Listing 2-3 demonstrates three techniques for creating a `basic_string` object.

Listing 2-3: Three Techniques for Creating a basic_string

```
#include <iostream>
#include <typeinfo>

using namespace std;

string operator"" _s(const char * str, unsigned len)
{
   return string{str, len};
}

int main()
{
    basic_string<char> StdString = "This is a standard string.";
    auto AutoString = "This is an auto string."_s;

    // Remove comment when your compiler supports C++ 14.
    //auto UDLString = "This is a UDL string."s;

    cout << StdString << endl << typeid(StdString).name() << endl;
    cout << AutoString << endl << typeid(AutoString).name() << endl;
```

(continued)

Listing 2-3 *(continued)*

```
// Remove comment when your compiler supports C++ 14.
//cout << UDLString << endl << typeid(UDLString).name() << endl;

    return 0;
}
```

This example performs three essential levels of conversion so that you can see the progression from one to another. In the first case, you see the straightforward method for creating a simple `basic_string` object, `StdString`. As you can see, it works just like any other template. The second case relies on a C++ 11 type operator definition to emulate the UDL that is included as part of C++ 14. The "Creating Your Own UDLs" section of this chapter tells you all the details about creating such an operator. All you really need to know for now is that the operator makes it possible to use a shortcut when creating `basic_string` objects. The third case shows the C++14 version of the same `_s` definition, but this one is built right into the Standard Library so you don't have to do anything special to use it. In all three cases, you create the same `basic_string` object type, but the technique differs each time. When you run this example, you see the following output:

```
This is a standard string.
Ss
This is an auto string.
Ss
This is a UDL string.
Ss
```

This output shows the mangled form of the `name()` function output. The fact that all three strings are the same tells you they're the same object type. If you want to see the unmangled names, you can use the `Demangle()` function provided in Listing 2-1.

There seems to be some confusion online as to how the raw and cooked versions of `basic_string` should work. In looking at the `_s` and `s` operators, the code already provides both raw and cooked implementations. For example, if you used this code with the `_s` operator:

```
auto RawString = R"(This is a\r\nraw string.)";
auto CookedString = "This is a\r\ncooked string.";

cout << RawString << endl;
cout << CookedString << endl;
```

you'd see the following output:

```
This is a\r\nraw string.
This is a
cooked string.
```

The `s` operator works in the same manner. So, you can use either raw or cooked strings with the same operator and receive the appropriate results.

std::complex

You may or may not remember complex numbers from school. A *complex number* consists of a real number and an imaginary number that are paired together. (Just in case you've completely forgotten about complex numbers, you can read about them at http://www.mathsisfun.com/numbers/complex-numbers.html.) Real-world uses for complex numbers include:

✦ Electrical engineering

✦ Fluid dynamics

✦ Quantum mechanics

✦ Computer graphics

✦ Dynamic systems

There are other uses for complex numbers, too, but this list should give you some ideas. In general, if you aren't involved in any of these disciplines, you probably won't ever encounter complex numbers. However, the Standard Library provides full support for complex numbers, just in case you do need them.

As with the BasicString example, this example shows the progression from a standard declaration to the C++ 14 suffix. The ComplexNumber example in Listing 2-4 demonstrates all three stages so you can see how both the C++ 14 suffix and the C++ 11 UDL forms work.

**Book VI
Chapter 2**

Working with User-
Defined Literals
(UDLs)

Listing 2-4: Three Techniques for Creating a complex Number

```cpp
#include <iostream>
#include <complex>

using namespace std;

complex<long double> operator"" _i(long double Value)
{
    return complex<double>(0, Value);
}

int main()
{
    complex<double> StdComplex(0, 3.14);
    auto AutoComplex = 3.14_i;

    // Remove comment when your compiler supports C++ 14.
    //auto UDLComplex = 3.14i;

    cout << StdComplex.real() << " " << StdComplex.imag() << endl;
    cout << AutoComplex.real() << " " << AutoComplex.imag() << endl;

    // Remove comment when your compiler supports C++ 14.
    //cout << UDLComplex.real() << " " << UDLComplex.imag() << endl;

    return 0;
}
```

The example declares variables of all three types and assigns values to them. It then displays both the real and imaginary parts of the number. When you run this example, you see the following output:

```
0 3.14
0 3.14
0 3.14
```

You can create three kinds of complex numbers. The following list shows the suffixes used for each type:

✦ **i:** `double`

✦ **if:** `float`

✦ **il:** `long double`

std::chrono::duration

The `chrono::duration` class serves to mark the passage of time. It answers the question of how much time has elapsed between two events. Developers use it for all sorts of time-related purposes.

A `chrono::duration` object relies on a second as the standard duration between ticks. A *tick* is a single time duration interval. Using the standard setup, each tick equals one second. However, you can use the `ratio` object to define a new tick duration. For example, if you define `ratio<60>` each tick lasts one minute. Likewise, defining `ratio<1, 5>` sets each tick to last one fifth of a second.

It's also possible to change one interval to another using `duration_cast` with either a standard interval, such as `chrono::seconds`, or any interval `typedef` that you want to create. For example, `typedef chrono::duration<double, ratio<1, 5>> fifths;` defines an interval called fifths.

There is a lot more to talk about with the `chrono::duration` class, but you now have enough information to work with the `Duration` example shown in Listing 2-5. As with previous examples, this one shows a progression from defining a variable directly, to using a custom UDL, and finally the built-in support that C++ 14 provides.

Listing 2-5: Three Techniques for Creating a `chrono::duration`

```
#include <iostream>
#include <chrono>

using namespace std;
```

```
chrono::duration<unsigned long long> operator"" _m(
    unsigned long long Value)
{
    return chrono::duration<int, ratio<60>>(Value);
}

int main()
{
    // Define an interval of 20 minutes.
    chrono::duration<int, ratio<60>>StdTime(20);
    auto AutoTime(20_m);

    // Remove comment when your compiler supports C++ 14.
    //auto UDLTime(20min);

    // Output the time in seconds.
    cout << chrono::duration_cast<chrono::seconds>(StdTime).count()
        << endl;
    cout << chrono::duration_cast<chrono::seconds>(AutoTime).count()
        << endl;

    // Remove comment when your compiler supports C++ 14.
    //cout << chrono::duration_cast<chrono::seconds>(UDLTime).count()
    //     << endl;

    return 0;
}
```

The example demonstrates a few features of the chrono::duration class. However, it focuses again on the progression from defining the variable by hand to using a shortcut to perform the task. Notice that the UDL relies on an integer value in this case, rather than a floating-point type. The value of 20 minutes is converted to seconds for output. As a result, you see these values when you run the application:

```
1200
1200
1200
```

The Standard Library supports a number of suffixes for chrono::duration when you use C++ 14. The following list shows the individual suffixes and tells you what they mean:

✦ **h:** Hours

✦ **min:** Minutes

✦ **s:** Seconds

✦ **ms:** Milliseconds

✦ **us:** Microseconds

✦ **ns:** Nanoseconds

Creating Your Own UDLs

The Standard Library, coupled with the built-in features of C++, provide you with an interesting array of literals. However, the true value of literals becomes more obvious when you create your own. There are many different needs you can address using UDLs, but three common needs are supporting data conversions, making custom types easier to work with, and obtaining desired side effects without the usual number of coding problems.

Although built-in or Standard Library literals come in both prefix and suffix form, you can only create the suffix form when defining your own literals. In addition, the suffix must begin with an underscore. The underscore serves to help prevent conflicts with existing suffixes and to ensure other developers know that the literal is a custom (nonstandard) form.

Developing a conversion UDL

It's possible to encapsulate conversions within a UDL. All you need to do once you create such a UDL is provide the appropriate suffix when defining the constant to obtain the result you want. The CustomUDL01 example in Listing 2-6 demonstrates a technique for defining a conversion that changes the radius input to the area of a circle in the constant.

Listing 2-6:   Defining a Data Conversion UDL

```
#include <iostream>

using namespace std;

constexpr long double operator"" _circ ( long double radius )
{
    return radius*radius*3.141592;
}

int main()
{
    double x = 5.0_circ;

    cout << "The circle's area is: " << x << endl;
    return 0;
}
```

In order to create the UDL, the example relies on a constexpr with a return value of a long double and an input value, radius, of a long double. The equation for computing the area of a circle is πr^2. As you can see, the example performs the correct computation as part of the constexpr.

Whenever you create a custom UDL, the compiler forces you to use the largest type for the conversion. What this means is that you must use a long double for floating point literals and unsigned long long for integer literals. Even if you later choose to use a smaller type, as is done in this example by declaring x as a double, the literal itself must employ the largest possible type.

To declare a UDL of the new type, the example creates x, which uses the _ circ suffix. It then outputs the result onscreen. When you run this example, you see that the correct value has been placed in x, as shown here:

```
The circle's area is: 78.5398
```

Developing a custom type UDL

A lot of the code you encounter relies on custom types that are hard to follow and understand. Creating a UDL to simplify the code makes things clearer and reduces the potential for error. The CustomUDL02 example in Listing 2-7 shows a custom type, the operator used to create the UDL, as well as how the UDL is used to define a literal.

Listing 2-7: Creating a UDL for a Custom Type

```cpp
#include <iostream>

using namespace std;

struct MyType
{
    MyType (double Input):Value(Input){}
    double Value;
};

MyType operator"" _mytype (long double Value)
{
    return MyType(Value);
}

int main()
{
    auto UDLType = 145.6_mytype;

    cout << UDLType.Value << endl;

    return 0;
}
```

In order for this technique to work, you must create a constructor for your type that accepts the number of inputs required to configure the type. At minimum, the constructor must accept one type or the input value the user provides is lost. The custom type need not support the same size data type as required by the operator, but they must be of the same sort. For example, you couldn't transition a long double to an int.

When you run this example, you see an output value of 145.6, which is the value you input to the custom type. It's possible to handle fairly complex setups using this approach. The user of your custom type obtains the capability to create clear code that's easy to follow and interpret, even when the underlying types are complex.

Using a custom UDL for side effects

One of the most interesting uses for UDLs is to create *side effects* (an operation other than the usual or normal operation, either to make the application shorter and more efficient or to provide added flexibility). You want to define a certain kind of operation that takes place as a result of defining the literal. What you get is still a literal, but a literal that doesn't necessarily denote a value that you plan to use later. The CustomUDL03 example in Listing 2-8 shows one such non-traditional use.

Listing 2-8:   Using UDLs to Create an Interesting Side Effect

```
#include <iostream>

using namespace std;

void operator"" _countdown (unsigned long long Value)
{
    for (int i = Value; i >= 0; i--)
        cout << i << endl;
}

int main()
{
    10_countdown;

    return 0;
}
```

Notice that the _countdown operator isn't attached to something that you'd normally associate with a value. In fact, it doesn't return a value at all. What you get instead is a side effect. When you run this example, you see this output.

```
10
9
8
7
6
5
4
3
2
1
0
```

What has happened is that the compiler has replaced 10_countdown with individual cout statements, one for each iteration of the loop. What you end up with is 11 cout statements that output the values between 10 and 0 (in reverse order). The side effect UDL opens all sorts of interesting possibilities for creating code that simplifies certain repetitive tasks in a manner that makes their use obvious.

Chapter 3: Building Original Templates

In This Chapter

✔ **Determining when to create a template**

✔ **Understanding the elements of good template design**

✔ **Developing a basic math template**

✔ **Creating a structure template**

✔ **Defining a class template**

✔ **Using template specialization to your advantage**

✔ **Building a library of templates**

✔ **Using your custom built template libraries**

C++ has been around for many years. Because of its longevity, C++ templates abound. In fact, it may seem that there is a template for every practical purpose. However, the templates that are available to the developer community through standardized and third-party resources usually reflect generalized needs. The individual company you work for (or you as a developer) may have specialized needs that a generalized template can't address.

Every programming tool in existence offers a certain amount of flexibility. The reason why you see so many generalized tools is that someone developed them and the community as a whole decided to adopt them. Never think that you can't create your own tools. After all, someone created the generalized tools you work with daily — creating a custom tool requires nothing special, just time and thought on your part.

The trick to creating a customized tool is to think the process through, just as you would for any application you create. The fact that you'll use this customized tool to create multiple applications means that you must apply a higher standard to its design and the code it contains than you would for one-time applications. A mistake in a customized tool can spell errors in every application you create using it, so this code must work well.

This chapter addresses the thought process behind templates first and then shows some typical template examples. The examples will help demonstrate ways in which you can use templates to create better applications that require less code because the templates you create meet your needs more completely than any generalized template can. After you see the template examples, you discover the techniques used to place a number of templates in a library. Finally, you discover how to use the template library to create applications.

Deciding When to Create a Template

The first step in creating a template is deciding whether your idea will generate a useful template. Most developers have thousands of creative thoughts that translate into ideas during their careers; however, only a few of these ideas are exceptionally useful. By determining whether the template you want to create is a good idea at the outset, you waste less time on bad ideas and have more time to create that truly useful idea that will help you ascend to the pinnacle of development notoriety (and the astronomical amount of cash that such as position tends to generate).

Before you begin creating the next template to awe and inspire developers everywhere, consider the following questions:

✦ **Is there a generic template that is close enough to meet your needs?** A good template idea is unique — it does something more than perform a useful task; it performs a new kind of useful task. Template ideas that fail the uniqueness test usually consume many resources for a small payoff.

✦ **Will you use the template more than once?** Some template ideas are so tuned to a particular project that the developer ends up using them precisely once, which means that the template never provides a payback on the investment to create it.

✦ **Will the template save more time than you use to create it?** Templates can become complex. In fact, some templates are complex enough that you'd save time by not writing them at all. The reason to use templates is to save time and effort, so a complex template tends to require a larger payback period than a simple one.

✦ **Is there a third-party template you can buy (or, better yet, obtain free) that nearly meets your need?** Someone else may have already had your good idea. Before you invest time in creating a template, you should spend time researching online. Someone else may have created a template that nearly matches your idea. Obtaining a third-party template that's close to what you want is always more time efficient than creating a custom template on your own.

✦ **How generic is the template you want to create?** Many good template ideas are simply too specific, which limits their adaptability to other situations. You want to create a unique template, but a unique template that can meet a range of organizational needs.

✦ **Is your template concept complete?** Developers often envision only a piece of a template. For example, if you create a math template, you should actually create a library that contains all the equations you plan to use with your applications. Designing a template that contains a single equation is never worthwhile because other developers will have to finish the work you started.

✦ **Do you have the skills to create the template?** Not everyone is a good template designer. A template designer must define a template that goes beyond the original expectations because someone will almost certainly use the template in unexpected ways. The best templates adapt to new situations that the originator never considered. Consequently, creating a template requires a different sort of mindset than creating an application.

A little research at the outset can save significant time, effort, and replicated development. C++ has been around for a long time (at least in computer terms) so you can choose from a wealth of existing code. Always determine in advance whether the template you want to create is worth the effort and will make life easier for other developers.

Defining the Elements of a Good Template

Book IV, Chapter 5 provides you with some insights into basic template creation techniques. However, this introductory chapter doesn't address what makes for a good template. After all, you don't want to appear like the guy who builds in his garage. The template you create has to look professional and work as expected.

The first decision you have to make is what kind of template to create. You can choose among these three types:

✦ **Function:** A function represents the simplest way to create a template and eases debugging requirements. You can group functions in libraries to make them easier to access. However, functions often lack depth and you can't coordinate activities between them as easily as you can between the elements of an object.

✦ **Structure:** A structure provides the best speed in many cases and can reduce the amount of system resources required, depending on how you define the structure. Remember that C++ allocates memory for the entire structure, but structures also present opportunities for optimization that you don't get with a class.

✦ **Class:** A class provides the greatest flexibility because you can express the template using all the elements that a class can provide — methods, properties, and events. You can inherit classes to create new classes. In short, if you have a complex idea to implement, classes are the way to do it.

The second decision you have to make is how to weight design factors when creating the template. C++ offers myriad ways to accomplish any given task. For example, you have multiple ways to create a function. However, one method is normally superior to the others simply because it offers some particular benefit. Consider these requirements when choosing the kind of template to create:

✦ **Security:** "Simplicity" often translates into "easier to secure." In general, functions are easier to secure than structures, which are easier to secure than classes. However, you can easily write an insecure class if you use the wrong approach. Secure templates often require additional checks that can affect reliability (the template tends not to allow specific actions when these actions affect security) and speed (additional code always slows template execution).

✦ **Reliability:** The options you choose will affect the reliability of the template you create. A reliable template produces consistent results for any data type supplied to it. In some cases, ensuring reliability means adding checks to the template, which increases complexity. The additional code affects both the security and the speed of the template.

✦ **Speed:** Templates save the developer time. However, if the resulting template produces slow code, you can be sure that users will complain and the developer will end up rewriting some code to improve application speed. A fast template is usually small and performs the task precisely. The additional checks required to ensure secure and reliable operation always affect speed negatively, so you must work to achieve a balance.

✦ **Usage:** Some templates are so difficult to use that we doubt very much that even the originator uses them. If a developer can't determine how to use your template, no one will ever use it and your effort is wasted. Consequently, you must design the template such that it meets security, reliability, and speed goals without becoming overly difficult to use.

✦ **Time:** Every time you design a new piece of software, there is a time element involved. It's essential to decide whether the template will ultimately save enough development time to offset the development cost of creating and testing it. A template that you only intend to use a few times may not be worth the effort.

✦ **Maintenance:** Someone will have to maintain the code used to create the template. A good template is one in which the code is relatively straightforward. Of course, you need to add comments to the code that explain how the code works — and fully document the template design. Most templates see some level of redesign during their lifecycles — they evolve as developers use the template and discover new ways to incorporate it into applications.

The best template is the one that seems obvious. We were recently reading an article about the invention of the safety pin. The safety pin seems obvious, but someone still had to invent it because no one else had thought about it. When you create a template and someone tells you that it seems like an obvious idea, don't get mad. Be glad. You've joined the ranks of people who thought of something that fulfills an obvious need, but no one thought about it before you did.

The third decision you must make is how inclusive to make the template. In some cases, you want to create a template that can handle a range of situations. However, a template can quickly become unwieldy and difficult to manage. A good template is balanced — it includes the elements you need, but nothing beyond.

Creating a Basic Math Template

With a math template, you usually need access to a wealth of calculations but may only use one or two of those calculations at a time. For example, if someone is calculating your mortgage, he or she doesn't need to know the amortization calculation. However, the person might need the amortization calculation when working with the next customer. In short, the calculations all have a purpose and you need them all, but you don't need them all at the same time. Because of the way you use math templates, they work best as a series of function templates. The `MathTemplate` example in Listing 3-1 shows how to create the series of functions.

Book VI
Chapter 3

Building Original
Templates

Listing 3-1:   Defining a Series of Function Templates

```
#include <iostream>
#include <cmath>

using namespace std;

template<typename T>
T Area(T height, T length)
{
    return height * length;
}

const double PI = 4.0*atan(1.0);

template<typename T>
T CircleArea(T radius)
{
    double result;

    result = PI * radius * radius;

    // This version truncates the value.
    return (T)result;
}

template<typename T>
T TriangleArea(T base, T height)
{
    double result;

    result = base * height * 0.5;

    return (T)result;
}
```

(continued)

Listing 3-1 *(continued)*

```
int main()
{
    cout << "4 X 4 Areas:" << endl;
    cout << "Square: " << Area<int>(4, 4) << endl;
    cout << "Circle: " << CircleArea<int>(2) << endl;
    cout << "Triangle: " << TriangleArea<int>(4, 4) << endl;
    cout << "Using a value of pi of: " << PI << endl;
    return 0;
}
```

The calculations could consist of any math calculation — the point of the example is that using functions makes each of the calculations discrete, easy to use, and easy to manage. When you run this example, you see the following output:

```
4 X 4 Areas:
Square: 16
Circle: 12
Triangle: 8
Using a value of pi of: 3.14159
```

Note that `CircleArea<int>(2)` uses half the value of the other calculations as input. That's because you calculate the area of a circle using the equation $\pi \times r^2$. If you want to see other area and volume equations, check out the website at `http://www.aquatext.com/calcs/calculat.htm`.

For consistency, you could change the circle equation to read like this:

```
radius = radius / 2;
result = PI * radius * radius;
```

Dividing the input by 2, essentially changing the diameter to a radius, means that you could call the equation using the same number as all the other area calculations: `CircleArea<int>(4)`. Whichever approach you choose, you need to document how the template works so that other developers know how to use it.

You should also note that the circle and triangle calculations perform a bit of type coercion to ensure that the user gets the expected results back by modifying the `return` statement to read `return (T)result;`. The type conversions are needed to keep your templates from generating warning messages. It's important to note that the approach used in the example truncates the result when the template returns an `int`.

Building a Structure Template

Structure templates have many interesting uses, such as creating a data repository that doesn't depend on a particular type. The `StructureTemplate` example in Listing 3-2 shows one such use.

Listing 3-2: Creating a Template from a Structure

```cpp
#include <iostream>

using namespace std;

template<typename T>
struct Volume
{
    T height;
    T width;
    T length;

    Volume()
    {
        height = 0;
        width = 0;
        length = 0;
    }

    T getvolume()
    {
        return height * width * length;
    }

    T getvolume(T H, T W, T L)
    {
        height = H;
        width = W;
        length = L;

        return height * width * length;
    }
};

int main()
{
    Volume<int> first;

    cout << "First volume: " << first.getvolume() << endl;

    first.height = 2;
    first.width = 3;
    first.length = 4;

    cout << "First volume: " << first.getvolume() << endl;

    Volume<double> second;

    cout << "Second volume: " << second.getvolume(2.1, 3.2, 4.3) << endl;
    cout << "Height: " << second.height << endl;
    cout << "Width: " << second.width << endl;
    cout << "Length: " << second.length << endl;

    return 0;
}
```

In this case, the structure contains height, width, and length data values that the code can use to determine volume. The structure includes a constructor to initialize the values, so even if someone calls `getvolume()` without initializing the structure, nothing bad will happen.

The structure allows independent access of each of the data values. You can set or get them as needed.

The `getvolume()` function is overloaded. You can call it with or without input values. The code in `main()` tests the structure thoroughly. Here's what you see as output from this example:

```
First volume: 0
First volume: 24
Second volume: 28.896
Height: 2.1
Width: 3.2
Length: 4.3
```

You can use structures for another interesting purpose. The C++ standard says you can't create a `typedef` template. For example, the following code produces an error when you try to compile it:

```
template<typename T>
typedef map<string, T> MyDef;
```

When you try to compile this code in Code::Blocks, you see the following error:

```
error: template declaration of 'typedef'
```

However, you can define a `typedef` within a structure template. The `Structure Template2` example code in Listing 3-3 shows a variation of the example found in Listing 6-3 of Book IV, Chapter 6.

Listing 3-3:   Using a Structure to Define a typedef

```cpp
#include <iostream>
#include <map>

using namespace std;

template<typename T>
struct MyDef
{
    typedef map<string, T> Type;
};

int main()
{
    MyDef<string>::Type marriages;

    marriages["Tom"] = "Suzy";
    marriages["Harry"] = "Harriet";

    cout << marriages["Tom"] << endl;
    cout << marriages["Harry"] << endl;

    return 0;
}
```

This example overcomes the C++ limitations by placing the `typedef` within the struct, `MyDef`. The same structure can hold any number of `typedef` entries.

TIP

Using a `typedef` in this manner makes it easier to work with `map`. All you need to worry about is the value type — the key type is already defined as `string`.

Except for the `marriages` declaration, this example works precisely the same as the example in Book IV, Chapter 6. It still outputs the following results:

```
Suzy
Harriet
```

Developing a Class Template

Class templates perform the heavy lifting of the template types. You use a class template to define objects of nearly any size. Classes are larger and more complex than the other techniques demonstrated in the chapter so far. In most cases, you use classes to represent complex objects or to perform tasks ill suited for function or structure templates.

REMEMBER

You normally code classes in a separate file using the name of the class as the filename. The class definition appears in a header file, while the code appears in a code file. To make things a bit easier to understand, this chapter eschews the normal setup and shows the entire example using a single file.

The example shows a specialized queue implementation. It includes many of the features of a standard queue and then adds a few features to meet special development needs. Queues and other containers tend to contain complex code, but you also need to use them with a variety of data types, making a class template the perfect implementation. The `ClassTemplate` example in Listing 3-4 shows the code for this example.

Listing 3-4:   Creating a Specialized Queue

```
#include <iostream>
#include <vector>

using namespace std;

template<typename T>
class MyQueue
```

(continued)

Listing 3-4 *(continued)*

```cpp
{
protected:
    vector<T> data;

public:
    void Add(T const &input);
    void Remove();
    void PrintString();
    void PrintInt();
    bool IsEmpty();
};

template<typename T>
void MyQueue<T>::Add(T const &input)
{
    data.push_back(input);
}

template<typename T>
void MyQueue<T>::Remove()
{
    data.erase(data.begin());
}

template<typename T>
void MyQueue<T>::PrintString()
{
    vector<string>::iterator PrintIt = data.begin();

    while (PrintIt != data.end())
    {
        cout << *PrintIt << endl;
        PrintIt++;
    }
}

template<typename T>
void MyQueue<T>::PrintInt()
{
    vector<int>::iterator PrintIt = data.begin();

    while (PrintIt != data.end())
    {
        cout << *PrintIt << endl;
        PrintIt++;
    }
}

template<typename T>
bool MyQueue<T>::IsEmpty()
{
    return data.begin() == data.end();
}

int main()
{
    MyQueue<string> StringQueue;
```

```
        cout << StringQueue.IsEmpty() << endl;

        StringQueue.Add("Hello");
        StringQueue.Add("Goodbye");

        cout << "Printing strings: " << endl;
        StringQueue.PrintString();
        cout << StringQueue.IsEmpty() << endl;

        StringQueue.Remove();
        cout << "Printing strings: " << endl;
        StringQueue.PrintString();
        StringQueue.Remove();
        cout << StringQueue.IsEmpty() << endl;

        MyQueue<int> IntQueue;

        IntQueue.Add(1);
        IntQueue.Add(2);

        cout << "Printing ints: " << endl;
        IntQueue.PrintInt();

        return 0;
}
```

The example starts with the class `MyQueue`. Note that `data` is a `vector`, not a `queue` as you might expect. A `queue` is an adapter — as such, it doesn't provide support for many of the features found in containers, such as `vector` — one of which is the use of `iterators`.

This example uses an `iterator` for printing, so it relies on a `vector`, rather than a `queue` as a starting point. Whenever you create your own specialized version of a common construct, make sure you begin with the right object. Otherwise, you might find the experience of creating the new class frustrating at a minimum, impossible in the worst case.

`MyQueue` includes the capability to add, remove, and print elements. In addition, you can check whether a queue is empty or full. You have already seen the code for these tasks in other parts of the book.

You might wonder about the code used for printing. The example includes separate methods for printing strings and integers, which might seem counterintuitive. After all, why not simply declare the iterator as follows so that it accepts any data type:

```
vector<T>::iterator PrintIt = data.begin();
```

The problem is that the iterator requires a specific data type. Consequently, you must declare it as shown in Listing 3-4. Otherwise you get this unhelpful error message:

```
error: expected ';' before 'PrintIt'
```

At some point, you want to test this new class using steps similar to those found in `main()`. The test checks whether the queue actually does detect the empty and filled states, how adding and removing elements works, and whether the print routines work. Here is the output from this example:

```
1
Printing strings:
Hello
Goodbye
0
Printing strings:
Goodbye
1
Printing ints:
1
2
```

Considering Template Specialization

Some templates don't go together quite as easily as you might expect because they express a concept that doesn't translate the same way for every data type. For example, when you use `stringify` to turn a data type into its string representation, the technique differs based on data type. For example, when you want to use `stringify` on an `int`, you might use the following template (as shown in the `StringifyInt` example):

```cpp
#include <iostream>
#include <sstream>

using namespace std;

template<typename T> inline string stringify(const T& input)
{
    ostringstream output;
    output << input;
    return output.str();
}

int main()
{
    // This call works as expected.
    cout << stringify<int>(42) << endl;

    // This call truncates.
    cout << stringify<double>(45.6789012345) << endl;

    return 0;
}
```

The `stringify()` function accepts any data type and simply uses an `ostringstream` to convert `input` to a `string`. This approach works fine for the first call in `main()`, which is an `int`. However, when the code uses it for a `double`, the result is truncated as shown here:

```
42
45.6789
```

You can fix this problem by adding special handling for a `double`. Here is the modified form of the example (as shown in `StringifyDouble`) that accommodates a `double`.

```
#include <iostream>
#include <sstream>
#include <iomanip>
#include <limits>

using namespace std;

template<typename T> inline string stringify(const T& input)
{
    ostringstream output;
    output << input;
    return output.str();
}

template <> inline string stringify<double> (const double& input)
{
    ostringstream output;
    const int sigdigits = numeric_limits<double>::digits10;
    output << setprecision(sigdigits) << input;
    return output.str();
}

int main()
{
    cout << stringify<int>(42) << endl;
    cout << stringify<double>(45.6789012345) << endl;
    return 0;
}
```

**Book VI
Chapter 3**

**Building Original
Templates**

When you run this example, you see the expected result because the `double` form of the template uses `setprecision` to modify the `ostringstream` value. As a result, you see the following output:

```
42
45.6789012345
```

As things sit with C++ today, you must create a special template for each data type that requires it. Theoretically, if C++ ever gets a `typeof()` function, you could detect the data type and add a `switch` to perform specialized processing within a single template. The `typeid()` function demonstrated in the "Prefixes and suffixes" section of Book VI, Chapter 2 could work as a substitute for `typeof()`, but it's vendor-specific and not implemented in every version of C++. If you choose to use the `typeid()` function, make sure you know which compiler your organization will use to compile the application code.

You may have also noticed the `inline` keyword used for the template in this example. The `inline` keyword tells the compiler to place the code created by the template in line with the code in which it appears, rather than out of line as a separate function call. In some cases, such as this `stringify()` function, the result is code that executes faster. The compiler is under no obligation to comply with the `inline` keyword. In addition, you want template code placed out of line when it must perform some level of instantiation or it doesn't represent critical path code that the application can call often.

Creating a Template Library

You won't normally create a template and stick it in your application project file. The previous examples in this chapter put everything together for ease of explanation, but in the real world, templates usually reside in a library. Code::Blocks provides several kinds of library projects. This chapter looks at the *static library* — a library that is added into the application. Templates always reside in static libraries.

Code::Blocks also supports dynamic link libraries (DLLs) and shared libraries that more than one application can use at a time. However, you can't place template code inside a DLL or shared library unless you create specific instances of the template because templates require the preprocessor to work and DLLs are pre-compiled code. Working with DLLs and shared libraries is more complex than working with static libraries, and you won't normally need the ability to share the library when creating a console application. See the "Defining your first project" section of Book I, Chapter 2 for details about the various project types that Code::Blocks supports.

Defining the library project

Creating a library project is only a little different than creating a console application. The following steps describe how to create a library project:

1. **Choose File➪New➪Project.**

You see the New From Template dialog box shown in Figure 3-1.

Figure 3-1: Provide a description of your project for Code:: Blocks.

2. Highlight the Static Library icon on the Projects tab, then click Go.

You see the Welcome page of the Static Library wizard.

3. Click Next.

You see a list of project-related questions, as shown in Figure 3-2. These questions define project basics, such as the project name.

Figure 3-2:
Provide a description of your static library for Code:: Blocks.

4. Type a name for your project in the Project Title field.

The example uses `MathLibrary` as the project title. Notice that the wizard automatically starts creating an entry for you in the Project Filename field.

5. Type a location for your project in the Folder to Create Project In field.

6. (Optional) Type a project filename in the Project Filename field.

7. Click Next.

You see the compiler settings shown in Figure 3-3. This example uses the default compiler settings. However, it's important to remember that you can choose a different compiler, modify the locations of the debug and release versions of the project, and make other changes as needed. Code::Blocks provides the same level of customization for libraries as it does for applications.

Figure 3-3:
Change the
compiler
settings to
meet your
project
needs.

8. **Change any required compiler settings and click Finish.**

The wizard creates the application for you. It then displays the Code::Blocks IDE with the project loaded. Note that the Static Library project includes some sample code to get you started. You could compile this library and test it now.

Configuring the library project

The static library starts with a standard C file. To make this library work well with templates, you need to delete the C file, add a C++ file, and add a header file. The following steps describe how to perform this process:

1. **Right-click main.c in the Projects tab of the Management window and choose Remove File From Project from the context menu that appears.**

Code::Blocks removes the file from the project tree.

2. **Choose File⇨New⇨File.**

You see the New from Template dialog box shown in Figure 3-4.

3. **Highlight the C/C++ Header icon and click Go.**

You see the Welcome page of the C/C++ Header wizard.

4. **Click Next.**

The wizard asks you to provide the header configuration information (see Figure 3-5).

Figure 3-4:
Add new files using the New from Template dialog box.

**Book VI
Chapter 3**

Building Original
Templates

Figure 3-5:
Define the header require-ments.

5. **In the Filename with Full Path field, type** MathLibrary.h, **click the ellipses button, and then click Save.**

Code::Blocks adds the complete project path to the filename you chose. Notice that Code::Blocks also supplies an entry for the Header Guard Word field. This word ensures that the header isn't added more than once to a project.

6. **Click All, and then click Finish.**

    The C/C++ Source wizard adds the file to your project. You're ready to begin creating a template library.

Coding the library

At this point, you have what amounts to a blank header file in a static library project. Your static library could conflict with other libraries, so it's important to add a namespace to your code. The example uses `MyNamespace`, but normally you'd use something related to you as a person or your company. After all, you should take pride in the library you've created! The `MathLibrary` heading in Listing 3-5 shows what you need to create the library used for this example.

Listing 3-5:   Creating a Static Library

```
#ifndef MATHLIBRARY_H_INCLUDED
#define MATHLIBRARY_H_INCLUDED

#include <iostream>
#include <cmath>

using namespace std;

namespace MyNamespace
{

template<typename T>
T Area(T height, T length)
{
    return height * length;
}

const double PI = 4.0*atan(1.0);

template<typename T>
T CircleArea(T radius)
{
    double result;

    result = PI * radius * radius;

    // This version truncates the value.
    return (T)result;
}

template<typename T>
T TriangleArea(T base, T height)
{
    double result;

    result = base * height * 0.5;

    return (T)result;
}

}

#endif // MATHLIBRARY_H_INCLUDED
```

As you can see, this is a portable form of the math library discussed in the "Creating a Basic Math Template" section of the chapter. Of course, the library form has changes. You have the usual #define statements and the use of a namespace to encapsulate all the code. Notice that the namespace comes after all the declarations.

Using Your Template Library

You have a shiny new template library. It's time to test it. The MathLibrary Test console application uses MathLibrary to display some area information. The output is the same as in the "Creating a Basic Math Template" section of the chapter. Listing 3-6 shows the test code used for this example.

Listing 3-6:   Testing the Static Library

```
#include <iostream>
#include "..\MathLibrary\MathLibrary.h"

using namespace std;
using namespace MyNamespace;

int main()
{
    cout << "4 X 4 Areas:" << endl;
    cout << "Square: " << Area<int>(4, 4) << endl;
    cout << "Circle: " << CircleArea<int>(2) << endl;
    cout << "Triangle: " << TriangleArea<int>(4, 4) << endl;
    cout << "Using a value of pi of: " << PI << endl;
    return 0;
}
```

When you use your own libraries, you need to tell the compiler where to find them. Because it's likely that you created the example library in the same folder as the test application, you can use the simple path shown in Listing 3-6.

Because the library relies on a namespace, you must also include using namespace MyNamespace; in the example code. Otherwise you'll spend hours trying to figure out why the compiler can't locate the templates in your library. Otherwise, you access and use the template library much as you did before.

Chapter 4: Investigating Boost

In This Chapter

✔ Considering what Boost can do for you

✔ Getting Boost and installing it

✔ Building the Boost tools

✔ Interacting with Boost.Build

✔ Using Boost Regression

✔ Working with the Boost Inspect tool

✔ Using the BoostBook document format

✔ Integrating the Boost QuickBook add-on

✔ Working with the Boost bcp tool

✔ Working with the Boost Wave tool

✔ Creating your first application using Boost

*A*s your skill with C++ improves, you find that you need additional functionality that doesn't come with the Standard Library or with the Standard Template Library (STL). For example, the simple act of checking a string for specific character sequences (such as a telephone number pattern) can prove difficult. You can do it, but most developers will think that someone else has certainly crossed this bridge before. The answer to the question of where to find the additional code you need is third-party libraries. One of the most popular C++ libraries is Boost, which is the topic of this chapter and the next.

Two book chapters can't serve as a complete reference to an entire library — especially not a set of libraries the size of Boost. This particular chapter (Chapter 4) has a set of more limited goals. It introduces you to Boost, and helps you understand why Boost may be helpful to your development efforts. It also shows you how to obtain and install Boost, demonstrates some Boost tools, and finally helps you create your first application using Boost. Chapter 5 picks up where this chapter leaves off and helps you use Boost to build some interesting applications. In short, these two chapters combined provide you with an overview of a library that you should consider spending more time discovering.

Libraries are simply repositories of code. Consequently, any library can help you produce applications faster and with fewer errors. However, not all libraries are created with the same quality of code. Many developers use the Boost libraries because it provides high-quality code — so high quality that some of Boost is being standardized for inclusion in the Standard Library. The bottom line is that you must choose the libraries you want with care and look at both quality and price (when price is an issue).

Understanding Boost

One of the best things about Boost is that the library itself is free. The Boost website, `http://www.boost.org/`, makes a point of letting developers know that they won't pay anything for using Boost, even in a commercial setting. In addition, Boost doesn't have any expenses, so you probably won't ever need to pay for it. You need to download boost from the `http://www.boost.org/` site before proceeding with the rest of this chapter and you should probably read the associated Getting Started guide so you know how to perform the installation for your platform. A number of people and organizations contribute to Boost, including (but not limited to)

✦ Open Systems Lab at Indiana University

✦ SourceForge

✦ Boost Consulting

✦ MetaCommunications

✦ Individuals, companies, and other organizations that run the regression tests

However, don't get the idea that Boost is completely free. If you want commercial-level support, you'll pay for it, just as you would with any other product. Only the library itself is free. The following sections describe some of the details of Boost.

Boost features

You might think that Boost couldn't really be all that complete if you can get it free. Actually, Boost includes a significant number of features — far more features than the average developer will use in writing typical applications. It's interesting to note that you probably have an application on your system that relies on Boost, Adobe Acrobat. That's right, major applications do rely on Boost because it's a feature-rich application development library. In fact, you can see entire lists of applications you know and use at `http://www.boost.org/users/uses.html` (simply choose one of the categories, such as Shrink Wrapped Boost, to see the applications in that category).

Ensure your compiler is supported

Boost constantly adds new libraries and functionality. In order to provide these new features, the developers who create Boost have to make some hard decisions. One of the hardest decisions is whether to continue supporting older compilers (and possibly hold Boost development back) or to drop support for some compilers in order to make Boost better.

Boost 1.55.0 is the current version as of this writing. This version no longer supports Digital Mars 8.41, GCC 3.3, Intel 6.0, and Visual C++ 7.1 (or earlier versions of these compilers). The group is also considering removing support for Metroworks C++, SunPro 5.7 (and earlier), and Borland C++ Builder 2006 (and earlier). As a result, if you're using this book with an older compiler, the examples in this chapter and Chapter 5 may not work. (In fact, they probably won't.) You can find information about these

sorts of updates on the main Boost page at `http://www.boost.org/` in the News column. If you plan to use Boost extensively, it pays to subscribe to their RSS feed for additional information.

In addition to the Boost-specific information, please be sure to check for book-specific information on my blog at `http://blog.johnmuellerbooks.com/categories/263/c-all-in-one-for-dummies.aspx`. I'll provide you with updates as readers bring issues to my attention. In addition, my blog is the place to look for information regarding the effect of Boost updates on book examples and so on. Please be sure to contact me at `John@JohnMuellerBooks.com` with your questions and concerns regarding book examples.

The current version of Boost contains in excess of a hundred libraries in categories that meet an incredible number of needs (new libraries are added all of the time). In some cases, you'll need only Boost to meet all your development needs. Because these libraries meet specific conformity requirements, you never find yourself calling a function one way with one library and another way when using a different library.

In addition to libraries, Boost also provides a number of tools to make your development experience more enjoyable. Most of this chapter discusses these specialized tools. Because you get the source code for all the tools, you can build a version of the tool for every platform in your organization, which means that every developer can use the same toolset. Using a common toolset reduces training time and tends to improve the consistency of development output.

Licensing

The Boost license is friendly to individual users, consultants, and organizations. Even if you work in an enterprise environment, you can use Boost for free. The developers behind Boost are concerned enough about legal matters that they continue working on the license so that usage requirements are easy to understand. You can find a copy of the current license at `http://www.boost.org/users/license.html`.

The Boost license and the GNU General Public License (GPL) differ in some important ways. The most important consideration for organizations is that the Boost license lets you make changes to the libraries without having to share these changes with anyone. You get to keep your source code secret, which is a big plus for organizations that create commercial applications.

Paid support

When working with Boost, you gain access to the source code and community support. For some organizations, the lack of a formal support mechanism is a problem. Fortunately, you can also get paid support from BoostPro Computing (`https://github.com/boostpro`). Most importantly, BoostPro Computing offers formal training in using Boost, which means your organization can get up to speed quickly. You can find additional companies that provide Boost support at `http://www.boost.org/support/index.html`.

Obtaining and Installing Boost for Code::Blocks

Before you can use Boost, you need to download it. The examples in this chapter rely on version 1.55.0 of the library, which you can obtain at `http://www.boost.org/users/history/version_1_55_0.html`. You get the entire Boost library in a single 99 MB download (when obtained in `.zip` format). There are downloads for Windows and Unix (which you can use for both Mac and Linux development).

The Boost documentation is a separate download that you obtain at `http://sourceforge.net/projects/boost/files/boost-docs/1.55.0/`. In addition, it's possible to download binaries for Windows systems, should you want the library pre-built. However, the link on the main page for the binary download is incorrect, at least as of this writing. You need to go to `http://sourceforge.net/projects/boost/files/boost-binaries/1.55.0-build2/` to download the binaries.

Boost for the Visual Studio developer

Boost works with a wide variety of programming products, so you shouldn't get the idea that just because we use Code::Blocks in this chapter that you can't use Boost with other products such as Visual Studio. In fact, there is special support for other development products.

Visual Studio developers often find that their development environment is complex enough that getting a good Boost install is difficult. BoostPro Computing remedies this problem by providing the BoostPro Installer (`https://github.com/boostpro/installer`). Download this product and follow the installation instructions on the website to get a better Visual Studio installation for Boost.

Unpacking Boost

The first step in gaining access to Boost is to unpack the Boost 1.55.0 library file (`boost_1_55_0.zip`) that you downloaded earlier. When working with Code::Blocks, you'll want to unpack this library into the `\CodeBlocks\ boost_1_55_0\` folder for ease of access. The documentation often refers to the `boost_1_55_0\` folder as the Boost root directory or `$BOOST_ROOT`. When you unpack the ZIP file, you see the following folders (some of the folders, such as `lib\`, will be empty):

✦ **boost\:** Contains all the Boost header files.

✦ **doc\:** Provides a subset of the Boost documentation. If you want complete documentation, you must either download the separate Boost Docs file or use the website directly.

✦ **lib\:** Contains all the Boost precompiled libraries after you build them. This folder won't contain any files (or may not even exist) when you unpack the Boost library.

✦ **libs\:** Provides a root folder for all the Boost library headers.

- **libs\accumulators\:** Contains a library of incremental statistical computation functions. In addition, you use this library for general incremental calculations.

- **libs\algorithm\:** Contains algorithms that build on the string functionality found in the Standard Library. These algorithms provide functionality such as trimming, case conversion, predicates, and find/replace functions. You'll also find a min/max library that lets you determine the minimum and maximum of an expression in a single call (among other things).

- **libs\any\:** Contains a library that helps you interact with variables in a manner reminiscent of scripting languages. You don't need this capability all the time, but it's handy when you want to do things such as convert between an `int` and `string` using a simple `lexical_cast`.

- **libs\array\:** Provides an extension to basic `array` functionality so that you get some of the advantages of using a `vector` without the performance hit that using a `vector` can introduce.

- **libs\more libraries:** Boost contains over a hundred libraries. You'll want to check them all out.

✦ **more\:** Holds policy and other important documents. The most important document at the outset is `getting_started.html`, which provides essential information for getting started using Boost. The `index. htm` file provides access to basic information about Boost, such as the licensing policy.

✦ **status\:** Provides access to a Boost-wide test suite. Generally, you won't need the contents of this folder unless you plan to augment the Boost libraries in some way.

✦ **tools\:** Contains a wealth of tools you use when working with Boost. Much of this chapter tells you about these tools. You must build the tools before you can use them. Each folder contains complete instructions, but you'll also find an example of building the tools later in this section.

Using the header-only libraries

No matter which platform you work with, the header-only libraries are ready for use immediately after you unpack Boost. These libraries appear in the `boost_1_55_0\boost\` directory. Each library is contained in a separate subdirectory and you access the library through its header file. Boost 1.55.0 supports 97 different header-only libraries that address all sorts of issues, such as incremental statistical computation. (That particular area is covered by the accumulators library, which is found in the `accumulators\` subdirectory.)

Having access to the library doesn't mean you'll know how to use it right out of the box, but the Boost folks do make an effort to provide you with good documentation so you can discover how to use Boost. Look in the `boost_1_55_0\libs\` directory and you see another set of subdirectories containing the names of libraries, such as `accumulators\`. Each of these subdirectories contains a minimum of three subdirectories:

✦ **doc:** The documentation for understanding and using the library. Access the documentation for an individual library by opening the `index.htm` file in its subdirectory. Access the documentation for Boost as a whole by opening the `libraries.htm` file found in the `boost_1_55_0\libs\` directory.

✦ **example:** A somewhat simple application that demonstrates how to use the library. (The example is designed to show both usage and functionality, so some complex libraries have larger examples to demonstrate them.) Some libraries include multiple examples to fully demonstrate the library's functionality.

✦ **test:** A test suite you can use to ensure that any changes you make to Boost won't break the library or cause undesirable side effects.

Depending on the needs of the library, you may find additional subdirectories that contain other information or resources, such as tools. Some of the libraries require additional processing before you can use them. The next section of the chapter describes the building process so that you have a complete Boost installation. Make absolutely certain that you build the libraries before you proceed.

Building the libraries

The Boost library relies on code in headers. Using this approach means that if you include the header in your code, you already have everything you need to use the Boost library. However, these few Boost libraries require separate compilation:

+ Boost.Chrono

+ Boost.Context

+ Boost.Filesystem

+ Boost.GraphParallel

+ Boost.IOStreams

+ Boost.Locale

+ Boost.MPI

+ Boost.ProgramOptions

+ Boost.Python (See the Boost.Python build documentation before building and installing it.)

+ Boost.Regex

+ Boost.Serialization

+ Boost.Signals

+ Boost.System

+ Boost.Thread

+ Boost.Timer

+ Boost.Wave

Book VI
Chapter 4

Investigating Boost

If you have used previous versions of Boost, throw out everything you know because this latest version uses a completely different (and much easier) process to build the libraries — and it works the same on any platform. The process isn't any faster, unfortunately, but then again, Boost is a huge library.

The following steps help you build the libraries and creating a centralized store of Boost information for your applications. These steps assume that you're using CodeBlocks as your IDE and that you've installed it using the instructions in Book I, Chapter 1. You may need to modify the steps if you used some other installation process or rely on a different IDE.

1. **Open a command prompt or terminal window using the technique appropriate for your platform.**

   For example, when working with Windows, you choose Start⇨Programs⇨ Accessories⇨Command Prompt. When working with a Mac you navigate to the /Applications/Utilities window and double click Terminal. The method of opening a terminal window in Linux varies with the distribution you use.

2. **Type** CD /CodeBlocks/boost_1_55_0 **and press Enter.**

   The command processor takes you to the Boost directory.

3. **(Optional) If you haven't already created a path to the CodeBlocks compiler at the command line or terminal, create one.**

   For example, when working with Windows, type **path = C:\CodeBlocks\ MinGW\bin;%path%** and press Enter.

4. **Type** bootstrap gcc **and press Enter.**

   You see a message, Building Boost.Build engine, at the command prompt or terminal window for a few seconds. Once the Boost.Build Engine is complete, you see additional text telling you how to use the resulting B2 command.

5. **Type** b2 –toolset=gcc **and press Enter.**

   Go get a cup of coffee. The installation process takes between 5 and 20 minutes depending on your system. This command prompt installs Boost using the default options and in the default directory. For example, you find Boost installed in the C:\Boost directory on a Windows system. It appears in the /usr/local/Boost directory on Mac and most Linux systems. When the process is complete, you find the new Boost folder complete with header and library files appropriate for your system.

Testing the installation

At this point, you have the unpacked Boost files as a subdirectory under your Code::Blocks installation and a set of built libraries in the Boost directory (wherever it might appear on your system). You may initially think you can get rid of one or the other set of files, but this isn't the case. The files you unpacked include documentation and example code that isn't part of the built libraries. The following steps help you test your installation by building the Boost.Timer library, which relies on both sets of files, so it's important that you have both sets in place. (You can modify these instructions to build other libraries as well.)

1. **Locate the** \CodeBlocks\boost_1_55_0\libs\regex\example\ timer **folder on your system.**

2. **Double-click the** regex_timer.cpp **file.**

Code::Blocks automatically opens the file for you. If you attempt to compile the file at this point, Code::Blocks will display a considerable number of errors. The errors aren't due to problems with the code, but with issues in the configuration. You need to configure Code::Blocks to work with this example.

3. **Choose Settings⇨Compiler.**

You see the Compiler Settings dialog box shown in Figure 4-1. You need to perform three configuration tasks in order to make the example usable:

- Tell Code::Blocks where to find the Boost include (header) files.

- Tell Code::Blocks where to find the Boost library files.

- Configure Code::Blocks to add the required libraries to the application.

Figure 4-1:
Use the
Compiler
Settings
dialog box
to configure
Code::
Blocks to
use Boost.

4. **Select the Search Directories tab.**

   You see three sub-tabs: Compiler, Linker, and Resource Compiler.

5. **Click Add in the Compiler sub-tab.**

   You see an Add Directory dialog box like the one shown in Figure 4-2.

Figure 4-2:
Add appropri-ate search directories for Boost header and library files.

6. **Type the location of the Boost header files in the Directory field.**

   As an alternative, you can click the Browse button to use a Browse for Folder dialog box to find them. The files are normally located in the `\Boost\include\boost-1_55 folder`.

7. **Click OK.**

   You see the search folder added to the Compiler tab, as shown in Figure 4-3.

8. **Click Add in the Linker sub-tab.**

   You see the Add Directory dialog box (refer to Figure 4-2).

9. **Type the location of the Boost library files in the Directory field and then click OK.**

   The Boost library files are typically located in the `\Boost\lib` directory. After you click OK, you see the directory added to the Linker tab.

10. **Select the Linker Settings tab.**

    This tab contains two lists — one for link libraries and another for linker options.

11. **Click Add.**

    Code::Blocks displays the Add Library dialog box shown in Figure 4-4. This example requires use of the `libboost_regex-mgw47-mt-1_55.a` library file.

Figure 4-3:
The Search
Directories
tab will
display any
compiler,
linker, or
resource
compiler
search
locations.

Figure 4-4:
The
example
requires use
of a special
library.

12. Type the location of the library in the File field.

The `libboost_regex-mgw47-mt-1_55.a` library is normally found in
the `\Boost\lib` directory. As an alternative, you can locate the file by
clicking the Browse button next to the File field.

13. Click OK.

You see the library file added to the Link Libraries list as shown in
Figure 4-5.

Figure 4-5:
The needed
file appears
in the Link
Libraries
list.

14. Click OK.

The Compiler Settings dialog box closes.

15. Build the application by choosing Build⇨Build.

The application should build without warnings or errors. If you see warnings or errors, ensure you've added both header and library search paths, and the required library file.

At this point, you have a shiny new application to try. This is an example application that is provided as part of Boost that shows how to work with regular expressions. (It serves to test the development environment to ensure everything works.) Now it's time to see the application in action.

1. Click Run.

You see the example start. The example asks you to type an expression. A simple string will work fine.

2. Type Hi when asked to enter an expression and press Enter.

The example will ask you to provide a search string.

3. **Type** Hi there! **and press Enter.**

You see the results shown in Figure 4-6. The times may be different because they depend on the processing speed of your system and a number of other factors.

C:\CodeBlocks\boost_1_55_0\libs\regex\example\timer\regex_timer.exe

```
Enter expression (or "quit" to exit): Hi
Enter string to search (or "quit" to exit): Hi there!
regex time: 1.09us
        match 0: "Hi" (matched=1)
        match $`: "" (matched=0)
        match $': " there!" (matched=1)

wregex time: 1.09us
        match 0: "Hi" (matched=1)
        match $`: "" (matched=0)
        match $': " there!" (matched=1)

regex time (search over std::deque<char>): 1.38571us
        match 0: "Hi" (matched=1)
        match $`: "" (matched=0)
        match $': " there!" (matched=1)

POSIX regexecA time: 0.455556us
        match 0: "Hi" (matched=1)
        match $`: "" (matched=0)
        match $': " there!" (matched=1)

Enter string to search (or "quit" to exit): _
```

Figure 4-6:
The example displays the result of the search.

4. **Type** quit **and press Enter.**

5. **Type** quit **(a second time) and press Enter twice.**

The application ends. At this point, you know you can create, build, and use Boost applications on your system. You can close Code::Blocks without saving anything.

Creating the Boost Tools

It's always nice when a vendor provides tools for making it easier to work with a product and Boost is no exception. You find these tools in the \boost_1_55_0\tools directory. The sections that follow this one describe a number of these tools in detail, but here is a quick list of the tools you get:

✦ **Boost.Build:** Helps you build applications that use Boost by automating some of the process from the command line. This product is actually an add-on for an updated version of Boost.Jam, which used to appear as a separate product. (In fact, you can still get it as a separate product from http://www.boost.org/doc/libs/1_31_0/tools/build/jam_src/index.html, but it's probably best if you use Boost.Build instead because Boost.Build is easier to use.)

✦ **Regression:** Performs regression testing on your Boost configuration and provides reports that tell you whether any changes you've made are working correctly.

✦ **Release:** Creates tarballs and zips of any applications that you create using Boost. This tool helps ensure that the package you create is complete so that someone using your application doesn't experience problems due to a lack of supporting libraries.

✦ **Inspect:** Determines if there are any errors in the Boost directory hierarchy. Errors in the directory hierarchy can cause the automatic Boost features to work incorrectly.

✦ **BoostBook:** Provides the developer with a fast and easy method for accessing the Boost documentation. It relies partially on DocBook (`http://www.docbook.org/`), the eXtensible Stylesheet Language (XSL), and some Boost functionality. This tool is used by some Boost libraries.

✦ **bcp:** Extracts subsets of Boost for use with your application. In order to perform this task, bcp also provides a method for determining which parts of Boost your code relies upon and it also makes it possible to print reports of Boost usage (including any required licensing information).

✦ **QuickBook:** Generates BoostBook XML files. This tool provides a WikiWiki (wiki) style documentation geared towards C++ documentation requirements. It relies on simple rules and markup for providing output formatting.

✦ **Wave:** Preprocesses your C/C++ application code. You can use it with any compiler. The main purpose of the Wave preprocessor is to check the expansion of macros in your code as part of the debugging process. You can also use it as a preprocessor replacement if you don't like how the preprocessor supplied with your compiler works.

✦ **AutoIndex:** Creates indexes for BoostBook and DocBook documents.

All of these tools come in source code format as part of your Boost installation. They're not ready for use when you unpack Boost. Of course, the lack of executable code makes sense considering the number of platforms that Boost supports. In order to use the tools, you must first build them.

The first task is to create a version of Boost.Build for your system. You use Boost.Build to build all of the other tools. The following steps describe how to build Boost.Build.

1. **Open a command prompt or terminal window using the technique appropriate for your platform.**

For example, when working with Windows, you choose Start⇨Programs⇨ Accessories⇨Command Prompt. When working with a Mac you navigate to the /Applications/Utilities window and double-click Terminal. The method of opening a terminal window in Linux varies with the distribution you use.

2. **Type** CD \CodeBlocks\boost_1_55_0\tools\build\v2 **and press Enter.**

The command processor takes you to the Boost.Build version 2 directory.

3. **(Optional) If you haven't already created a path to the CodeBlocks compiler at the command line or terminal, create one.**

For example, when working with Windows, type **path = C:\CodeBlocks\ MinGW\bin;%path%** and press Enter.

4. **Type** bootstrap gcc **and press Enter.**

You see a message, Bootstrapping the build engine, at the command prompt or terminal window for a few seconds. Once the Boost. Build compilation is complete, you see additional text telling you how to use the resulting B2 command.

5. **Type** b2 install toolset=gcc –prefix=*DIR* **and press Enter.**

You must replace the placeholder text *DIR* shown above with the location you want to use to install Boost.Build. For example, if you have a Windows system and want to install Boost.Build in C:\Boost.Build, then you'd type **b2 install toolset=gcc --prefix=C:\Boost.Build** and press Enter.

6. **Add Boost.Build to the path using the command for your particular platform.**

For example, when working with Windows, type **path=C:\Boost.Build\ bin;%path%** and press Enter.

Now that you have an application to build the Boost tools, you can build the tools themselves. A number of the tools come with build directories or build files in their main directory. In those directories are the instructions required to create the tools. For example, look in the \CodeBlocks\boost_1_55_0\ tools\auto_index\build directory and you see a Jamfile.v2 file. This is the file that contains the instructions for building the AutoIndex tool. Likewise, you find a Jamfile.v2 file in the \CodeBlocks\boost_1_55_0\ tools\bcp folder. (The file is in the main directory, rather than a build directory in this case.). No matter where the Jamfile.v2 file is located, you use it to build the associated tool.

However, the easiest method to build the tools is to build them all at once. A special `Jamfile.v2` file is located in the `\CodeBlocks\boost_1_55_0\tools` directory. You use it to create all the tools at once, using the following steps.

1. **Open a command prompt or terminal window using the technique appropriate for your platform.**

2. **Type** CD \CodeBlocks\boost_1_55_0\tools **and press Enter.**

   The command processor takes you to the main tools directory.

3. **(Optional) If you haven't already created a path to the CodeBlocks compiler at the command line or terminal, create one.**

   For example, when working with Windows, type **path = C:\CodeBlocks\ MinGW\bin;%path%** and press Enter.

4. **(Optional) If you haven't already created a path to Boost.Build at the command line or terminal, create one.**

   For example, when working with Windows, type **path=C:\Boost.Build\ bin;%path%** and press Enter.

5. **Type** b2 toolset=gcc **and press Enter.**

   Be patient; the build process will take several minutes. The executable files for Regression (both `library_status.exe` and `process_jam_log.exe`), Inspect (`inspect.exe`), bcp (`bcp.exe`), QuickBook (`quickbook.exe`), Wave (`wave.exe`), and AutoIndex (`auto_index. exe`) will automatically appear in the `\CodeBlocks\boost_1_55_0\ dist\bin` directory on your system once the build process is complete. BoostBook content appears in the `\CodeBlocks\boost_1_55_0\ dist\share\boostbook` directory. Release is the only utility that isn't actually built; it consists of a number of batch files that you find in the `\CodeBlocks\boost_1_55_0\tools\release` directory.

Using Boost.Build

Boost.Build is a complex tool that helps you create fully functional applications that rely on Boost using your compiler, such as GCC. It provides an automated command line approach to performing tasks that some developers prefer, especially when performing repetitive tasks where the IDE simply gets in the way. You have already used Boost.Build several times in this chapter to build the Boost libraries, a specific version of Boost.Build for your compiler, as well as the Boost tools. The following sections provide some helpful hints and tips for working with Boost.Build.

Getting a successful build

Every time you use the B2 command at the command prompt or terminal window, you use Boost.Build. A few rules to remember when using Boost.Build are

✦ Ensure that you have a path set up to your compiler.

✦ Ensure that you have a path set up to Boost.Build.

✦ Specify the `toolset` property to ensure Boost.Build uses the correct compiler options.

✦ Use the --prefix option to place the output in a specific directory.

If you know these rules, you'll avoid the problems that plague many developers who are new to Boost.Build. The `bbv2.html` file contained in the \ `CodeBlocks\boost_1_55_0\doc\html` directory contains complete documentation for Boost.Build. This is where you find a complete list of the Boost.Build properties and options. In addition, the documentation tells you how to perform various build types, such as applications and libraries.

Using the examples

Reading the Boost.Build documentation will tell you a lot about the product, but working through the examples will give you hands-on experience. The `\Boost.Build\share\boost-build\example` directory contains a number of examples you can work with to build your knowledge of Boost.Build. The `Hello` example (found in the `hello` subdirectory) is the best place to start. Try this example out using the following steps.

1. **Open a command prompt or terminal window using the technique appropriate for your platform.**

2. **Change directories to the** `\Boost.Build\share\boost-build\` `example\hello` **directory on your system.**

3. **(Optional) Create a path to the CodeBocks compiler directory.**

4. **(Optional) Create a path to the Boost.Build directory.**

5. **Type** b2 toolset=gcc release **and press Enter.**

   You see the following information presented at the command prompt telling you that Boost.Build has created a release version of the `Hello` example using the GCC compiler:

   ```
   ...found 8 targets...
   ...updating 5 targets...
   common.mkdir bin
   common.mkdir bin\gcc-mingw-4.7.1
   common.mkdir bin\gcc-mingw-4.7.1\release
   gcc.compile.c++ bin\gcc-mingw-4.7.1\release\hello.o
   gcc.link bin\gcc-mingw-4.7.1\release\hello.exe
   ...updated 5 targets...
   ```

**Book VI
Chapter 4**

Investigating Boost

6. **Type** cd bin\gcc-mingw-4.7.1\release **and press Enter.**

    You are taken to the output directory for the Hello example. When working with Boost.Build to create an application, the application hierarchy starts with the bin directory, followed by a compiler-specific directory, followed by the kind of output (such as debug or release).

7. **Type** hello **and press Enter.**

    You see Hello! as the application output.

The other examples provided with Boost.Build work approximately the same way. You open the command prompt or terminal window, create the appropriate environment, build the example, and then test it. Some examples require a special setup. You can find details of the setup requirements in the readme.txt file for each example.

Using Regression

Regression is an add-on for Boost.Build that lets you perform regression testing as part of the build process. *Regression testing* ensures that your application meets specific requirements and that changes you make to your application don't add potential bugs. Larger organizations usually employ regression testing as part of major application projects because the testing environment becomes so complex. You never need a product of this sort for smaller applications or for discovering new C++ features.

As with Boost.Build , you get Regression when you install Boost according to the instructions found in the "Obtaining and Installing Boost for Code::Blocks" section of the chapter. Regression is an advanced tool that requires that you know a little something about Python as well as C++. Because Regression is such a complex tool, incomplete, and currently in beta, it's well outside the scope of this book to describe. However, you can find the requirements and step-by-step instructions for using Regression at http://beta.boost.org/development/running_regression_tests.html.

The Regression add-on provides a number of specific capabilities that you may want to know about. The main Regression website at http://www.boost.org/doc/libs/1_55_0/tools/regression/doc/index.html provides access to this information. If you do decide to try Regression, make sure you obtain the correct version of Python and perform all required setup testing.

Using Inspect

Many organizations want to make changes to the Boost library to ensure that the library meets their needs or to augment the Boost library to meet a new requirement. Whenever you change something, there is a chance that the change will cause compatibility issues because it doesn't meet the Boost library guidelines. In addition, it's possible for a developer to introduce errors into the Boost library that others will find difficult to fix. The Inspect utility makes it possible for you to scan for potential Boost library errors after you make a change to it.

Start Inspect from the directory that you want to check. To make this process more efficient, make sure you set a path to the copy of Inspect that you built in the "Creating the Boost Tools" section of the chapter using the method appropriate for your platform. For example, when working with Windows, you type **path = C:\CodeBlocks\boost_1_55_0\dist\bin;%path%** and press Enter.

Inspect looks for errors in the current directory and all subdirectories. You can try it out by checking the library files you built earlier in the "Building the libraries" section of the chapter. These files usually appear in the \ Boost\lib directory. Normally, Inspect performs a complete check of the libraries. However, you can modify Inspect behavior using the following command-line switches to perform specific tests:

**Book VI
Chapter 4**

Investigating Boost

+ `-license`
+ `-copyright`
+ `-crlf`
+ `-end`
+ `-link`
+ `-path_name`
+ `-tab`
+ `-ascii`
+ `-apple_macro`
+ `-assert_macro`
+ `-deprecated_macro`
+ `-minmax`
+ `-unnamed`

You can use any number of these command-line switches. If you forget the Inspect command-line switches, type **Inspect -help** and press Enter. Inspect shows you a list of the command-line switches you can use for testing.

Inspect also provides a number of command-line switches that affect how it performs tests. The following list describes these command-line switches:

✦ -cvs: Performs a check of only the cvs directory and ignores all other files.

✦ -text: Outputs the results in pure text format. This option is especially useful when you want to save the results to a text file for later analysis. Otherwise, Inspect formats the output as HTML. Figure 4-7 shows a typical report. Click on the links to see details about a particular test, such as the licensed status of each file within a particular directory.

Inspect outputs information to the default output device, which is normally the console (your display). Seeing HTML in text form on a display isn't particularly helpful. Most platforms offer some type of redirection feature so that you can see the output to a file. For example, on a Windows system you can type **Inspect > MyReport.html** and press Enter to output the results to a file named MyReport.html.

✦ -brief: Reduces the amount of output text to the minimum required to indicate success or failure of the various tests.

Inspect is sensitive about the ordering of command-line switches. You must place the -cvs, -text, or -brief command-line switch first, and then the test switches; otherwise Inspect displays an error message. The website at http://www.boost.org/doc/libs/1_55_0/tools/inspect/index. html tells you more about working with Inspect.

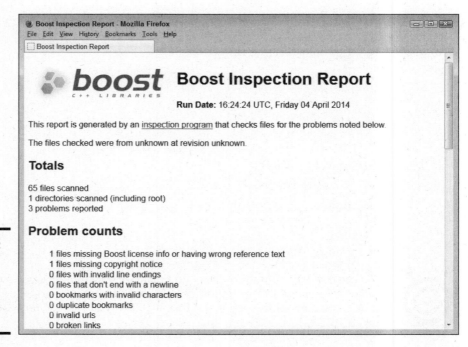

Figure 4-7:
Inspect normally outputs its reports as HTML.

Understanding BoostBook

The world abounds with documentation formats — everything from .docx files produced by Word to the seemingly ubiquitous .pdf file. Of all the documentation formats, the most universal and compatible is the lowly .txt file. However, .txt files lack formatting, which means they limit you solely to words, which may not be enough to describe your documentation. Because you can choose from so many different file formats and formatting code can prove especially difficult, the Boost library relies on a special document format called BoostBook.

Documentation seems to be the bane of developers everywhere. No one seems to want to write the documentation, and the attempts at documentation often leave readers with more questions than answers. BoostBook won't make you a good writer. While it does help you produce highly formatted documentation with a standardized format, it can't overcome deficiencies in writing skill. When creating documentation for your project, the best writer in your group is still the unsurpassed choice for documentation tasks.

If you have installed the Boost library using the instructions in the "Obtaining and Installing Boost for Code::Blocks" section of this chapter, you already have access to BoostBook. However, as with some other Boost utilities, you need to know a bit about Python to use this feature. In addition, you need an Apache server setup and must also download a number of other utilities. In short, even though BoostBook is accessible from a Boost library perspective, you still need to do some work to make this feature useful. The instructions at http://www.boost.org/doc/libs/1_55_0/doc/html/boostbook/getting/started.html describe the additional steps you need to perform.

BoostBook relies on XML to hold the content you want to place in the document. The use of XML is the reason you must install the DocBook eXtensible Stylesheet Language (XSL) (http://docbook.sourceforge.net/) and DocBook Document Type Definition (DTD) (http://www.oasis-open.org/docbook/xml/4.5/) support. You can see the XML used for BoostBook at http://www.boost.org/doc/libs/1_55_0/doc/html/boostbook/documenting.html. Check the main BoostBook page at http://www.boost.org/doc/libs/1_55_0/doc/html/boostbook.html for additional information.

If you performed the steps in the "Creating the Boost Tools" section of the chapter, you already have access to all the functionality needed to use BoostBook. The files you require appear in the CodeBlocks\boost_1_55_0\dist\share\boostbook directory of your system. These files help you perform the required formatting.

TIP

Even if you choose not to use BoostBook for your project, you do need to create a common documentation format. Using BoostBook may prove complicated for the Windows developer — it seems that the originators meant this documentation format more for Unix and Linux developers. However, it's still a useful documentation format and you should consider it. If you find BoostBook lacking, you need to create a custom format or suffer the consequences of a poorly documented application.

Using QuickBook

QuickBook is an add-on for BoostBook. This utility started as someone's weekend project. Originally, QuickBook outputted simple HTML documents. However, now it outputs XML in BoostBook format so that you can quickly generate documentation that links with the rest of the documentation for your project. As described by the author at `http://www.boost.org/doc/libs/1_55_0/doc/html/quickbook.html`, QuickBook is a WikiWiki style documentation tool. It's important to note that some people simply call it a Wiki (`http://en.wikipedia.org/wiki/Wiki`) or Wiki-Wiki or even Wiki Wiki. All the terms mean the same thing.

Before you use QuickBook, you generate a documentation file. You can see an example of such a file at `http://www.boost.org/doc/libs/1_55_0/tools/quickbook/doc/quickbook.qbk`. For a complete syntax summary for QuickBook, look at `http://www.boost.org/doc/libs/1_55_0/doc/html/quickbook/syntax.html`.

At this point, you're probably wondering why you should use QuickBook at all, since you have to generate a document file for it anyway. Here are the reasons why many developers use QuickBook instead of relying on BoostBook directly:

✦ The QuickBook syntax is easier to read and use than writing XML.

✦ You can use QuickBook to generate non-Boost documentation.

✦ It's relatively easy to convert other documentation formats into QuickBook syntax.

QuickBook is a command-line utility. You find it in the `\CodeBlocks\boost_1_55_0\dist\bin` directory after generating the Boost tools. (See the "Creating the Boost Tools" section of the chapter for details.) Here are the command-line switches you can access when working with QuickBook:

✦ **--help:** Displays a help message showing all the command-line switches, as well as the command-line syntax.

✦ **--version:** Displays version information about QuickBook.

✦ **--no-pretty-print:** Disables XML printing and uses plain text instead.

✦ **--indent** *arg*: Defines the number of spaces to use for indents (as specified by arg).

✦ **--linewidth** *arg*: Defines the number of characters in a single line.

✦ **--input-file** *arg*: Specifies the name of the input file.

✦ **--output-file** *arg*: Specifies the name of the output file.

✦ **--debug:** Places QuickBook in debug mode (useful only for developers who want to tinker with the executable).

✦ **--ms-errors:** Specifies that QuickBook should use the Microsoft Visual Studio style of errors and warnings in the output message format. This option can make QuickBook easier for Microsoft Visual Studio developers to use and understand.

Using bcp

The bcp (Boost copy) utility helps you make Boost more manageable. You can use it to

✦ Copy one or more Boost modules to another location so that you can use a subset within an application.

✦ List all the elements within a module.

✦ Create an HTML report about module content that includes:

• License information

• Files without licensing information

• Files without copyright information

• Copyright information

• Dependency information for individual files

Theoretically, you can also use bcp to scan your application for a listing of elements needed to run the application. The output report includes all the information in a standard bcp report for a Boost module. You use one of four command-line syntaxes to work with bcp, as shown here:

```
bcp [options] module-list output-path
bcp --list [options] module-list
bcp --list-short [options] module-list
bcp --report [options] module-list html-file
```

Each of these command-line syntaxes performs a different task: copy, listing, short listing, and reporting. These command lines can accept a number of options, as described in the following list:

✦ **--boost=*path***: Defines the path to the Boost library.

✦ **--scan:** Treats the modules as a non-Boost file for the purpose of scanning file dependencies. You always use this option with your own applications.

✦ **--cvs:** Copies only files under Concurrent Versions System (CVS) version control.

✦ **--unix-lines:** Uses Unix-style line endings for the output. You won't ever use this command-line switch on a Windows system but may need it on Unix, Linux, and Macintosh systems.

Using bcp is relatively straightforward. For example, if you want a listing of files for the regex library, change directories to \CodeBlocks\boost_1_55_0, and then use the following command line:

```
bcp --list regex > Out.txt
```

The bcp utility looks in the \CodeBlocks\boost_1_55_0 directory for Boost. In this case, the output appears in Out.txt. You should always use file redirection because the output is too large to read at the command prompt.

Let's say you want a report about the regex module instead of a simple listing. In this case, you use the following command line:

```
bcp --report regex MyReport.html
```

Creating a report can take a while. Eventually, you see an HTML report like the one shown in Figure 4-8. You can discover more about bcp at http://www.boost.org/doc/libs/1_55_0/tools/bcp/doc/html/index.html.

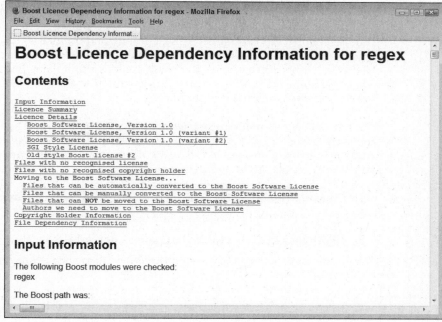

Figure 4-8:
The bcp utility can output some nice-looking reports about Boost modules.

Using Wave

The Wave utility is a preprocessor for the Boost library. Using a preprocessor can significantly speed the compilation process because a preprocessor compiles the library portion of the application. After you compile it the first time, you need not compile the library again. Theoretically, you can use Wave with any C++ compiler; however, you probably won't need it with compilers such as Code::Blocks and Microsoft Visual Studio because these products include their own preprocessor. You can find more information about the Wave utility at `http://www.boost.org/doc/libs/1_55_0/libs/wave/doc/wave_driver.html`.

There is more to the Wave utility than meets the eye, however. The Wave utility relies on the Wave library. This library ships as part of Boost and you can use it in your applications as you do any other library. The website at `http://www.boost.org/doc/libs/1_55_0/libs/wave/index.html` tells you more about the Wave library.

Building Your First Boost Application Using Date Time

Enough information about licensing, content, and utilities — it's time to use the Boost library for something interesting. This section shows a simple date/time example that you can't easily build without using Boost. You also discover some interesting setup requirements that are good to know when you work with other third-party libraries.

As normal, this example begins with a console application. The example uses the name `FirstBoost`. After you create the console application following the steps you've used to create all of the other console applications in the book, perform these setup steps:

1. **Choose Project⇨Build Options and select the Search Directories tab.**

You see the Project Build Options dialog box.

2. **Highlight FirstBoost in the left pane. Click Add.**

Code::Blocks displays the Add Directory dialog box shown in Figure 4-9.

Figure 4-9:
Select
the Boost
library
directory.

Figure 4-9: Select the Boost library directory.

3. **Click the ellipses button to display the Browse for Folder dialog box and highlight the `\CodeBlocks\boost_1_55_0` folder on your hard drive. Click OK.**

A dialog box appears asking whether you want to maintain the entry as a relative path. *Relative paths* specify a location using the current location as a starting point. The alternative is an *absolute path*, which specifies a location based on the root directory of your hard drive. In most cases, absolute paths are less likely to get broken.

4. **Click No.**

Code::Blocks adds the folder you selected to the Add Directory dialog box.

5. **Click OK.**

You see the folder for the Boost library as shown in Figure 4-10. (Your path could vary from the one shown in the screenshot, depending on the platform you use and how your copy of Boost was set up). Make sure you select the correct folder; otherwise the compiler won't be able to find the Boost library or the headers won't compile correctly because they point to the wrong location on the hard drive.

6. **Click OK.**

   The application environment is ready to use with the Boost library.

Now that you have the environment configured, you can begin working with Boost. Listing 4-1 shows a date/time example that displays the current time and then a modified date/time.

Figure 4-10:
Make sure you set the environment to use Boost.

Listing 4-1: Using Boost to Create a Simple Date/Time Example

```
#include <iostream>
#include "boost/date_time/posix_time/posix_time.hpp"

using namespace std;
using namespace boost::posix_time;
using namespace boost::gregorian;

int main()
{
    // Obtain the current date and time.
    ptime Now = second_clock::local_time();
    cout << Now << endl;
```

(continued)

Listing 4-1 *(continued)*

```
    // Get the date and adjust it for tomorrow.
    date TheDate = Now.date() + days(1);

    // Get the time and adjust for an hour from now.
    time_duration TheHour = Now.time_of_day() + hours(1);

    // Create a new date/time and output it.
    ptime NewDateTime = ptime(TheDate, TheHour);
    cout << NewDateTime << endl;

    return 0;
}
```

As with any other added capability, you must include the proper library files. Note that Boost headers use an .hpp extension, which makes it harder to confuse them with some other header type. To define what to include as the path to your library, simply look at the hierarchy in Windows Explorer. Locate the .hpp file you want to use and then copy that information from the Address bar.

Boost provides namespaces for each of the libraries. In this case, the ptime and time_duration classes appear in the boost::posix_time namespace and the date class appears in the boost::gregorian namespace. If you find that your application won't compile, it usually means that you've missed a namespace and need to consider where each of the classes in your application comes from.

The application code begins by creating a variable, Now, that contains the current time, which you obtain using the second_clock::local_time() method. It then displays the current time. The ptime class includes methods for interacting with every time element: years, months, days, hours, minutes, seconds, and so on. The example shows a few of the interactions you can perform. When you run this application, the second time you see is one day and one hour ahead of the current time.

Chapter 5: Boosting up a Step

In This Chapter

✔ **Using RegEx to parse strings**

✔ **Using Tokenizer to break strings into tokens**

✔ **Converting numbers to other data types**

✔ **Using Foreach to create improved loops**

✔ **Using Filesystem to access the operating system**

The Boost library is vast. It's doubtful that a typical developer will ever use everything that Boost has to offer. Of course, before you can pick and choose what you want to use, you need to know it exists. Browsing through the help file can reveal classes that you need to add to your toolkit to produce good applications. This chapter helps by taking you on a whirlwind tour of the major Boost categories. Don't expect this chapter to discuss everything — Boost is simply too large for that. If you want to see a list of what Boost has to offer, check out

✦ **All classes in alphabetical order:** `http://www.boost.org/doc/libs/1_55_0`

✦ **Categorized list:** `http://www.boost.org/doc/libs/1_55_0?view=categorized`

In addition to reviewing the examples in this chapter and looking through the help file, it also pays to browse the Boost directory for examples. For example, if you look at the `\CodeBlocks\boost_1_55_0\libs\regex\example` directory, you find three examples of how to use RegEx, one of which is demonstrated in the "Testing the installation" section of Book VI, Chapter 4. Every example directory contains a `Jamfile.v2` you can use to build the examples using Boost.Build. If you still haven't found the example you need, check online for more examples — Boost is extremely popular. Even Microsoft has gotten into the act by providing examples at `http://msdn.microsoft.com/library/aa288739.aspx`.

Before you begin working through the examples in this chapter, make sure you know how to configure your development environment to use Boost. The "Testing the installation" and "Building Your First Boost Application Using Date Time" sections of Book VI, Chapter 4 tell how to configure Code::Blocks to use Boost. The "Building Your First Boost Application Using Date Time" section also provides you with a simple example that gets you started working with Boost.

Parsing Strings Using RegEx

Regular expressions are an important part of today's computing environment. You use them to perform *pattern matching,* where the application finds a series of matching characters in a string. For example, if you want the user to enter values from 0 through 9 and nothing else, you can create a pattern that prevents the user from entering anything else. Using patterns in the form of regular expressions serves a number of important purposes:

✦ Ensures that your application receives precisely the right kind of input

✦ Enforces a particular data input format (such as the way you input a telephone number)

✦ Reduces security risks (for example, a user can't input a script in place of the data you wanted)

Some developers make the mistake of thinking that a regular expression can prevent every sort of data input error. However, regular expressions are only one tool in an arsenal you must build against errant input. For example, a regular expression can't perform range checking. If you want values between 101 and 250, a regular expression will ensure that the user enters three digits; however, you must use range checking to prevent the user from entering a value of 100.

Defining the pattern

The RegEx library provides a number of methods for creating a pattern. For example, if you want the user to input only lowercase letters, you can create a range by using [a-z]. The example in this chapter shows how to create a simple three-digit numeric input. However, you can create a pattern for nearly any use. For example, a telephone number pattern might appear as ([0-9] [0-9] [0-9]) [0-9] [0-9] [0-9]- [0-9] [0-9] [0-9] [0-9], where a telephone number of (555) 555-5555 is acceptable, but a telephone number of 555-555-5555 isn't. The RegEx library reference appears at http://www.boost.org/doc/libs/1_55_0/libs/regex/doc/html/index.html.

This chapter doesn't provide you with a full explanation of all the patterns you can create.

The best place to start discovering the basics of patterns is at http://www.boost.org/doc/libs/1_55_0/libs/regex/doc/html/boost_regex/syntax.html. It's important to note that older versions of Boost only supported the Perl syntax — newer versions support POSIX basic and POSIX extended syntax as well. Boost provides a wealth of pattern types.

How you use the pattern is just as important as how you create the pattern. For example, you can use RegEx_match to obtain a precise match. However, if you want to only search for a value, you use RegEx_search instead. The usage reference appears at http://www.boost.org/doc/libs/1_55_0/libs/regex/doc/html/boost_regex/ref.html.

Defining the pattern for a regular expression can prove time-consuming. However, once you create the pattern, you can use it every time you must check for a particular input pattern. The following sections describe how to work with the RegEx (*regular expressions*) library.

Adding the RegEx library

Most of the Boost library works just fine by adding headers to your application code. However, a few components, such as RegEx, require a library. Before you can use a library, you must build it. The instructions for performing this task appear in the "Building the libraries" section of Book VI, Chapter 4. After you build the library, you must add it to your application.

There are two techniques for adding the required headers and libraries to an application. The first technique is to add it to the compiler settings, as you did for the "Testing the installation" section of Book VI, Chapter 4. The second technique is to add the settings to a specific project. You use the first technique when you work with Boost for a large number of projects and require access to all libraries. The second technique is best when you use Boost only for specific projects and require access only to specific libraries. The following steps show you how to perform the project-specific setup for any library, not just the RegEx library:

1. **Use the Project wizard to create a new project.**

Nothing has changed from the beginning of this book — every application begins with a new project.

2. **Choose Project⇨Build Options.**

Code::Blocks displays the Project Build Options dialog box.

3. **Select the Linker Settings tab.**

You see a number of linker settings, including a Link Libraries list, which will be blank.

4. **Click Add.**

Code::Blocks displays the Add Library dialog box shown in Figure 5-1.

**Book VI
Chapter 5**

Boosting up a Step

Figure 5-1:
Select the library you want to add.

5. **Click the Browse button — the button sporting the ellipses.**

You see the Choose Library to Link dialog box.

6. **Using the dialog box, navigate to the `libboost_regex-mgw47-mt-1_55.a` library (the release version of the library), select the library, and then click OK.**

   The Boost library files are typically located in the `\Boost\lib` directory. When you click OK, you see a dialog box that asks whether you want to keep this as a relative path.

   Relative paths specify a location using the current location as a starting point. The alternative is an *absolute path*, which specifies a location based on the root directory of your hard drive. In most cases, absolute paths are less likely to get broken.

7. **Click No.**

   You see the absolute path for the `libboost_regex-mgw47-mt-1_55.a` library added to the File field of the Add Library dialog box.

8. **Click OK.**

   After you click OK, you see the absolute path for the library added to the Linker Settings, as shown in Figure 5-2.

Figure 5-2:
Add the library to the application.

9. **Click the Search Directories tab.**

   You see three sub-tabs: Compiler, Linker, and Resource Compiler.

10. **Click Add in the Compiler sub-tab.**

You see an Add Directory dialog box like the one shown in Figure 5-3.

Figure 5-3:
Add
appropriate
search
directories
for Boost
header and
library files.

Add directory

Directory: `C:\CPP_AIO\BookVI\Chapter05\RegEx\`   ...

OK   Cancel

11. **Type the location of the Boost header files in the Directory field.**

As an alternative, you can click the Browse button to use a Browse for Folder dialog box to find them. The files are normally located in the `\Boost\include\boost-1_55` folder.

12. **Click OK.**

You see the search folder added to the Compiler tab as shown in Figure 5-4.

Figure 5-4:
The Search
Directories
tab will
display
the search
location
for any
compiler,
linker, or
resource
compiler.

13. **Click Add in the Linker sub-tab.**

You see yet another Add Directory dialog box (refer to Figure 5-3).

14. **Type the location of the Boost library files in the Directory field and then click OK.**

The Boost library files are typically located in the \Boost\lib directory. After you click OK, you see the directory added to the Linker tab.

15. **Click OK.**

The RegEx library is now ready for inclusion in your application.

Creating the RegEx code

Using a regular expression is relatively straightforward. All you do is create the expression and then use it with a function to perform specific kinds of pattern matches. The function you choose is important because each function performs the pattern matching differently. The RegEx example code in Listing 5-1 demonstrates how to create a regular expression and then use it in two different ways to determine whether user input is correct.

Listing 5-1:   Performing Matches and Searches Using RegEx

```cpp
#include <iostream>
#include "boost/regex.hpp"

using namespace std;
using namespace boost;

int main()
{
    // Obtain an input from the user.
    char MyNumber[80];
    cout << "Type a three-digit number: ";
    cin >> MyNumber;

    // Define the regular expression.
    regex Expression("[0-9][0-9][0-9]");

    // Create a variable to hold the matches.
    cmatch Matches;

    // Perform a matching check.
    if (regex_match(MyNumber, Matches, Expression))
    {
        cout << "You typed: " << Matches << endl;
    }
    else
    {
        cout << "Not a three-digit number!" << endl;
    }
```

```
    // Perform a search check.
    if (regex_search(MyNumber, Matches, Expression))
    {
        cout << "Found: " << Matches << endl;
    }
    else
    {
        cout << "No three-digit number found!" << endl;
    }

    return 0;
}
```

In this case, the code begins by adding the proper header, RegEx.hpp, and the proper namespace boost. In many cases, you can get by without doing much more than performing these two steps in your code.

**Book VI
Chapter 5**

Boosting up a Step

The first step in the code is to get some user input. Even though the prompt tells the user to enter a three-digit number, C++ doesn't enforce this requirement.

The second step is to create the regular expression. What we need for this example is a set of three ranges for numbers: [0-9][0-9][0-9]. Using ranges works well for a number of tasks, and you use them often when creating a regular expression.

The third step is to perform the pattern match. The example uses RegEx_match(), which performs a precise match, and RegEx_search(), which looks for the right characters anywhere in the input. Both functions require three input values: the value you want to check, an output variable of type cmatch that tells where the match is found, and the regular expression.

To see how this code works, you must perform a series of three tests. First, run the application and type **0** as the input. Naturally, typing 0 means that the code will fail and you see this output:

```
Not a three-digit number!
No three-digit number found!
```

Second, let's see a success. Run the application again and type **123** as the input. This time you see

```
You typed: 123
Found: 123
```

So far, there isn't much difference between the two functions, which is why you need the third test. Run the application a third time and type ABC123XYZ as the input. Now you see the difference between a match and a search:

```
Not a three-digit number!
Found: 123
```

This final test shows that the `RegEx_search()` function finds the three-digit value in the string. Obviously, the `RegEx_search()` function is great when you need to locate information but not good when you need to secure it. When you need a precise pattern match, use `RegEx_match()` instead.

Breaking Strings into Tokens Using Tokenizer

As humans, we view strings as a sentence or at least a phrase. Mixtures of words create meaning that we can see in a moment.

Computers, on the other hand, understand nothing. A computer can perform pattern matching and do math, but it can't understand Kipling (read more about this fascinating author at `http://en.wikipedia.org/wiki/Rudyard_Kipling`). It's because of this lack of understanding that you must tokenize text for the computer. A computer can perform comparisons on individual *tokens*, usually single words or symbols, and create output based on those comparisons.

The compiler you use relies on a *tokenizer*, an application component that breaks text into tokens, to turn the text you type into machine code the computer can execute. However, the tokenizer appears in all sorts of applications. For example, when you perform a spelling check on a document, the word processing application breaks the text into individual words using a tokenizer, and then compares those words to words in its internal dictionary.

The `Tokens` example in Listing 5-2 shows a method for creating tokens from strings. This basic technique works with any phrase, string, or series of strings. You'll normally process the tokens once you finish creating them.

Listing 5-2:   Creating Tokens from Strings

```
#include <iostream>
#include "boost/tokenizer.hpp"

using namespace std;
using namespace boost;

int main()
{
    // Define the test string.
    string MyString = "This is a test string!";

    // Obtain tokens from the string.
    tokenizer<> Tokens(MyString);

    // Display each token on screen.
    tokenizer<>::iterator Iterate;
    for (Iterate = Tokens.begin(); Iterate != Tokens.end(); Iterate++)
        cout << *Iterate << endl;

    return 0;
}
```

The `tokenizer` template places the tokenized form of `MyString` in `Tokens`. The application now has a set of tokens with which to work. To see the tokens, you must iterate through them by creating a `tokenizer<>::iterator`, `Iterate`. The application uses `iterator` to output the individual tokens. When you run this application, you see the following output:

```
This
is
a
test
string
```

This example shows a basic routine you can use for just about any need. However, you might need some of the extended capabilities of the `tokenizer` class. Check out the materials at `http://www.boost.org/doc/libs/1_55_0/libs/tokenizer/index.html` for more information about both the `tokenizer` and the `tokenizer<>::iterator`.

**Book VI
Chapter 5**

Boosting up a Step

Performing Numeric Conversion

Numeric conversion isn't hard to perform — it's *accurate* numeric conversion that's hard to perform. Getting the right result as you move from one type of number to another is essential. Sure, you probably won't notice too much if your game score is off by a point or two, but you'll definitely notice the missing dollars from your savings account. Worse yet, when you finally get to take that rocket into space, a rounding error can definitely ruin your day as you head off toward the sun, rather than Planet Earth.

The Boost library includes the `converter` template, which makes converting from one kind of number to another relatively easy. The `converter` template includes all kinds of flexibility. The `Convert` example shown in Listing 5-3 presents two different levels of converter template usage, but really only scratches the surface of an infinitely more complex Boost library feature.

Listing 5-3:   Converting from double to int

```
#include <iostream>
#include "boost/numeric/conversion/converter.hpp"

using namespace std;
using namespace boost;
using namespace boost::numeric;

int main()
{
    // Create the converter.
    typedef converter<int, double> Double2Int;
```

(continued)

Listing 5-3 *(continued)*

```cpp
    // Define the variables for the example.
    double MyDouble = 2.1;
    int MyInt = Double2Int::convert(MyDouble);

    // Display the results.
    cout << "The double value is: " << MyDouble << endl;
    cout << "The int value is: " << MyInt << endl;

    // See what happens with a larger value.
    MyDouble = 3.8;
    MyInt = Double2Int::convert(MyDouble);
    cout << "The double value is: " << MyDouble << endl;
    cout << "The int value is: " << MyInt << endl;

    // We don't want truncation, so let's round.
    typedef conversion_traits<int, double> Traits;
    typedef converter<int, double, Traits, def_overflow_handler,
                      RoundEven<double> > Double2Rounded;
    MyInt = Double2Rounded::convert(MyDouble);
    cout << "The int value is: " << MyInt << endl;

    return 0;
}
```

TECHNICAL STUFF

Why numeric conversion is necessary

Humans don't differentiate between one kind of number and another — seeing 1 is about the same as seeing 1.0. The computer, however, does make a differentiation between numbers at two levels:

- Integer versus floating-point

- Size

The integer part of the equation comes into play because of the early processors in PCs, which could perform only integer math. For floating-point math, you had to buy a separate math coprocessor. Today, the math coprocessor comes with the processor, but integer and floating-point math still occur in different areas of the processor. When the processor performs integer math, it uses different registers and capabilities than when it performs floating-point math. So the conversion between integer and floating-point data is more than philosophical — it involves using physically different areas of the processor.

The size issue determines how large the integer or floating-point value is. Again, the difference is physical. Early processors could handle only 8 bits of data at a time, then 16 bits, and on to 32 bits, and finally the 64 bits of today. Using larger numbers in older processors required a number of additional tasks in software, so using larger numbers incurred a significant performance penalty.

Today, with memory and processor register size no longer a concern, large numbers are also no longer a concern, except that you must observe the historical reasons for using numbers of a specific size. In addition, there are sometimes benefits from a reliability, security, or speed perspective in using a smaller number. The important consideration in working with numbers is that you must observe the correct conversion techniques when you want to obtain the correct results.

The example begins by creating a `converter` object, `Double2Int`. This first object shows the minimum information you can provide — the target (`int`) and source (`double`) values. The default setting truncates floating-point values (`float` and `double` among them) to obtain an `int` value. To perform a conversion, the code relies on the `convert` method, which requires a variable of the required source type as an argument.

The `converter` template includes support for four kinds of rounding. You must use the correct kind of rounding to match your application requirements. Imagine what would happen to calculations if you used truncation when rounding is really the required operation. The following list describes all four kinds of rounding that `converter` supports:

✦ `Trunc`: Removes the decimal portion of the value (rounds toward 0)

✦ `RoundEven`: Rounds values up or down as needed

✦ `Ceil`: Rounds the value up toward positive infinity when the decimal portion is greater than 0

✦ `Floor`: Rounds the value down toward negative infinity when the decimal portion is greater than 0

The second `converter` object, `Double2Rounded`, shows the template requirements to choose the kind of rounding that the object performs. In this case, you supply five arguments to the template (the `converter` template actually accepts up to seven arguments, discover more about them at http://www.boost.org/doc/libs/1_55_0/libs/numeric/conversion/doc/html/boost_numericconversion/converter___function_object.html):

✦ Target

✦ Source

✦ `conversion_traits`, which include the target and source types as a minimum

✦ Overflow handler, which determines how the object handles conversions that result in an overflow (the default is `def_overflow_handler`)

✦ Rounding template object (which includes the rounding source type)

The process for using the extended form of the `converter` template is the same as the simple form shown earlier in the example. However, you must now create a `conversions_traits` object (`Traits` in this case) and provide the required input information. (See more examples of using `conversion_traits` at http://www.boost.org/doc/libs/1_55_0/libs/numeric/conversion/doc/html/boost_numericconversion/conversion_traits___traits_class.html.) As before, you rely on the `convert` method to perform the conversion process. Here is the output you see when you run the application:

```
The double value is: 2.1
The int value is: 2
The double value is: 3.8
The int value is: 3
The int value is: 4
```

Note that the last two lines show the difference in rounding the value 3.8. In the first case, you see the default `Trunc`, and in the second, you see the effects of `RoundEven`. Discover more about performing numeric conversion using Boost at `http://www.boost.org/doc/libs/1_55_0/libs/numeric/conversion/doc/html/index.html`.

Creating Improved Loops Using Foreach

Writing efficient loops is a requirement if you want your application to perform optimally. Interestingly enough, many loops use a certain amount of *boilerplate* code (code that is essentially the same every time you write it, but with small nuances).

Templates and other methodologies described in this book provide a means to overcome the boredom of writing essentially the same code. However, none of the examples to date has shown a tried and true method, macros. A *macro* is essentially a substitution technique that replaces a keyword with the boilerplate code you'd normally write. Macros normally appear in uppercase, such as `BOOST_FOREACH`, which is the macro used in this section of the chapter. Instead of typing all the code associated with a macro, you simply type the macro name and the compiler does the rest of the work for you.

The magic behind the `BOOST_FOREACH` macro is that it creates all the iteration code you normally create by hand. In other words, you aren't providing any less code to the compiler, you simply let the macro write it for you. The Boost library still relies on the Standard library `for_each` algorithm; you simply avoid writing all the code you used to write when using the algorithm. You can discover more about the `BOOST_FOREACH` macro at `http://www.boost.org/doc/libs/1_55_0/doc/html/foreach.html`.

You may recognize the `ForEach` example in Listing 5-4 partially from Listing 6-1 in Book IV, Chapter 6. However, instead of choosing specific items, the example now uses a `BOOST_FOREACH` loop to iterate through the `vector`.

Listing 5-4: Creating a BOOST_FOREACH Loop

```
#include <iostream>
#include <vector>
#include "boost/foreach.hpp"
```

```
using namespace std;
using namespace boost;

int main()
{
    // Create a vector and store values in it.
    vector<string> names;

    names.push_back("Tom");
    names.push_back("Dick");
    names.push_back("Harry");
    names.push_back("April");
    names.push_back("May");
    names.push_back("June");

    // Iterate through the vector.
    BOOST_FOREACH(string Name, names)
        cout << Name << endl;

    // Iterate backward, too!
    cout << endl << "Backward:" << endl;
    BOOST_REVERSE_FOREACH(string Name, names)
        cout << Name << endl;

    return 0;
}
```

This example begins by creating a vector. In fact, it's the same vector as the one used for the example in Book IV, Chapter 6, Listing 6-1. In this case, the example then creates a `BOOST_FOREACH` loop that iterates through `names`. Each iteration places a single value from `names` into `Name`. The code then prints the single name.

An interesting feature of the Boost library is that you can reverse the order of iteration. In this case, the code uses a `BOOST_REVERSE_FOREACH` loop to go in the opposite direction — from end to beginning. The technique is precisely the same as going forward. Here is what you see when you run this application:

```
Tom
Dick
Harry
April
May
June

Backward:
June
May
April
Harry
Dick
Tom
```

As you can see, iterating forward and backward works precisely as you expect. The BOOST_FOREACH and BOOST_REVERSE_FOREACH macros support a number of container types:

✦ Any Standard Template Library (STL) container

✦ Arrays

✦ Null-terminated strings (char and wchar_t)

✦ STL iterator pair (essentially a range)

✦ boost::iterator_range<> and boost::sub_range<>

The macro STL container support is generalized. Any object type that supports these two requirements will work:

✦ Nested iterator and const_iterator types

✦ begin() and end() member functions

Accessing the Operating System Using Filesystem

Working with files and directories is an important part of any application you create. Book V shows some standard techniques you use to work with both files and directories. However, these methods can become cumbersome and somewhat limited. Boost augments your ability to work with the file system using the Filesystem library. Creating and deleting both files and directories becomes a single call process. You can also perform tasks such as moving and renaming both files and directories.

The most important addition that Boost makes is defining a method to obtain error information from the operating system. This feature is found in the System library, which you must include as part of your application. Among other capabilities, the System library makes it possible to convert a numeric error that the operating system returns into a human readable form. Unfortunately, the System library is still a work in progress, so this chapter can't demonstrate how to use it in any great detail.

You must add references to the libboost_filesystem-mgw47-mt-1_55.a and libboost_system-mgw47-mt-1_55.a files using the technique found in the "Adding the RegEx library" section of this chapter for the example to work. The project file may require that you change the library setting to match your system. When you set up this application properly, you should see two libraries on the Linker Settings tab of the Project Build Options dialog box, as shown in Figure 5-5.

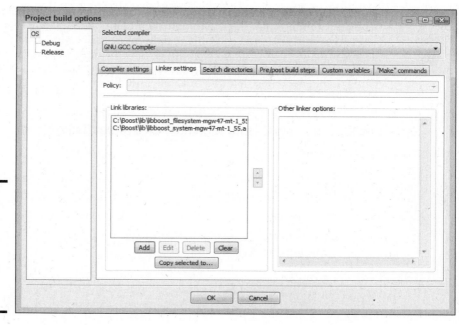

Figure 5-5:
Using the
Filesystem
library
requires
the System
library as
well.

The Filesystem library and the Standard library

The developers of the Boost library continuously add to its capabilities. Some of the additions developers make are so useful that they end up in the Standard library. The Filesystem library is one of these useful elements. You can see the proposal for adding the Filesystem library to the Standard library at `http://www.open-std.org/jtc1/sc22/wg21/docs/papers/2006/n1975.html`.

Of course, standardized libraries require discussion from multiple groups, not just the Boost developers. Consequently, the Boost library you use today may not be precisely the same library you see added to the Standard library. It's important to keep up with the proposed technical changes to the Boost library as they move to the Standard library by reviewing the documentation online.

The Boost library documentation appears at `http://www.boost.org/doc/libs/1_55_0?view=categorized`.

The movement of code from one setting to another tends to confuse developers because they suddenly find that a favorite library has seemingly disappeared. These developers also question whether they should continue using the old library or move to the new one. In all cases, you want to use the Standard library when you can because the Standard library is fully supported by a standards group, and well, standard. Consequently, when the Filesystem library finally makes the move to the Standard library, be prepared to make a change in how you work with it and update your code as needed to ensure full compliance with the code everyone else creates.

The OS example in Listing 5-5 shows only a modicum of the capabilities of the Filesystem library. The big thing to remember when using this example is that it requires both Filesystem and System libraries since the System library provides error-handling support. The example begins by creating a directory and a file, adding data to the file, reading the file back in and displaying it, and then deleting both file and directory.

Listing 5-5:   Interacting with the File System Using Boost

```
#include <iostream>
#include "boost/filesystem.hpp"

using namespace std;
using namespace boost::filesystem;

int main()
{
    // Check for the existence of the directory.
    if (! exists("Test"))
    {

        // Create the directory.
        create_directory(path("Test"));
        cout << "Created Directory Test" << endl;
    }
    else
        cout << "Directory Test Exists" << endl;

    // Check for the existence of the file.
    if (! exists("Test/Data.txt"))
    {
        // Create the file.
        ofstream File("Test/Data.txt");
        File << "This is a test!";
        File.close();
        cout << "Created File Data.txt" << endl;
    }
    else
        cout << "File Data.txt Exists" << endl;

    // Read the file.
    if (exists("Test/Data.txt"))
    {
        cout << "Data.txt contains " << file_size("Test/Data.txt")
            << " bytes." << endl;

        ifstream File("Test/Data.txt");
        string Data;

        while (! File.eof())
        {
            File >> Data;
            cout << Data << " ";
        }
        cout << endl;

        File.close();
    }
```

```
    else
        cout << "File Data.txt Doesn't Exist!" << endl;

    // Delete the file and directory.
    if (exists("Test/Data.txt"))
    {
        remove(path("Test/Data.txt"));
        cout << "Deleted Data.txt" << endl;
    }

    if (exists("Test"))
    {
        remove(path("Test"));
        cout << "Deleted Test" << endl;
    }
}
```

The first feature you should notice about this example is that it constantly checks to verify that the file or directory exists using the exists() function. Your applications should follow this pattern because you can't know that a file or directory will exist when you need to work with it, even if your application created it. A user or external application can easily delete the file or directory between the time you create it and when you need to work with it again.

To create a directory, you use create_directory(), which accepts a path as input. You create a path object using path(). Many of the other Filesystem library calls require a path object as well. For example, when you want to remove (delete) either a file or directory, you must supply a path object to remove(). Interestingly enough, remove() does remove a file without creating a path object, but it won't remove a directory. The inconsistent behavior can make an application that incorrectly uses remove() devilishly difficult to debug.

You won't throw elements of the Standard library out when working with the file system. For example, you still use ofstream and ifstream to work with file content, just as you did in Book V, Chapters 2 and 3. The Filesystem library only augments what you already have available. Here is what you see when you run this application:

```
Created Directory Test
Created File Data.txt
Data.txt contains 15 bytes.
This is a test!
Deleted Data.txt
Deleted Test
```

One final element to look at in this example is file_size(), which reports the size of the file in bytes. The Filesystem library provides a number of helpful statistics you can use to make your applications robust and reliable. As previously mentioned, you want to spend time working with this library because it contains so many helpful additions to the standard capabilities that C++ provides.

Appendix: Automating Your Applications with Makefiles

In This Appendix

✔ Compiling and linking your applications

✔ Automating your work

✔ Implying work with inference rules in your Makefiles

✔ Getting the most out of Makefiles

S ince the beginning of time, or at least since the beginning of the Unix operating system, programmers have used a utility called make to build their applications. And it's still often used today. The make utility looks at which of your source code files have changed and decides what needs to be compiled and built.

Development tools, such as Code::Blocks and Microsoft Visual C++, don't require you to use a make utility, because they have such decision-making features built in. But many free compilers use them. Fortunately, the process for creating and using make files is no longer as difficult as it once was. Third-party libraries come with make utilities (such as the Boost library's Boost.Build; see Book VI, Chapter 4) that greatly reduce the complexity of creating and using make files.

Before using make, understanding the compile and link processes is important. In this appendix, we cover the compile and link processes and advise how to use make to automate your building. Please note, however, that make itself is a complex tool, and enough information is available about it to fill an entire *For Dummies* book. Therefore, we suggest that you don't worry about mastering make and what are called Makefiles. Instead, read this appendix so that you understand them. Then, if you work with Makefiles in your projects, start with an existing one. If you understand it, you can easily modify it for your project.

Compiling and Linking

When you create an application, you write your code in various source code files. For one application, you can have many different source code files. Some large corporate projects may have hundreds (or even thousands) of source code files with dozens of programmers working on the different files.

As you can imagine, dozens of strong-willed programmers working together makes for quite an adventure; but by using tools like make, these programmers are able to easily work together without a single disagreement ever taking place. Okay, we lied. But nevertheless, make makes their lives easier.

To transform these source code files into a single application, you need to compile and link them.

Compiling means transforming your C++ code (or whatever language you are using) into a machine-readable language called Assembler. The Assembler language differs among types of processors. Most of you reading this book are probably working on some version of an AMD or Intel processor, so the C++ compilers you use normally translate your applications into assembler code (also called machine code) that's appropriate for the processor on your system. (You can also tell the compiler to target some other processor in many cases.) The compiler stuffs all this assembler code into a file called an *object file* and typically names the file the same as the original source code file but with an .obj or .o extension. For each source code file, the compiler makes a single object file.

After you have compiled all your source code files, you run the linker. The *linker* takes the object files and combines them into a single file that you can run on your computer. This single file usually gets an .exe extension, which stands for *exe*cutable. The origin of this term comes from *execution,* which refers to the running of an application and probably had something to do with what the user of the first computer application wanted to do to the programmer after using the application. But we're only guessing.

The linker can produce other kinds of output files. For example, you can create a .lib (library) or .dll (Dynamic Link Library, or DLL) file. These files contain executable code, just as the .exe file does, but you don't execute them as stand-alone files — an .exe file normally loads them and uses the executable code they contain.

The compiler also inserts into the object files a great deal of information in addition to the assembler code. For example, when you are still in the process of developing your application, you can instruct the compiler to put debug information in the file. (Although sometimes the debug information goes in a separate file; it depends on the compiler.) Debug information includes the names of your variables and the line numbers of the source code. When you use a debugger tool, that tool knows about your code by looking at the debug information.

The compiler also puts information about the code, such as the names of items that occur, in other source code files. For example, if you are writing code that calls code in another source code file, the compiler includes the name of that code in the object file. That way, the linker can connect the two.

Understanding external linkage

An example of where you may encounter external linkage is when code in one source code file calls a function in another source code file. When the compiler compiles the first source code file, it doesn't know where in the compiled assembler code the routine will be when it compiles the second source code file. And even if the second source code file is already compiled, the compiler isn't particularly interested in digging around the other object file to figure out where it is. So instead, the compiler simply creates a *reference* to the routine. It places this reference inside the first object file.

Later, the linker replaces the reference with the address of the call, and that address is what will end up in the final executable. This address, however, is just temporary and serves as a placeholder until the final application is loaded into memory. When you run the

executable and the application gets loaded into memory, a special application called the *loader* replaces the address with the actual memory address where the routine is located. Whew!

Your code may also call code that lives outside your application, such as a routine in a DLL. In that case, the compiler still puts the name of the routine inside the object file. But at link time, the linker includes a placeholder that notes the name of the item (or perhaps a unique number) and the name of the DLL file. The linker puts that information inside the executable file. When you run the executable file and the application gets loaded into memory, the computer first makes sure that the DLL is loaded (following the same steps here that it's using to load the executable! Oh my!) and then replaces the information with the real live address of the DLL's routine. Again, whew!

Finally, a compiler can add resources to the object files, such as graphics and sounds that your application requires. These resources appear as data that the application accesses later. Data appears in separate areas from executable code within the file, but you don't need to worry about the object file organization — the compiler takes care of managing both code and data for you.

Automating Your Work

When you're developing an application and working with, say, ten different source code files and you're ready to compile and link your work, you could compile each source code file separately and then link them all together. However, it would be nice if you had to compile only the source files that have changed since the last time you compiled. After all, if one of the source code files was compiled to an object file earlier and hasn't changed since the last compile, why bother compiling it again?

The solution is to use some kind of special application that checks to find out which source files have changed and compiles only those. Or if none of the source files has changed, the special application checks only to see whether any external libraries have changed and, if necessary, does only a link. Or if nothing has changed at all, do nothing and call the application up to date.

That is exactly what the make utility does. Using make, you can be sure that only the object files and executables that are out of date get updated. How does make do this? It simply compares the dates on the files, that's all. It looks at a source code file and its associated object file. If no object file is associated with the source code, it definitely compiles the source code files. If an object file is available, and the object file is newer than the source code file, make knows that the source code file hasn't changed since the last compile, and therefore there's no reason to recompile it. But if the source code file is newer than the object file, it must have changed since the last compile, and thus the make utility compiles it.

To build your application by using make, you just type this at the console (that is, either the terminal on Mac or Linux computers or the command prompt on Windows computers):

```
make
```

Note that different make applications have different names. For example, Microsoft provides the nmake utility that you can read about at http://msdn.microsoft.com/library/dd9y37ha.aspx. When using these other kinds of make utilities, simply type its name instead of make.

If anything in your project needs building, make will do it. Otherwise, it prints the simple but sweet little message:

```
make: 'myprogram' is up to date.
```

Well, this is all fine and dandy, except for one little catch: the make utility needs something called a Makefile. The Makefile lists information about what exactly it's supposed to make. Unfortunately, Makefiles aren't exactly simple. The make utility (and its Makefile concept) was, after all, invented something like 30 years ago, back in the dark ages when computers were made of stone and cars had square wheels. But that's okay. Today's computers still handle Makefiles, and you can find out how to use them. The next section covers what exactly goes inside these animals. The things in the files are themselves interesting little animals called *inference rules*.

Implying with Inference Rules

Everybody loves rules, and so does the make utility. Before make knows what to make, you need to supply it with a set of rules. Programmers have decided to call these rules *inference rules,* for lack of a better term. Well, actually, tons of better terms that take up less space are available. But they chose *inference* because the make utility will infer what it's supposed to do based on the rules implied by the Makefile.

In general, an inference rule specifies the file you want to create (such as an object file) and the file or files it depends on (such as its associated source code file). Next the rule states how exactly to create that file. For example, if you have an object file that depends on a source code file, the way to create it is by running the compiler command.

A typical inference rule looks like this. The first line specifies the name of the file you want to create, then it has a colon, and then the files it *depends* on are listed. The next line starts with a tab and then lists the commands to run to create that new file, with one command per line. The following example is a rule for creating a text file:

```
test.out: test.txt
    cp test.txt test.out
    echo WORKED >> test.out
```

The first line means that we want to create a file called test.out, and it depends on the file called test.txt. If test.txt is newer than test.out (meaning it has changed since the last time this rule was run), make executes the two commands that follow. In this case, the first one copies test.txt into the test.out file, and the second one appends the word WORKED at the end of test.out.

You may notice something interesting about the preceding inference rule. Instead of using the usual copy command, here we used the cp command, which is the equivalent under Unix. Many of the free make utilities on the market, such as Cygwin, rely on Unix-style commands. If you prefer to work with the MinGW compiler or the Borland compiler, you can use the copy command instead.

If you want to try out this Makefile business, create a text file called Makefile and put the following in it:

```
test.out: test.txt
    cp test.txt test.out
    echo WORKED >> test.out
```

(Note that the second and third lines begin with a single tab; do not start the first line with any tabs.) Next, make a text file in the same directory and call the file `test.txt`. Finally, while in the same directory, type the following command:

```
make
```

Note that you will need to have a `make` command installed. For example, you can obtain Cygwin at `http://www.cygwin.com/`. Book VI, Chapter 4 describes the Boost.Build compiler. You can also obtain the Borland compiler from `http://www.embarcadero.com/downloads`.

If you do some exploring, you are likely to discover that you can, optionally, name your `Makefile` something other than `Makefile` and then specify your filename in the `make` command. For most versions of `make`, you do this by typing

```
make -f filename
```

However, we do not recommend doing this. Most programmers always use the filename `Makefile`, and if you call yours something different, you are likely to rattle their chains a little. Computer people are not known for their flexibility; and if you do this, your coworkers probably won't pay for your pizza this Friday.

Using rules that depend on other rules

Some special situations arise when working with inference rules. For example, `test.out` may not exist at all. In that case, the commands will definitely run because the idea is that this rule tells how to create a `test.out` file.

Another special situation deals with `test.txt` itself in the previous examples. Does *it* depend on anything? For example, another rule may say this:

```
test.txt: originalfile.txt
    cp originalfile.txt test.txt
```

This rule states that `test.txt` depends on `originalfile.txt`. If `originalfile.txt` has changed, `make` creates `test.txt` based on the command, which is a `cp` command.

As it turns out, `make` is surprisingly smart for such an old computer tool. Before it ventures into the rule to create `test.txt`, it sees that `test.txt` depends on `originalfile.txt`, and checks to see whether `originalfile.txt` has any rules. If so, `make` keeps tracing backward until it gets to a rule with no prior dependencies.

So these two rules would all be lumped together into a single `Makefile`:

```
test.out: test.txt
    cp test.txt test.out
    echo WORKED >> test.out
test.txt: originalfile.txt
    cp originalfile.txt test.txt
```

You can have multiple rules in your `Makefile`, and they don't all have to depend on each other. If you have multiple rules without such interdependencies in your file, however, `make` starts by running the first rule that it encounters.

Making specific items

When you have a `Makefile` filled with all sorts of rules, you may want to build only one particular item inside it. For example, if you have dozens of source code files, you may want just to compile the source code file you're working on, without building the whole shebang all the way to the final executable.

To specify exactly *what* you want to build, just throw in the name of the item after the word `make`:

```
make test.txt
```

If you are working with the `Makefile` with rules for both `test.out` and `test.txt`, then when you issue this command, you create only `test.txt`; you will not create `test.out`. However, if `make` requires other rules to be built before this rule can run, it will run those rules.

So with the example we give regarding multiple source code files, if you want to compile only the one called `NiftyFeature.cpp`, you would type

```
make NiftyFeature.o
```

Note that the file extension in this line is `.o`. The reason is that, although you're compiling the source file (`NiftyFeature.cpp`), you are *making* the object file (`NiftyFeature.o`). Therefore, you specify the name of the object file in the `make` command when you want to compile a particular source file.

Depending on multiple files

Not only can you have multiple rules in your `Makefiles`, but you can have one rule that depends on multiple files. This is common when building files, particularly in the link step. For example, the final application itself, such as `myprogram.exe`, is going to depend on many files, including all the object files in your project, as well as any libraries.

To list multiple dependencies, you create your `Makefile` rule, listing all the dependencies on the right of the colon, separated by spaces, as in the following example (don't use commas or semicolons to separate them):

```
test.out: test1.txt test2.txt
    echo hello > test.out
```

Here, `test.out` depends on both `test1.txt` and `test2.txt`. When you run `make`, if either of these two latter files has changed since the last time you ran `make`, the echo line executes.

If you have lots of files to the right of the colon, you can put them on multiple lines if you prefer by ending each line (except the final one) with a backslash (`\`), as in the following example:

```
test.out: test1.txt \
 test2.txt
    echo hello > test.out
```

Often, people indent the following lines with a single space, as we did there, primarily for readability. Although using a tab here is okay, we don't recommend doing that. The tabbed line makes it harder for us mere humans to read, because the tabbed line will be aligned with the commands that follow.

If a header file changes and your source code file uses it, you will want your source code file to be rebuilt the next time you run `make`. Therefore, including header files in your list of dependencies is a good idea. But it can be difficult to figure out what header files your source file depends on. It turns out that there's a nifty little trick that can help you do this. Compilers such as Cygwin and MinGW can build such a list for you. To do this, you use the `-M` option, as in the following example:

```
g++ -M main.cpp
```

When we ran this on one of our source code files, we saw the following appear on the screen:

```
main.o: main.cpp /usr/include/g++-3/iostream.h \
 /usr/include/g++-3/streambuf.h /usr/include/g++-3/libio.h \
 /usr/include/_G_config.h \
 /usr/lib/gcc-lib/i686-pc-cygwin/2.95.3-5/include/stddef.h \
 /usr/include/sys/cdefs.h main.h
```

Notice to the left of the colon is the object file, `main.o`. To the right are the files it depends on, starting with our source code file (`main.cpp`). The several header files follow, including their paths. To use these, you would then paste them into your `Makefile`; they represent the first line of the rule.

If you want to use the -M option to generate your dependencies (but only want to list the header files in your project and not all those other bizarre ones that live inside the main include directory), you can throw in an extra *M:*

```
g++ -MM main.cpp
```

When we run this, we see only the header files in our project. Here's the output we get:

```
main.o: main.cpp main.h
```

Often, this is more useful because it's rare that the system header files change.

Compiling and linking with make

To really use make in your projects, you need rules that tell make to run the compiler. For each of your source code files, you want to build an object file; and from there, you want to link the object files into a single executable. You can write a Makefile that specifies these rules, such as the following:

```
mystuff.o: mystuff.cpp
    g++ -c mystuff.cpp -o mystuff.o
```

The first line says that our object file depends on the source file. The second line is the command to run to create the object file.

Linking is a bit more complex because to successfully link an application, you need to include several libraries. Which libraries you include depends on which compiler you use.

The beauty of using Makefile, however, is that after the information for compiling and linking is there, you don't need to do anything else. When it's time to build your application, you simply type

```
make
```

Certainly, you will be compiling and linking. Remember that with Makefiles, the best way to use them is to simply understand them. That way, you can take an existing one and fix them up so that they work with your particular project. Writing one from scratch requires a strong knowledge of the intricate workings of the inference rules. Toward the end of this appendix (in the sidebar "Discovering more about make"), we tell you where you can find that information if you really want to study it.

Cleaning up and making it all

When you have a `Makefile` and a huge project, you may want to periodically start fresh, cleaning out all your object files and the final executable, before you do a build. For example, you may be working on a project, and so much has changed that you would prefer to start fresh with your next build. To do this, you can include a `clean` section in your `Makefile` that looks like this, if you're using Cygwin:

```
clean :
    rm -f *.o
    rm -f *.obj
    rm -f myprogram.exe
```

Note that no files are listed after the colon. Thus, when you type

```
make clean
```

the `rm` commands (which delete the files) will always run.

If you're using either the MinGW or Borland compiler, you want your `clean` section to look like this:

```
clean :
    del *.o *.obj myprogram.exe
```

Using macros

Environment variables can include macros. A *macro* is basically a word that represents something else that is probably more complicated. For example, you may have something like this:

```
MYFILES = one.cpp two.cpp three.cpp four.cpp
```

Then, any place in your `Makefile` where you want to refer to the four files `one.cpp`, `two.cpp`, `three.cpp`, and `four.cpp`, you can instead simply write

```
$(MYFILES)
```

When you access a macro, you precede it with a dollar sign ($), and you put the name inside parentheses. The `make` utility then knows that this is a macro and needs to be expanded.

Discovering more about make

If you want to be a serious, diehard, late-into-the-night, big-time "maker," you can read its online manual. You can do tons and tons of things with make, and you could easily stay up all night playing with it all — or, at least, trying to learn it all. You may not ever have a need for all the things you learn, but you never know. Here's the site: http://www.gnu.org/manual/.

Scroll down to find the entry on make. (make will be followed by a hyphen and some numbers representing the version number.) When you click it, you will see an enormous page filled with the wonders of make. Trust us: It's long and boring.

Getting the most out of Makefiles

Here are some other features you can use when working with Makefiles:

✦ If your lines run long and you want to continue them on the next line without confusing poor old make, you can end a line with a backslash (\) and then continue it on the next line.

✦ Your best bet when working with Makefiles is to start with one that you know works and then change it so that it applies to your current project. The truth is, almost no programmer creates a Makefile from scratch. Programmers don't like to work that hard on auxiliary projects like messing with Makefiles. They'd rather get to their programming. So if you need a starting point, you can find a sample in this appendix.

✦ Most Makefiles will have a rule called all. The idea behind this rule is that it encompasses all the other rules. When you type **make all**, you can build your whole project.

✦ You can include comments in your Makefiles by starting them with a # character. These comments are not used by the Makefile.

✦ Makefiles can include what are called *implicit rules,* which are rules that pertain to a whole set of files with the same file extension (such as .cpp). These comments can help you understand the Makefiles when working with them.

✦ If you don't like Makefiles, you don't have to use them. Development environments such as Code::Blocks and Microsoft Visual C++ make it possible to create great applications without ever touching a Makefile.

Index

O

U

About the Authors

John Mueller is a freelance author and technical editor. He has writing in his blood, having produced 94 books and over 300 articles to date. The topics range from networking to artificial intelligence and from database management to heads-down programming. Some of his current books include a Windows command line reference, books on VBA and Visio 2007, a C# design and development manual, and an IronPython programmer's guide. His technical editing skills have helped more than 63 authors refine the content of their manuscripts. John has provided technical editing services to both *Data Based Advisor* and *Coast Compute* magazines. He has also contributed articles to magazines such as *Software Quality Connection*, *DevSource*, *InformIT*, *SQL Server Professional*, *Visual C++ Developer*, *Hard Core Visual Basic*, *asp.netPRO*, *Software Test and Performance*, and *Visual Basic Developer*. Be sure to read John's blog at http://blog.johnmuellerbooks.com/.

When John isn't working at the computer, you can find him outside in the garden, cutting wood, or generally enjoying nature. John also likes making wine and knitting. When not occupied with anything else, he makes glycerin soap and candles, which comes in handy for gift baskets. You can reach John on the Internet at John@JohnMuellerBooks.com. John is also setting up a website at http://www.johnmuellerbooks.com/. Feel free to take a look and make suggestions on how he can improve it.

Jeff Cogswell is an experienced teacher, writer, and software engineer. He worked 15 years as a professional programmer and software engineer before leaving that field to write and edit full time. He is currently a senior editor with Ziff Davis Enterprise, writing and editing for DevSource.com and eWEEK.com. His skills include C++ as well as several other languages and platforms, such as C# and ASP.NET. In his spare time he enjoys traveling, playing the guitar, and photography.

Dedication

Some people are meant to touch our lives for a while and then go away —
leaving an impression that lasts forever. This book is dedicated to the endur-
ing spirit of my wife, Rebecca, who will always remain by my side.

— John Paul Mueller

To my wife Angie, and my son Dylan, with love.

— Jeff Cogswell

Authors' Acknowledgments

Thanks to my wife, Rebecca, for working with me to get this book completed. I really don't know what I would have done without her help in researching and compiling some of the information that appears in this book. She also did a fine job of proofreading my rough draft. Rebecca keeps the house running while I'm buried in work.

Russ Mullen deserves thanks for his technical edit of this book. He greatly added to the accuracy and depth of the material you see here. Russ is always providing me with great URLs for new products and ideas. However, it's the testing Russ does that helps most. He's the sanity check for my work. Russ also has different computer equipment from mine, so he's able to point out flaws that I might not otherwise notice.

Matt Wagner, my agent, deserves credit for helping me get the contract in the first place and for taking care of all the details that most authors don't really consider. I always appreciate his assistance. It's good to know that someone wants to help.

A number of people have read all or part of this book to help me refine the approach, test the coding examples, and generally provide input that all readers wish they could have. These unpaid volunteers helped in ways too numerous to mention here. I especially appreciate the efforts of Eva Beattie, Glenn A. Russell, Austin Jonas, Osvaldo Téllez Almirall, Dave Taylor, Emanuel Jonas, and Michael Sasseen, who provided general input, read the entire book, and selflessly devoted themselves to this project.

Finally, I would like to thank Connie Santisteban, Paul Levesque, Becky Whitney, Barry Childs-Helton, and the rest of the editorial and production staff at Wiley.

— John Paul Mueller

I first want to thank John Mueller for continuing his good work on the third edition of this book. Yet another book brings another big thanks to my agent and friend, Margot Hutchison, for the usual great work. And special thanks to Connie Santisteban and editors Paul Levesque, Becky Whitney, and Barry Childs-Helton for their meticulous work in making this project a reality. Finally, thanks to my wife Angie and my son Dylan for supporting me in all my projects.

— Jeff Cogswell

Apple & Mac

iPad For Dummies,
6th Edition
978-1-118-72306-7

iPhone For Dummies,
7th Edition
978-1-118-69083-3

Macs All-in-One
For Dummies, 4th Edition
978-1-118-82210-4

OS X Mavericks
For Dummies
978-1-118-69188-5

Blogging & Social Media

Facebook For Dummies,
5th Edition
978-1-118-63312-0

Social Media Engagement
For Dummies
978-1-118-53019-1

WordPress For Dummies,
6th Edition
978-1-118-79161-5

Business

Stock Investing
For Dummies, 4th Edition
978-1-118-37678-2

Investing For Dummies,
6th Edition
978-0-470-90545-6

Personal Finance
For Dummies, 7th Edition
978-1-118-11785-9

QuickBooks 2014
For Dummies
978-1-118-72005-9

Small Business Marketing
Kit For Dummies,
3rd Edition
978-1-118-31183-7

Careers

Job Interviews
For Dummies, 4th Edition
978-1-118-11290-8

Job Searching with Social
Media For Dummies,
2nd Edition
978-1-118-67856-5

Personal Branding
For Dummies
978-1-118-11792-7

Resumes For Dummies,
6th Edition
978-0-470-87361-8

Starting an Etsy Business
For Dummies, 2nd Edition
978-1-118-59024-9

Diet & Nutrition

Belly Fat Diet For Dummies
978-1-118-34585-6

Mediterranean Diet
For Dummies
978-1-118-71525-3

Nutrition For Dummies,
5th Edition
978-0-470-93231-5

Digital Photography

Digital SLR Photography
All-in-One For Dummies,
2nd Edition
978-1-118-59082-9

Digital SLR Video &
Filmmaking For Dummies
978-1-118-36598-4

Photoshop Elements 12
For Dummies
978-1-118-72714-0

Gardening

Herb Gardening
For Dummies, 2nd Edition
978-0-470-61778-6

Gardening with Free-Range
Chickens For Dummies
978-1-118-54754-0

Health

Boosting Your Immunity
For Dummies
978-1-118-40200-9

Diabetes For Dummies,
4th Edition
978-1-118-29447-5

Living Paleo For Dummies
978-1-118-29405-5

Big Data

Big Data For Dummies
978-1-118-50422-2

Data Visualization
For Dummies
978-1-118-50289-1

Hadoop For Dummies
978-1-118-60755-8

Language & Foreign Language

500 Spanish Verbs
For Dummies
978-1-118-02382-2

English Grammar
For Dummies, 2nd Edition
978-0-470-54664-2

French All-in-One
For Dummies
978-1-118-22815-9

German Essentials
For Dummies
978-1-118-18422-6

Italian For Dummies,
2nd Edition
978-1-118-00465-4

Available in print and e-book formats.

Available wherever books are sold. **For more information or to order direct visit www.dummies.com**

Math & Science

Algebra I For Dummies,
2nd Edition
978-0-470-55964-2

Anatomy and Physiology
For Dummies, 2nd Edition
978-0-470-92326-9

Astronomy For Dummies,
3rd Edition
978-1-118-37697-3

Biology For Dummies,
2nd Edition
978-0-470-59875-7

Chemistry For Dummies,
2nd Edition
978-1-118-00730-3

1001 Algebra II Practice
Problems For Dummies
978-1-118-44662-1

Microsoft Office

Excel 2013 For Dummies
978-1-118-51012-4

Office 2013 All-in-One
For Dummies
978-1-118-51636-2

PowerPoint 2013
For Dummies
978-1-118-50253-2

Word 2013 For Dummies
978-1-118-49123-2

Music

Blues Harmonica
For Dummies
978-1-118-25269-7

Guitar For Dummies,
3rd Edition
978-1-118-11554-1

iPod & iTunes
For Dummies, 10th Edition
978-1-118-50864-0

Programming

Beginning Programming
with C For Dummies
978-1-118-73763-7

Excel VBA Programming
For Dummies, 3rd Edition
978-1-118-49037-2

Java For Dummies,
6th Edition
978-1-118-40780-6

Religion & Inspiration

The Bible For Dummies
978-0-7645-5296-0

Buddhism For Dummies,
2nd Edition
978-1-118-02379-2

Catholicism For Dummies,
2nd Edition
978-1-118-07778-8

Self-Help & Relationships

Beating Sugar Addiction
For Dummies
978-1-118-54645-1

Meditation For Dummies,
3rd Edition
978-1-118-29144-3

Seniors

Laptops For Seniors
For Dummies, 3rd Edition
978-1-118-71105-7

Computers For Seniors
For Dummies, 3rd Edition
978-1-118-11553-4

iPad For Seniors
For Dummies, 6th Edition
978-1-118-72826-0

Social Security
For Dummies
978-1-118-20573-0

Smartphones & Tablets

Android Phones
For Dummies, 2nd Edition
978-1-118-72030-1

Nexus Tablets
For Dummies
978-1-118-77243-0

Samsung Galaxy S 4
For Dummies
978-1-118-64222-1

Samsung Galaxy Tabs
For Dummies
978-1-118-77294-2

Test Prep

ACT For Dummies,
5th Edition
978-1-118-01259-8

ASVAB For Dummies,
3rd Edition
978-0-470-63760-9

GRE For Dummies,
7th Edition
978-0-470-88921-3

Officer Candidate Tests
For Dummies
978-0-470-59876-4

Physician's Assistant Exam
For Dummies
978-1-118-11556-5

Series 7 Exam For Dummies
978-0-470-09932-2

Windows 8

Windows 8.1 All-in-One
For Dummies
978-1-118-82087-2

Windows 8.1 For Dummies
978-1-118-82121-3

Windows 8.1 For Dummies,
Book + DVD Bundle
978-1-118-82107-7

Available in print and e-book formats.

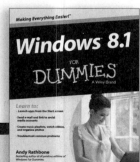

Available wherever books are sold. For more information or to order direct visit www.dummies.com